A DICTIONARY OF
MODERN AMERICAN
USAGE

A Dictionary

OF

MODERN AMERICAN

USAGE

BY

H. W. HORWILL

SECOND EDITION

OXFORD

AT THE CLARENDON PRESS

Oxford University Press, Ely House, London W.1

GLASGOW NEW YORK TORONTO MELBOURNE WELLINGTON
CAPE TOWN SALISBURY IBADAN NAIROBI LUSAKA ADDIS ABABA
BOMBAY CALCUTTA MADRAS KARACHI LAHORE DACCA
KUALA LUMPUR HONG KONG

FIRST PUBLISHED 1935
REPRINTED SEPTEMBER 1935
SECOND EDITION 1944
REPRINTED 1946, 1949, 1952, 1954, 1958, 1965

PRINTED IN GREAT BRITAIN

PREFACE

THE title of this book has obviously been suggested by that of H. W. Fowler's *Dictionary of Modern English Usage*, but the two books are radically different in their purpose. Mr. Fowler's ambition was to help English people to use their own language more correctly. Mine is certainly not to teach Americans how to write or speak American.

The present volume is intended for the benefit of three classes of readers. (1) It is primarily designed to assist English people who visit the United States, or who meet American friends, or who read American books and magazines, or who listen to American 'talkies'. Few of us, perhaps, realize what a subtle and frequent cause of misunderstanding lurks in the fact that so many familiar words are used in America with a different meaning, or at any rate with a different implication, from that which they bear in England. On both sides of the Atlantic we speak a common language, but if that common language has not always a common meaning its employment as a means of communication is beset by many pitfalls. The object of this book is to set forth and explain these differences of linguistic idiom, many of them unsuspected by the ordinary man.

(2) Its value, I hope, will be scarcely less to Americans. They will learn from it much that will interest them respecting the stamp that has been impressed upon the language by the American environment and American conditions of life. It will also, incidentally, make English speakers and writers more intelligible to them, as I have included, for their benefit, fuller particulars of the normal usage in England than would be required by English readers. I have not thought it necessary, however, to give English usages anything like an exhaustive treatment. The few readers who may require such a complete account can turn for it to the *Oxford English Dictionary* or some other source of detailed information. It has seemed to me sufficient to set down the meanings that are attached to a word by an ordinary educated Englishman in his everyday use of it, without troubling, for example, about its signification in a local dialect or in the special vocabulary of a particular trade. In matters of English usage I have taken the *Oxford English Dictionary* and its *Supplement* as an authoritative standard.

(3) Apart from the service it may render in facilitating intercourse between England and the United States, this book is intended also to provide material for any student of language, whatever his nationality, who concerns himself with tracing the changes in

signification to which words are subject in the course of a long history.

The words dealt with in this dictionary may be divided into the following classes, which are not, however, mutually exclusive:

(1) Words whose meaning in America is entirely different from their meaning in England; as *billion, precinct, ruby type, solicitor*.

(2) Words whose general meaning is the same in both countries, but which, in America, have acquired a specific meaning in addition; as *brotherhood, commute, dues, fit, homestead, senior*.

(3) Words whose normal use has, in America, been extended to cover certain adjacent territory; as *freight, graduate, hunt*.

(4) Words that, in America, have acquired different shades of meaning and therefore carry different implications; as *jurist, politics*.

(5) Words that retain in America a meaning now obsolete in England; as *apartment, citizen, conclude, tardy, thrifty, town*.

(6) Words that, in America, have acquired a figurative meaning not in current use in England; as *gridiron, knife, pork, stripe, timber*.

(7) Words that, in America, commonly take the place of synonyms that are more generally used in England; as *faucet* (for *tap*), *hog* (for *pig*), *line* (for *queue*), *mail* (for *post*), *two weeks* (for *fortnight*).

(8) Words of slightly varying forms, of which one form is preferred in America and another in England; as *aluminum* (*aluminium*), *acclimate* (*acclimatize*), *candidacy* (*candidature*), *deviltry* (*devilry*), *telegrapher* (*telegraphist*).

(9) Words that, in America, go to form compounds unknown in England; as *blue, night, scratch, thumb*.

It will thus be seen that this does not profess to be a dictionary of Americanisms. For the achievement of an enterprise of so wide a scope we must wait until Sir William Craigie and his collaborators have completed the great work—*The Historical Dictionary of American English*—on which they are now engaged at the University of Chicago.[1] I have taken into account here such words only as are common to the vocabularies of both England and the United States. Except in special cases I have not included words that are purely American in their origin (e.g. *chautauqua*), or words adopted into current American speech from foreign languages (e.g. *mesquite*). The special cases arise when a word of native origin has been acclimatized in England but with a different meaning from that which it bears in the United States (e.g. *caucus*), or when a foreign word adopted in America is likely to be confused with an English word of similar form (e.g. *stoop*). I have not included a word merely because it is spelt or pronounced differently in America,

[1] The last parts were published 1944.

but I have incidentally noted differences of spelling or pronunciation in the case of words included for other reasons.

The present volume is not based upon other dictionaries but upon material I have collected independently during more than thirty years, six of which were spent in the United States. (It would be quite impossible to compile, from dictionaries alone, a satisfactory record of national differences in verbal usage. For example, our English dictionaries give both *crematorium* and *crematory*, but you never hear an Englishman speak of a *crematory*.) At the same time, I have checked my own work by reference to such authorities as the *Oxford English Dictionary* (including the Supplement), the *Century Dictionary*, *Webster's Dictionary*, and the *Standard Dictionary*. I have also profited from consulting the *Encyclopedia of the Social Sciences*—a valuable work which is not as well known in England as it deserves to be—for authoritative information respecting the technical terms within its field.

As far as possible I have illustrated my account of American usages by examples I have myself met with—none of my quotations are at second-hand—in the course of my reading of (1) American newspapers and periodicals and (2) American books. In the case of newspapers and periodicals, it has seemed to me unnecessary to take up space by citation of names. Whether a quotation appeared originally in the *Cincinnati Enquirer* or the *Topeka Capital* is of no real significance. Accordingly, where an example is given without mention of its source, the reader may assume that it is taken from an American newspaper or magazine. The purpose of these quotations is to provide illustrations of the American use of the word or expression in question, or, in some instances, to supply such information about the thing it denotes as would make it more intelligible to the English reader. I have not attempted the more ambitious task of tracing, by means of dates, the historical development of the use of the term. Other things being equal, I have utilized the most recent examples in my collection, but, if an example dated 1900 casts a clearer light upon the American use of a word than one dated 1930, I have preferred the earlier passage to the later. Whatever the date of the example, however, the reader may be assured that the idiom illustrated is still in current use. In the case of passages extracted from books, it should be remembered that books sometimes bear a different title in the United States from that under which they are published in English editions. I have reproduced the American spelling as an essential part of a quotation. So, too, the insertion or omission of a hyphen in (more or less) compound words corresponds to the practice followed in the original text. In consequence, a term may appear in consecutive quotations as two separate words, as a single word, and as hyphenated. In such matters the American practice is no less go-as-you-please than the English.

There are three problems, in especial, that confront the compiler of such a dictionary as this. In the first place, he must beware of hasty generalization; that is to say, he must be careful not to mistake an idiosyncrasy of a single writer for an example of a general usage. Possibly I have sometimes fallen into this error, but at any rate I have tried to avoid it. In most cases the examples quoted are only a selection from a much larger number recorded in my notes.

Again, it has not been my intention to include slang words and expressions, but in practice I have often found it difficult to draw the line between slang and colloquialisms. The difficulty is enhanced by the fact that many words, originating as slang, soon establish a claim to a reputable place in the permanent vocabulary of the language. When I have found that a word, though labelled as slang in the dictionaries, is used in serious treatises by university professors, I have not hesitated to include it.

My third problem is by far the most difficult. It arises from a process which is rapidly going on, almost unnoticed, all the time that one's book is in preparation. Usages that to-day are peculiar to America are to-morrow adopted by English writers and speakers, frequently without the least suspicion of their transatlantic origin. A striking example has recently offered itself. Many of my readers will doubtless be surprised to learn that the use of *cut* in the sense of *reduction* is a neologism imported from the United States during the fourth decade of the present century. As late as 1929 it was not yet recognized in the *Concise Oxford Dictionary*—it appears, of course, in the 1934 edition of that work—although, as examples in my MS. notes prove, it was commonly so used in America as long ago as 1904 at least. Its general use in England dates from the financial and economic crisis of 1931. It had begun to creep into the headlines a few years before, being found in newspaper offices to be much easier than *reduction* to manipulate in a small space. During the discussions, in Parliament and the press, of the budget of September, 1931, public speakers and leader-writers, who had occasion to refer again and again in a speech or article to the reductions in the unemployment allowances, &c., came to appreciate the convenience of the shorter word. For a time it appeared within inverted commas—as, for example, in *Whitaker's Almanack* for 1932, pages 175 and 881—but before long, like the use of the title *General* for the head of the Salvation Army, it lost the half-apologetic suggestion implied by these marks.

It so happens that I possess exceptional means of ascertaining what linguistic usages, now more or less acclimatized in England, have been taken over from America during the present century. My first period of residence in the United States was between 1900 and 1905. After I had spent a year or two in New York, I found myself becoming impressed by the unexpectedly large number of differences between English and American idiom, and it occurred to me that it might be worth while to jot down instances that I came across of an American linguistic usage that was unfamiliar to me. Accordingly, I began, some time in 1902, to make notes of them. Several of these usages have since come to be so frequent in this country that scarcely any Englishman regards them to-day as importations, and, if I trusted to my memory alone, I doubt whether I should myself think of them as originally American. But when I find examples of them set down in black and white, with dates, in my notes, I know for a certainty that, in the early years of the century, they struck my attention as not being then in use at home. This conclusion is confirmed when, as commonly happens, I find the usage in question not recognized in the dictionaries published in England at about that period.

I have decided that, in such cases, the recent acclimatization in England of a usage previously peculiar to America should not debar it from recognition in this dictionary. While an interpretation of it may no longer be necessary in order to help English readers to understand American books, it will at any rate be of service to students of the development of language to find a record here of the American origin of such variations from the normal English practice of a few years ago. At the same time, it seems desirable to give some indication of the changes that have been taking place. I have therefore marked with a dagger (†) those words and usages which seem to me now on the way towards being naturalized in England and with a double dagger (††) those whose naturalization here is by this time complete. In such matters the judgement of any individual is, of course, not infallible, and I shall not be surprised to find that some critics think me too sparing of my daggers while others consider me too liberal with them.

March, 1935.   H. W. H.

NOTE TO SECOND EDITION

ONE of the publications of the Society for Pure English is a pamphlet, entitled 'American Variations' (S.P.E. Tract, No. XLV), in which the author of this dictionary has discussed the question of the differences between English and American idiom as regards both vocabulary and grammatical usage. It brings together and classifies, in the form of a general survey of the subject, the specific instances, recorded in this volume under their several headings, of the variations in the English and American uses of words that are part of our common speech on both sides of the Atlantic. Such a conspectus, it is thought, might appropriately serve as an introduction to the present edition of the dictionary proper, and the greater part of it is accordingly reprinted here for that purpose.

August 1943   H. W. H.

ACKNOWLEDGEMENTS

I MUST publicly offer my hearty thanks to several persons whose generous help, both in suggestion and in correction, has saved me from many faults of omission and commission. The whole dictionary was read in typescript by Lieut.-Col. H. G. Le Mesurier, C.I.E., joint editor of the latest edition of the *Concise Oxford Dictionary*. The proofs were subsequently read in Chicago by Mr. M. M. Mathews, a member of Sir William Craigie's Dictionary staff, and in Oxford by Dr. R. W. Chapman and other members of the staff of the University Press. Professor A. L. Goodhart has revised my definitions of certain legal and other terms. The book has greatly profited by the comments of all these scholarly critics. I must also gratefully recognize the kindness of several personal friends who have assisted me in various matters of English or American usage; especially Miss Mary K. B. Honey, Miss N. V. D. Skillman, and Miss R. J. Coffin. I cannot fully express the debt I owe to my wife, whose co-operation has been of great service to my work in all its stages. It will, of course, be understood that I alone am responsible for the opinions pronounced or implied in the book on doubtful or controverted points as well as for any defects that may still be found in it.

INTRODUCTION

'WHEN we Americans are through with the English language, it will look as if it had been run over by a musical comedy.' In making this sensational prediction, 'Mr. Dooley' forbore to speculate as to the date when this critical stage of linguistic history was likely to be reached. Meanwhile, a less startling analogy derived from the arts would seem appropriate to describe what has so far happened to the English language in the United States. In their use of English speech, Americans have not abandoned the original tunes, but are playing them with variations.

The language spoken and written in the United States to-day presents many striking differences from that current at home. This distinction is much more strongly marked than the difference between the English of the mother country and that of the overseas dominions and colonies—with the exception, of course, of Canada, whose speech has been strongly affected by contact with her neighbour. One explanation that naturally suggests itself is that immigration into Australia or New Zealand, for instance, has been almost exclusively British, whereas in America not only were the first settlers in regions of considerable extent French or Spanish, but, over a long period, the country as a whole received many millions of immigrants from other than English-speaking lands. This immense volume of foreign immigration might have been expected to leave many traces on the language. Actually, its influence has been comparatively slight. While the new-comers have shown great activity in producing periodicals and newspapers in their native tongues, they have been content to take the language of their adopted country as they have found it.

French exploration is recalled by a few place-names, such as Baton Rouge and Terre Haute, and by the use of *bad lands* to denote a barren region in the West which the French called *mauvaises terres*. There are, moreover, a few English words whose meaning in the United States corresponds more closely to that of their French counterparts than to their meaning in England; e.g. *apartment, ascension, billion, carousal, chicory* and *endive, circulate, diction, exposition, museum, name* (verb), *professor, proposition, recite, tardy,* and *theme*. It would not be safe, however, to conclude that all these are products of French influence, for, in the case of some of them, examples of what is now the American use might be found in Shakespeare or Evelyn.

Spanish, too, has contributed several place-names, such as Los

Angeles and San Francisco. The words it has contributed to the vocabulary are mainly terms relating to the fauna, flora, and other natural features of certain regions, and outside these regions they are in little use. A man you might happen to meet on Boston Common would be as little likely to know what was meant by a *mesa* or a *coyote* as any one casually encountered in Hyde Park. It would be difficult, if not impossible, to discover an instance of Spanish influence affecting the meaning of an English word.

Although New York was once New Amsterdam, Dutch has had a very slight influence on the language. The Stuyvesants, Van Cortlandts, and Bleeckers of that period may have left memorials in the names of some of the city streets, but they have made no greater impression upon the language than the Boers of South Africa. More words have been introduced into the English vocabulary from Arabic than into the American vocabulary from Dutch. Yet no one ever thinks of Arabic as having appreciably affected the development of the English language.

With German it is a different matter. The words *dumb* and *fresh* are common in America in the sense of *dumm* and *frech*. The use of *eat* for *take one's meals* reminds one of the German *essen*, but it may be found in the Authorized Version of the English Bible. There are similarities, to say the least, between American and German practice in the compounding of words; e.g. the omission of the hyphen in *coworker* (cf. *Mitarbeiter*) and the preference for *cook-book* (cf. *Kochbuch*) and *sail-boat* (cf. *Segelboot*) over the English *cookery-book* and *sailing-boat*. Americans, too, speak not of a *barber's shop* but of a *barber shop* (cf. *Barbierstube*). It is, perhaps, more than an accident that the American use of certain prepositions corresponds more nearly to German than to English practice. In the United States, again, as in Germany (but not in England), the office a man holds commonly serves as a title; e.g. Secretary of the Interior Bliss. It is doubtful, however, whether such influence as the German language has exercised over American idiom is wholly, or even mainly, to be attributed to immigration from Germany. It is more likely to be a by-product of the fact that, for more than a single generation, the only Americans who studied abroad studied in Germany. Accordingly the literary style of many American scholars, teachers, and writers came to be affected by German rather than English practice.[1]

On the whole, then, it is safe to say that foreign influences have had little to do with the divergences of American from English

---

[1] What has been said of the slight influence of the European languages applies also to the Indian dialects, which contributed a large number of place-names and a few additions to the everyday vocabulary.

speech. One of the most important causes of these differences is American conservatism. When 'Mr. Dooley', as quoted above, used the locution *through with*, he was not an innovator but a diehard, firm in his determination to keep Chicago faithful to the idiom of sixteenth-century Stratford-on-Avon.[1] Many English words, forms, and meanings have been retained in the United States long after they have become obsolete in the mother country, just as the procedure of American law-courts to-day embodies technicalities that legal reform banished from English tribunals long ago. In his chapter on 'The American Intellect' in *The Cambridge Modern History* Professor Barrett Wendell suggests that the conflict between Englishmen and the rebellious colonists in 1775 may have been largely due to the fact that the latter, far more than the former, preserved traits which had ceased to be fully characteristic of England a hundred years before. This remark certainly applies to the language. A distinguished American once coined the happy phrase 'our contemporary ancestors' to denote the hill population of Kentucky and Tennessee, in recognition of their observing certain social customs that are commonly described as Elizabethan. Linguistically, the American people as a whole sometimes seem to be our contemporary ancestors rather than our cousins. In a later section of this essay will be found some examples of the survival in America of grammatical usages now obsolete in England. As regards the meaning and use of words, a complete list of American survivals of earlier English practice would be of startling length. I cannot hope to have noted them all in the body of the Dictionary, but examples will be found under the headings *accommodation, administration, admire, after, aim, apartment, appeal, avail, baggage, barker, belie, bit, blank, bosom, bug, bully, bunch, bushel, cabin, carom, chambermaid, choice, citizen, cockney, commissary, common, conclude, copy, councilman, cricket, decedent, deck, declination, develop, drouth, Dutch, eat, enlarge, fair, fall, fill, fleet, font, foot, fore, gallon, goody, gore, guess, hack, halt, inn, jag, jar, jeer, know, lay, ledger, loan, loft, mad, maybe, merchant, mighty, nasty, oar, overly, parley, peek, pig, pitcher, platter, plenty, preceptor, proponent, quit, rare, register, remember, right, rod, say, sheepman, sick, skill, slim, slur, snarl, spell, squint, stall, sulky, tally, tardy, thrifty, through, town, tradesman, try, valise, well, wheel,* and *wise.* These words (or certain compounds of them) are either obsolete in England—except, in some cases, in dialect —or have lost in England a meaning which they retain in America. A cautionary note is perhaps necessary here. It is possible that,

[1] 'If a man is through with them in honest taking up, then they must stand upon security.'—*2 Henry IV*, Act I, Scene 2.

in some instances, an American usage which coincides with an earlier English usage is an example not so much of a survival as of a revival. That is to say, it has not actually persisted in America through the centuries, but has been abandoned there, as at home, and has subsequently been brought once more into current use. For an authoritative decision on such points we must await the chronological data that will be provided by Sir William Craigie's forthcoming *Historical Dictionary of American English.*

Closely akin to these usages are those which appear to have been introduced into America from various dialects of the British Isles and which to-day are part of the common American idiom. For examples see the Dictionary under the headings *aisle, allow, any, back, bottom, buck, bugaboo, butt, cake, candy, chuck, clear, clip, deviltry, dove, grist, have, hustle, make, meat, nip, none, pin, pointer, raft, raise, rooster, shade, smell, some, spool, sun,* and *tout.*

Many divergences from English meanings have an historical explanation. To an American the word *colonial* carries widely different associations from those it bears for an Englishman. In the United States it refers specifically to the period of the national life before the Revolution, and may thus sometimes come to be almost a synonym for *antique,* as when one speaks of colonial furniture or colonial architecture. With this we may compare the attributive use of *mission* in such terms as mission furniture and mission architecture, denoting the styles which take as their pattern the type found in the buildings erected by the early Spanish missions in California and elsewhere. Another relic of pre-Revolutionary days is the use of *Quaker* as a reminiscence of the part played by William Penn and his associates in the foundation of Pennsylvania. To-day the mention of a Quaker policeman or a Quaker football team has not an ecclesiastical but a geographical signification. The conditions of life among the early settlers gave *frontier* a special meaning which it still retains. The only boundary in those days was the informal line that separated their settlements from the land still occupied by the Indians. This boundary was therefore virtually equivalent to the limit reached by the spreading of the white population. Accordingly, *frontier* came to be applied specifically to an imaginary line, moving constantly farther and farther West, which marked the farthest point reached by the adventurous pioneer. When an American wishes to refer to the line which divides one nation from another, he invariably uses *boundary,* not *frontier.*

From the Revolutionary era comes *Hessian* as a synonym for *mercenary,* thus recalling the hiring of Hessian troops to fight on the British side in the War of Independence. During the same period *Tories* and *Whigs* acquired a novel meaning, being used to denote respectively those who opposed and those who favoured the severing of the connexion with Great Britain. (Later, the name of *Whig* was given also to the party that opposed Andrew Jackson.) The term *Bill of Rights*, as employed in the United States, seldom refers to the famous English statute of 1689. The name is commonly given to the first nine (or ten) Amendments to the United States Constitution which were adopted in 1791 in order to prevent the Federal Government from encroaching upon the liberties of the people. The Civil War gave *Unionist* the special meaning of an opponent of the secession of the Southern States. In the period immediately following, the term *reconstruction* was specifically applied to the process by which the States that had seceded were restored to the rights and privileges of membership of the Union. A Southerner who, after this restoration, continued to cherish the sentiments common in the South during the war, is sometimes described as *unreconstructed*. During the reconstruction period a Republican who went down from the North to seek office or political influence in the South was called a *carpet-bagger*, while a white Southerner who co-operated with the Republican party was dubbed a *scalawag*. The fact that in the United States for several generations protectionism has been the normal fiscal policy has given to *tariff reform* a precisely opposite meaning to that which became familiar in England during the period of Joseph Chamberlain's propaganda.

The difference between the political systems of England and America has left its traces upon the vocabulary. Thus, *elector* and *voter* are by no means synonymous in the United States, where the former term has a signification which reminds one of the 'Electors of Hanover'. It denotes one of the persons who, according to the Constitution, are chosen in the several States to perform the function—now purely formal, for the decision has already been virtually made by popular vote—of electing the President. The members of the President's Cabinet are popularly known not as the *government* but as the *administration*. There is good reason for the difference, for while the British Cabinet, through its control of the legislative body, can exert a dominating influence on the passing of laws, the American, being outside Congress, is charged only with the duty of administering them. In England the first minister of the Crown is naturally called the *Prime Minister* or *Premier*. In America the *Premier* is the person who ranks first among members of the Cabinet; i.e. the Secretary of State, whose principal functions are those of a Foreign Minister. The development in America of a system of government different from that of the mother country accounts for the different use of many other specific terms; e.g. *convention, expansion, franchise, hyphenate, lobby, marshal, message, moderator, nullification, ordinance, organize, police power, radical, recall, secret service, sheriff, supervisor, surrogate, territory.* The word *politics* itself has come to bear so peculiar a signification in the United States that its use has been the cause of frequent misunderstandings.

The educational history of America explains certain striking differences between English and American practice in the use of educational terms. In England we still call Eton and Harrow *public schools,* although most people would find it difficult to give a reason for the adjective to-day. In America, whose educational system started with a clean slate, the term was naturally applied to such schools as were established and maintained by public authorities and administered under public control. Accordingly, the *public school* (often known as a *common school*) of the United States corresponds to the English *council school* or former *board school,* and the term *private school* is applied to hundreds of schools that would not come within this category in England, where it denotes a school carried on for the profit of the owner. Thus, Eton and Harrow would be considered private schools in America. In the field of higher education also the difference between the systems of the two countries accounts for differences in the vocabulary. At American colleges and universities honours are not awarded, as at Oxford and Cambridge, to students who pass a more advanced examination than the rank and file, and *honor system* denotes the practice, adopted at certain institutions, of conducting written examinations without supervision, the candidates being put upon their honour to use no illegitimate aids. As there is no special examination for honours in America, the division of successful candidates into classes is absent also, and a *class* consists of the whole body of students completing their course in the same year. Thus, the class of 1936 at Harvard consists of all the students who entered in 1932 and will graduate (or, as they prefer to say in America, *be graduated*) in 1936. The development of student organizations in America on different lines from those of English colleges and universities has given a specific meaning to *fraternity* and *chapter.*

The frequent use in America of *road* in the sense of *railroad* was explained by Freeman as due to the historical circumstance that —whereas in England we had roads before we had railroads, so that the railroad needed a qualifying syllable to distinguish it from the older and better-known kind of road—in a large part of America the railroad is actually the oldest road, so that there was no such need to distinguish it from any other. In England, moreover, we adapted the familiar terms of the stage-coach era for use in the new method of transport. In America the independent development of the new method led to the use of *car, engineer, conductor,* and *ticket-office* in place of our *coach, driver, guard,* and *booking-office.* A notable feature of American terminology is the extension to land transport of many terms that properly indicate transport by sea; e.g. *aboard, bill of lading, board, freight,* and *ship* (verb). We shall find in the industrial history of America the reason for the specific American use of various other words, such as *express, pack,* and *stores.*

There is another class of words whose peculiar American meaning has an historical explanation. The early English settlers found themselves in a country whose vegetable and animal life presented several novel features.

'One of the chief articles of food among the Indians was corn. The colonists had not seen any grain just like this before, so they were somewhat puzzled to know what name to give it. For some reason they did not adopt the Indian name, whatever that was, nor did they at first employ the name *maize* which the Spaniards had already taken over from a native dialect in Cuba. Instead, the Puritans used the expression *Indian corn* and for some time they distinguished the corn in America from that in England by the terms *Indian corn* and *English corn.* They kept this distinction in speaking of the meal produced from corn and used the terms *Indian meal* and *English meal.* After a time, however, it was no longer necessary or desirable to keep up the distinctions; the single word *corn* came to mean in this country *Indian corn,* and *meal* has no distinguishing word used with it.'[1]

In a few cases—e.g. *hickory, persimmon, squash*—the new-comers adopted the native name, but they frequently applied to the unfamiliar tree, plant, flower, or fruit (as did the early settlers in Australia when confronted by a similar problem) the name of some English growth to which it seemed to bear a resemblance. Sometimes this resemblance was purely superficial, so that a botanist would be horrified by such a suggestion of identity. In this way *bay, beech, cowslip, cucumber, hemlock, laurel,* and *walnut* have come to bear a different meaning in certain parts of the United States. In the animal world a similar process of analogy has given a different signification to *blackbird, night-hawk, lark, oriole, partridge, pheasant, robin,* and *swallow.*

The history of English in America illustrates certain tendencies which are constantly at work in all languages. Many examples present themselves of the figure which grammarians call Synecdoche, by which a word denoting a part is to be understood as

[1] M. M. Mathews, *The Beginnings of American English,* p. 1.

referring to the whole, or a word properly applicable to a species is used of a genus, or vice versa. Thus, *aisle* may denote almost any kind of gangway, whether in a train or a theatre or a shop; a *ballot* taken at a political nominating convention is simply a vote, having lost its distinctive meaning of a vote given in secret; *bug* is in America virtually a synonym for *insect*; *can* and *pail* are not restricted to vessels that hold liquids; *candy* has become a general name for everything included in the English *sweets* (except in the sense of the sweet course at a meal); a *cane* need not be slender but may be a stick of any size and thickness; a *card* may be any kind of printed announcement, not necessarily on cardboard; *cow*, in many compounds, has the meaning of *cattle*; and *wheel* often means *bicycle* or *tricycle*. So, too, a case in an American court is said to be *tried* not only by the judge and jury—the only persons whose function it is to decide the question by consideration of the evidence—but by the lawyers who plead on either side.

In several other instances a word has been liberated in America from the restrictions that limit its application in England; for example, *aboard, accent, Anglican, apt, avenue, bakery, barn, bid, bill of lading, blockade, board, bunch, captain, chambermaid, claim, clergyman, clerk, compensation, conservative, crew, crowd, dedicate, dissenter, extended, freight, home, hunt, institute, liable, lieutenant, limit, locate, lunch, market, merchant, mileage, office, outfit, parish, park, parley, parole, patrol, penitentiary, platoon, recitation, rent, robe, salesman, shape, ship, squad, stage, stock, story, team, vacation, veteran, visit, waitress.* An incidental consequence of these changes in the use of words is that many useful distinctions that are preserved in England are obscured, or even disappear altogether, in American usage. On the other hand, American writers invariably contrast *avocation* and *vocation*, which in England are nowadays commonly regarded as synonyms, and they observe a more definite distinction than we do between *basin* and *bowl*. For another example of discrimination see under *majority*.

An example has been given above of the American employment of the word for a genus to denote a species; i.e. *corn*, which in England is collectively used for any kind of grain, but in America always denotes Indian corn or maize and is never applied to wheat, rye, barley, or oats. The frequent use of *road* for *railroad*, also noted above, is a further illustration of the same process. Other examples of specialization are: *amalgamation*, which denotes the racial admixture of whites and Negroes; *dry goods*, the name given in American stores to articles of drapery, mercery, and haberdashery, as distinct from groceries, hardware, &c.; a *homestead*, which is not any kind of farmstead but a piece of land allotted to a settler under the conditions of the Homestead Act; and *pre-emption*, which has also a specific meaning in connexion with the acquisition of public land. Several words which have become specialized in England have passed through the same process in America, but in the latter country it has taken a different turn. Thus, a *corporation* is not a municipal body but a business company; *franchise* rarely means the right to vote but usually denotes a commercial privilege or concession; the *life guards* are not cavalry regiments but men employed in rescuing persons in danger along the coast; the *pavement* is not the sidewalk but the roadway; a *roundsman* is not a tradesman's employee but a police-officer; and a *subway* is not a tunnel for pedestrians but an underground railway. In a much larger number of instances a word, while not losing its general meaning, has acquired in America a specific meaning in addition; for example, *appropriate, available, brotherhood, button, colloquy, commute, concourse, deal, dispensary, dues, fit* (verb), *husky, joint, junior, levee, mat, notion, opening, parquet, pennant, pit, point, policy, portfolio, post, procurement, prudential, racket, register, regular, release, repeater, required, reservation, rest* (verb), *rig, rustle, saloon, section, senior, squat, stockade, stub, tabloid, target, tipple, traction, transfer, transient, transportation, usher, utility, wad, zone.*

In American usage there is one curious instance of the transference of an adjective from the person who has the quality it denotes to some object with reference to which he manifests that quality. A person who fails to pay his taxes may properly be said to be *delinquent* in respect of that obligation. In America, however, the taxes themselves may be described as delinquent in virtue of his omission. As though to restore the balance the delinquent person in such a case is commonly said to be himself *derelict*, although that word applies rightly not to the offender but to the duty he has failed to perform. Verbs may also be subject to similar shifts of meaning. An American farmer does not *feed* horses on oats, but feeds oats to horses. So, too, in America you do not *shower* missiles or compliments on a person, but you shower him with missiles or compliments. A peculiar example of transference is the use of *penalty* in the term *penalty envelope*, the term denoting an official envelope which carries, without a stamp, a communication sent by one of the executive departments of the Federal Government. It derives its name from the fact that a penalty is imposed for its unauthorized use.

In the United States, as in every other country, euphemism has been responsible for many changes of meaning. The inferior status of the domestic servant is disguised by the term *help*, and the shop assistant prefers to be called a *clerk*. The misdeeds of the desperado of the West are somewhat palliated when he is called merely a *bad man*, and the modern gangster appears in an even friendly light when he takes his victim *for a ride*. In America a *jail delivery* means not, as in England, the clearing of a jail of prisoners by bringing them to trial, but the concerted escape of several convicts. Perhaps the most extreme example of euphemism is the use of *cadet* to denote a procurer. The Civil War has often been spoken of as *the late unpleasantness*, and the expression has been adopted to apply to the Spanish-American War and the Great War (in America, the World War). The suggestion of recklessness implied in running risks disappears when one simply *takes chances*. The kind of interview which includes the passing of a bribe becomes more respectable when the briber merely *sees* the corrupt legislator and when the recipient of the bribe *takes care of* the interests that have bought his services. To be *tired* is often equivalent to being bored. The prejudice that many people feel against advertising is likely to be dispelled if they can be made to believe that it is no more than *publicity*. American optimists scored a great victory when they induced their fellow countrymen to speak of the results of the economic and financial *débâcle* of 1929 as *the depression*.

Litotes, or under-statement, is illustrated in the colloquial use of *no conjurer* to denote a stupid person, and of *have no use for* to indicate actual dislike or disapproval. As a New York paper once remarked, the foreigner invited to stay at a *cottage* at Newport would go sadly wrong if he adjusted his wardrobe to his natural expectations of the environment in which he would find himself. Perhaps the best-known example of American under-statement is *guess*, but this is a survival of an earlier English usage.

The vocabulary of every language is affected, in the course of its history, by the tendency to use certain nouns as verbs, adjectives as nouns, &c. The American variety of English has been especially prolific in examples of this practice. In 1789 Benjamin Franklin, writing to Noah Webster, complained that during his absence in Europe there had been introduced 'into our parliamentary language' the use of the substantives *advocate*, *notice*, and *progress* as verbs also. He hoped that Webster would reprobate them. Webster incorporated the innovations in the 1828 edition of his dictionary without the 'discountenancing mark' which Franklin had suggested, but it took some time for them to be accepted in England also. In 1845 Sir James Stephen, writing to Dr. Robert Vaughan, uses *progress* as a verb, and adds in parenthesis: 'The Yankees should be thanked instead of ridiculed for the word.' Since then, the same process has been continuing in America at a rate which outstrips the English capacity for naturalization. We have adopted *class, glimpse, list, sense, stress,* and *voice,* but we still regard as alien the verbs *accession, clerk, contact, district, muscle, package, proselyte, railroad, recess, room, route, scab,* and *trustee.* All these are in common use, but the list might be greatly extended if we included examples taken from individual writers. It would scarcely be an exaggeration to say that an American writer never hesitates to turn a noun into a verb if it will serve his purpose. In various American books and periodicals I have come across the verbs *anguish, antidote, archipelago, bill of sale, candidate, climax, commentary, convenience, culture, detour, fellowship, grit, hothouse, language, lesson, message, metre, pedestal, suicide, suspicion, ultimate,* and *wharve.*

For examples of adjectives used as nouns I may refer to my dictionary under the headings *alternate, centennial, dry, high, hostile, local, low, mural, postal, sociable, salutatory, spiritual, tough, transient, trusty,* and *wet.* In *jolly* we have an example of an adjective used as a verb, and in *any, mighty, real,* and *some* examples of adjectives used as adverbs. The only instances I have noted of a verb sometimes used as a noun are *divide* and *raise.* (One may ignore the vulgarism *eats.*) The most frequent case of the acquisition of an additional meaning by a verb is the use of a transitive as an intransitive (e.g. *hustle, locate,* and *substitute*) or vice versa (e.g. *appeal, battle, head, hop, protest, rank, step,* and *swarm*). Many other examples of the same tendency might be quoted from individual writers.

A feature of every language is the tendency to shorten words that are found inconveniently long for everyday use. E.g. we commonly speak of a *cab,* not a *cabriolet,* and of a *piano,* not a *pianoforte.* In America the list of curtailed words has received several additions; for example, *auto* (from *automobile*), *coon* (from *raccoon*), *cute* (from *acute*), *gas* (from *gasoline*), *lot* (from *allotment*), *most* (from *almost*), *pep* (from *pepper,* in the figurative sense), and *possum* (from *opossum*).

The extension of the meaning of words by their metaphorical use is too large a subject to be dealt with here. Its adequate treatment would demand a separate treatise. American slang is especially rich in metaphor, and many figurative uses of words that originated in slang have established within a short time a claim to a reputable place in the permanent vocabulary. Examples will be found on almost every page of my dictionary. The great variety of American metaphor may be illustrated by the large number of figurative terms associated with more or less discreditable political manœuvres; e.g. *colonizer, deal, filibuster, floater, fry the fat, graft, gumshoe, knife, log-rolling, peanut politics, pie counter, pipe-laying, plum-tree, pork barrel, pussyfoot, rake off, sawing wood, slaughter, slush fund, soft pedal, spoils, straddle, with a string,* and *take to the woods.*

There are other changes which are neither examples of processes that can be observed in all languages nor results of causes associated with the history of the American people. It would perhaps be too much to say that they spring from peculiarities of the American character, but at any rate they illustrate certain popular tendencies that are especially noticeable in the United States. Mr. Christopher Morley has come nearest to a precise account of them in referring to them as illustrations of 'temperamental discrepancy'. One may observe in America a tendency to magnify an office by the use of complimentary terms—the tendency, especially common in democratic countries, to give everybody a measure of distinction. In the United States no exceptional eminence is implied by the term *Solon,* which in the vocabulary of some newspapers is no more than a synonym for *Congressman. Judge* does not necessarily carry with it in America the dignified associations it possesses in England. The title is often given to a police-court magistrate. This peculiarity, by the way, sometimes leads to misunderstandings. In September, 1935, an inordinate significance was attached in Berlin to certain comments on the Nazi régime made by a Brooklyn magistrate whom the cablegrams described as a judge. Even more important is the divergence between the English and American uses of *jurist,* which is not restricted in the United States to the meaning of an expert in the science of law. It is commonly applied to any one who has obtained the qualifications required for legal practice. In one instance, at least, this difference had serious consequences. When, after refusing arbitration, the United States consented to refer the Alaskan Boundary dispute to a Joint Commission consisting of three American and three British representatives, it was provided by the treaty that this tribunal should consist of 'impartial jurists of repute'. Two of those chosen by the United States were admittedly jurists in no other sense than that they had been admitted to the Bar. They were not, as were the British representatives, authorities on questions of law, and even their active careers had been in politics rather than in legal practice. The title *president,* too, decorates in America many a man who in England would have to be content with a more commonplace designation. It is the commonly accepted term for the head of any railway, bank, or almost any other kind of business organization. One may come across references in the newspapers to the president of a labour union, of a baseball league, or of an association of pushcart men (i.e. costermongers). In the business world, again, *executive* is the name given to an official of a firm whose functions in England would be indicated by *manager*. In American newspaper offices, a member of the staff who is in charge of a single feature or department is dignified by the title of *editor*. This practice is being introduced into English journalism, but not without protest. In the life of C. P. Scott of the *Manchester Guardian* we are told that he strongly objected to it, and that when a list of all the editors on a great New York daily was read out to him he was much amused, and remarked: 'I wonder what on earth they all find to do.' The term *contributing editor* has even been invented to glorify the functions of a person who edits nothing but has merely been engaged to contribute articles or correspondence. An American *professor* may not be the occupant of a chair at a college or university. He may be the principal of a secondary school.

Akin to this tendency is the marked preference of American taste for the grandiloquent. A fine-sounding word, especially if it has a touch of the classical or pseudo-classical about it, is preferred to a commonplace synonym. As *The Times Literary Supplement* has happily put it, 'Things are commonly dignified in America by the grandest term they will bear.' Many illustrations of this preference may be described as examples of what H. W. Fowler calls 'anti-Saxonism'. Thus *automobile* takes the place of *motor-car*, *chiropodist's knife* of *corn-knife*, *commutation ticket* of *season ticket*, *cuspidor* of *spittoon*, *data* of *facts*, *elevator* of *lift*, *expectorate* of *spit* (cited by H. W. Fowler as an example of 'Genteelism'), *faucet* of *tap*, *graduate* of *complete a school course*, *intermission* of *break* (at school), *intersection* of *street-crossing*, *janitor* of *caretaker*, *locomotive* of *engine*, *mucilage* of *gum*, *making a reservation* of *booking a room*, *schedule* of *time-table*, *semi-annual* of *half-yearly*, *stenographer* of *shorthand-writer*, and *vacation* of *holiday*. Similarly *auditorium*, *antagonize*, *operate*, and *proposition* have a vogue in America that goes far beyond their deserts. Miss Vera Brittain, recounting her experiences on a lecture tour in the United States, notes that the questions put by members of the audience at the close of an address are elevated to the dignity of a *forum*.[1]

In mitigation of this indictment Americans may plead that they prefer *baby carriage* to *perambulator* and *draft* to *conscription*. They may also call attention to the effect upon their vocabulary of the importance attached to the headline in American journalism. A short word is much easier than a long one to manipulate in a small space. Accordingly, the member of a newspaper staff who is responsible

[1] *Atlantic Monthly*, June, 1935.

for writing the headlines prefers *ban* to *prohibit* or *prohibition*, *cop* to *policeman*, *crash* to *collision*, *cut* to *reduction*, *foe* to *enemy*, *gems* to *jewels*, *hit*, *rap*, or *score* to *criticize*, *jobless* to *unemployed*, *kin* to *relatives*, *nab* to *arrest*, *probe* or *quiz* to *investigation*, *sleuth* to *detective*, *sue* to *prosecute*, *thug* to *highwayman*, *troth* to *engagement*, and *wed* to *marry*. It will be noted that in some of these instances the demand for brevity has led to the revival of a word that in normal use had become, or was becoming, archaic. For a similar reason the writer of headlines suppresses articles and auxiliary verbs wherever possible. He also prefers the present tense to the past and the active voice to the passive. As newspaper headlines are more widely read in America than anything else that appears in print, their style cannot be without influence on popular literary usage.

In the case of a large number of words there is no obvious explanation of the difference between their English and their American use. It would be possible to compile a long list of words which denote in the United States something entirely different from what they signify in this country, but whose change of meaning cannot be attributed to any definitely known cause. How has it come about, for instance, that *biscuit*, *boot*, *muslin*, and *ruby type* have suffered such radical changes in meaning through crossing the Atlantic? The American preference for a certain term over a synonym more usually employed in England is equally mysterious in a large number of instances. Why has American practice decided in favour of *clipping bureau* rather than *press-cutting agency*, or *white-collar worker* rather than *black-coated worker*, or *guard* rather than *warder*, or *silent partner* rather than *sleeping partner*? It is possible, of course, that future research into the history of American English may throw light on such problems, but at present any attempt to solve them must be mere guess-work.

It is unnecessary to deal at length with the additions that America has made to the vocabulary by the coinage of new words or new compounds. This subject has already been treated by Sir William Craigie in No. XXVII of the S.P.E. Tracts. One may supplement what he has there said, however, by remarking that American writers, of all grades, habitually exercise much greater freedom than English writers in the creation of new words, even when words that would precisely express their meaning are already at their service. Prof. Brander Matthews[1] says that *indorsation* is not an Americanism but an Edisonism. That is perfectly true, but the tendency illustrated by Edison's practice of the art of invention outside his normal field of experiment may itself not unfairly be

[1] *Parts of Speech*, p. 104.

called an Americanism. Even in so distinguished a writer as William Dean Howells we may find *chasmally, knowledgefully, replylessly,* and *indigeneity.* University professors and other persons of literary or academic reputation have been responsible for such coinages as *inhabitancy, civilizationdom, inspirator,* to *intervent, areal, seasonality,* and *relishingly.* Americans seem especially addicted to the creation, or at any rate the use, of unnecessary words in *-ment.* With *abolition* ready to hand, *abolishment* is surely a superfluity, but it may frequently be encountered in American publications. One may also meet such words as *arousement, bequeathment, consolement, demolishment, denouncement, denotement, devotement, extinguishment, lavishment, pertainment,* and *revealment.*

So far we have been considering divergences that might be set down under the general heading of Vocabulary. It remains to note differences in grammatical usage. The definite article is often omitted in America after *all* in cases where it would be considered necessary in England. We say 'all day' and 'all night'. In America they say also 'all morning', 'all week', and 'all summer'. Another type of omission is illustrated in 'day before yesterday', 'day after to-morrow', and 'month after next'. There is a general tendency, too, to omit either the definite or the indefinite article where the omission can result in no ambiguity or misunderstanding. Thus, a notice in a Washington street-car runs: 'Motorman's duties require his full attention. He is not allowed to talk to you while car is in motion.' The following examples are taken from reputable historical works by university professors. 'That he kept these divergent elements together is indication of the President's greatness.' 'Sight of better implements filled the Indians with amazement.' 'Substitution of iron for wood hastened the decline of the sailing vessel.' 'Size, shape and position of Asiatic countries all combine to produce climatic variations.' A difference in the order of words may be noted in the use of the indefinite article. An American says 'a half dozen' or 'a half hour', whereas an Englishman says 'half a dozen' or 'half an hour'.

In America the mark of the plural may be added to several nouns which do not take it in England; e.g. *accommodations, beets, buckwheats, buntings* (in the sense of *flags*), *candies, cramps,* and *doggerels.* On the other hand, *innings,* when used with the singular meaning, appears as *inning.* The question of certain Latin plurals deserves notice. In England *agenda* is commonly treated as a singular, being regarded as virtually a collective term, equivalent to *list of business.* It is probably for a similar reason that a catalogue, issued in the autumn of 1935 by one of the leading American university presses, mentions, as one of the merits of a certain book, that it contains *an invaluable addenda*. These appendices appear to be regarded as a group. The same consideration, however, is scarcely applicable to the occasional American use of *strata*, and the habitual American use of *data*, as singular nouns. A peculiar use of the plural form is illustrated in 'The operatic tenor Campanini was engaged to sing mornings', and 'A niece of theirs had earned her way through College by waiting on the Atkins-Smythes' table, summers'. This usage is said to be a relic of the old adverbial genitive.

In his presidential address to an educational conference several years ago Sir Henry Hadow warned his hearers against the adjectival use of substantives, as in such newspaper headlines as 'Election Returns' and 'Reparations Expert'. This practice is far more common in America than in England. For example, there was published in 1935 a volume in which the problems of American secondary education were discussed by several writers who hold influential positions in American schools and colleges. In this book we find such expressions as *neighborhood projects, music experiences, language usage, shop activities, teacher effort, teacher guidance, pupil activities, pupil use, pupil participation, pupil co-operation, child command, child guidance, tool subjects,* and *tool activities.* This fashion of writing often involves ambiguity. In *teacher guidance* is the teacher the person who guides or the person who is guided? The context shows that the former meaning is intended. Precisely the same idea, however, is expressed in another passage of the same book by *child guidance. Child command,* on the other hand, has nothing to do with giving orders to children. The complete phrase runs: 'To give child command over important tools.' In other books by reputable American authors I have come across *weevil damage* (damage by weevils), *Hoover agitation* (agitation carried on by Mr. Hoover), *employee morale* (the morale of employees), *employee ownership* (ownership by employees), *owner farms, employer responsibility, energy resources,* and *vessel excellence.* The following sentences occur in articles appearing in a single issue of the *Atlantic Monthly* (October 1935): 'The fallacy of this theory that consumer spending will cure unemployment.' 'Corporate profits flow from consumer satisfaction and public goodwill.' 'Consumer preference in automobile styling is carefully studied.' 'There has been little consumer encouragement to fundamental improvement.'

In the conjugation of verbs certain forms now obsolete in England still persist in America, notably *dove* (from *dive*), *gotten* (which survives in England in the compounds *begotten* and *forgotten* and in the technical vocabulary of mining), *proven,* and *stricken.* In some points American usage differs from English as regards the use of auxiliaries. There is an ellipsis of the verb *to be* after *order* and other verbs with a kindred meaning. For example: 'The work on the frigates had progressed so far that it was ordered completed.' 'Committee chairmen desire a meeting called.' 'As soon as his ballot was announced voted, Hearst left the shop hurriedly.' The use of *do* as an auxiliary with *have* is frequent in America in instances where it would not be permitted by English idiom. According to Dr. H. Bradley, 'the use of the auxiliary *do* is correct English only when *have* expresses something occasional or habitual, not when the object is a permanent possession or attribute. It is permissible to say, "Do you have breakfast at eight?" or "We do not have many visitors", but not "Does she have blue eyes" or "He did not have a good character".'[1] This distinction is obliterated in America; e.g. 'Her later works do not have the charming spontaneity of her romances of the Tennessee mountains.' The *Springfield Republican*, in reviewing Professor G. P. Krapp's work, *The English Language in America*, headed its article, 'Does America Have a Language of Its Own?'. Another American peculiarity in the use of auxiliaries is the preference—not general, but common enough to deserve noting—of *would better* over *had better*; e.g. 'If this be our national genius, we would better accept it with all its limitations.'

A few verbs are used in America in a different construction from that which is idiomatic in England. Thus, *aim*, in the figurative sense, is followed (according to a usage now obsolete in England) by *to* with the infinitive instead of *at* with the gerund. Thus, 'It aims to provide a brief introduction to Mohammedan law.' Here the English usage would be 'aims at providing'. Again, to *charge that* is a locution common in America. In England a man may be charged with having committed an offence. In America one may charge that he committed an offence.

The adverb, on the whole, plays a more important part in America than in England. It is frequently used to intensify verbs which, one might suppose, could do very well without its aid. Thus we find *beat up*, *check up*, *close* or *shut down*, *figure out*, *give out* (an interview), *lose out*, *rest up*, *start in* or *out*, *try out*, *watch out*, and *win out*. In some instances, e.g. *try out*, this is a revival of good Elizabethan English.

This use of adverbs whose function is merely intensive must be distinguished from the addition of an adverb that entirely alters the meaning of a verb; e.g. *call down*, *count out*, *get away* (*with*), *get behind*, *get there*, *go out*, *knock down*, *lay off*, *let up*, *pass up*, *put*

[1] *The Making of English*, p. 71.

across or *over*, *round up*, *slip up*, *stop by*, *off*, or *over*, *take in*, *throw down*, *turn down*, and *walk out*. These are examples of a distinctive feature of American idiom—the preference of a combination of verb and adverb to a single verb or to a more roundabout expression. Thus, we have *go out* for *collapse*, *throw down* and *turn down* for *reject*, *pass up* for *decline*, *let up* for *desist*, and *slip up* for *err*, while *put across* is equivalent to *secure the adoption of* and *stop off* to *break one's journey*. Sometimes the difference lies in the use of a different adverb, as *come out* for *come off*, *fill out* for *fill up*, *get by* for *get through*, *melt up* for *melt down*, and *take out* for *take in* (to dinner); sometimes in the use of a different verb, as *crowd out* for *drive out* and *fetch up* for *finish up*; and sometimes in the use of both a different verb and a different adverb, as *come by* for *look in*. Such instances as *pass up* for *decline* and *turn down* for *reject* go some way to counterbalance that American preference for the Latin word which was noted on a previous page. The advantage of the American idiom is that it preserves the vividness of the metaphor, while in the English idiom one has almost come to forget that the term employed involves any metaphor at all.

It is sometimes alleged that in America prepositions are employed to a greater extent than in England. Such examples as *fall for*, *stand for*, *up against*, and *up to* are frequently cited as illustrations, but it is difficult to see how they exhibit a greater fondness for prepositions than their English synonyms *be captivated by*, *be responsible for*, *confronted with*, and *incumbent on*. There are, it is true, a few instances in which an unnecessary preposition may occasionally be found in American speech or writing, e.g. *all of*, *feel of*, *off of*, *remember of*, *smell of*, and *visit with*. Most of these are survivals of an old partitive genitive. On the other hand, so many prepositions are eliminated by the American use of certain intransitive verbs as transitives (see p. xxi) that one may reasonably doubt whether prepositions are actually more frequently used in America than in England.

In the matter of prepositions the real difference between English and American idiom lies in the choice of the preposition to use in certain connexions. Thus we find sales *at* (not *by*) auction and *at* (not *by*) retail, imprisonment *at* (not *with*) hard labour, to name *for* (not *after*), the worst accident *in* (not *for*) years, to want *of* (not *with*), five minutes *of* (not *to*) or *after* (not *past*) three, *on* (not *at*) hand, a new lease *on* (not *of*) life, a monopoly *on* (not *of*), taking notes *on* (not *of*), the man *on* (not *in*) the street, statistics *on* (not *about*), playing *on* (not *in*) the eleven, the laugh was *on* (not *against*) him, and all there is *to* (not *about*) it. When an American takes a railway journey he speaks of himself as *on* the train, not *in* it. Both expressions may doubtless be defended, but there is something to be said for the suggestion some one has offered, that being in a train is safer, more comfortable, and less draughty than being on a train. The explanation of the American use of *in, with,* and *among* after *belong,* which in England is invariably followed by *to,* seems to be that *belong* may be used in America in a sense unknown in England. On the whole, one may perhaps say that an American writer tends to use prepositions more loosely than an English writer. He seems sometimes to catch up the first one that occurs to him, whether it fits the case precisely or not. Thus, 'A great aversion *of* anything that may be called a drug.' 'An investigation *into* the status of the teaching of almost all subjects.' 'New tests *on* the molasses-arsenate treatment.' 'I apologized for asking for impressions *on* America.' 'The author wishes to express his appreciation *for* the aid received.' 'The explanation *for* the marked drop in the Pacific cargoes.' 'The similarity of his fundamental ideas *with* those of Adam Smith.'

Is the divergence between American and English usage increasing or diminishing? That question is difficult to answer owing to the impossibility of devising a conclusive test. One's general impression, however, is that the usage of the leading American writers of the period of Lowell and Holmes was more closely akin to that of the English writers of their day than is that of the twentieth-century American writers to their contemporaries in England. English readers to-day have greater need of a glossary for Theodore Dreiser than their fathers or grandfathers had for Nathaniel Hawthorne. Possibly the ambition of so many American writers of the present generation to emancipate themselves from Old World models has something to do with this.

On the other hand, there cannot be the slightest doubt that the naturalization of American usage in England, especially in the matter of vocabulary, is a process that never slackens. It can be noted with respect to several of the features of American English to which attention has been called in previous pages. (1) The use of adverbs to intensify the meaning of verbs—e.g. *close down, test out*—has made rapid headway among English writers and speakers since the beginning of the present century. (2) There is also an increasing tendency to adopt those combinations of verb and adverb which Americans prefer to a single verb or to a more roundabout expression, e.g. *turn down* rather than *reject,* and *put across* rather than *secure the adoption of.* (3) Those sections of the English daily press which have been becoming more and more Americanized in other respects are now following the American example in the choice of short words for headlines. (4) Certain uses of familiar words, which at the beginning of the century (or, at the outside, fifty years ago) were peculiar to the United States, are now either completely naturalized in this country or evidently on the way to naturalization. Numerous examples will be found by noting the words to which daggers are prefixed in my Dictionary. (5) Many words and locutions invented in America find their way, sooner or later, into everyday speech and writing in England. This is by no means a recent phenomenon. Generation after generation, English purists have protested against the admission of these aliens, but their demands for the enforcement of an embargo on them have usually been in vain. To-day many of these importations have become so thoroughly incorporated in the language that few of us are aware that they are actually American coinages. Every one recognizes, of course, that such terms as *banjo, blizzard, bogus, bunkum,* and *lynch law* came to us from across the Atlantic, but it would surprise most Englishmen to be told that they owe to America *belittle, boarding-house, business man, governmental, graveyard, hurricane deck, law-abiding, lengthy, overcoat, telegram,* and *whole-souled.*

If we ask what are the principal causes of the adoption in England of linguistic usages originating in America, the answer commonly given is that it has been mainly due, in recent years, to the influence of the 'captions' of American silent films and the speech of American talkies. These, no doubt, have had a widespread effect, but it is easily possible to exaggerate their importance. If we look outside the cinema for an explanation, we shall find it, in part, in the increasing attention that is paid in England to American books and magazines. It is almost impossible for any one who does much reading in American publications to escape altogether the influence of this literary environment.

A still greater contributory cause is to be found in the fact that nowadays so many members of the staffs of English newspapers are either Americans or English journalists who have spent several years in the practice of their profession in the United States. Without any deliberate intention to modify English idiom they naturally use in their own writing expressions to which they have become accustomed in America, and thus make them familiar to a multitude of English readers. It is through the daily press that most neologisms are introduced to the English public. The rate of naturalization varies greatly. Sometimes the process takes a long while. For instance, in the year 1818 there was an immense fall of cliff between Shanklin and Ventnor in the Isle of Wight. At the time, in accordance with normal English usage, this was called a *landslip,* and the place where the fall occurred bears the name of The Landslip to this day. Similar falls, not many miles away, in 1928 and 1935 were described in most newspaper reports as *landslides*. The American term, however, has not yet become completely naturalized here, for the most recent English encyclopaedias, in their geological articles, still hold to *landslip*. On the other hand, the adoption of the Americanism *cut* in the sense of *reduction* took place almost overnight in connexion with the financial crisis of 1931.

In spite of this process of naturalization, the English spoken and written in America remains, and will remain, different in many respects from that spoken and written in England. Many distinctive American usages are, in their nature, unsuitable for export. All the while, too, American ingenuity is adding to the list. While one Americanism is on its journey across the Atlantic, another is springing out of the fertile linguistic soil of the Middle West to restore the balance. These differences, however, are far from making the speech of America a new and independent language. They are no more than variations of the English theme. At times their diversity is so great that it is hard to recognize the original tune, and some of us may resent them as distortions of it. But after all, the fact that the English tongue shows itself capable of being adapted to so many novel purposes, while losing none of its dominant characteristics, may be regarded as a welcome evidence of its flexibility and vitality.

ABBREVIATIONS

in addition to those in ordinary use

abbrev.	abbreviate(d), abbreviation(s)	**infin.**	infinitive
acc.	according	**intrans.**	intransitive(ly)
adj.	adjective, adjectival	**lit.**	literal(ly), literature
adv.	adverb(ial)	**metaph.**	metaphor(ical)
advt.	advertisement	**mod.**	modern
Am.	America(n)	**neg.**	negative
attrib.	attributive(ly)	**O.E.D.**	Oxford English Dictionary
autobiog.	autobiography	**obs.**	obsolete
betw.	between	**orig.**	original(ly)
biog.	biography	**pass.**	passive
colloq.	colloquial(ly)	**plur.**	plural
conj.	conjunction	**polit.**	politics, political
Dem.	Democrat(ic)	**pref.**	preface, prefix
dial.	dialect(s), dialectal	**prep.**	preposition
dict.	dictionary	**Pres.**	President
eccl.	ecclesiastical	**pres.**	present
encycl.	encyclopaedia	**refl.**	reflexive
Eng.	England, English	**Rep.**	Republican
equiv.	equivalent	**sci.**	science(s)
esp.	especially	**sing.**	singular
etym.	etymology	**soc.**	social
exc.	except	**spec.**	specific(ally)
fig.	figurative(ly)	**suppl.**	supplement
fut.	future	**trans.**	transitive(ly)
hist.	history	**vocab.**	vocabulary
indef.	indefinite	**=**	is equivalent to

† denotes that the word or usage thus marked is apparently becoming naturalized in England.

†† denotes that the word or usage thus marked has become naturalized in England since the beginning of the present century.

SMALL CAPS: the printing of a word in small capitals indicates that further information will be found under that heading.

A Dictionary of

AMERICAN USAGE

A. Am. *A No.* 1 = Eng. *A.* 1.
'Confession has come to be reckoned A No. 1 as a fad among certain soul throbbers.'

aboard. In Am. this word has lost its exclusively nautical flavour. When a train is starting, 'All aboard!' = Eng. 'Take your seats, please!' 'She got a seat in one of the cars, and, just as the train was to pull out, her husband came running along and climbed aboard.' 'When the morning train rattled up to the Marietta station, the McAdoo family climbed aboard' (W. G. McADOO, *Crowded Years*, 7). See BOARD.

academy. The current uses of the word in Great Britain are (1) a society for cultivating art, literature, &c.; e.g. the Royal Academy, the British Academy, the Royal Scottish Academy, the Royal Academy of Music; (2) a training school for army officers, as the Royal Military Academy, Woolwich; and (3) in Scotland, a day school of high school rank; e.g. the Edinburgh Academy, the Glasgow Academy. (Its use to denote a pretentious private school, such as that attended by Becky Sharp, is now practically obs.) Two of these uses are paralleled in Am.: (1) in the Am. Academy of Arts and Letters, the National Academy of Design, and the National Academy of Sciences; and (2) in the U.S. Military Academy at West Point and the U.S. Naval Academy at Annapolis. As a secondary school, however, the academy in Am. differs from the Edinburgh Academy in being mainly a boarding school. Many of its best-known examples were established in Revolutionary or pre-Revolutionary times.

The name is rarely given to a school of recent foundation.

In addition to West Point there are in Am. many so-called *military academies* whose character is likely to be misunderstood in Eng. as they are private institutions and do not always aim at preparing their pupils for a military career. Their assumption of the term *military* means simply that they are conducted in a military way. The students wear uniforms and are organized in companies, with captains, sergeants, &c. Such schools lay special stress upon discipline and are accordingly in favour with the parents of boys who are difficult to manage at home. Here are significant extracts from advts. of various military academies in a recent issue of the *Atlantic Monthly*. 'One of California's finest private schools.' 'Superb disciplinary training equaled by academic excellence. Prepares thoroughly for all colleges and for citizenship.' 'The American Rugby.' 'Nationally recognized for progressive educational methods, college preparation and stalwart character training.' Lincoln Steffens tells us in his Autobiog. (i. 102) that his father took him away from the grammar school and sent him to 'a private school, the military academy at San Mateo', because he seemed to need a school where there was enough discipline to compel him to work. He was then about 15 years old.

accent. In Eng. (see H. W. Fowler's *Modern English Usage*) the verb *accent* is commonly used in the literal sense, i.e. sound or write with an accent, while *accentuate* is preferred in fig. senses. This distinction is **not**

always observed in Am. 'This little group accented every happy feature of Indian life.' 'Lack of money accents every other distress' (RUTH HALL, Pine Grove House, 272). 'Though occasional cities were to be found in the Great West and the South, their existence merely accented the general rural character of the civilization which encompassed them' (Prof. A. M. SCHLESINGER, The Rise of the City, 57).

accession. Books added to a library are technically called *accessions* to it. The noun has given rise in Am. to a verb *accession*, to denote the act of entering a book on a list of such additions. 'Material received by the Smithsonian through its own exchanges is first accessioned there' (Report of Librarian of Congress). 'He sometimes used to work in that library accessioning books, as a way of earning pocket-money' (CHRISTOPHER MORLEY, John Mistletoe, 22).

acclimate. In Am. the form *acclimate*, derived from the French *acclimater*, is preferred to *acclimatize*, which is now usual in Eng. (It is accented on the first and last syllables.) 'Most of the teachers have become acclimated and used to life in the Philippines.' 'Fifteen Head of Fresh Country and Acclimated Horses' (Advt.). 'Milnes's social method was the breakfast, and nothing could be more agreeable in England; we cannot acclimate it here' (JULIAN HAWTHORNE, Hawthorne and his Circle, 218).

Hence, Am. *acclimation* = Eng. *acclimatization*. 'The life of a poor girl art student in the Latin quarter of Paris during the winter is not very comfortable. Acclimation is a long process there.'

accommodation. The plur., *accommodations*, though used by Defoe, Boswell, and Jane Austen, is now unknown in Eng. but is still common in Am. in many senses of the word. 'Mr. Walter's plan was to build out the east front and incidentally to provide additional office accommodations.' 'If it does not buy goods, it must buy services—that is, freights, insurance, tourists' accommodations, &c.' 'In at least two states it is forbidden by law to sell Pullman accommodations to Negroes' (R. R. MOTON, What the Negro Thinks, 75). 'In Liverpool, luckily I secured accommodations at the Adelphi Hotel. . . . Col. Stair had secured accommodations for me on the "Belgic"' (Dr. FRANKLIN H. MARTIN, The Joy of Living, ii. 465). 'No expenditure of Treasury funds means so much for national welfare as the contributions for postal accommodations' (C. KELLY, U.S. Postal Policy, 235). 'This bank offered few accommodations outside the immediate vicinity. Its capital was subscribed in large part by local merchants, and this fact caused the directors to take care of their requests in preference to those of others' (G. T. STARNES, 60 Years of Branch Banking in Virginia, 23).

An *accommodation train*, in Am., is a train that carries both passengers and goods, and stops at all, or nearly all, the stations on its route. 'The care to keep out the air of the tunnel appears to be greater upon the express trains than it is upon accommodation trains.' R. DE BARY (Land of Promise, 63) explains that this kind of train earns its name by 'obliging all the world it meets upon the journey'.

account. In Am. *of no account* is often abbrev. to *no account*, which then becomes a hyphenated adj., in the sense of *valueless*, *worthless*. 'To-day she throws aside the old-time no-account steed, and insists on a horse that is good looking.' 'What no-account characterless people do in these concerns does not matter so much, because their example carries little weight.'

acquainted need not, in Am. colloq. use, be followed by *with* and mention of the persons whose acquaintance is made. Thus, the writer of an account of the Chicago Rotary Club refers to the difficulty, in a club with a large membership, of 'getting new members acquainted'. What he means is the difficulty of making them feel at home by becoming acquainted with their fellow members. He similarly remarks that a new member feels 'lost' if his sponsors do not assume responsibility 'for getting him acquainted'.

††across. The Am. expression *put across* is said to have been borrowed from the vocab. of the stage; e.g. 'Only action can get across the footlights to the girl with the gumdrop' (F. J. STIMSON, My U.S. 153). Thus *put across = secure the adoption of, pass off*. 'Every one of them admitted that only fear of unions had enabled them to put these measures across with directors and stockholders' (NORMAN THOMAS, America's Way Out, 252). 'The wisest politician is one who knows when to yield or appeal, what he can "put across", what the marginal voters necessary to his triumph are thinking and feeling' (C. A. and W. BEARD, The Am. Leviathan, 107). 'The adventitious aids which religion must call to its service to put its messages across' (J. T. FLYNN, God's Gold, 397).

adjunct is spec. used in Am. in the title *adjunct professor*, which denotes the holder of an academic post slightly inferior in rank to a full professorship. 'As a reward my title was advanced to adjunct professor' (Prof. M. PUPIN, From Immigrant to Inventor, 291). 'The next year he was made adjunct professor and in 1857 he was appointed professor of the Eng. language' (Dict. Am. Biog. xii. 269). See ASSOCIATE.

administrate. Where *administer* would be used in Eng., *administrate* is sometimes preferred in Am. The latter word is so rarely used in Eng. that it is not even mentioned in the *Shorter O.E.D.* The *O.E.D.*, whose latest example is dated 1855, describes it as a by-form of *administer*, but only when followed by such words as *sacrament, oath, medicine*. In Am., as the following quotations show, it may have the meaning of *manage, control*. 'The Dominican commission to administrate the debts of the island.' 'The expenses of administrating the land grant had been enormous' (Prof. J. B. HEDGES, Henry Villard and the Railways of the North West, 10). 'Several weeks later he handed me a full accounting of some small funds which he had been hoarding and administrating for the department' (Prof. A. G. KELLER, Reminiscences of William Graham Sumner, 108).

administration. In Eng. what is now called the *Government* was once known as the *Administration*. (The *O.E.D.* gives quotations in this sense dated 1731, 1783, 1790, and 1840.) The latter word is still in occasional use among writers and speakers on public questions, but the man in the street nowadays would not know what you meant if you asked him whether he was for or against the Administration. The earlier practice has survived in Am., where the term is applied to the President and his Cabinet. Thus, one speaks of the MacDonald Government but of the Roosevelt Administration. An Am. college professor complained some years ago that when he announced a course of lectures on 'Administration' nobody knew what he meant. The word had so generally come to indicate the personnel of the executive department that its prior meaning, as denoting the art of conducting the business of government, had been forgotten. In his *Politics and Administration* Prof. F. J. Goodnow suggests that there is a reason why the Eng. ministry is called a government and the Am. an administration. 'For the one,' he says, 'through its control of Parliament makes as well as administers laws;

the other merely administers laws made by Congress. The one expresses as well as executes the will of the State; the other merely executes it.' Hence we find such compounds as *administration senator* and *administration journal*, meaning a senator and a journal supporting the administration of the day. Similarly, *administration measure*. 'The weak-minded President was prevailed upon to make the bill an administration measure, and to bring to its support the full power of that legalized bribery known as "patronage"' (U. SINCLAIR, Manassas, 83).

Ministry is not used in Am. as a synonym for *administration* in this sense. See CABINET.

admire is still occasionally used colloq. in Am. in the sense of *be pleased, very much like*, now obs. in Eng., exc. in dial. '"Well, gentlemen," said the sheriff, "I'll be all ready to start for the North Fork in 15 minutes, and I'd admire to have you all go along"' (ANDY ADAMS, The Outlet, 202).

admit. An Am. lawyer is not *called* to the bar but *admitted* to it. 'Bill 322 has been prompted by a sincere purpose to stiffen the test of qualification for admission to the bar.' 'In January, 1885, I was admitted to the bar at Chattanooga' (W. G. McADOO, Crowded Years, 40). 'He studied law and was admitted to the bar' (E. D. ADAMS and J. C. ALMACK, Hist. of U.S. 384).

adviser is a technical term at Harvard. J. Corbin, in a comparison of methods at Oxford and Harvard (An Am. at Oxford, 277), says of Harvard: 'A board of advisers has been established, each member of which is supposed to have a helpful care of 25 freshmen. . . . His first duty is to expound to his charges the mysteries of the elective system, and to help each student choose his courses. . . . When, as often happens, a proctor is also a freshman adviser,

he unites the two administrative duties of an Eng. tutor.'

affiliate and **affiliation** are rarely used fig. in Eng. except to denote the relationship of colleges to a university and of branch societies to a central society. In Am. they are rarely used except fig. 'I have not sought to find out the politics of a single one of you, and indeed as to the majority of you I have not the slightest idea what your political affiliations are' (Pres. THEODORE ROOSEVELT in a letter to the Panama Canal Commission). 'Few of the settlers affiliated with the Catholic Church' (Prof. A. E. MARTIN, Hist. of U.S. i. 270). 'Walter Page in the U.S. and Mr. Arthur J. Balfour in Great Britain were among those who seized the Venezuelan crisis of 1896 and the Spanish-Am. crisis of 1898 as events upon which to base strong affiliations between the two great Eng.-speaking peoples' (B. J. HENDRICK, The Earlier Life of Walter H. Page, 261). 'She found the South uncongenial; she did not understand or affiliate with its people' (MARIE VAN VORST, Amanda of the Mill, 115). In the last two examples the idea of a filial relationship seems to have been entirely superseded by that of association. Indeed, the Am. *affiliate* might frequently be represented in Eng. by *fraternize*. As the above examples show, it is followed by *with*, not *to*. It is sometimes trans. also. 'His views on government naturally affiliated him with the Federalists' (J. TRUSLOW ADAMS, Hist. of the Am. People to the Civil War, 188).

after. Maria Edgeworth (Mme de Fleury, c. 1) has: 'It was now half after four.' Nowadays, in Eng., exc. in a few dial., this would be 'half-past four'. In Am. *after* is still used in such connexions. 'About half after twelve the roof of the building fell in.' See OF.

agate. In Eng. used only as the

name of a precious stone. In Am., also the printer's term for the type, intermediate between nonpareil and pearl, known in Eng. as *ruby*. 'Rate $1.00 an agate line' (Advt.). 'The eye-ruining job of setting up a New Testament in agate with notes in pearl' (Dict. Am. Biog. vii. 528). See RUBY.

agent is used in Am. in certain combinations with meanings unknown in Eng. *Business agent*, which has only a general signification in Eng., is employed spec. in Am. 'Business agent is the title usually given to the general executive officer, formerly called the "walking delegate", who represents a local [trade] union or council in its daily business and whose work consists for the most part in enforcing union standards and verbal or written agreements with the employer' (Encycl. Soc. Sci. iii. 91). 'As a business agent he finds that he cannot go around denouncing the employers all the time: he must bargain with these employers every day' (P. BLANSHARD, Outline of the British Labor Movement, 132).

Am. *road agent* is a euphemistic term for a *highwayman*. 'It was thought he had considerable treasure on the stage, when, as a matter of fact, he had none. Road agents stepped out and stopped the team.' 'The combination of mountain solitudes and valuable freighter lines inevitably produced sets of "road-agents" or highwaymen' (A. NEVINS, The Emergence of Modern Am. 140).

Am. *station agent* = Eng. *station master*. 'Many of those who were already on the platforms demanded their money back. The station agents, who are not permitted to refund, issued "blockade tickets".' 'A belief that it is proper to tip waiters, taxicab drivers, and barbers, but under no circumstances station agents and ushers' (W. LIPPMANN, Public Opinion, 99). 'Himself a lover of things beautiful, he offered a prize annually to the station agent who should pro-

duce the most attractive grounds' (Dict. Am. Biog. x. 143).

Am. *ticket agent* = Eng. *booking clerk*. 'In some places ticket agents refused to sell to Negroes railroad tickets to any Northern point' (R. R. MOTON, What the Negro Thinks, 58).

See also CLAIM.

The Eng. *newsagent* is called in Am. a *newsdealer*. See NEWS.

†**aim.** In its fig. sense the verb *aim* is followed in Eng. by *at* with the gerund. Am. retains the usage, now obs. in Eng., exc. in dial., of following it by *to* with the infin. 'It aims to provide a brief introduction to Mohammedan law.' 'Johnson had aimed to settle down to the peaceful life of a small parish' (Prof. H. W. SCHNEIDER, The Puritan Mind, 171). 'Mr. and Mrs. Adams aimed to create a social centre for New Englanders' (The Education of Henry Adams, 101).

air. In Am., long before the days of aviation, *air line* was a term in common use. It denoted the shortest distance between two points; i.e. a *bee line*. 'The judge held that distance was to be measured by air line or "as the crow flies", not as the main traveled road leads.' 'As an air line the distance between the terminal ports of Sandy and Beaver canal was some 40 miles, but this stretch was increased to 60 by the necessity of following the watercourses and dodging hills' (H. CROLY, Life of M. A. Hanna, 30). Hence certain railways were commonly called *air lines* because of the directness of their routes. 'The public regards the purchase of the Seaboard Air Line as another serious step in the direction of railroad consolidation.' 'Thousands speculated without the slightest knowledge of the nature of the company upon whose fortunes they were relying, like the people who bought Seaboard Air Line under the impression that it was an aviation stock' (F. L. ALLEN, Only Yesterday, 315, in an account of the speculation craze of 1929).

††The Am. fig. term *hot air* corresponds to the Eng. *mere vapouring*. 'A prominent Dem. senator who always makes it a point to tell the truth whenever he says anything, and will not give out "hot air" interviews.' 'When the Negro has met with discriminations and with difficulties because of his race, he has invariably tended to get up more steam. When this steam has been rightly directed and controlled, it has become a great force in the upbuilding of the race. If, on the contrary, it merely spent itself in fruitless agitation and hot air, no good has come of it' (BOOKER WASHINGTON, My Larger Education, 4).

In Am. the compound *airplane* is invariably preferred to *aeroplane*. 'In 1903 the first flight of more than 500 feet was made by an airplane' (C. A. and M. R. BEARD, The Rise of Am. Civilization, ii. 754).

aisle is used in Eng., exc. in a few dial., only of a division of a church or of a passage betw. rows of pews. In Am. it may denote almost any kind of gangway, whether in a train (where it corresponds to the Eng. *corridor*), or a theatre, or a shop. In a report of a railway accident occurring at night, one reads that passengers 'were thrown from their berths into the aisles'. 'The British fashion of having railway compartments instead of an undivided car with a nice long aisle' (SINCLAIR LEWIS, Dodsworth, 57). A theatre-goer is described as 'sailing down the aisle just before the curtain rose for the matinee'. An Am. biog. sketch of H. G. Wells tells us that 'his mother possessed no greater ambition for her sons than the aisles of a draper's shop'.

alderman. The alderman in an Am. municipality differs in important respects from the Eng. alderman. In Eng. he is elected by the councillors, but in Am. by popular vote, as representative of some particular ward. In Eng. the aldermen sit with the councillors as members of a single body. In many Am. cities they constitute a separate body, known as the board of aldermen, which serves as an upper house of the municipal government. The Am. alderman usually possesses some judicial powers also.

all. In Am. usage *the* is often omitted where it would be required in Eng. after *all*. 'The senator has been troubled with lumbago all summer.' 'People who had waited all morning for the sun to appear.' 'I had written hard all morning' (E. POOLE, The Harbor, 221). 'Dick Pye would be there all week' (SINCLAIR LEWIS, Work of Art, 332). In Eng., however, one says 'all day' and 'all night'.

As though to compensate for this omission, *of* is inserted after *all* where it would be considered unnecessary in Eng. 'Nowadays all of the nations of the world are neighbors one to the other' (from an executive order issued by President THEODORE ROOSEVELT). 'All of Herrick's geese were swans' (T. B. ALDRICH, Ponkapog Papers, 169). 'We find all of these influences active in increasing the modern vocabulary' (J. B. GREENOUGH and G. L. KITTREDGE, Words and Their Ways, 23). 'There were insufficient Am. vessels to handle all of the traffic' (Dr. J. H. FREDERICK, Development of Am. Commerce, 77).

†Am. *all of* = Eng. *fully, as much as*. 'He could hire a bomber to do an ordinary routine job with a black-powder bomb for $100, but a risky job with a dynamite bomb might cost him all of $1,000' (F. L. ALLEN, Only Yesterday, 268).

Am. *all over* = Eng. *everywhere*. This is apparently an abbrev. of *all over the world, all over the place*. 'News Flashes From All Over' (Newspaper headline for a column of miscellaneous items). 'They were so delighted to see her, they never scolded her a bit, for they'd been out hunting all over for her.'

The expression *all the time* is idiomatic in Eng., as Mr. H. W. Fowler points out in his *Modern Eng. Usage*, only when the time in question is a definite period fixed by the context. In Am. it is a synonym for *always*. 'It solemnly and all the time supports the Rep. party.' 'First, last, and all the time' is a common political slogan.

See also AROUND.

alley, in the Eng. sense of a *narrow street*, is commonly represented in Am. by *alleyway*. Acc. to the *O.E.D.*, *alley* in Am. means a back-lane running parallel with a main street. Acc. to Dr. G. P. Krapp, in Am. *alley* commonly means 'a narrow driveway between two rows of houses upon which there are stables, &c., sometimes spoken of as a *back alley*' (Comprehensive Guide to Good Eng. 31). 'A little street, or alleyway, is called (in Mexico) a callejon.' 'Our side of the cab is quite cut off from the fireman's side by a swelling girth of boiler, which leaves an alleyway at right and left wide enough for a man's body' (C. MOFFETT, Careers of Danger, 382).

allow is sometimes used colloq. in Am. in the sense of *assert, declare, affirm*. 'Absalom Magoffin [an undertaker] would buttonhole you on the street and allow that, while he wasn't a doctor, he had had to cover up a good many of the doctor's mistakes in his time, and he didn't just like your symptoms' (G. H. LORIMER, Old Gorgon Graham, 38). Acc. to Wright's *Dialect Dict.* an approach to this meaning may be found in certain Eng. dialects, where it = *suppose*.

almost is used in Am. with the neg., where in Eng. one would say *scarcely* (or *hardly*) *any, scarcely* (or *hardly*) *ever*, &c. 'The Act went through Congress with almost no one appreciating its true significance' (Prof. N. W. STEPHENSON, Life of N. W. Aldrich, 189). 'One of those Patricks who are almost never called Pat' (S. O. JEWETT, The Queen's

Twin, 73). 'In this new outburst of municipal greed almost nothing escaped' (Prof. C. E. MERRIAM, Chicago, 60).

almshouse. 'In the U.S. this term denotes a public institution for indoor relief of the poor. This type of institution originated in Eng., where it is known as the *workhouse*; *almshouse* in Eng. refers to the private endowed home for aged indigents' (Encycl. of the Social Sciences, ii. 8). The same article adds that, while *almshouse* is the generic term in Am. for public institutions for poor relief, the actual names vary according to locality. Thus, although *almshouse* is the legal name in New Eng. and is fairly consistently found in the East and South, in Ohio it is *infirmary*, in Indiana *asylum*, and in the Middle West *poor house, poor farm, county farm,* or *county house*. See WORKHOUSE.

alternate. Used in Am. as a noun, in the sense of a duly accredited substitute for a delegate. In electing representatives to political or religious conventions it is customary to provide each member with an *alternate* to take his place in the event of his being unable to attend. The alternate does not fill any gap that happens to arise, but only that caused by the absence of the particular member for whom he is, so to speak, an understudy. While that member is present, the alternate may attend the sessions, but without the right to speak or vote. Thus, in a report of the General Assembly of the Presbyterian Church we read that 'nearly the entire body of commissioners, numbering 750, and their alternates of equal number, were present.' 'I knew that, as an alternate, I would not have a vote, but I would have a seat on the floor of the convention and be close to whatever happened' (W. G. MCADOO, Crowded Years, 37). *Substitute delegate* is the official term denoting a person appointed to attend the League of Nations Assembly on similar conditions.

From this use the word has come to have sometimes the general meaning of *substitute* or *alternative*, as when Prof. T. R. Lounsbury (The Standard of Pronunciation in English, 231) says that 'the pronunciation of the final *t* of *trait* . . . appeared as an alternate in the dictionary of Latham'.

aluminum. The name invariably given in Am. to the metal known in Eng. as *aluminium*. Acc. to the *O.E.D.* it was for some time current in Eng., but ultimately the termination *-ium* came to be preferred as harmonizing best with such other names of elements as potassium, magnesium, &c. 'Aluminum is a metal that combines strength and lightness.' 'The strange feather-weight metal called aluminum' (A. NEVINS, Life of Henry White, 17).

alumnus. In Eng. this word is rarely used, but in Am. it is the recognized term for a college graduate. 'Tuesday was alumni day at Yale, when hundreds of old graduates gathered in Alumni Hall to listen to the annual report.' 'All the leading citizens of the town are alumni of the college' (L. LEWISOHN, Up Stream, 99). 'Alumni of Cambridge were liberally represented among the clergy [originally settling in Massachusetts], together with a few from Oxford' (M. GRANT, Conquest of a Continent, 83). 'This attitude resulted in a devotion to the colleges and universities in Am. on the part of their alumni' (Prof. A. H. QUINN, The Soul of Am. 117). All these quotations would be quite un-English though not, perhaps, un-Scottish, for a periodical issued from St. Andrews is called an *Alumnus Chronicle*.

In Am. the term is also used of a school pupil who has completed his course. One may even come across a report of a reunion of the alumni of a Sunday school. 'A man, not an alumnus of the school, once gave his impression of a typical St. Paul's boy' (F. J. KINSMAN, Salve Mater, 20).

The feminine form *alumna* is equally common. 'He talked to the Radcliffe alumnae on Jan. 13' (E. C. MARTIN, Life of J. H. Choate, ii. 314). 'Those lean and spinster fowls who ran away from home, like ambitious young alumnae' (CHRISTOPHER MORLEY, John Mistletoe, 46). 'She was one of the members of the class of 1902 to return for the alumnae fete in June 1930' (R. W. BABSON, Washington and the Revolutionists, 89).

amalgamation is spec. used in Am. to denote the racial admixture of whites and Negroes. 'He is attempting to show the awfulness of amalgamation, and, like most Southern writers upon that subject, he assures you on the one side that the Negro is so far below the white that amalgamation is an unthinkable evil, and at the same time in many pages warns his countrymen that amalgamation is a positive danger.'

ambulance. The meaning of the Am. term *ambulance chaser* is evident from the following quotations. 'The receiver of one of the traction companies is leading a movement against the so-called "ambulance chasers", or lawyers who make a business of promoting damage suits against railroads and street railways on the basis of contingent fees, which run from 20 to 50 per cent. of the amount of damages sought to be recovered.' 'Six lawyers visited the home of a child run over and killed by an express wagon and importuned the parents for permission to bring suit for damages against the company. The body of the unfortunate child had hardly been brought to the house before the "ambulance chasers", as lawyers of this class are called, began to arrive.' 'A group of men, called "common law" lawyers, were accustomed to group themselves around the portals of St. Paul's Cathedral, somewhat in the manner of the ambulance chaser of the present day, to ask employment from any litigant who needed a lawyer' (Dr. J. M.

Beck, May it Please the Court, 112).

angel. The Am. terms *angel cake* and *angel food* do not mean ambrosia, but a kind of spongy confectionery made of flour, sugar, and whites of eggs. 'Angel cake, sponge cake, and ice-cream cake have conspired to relegate the seed cake to practical oblivion.' 'Angel food and sunshine cake, baked in pans made for the purpose, require a cool oven' (Mrs. Rorer's New Cook Book, 19).

Anglican means in Eng. *pertaining to the Church of England*, but in Am. it may mean *English*. Thus *Scribner's Mag.* describes Rhodes scholars from the Dominions as better prepared for Oxford than those from the U.S. inasmuch as they have been educated 'acc. to the Anglican tradition'. A character in one of Ruth Hall's novels 'cultivated a throaty voice which she flattered herself was Anglican'. 'In the United States a traveler may find at least three regions which are suitable abodes for country gentlemen in the strictly Anglican sense of the expression' (Prof. C. E. Cason, in Culture in the South, 490).

†**antagonize.** Though *antagonist* is quite common in Eng., *antagonize* is seldom used by good writers. In Am. it is in common use in the sense of *oppose*. In Eng., acc. to the *O.E.D.*, antagonizing forces must be of the same kind, but in Am. a person may antagonize an impersonal force. 'Dr. Bushnell antagonized theology and denied the rational possibility of it' (Prof. L. O. Brastow, Representative Modern Preachers, 148). It may also mean *alienate, provoke the opposition of*. 'Lincoln antagonized the radicals further by refusing to permit the enlistment of fugitive slaves' (Prof. A. E. Martin, Hist. of U.S. i. 717). 'He had antagonized his benefactor by opposing his views in reference to the conduct of the Civil War, and by other similar indiscre-

tions was making new enemies almost every day' (Marian Gouverneur, As I Remember, 247). 'Efficient though he was as a propagandist, Garrison had a talent for antagonizing even his supporters' (Dict. Am. Biog. vii. 170). See H. W. Fowler's discussion of this word in *Modern Eng. Usage*.

ante-bellum. Acc. to the *O.E.D.* Suppl., the term *ante-bellum*, when used in Eng., refers spec. to either the South African War or the European War. In Am. it refers to the Am. Civil War. 'The best pictures extant of Southern life in the ante-bellum days.' 'One day, when we were holding a meeting to secure funds for its erection, an old, ante-bellum colored man came a distance of 12 miles, and brought in his ox-cart a large hog' (Booker T. Washington, Up from Slavery, 140). 'I remember among these an accomplished gentleman, who worked in Am. in the anti-slavery cause, in ante-bellum days' (Dr. E. E. Hale, Lowell and his Friends, 138). 'He wears a black ante-bellum bow tie' (E. Wilson, The Am. Jitters, 23).

anxious. Am. *anxious seat* or *anxious bench* = Eng. *penitent form*. 'It was among the young men that Weld chiefly labored in the revivals, admonishing them at the anxious seat' (Prof. G. H. Barnes, The Anti-slavery Impulse, 13). The term has supplied Am. with a common metaphor; thus, *on the anxious seat = on tenterhooks.* 'All the men present were on the anxious seat, seeking to learn whether their new judge was "easy" or "tough".' 'They have enough formidable submarines to keep England on the anxious seat.'

any. In addition to its normal uses, *any* in Am. may mean *at all*, as also in certain Eng. dial. 'An interesting speech followed which did not help matters any.' 'It is doubtful if his present condition could be bettered any.' 'Costa did not mind this **any**'

(Dr. H. P. FAIRCHILD, Greek Immigration to U.S. 101). 'Sumner was abused enough, and we all knew it. It failed to hurt him any, in our eyes' (Prof. A. G. KELLER, Reminiscences of William Graham Sumner, 44).

††Am. *anyway* = Eng. *anyhow*, in the sense of *at any rate, in any case.* 'That is something gained, anyway.' 'Classical scholarship is not attainable anyway in the secondary school' (Prof. H. P. HANUS, A Modern School, 23). 'Anyway, they were learning the language' (The Education of Henry Adams, 76). 'The real distinction between the two is not of great importance anyway' (G. R. SHERRILL, Criminal Procedure in N. Carolina, 25). 'German representatives had to be in Geneva anyway to attend the sessions of the League' (W. LIPPMANN, The U.S. in World Affairs in 1932, 254).

apartment. In Eng. an *apartment* was once a suite of rooms. The *O.E.D.* quotes Evelyn, the diarist, as describing in 1641 his 'new lodgings' as 'a very handsome apartment'. Nowadays an *apartment* is in Eng. a single room, and the original sense of the word is expressed by the plur. Thus, landladies at the seaside advertise 'Apartments to Let'. The Am. *apartment* retains the earlier sense, and corresponds to the Eng. *flat*, while the Am. *apartment hotel* is what would be called in Eng. a *block of service flats*. 'The tendency toward co-operative living, whether it be shown in boarding-house, hotel, and apartment living, or in the community co-operative kitchen.' 'The apartment hunter now has the selection of two modes of a life; the everyday housekeeping apartment and the apartment hotel.' Accordingly, the Am. *apartment* and the French *appartement* mean the same thing. Prof. Félix Boillot, however, tells us (Le Vrai Ami du Traducteur, 52) that some French hotels are beginning to call a single room *un appartement*. This Anglicism,

he notes, usually carries with it a considerable inflation of the bill.

appeal. In Am. the verb *appeal* is trans. as well as intrans. This use is obs. in Eng., as may be inferred from the fact that the latest example of it given by the *O.E.D.* is dated 1590. 'They do not improve their position by undertaking to appeal the rebating case on various grounds.' 'Important suits are likely to be appealed the second time from the middle courts to the State Supreme Court' (Prof. A. B. HART, Actual Government, 160). 'Five times he appealed the case, always losing' (Dict. Am. Biog. vi. 531). 'These are the cases most often appealed to the Supreme Court' (G. R. SHERRILL, Criminal Procedure in N. Carolina, 3).

appearing. 'He is a very youthful appearing man.' 'An address by a very youthful appearing man of science' (MARK SULLIVAN, Our Times, iii. 290). 'As rough-appearing as her husband' (H. JUSTIN SMITH, Chicago, 27). This use of *appearing*, occasionally met with in Am., is unknown in Eng., where *looking* would be substituted.

†**appointive.** In Am. a post that is filled by appointment, in contrast with election, is described as *appointive*. 'High appointive posts under the federal government.' 'The Republicans bitterly resented Ellsworth's resignation [of the Chief Justiceship], which had snatched from their very grasp the highest of appointive offices' (Dict. Am. Biog. xii. 319).

appraiser. A spec. use of this word in Am. is as the technical term for a Customs officer who appraises the value of goods subject to duty. 'It falls to the appraiser's office in each port to examine the goods, to see that they correspond with the invoices in quantity and quality, and that they are stated at their true values. The appraiser's work is the most delicate in the whole system. By the act of

1890 was created a body of general appraisers. A board made up of three of these appraisers has a final decision on the value of imported goods: from them no appeal can be taken, either to the secretary of the treasury or to the courts' (Prof. A. B. Hart, Actual Government, 400).

appreciate. In Am. often directly followed by *that.* 'He appreciated that the existing laws, however sound in purpose, were working an economic injustice' (Prof. A. B. Darling, Public Papers of F. G. Newlands, i. 89). Acc. to Eng. idiom, this would be 'He appreciated the fact that'. 'I appreciate that, if this were a juridical question, these provisions would not be applicable' (J. M. Beck, May it Please the Court, 314).

appropriate. 'It is only a few years since the fact that a billion dollars had been appropriated by one Congress aroused the nation' (H. L. West, in the Forum, April 1904). No wonder that the country should be stirred, an Englishman might naturally reflect, if Congress stole so big a sum as that. His poor opinion of the honesty of Congressmen would be confirmed on finding Prof. R. T. Ely (The Evolution of Industrial Society, 317) expressing his 'doubt whether we shall ever again see a Congress appropriating so small a sum as 1,000 million dollars'. A correct understanding of what is meant, however, leaves Congress without a stain on its character. It had simply been voting public money for various public purposes. In Eng. *appropriate* and *appropriation* are sometimes used in the same sense, but only with an indication of the purpose to which the money is devoted. To *appropriate,* without such qualification, is to *take for oneself.*

The word *appropriation* is so commonly understood to mean a vote of money by Congress that it may even be used without any mention of Congress at all. Thus, in one of his annual reports, the Librarian of Congress says:

'The following table exhibits the appropriations and expenditures of the Library for the fiscal year.' Here *appropriations* practically = *income,* for it means the financial provision made by Congress for the upkeep of the Library. It was not the Library, but Congress, that appropriated this money in the Am. sense.

apt. 'When these reverend gentlemen appear at the bar of God, in company with Booker Washington, which of them will be the most apt to receive the golden crown?' 'The incident is not apt to be followed by international complications.' 'The disaster is apt to result in a system of inspection that will inspect.' In each of these instances an Eng. paper would have used *likely* instead of *apt.* In Eng. *apt* always suggests a general or habitual tendency. It is not used in a hypothetical prediction of what will happen in a particular case. Thus, an Englishman would say, 'I am apt to catch cold if I go out without my overcoat', but, 'I shall be likely to catch cold if I go out to-night without my overcoat'.

arbo(u)r. In every State of the Union, as well as in the District of Columbia, there is observed every year, either by Governor's proclamation or by law, an *Arbor Day,* distinguished by the planting of trees, esp. in connexion with schools. 'Arbor Day is being celebrated in the schools of Greater N.Y. to-day, as well as throughout the State. In the suburbs and at other schools where there is space about the buildings, trees were set out, or shrubs, where the space is limited. In the East Side and other congested districts, where there is no room for anything but the building and paved playgrounds, flower seeds were planted in window boxes, that the object of the day, the inculcation in the children's minds of a love for natural scenes and objects, might be furthered.' 'Arbor Day was first observed in Nebraska, on April 10, 1872, on which occasion more than 1,000,000 trees were planted' (World Alm. for 1933, 71). A similar celebration, bearing the same name, has since been adopted in South Australia.

arctic sometimes means in Am. a kind of overshoe, esp. suitable for wearing when snow is on the ground. It is mainly of rubber, but with a cloth top. 'The citizen who thought a big fall of snow was impending and went out to invest in a new pair of arctics.'

Argonauts. In Am. this name has been borrowed from classical legend to denote the adventurers who made their way to California during the gold rush of 1849. A book of Bret Harte's about them was entitled 'Tales of the Argonauts'. This use of the word was more appropriate than one might perhaps suppose, for at that time three of the routes to the goldfields from the Eastern States involved passages by water—one of them a voyage round the Horn, occupying from six to nine months. In more recent times the name has been given to the adventurers who sought for gold in the Klondike. It is in this sense that it is employed in the following passage: 'Taxing all available means of water transport northward, the argonauts braved incredible hardships presented by a frozen and forbidding country in order to reach the new El Dorado' (Prof. A. M. SCHLESINGER, The Rise of the City, 430).

armo(u)ry. In Eng., a *place where arms are stored*. In Am., also a place where arms are made, a *gun factory* or *gun foundry*. 'Nearly all local historians have given Gen. Washington the credit for the selection of the present site for the armory, but from the letters discovered it appears that he selected the town as a proper place for the making and storage of munitions of war, rather than to indicate the site of the plant.' 'He became superintendent of the armory of the

Providence Tool Co. In the course of his service he brought the manufacture of Springfield rifles to a high point of efficiency' (Dict. Am. Biog. ix. 286).

An Am. *armory* also serves the purposes of an Eng. *drill hall*. 'Allan discussed it one night with his cousin Jack, chancing to meet him coming home from the armory. He was on his way home from drill' (U. SINCLAIR, Manassas, 249). The word is often used in this sense in India.

army. It is important not to confuse the U.S. Army with the *Grand Army of the Republic* (or *Grand Army*), which is something entirely different. The latter is an organization of ex-soldiers who fought on the Union side in the Civil War. It has sometimes exerted great political influence. 'In every city or town where a Grand Army post is located, the veterans marched to the cemeteries and held memorial exercises.' 'Most politicians would as soon think of hara-kiri as offending the Grand Army by vetoing a pension bill.' 'The million or more soldiers who had fought for the Union, organized into the Grand Army of the Republic, became a political unit' (Prof. A. H. QUINN, The Soul of Am. 91). 'I never had a better time than in 1888 when the Grand Army of the Republic spent a week with us. There were 70,000 of them in Columbus that throbbing hot September' (JULIA B. FORAKER, I Would Live it Again, 111).

around. In Eng. *around*, as an adv., means *on every side, in every direction*, and, as a prep., *on all sides of, in every direction from*. In Am. it is also used where *round* would be used in Eng., as in 'The Little Church Around the Corner'.

Hence Am. *all-around* = Eng. *all-round*. 'The all-around lawyer still exists, but the most eminent lawyers are those who have specialized.' 'The most comprehensive and the best all-around Am. city school exhibit is undoubtedly that of N.Y.' 'The all-around experience which goes to make up the skilled journalist' (WILLIS J. ABBOT, Watching the World Go By, 41).

Another special Am. use is as an equivalent for *about*. 'Around 600,000 copies were sold' (Dict. Am. Biog. vi. 102). 'The convention adjourned around 4 o'clock' (W. G. McADOO, Crowded Years, 158).

ascension. In Eng. one speaks of a balloon *ascent*, but in Am. of a balloon *ascension*. 'The boy balloonist made an ascension this evening in spite of an injunction secured by his parents to restrain him.' 'On a certain Sunday afternoon there was to be a balloon ascension at the great pleasure park' (C. MOFFETT, Careers of Danger and Daring, 125). 'In the 1880's almost every circus that visited the little Southern towns made a big feature of a balloon ascension' (W. G. McADOO, Crowded Years, 521).

In other connexions also, *ascension* seems to be the Am. preference. 'The final steps which led to the wrecking of his party and the ascension to power of Woodrow Wilson' (H. F. PRINGLE, Theodore Roosevelt, 545).

aside. Am. *aside from* = Eng. *apart from, in addition to, except for.* 'Others aside from Mr. Markham might confess their indebtedness to certain appreciative reviewers.' 'Aside from a severe fright, Mr. Houghton was uninjured.' 'The Department is without information concerning the unsettled condition in Cuba, aside from press dispatches.' 'Aside from the wars in Europe which brought on wars in Am., the history of the colonies during the first part of the 18th century is uneventful' (Prof. H. E. BOURNE, The Teaching of History, 303). The Christian Endeavour Society unconsciously proclaimed its Am. origin by requiring from its members a pledge to take some part 'aside from singing' in every meeting.

Assembly is the name of the Lower House of the Legislature in several of the Am. States. A member of such a House is called an *Assemblyman.*

assignment is often used in Am. where *appointment* or *commission* would be used in Eng. 'He had the missionary instinct and went into the Presbyterian ministry, receiving assignments in various parts of the mining camp West.' 'His War assignments included official missions to Archangel and Vienna, service with the Peace Conference at Versailles, and the post-War famine-relief expedition to Moscow' (H. J. COOLIDGE and R. H. FORD, Archibald Cary Coolidge, viii). 'He persuaded her to write a life of Napoleon. Her researches had familiarized her with the background of the period, and she accepted the assignment' (Dr. C. C. REGIER, The Era of the Muckrakers, 122).

†The word is esp. used of a spec. task allotted to a newspaper reporter. 'The first "assignment" I ever had as a N.Y. reporter was to go to Delaware to see a woman whipped' (JULIAN RALPH, The Making of a Journalist, 126). 'One of his early assignments was to interview Coxey' (Dr. C. C. REGIER, op. cit. 147). 'After finishing his afternoon assignment and getting a hasty dinner, the reporter usually receives an evening assignment' (E. L. SHUMAN, Practical Journalism, 51).

In Am. colleges *assignment* denotes a course of reading or some other spec. piece of work that a student is instructed to carry out. 'Our present-day fashion of giving the undergraduates their assignments of reading in homeopathic doses.' 'College libraries, where young men, after they had read the assignments in the Puritan classics required by their innocent old tutors, discovered a totally different learning in the best Eng. authors of the day' (Prof. H. W. SCHNEIDER, The Puritan Mind, 158). 'Enough material is presented to form a complete course, although the references at the end of each chapter will be found useful for class assignments' (Dr. J. H. FREDERICK, The Development of Am. Commerce, pref.).

The term *assignment of wages* is peculiar to Am., and denotes a distinctively Am. practice, by which part of his future earnings is mortgaged, so to speak, by a working-man to a creditor. 'A grocer has advanced credit to a railway worker and has taken as security an assignment of the workman's future wages.' 'His office [the office of a money-lender] had a record of some 800 assignments of wages in one year, most of which are made by young, unmarried men.'

associate. Frequently applied in Am., esp. in the compounds *associate editor* and *associate professor*, to an official junior who is regarded as a colleague rather than a subordinate. It therefore denotes a higher status than that of an assistant. 'The board of trustees of the City College has divided the teaching force into five classes, as follows: Professors, associate professors, assistant professors, instructors, and tutors.' 'He will be called as Extraordinarius (reader or lecturer, as the Eng. would say, associate professor, as one would say in Am.) to Tübingen or Graz' (Dr. A. FLEXNER, Universities, 324). The succession of grades may be traced in some of the careers recorded in *Who's Who in Am.*; e.g. 'on editorial staff of St. Nicholas since 1873; assistant editor, 1878; associate editor, 1893–1905, and editor in chief since 1905.' See ADJUNCT.

at. The Am. jocose use of a superfluous *at* is illustrated in the following examples. 'The business world wants rest. It wants to know where it is at.' 'Suppose a subway should happen to be filled with the requisite combination of gas and air for an explosion, and defective insulation or a short circuit should furnish a connecting link—where would we passengers be at?' 'It is amazing that Dem. leaders could have allowed themselves and their organization to be brought to this pass without knowing where they were at.'

Am. *at auction* = Eng. *by auction.* 'The property was recently sold at auction for non-payment of taxes.' 'A collection of books that was to be sold at auction' (Prof. N. W. STEPHENSON, Nelson W. Aldrich, 424). 'The trustees must sell the property at auction' (Prof. L. J. SHERRILL, Presbyterian Industrial Schools, 95).

Am. *at retail, at wholesale* = Eng. *by retail, by wholesale.* 'For the one farmer who sells vegetables at retail, there are 50 who sell at wholesale' (L. F. CARR, Am. Challenged, 248).

attorney is a word in much more frequent use in Am. than in Eng. It must be remembered that in Am. the legal profession is not divided, as in Eng., into *barristers* and *solicitors.* The word *barrister* is unknown, and SOLICITOR (q.v.) is not used in the Eng. sense. The technical designation of a fully qualified lawyer in Am. is 'attorney and counselor-at-law'. 'Then it was that he seriously undertook the practice of law, receiving his appointment as attorney and counselor at law' (B. A. KONKLE, Life of Joseph Hopkinson, 6). 'I had reported trials in courts while seeing and hearing the judges, the attorneys, and the prisoners' (L. STEFFENS, Autobiog. 662).

The Am. *district attorney* or *circuit attorney* is a *public prosecutor.* 'Both the present district attorney in N.Y. City and the circuit attorney in St. Louis have earned a well-deserved reputation by obtaining evidence on their own initiative against gamblers, blackmailers, and other criminals, in addition to performing their ordinary duty of presenting that evidence to the courts.' 'He became circuit attorney, the prosecuting officer of the St. Louis district' (L. STEFFENS, Autobiog. 369).

The status and functions of the

Attorney-General of the U.S. differ in important respects from those of the Eng. Attorney-General. (1) He is always a member of the President's Cabinet, in which he ranks after the Secretaries of State, War, and the Treasury. He is accordingly disqualified from membership of either House of Congress. (2) Since 1870, in addition to his duty of advising the President on legal points and his responsibility for prosecuting all Supreme Court suits in which the U.S. is concerned, he has been the head of a Department of Justice.

Each State has also an *Attorney-General*, who gives legal advice to the Governor and other State officers, and appears for the State in civil and criminal cases. In most instances he is directly elected at the general State elections.

The title is also sometimes loosely applied to officers of much less dignity and importance. Thus, a former Governor of the Philippines, Luke E. Wright, is sometimes said to have previously been Attorney-General of Tennessee. 'Hon. Luke E. Wright', a Nashville paper explains, 'was for eight years State's Attorney of the Criminal Court of Shelby County. It is a practice peculiar to Tennessee to dub all State's Attorneys Attorneys-General.'

auditorium is seldom used in Eng. exc. in connexion with theatres. If, on entering an Eng. building that contained a concert hall, one were to ask to be directed to the auditorium, the chances are that one would not be understood. In Am. it is the normal term for a hall in which performances are given or meetings are held. 'The auditorium of the City Hall is thought to be large enough for the convention itself.' 'The interior of the church is divided into an auditorium, Sunday school-room, and pastor's study on the first floor.' 'The large auditorium was used for lectures, concerts and various public meetings.' 'As a rule, all the pupils

of the ordinary city school do the same thing at the same time. In the morning, they meet in the auditorium for general exercises' (Dr. C. C. BOYER, Hist. of Education, 447).

automobile. In Am., *automobile* is commonly preferred to *motor-car*, the term which is in general use in Eng. (In Am., however, *car*, without prefix, is common in this sense.) The word may sometimes be found as a verb. 'Here is a hat for the skating girl and the automobiling woman.'

It is often abbrev. to *auto*. 'The things that money will buy—food, clothing, autos, houses, lands and all the rest' (E. B. CHAFFEE, The Protestant Churches and the Industrial Crisis, 86).

Hence Am. *auto-bus* = Eng. *motor-bus*, and Am. *autoist* = Eng. *motorist*. 'In Paris, Berlin and London the auto-bus has come into extensive use as a means of transportation' (H. M. POLLOCK and W. S. MORGAN, Modern Cities, 6). 'The young lawbreakers who stone autoists.'

avail. Am. *avail of* = Eng. *avail oneself of*. 'The anxiety of sellers to avail of prices which look very high.' 'The amount of sulphuric acid availed of by a country is a very fair measure of its civilization.' 'The class availed of the departing professor's hospitality' (M. A. DE W. HOWE, Life of Barrett Wendell, 28). This usage may be found in Shakespeare (Measure for Measure, III. i), but it is now commonly regarded as a solecism in Eng.

In Am. *available* and *availability* (together with *unavailable* and *unavailability*) have two spec. meanings unknown in Eng. (1) The term *available* is applied to a MS. which an editor is willing to accept. 'All you get is his printed slip of regret that your matter is not quite available.' An Eng. editor would reply that it was *unsuitable*. 'A leading activity of the Post Office is the carrying of unsolicited and unavailable manuscripts.' 'Those members of the editorial tribe whose lot it is to receive and decide upon the availability of manuscripts sent in by authors.' (2) In Eng. if it is said that a certain person is not available as a candidate for Parliament or for a particular office, the meaning is that either he lacks certain prescribed qualifications or that he is precluded from becoming a candidate by ill health, the obligations of his business, or what not. It often happens that the man thus described would be the strongest possible candidate if circumstances allowed him to stand. In Am., on the other hand, a politician is pronounced unavailable—though he may be quite free and anxious to enter the contest—if he is considered unlikely to be a popular candidate. 'The reluctance of both Democrats and Republicans to nominate him has been an illustration of the way in which what is called availability is preferred to character and efficiency.' 'Root's speech put an additional weight of unavailability on Root as a Presidential possibility' (MARK SULLIVAN, Our Times, iii. 281). 'It is a commonplace of our modern politics that nothing is more likely to make a distinguished and very able man unavailable, as the saying is, as candidate for the presidency than to have shown marked capacity for leadership and to have taken a pronounced stand on any important question which excites difference of opinion and arouses popular feeling' (Dr. N. M. BUTLER, Between Two Worlds, 367).

avenue. In an address reported in *The Times* of July 12, 1933, Sir William Beach Thomas deplored the 'urban mind', which prefers the cinema to the nightingale and prefers streets to avenues. This distinction would scarcely be understood in Am., for while in Eng. the name of *avenue* is usually reserved for a road bordered by trees, in Am. any wide street, though quite bare of trees, may bear this name. In a considerable part of N.Y., for instance, the main purpose of the term seems to be to mark the distinction between thoroughfares running N. and S., which are called *avenues*, and those running E. and W., which are called *streets*.

avocation. In Eng. often incorrectly used as a synonym for *vocation*. In Am. always used in its proper sense of a pursuit apart from a man's occupation or calling. 'Ten volumes in ten years is not a bad record, when we consider that their author was by vocation a journalist and a man of letters only by avocation' (W. M. PAYNE, Editorial Echoes, 281). 'Avocations held a considerable place in Mr. McLaughlin's life. He delighted in hunting, fishing, fine dogs, and flowers' (Dr. H. ZINK, City Bosses in U.S. 192). 'In England men have more avocations, more amusements, more interests outside of the daily round of pressing business than with us. These avocations demand leisure' (PRICE COLLIER, England and the English, 147). In the same book we are told of London society that, while its vocation is amusement, its avocation is politics.

away. Am. *away* = Eng. *a long way* in such expressions as *away behind, away down, away off, away up.* 'Manufacturers of all good cars are away behind in their deliveries.' 'While New York stands an easy second, Boston is away down in the 21st place.' 'Away off on the coast of Norway.' 'Turkeys are away up in price.' See WAY.

Am. *away back* = Eng. *as long ago as.* 'Away back in February bids were asked for the construction of a preliminary plant.' 'He insisted upon this away back in the Revolution' (W. F. JOHNSON, A Century of Expansion, 81).

See also GET, GIVE.

B

baby. †For *baby carriage* and *baby coach*, see the following quotations. 'It gave a chance for a lot of jokes which were so distinctively British that a baby carriage was called a "perambulator".' 'Eng. baby coaches. For Eng. babies, Am. babies, or any other kind. But the carriages are a distinctly Eng. idea—they dub them "Perambulators"' (Advt.). 'Another room serves as a storehouse for bicycles and baby-carriages' (H. M. POLLOCK and W. S. MORGAN, Modern Cities, 50).

In Am. *plead the baby act* = *plead infancy as a legal defence.* The expression is sometimes used fig. in the sense of excusing oneself on the ground of professed inexperience. 'One minute reading the riot act of manly independence, and the next pleading the baby act of thoughtless irresponsibility.'

back. Am. *back and forth* = Eng. *to and fro, backwards and forwards.* 'How our great men do switch back and forth!' 'The railroad made it possible for Mr. Cook to go back and forth to his law office' (S. GLASPELL, The Road to the Temple, 14). 'Invectives were thrown back and forth across the chamber by Northern and Southern members' (Prof. A. E. MARTIN, Hist. of U.S., i. 609). In Eng. *forth* is now somewhat archaic, but the expression *forth and back* is in use in certain Eng. dial.

Am. *back of* = Eng. *at the back of, behind.* 'Each speaker told what the organization back of him wanted.' 'Various motives were back of this reversal of policy' (Prof. H. ROBINSON, Development of British Empire, 25). 'The security back of the debentures of the intermediate banks' (Prof. E. S. SPARKS, Agricultural Credit in U.S. 387). 'Back of this contest was the belief of the Eng. people that etc.' (J. M. BECK, May it Please the Court, 309). Acc. to Dr. Fitzedward Hall (N.Y. Nation, May 25, 1893) this usage crossed the Atlantic from Ireland.

In Am. *back* is used much more than in Eng. in compound words, with or without a hyphen.

Am. *back district* = Eng. *country district, out-of-the-way district.* 'Rugs made by country women in the back districts.'

The Am. term *backfire* is defined by Webster as a fire started ahead of a forest or prairie fire to burn only against the wind, so that when the two fires meet both must go out for lack of fuel. It is often used fig. 'The backfire at the labor leader is the shrewdest kind of political tactics.' 'Neither suggestion seems to have been made very seriously, exc. in so far as a hope is entertained that a backfire may be started against the movement for the election of senators directly by the people.'

A big log placed at the back of an open fire is called in Am. a *backlog.* The word is often used fig. 'Once upon a time, in a good old-fashioned country home, the father in a rather peremptory fashion ordered his son to go out and bring in the backlog.' 'It should be quite as bad form to leave a will without mention of some benevolent institution as in more conservative days it was to transfer an estate unprovided with some modest "backlog" of Government bonds.'

††To be *a back number* is to be *out of date, on the shelf.* 'He was told by some astute Hill men that he really ought to remain at the head of the committee, and that the talk about his being a back number was manufactured by Republicans.'

Am. *back pay* = Eng. *arrears of pay.* 'He gives a pathetic account of the sufferings of the circus employees, and adds that nearly 200 claims for back pay have been left with the consulate.' 'He had to go into hiding to escape a band of Revolutionary soldiers who had not received their back pay' (Prof. T. J. GRAYSON, Leaders and Periods of Am. Finance, 37).

Am. *back rent* = Eng. *arrears of rent.* 'Smith urged that houses used by the Government should be returned to their owners, and he advised the payment of back rent to help the sufferers and to stop evil reports' (Dr. O. T. BARCK, N.Y. During the War for Independence, 88).

Am. *back salary* = Eng. *arrears of salary*. 'It is a disgrace to the city that he should be compelled to sue for back salary.' 'Gruett was seeking $28,000 from Pierce in alleged back salary' (S. H. ACHESON, Joe Bailey, 214).

In Eng. a *backstop* (more frequently *long stop*) is a cricketer who, in fielding, is placed at a considerable distance behind the wicket-keeper. In Am. baseball it denotes a barrier placed behind the catcher to stop balls that he fails to catch. 'Anybody who wishes to see the scores can find them painted up on the backstop of the baseball field.'

Am. *back taxes* = Eng. *arrears of taxes*. 'The various corporations in this city which have been fighting the law owe in back taxes and accrued interest $24,008.' 'Much of the money was used to pay up back taxes, which were required to be paid before a citizen could vote' (D. L. COLVIN, Prohibition in U.S. 346).

The Am. expression *back and fill* = Eng. *shilly-shally, vacillate*. This is a nautical metaphor. Its original sense is thus defined by the *Century Dict.*: 'To get a square-rigged vessel to windward in a narrow channel, when the wind is against the tide and there is no room for tacking, by alternately filling and backing the sails so as to make the ship shoot from one side of the channel to the other while being carried on by the tide.' 'This time the editor backed away, but filled and came up with his answers.' 'The engine was backing and filling on a side-track.' 'A decade had now been consumed in useless backing and filling on the money question' (Prof. D. C. BARRETT, Greenbacks and Specie Payments, 180). 'It seems absurd now in reviewing the correspondence to see how much backing and filling there was, with varying opinions and suggestions, before the

final title was adopted' (H. J. COOLIDGE and R. H. LORD, Archibald Cary Coolidge, 311).

bad. Used in Am. in two special senses. The *Bad Lands* are a certain barren region in the West, to which the name of *mauvaises terres* was given by the early French explorers. 'He returned yesterday from a trip of three months spent in the "Bad Lands" of Dakota and Wyoming, searching for the remains of extinct animals and fishes.' 'A blizzard of Bad Lands intensity.'

The term *bad man* is also of Western origin. It denotes a *desperado*, who is given to a free use of his 'gun'. 'I was reminded of the way in which Western "bad men" make a tenderfoot dance by shooting all around his feet.' 'He even appointed a typical "bad man"—that is, manslayer—to office as proof of his fondness for Arizona and his thoroughly democratic sympathy with the man who is down.' 'He had been in the West for only a short time when he had his first encounter with a bad man. . . . The bad man advanced brandishing his six-shooter' (H. F. PRINGLE, Theodore Roosevelt, 101).

bag. *To set one's bag* seems to be the Am. equivalent of the Eng. *to set one's cap*, except that the ambition is political rather than hymeneal. 'Lundin urged him to set his bag for the office of mayor and promised to direct the campaign if he would run' (Dr. H. ZINK, City Bosses in U.S. 281). 'The office of coroner paid handsomely in the seventies of the last century; therefore, Croker set his bag for the office and in 1873 received election' (op. cit. 131).

baggage. The *O.E.D.* gives quotations for this word ranging from 1430 to 1766. In Eng., though remaining in use among military men, it has otherwise become obs., having been superseded by *luggage*, but in Am. it is still the normal term for a traveller's belongings. 'The large amount of baggage which the Am. traveler is allowed to carry puts a heavy burden upon the railroad.' See BLIND.

Hence *baggageman, baggage-smasher* (a facetious term for the same person), *baggage-master, baggage-car, baggage-check,* and *baggage-room.* 'A Minnesota university man's trunk was so chock full of learning that it blew up in Kansas City and bruised a baggageman.' 'I went to work at one of the steamboat piers as a baggageman—sometimes lovingly referred to as a "baggage-smasher"' (OWEN KILDARE, My Mamie Rose, 242). 'The baggage-master, spinning a trunk dexterously into rank with its fellows' (R. W. CHAMBERS, The Fighting Chance, 2). 'The baggage car was derailed and badly split.' 'Piled high in the baggage-room is a multitude of trunks.' See LUGGAGE.

bakery denotes in Am. not only a place where baking is done but a place where baked products are sold. 'I bought my luncheon at a different bakery every day' (KATE DOUGLAS WIGGIN, My Garden of Memory, 112). 'I ate nothing till evening when I went into a bakery' (L. LEWISOHN, Up Stream, 122).

balance. The *O.E.D.* describes balance as 'commercial slang' when meaning the *remainder,* the *rest.* In Am. this use has gained a higher status. 'About 1890 he retired from business. He spent the balance of his life in travel' (Dict. Am. Biog. vi. 129). 'A settler could buy smaller tracts of land, paying down only 50 cents an acre, the balance of a dollar and a half an acre being nominally spread over four years' (J. TRUSLOW ADAMS, The Epic of Am. 126).

balcony. For Am. use, see quotation. 'The dress circle [in an Eng. theatre], analogous to our balcony, has stall seats at ten and six, with the rear ones slightly cheaper.'

ball is often used attrib. in Am. instead of *baseball;* less frequently, instead of *football.* 'The tariff set an apathetic House cheering like rooters at a ball game.' 'The ball park was crowded with spectators when the game between Louisville and Toledo was called.' 'I went to my desk every morning with the eagerness of a boy going to a ball game' (W. G. MCADOO, Crowded Years, 445).

'They used to tell me that Napoleon Bonyparte was a champeen chess player, but Hogan says he was on'y good because annybody that bate him might as well go down and be measured f'r his ball an' chain' (F. P. DUNNE, Mr. Dooley's Opinions, 80). This remark needs interpretation to those who do not know that the *ball and chain* is one of the penal devices of the U.S. It is defined by the *O.E.D.* as 'a heavy metal ball secured by a chain to the leg of a prisoner or convict, to prevent escape'. 'Hammonton has resolved to see what the ball and chain gang system will do in the way of driving off the tramps and vagrants. The town council has asked the county Board of Freeholders to provide the shackles, and all men caught wandering around, begging and having no visible means of support, will be chained and set to work digging gravel or mending the roads.' 'Tammany was against his nomination from the first, but was beaten to the ground, then whipped into line, and made work for him under ball and chain, and in stripes, to the end.' 'Prisoners at work on the streets . . . who have bad reputations or give trouble, those who are under large fines and do not belong to the community, and those having other charges pending are forced to wear a 25 pound ball and chain attached to one ankle' (F. W. HOFFER, D. M. MANN, and F. N. HOUSE, The Jails of Virginia, 49). See also CHAIN.

ballot. By a curious perversion of its proper and distinctive meaning, this word has come to be generally used in Am. to denote the open voting at a national party convention when a candidate for the Presidency is being nominated. Thus, the histories and year-books, as well as the contemporary newspapers, tell us that in 1924 Coolidge was nominated by the Republicans on the first ballot and Davis by the Democrats on the 103rd ballot. Actually, the spokesman of each State delegation announces its choice publicly—indeed, this choice is shouted in the ears of several thousand people—but the voting thus conducted without the least pretence of secrecy is nevertheless called a ballot. 'The disturbance which followed the La Follette speeches became so prolonged and annoying that Senator Lodge [the chairman of the convention] was compelled to order the roll call of States on the final ballot many minutes before anybody could be heard 20 feet away.'

'Issues of paramount significance were lacking during his governorship, although it was then that Minnesota adopted the Australian ballot' (Dict. Am. Biog. xii. 554). What peculiar method of voting, one naturally asks, is this *Australian ballot*? There is really nothing strange or mysteriously antipodean about it, for this is the name given in Am. to the method of voting which has been familiar in Eng. ever since the first adoption of the ballot in public elections; i.e. the names of all the candidates are printed on an official voting-paper and the voter marks a cross against the names of the candidates of his choice. In Am., before the Australian ballot was introduced, no official voting-paper was provided, but each voter handed in a paper on which was printed or written his own selected list of names—usually supplied to him, of course, by the agents of his own party. This primitive system, which greatly discouraged independence on the part of the voter, was not generally superseded until the 'nineties. The Australian ballot derived its name from its country of origin, as it is said to have been

devised by William Robinson Boothby, Sheriff and Returning Officer for the Province of South Australia.

In Am., when the election of a person to an office—other than public offices—is obviously a mere formality, or when it is desired to pay the compliment of unanimous election to a candidate who has just been chosen after a contest, the secretary of the electing body is sometimes instructed to *cast a single ballot* for him. 'At last a lay deputy from Mississippi said: "We all second him", which was quite evidently the case, so, to save time, the first assistant secretary cast a single ballot as the unanimous vote of all for Dr. McKim' (N.Y. Churchman in a report of the triennial Protestant Episcopal Convention).

band. Only an exceptional man can make himself heard above the noise of a band. Hence the Am. metaphor, *to beat the band*, which is not limited to competitions in sound. 'I overheard one man telling another that he had just given his mother-in-law "a dandy funeral" and that enough flowers had been sent "to beat the band".' 'She is built on the skyscraping plan of the new girl, with shoulders and a neck to beat the band' (W. D. HOWELLS, Letters Home, 53).

An old-fashioned circus procession in Am. is headed by a band. Hence the political metaphor of the *band wagon*. 'Democratic politicians like to be on the winning side, or "get into the band wagon", to use a favorite metaphor of politics.' 'He is no leader of forlorn hopes. He wants the front seat in the band wagon.' 'The crowd that rushed for the band wagon is quite as capable of being stampeded in the opposite direction when the musicians' wind is exhausted.' 'The offer of the governorship was the same thing as a gracious assurance that he might have his place in the sun—or, in home-spun Am., the band wagon' (Prof. N. W. STEPHENSON, Life of Nelson W.

Aldrich, 4). 'A victory in this early election would attract the so-called "band-wagon" voter, whose chief interest in an election is to align himself with the winning side' (C. E. ROBINSON, Straw Votes, 27).

†**bank.** The Am. metaphor *bank on = count on, rely on* is said to have nothing to do with high finance, but to be derived from the forming of a bank at a gaming table. 'A February without zero weather is miraculous. Let us not bank too confidently on such remote precedents as those of 1876–77 and 1857–58.' 'Strings of titles appended to every instructor's name on a college programme do not establish ability to teach. Are the colleges banking on parents who do not know this?'

See also EXAMINER.

banner. In Am. an adj. as well as a noun, meaning *principal, foremost, first-rate*; i.e. worthy to carry the banner. 'New construction is a banner investment, better even than buying low-cost securities.' 'The earnings of all Vanderbilt lines had a banner month in August' (i.e. a record month). 'Everybody detests Mrs. Chittenden, but as the banner patient of the sanitarium she must be treated with respectful consideration.' 'As foreman of Lovell's beef ranch I spent five banner years of my life' (ANDY ADAMS, The Outlet, 371). 'Massachusetts is still the banner state of the Union, when we take into account not only the number of points covered, but the methods of carrying out the law' (Prof. R. T. ELY, Evolution of Industrial Society, 357).

banquet. Often used in Am. of much less sumptuous repasts than those to which it is restricted in Eng. In its account of the opening of a new Congregational Church in a small New Eng. town, a Boston paper reports that 'there is a banquet room and a kitchen in the basement'. A N.Y. paper, recording a visit paid by Sir H. M. Stanley to 'the poorhouse where his definitely ascertained history begins' says that he 'banquetted the children there'. Advts. of books and correspondence courses that profess to teach the art of public speaking call attention to the importance of being able to express oneself effectively at banquets, whereas a similar Eng. advt. would refer to public dinners.

bar. The *barman* of an Eng. public-house is the *bartender, barkeeper,* or *barkeep* of an Am. saloon. 'The fraudulent votes of liquor dealers, bartenders, and city job-holders illegally registered in his ward' (Dr. H. ZINK, City Bosses in U.S. 83). 'He was expected to lend the distinction of his presence to the barkeepers' annual ball' (W. A. WHITE, Masks in a Pageant, 11). 'Think of walking up to a bar, and then asking the barkeep for an ice-cream soda!' (L. STEFFENS, Autobiog. 101).

†**bargain.** The term *bargain counter* is of Am. origin, and denotes a counter or department of a store where articles are offered at esp. reduced prices. 'Every book should have its chance to sell at a living price, before it is dumped on the bargain counter.' The term is often used fig. 'The fact that the investments of the East Side are in real estate explains why it did not rush to the Wall Street bargain counter.' 'The $3,000,000 palace W. C. Whitney ransacked the world to adorn was on the bargain counter and sold to a rich new-comer at half price within five years after it was completed.' 'The group of men who have lost good jobs and are on the "bargain counter" of the employment market' (M. A. ELLIOTT and F. E. MERRILL, Social Disorganization, 318).

barge may denote in Eng. the second boat of a man-of-war, a large ornamental oared vessel for state occasions, or the house-boat of an Oxford or Cambridge college boat-club, but the word is most frequently applied to a flat-bottomed vessel conveying coal and other freight, mainly along the canals. In Am. vessels of a similar build and with the same name carry passengers on pleasure excursions. They are double-decked and are usually without sails or power, being towed by steamers or tugs. 'The steamer was coming down the North River, towing three barges crowded with excursionists.'

There is a startling suggestion of Noah's Ark on Ararat in a report of visitors being 'conveyed in barges to the crest of High Pole Hill'. In this instance the *barge* is actually a New Eng. vehicle, defined in the *Century Dict.* as 'a large wagon, coach or omnibus for carrying picnic parties or conveying passengers to and from hotels'. A Springfield (Mass.) paper describes a Sunday School outing where the excursionists were accommodated in 'ten four-horse barges and four two-horse rigs'.

bark. In Eng. a person of unpolished manners is sometimes called a *rough diamond*. In Am. a different metaphor finds favour. He is described as a man *with the bark on*. 'Your Westerner with the bark on is fond of strong and picturesque figures of speech.'

barker. The *O.E.D.* gives a quotation from Hazlitt, dated 1822, illustrating the use of this word to denote a tout for an auction-room or shop. It is now obs. in this sense in Eng., but still common in Am. 'He was today sentenced in Police Court to serve 105 days in jail for attacking a "barker", who accosted him in front of a second-hand store. He claimed that the "barker" grabbed hold of him, and tried to make him buy, and he resented the "quick-sale" tactics.' 'Conditions were so dull that barkers had to be enlisted to call the public's attention to the boats tied up along the water front.' 'The secretary was a man of pugilistic build, with the voice of a side-show barker' (H. A. FRANCK, Vagabond Journey, 276).

'Across the street a barker shouted the virtues of an old Charlie Chaplin film' (L. ADAMIC, Laughing in the Jungle, 196).

The French *aboyeur* seems to be used in a somewhat similar sense.

barn. On Am. farms the covered buildings in which grain and hay are stored are often used to house horses and cattle also. *Barn* thus becomes equivalent to *stable* or *cowshed*, and a familiar proverb accordingly takes a new form, as when Dr. J. M. Beck (Our Wonderland of Bureaucracy, 207) speaks of the necessity of locking the barn door before the horse is stolen. In his learned treatise on 'The Proverb' Prof. Archer Taylor also gives it in this form. During a severe winter one may read of cattle being 'found frozen stiff in the barns'. The contents of an old barn that takes fire include 'four horses, two pigs, a new hack and livery stock in general'. Hence the terms *cow-barn* and *horse-barn*. William Dean Howells, writing in *Harper's Monthly* of July 1906, describes a vast, stately structure which 'is now used for the cow-barn of a dairy farmer'. A less usual compound is *animal barn*, which seems, as in the following extract from a New Eng. paper, to mean a small menagerie: 'The main animal barn at Forest Park was partly destroyed by fire. Quick work on the part of the park employees and the firemen saved the collection of more than 100 birds, a dozen monkeys, two leopard cats . . . from complete destruction.' The great Chicago fire of 1871 is commonly attributed to the kicking over of a lighted oil lantern by a cow 'in a barn'.

The tramway depot, in which cars are housed when not running, becomes in Am. a *barn* or *car barn*. 'The signal to go ahead was given, and the car shot into the barn.' A technical treatise describes a certain type of apparatus as being employed 'when the car-barn is provided with pits below the tracks'.

baron. †Though there is no peerage in Am., the word *baron* is in frequent use, in very much the same sense as the Eng. *magnate*. 'Between the cattle barons and the beef trust the long-suffering public is not likely to get much but bone.' 'The ice "barons" of this city have again raised the price of ice to the dealers.' 'Safe within my social uniform I mixed undistinguishedly with the coal barons and college presidents of my native land' (HAMLIN GARLAND, Roadside Meetings, 473). 'The daughters of rich beef and soap and sausage barons began giving their hands to titled European vagabonds' (J. T. FLYNN, God's Gold, 280).

Hence *barony* in a corresponding sense. 'He was to see John D. Rockefeller collect into a mighty barony the wide-spread and disunited oil companies' (Prof. T. J. GRAYSON, Leaders and Periods of Am. Finance, 477).

barrel. In Am. politics the money with which a campaign is financed is often called a *barrel* (i.e. of dollars). 'Others informed the Rep. representatives that the situation was nothing like what it was at the last election, and that there was now no call for a big barrel.' See also PORK.

A low-class drinking-place is sometimes called a *barrel house* or *barrel shop*. 'The tramp could go his way in the morning to the barrel house or the beer saloon.' 'The deaths were caused by drinking a poisonous substitute for whiskey sold in the low "barrel shops" along Tenth-avenue.'

For *garbage barrel*, see GARBAGE.

basket. The Am. *basket dinner* or *basket lunch* = the Eng. *picnic*, esp. when organized by a church or society. 'Capt. Glenn is to deliver an address to the excursionists, and after the speech a basket dinner will be enjoyed by the picknickers.' 'At noon a bountiful basket lunch was served under the trees.' The term *basket picnic* is also used. 'A monster basket picnic and reception has been arranged by the local Presbyterians.'

battery. A specific Am. use of this word is to denote the pitcher and catcher together in a baseball team. 'A former member of Yale battery.'

battle. In Am. *battle* is a trans. as well as an intrans. verb. 'The significance and value of Dr. Bushnell for the Christian Church is in his battling a theology that had a false philosophical basis' (Prof. L. O. BRASTOW, Representative Modern Preachers, 148). 'He went forth to battle Gouldism and all that Gouldism represented' (J. K. WINKLER, Life of J. Pierpont Morgan, 102). 'Battling the Crime Wave' is the title of a book by Prof. H. Elmer Barnes.

Am. *sham battle* = Eng. *sham fight*. 'The sham battle will take place tomorrow afternoon; the exact time or the location is known to the officers only.'

bawl. The Am. *bawl out* means much more than *bawl at*. It implies not merely a loud tone of voice but a reprimand, delivered in a bullying fashion. One may cf. the Eng. expression *tell off*. 'The common scolding or "bawling out" of traffic offenders instead of polite warning or firm arrest and punishment is a typical case of vicious police administration' (Prof. C. E. MERRIAM, Chicago, 40). 'He used to bawl Otto out in front of the people he was waiting on' (E. WILSON, The Am. Jitters, 123).

bay. In Eng. this name is given to a variety of laurel, the *Laurus nobilis*, but in Am. to the *Magnolia glauca*. In Am. *bayberry* not only denotes the fruit of the bay, but is the name given to a quite different tree, the wax myrtle, or *Myrica cerifera*, and to its fruit. 'The bayberry dips are made by boiling bayberries down to a thick wax and dipping cords into the mixture.'

beat. The verb *beat*, used in Eng. as a synonym for *overcome, surpass*, has acquired a bad sense in Am. where it often means *get the better of by illegitimate means, cozen, cheat*. 'The lawyer who considers it inconsistent with his professional integrity to help a fellow-creature beat a statute is a rare person.' 'The people who try to beat the street car conductors out of their fare.' 'Respectable citizens who would not dream of beating a grocer's bill will try to cheat their way on to Uncle Sam's pay roll' (F. J. HASKIN, The Am. Government, 380). A *beat* is a man who is given to such practices. 'He knows more about the ways and schemes of the hotel "beats" than any other man in the country.'

In Am. journalism *beat* is used, as an alternative to *scoop*, to denote a piece of news which a reporter has gained in advance of his rivals and which is accordingly published in his own paper exclusively. 'In the earlier parts [of Stanley's book on his discovery of Livingstone] one gets chiefly the alert and jaunty newspaperman, intent on his beat.' 'I made a bargain with the authorities by which I left them to obtain the confession anew for themselves, while I secured what is called a "beat" for my paper—a "beat" being an exclusive piece of news, and the getting thereof being the highest aim and the proudest achievement of a correspondent' (J. RALPH, The Making of a Journalist, 56).

†To *beat up* does not seem to differ from to *beat*, in the ordinary sense, except in suggesting that the drubbing described is more severe. 'He became a marked man and eventually was beaten up or assassinated' (L. ADAMIC, Dynamite, 15). 'If a white man stood up for a Negro in a race quarrel, he might be kidnapped and beaten up' (F. L. ALLEN, Only Yesterday, 68).

The Am. expression *beat one's way* carries with it an implication that is lacking in *make one's way*. It suggests that the journey is accomplished by tramping the roads or by stowing away on freight trains. 'While posing as a tramp he told many conflicting stories, but stuck to one finally—that he had come from the West, and had

beaten his way by trains and turnpike.' 'He walked to N.Y., drifted to Buffalo, and beat his way to Chicago on a lake vessel' (Prof. T. J. GRAYSON, Leaders and Periods of Am. Finance, 401).

†Am. *beat it* = Eng. *make off*. 'It never failed to work up a cracking shower in the late afternoon. Most of the crowd would beat it up to the hall for cover' (G. REYNARD, in Life in the U.S. 316). 'The murderer beat it, leaving him for dead' (ELLERY QUEEN, The Siamese Twin Mystery, 96).

bed. The compound *bedfast* is not unknown in Eng., but it is nowadays only dial., and much less common than *bedridden*. In Am. *bedfast* is in current use, chiefly among doctors and nurses. 'He had been failing in health for the past two years and for the past week has been bedfast.' 'On his annual visitation to the State Tuberculosis Sanatorium the Bishop of Harrisburg administered confirmation to two bedfast patients.'

††In Am. the compound *bed-rock* is often used fig. 'The price of shingles in the central west has been driven to a bed-rock basis by shipping into the territory great quantities of shingles from the Pacific Coast.' 'Study and reflection culminated in that year. Both sides got down to bed-rock, and in this period we find the best and strongest pamphlets' (S. G. FISHER, True Hist. of the Am. Revolution, 126).

See also BUG.

bee. A special Am. use is defined by the *Century Dict.* as 'an assemblage of persons who meet to engage in united labor for the benefit of an individual or a family, or in some joint amusement; so called from the combined labor of the bees of a hive'. The *O.E.D.* also says that the word is so used 'in allusion to the social character of the insect'. If this be the explanation, it seems strange that the word *bee* should not be applied to an individual member of the gathering but to the gathering as a whole. for which *hive* would surely be a more appropriate metaphor. 'The Martha Washington Benevolent Society met the other day for its annual spinning bee. Old-fashioned spinning wheels were in actual use.' 'A bride who is to be married this month has just given a ribbon bee to her bridesmaids. The girls passed their time in threading ribbons through the bride-elect's lingerie. After the trousseau was gayly dressed, refreshments were served.' 'The *Cleveland Plain Dealer* notes the change that has come upon the husking bee within a decade or so. It used to take place in a dimly-lighted barn, and the discovery of a red ear conferred a traditional privilege of kissing the girl at one's side. Corn was really husked in large quantities, and the dance and cider and doughnuts were pastime and refreshment earned by toil. Now the farmyard is decorated with Japanese lanterns and people arrive in motor cars and stand about a pile of corn shucks which the farm hands have arranged to give "color" to the entertainment.' 'A stalwart young farm hand striding down the road, pitchfork on his shoulder, making his way to a threshing bee' (HAMLIN GARLAND, Roadside Meetings, 177). In volumes of recollections of Am. rural life in the last century, one may find mention also of log-rolling bees, apple-paring bees, and quilting bees.

In the following quotations the use of the word is considerably extended. 'If we don't stop the Banking Department investigation, we can never head off the probing of the Railroad Commission or any other State department, and such an investigation bee spells ruin.' 'After having cheated a possible lynching bee out of its victim yesterday, Sheriff Christopher decided to refuse all visitors admittance to the jail.' 'Big Hanging Bee is now on in Chicago' (Newspaper headline above a report of the hanging of eight murderers within a few days).

The only Eng. use of *bee* in the Am.

sense is in the compound *spelling-bee*, denoting a competition in spelling. Both the thing and the word were introduced from Am. in the 1870's, and had a considerable vogue for a few years.

beech. The Eng. *beech* is *Fagus sylvatica*. The Am. is *Fagus ferruginea*. The bark of the Eng. tree is a dark slaty grey, while that of the Am. is a very light grey. The margin of the Eng. leaf is so obscurely toothed that the leaf is practically entire, while that of the Am. is very strongly toothed.

beet. In Eng. the plur. *beets* was once in common use, like *beans, greens,* &c., but nowadays it has been entirely superseded by *beetroot*. In Am. the older usage is retained. 'Cold chopped beets with lettuce make a good supper salad.' 'When young and tender, red beets are easily cooked, palatable and fairly digestible' (Mrs. RORER's New Cook Book, 358).

†**begin.** An idiomatic Am. use of *begin to*, with a negative, is illustrated in the following quotations. 'No criminal trial of recent years has begun to arouse so wide a public interest as this one;' i.e. has aroused anything like so widespread, &c., has aroused an interest at all approaching, &c. 'The criticism does not begin to be as subtle as that of Mr. Raleigh's study;' i.e. is nothing like so subtle. 'The statement doesn't begin to be comprehensive enough;' i.e. is far from being. 'The social scientist cannot begin to offer the assurance of a laboratory test' (W. LIPPMANN, Public Opinion, 372). 'Even New Orleans does not begin to compare in size with a dozen cities scattered over other sections of the U.S.' (Prof. E. W. PARKS, in Culture in the South, 505).

beho(o)ve. While the form *behove* is in common use in Eng., *behoove* is preferred in Am. Webster gives *behove* a secondary place, and the

Century Dict. mentions it as the less correct spelling. 'It behooves the northenders to appoint a health officer.' 'A sort of Providence had entered into their life, which it behooved them to accept without further concern.' 'The lesson is that it behooves us to look less at the politician and more closely at ourselves' (Dr. N. M. BUTLER, Between Two Worlds, 124).

belie is no longer used in Eng. in the sense of *give the lie to*. The last example given by the *O.E.D.* is dated 1649. That this use is still retained in Am. is shown by the following extract from a book published in 1931. 'He was deficient in judgment about other men and was inclined to abuse and belie those who disagreed with him' (Prof. A. E. MARTIN, Hist. of U.S. ii. 103).

†bell. In Am. there are two compounds, *bellboy* and *bellhop*, each of which denotes an employee who attends to the needs of guests in a hotel when summoned by a bell. 'The clerk sent a bellboy to the room at the time stated, but repeated knocks on the door brought forth no answer.' 'In Pittsburgh the leading hotels lost their entire force of waiters and bellboys within a few days' (Prof. A. E. MARTIN, Hist. of U.S. i. 576). 'The hotel bellhop running to Room 417 with another order of ginger ale and cracked ice' (F. L. ALLEN, Only Yesterday, 253). 'A senator is expected to do simultaneously the work of a college professor and of a bellhop' (G. W. PEPPER, In the Senate, 25).
The Am. *bellboy* may be of either sex. 'A girl may not become a bellboy in Ohio or Washington' (M. A. ELLIOTT and F. E. MERRILL, Social Disorganization, 290).

belong. In Eng., when *belong* is followed by a preposition, that preposition is invariably *to*. In Am. it may be (1) *in*, (2) *with*, or (3) *among*. (1) 'Both books, by virtue of their literary quality, belong in the notable group of Eng. impressions which includes etc.' 'The elaborate treatises on rhythm are analytic, not synthetic, and belong in the study, not the writing, of poetry' (H. S. CANBY, Better Writing, 133). 'I freely admit that this letter belongs in the archives of New Eng.' (Dr. A. S. W. ROSENBACH, Books and Bidders, 287). (2) 'Cheese belongs with salad quite as much as it does with coffee.' 'The name of Robert Koch belongs with that of Pasteur in the history of medical science.' 'In general he belongs for me with George Eliot, Dickens, and Thackeray as an author to whose personality I cannot attach myself' (Letters of W. P. Garrison, 84). (3) 'The friend naturally belongs among those who habitually read book advertisements.' 'It belongs among the small number of Am. medical schools to which great praise is due' (Dr. A. FLEXNER, Universities, 112).
Evidently the explanation of this difference in idiom is that *belong* may be used in Am. in a sense unknown in Eng. It would not have been used by an Eng. writer in any of the above extracts. He would have substituted some such expression as *find their place* or *should properly be included*, in which case *in* or *with*, not *to*, would naturally have followed. The difference in meaning between *belong to* and *belong in* is especially noticeable in the quotation from Dr. Rosenbach. His suggestion is that the archives of New Eng. would be an appropriate home for the letter in question. *Belongs to* would have meant that the letter was already deposited there.

belt is commonly used in Am., where *zone* would be used in Eng., to denote a district or region, generally with some distinctive prefix. 'A wet heavy snow swept over the N. Central States to-day . . . Milwaukee and Lansing were at the north end of the storm belt.' 'This is the time of year when the far-famed Michigan fruit belt has to let itself out several holes in order to make room for its crop.' 'There is a man in New Jersey who has not slept in 20 years. He might try crossing the Delaware and getting out of the mosquito belt.' 'Illinois is divided into a wheat belt, a corn belt, and the city of Chicago' (Prof. A. B. HART, Actual Government, 116). 'Victorian ways have survived beyond their appointed time in the Bible belt' (JOSEPHINE PINCKNEY, in Culture in the South, 40).

The term *Black Belt* is frequently used in discussions of the Negro problem. 'I have often been asked to define the term "Black Belt". So far as I can learn, the term was first used to designate a part of the country which was distinguished by the colour of the soil. The part of the country possessing this thick, dark, and naturally rich soil was, of course, the part of the South where the slaves were most profitable and consequently they were taken there in the largest numbers. Later, and especially since the [civil] war, the term seems to be used wholly in a political sense—that is, to designate the counties where the black people outnumber the white' (BOOKER T. WASHINGTON, Up from Slavery, 108).

The term *belt line* is applied in Am. to a tram-line which takes a circular route. It is also used fig. 'George B. McClellan and Edward M. Grout were scheduled for a belt line tour of speech-making last night.'

bench. In Am. a geological term in popular use, defined by the *O.E.D.* as 'a level tract between a river and neighbouring hills'. 'We live in a depression, or small valley, on this shelf or bench.' Hence, *benchlands*. 'He turned his herd loose among the bottoms and foothills and benchlands.'

In Am. papers one may sometimes read reports of a *bench show*. The context will make it clear that this does not mean an exhibition of benches, but what in Eng. is called a *dog show*. Thus: 'The opening of the annual bench show of the Westminster Kennel Club.' The term originates in the practice on such occasions of arranging the dogs on benches or platforms so that their physical points may be compared. It marks the distinction between such a competition and a *field show* or *field trial* where awards are made for performance.

bends. The noun *bend* is used in Am. in the plur. to denote an industrial disease to which workers in caissons are liable. 'A laborer in Long Island City tunnel died to-day just as he had finished work. He was about to ascend the shaft, when he was seized with the "bends". Comrades hurried him to the mouth of the shaft, but he was dead when a doctor arrived. The "bends" is the popular name for the collapse of the spinal cord caused by the heavy artificial air pressure in these tubes far under water.' Acc. to a correspondent of the N.Y. *Nation* (Feb. 13, 1908) this disease was first closely observed when the piers of the St. Louis bridge were sunk in 1869–72. When the men came up, they would hold their hands against their stomachs, bend over, and in a curved attitude walk slowly and painfully to shore. At this time there was among women a fashion of walking called *the Grecian bend*. One workman would say of another, when he showed symptoms of caisson disease, 'He has got the Grecian bend'. When the St. Louis workmen migrated to other bridges, tunnels, &c., they carried the name with them, but in course of time dropped *Grecian*.

A writer in the *Atlantic Monthly* of April 1932 uses the same term to denote a similar trouble afflicting the divers in Florida sponge fisheries: 'The boats frequently bring men up from 20 fathoms very sick with the bends.'

best Am. *get the best of* = Eng. *get the better of*. 'The True Story of a Man Who Got the Best of the Standard Oil Company' (Newspaper headline). 'I was at war with the British Government, and it had got the best of me' (FRANK RONEY, Autobiog. 139).

bid is used in Am. both in the sense of the Eng. *bid*, an offer of a price by a prospective purchaser, especially at an auction, and of the Eng. *tender*, a statement of the price at which one is prepared to undertake a certain piece of work or to supply certain goods. 'Sealed bids for the construction of the federal building will be opened on Jan. 23 at the architect's office.' 'Under the contract system the plans and specifications are prepared by city authorities; then bids are asked from private contractors. The contractor whose bid is accepted furnishes the materials and manages the labor forces' (Dr. C. C. MAXEY, Outline of Municipal Government, 205). 'The Serbian Government cabled me to make a contract for 5,000 tons of lard. I called up representatives of Swift and of Armour, requesting them to file their bids in 48 hours' (Prof. M. PUPIN, From Immigrant to Inventor, 344). See PROPOSAL.

bill. In Eng. to be presented with a bill ordinarily means to receive a statement of what one owes for goods purchased or services rendered. In Am. it may represent an addition to the credit instead of the debit side of one's accounts. For the Am. *bill* corresponds to the Eng. *note* in the sense of paper money. 'The bills were of the $2 denomination.' 'A dime makes as much noise on a collection plate as a quarter, and both make more noise than a bill. If you don't want your left hand to know what your right hand doeth, put in a bill.' Accordingly, *bank-bill* = Eng. *banknote*. 'Ripping up old pocket-books in the firm belief that bank-bills to an immense amount were hidden in them' (O. W. HOLMES, Autocrat of the Breakfast Table, 186). A pocketbook in which such bills are kept is sometimes called a *billbook*. 'In a

billbook in an inside pocket were many checks for various sums on Plainfield banks.'

††The **Am.** metaphor *fill the bill* = *meet all requirements, do all that is needed*. 'There are fewer and fewer places in the church where a mediocre man can fill the bill.' 'The gasoline vehicle has been so much improved in all its details that it would seem to fill the bill for all classes of work.'

†In the sense of *placard*, this word has given rise in Am. to the verb *bill* = *announce, promise*. 'Its big annual dinner is billed for Oct. 19.' 'If he is all that he is cracked up to be, Missouri is certainly billed for some good government.' 'He remarked: "I ain't ever billed this promenade as a Coney Island picnic"' (FRANK NORRIS, A Deal in Wheat, 162).

In Eng. a *billboard* is a board on which a newsagent displays the contents bill of a newspaper. In Am. the newspapers issue no contents bills, and *billboard* = Eng. *hoarding*. 'An ordinance demands that no billboard be erected on a residence street without the consent of three fourths of the frontage in the block concerned.' 'For a long time the residence sections of the city have been disfigured by hideous billboards' (Am. Year Book for 1919, 255). 'The modern newspaper tends towards the billboard and pictorial effect' (Prof. C. E. MERRIAM, Chicago, 168).

In Eng. a *bill of lading* is a receipt given for goods shipped on board a vessel. In Am. the name is also used in the case of goods delivered to a carrier for transport by land. On Am. railroads, accordingly, *bill of lading* denotes what on Eng. railways is called a *consignment note*. 'In theory each state enjoys full power to regulate the business of railroads within its boundaries. In practice this power is limited by the mere fact of national regulation of interstate business. For example, the national commission prescribes a system of accounting or a uniform bill of lading for interstate business' (Prof. H. L. McBAIN, The Living Constitution, 46). See FREIGHT, SHIP.

A reference in an Am. publication to the *Bill of Rights* rarely has anything to do with the famous Eng. statute of 1689. This name is commonly given to the first nine (or ten) Amendments to the U.S. Constitution, which were added in 1791 to the fundamental law of 1787 in order expressly to prevent the Federal Government from encroaching upon the liberties of the people. It may also denote a similar section of a State Constitution. 'I commend to my distinguished colleague a re-reading of the Bill of Rights, as set forth in the first nine amendments to the Constitution' (Dr. J. M. BECK, May it Please the Court, 211). 'The World War and its anti-red aftermath resulted in laws and decisions which mean that in an emergency the Bill of Rights which we had supposed was written by amendment into our Constitution is scarcely more than a scrap of paper' (NORMAN THOMAS, America's Way Out, 18). 'The Bill of Rights—our forefathers' listing of unalienable liberties and personal securities—was written a century and a half ago' (HERBERT HOOVER, The Challenge to Liberty, 195).

For *bill of equity*, see EQUITY.

billion, in Eng. = a million millions, but in Am. = a thousand millions, i.e. the Eng. *milliard*. This is the only example, some one has said, of a thing that is bigger in Eng. than in Am. 'Too many of those who comment with gratitude and pride on the announcement that the trust funds in the Am. Treasury have now reached the unexampled sum of over a billion dollars overlook the fact that nearly 480 millions of this, almost one-half, are standard silver dollars.' 'A generation ago, comment was made because we had in the U.S. what was called a "billion-dollar Congress"— that is, a Congress which in its two

years of power voted a billion dollars for the maintenance of the national government. That meant 500 million dollars each year' (Dr. N. M. BUTLER, Looking Forward, 170) See also TRILLION.

According to the *O.E.D.*, the word was coined in the 16th century to denote the 2nd power of a million, *trillion* and *quadrillion* being similarly formed to denote its 3rd and 4th powers. The application of the word was changed later by French arithmeticians, figures being divided in numeration into groups of threes instead of sixes. Hence in France, followed by Am., *billion* now denotes not the 2nd power of a million but 1,000 millions. Eng. retains the original and etymological use.

billy. 'A highwayman's club' is one of the definitions of this word given in the *O.E.D.* In Am. it may also mean a club, but a policeman's, called in Eng. a *truncheon.* 'Eight men set upon a policeman this morning, and, after taking his revolver and billy away from him, kicked and beat him.'

biscuit. The Eng. *biscuit* has become a *cracker* in Am. though, oddly enough, an Am. firm which manufactures it on a large scale calls itself the National Biscuit Co., not the National Cracker Co. The Am. *biscuit* is quite different. It is soft, not hard, and is something in the nature of an English scone, but much lighter, never sweet, and always served piping hot with plenty of butter. It is made of dough, raised with yeast or soda, and sometimes shortened with lard. 'Did he never spread cream ham gravy on his hot biscuits , when taste and delicious odor united to delight his palate?' 'His mother stood by the breakfast-table. The coffee-pot was at her hand, a plate of hot biscuits near it' (MARIE VAN VORST, Amanda of the Mill, 56). The plur. is *biscuit*, as well as *biscuits*. See RAISE.

bit. It is only in such compounds as *threepenny bit* and *sixpenny bit* that *bit* survives in Eng. as a synonym for a small coin. In Am.—principally in the West and South—it denotes either (1) a silver coin, now obs., worth 12½ cents, or (2) the sum of 12½ cents. 'The individual who could shovel two dollars' worth of sand a day could not pick two bits' worth of hops in the same time.' 'Jim was smoking two-bit cigars' (G. H. LORIMER, Old Gorgon Graham, 287).

A *short bit* is a ten-cent piece. 'The dime, or "short bit", became the minimum coin of general circulation in the nineties.'

black. 'If we can thus start a strong sound upward spiral of business activity our industries will have little doubt of black-ink operations in the last quarter of this year' (Pres. FRANKLIN D. ROOSEVELT, On Our Way, 110). For the explanation of this spec. Am. use of *black ink*, see RED.

The Eng. *blackbird* is a species of thrush, *Turdus merula.* In Am. the name is given to other birds, e.g. *Gracula quiscala* and *Oriolus phoeniceus*, which are more nearly related to the Eng. *starling.*

The Am. compound *blackjack* denotes a weapon, used as a bludgeon, such as is described in the first quotation. 'The blackjack recovered by the police consists of a piece of lead, egg-shaped, weighing a pound and a half, set snugly in a network of narrow strips of leather.' 'This position, the coroner said, was not such as the body would have taken had Newman been struck with a blackjack or other weapon.' 'Knives, blackjacks and fists drove reputable citizens from the ballot-boxes' (S. B. WHIPPLE, Noble Experiment, 99).

See also BELT.

blank. The *O E.D.* marks as obs. the use of *blank* for 'a document, "paper", or "form", with spaces left blank to be filled up at the pleasure of the person to whom it is given.' The illustrative quotations range from 1586 to 1780, and include one from Shakespeare. In Am. *blank* is still ordinarily employed in this sense, where it is the equivalent of the Eng. *form.* Tenders for the supply of goods to Government offices have to be made out on prescribed blanks; telegrams are written on telegraph blanks; and, when a donation is made to a charity, the amount of the gift is stated on a subscription blank. 'The muddle in the count of the vote on Tuesday, resulting from the erroneous form of the return blanks sent out to the election officers.' 'By means of question blanks sent to the parents, much information concerning each child is secured by the teachers' (Prof. PAUL H. HANUS, A Modern School, 128). 'Stacks of fresh clean telegraph blanks' (CHRISTOPHER MORLEY, John Mistletoe, 181).

The verb *blank*, now obs. in Eng., is still current in Am. in the sense of *beat hollow, smash utterly.* Thus 'Yale Blanks Princeton in Football Battle' is the headline of a newspaper report of a match in which Yale defeated Princeton by 12 to 0.

blanket is often used attrib. in Am. in a fig. sense. The metaphor is not connected with the idea of extinguishing, but suggests the function of covering. Thus, a *blanket clause* is defined by the *Century Dict.* as 'a general or indefinite clause formed so as to provide for a number of contingencies'. 'The Bureau of Construction has received a "blanket" order to do everything which is absolutely necessary to place the flagship in the best of trim.' 'Roosevelt had been approached by Taft supporters to give a blanket endorsement of the new Administration' (L. EINSTEIN, Roosevelt, 192). 'Section 251, Revised Statutes, gives almost blanket authority to the Secretary of the Treasury to issue regulations for collecting taxes' (Dr. J. M. BECK, Our Wonderland of Bureaucracy, 166). In the early days of President Franklin Roosevelt's administration, one heard a great deal of his *blanket code*; i.e. a code by which all Am. industry was to be regulated, pending the adoption of specific codes for individual industries.

A *blanket tribe* is a tribe of Indians still adhering to tribal customs, as illustrated by their continuing to wear blankets. 'On our left was the reservation of three blanket tribes of Indians' (ANDY ADAMS, The Outlet, 81).

For *blanket-shawl* see the following quotation. 'When I fling a Bay-State shawl over my shoulders, I am only taking a lesson from the climate that the Indian had learned before me. A blanket-shawl we call it, and not a plaid; and we wear it like the aborigines, and not like the Highlanders' (O. W. HOLMES, Autocrat of the Breakfast Table, 18).

The verb *blanket* is a yachtsman's term in use both in Eng. and in Am. in the sense of *take the wind out of the sails of*. Its fig. use seems to be peculiar to Am. 'Some men who had been contributors to the Rep. cause said they had first been approached by representatives of the Citizens' Union, who, presenting the theory that the cause was a common one, bagged the contributions. In this way the Rep. campaign was blanketed.' 'But it so happened that Mr. Taft was completely blanketed by the San Francisco earthquake. That catastrophe occurred the very day he began his testimony and so occupied public attention that the mere fact of his having appeared before the Senate committee was either completely overlooked **or** speedily forgotten.'

bleacher. In Eng. a person who bleaches or a vessel used in bleaching. In Am., spec. applied, usually in the plur., to roofless benches for spectators at outdoor games; presumably because they are exposed without shelter to the rays of the sun. 'The bleachers of the club grounds have been so enlarged this season as to

accommodate about 12,000 persons, but over not one of these seats is the slightest protection from the sun's rays.' 'The many who sit on the bleachers smoking, or lying idling round' (Prof. H. H. HORNE, Philosophy of Education, 85). 'The spectator at the play or before the screen or upon the bleachers' (G. W. PEPPER, In the Senate, 20).

blind. In Eng. an alley closed at one end is called a *blind alley*. Similarly a railroad car having no door in the end nearest the engine is called in Am. a *blind car*, and the baggage carried therein is called *blind baggage*. 'Turning hobo, he traveled through every State in the Union. He knew the secrets of the "blind baggage" and the ways of railroad "bulls"' (H. A. FRANCK, Vagabond Journey, 361).

A *blind pig* or *blind tiger* is an illicit drinkshop. 'Six non-commissioned officers have been reduced to the ranks for running what is technically known as a "blind pig", or unlawful canteen.' 'Some effort was made to suppress blind tigers, which were then chiefly supplied by moonshine stills' (D. L. COLVIN, Prohibition in U.S., 297). Hence *blind pigger*. 'The blind pigger in wet territory can procure his liquor shipments without exciting suspicion' (D. PICKETT, Cyclop. of Temperance, 1917, ed., 55).

The history of this curious term is thus related. 'It originated from the idea of a shrewd Yankee who thought to evade the law by giving away his liquor, since there was then no statute expressly forbidding such gifts. This original, therefore, bought a blind pig, established it in a comfortable box within a tented enclosure, and advertised to the world that it might "Look at the Blind Pig—Ten Cents a Look". With every "look", he gave away a drink of rye or bourbon, dependent upon the pig-fancier's personal taste' (S. B. WHIPPLE, Noble Experiment, 19).

In Am. the derivative *blinder* **is**

commonly preferred to *blinker*. 'If they'd put blinders on th' mules, they wudden't be scared' (F. P. DUNNE, Mr. Dooley in Peace and War, 16). 'I plead with the young writer to pull off the blinders which ruling-class propaganda seeks to fasten over his eyes' (UPTON SINCLAIR, Money Writes, 212). The term is found in some Eng. dial.

block. In Eng. a *block* is a tall and massive building, usually consisting of several self-contained sections occupied by various tenants; e.g. a block of flats, a block of offices. A building or continuous series of buildings of lower elevation is called a *row*; e.g. a row of artisans' dwellings, a row of shops. An Am. *block* is not a building at all, but a unit of space measurement. It may be either (1) a rectangular area bounded by four streets, or (2) such portion of a street as lies between one intersecting street and the next. (1) 'Pies are cut into slices, cities into blocks.' 'The Treasury Department occupies a four-story building a block square.' 'An entire block along the Hudson River front, between 54th and 55th Streets, from 11th to 12th Avenue, has been purchased by the N.Y. Hospital.' (2) 'It is convenient to leading hotels—a block south of the Sherman, a block north of the Morrison, and a block east of the La Salle' (Advt.). 'Not three blocks removed from the heart of the theatre district' (C. S. JOHNSON, The Negro in Am. Civilization, 199). 'The cheering crowd covered many solid blocks' (M. HILLQUIT, Loose Leaves from a Busy Life, 111).

Thus if, in Am., you inquire for Mr. Smith's office and are directed to the next block, this means that it is just beyond the next corner. If, in Eng., you get the same answer, you will find the office in the next big building, whether beyond the next street corner or on this side of it.

blockade. In Eng. used only in the well-known naval or military sense.

In Am. used also of any cessation of progress when due to some kind of obstruction. 'When a drawbar on the middle car of a Third Avenue elevated train broke at Canal Street this morning, a long blockade began.' 'Plans for relieving the tremendous railroad congestion, particularly the blockade of traffic on the Pennsylvania and the Baltimore and Ohio Railroads' (W. G. McADOO, Crowded Years, 470). In Eng. a congestion of this kind would be called a *block*.

blood. As long ago as 1857 Oliver Wendell Holmes wrote: 'Let me beg you not to speak of a "thoroughbred" as a "blooded" horse, unless he has been recently phlebotomized. I consent to your saying "blood horse" if you like' (Autocrat of the Breakfast Table, 33). Little attention seems to have been paid to his appeal, for we find even such a distinguished man of letters as W. D. Howells writing (in *Harper's Monthly*, June 1906) of 'the blooded hunters or racers to whose breeding that great nobleman is said to be mostly affectioned'. 'Fleischmann bought a string of expensive blooded horses' (Dict. Am. Biog. vi. 459). 'He was never so happy as when his blooded horses were winning an international steeplechase' (H. O'CONNOR, Mellon's Millions, 244).

In Am. *waving the bloody shirt* is fig. and spec. used to signify the stimulation of revengeful feelings by reviving, for political purposes, the memories of the Civil War or of the Reconstruction period. 'Memories of the Civil War were still rife, and to wave the bloody shirt in political assemblies was a not infrequent practice' (G. T. CLARK, Leland Stanford, 455). 'The Rep. party had fattened on the hatreds of the Civil War through persistent waving of the bloody shirt' (H. F. PRINGLE, Theodore Roosevelt, 73). The origin of this metaphor is variously attributed to (1) an alleged practice in Corsican vendettas, of waving the blood-stained shirt of a wounded man as an incitement to revenge, and (2) a passage in which Gibbon says: 'The sacred duty of pursuing the assassins of Othman was the engine and pretence of his ambition. The bloody shirt of the martyr was exposed in the mosque of Damascus.' The former explanation seems the more likely, as Gibbon is not, as a rule, the favourite reading of Am. politicians.

bloomer. In Am. this word, in addition to its ordinary meanings, may denote a type of tram-car. 'Attempting to board a moving Crescent Park bloomer car caused him to lose both feet and may cost him his life. The car was one of the new eight-wheel bloomers.'

blotter. In Am. the technical term for an official record at a public institution, esp. a police station (where it often corresponds to the Eng. *charge-sheet*). 'A long and elaborate report of the affair, which covers ten pages of the big blotter at the Ardmore Police Headquarters.' 'They also discussed the commissioner's position in refusing to throw the police blotters open to the [street railway] company and to citizens in the matter of damage suits for accidents.' 'While the action of the sun in melting snow has reduced the liability of injury to pedestrians, the injury list is still growing, and three more additions were made yesterday on the hospital blotter.' 'It was necessary, when the question of priority arose, to examine the day-book or blotter in the chief clerk's office [at the Patent Office] to determine the exact time of day when the respective papers were filed.'

††**blow.** 'What wind brought you here?' is a question one sometimes puts to a person who appears suddenly and unexpectedly. The Am. fig. use of *blow in* seems to be an analogous idiom. It usually corresponds to the Eng. *turn up*. 'As she opened the vestibule door he blew in, most literally, on a drenching gust of

Arctic cold.' 'Yesterday your old college friend, Clarence, blew in from Monte Carlo' (G. H. LORIMER, Old Gorgon Graham, 47). See also BREEZE.

blue. In the Am. Civil War the Union soldiers wore a blue uniform and the Confederates a grey. Accordingly, Pres. Theodore Roosevelt, speaking to an audience of Northern veterans, addressed them as 'you who wore the blue in the great years from '61 to '65' and referred to 'your gallant foes who wore the grey'. 'Until recently the survivors of either the Union or the Confederate armies —the wearers of the blue or gray— were conspicuous citizens in nearly every Am. hamlet' (L. M. HACKER and B. B. KENDRICK, The U.S. since 1865, 3).

In inter-university athletics blue is the Yale colour. 'If you are going to bet, I should say, put your money on the Blue. Yale has a splendid team, and I look for a victory.'

The term *blue laws* is used in Am. primarily to denote certain restrictive regulations popularly supposed to have been imposed by their Puritan governments upon the early settlers in New England. Hence it comes to be employed also as a convenient term for any laws that restrict personal liberty in such matters as Sunday observance, the drinking of intoxicants, &c. 'They say that the people prefer Tammany corruption coupled with personal liberty to good government and the enforcement of blue laws.' 'It is a widespread belief that "blue laws" were an invention of the Puritans, but in reality they began in antiquity and continued through the Middle Ages into modern times. Sumptuary laws were repeatedly enacted in the cities of Switzerland before the Reformation' (Prof. S. M. JACKSON, Life of Zwingli, 22). 'Our law books are cluttered with blue laws that are dead but unrepealed' (L. STEFFENS, Autobiog. 858). 'In California, in 1883, the legislature repealed all the Sabbath blue laws' (Prof. A. M. SCHLESINGER, The Rise of the City, 334). 'As far as morals and legislation go the Blue Laws of Connecticut could be duplicated in Virginia' (J. TRUSLOW ADAMS, America's Tragedy, 5).

One must be careful to distinguish *blue laws* from *blue sky laws*, which are entirely different. 'Blue sky laws are an Am. device for the protection of the inexperienced investor against fraud and misrepresentation in the sale of corporate securities . . . There have been two principal kinds of blue sky laws, regulatory acts and fraud acts' (Encycl. Soc. Sci. ii. 602). For full details, see the article quoted. 'Idaho has in its Department of Finance what is officially known as the Bureau of Blue Sky, which analyses applications to sell stock, shares or bonds in Idaho, and none may be sold by companies or corporations issuing them except on a permit issued by it' (World Alm. for 1931, 871). 'The greater number of these organizations were blue sky ventures brought into being to sell gold, silver and oil stock to the unwary' (J. T. FLYNN, God's Gold, 138). 'In 1917 "Blue Sky" laws of three States were upheld by the Supreme Court. It was declared that in requiring dealers in securities to obtain licenses, and in giving to an administrative officer the authority to revoke licenses on certain grounds named, the statutes were within the police power to protect the public from fraud' (Prof. C. K. BURDICK, Law of the Am. Constitution, 575).

The Am. *bluebird* is a bird, so called from its colour, of the percher type. 'If they are constantly and regularly fed, robins, bluebirds, sparrows and others of the house-haunting tribes are said to become fearless, and even affectionate.' 'Sweeter than any other sound to his heart was the bluebird's clear and confiding tremolo in the misty aisles of the woodland' (E. C. WALTZ, Pa Gladden, 209).

A *blue book* is in Eng. a Parliamentary or other Government report, but in Am. a register of Civil Servants. In the 1912 edition of his work on 'The Am. Government' F. J. Haskin points out that 'a graphic illustration of the growth of the civil service of the U.S. is afforded by a contrast of the Government Blue Books published in 1816 and 1905. The one published in 1816 is not much larger than a child's "reader", and had but 176 pages. The one for 1905 had 4,219 pages.' For another use of the term compare the following newspaper extract: 'Some day the people will wake to the fact that the last Legislature spent a lot of money, that measures which would have been blocked under a properly careful and economical administration got through unchallenged, were not halted in the executive chamber, and reached the blue book.'

The name *bluefish* is given to several Am. fish which are desirable for their eating qualities. 'We need not jump to the conclusion that the codfish, shell fish and bluefish are going to the dogfish.'

A variety of Poa which flourishes esp. in Kentucky, where it is highly valued for pasturage and hay, is called *blue grass*. 'Reports from Lexington, Kentucky, indicate that blue laws in the blue grass region make the bluebloods there feel blue.' 'The wind shook the happy leaves and trembled through the budding heads of blue grass' (JOHN FOX, Little Shepherd, 385).

A drug of which blue pills are made is called in Am. *blue-mass*, being prepared by rubbing mercury with glycerine, honey, confection of rose, &c., until a mass is formed. 'About the only things the average rural citizen had to buy [in 1781] were hats, shoes, gunpowder, muskets, the Holy Bible, quinine, and blue-mass' (Prof. T. J. GRAYSON, Leaders and Periods of Am. Finance, 29).

Blue-nose is a colloq. designation of a native of Nova Scotia. Acc. to the *Century Dict.* it is an allusion either to the hue given to the noses of its inhabitants by its severe winter or to a kind of potato so named which is largely produced there. 'The "Blue-noses" who come down from Nova Scotia to work in competition with Am. carpenters.' 'The green waters of the Back Bay, where the Provincial blue-noses are in the habit of beating the "Metropolitan boat-clubs"' (O. W. HOLMES, Autocrat of the Breakfast Table, 59).

The name of *blue-stem* is given in Am. to various coarse but useful grasses, chiefly *Andropogon furcatus*. 'On the high prairie where the grassy stretches extend for miles on an almost unvarying level, the settlers found queer little oases of rank bluestem, showing up in marked contrast against the buffalo grass' (P. H. PEARSON, Prairie Vikings, 24).

board. In Am. one may *board*, or *get on board*, a train or car as well as a vessel. 'The train will make stops at all the principal cities in order that delegates from the adjacent Congressional districts may board it.' 'Three private detectives were on board the train when it left Boston.' 'Robert Louis Stevenson boarded a transcontinental immigrant train in 1879' (Prof. A. M. SCHLESINGER, The Rise of the City, 27). See ABOARD.

This Am. use of the word has had an important effect on business terminology, as thus explained by an Eng. writer. 'In this country F.O.B. means free on board the steamer—namely, the ocean-going vessel. Yet, in the U.S., F.O.B. means free on board the railway truck, because business men in the U.S. instinctively think primarily in terms of railway transport. Thus, if goods are bought in Chicago "F.O.B. San Francisco", for destination to the Far East, the interpretation in the U.S. would be that the seller had fulfilled his part of the contract when he had placed the goods free on board the railway truck at Chicago, and had paid for

the long transport to San Francisco, leaving the buyer to pay the costs of shipping the goods at that port' (CUTHBERT MAUGHAN, Trade Term Definitions, 59).

In Am. *board* in the sense of *provide* (or *receive*) *food and lodging* may be used concerning horses as well as human beings. 'The owner of a large stable said tha t,being near the park, he had recently had some 70 horses to board.' 'Many horses were suffocated and burned to death early this morning when fire destroyed the two-story boarding stable.' 'Boarders wanted at Rockville Boarding Stable' (Advt.). Accordingly the Am. *boarding stable* = the Eng. *livery stable* in one of its meanings.

The word *boardwalk* has been invented in Am. to denote a promenade, frequently at the seaside, constructed of wooden boards. 'The most elaborate decoration will naturally be on the boardwalk, one detail of which will be a continuous arch of electric lights along a distance of at least three miles.' 'The Anglo-Am. mind hides the edges of the sea of life with a board-walk of ethical concepts' (L. LEWISOHN, Up Stream, 116). 'Fire at Coney Island destroyed four blocks of the boardwalk' (World Almanac for 1933, 111).

Board of Trade. In Eng. a Government Department responsible for matters relating to trade and industry, and thus largely corresponding to the U.S. Department of Commerce. In Am. an unofficial local association of business men, akin to a chamber of commerce. 'A committee from the New Orleans Board of Trade has been touring the country to examine the grain conditions.' 'Chambers of commerce, boards of trade, and merchants' associations are organized primarily to promote the interests of business within their respective communities' (Encycl. of the Social Sciences, iii. 501). There seems to have been some misconception of the constitution of the Eng. body of this name in the statement of the N.Y. *Independent*

(13 Aug. 1903) that 'it will be impossible for Mr. Chamberlain to buck against the unanimous Eng. Board of Trade'.

bob has in Am. the additional meaning of a *runner* on which a load is drawn. 'Spruce and hemlock logs drawn on bobs.' It is esp. used of the runner of a sleigh or sled, which may accordingly be called a *bobsleigh* or *bobsled*. 'Daddy drove the old horse and we sat on some boards nailed on the front bob of his old bobsled.' 'Three boys are in Englewood Hospital as the result of a collision between two bob sleds.' Of recent years these words have come to some extent into Eng. use through the popularity of winter sports in Switzerland, and are consequently described by the *Concise Oxf. Dict.* as Anglo-Swiss.

In allusion to its short tail the *bay lynx* (*Lynx rufus*) is called in Am. a *bobcat*. 'Virgin soil, where for centuries the wolves, bobcats and Indians had leisurely roamed.'

The term *bob veal* is used in Am. of veal unfit for food. 'A butcher was sentenced to pay a fine for having violated the Meat Inspection act by shipping in interstate commerce the carcasses of five bob veal calves to this city.'

boil. In Am., esp. in New Eng., the name of *boiled dinner* is spec. given to a meal which, according to a description given by the *Springfield Republican*, is mainly 'a symposium of vegetables and meats—corned beef, cabbage, hunks of pork, potatoes, turnips, carrots, and onions—all potted together in appetizing contiguity, and boiled in a large iron pot hung by an S hook on the crane in a large open fireplace'. When all was done, 'the entire mess was piled upon one great platter and set in the center of the table, pot liquor and all'. This was followed by 'the Indian pudding, made of rich yellow corn meal fresh ground from the local grist-mill, and boiled in a bag'. 'He never ceased to insist, once a week,

on having for himself only an old-fashioned New Eng. boiled dinner' (Prof. N. W. STEPHENSON, Life of N. W. Aldrich, 144). 'Once seated, habit asserted itself and he attacked the boiled dinner with a ferocity which should have been exercised against Jethro' (WINSTON CHURCHILL, Coniston, 120).

†A white or linen starched shirt is sometimes colloq. called in Am. a *boiled shirt*. 'Tammany Hall has progressed from shirtsleeves to the "boiled shirt".' 'A man in store-clothes—boiled shirt and derby hat, a flashy tie, a pair of gloves; to the eyes of all save Euston a gentleman' (MARIE VAN VORST, Amanda of the Mill, 27). 'The long-tailed black undertaker's coat, the boiled white shirt, the resplendent black tie' (Dr. H. ZINK, City Bosses in the U.S. 283).

bolt. The announcement that Mr. Smith has bolted his ticket would naturally be interpreted by an Eng. reader as meaning that Mr. Smith has gulped down a bit of pasteboard without chewing it. It actually means that Mr. Smith has deserted the candidates of his party. (See TICKET.) The verb *bolt* is used in Eng. as well as in Am. in the sense of *rush away*, but its trans. use is unknown in Eng. exc. in the sense of *fasten*. An Englishman bolts *from* anything that he wishes to leave in haste and without ceremony. An Am. bolts it direct, without an intervening preposition. When, several years ago, the members of the Opposition walked out of the House of Commons *en bloc* as a protest against the moving of the closure, an Am. paper headed its report of this proceeding: 'Bolted Commons During Debate.'

This use of the word is esp. common in connexion with Am. politics at election time. 'Butler, who had all along voted for Jefferson Davis as the nominee, bolted the convention because of this slave-trade speech.' 'It was Roosevelt's intention to bolt the party when he arrived in Chicago'

(H. F. PRINGLE, Theodore Roosevelt, 564). 'Though a bimetallist, I bolted Bryan' (F. J. STIMSON, My U.S. 64). The noun *bolt* is used in a corresponding sense. 'The nomination of Mr. Taft might hang upon preventing a Western bolt on the issue of the monetary bill' (Prof. N. W. STEPHENSON, Nelson W. Aldrich, 328).

bond. See DEBENTURE. 'Insistent demands for dividends, bond interest, and other fixed charges.' 'The public no longer wanted anything so stale and profitless as bonds, it wanted securities which would return profits. Company after company was taking shrewd advantage of this new appetite to retire its bonds and issue new common stock in their place' (F. L. ALLEN, Only Yesterday, 312). 'The banker's profit on underwriting the new stocks and bonds' (L. STEFFENS, Autobiog. 191).

Hence *bond salesman*. 'Bond salesmen seldom get rich by investing in the securities which they so warmly recommend.' 'The less active intellect of the bond salesman about to construct a letter' (H. S. CANBY, Better Writing, 12). 'A group of 400 bond salesmen, organized in teams, made a house-to-house canvas in N.Y. City' (W. A. BROWN, in The N.Y. Money Market, iv. 312).

In Eng. a warehouse, in charge of Custom House officials, in which goods liable to duty are stored until they are needed for sale, is called a *bonded warehouse*. A different Am. use of the term is thus described: 'In its efforts to standardize and organize the whole process of marketing produce, Congress has provided, by the Warehouse Act of 1916, for the regulation of concerns engaged in the storage of agricultural commodities entering interstate or foreign commerce. Federal control in this sphere is designed primarily to safeguard growers against fraud and discrimination. With this end in view, every person who wishes to operate a warehouse coming within the terms of the Act is required to satisfy the Secretary of Agriculture that his physical plant is adequate and to post a satisfactory bond demonstrating his ability to meet the obligations imposed by law. When approved by the Secretary such places are known as "bonded warehouses"' (C. A. and W. BEARD, The Am. Leviathan, 544).

bone. The Am. colloq. expression *bone up* = Eng. *swot up*. 'I have known Congressmen, when they were boning up on a subject, to study as they had not studied since they passed their final examinations' (W. LIPPMANN, Public Opinion, 291). For *bonedry*, see quotation. 'The term "bonedry", used in qualifying a prohibition law, indicates that the law prohibits the importation of liquor for beverage purpose whether or not it is intended that the liquor shall be sold' (D. PICKETT, Cyclop. of Temperance, 62).

Am. *boner* = Eng. *howler*. 'The only relief a teacher can be sure of in reading themes is the amusement which comes from some egregious "boner".' 'A recent book of boners gives this definition of a sincere friend taken from a boy's examination paper.'

The Am. compound *boneyard* denotes a place where the bones of dead animals are collected. It sometimes = Eng. *knacker's yard*. 'A dilapidated horse saved from the boneyard by the heroine of the story.' 'I have met men, Indians and hunters, who speak of "bone yards" which they have discovered—places where they can go at any time and be sure of finding a good set of caribou antlers' (W. J. LONG, Beasts of the Field, 70).

booby is commonly curtailed in Am. to *boob*. 'The boob who is too stupid to see that illegal driving is a two-edged sword.' 'Why should the revolt against dulness lead to the cult of smartness? Is the boob to be condemned and the smart-aleck enthroned?' (Prof. E. MIMS, Adventurous Am. 141). 'He [Jefferson] made a new acting version of *The Rivals* in which he elevated Bob Acres from a rustic boob to a quaint and whimsical eccentric' (Dict. Am. Biog. x. 16).

boom. ††The *O.E.D.* suggests that the Am. use of this word may be a particular application of *boom* in the sense of a loud deep sound with much resonance or humming effect, but with reference not so much to the sound as to the suddenness and rush with which it is accompanied. Whatever may be the explanation, the noun is a common term of the Am. business vocab. to denote a rapid advance or increase of activity. 'The textile industries are looking up, and, while nothing like a boom is in sight, their outlook is decidedly more favorable.' 'The demand for labor in the first boom was met in considerable part by the demobilized soldiers and the revived immigration' (Dr. E. E. LEWIS, Mobility of the Negro, 111). There is a corresponding verb *boom*, both trans. and intrans. 'The sudden scarcity of laborers created a panic among the farmers, and boomed the sale of all manner of farm machinery' (H. N. CASSON, Life of C. H. McCormick, 190). 'The merchants soon began importing freely again, and business began to boom at last after the hard years' (J. TRUSLOW ADAMS, Hist. of the Am. People to the Civil War, 98).

A *boom town* or *boom city* is one that is built up with a rush. 'Quite as melancholy as the moss-grown ruins of older civilizations are the frame-built boom towns of the West, located where the railroad was once expected to go but did not.' 'No boom city of the West can boast such a record of amazing and substantial growth.' 'In 1858 he was attracted to the boom town of Sumner' (Dict. Am. Biog. ix. 462).

A political *boom* is a concerted and strenuous effort to work up enthusiasm for a candidate for office. 'The launching of the Gorman boom for the Presidency.' In this sense, too, there is a corresponding verb. 'There are half a dozen Rep. lawyers mentioned and boomed for the vacancy on the Supreme Bench.'

boot. Hamlin Garland tells us in his autobiography (Roadside Meetings, 213) that when he went to Oakland to find Joaquin Miller a man said to him, 'Yes, I know Miller. He's a rough old fellow—wears boots.' So, too, the *Dict. Am. Biog.* (xiv. 520) describes a former Senator from Alabama as exhibiting 'a somewhat rustic and old-fashioned style of dress, his feet being clad in the only pair of boots then worn in the Senate'. Why should the habitual wearing of boots be regarded as a mark of uncouthness? The explanation is that in Am. *boot* is specialized to mean a *high boot* or *wellington*, while what is ordinarily known in Eng. as a *boot* is called a *shoe*. Some years ago a visitor at a Brighton hotel who was posing as a wealthy Am. was detected as a fraud through incautiously directing that plenty of cream should be used 'in doing my boots'. An employee, who knew good Am. when he heard it, became suspicious, and communicated his suspicions to the manager.

Inconsistently enough, an Am. calls the boy who shines his shoes a *boot-black*, while an Englishman calls the boy who blacks his boots a *shoe-black*. 'Nearly everybody in Am. takes part in it, down to boot-blacks and garage-boys' (C. A. and W. BEARD, The Am. Leviathan, 220). 'You can not even see a boot black's stand in München that is not full of kunst' (ANITA LOOS, Gentlemen Prefer Blondes, 146).

The Am. compound *bootlegger*, denoting an *illicit seller of liquor*, is now so familiar that it needs no illustrative quotations. It is said to have been originally applied to a man who surreptitiously conveyed liquor in his boot-legs.

This word, as well as the corresponding adj. *boot-leg*, may sometimes be used of other kinds of illicit traffic. 'Still carried on clandestinely after its legal abolition in 1808, conditions on the slavers when the trade became "boot-leg" were worse even than before' (J. Truslow Adams, America's Tragedy, 71).

bosom is still used in Am. in the sense, now obs. in Eng., of a *shirt-front*. 'The waiters did not wear dress coats, shirts with soiled bosoms, or white aprons.' 'Men's Unlaundered Shirts, made of good muslin over perfect-fitting models. Three-ply linen bosoms reinforced back and front' (Advt.). 'Annoying, is it not, to sit in your chair and have your shirt bosom rise up out of your waistcoat?' 'I bought broad-bosomed shirts' (Hamlin Garland, Roadside Meetings, 420).

boss, an adaptation of the Dutch *baas*, has long been in general colloq. use in Eng. in the sense of *master* or *foreman*. In Am., which introduced it into our language, it has also a spec. political meaning. It denotes a politician who, although he may hold no office, exercises a dominating influence in public life—dispensing patronage, settling disputes, deciding party tactics, and so on. 'The "boss", in the common acceptation of the term, is a man who concerns himself little with policies, and much with the bringing together of a majority which will enable him to keep his friends in office' (Prof. A. B. Hart, Actual Government, 101). There are several derivatives, such as *bossible*, *boss-ridden*, *bossdom*, *bossism*, and *boss-ship*.

bottom. A stretch of low-lying land by the side of a river is sometimes known in Am., as in Eng. dial., by the name of *bottom* or *bottom land*. 'We went down across the creek and entered a dark spruce bottom' (M. H. Hartwick, in Life in the U.S. 11). 'Slave-owners who had sufficient credit to secure many negroes generally were able to pur-chase the good lands that lay along the rivers. Thus the slave population was densest in the fertile bottom lands' (Prof. C. S. Sydnor, Slavery in Mississippi, 187).

boulevard. Greenough and Kittredge have noted that, in the planning of new residential districts in the suburbs of Am. cities, a *boulevard* will often be laid out 'without consideration of the original meaning of that term or its later derived sense' (Words and Their Ways, 318). Acc. to Brachet's *Etymological French Dict.*, this was originally a military term, meaning the *terre-plein*, or platform of ramparts. The boulevards of Paris were, in the time of Louis XIV, simply the line of fortifications round the city. This, planted with trees, became a fashionable walk, and the word *boulevard* came afterwards to mean any walk or street planted with trees. In Am. nowadays it means no more than a wide and well laid-out main street or road, and often = Eng. *arterial road*. 'The trotting horse, the bicycle, and the automobile combine to demand good roadways in cities; and hence have grown up systems of boulevards, broad, winding, and well-surfaced, reaching from park to park and often from city to city' (Prof. A. B. Hart, Actual Government, 328). 'They had already begun that system of parks and boulevards which later enclosed the city in a ring of verdure' (Willis J. Abbot, Watching the World Go By, 62). 'The tourist booming along the Kansas–Colorado boulevard sees only a stretch of monotony that burns his eyeballs' (M. McKernan, in Life in the U.S. 210).

bounce is spec. used in Am. in the sense of *dismiss from employment* or *eject violently*. Hence Am. *bouncer* = Eng. *chucker-out*. 'A minor pugilist and floor manager, otherwise "bouncer", in Bowery resorts.' 'The force of special "bouncers" employed by the Brooklyn Rapid Transit Co. to suppress rowdyism on its cars put in

their first Sunday's work yesterday.'
'The bartender and the bouncer
lifted him from the chair and threw
him into the street' (K. BERCOVICI,
Around the World in N.Y. 392).

bound. 'When I was lecturing in
Am. I was often told, in a radiant and
congratulatory manner, that such
and such a person was bound to come
and hear me lecture. It seemed a very
cruel form of conscription, and I could
not understand what authority could
have made it compulsory' (G. K.
CHESTERTON, What I Saw in Am.
279). Mr. Chesterton explains that,
whereas in Eng. 'he is bound to
come and see you' means that he is
obliged to come and see you, in Am.
it means that he is bent on coming
to see you, that he is irrevocably
resolved to do so, and will surmount
any obstacle to do it.

bourbon. The Bourbons, who forgot nothing and learnt nothing, have
supplied the vocab. of Am. politics
with a convenient epithet for an ultra-
conservative or die-hard. It was originally applied to a certain section of the
Dem. party, but it may now be used
of any kind of reactionary, whether a
Dem. or a Rep. 'Last week's Home-
Market Club demonstration of bourbon
resistance to any reduction of the
tariff.' 'The stand-pat bourbonism
of the Rep. machine.' 'On this
matter that section is to-day more
exclusive and bourbonish and reactionary than it was 30 years ago.'
'Often maligned as a Bourbon, a
reactionary throwback to days of less
social democracy, he always con-
tended that he was a better friend
to labor than many of labor's more
strident partisans in Congress' (S. H.
ACHESON, Joe Bailey, 201). The
term may be applied not only to
political conservatism but to religious
also. 'The Presbyterian [in the
South] is a Bourbon, as distrustful of
theological Whiggery as he is proud
of his well-won reputation for culture'
(E. McN. POTEAT, in Culture in the
South, 259).

bow. In Eng. many varieties of
bent things are called *bows.* Am. has
added to the list the sidesprings or
the frames of the lenses in a pair of
spectacles. In a biog. of Senator
Aldrich Prof. N. W. Stephenson
quotes him (p. 80) as saying in a
speech: 'The lowest-priced spectacles
I could find anywhere in Washington
were 25 cents per pair, and the man
who offered them for sale was candid
enough to say of them, "The glass is
window glass and the bows are
worthless".' 'Lincoln drew from his
pocket a pair of steel-bowed spectacles' (F. E. LEUPP, Walks about
Washington, 33).

bowl. The distinction between a
bowl and a *basin* is not very definite.
Acc. to the *O.E.D.* 'historically a
bowl is distinguished from a basin by
its more hemispherical shape; a basin
being proportionately shallower and
wider, or with the margin curved
outward, as in the ordinary wash-
hand basin'. 'But the actual use of
the words', the same authority adds,
'is capricious.' Certainly *bowl* is
commonly used in Am. for a receptacle that in Eng. would be called a
basin. 'For this amount of money she
can buy a bowl of milk and crackers.'
'The cost of filling the family sugar-
bowl in this way is about two cents
per pound' (W. E. SMYTHE, City
Houses on Country Lanes, 159). 'A
5-cent glass of beer with a bowl of
good soup thrown in' (Dr. H. ZINK,
City Bosses in U.S. 148). In Eng.,
however, one speaks of a *salad-bowl,
finger-bowl,* and *punch-bowl.*
The word may also denote an *amphi-
theatre.* 'Europe was bursting out
with stadiums after the World War,
and good-sized bowls were being
hollowed in various parts of Am.'
(H. JUSTIN SMITH, Chicago, 361).

box is spec. used in Am. baseball to
denote the rectangular space in which
the PITCHER (q.v.) stands. 'It was
a pitcher's battle, with Ewing in the
box for Cincinnati.'
The compound *box-car* denotes an

enclosed and covered freight-car, as contrasted with a FLAT-CAR (q.v.). For this use of *box* one may cf. the Eng. *horse-box*. 'An order has been issued for the building of 33 stations at different points along the line, where box-cars and old buildings are now being used.' 'One night several hundred box-cars in the Pittsburgh yards were soaked with oil and set on fire' (L. ADAMIC, Dynamite, 32). The Eng. *witness-box* becomes in Am. a *witness-stand*. See STAND.

Brahmin is commonly used in Am. in a sense sufficiently indicated by the following quotations. 'Dr. Holmes used to dwell rather too much on the qualities of what he styled "the Brahmin caste" in New Eng.; yet there was a certain truth in the distinctions he thus pointed out. Longfellow, for instance, as distinguished from Whittier, belonged to this Brahmin caste, inclining to conservatism, and in the days of King George to toryism . . . Very little toryism appeared either in Thoreau or Longfellow; but so far as ancestry went, at least on one side, both belonged to Holmes's Brahmin caste—devoted, that is, to culture and religion, rather than to money-getting.' 'The fact that Douglass was able to live in Boston bears testimony to the growing tolerance of New Eng., but it does not prove that the Brahmin clergy had by any means been driven from the field' (Prof. W. P. TRENT, Hist. of Am. Lit. 112). 'Lowell's democratic sympathies were separating him slowly yet imperceptibly from the "Brahmin" caste to which by inheritance he belonged' (F. GREENSLET, Life of Lowell, 46). 'New York, New Haven and Hartford stock at 140, and now Boston and Albany stock at 200! These are rough times for securities of the Brahmin New Eng. type.'

branch may denote in Am. a small brook, without any suggestion that it is a tributary of a larger stream. 'She always went to the little branch back of the church and washed her feet clean' (J. PETERKIN, Roll, Jordan, Roll, 197). 'Water is carried from a distant well or near-by branch' (J. W. HATCHER, in Culture in the South, 401).

†**brass.** The Am. expression *get down to brass tacks = come to the point, get down to details.* 'This bold sister was the first member of all the congregation who had taken the trouble to get down to brass tacks in a discussion of the scandal.' 'I cut it short there, and asked her to get down to brass tacks, as I was very busy' (G. H. LORIMER, Old Gorgon Graham, 217). 'Wilson had opened his campaign with a series of speeches aimed at corporations, turning many pretty phrases such as "guilt is personal", but not getting down to brass tacks on the pressing state issues' (J. KERNEY, Political Education of Woodrow Wilson, 65).

break. †In Am. this name is given to the kind of mistake that in Eng. is commonly denoted by the French term *faux pas.* 'Breaks and bulls were frequent in these speeches, for he always spoke extemporaneously.' 'He has to edit the candidate's letters and speeches; and goose-flesh comes out on him every morning as he picks up the newspaper, for fear that some unfortunate speech has been uttered, an indiscreet letter sent, or some other "break" made.' 'I've been afraid all along that you were going to spoil the only really sensible thing you've ever done by making some fool break' (G. H. LORIMER, Old Gorgon Graham, 91). 'Her spontaneous laughter at some of my foolish and strange breaks' (Dr. FRANKLIN H. MARTIN, The Joy of Living, i. 246). An Am. book entitled 'Breaks: Unintentional Humor by Tired Newspapermen and Others' is a collection of amusing misprints, slips of the pen, and newspaper 'howlers'.
In the vocab. of Am. politics *break* is commonly used where *split* would be preferred in Eng. 'The opposition

was sufficiently influential to produce a party break in the Senate' (Prof. H. J. FORD, Woodrow Wilson, 205).

Am. *an even break* = Eng. *quits*. 'What the Tombstone scribe wished to bring out was that the "Greaser" and the "Chink" are about an "even break" when it comes to illustrating tricks that are vain.'

A customer at the stores will find that Am. *broken lots* = Eng. *job lots* and Am. *broken sizes* = Eng. *odd sizes*.

breast-pin. Am. *breast-pin* sometimes = Eng. *brooch*. The Eng. *breast-pin* is commonly called in Am. a *stick-pin* or *scarf-pin*. 'Mrs. Aylshire raised and lowered a large gold breastpin with a deeply pneumatic sigh.' Cf. STICK.

breath. The common Eng. expression *take one's breath away* seems to have lost *away* in crossing the Atlantic. 'The daring campaign these men were waging took his breath' (T. DIXON, The Clansman, 351).

breeze. In Am. the verb *breeze* is used fig. in much the same sense as BLOW (q.v.), but carries with it a stronger suggestion of rapid movement. 'He breezed through the Louvre at such a pace that he broke all rapid sight-seeing records.' 'The Rough Riders had breezed into Washington almost a week ahead, with Western effervescence and exhibitionism' (H. F. PRINGLE, Theodore Roosevelt, 362). 'When he breezed into the office of *The Times* as its new owner' (WILLIS J. ABBOT, Watching the World Go By, 85).

brief. In the vocab. of the Eng. legal profession, a *brief* is a summary of the facts of a case, prepared by a solicitor for the instruction of the counsel who is conducting the case in court. It is, accordingly, a private document. In Am. the same word is used to denote a printed statement submitted to the court by a lawyer. It contains all his arguments, citations, &c.,

and sometimes it runs to over 1,000 pages. It thus corresponds largely to Eng. *pleadings*. 'The reargument [before the Supreme Court] took place on April 13, when Senator Pepper submitted a masterly brief and an eloquent oral argument in support of the constitutionality of the statute' (J. M. BECK, Our Wonderland of Bureaucracy, 60). In a volume published in honour of Mr. Justice Brandeis on his 75th birthday one of the contributors, referring to the period when that judge was practising at the bar, says that 'by a series of arguments and briefs he created a new technique in the presentation of constitutional questions'. Another contributor to the same volume says that the part played by Mr. Brandeis in the famous Five Per Cent. case is not forgotten, for 'the brief which he filed in that proceeding in his capacity as attorney for the Interstate Commerce Commission disclosed a thorough understanding of the railroad problem'. The official Style Manual of the Government Printing Office at Washington includes instructions for the printing of *court briefs*.

broadcloth. An Eng. visitor to Am. is sometimes startled by seeing advertisements of shirts made 'of Eng. broadcloth'. To him, *broadcloth* has always meant a dressed black cloth from which coats are made, and it seems strange to think that any one should wish to wear it next the skin. The explanation is that Am. *broadcloth* = Eng. *poplin*.

†**bromide.** For the fig. use of this word in Am. see the following quotation. 'Much talk [in 1907] about Gelett Burgess's whimsical division of human beings into "bromides" and "sulfites"—the bromides being the majority of mankind who "all think and talk alike", and "may be depended upon to be trite, banal, and arbitrary", while the sulfites were those who do their own thinking, who "eliminate the obvious from their conversation" and have surprises up

their sleeves' (MARK SULLIVAN, Our Times, iii. 515).

The utterances of such persons may also be called *bromides*. 'There was a dinner in his honor at which Roosevelt voiced a good many bromides about "pluck, honesty and private morality in public life"' (H. F. PRINGLE, Theodore Roosevelt, 72). Acc. to C. G. Ross (The Writing of News, 225) a bulletin issued by a N.Y. newspaper for its staff defines a bromide as 'a word, phrase or expression, or turn of style, that is esp. lacking in originality—overworked, hackneyed.'

Hence the adj. *bromidic*. 'The finest literary touch is of no value unless combined with a situation or an action which makes the most bromidic words then spoken splendid' (F. J. STIMSON, My U.S. 157).

The fig. application of these terms is, of course, suggested by the use of bromides as sedatives and sleeping-draughts.

broom. An Am. correspondent of the *Landmark* (June 1931, p. 368) states that what the Americans call a *broom* does not exist in Eng., while Eng. *brooms* are more like Am. *long-handled brushes*. The *Century Dict.* defines a *broom*, however, as 'a brush attached to a long handle for sweeping; made chiefly of broom-corn in the U.S. and commonly of bristles or hair in Eng.'

brotherhood as a spec. title usually denotes in Eng. one of the organizations that have been the outcome of the Pleasant Sunday Afternoon movement. In Am. the name has been adopted by the trade unions of railwaymen; e.g. the Brotherhood of Locomotive Engineers, the Brotherhood of Locomotive Firemen and Enginemen, and the Brotherhood of Railroad Trainmen. 'One effect of unemployment was to bring to the front the 5-day week movement and the demand by the railroad brotherhoods for the establishment of a basic 6-hour day.' 'The movement for

labor banking inaugurated by the Brotherhood of Engineers' (NORMAN THOMAS, America's Way Out, 265).

brown. The compound *brownstone*, denoting a variety of dark-brown sandstone, has in Am. a spec. implication. Until the fashion of living in APARTMENTS (q.v.) set in, many well-to-do, and even wealthy, families in Am. cities occupied houses built of this material. 'The theory that reputable citizens are more neglectful of the franchise than those who are careless of the moral obligations of citizenship is not sustained by the facts. The "brownstone vote", as it is called, is cast as completely as is the vote of the most crowded tenement house districts.' 'It was not till the late winter that the inhabitants of the brownstone districts, the prosperous minority in a word, received a revelation of the nature of Devery's rule and of the degree of its arrogance' (A. HODDER, A Fight for the City, 7). 'During the 1880's a dark brown tide swept up the avenue. The late A. T. Stewart's marble palace at the corner of 34th Street, long a magnet for sightseers, was eclipsed by the newer brownstone mansions of the Vanderbilts and others' (Prof. A. M. SCHLESINGER, The Rise of the City, 84). Cf. the opening lines of Oliver Wendell Holmes's verses entitled 'Contentment':

Little I ask; my wants are few;
I only wish a hut of stone,
(A *very plain* brown stone will do,)
That I may call my own.

brush may mean in Am. *a short and sharp contest*, esp. in sports. 'Mr. Dodge was driving north, and got into a brush with a passing horseman. In close order the two swept up the stretch . . . He was thrown on a grass plot, and his horse continued the brush for about 10 yards.' 'Apart from the annual regatta, there are endless minor "brushes" for the "fresh-water sailormen".' 'We were feeling pretty smart, as we had just had a brush down the river with several pairs of Middlebury College canoes, and passed them all by' (F. J. STIMSON, My U.S. 147). In describing (Atlantic Monthly, Oct. 1931) his Shakespearian discovery at the Public Record Office, Dr. Leslie Hotson writes: 'Our business at present is not with the brush between Justice Gardiner and Francis Langley in 1597 over the Privy Council's order, but with their quarrel in 1596 involving Wayte and Shakespeare.'

The verb *brush* is used in a corresponding sense. 'Excitement ran high on the Speedway yesterday morning, when two runaways occurred during the height of the brushing.' 'The drivers who were prevented from taking their usual Sunday morning spin turned out during the afternoon, and spent a couple of hours brushing their fast steppers on the upper stretch.'

In Am. *brush up*, in the fig. sense of *renew one's studies of*, is followed by *on*. 'If you wish to brush up on your English you will find nothing better than etc.' 'The ex-governor must brush up a bit on his ecclesiastical studies.'

buck. In addition to its other meanings, *buck* may be used in Am. to denote a male Indian or Negro. 'Crazy Snake [a chief of Creek Indians] has the moral support of 200 bucks, squaws, and children.' 'If a buck nigger should offer to escort a young white woman to church, her father, if he were a true Southern white man, would kill the brute as he would a mad dog' (From a speech by the late JEFF DAVIS, Governor of Arkansas). 'The young buck who graduated from Carlisle was not likely to return to the blanket of his forefathers or prefer a squalid tepee to a livable frame house' (Prof. A. M. SCHLESINGER, The Rise of the City, 373). In Eng. the term *buck nigger* is known, but *buck* is not used by itself in this sense.

The word may even be applied to a male fish. 'Roe shad were selling at $1.50 each this morning, and buck shad were bringing 75 cents.'

The verb *buck = butt, kick*, a dial. word in Eng., is in common use in Am. both trans. and intrans. 'If the mayor bucks the leaguer that has conquered so many other mayors, he will win official freedom during the remainder of his term.' 'There's no use bucking that idea' (G. H. LORIMER, Old Gorgon Graham, 307). 'It will be impossible for Mr. Chamberlain to buck against the unanimous Eng. Board of Trade.'

††**bucket.** The Am. compound, *bucket-shop*, does not denote, as one might suppose, a shop which offers buckets for sale. For its meaning see the following quotations. 'The chief difference between the bucket-shop and the regular brokerage house, where trading is done on margin, is that the former does not as a rule fill the customer's order, but takes it as a bet on the market, while the regular establishment does actually buy or sell the stock as ordered, carrying the same with its own or borrowed money at the expense of the customer who puts up the required cash margin.' 'In general it may be said that a bucket-shop is a brokerage office where orders are never executed, and the funds of the customers are fraudently appropriated.' 'Bucket-shop transactions are readily and correctly classified as gambling, since they are nothing but betting on changes of prices' (Encycl. Social Sci. vi. 556).

bud. In Am. a colloquial term for a *débutante*. A Philadelphia paper reports a young lady as having 'made her formal bow to society at a tea given this afternoon at the residence of the fair bud's grandmother'.

bug. This word, which in Eng. is specialized to mean the *Cimex lectularius*, has no offensive associations in Am., where (as in the Eng. of a few centuries ago) it is virtually a synonym for *insect*. Thus C. H. Sternberg could write (Life of a Fossil Hunter, 272): 'This superstitious fear which men and, even more, women have of snakes, lizards, and bugs, how cruel it is!' 'Setting Bugs to Catch Bugs' is the heading of a leading article on the use of beneficent insects to destroy mischievous insects. 'No man can sleep on St. Lucia till he gets used to the night song of bugs and frogs.' *Bug* may even be used as a synonym for *bacterium*. 'In the new milk regulations the Boston Board of Health places the limit on the number of bugs that a person should swallow with a glass of milk at about 100,000,000. The new article in the rules provides that no person shall bring into Boston for the purpose of sale any milk which contains more than 500,000 bacteria per cubic centimeter.' There is a suggestion of bacterial influence also in such statements as: 'Washington has had the roller-skating bug for the past three or four months.' 'Every one on the farm must have been bitten by the lazy bug.' The curious Am. term *bughouse* does not denote a building, but is an adj., meaning *demented*. Here the idea is that the person so described is inhabited by certain bacteria which produce lunacy. 'The soldiers out here [in the Philippines] are getting bughouse drinking the native wine.'

In Am. the insect known in Eng. as a *bug* is distinguished from other kinds of insect by the name *bed-bug*. 'The first few months in our new home were dominated by the pursuit of the bed-bug' (C. McCRAE, in Life in the U.S. 54).

The older meaning survives in Eng. in *bug-hunter*, a colloq. term for *entomologist*, and in *May-bug* = *cockchafer*.

Am. *lady-bug* (a term found also in Eng. dial.) = Eng. *lady-bird* and Am. *lightning-bug* = Eng. *fire-fly*. 'As an enemy of the dreaded San Jose scale, which dotes on peach trees, the lady-bug is a rank failure.' In *What America is Doing*, an Eng.

writer, Annette M. B. Meakin, tells us how she saw some children, in an Ohio town, chasing some brilliant fire-flies. Presently one of the little girls ran up to her, exclaiming, 'I have caught three lightning-bugs.'

The Am. term *fire-bug* denotes an *incendiary*. 'More than 50 lives were jeopardized yesterday when a fire-bug started a fire in a 5-story brick double tenement.'

Am. *rose-bug* = Eng. *rose-beetle* or *rose-chafer*. 'Then came armies of creatures to swarm over the tender rose leaves. What these left when satiated the rose-bugs appropriated.'

In Am. certain lighthouses have the name of *bug*—e.g. the Little Bug, Portland, Maine, and the Bug Lighthouse, Boston—but no one seems to know why.

The *bug-eye* is defined by the *Century Dict.* as 'a flat-bottomed centerboard schooner of small size decked over, and with a cabin aft, used in oyster-fishing in Chesapeake Bay'. 'He was about as well qualified for the post as the master of a Chesapeake Bay bug-eye would be to command the *Leviathan*' (The Mirrors of Wall Street, 226).

bugaboo. The Eng. *bugbear* is in Am. a *bugaboo*, a word now used in Eng. in dial. only. 'Thirty years ago Emerson was one of the bugaboos which were used to scare theological babies.' 'The white worker balks at the bugaboo of "social equality"' (S. D. SPERO and A. L. HARRIS, The Black Worker, 467). 'There is a new school of soothsayers who would frighten us with the bugaboo that independence of the Philippines would disturb the present balance of power in the Orient' (Sen. H. B. HAWES, Philippine Uncertainty, 202).

building. In Am., *building*, with the definite article, commonly takes the place of the Eng. *house* as part of the name of a block of business offices. Thus, the Equitable Building, the Woolworth Building, and the Empire State Building correspond in

N.Y. to Bush House, Australia House, and Imperial Chemical House in London. In Am. a structure bearing the name of *house* would be understood to be a hotel. See HOUSE.

Am. *building and loan association* or *building association* = Eng. *building society*. 'Building and loan associations and their Eng. counterpart, building societies, are cooperative or quasi-cooperative institutions engaged in financing through mortgage loans the building and purchase of houses' (Encycl. Social Sci. iii. 47). 'As a rule, building and loan associations have confined their loans to city real estate, but in a few states they have made farm loans' (Prof. E. S. SPARKS, Agricultural Credit in U.S. 187).

bulletin is used spec. in the Am. newspaper world as the technical term for 'a brief telegram covering the main facts of a story, complete in itself but usually followed by a detailed "add"' (D. GLASS, Writing for the Press, 39). 'The plan was that, as soon as the decisions were handed out, we would rush the boy down to the man in the booth with a bulletin to the office, and then we would dash across the street with the ruling itself' (The End of the *World*, 112). 'During the Hall-Mills murder trial, 60 leased wires carried bulletins to the newspapers of the country' (Prof. H. C. BREARLEY, Homicide in U.S. 37).

bully. The Shakespearian sense of *bully*, now obs. in Eng., is still current in Am., where the word signifies *first-rate, excellent, capital*. 'The Mayor was bronzed and in good spirits after his three weeks of idleness at the seashore. He said he felt bully.' 'The suggestion is made that he would make a bully headmaster of a big boys' preparatory school.' '"It's a bully fire", said the boy' (E. ORNE WHITE, Lesley Chilton, 84).

bumper. In addition to its Eng.

uses, *bumper* denotes in the vocab. of Am. railways the apparatus known in Eng. as a *buffer*. 'A car ran away and crashed into the bumper at the end of the line.' 'There will be from two to five men standing upright between the cars, riding the bumpers.' 'When a fellow can't get a free pass, and he has any sort of stuff in him, he'll usually hustle for his car fare, rather than ride through life on the bumpers of a freight' (G. H. LORIMER, Old Gorgon Graham, 255).

†**bunch** is freely used in Am., as formerly in Eng., to denote any kind of collection or group. In Eng. it is now generally restricted to a cluster or tuft of things growing or tied together, though there are recent signs that the older sense is returning. 'A bunch of horses', 'a bunch of maps', 'a bunch of leases', and 'a bunch of statistics' are examples from the Am. press. 'A big bunch of automobiles parked in a road' (L. STEFFENS, Autobiography, 855). In his novel, *The Harbor*, Ernest Poole describes one of his characters as buying 'a bunch of meal tickets' each week at a cheap restaurant. Acc. to the *Washington Post*, 'the diplomatic bunch' is the term by which Washingtonians 'offhandedly call the legation people'. 'Flavia had no inclination to eat lunch with a bunch of teachers' (L. N. WRIGHT, Limbs of an Old Family Tree, 120).

The verb *bunch* has in Am. a similar extension of meaning. 'In the meantime south-bound expresses often become bunched near the other end of the line.'

bunting. 'The clubhouse was decorated with buntings and flags.' In Eng. this would have been *bunting*, as the plur. form is unknown.

bureau. In English a *desk or writing-table with drawers*; an *escritoire*. In American a *dressing-table*. 'She looked on the table, then on the bed and bureau in the bedroom.' Hence *bureau-scarf*, meaning a *cover for a* *dressing-table.* 'She began embroidering a bureau-scarf and table-cover for Lily's room' (MARY E. WILKINS FREEMAN, By the Light of the Soul, 347).

Officially, a *bureau* is a division of an Am. government *department*, corresponding to a *department* of an Eng. *ministry.* (See DEPARTMENT.) Thus, while the Eng. Ministry bearing the name of the Board of Trade has its Mines Department, the Am. Department of Commerce has its Bureau of Mines. 'In 1862 the then Bureau of Agriculture was raised to the rank of a Department' (L. M. HACKER and B. B. KENDRICK, The U.S. since 1865, 178). In general, the word is often used in Am. where Eng. usage would prefer *office* or *organization.* Thus, Am. Weather Bureau = Eng. Meteorological Office. 'The Diocesan Committee has established a bureau where poor people can secure good, serviceable clothing at a nominal price.' 'William F. McCombs of his own motion started a bureau in aid of Wilson's candidacy' (Prof. H. J. FORD, Woodrow Wilson, 156).

Am. *bureau of information* = Eng. *inquiry office.* 'The same statement would appear quite natural if coming from the ticket agent or a boy at the bureau of information' (Dr. J. M. RICE, The People's Government, 34).

†**burn.** When it is said in Am. that some one possesses money (or whatever it may be) *to burn,* the suggestion is that he has so much that he might throw some of it into the fire without missing it. It is thus equivalent to saying that he has enough and to spare. 'The most bitter fight is being waged in the 29th district. There is campaign literature to burn there.' 'To say that the Arctic regions have mastodons to burn would be an extravagant statement of the case, but discoveries like that now reported from the upper Yukon are not unusual.' 'It is said that cremation is fashionable in Eng. But it has always been understood that they have

population over there to burn.' 'She has already had library experience to burn.' 'A supposed Miss Moneybags, who had dollars to burn' (E. L. BANKS, Autobiog. of a Newspaper Girl, 265).

For *burnsides,* see SIDE.

bus. In an account of a fire in the restaurant of the Capitol at Washington, a newspaper reports that 'about 23 bus boys and dishwashers fled from the building in terror as smoke filled the kitchen'. What were bus boys doing in the kitchen? Their work surely was in the stables or garage. The explanation is that the Am. *bus boy* or *bus girl* is a servant who goes round the tables at an eating-house and removes the trays and plates that the customers have finished with. 'Having started with Filipino bus boys, a local restaurant gradually substituted Filipino for white Am. workers in other departments of work' (BRUNO LASKER, Filipino Immigration, 46). 'For 8 or 9 months he worked as bus-boy in various restaurants, clubs and hotels' (E. WILSON, The Am. Jitters, 122).

In this sense, as in its normal Eng. sense, *bus* seems to be an abbrev. of *omnibus.* F. P. Grove (A Search for Am. 37) quotes a restaurant keeper as saying: 'I cannot put you on as a waiter at once. But I will take you on as an omnibus. You will have to help the regular waiters out, carry trays full of soiled dishes to the kitchen, help to clean the silver, and make yourself generally useful.'

bushel. The Eng. bushel is slightly larger than the Am. It has a capacity of 2,218·192 cubic inches. Am. retains the earlier Winchester bushel (superseded in Eng. in 1826 by the Imperial bushel), which has a capacity of 2,150·42 cubic inches.

business. For *business agent,* see AGENT. Am. *business suit* = Eng. *lounge suit.* 'A generation or so ago the average Congressman would no more have gone on the floor in a business suit than he would have followed Jerry Simpson's alleged example and appeared without socks.' 'Coolidge appeared in his first review of the Grand Fleet in a business suit and a yachting cap' (W. ALLEN WHITE, Masks in a Pageant, 451). 'I was having all sorts of fashionable clothes made for my start in life; morning suits, evening suits, sporting and even business suits' (L. STEFFENS, Autobiography, i. 166).

busy. †Am. *get busy* = Eng. *get to work, stir oneself, look alive.* 'He said he did not apprehend any great difficulty in clearing away the snow. "We are getting busy, right away," he said, "and have 3,000 men working."' 'The Lord helps those who help themselves, and Boston should get busy and give the matter of port development careful study without further delay' (F. J. STIMSON, My U.S. 92). 'An officer at the Station House told them that they better get busy and get bail or they would have to stay in jail all night' (W. B. and J. B. NORTHROP, The Insolence of Office, 47).
In the vocab. of the Am. telephone system *Line busy* = Eng. *Number engaged.*

butcher. 'The steward of the dining-car brought pots of steaming coffee, and the "butcher" brought baskets of fruit, and the train conductor brought real Scotch' (UPTON SINCLAIR, Money Writes, 124). What is a butcher doing in the personnel of a railway train? And why should he thus trespass, apparently, on the province of a fruiterer? The explanation is that, in Am., the word *butcher* may denote a vendor of miscellaneous articles on a train. Thus: 'When he was twelve, he put in his application to the news company and became a "train butcher" ... He was "candy butcher" two years.' 'In his waking hours the traveler is bullied by the chesty "train butchers" who regard all men and women who come within the sound of their rasping voices as

victims.' 'The peanut butcher on a train one day was trying to sell him Henry George's "Social Problems"' (L. STEFFENS, Autobiog. 475).

butt may denote in Am., as in Ireland, the stump of a partly smoked cigar or cigarette. 'Take the Brooklyn Bridge station. An examination of the roadbeds there at almost any time will find them covered with paper scraps, cigarette and cigar butts. Anybody who stands on the platform five minutes may see patrons tossing them upon the tracks.' 'Those who had eaten stood about for a few moments lighting cigarette butts.' 'I do not for a moment pretend that it [smoking] is anything but a rather unpleasant habit; butts, ashes, smell' (ALICE ROOSEVELT LONGWORTH, Crowded Hours, 62).

button. In Am. a *button* may be a *collar-stud* or *cuff-link.* In a biog. of his father, the famous evangelist, W. R. Moody illustrates his simplicity of life by telling us that he wore no jewellery and even dispensed with cuff buttons in later years. 'The others looked at him as if they were ready to swallow him, starched collar, necktie, collar-button, shoes and all' (K. BERCOVICI, Around the World in N.Y., 402).
The word also denotes a celluloid emblem worn on a coat lapel during election campaigns and bearing the favoured candidate's portrait. 'Representative Fitzgerald appeared in the House to-day wearing in the lapel of his coat a handsome button, on which was photographed the likeness of Judge Parker, and an inscription declaring his candidacy for the Presidency.' 'A large number of Hearst buttons were noted in the crowd.' 'The streets were strewn with the socialist party buttons, which voters had thrown away when the news came' (L. STEFFENS, Autobiog. 688). It seems that this use of the word was once common in Eng. Acc. to a quotation in the *O.E.D.* Suppl. it is traceable back to

Jacobite times, and Repeal buttons were highly favoured in Ireland during the closing years of O'Connell's ascendancy.

button-ball or *button-wood* is the popular Am. name for the Occidental plane-tree, so called from its round, pendent fruit. 'A large button-ball tree stands in front of the second house.' 'Walking slowly under the mottled branches of the button-woods.' 'The button-wood throws off its bark in large flakes' (O. W. HOLMES, Autocrat of the Breakfast Table, 138). 'The technique of investing funds had undergone changes in many details since the first informal selling under the buttonwood tree in Wall Street' (Dr. M. G. MYERS, The N.Y. Money Market, i. 37).

buzz. The Am. term *buzz saw* denotes a *circular saw*. It is so called from its characteristic noise when at work. 'John Hanson, who is employed at George A. Stevens's box shop, had the thumb of his right hand severely lacerated Saturday while at work with a buzz saw.' The term is often used fig. 'McLaughlin [a N.Y. political leader] and his men will know better next time than to monkey with the buzz saw.' 'The leaders of both the Dem. and Rep. parties will discover that municipal ownership is a dangerous buzzsaw, which they should leave severely to itself.'

by. The expression *by and large*, meaning *generally speaking, to all intents and purposes*, is rare in Eng. but common in Am. 'By and large, mankind had no serious use for master planning before 1800.' 'By and large, the work of the graduates of West Point has compared well in civic worth with that of the men of other colleges.' 'The paper which goes into the homes of the fairly prosperous is by and large the one which offers most to the advertiser' (W. LIPPMANN, Public Opinion, 323).

C

cabin. Mrs. Stowe's famous story, *Uncle Tom's Cabin*, has familiarized Eng. readers with the Am. use of the word, now obs. in this sense in Eng., to denote a small and roughly built cottage. 'The cabin was of the rudest sort, with a single room, a single window, a big fireplace, and a huge outside chimney' (W. E. CURTIS, The True Abraham Lincoln, 19).

cabinet. The term *cabinet minister* is unusual in Am., where *cabinet member* or *cabinet officer* takes its place. 'The youngest cabinet member since Alexander Hamilton's day' (Dict. Am. Biog. viii. 397). 'No man has ever been permitted to rise from the position of attorney in the Department of Justice to the position of a cabinet member' (Dr. J. M. BECK, Our Wonderland of Bureaucracy, 120). 'With him they swept out of office the whole crew of third-rate cabinet officers.' 'Present practice makes no provision whatever for the appearance on the floor of either house of Congress of that cabinet officer who would be best qualified to discuss the proposal' (Dr. N. M. BUTLER, Looking Forward, 142). 'A number of Wilson's cabinet officers, specifically Secretary of State Lansing, Secretary of the Interior Lane, and Attorney General Palmer, gave ready ear to the indignant charges of the interventionists' (L. M. HACKER and B. B. KENDRICK, The U.S. since 1865, 479). See FAMILY.

The difference between the Eng. and the Am. nomenclature is significant of a difference in fact. An Am. cabinet, though often called an ADMINISTRATION (q.v.) is not a *ministry* in the Eng. sense. In particular, it has no collective responsibility. It is composed of the heads of the Federal DEPARTMENTS (q.v.).

The term *cabinet* is sometimes loosely used in Am. to denote minor groups of official advisers. 'The chairmanships [of committees in the House of Representatives] being distributed in the discretion of personal favor of the speaker, carry with them a recognition of obligation to the speaker which gives him great influence over the action of committees. So great is this influence that some speakers have referred to the chairmen as "my cabinet".' 'Generally speaking a mayor may have the resignation of any of his cabinet' (Prof. C. E. MERRIAM, Chicago, 258).

caboose. In Eng. a kitchen on a ship's deck. In Am. a brake-van on a freight (goods) train, used by the conductor and the brake-men. 'He told how he had to get a permit to ride to his destination in a caboose, and of the vivid memory which he yet had of that terrible ride at the rear of a freight train.' 'The rest of the crew knew nothing of the accident until they saw from the caboose windows the bodies of their fellow-employees lying along the tracks.' 'Many a time when he was trying to get a little sleep in a wayside station, while waiting for a connection, or lay in a bunk in the caboose of a freight train, the special car of his opponent, decorated with flags and lithographs, would go sweeping by' (W. E. CURTIS, The True Abraham Lincoln, 113). 'Not wanting to be separated, the family decided to ride in the caboose of the train which carried their possessions' (W. F. DEXTER, Herbert Hoover and Am. Individualism, 9).

cadet. This term is sometimes used in Am., esp. in N.Y., as a euphemism for *procurer*. 'Disorderly houses multiply, and there are signs that the "cadet" infamy is again in existence.' 'The keeper of a brothel finds it a lucrative business. The cadet, panderer, and white slave dealer all find this business fascinating from the purely business view-point' (H. M. POLLOCK and W. S. MORGAN, Modern Cities, 320). 'The sidewalks in front of a burlesque show are thronged with pimps and panderers who offer to conduct the patrons of the show to a house of ill-fame. These cadets realize that the passions of the customers at the show have been highly aroused' (M. A. ELLIOTT and F. E. MERRILL, Social Disorganization, 635).

cage is a technical term in Am. baseball for the special enclosure in which batting practice is sometimes carried on. 'While the baseball men are learning to slide for bases in the cage' (J. CORBIN, An Am. at Oxford, 148).

cake. If an Eng. visitor to Am. asks for *cakes*, he is likely to be offered something very different from what he wants. *Cake* in Am. is very much the same as in Eng., but the plural form is reserved for a small portion of batter fried on a griddle—a kind of pancake—commonly of buckwheat. One may compare the Am. usage with the familiar appellation of Scotland as 'the land of cakes', i.e. not sweetened or fancy confectionery, but oatcakes. 'News, like buckwheat cakes, is not good for much after it becomes cold' (E. L. SHUMAN, Practical Journalism, 87). See also ANGEL, FLANNEL, HOE, LAYER, LOAF.

calamity is used in Am. in some curious combinations. A *calamity howler* is a pessimist, and his indulgence in gloomy forecasts is *calamity howling*. 'Common stock should be either eliminated entirely or dividends postponed for a period of not less than five years, so that it will not become the football of every calamity howler.' 'The most striking feature of his address is his direct reference to the failing business prosperity of the country. He is the first one among the leaders in the campaign to introduce what the other side may tersely call "calamity howling".' 'The only calamity howler with whom I conversed was an old fellow who discoursed upon the degeneration of youth.'

A *calamity issue* at an election is an issue that is likely to be disastrous to the party that raises it. 'Croker invited Bryan to see him for the special purpose of asking him to drop free silver and other calamity issues next year.'

calendar. The use of this term to denote a *cause-list* in the law courts is not limited in Am., as in Eng., to criminal trials. 'The calendar was loaded with all sorts of suits, most of them hinging on the question whether Sun Mountain contained one lode or many' (Dr. G. D. LYMAN, Saga of the Comstock Lode, 189).

It is also the normal term for the official agenda of Congress, thus corresponding to the *order paper* of the British Parliament. 'Shortly thereafter, the adjournment resolution was acted on, leaving the prohibition proposals hanging fire to go on the calendar for disposition at the opening of the December session.' 'The present Committee on rules controls the calendar and procedure' (J. M. BECK, Our Wonderland of Bureaucracy, 207). 'Stanford reintroduced the bill in December 1891, and in due course it was reported with an amendment by the committee and placed upon the calendar' (G. T. CLARK, Leland Stanford, 455).

In Am., CATALOGUE (q.v.) takes the place of the Eng. *calendar* to denote the official year-book of a college or university.

calico. The difference between the Eng. and Am. uses of this word is indicated by the complaint of an Am. woman writing to the *Manchester Guardian* of her difficulties in shopping in Eng. 'I go to the draper's shop', she says, 'for some unbleached muslin. I find I am buying calico, although my idea of calico is a cheap cotton print.'

call. Both the term *call loan* and the transaction it represents are peculiar to Am. N.Y. brokers obtain their funds through either time loans or call loans. The former are made for a specified date, whereas the latter can be terminated by either party at a day's notice. A call loan is made upon collateral which must have an aggregate market value of at least 20 per cent. above the face value of the loan. 'The most distinctive feature of the present-day money market in N.Y. is the call loan. In none of the European money centers has a similar type of loan reached such predominance or been utilized in the same degree. The demand loan secured by stocks and bonds is a peculiarly Am. product . . . The call loan made its appearance in N.Y. in close association with bankers' balances, and would never have become important if there had not existed these great reservoirs of funds available for just such a use' (Dr. M. G. MYERS, The N.Y. Money Market, i. 126).

For *call market* see quotation, which refers to the speculations of the late B. P. Hutchinson on the Chicago Board of Trade. 'He took the lead in organizing the "call market" for dealing in "puts and calls". This method of dealing consists in the sale by one operator to another of the option of buying from or selling to the person giving the option a future contract in grain or provisions within a range of prices and over the period intervening between the close and opening of the market' (Dict. Am. Biog. ix. 437).

The Am. colloq. expression *call down = challenge, reprove.* 'The President did a wise thing in calling down the aggressiveness of the labor organizations in the attempt made by some of them to declare that union labor only should be employed in the Government service.'

For *call to order*, see ORDER. For *calling card*, see VISIT. See also ADMIT.

camp. When an Am. tells you that he is going to a summer camp, it is not safe to assume that he intends to live the simple life under canvas.

'The word *camp* is ambiguous as applied to abodes in the Adirondack forest, for it may be used to designate a snug little cabin, with its modest half-acre of territory, or it may apply to an extensive establishment that represents the outlay of thousands of dollars, standing in the midst of a royal estate of 50,000 acres, including forests, mountains, and lakes.'

campaign. The military metaphor of a *campaign* is not unknown in Eng. as applied to the propaganda connected with a political election, but in Am. it is in much more common use. It has given rise to several specific terms peculiar to the U.S.

Thus, a *campaign biography* is a biography of a candidate (esp. for the Presidency) published shortly before the election and written with the special object of attracting votes. 'Probably no presidential nominee was ever wholly pleased with his campaign biography, no matter how eulogistic.' 'Howells was appointed as consul to Venice while still in his twenties—he won the appointment as a result of a campaign biography he had written of Lincoln' (V. F. CALVERTON, The Liberation of Am. Literature, 375).

In preparation for an election, each party issues an officially authorized *campaign book*, for the special benefit of writers and speakers on its own side. This is a substantial volume, which might be described as a storehouse of relevant facts, statistics, and arguments. 'The Rep. campaign book stands upon the record of the party, which is a record of promises made good. The Dem. campaign book also will have to stand upon the record of the party, but it is a record of broken promises and unfulfilled predictions.' 'On Monday the President is to see the manuscript of the Rep. campaign book which has been compiled for use in the Congressional elections.'

The more generic term *campaign document* may denote not only either of the two compilations above mentioned but any kind of electioneering literature. 'It does not appear that any effort will be made to prevent the distribution of the pamphlet as a campaign document, any more than a speech from some public man containing partisan material.' 'His extemporaneous address was so masterful and clever that it was selected by the state Rep. committee as a campaign document' (Prof. D. C. BARRETT, The Greenbacks and Specie Payments, 225). 'He delivered a rollicking speech against Cass which was essentially a campaign document' (Dict. Am. Biog. xi. 245). 'In 1857 Hinton R. Helper published a violent attack on slavery in a volume which has been said to have sold or been given away to the extent of about a million copies in the next four years, having been used as a Rep. campaign document in 1860' (J. TRUSLOW ADAMS, America's Tragedy, 134).

The term *campaign chairman* is explained by the following quotation. 'Experience has shown that it is the candidate, and not the chairman of the campaign committee, who leads his party to defeat or victory. Blaine's failure to reach the Presidency and Harrison's success were equally independent of the campaign chairman.'

A *campaign club* is an organization of supporters of a candidate, formed in order to promote his election by a variety of means. For an excellent sketch of the work of such clubs see the chapter on 'The Presidential Campaign' in Bryce's *Am. Commonwealth*.

A *campaign emblem* is a party symbol; e.g. the Rep. eagle and the Dem. cock (or rooster, as it is called in Am.). It usually appears on a ballot paper at the head of the list of candidates nominated by the party that has adopted it. It may also be frequently seen on banners and personal badges. It must be distinguished from the zoological figures which cartoonists have popularized; e.g. the Rep.

elephant and the Dem. donkey. In the following passage the term is used in a slightly different sense: 'The rails [split by Lincoln in his early days] were taken to the National Convention at Chicago and had a prominent place at the Illinois head-quarters. Later in the campaign they were sent from place to place in the country, and other rails from the old farm were also used as campaign emblems' (W. E. CURTIS, The True Abraham Lincoln, 27).

can. In Eng. a *can* is a vessel for holding liquids. In Am. it has a much wider signification, being practically equivalent to the Eng. *tin* in the sense of a metal container, esp. for preserved foods. 'The story of the salmon from the spawn to the labelled can that sits upon the shelf of a grocery store.'

†Hence the verb *can* and the nouns *canner* and *cannery.* 'The great trusts which control the output of meats, sugar, oil, canned goods.' 'Canned meat and canned fish are not on a par with fresh articles' (Dr. R. L. ALSAKER, Eating for Health and Efficiency, 41). 'The short supply of fruits is bothering canners.' 'Much of the garden product of the colony is canned at a near-by cannery.' 'During the year some 3,000 of the Chinese were employed in the salmon canneries' (J. W. JENKS and W. J. LAUCK, The Immigration Problem, 219).

The double meaning of the verb *can* is illustrated in the reply of a resident in a fruit-growing district who was asked what the growers did with all their products. 'We eat all we can,' she answered, 'and we can what we can't.'

Acc. to Webster the noun *can* may be used of a glass or earthenware jar in which food is preserved. At any rate, food so preserved may be in-cluded among *canned* goods, so that *canned* may be a synonym not only for *tinned* but for *bottled.*

For *garbage can,* see GARBAGE.

candidacy is preferred in Am. to *candidature,* which is the usual term in Eng. 'The candidacy would be an excellent advertisement.' 'A minority supported the candidacy of "Little Tim" Sullivan for vice-chairman' (Dr. H. ZINK, City Bosses in U.S. 165). 'These things help his candi-dacy quite as much as any qualities of intellect' (PRICE COLLIER, England and the English, 249).

candle. There is an Am. compound *candlewick,* which denotes a particular style of embroidery for bedspreads. It is considered esp. suitable for old-fashioned four-posters. 'The candle-wick spread on the four-poster' (SINCLAIR LEWIS, Work of Art, 335). 'A French knot candlewick bedspread done on cotton cloth spun and woven by her mother-in-law' (A. H. EATON, in Culture in the South, 303).

candy is in Eng., exc. in certain dial., a particular form of sweetmeat, defined by the *O.E.D.* as 'crystal-lized sugar, made by repeated boiling and slow evaporation'. It is more fully called *sugar candy,* and has no plural form. In Am. *candy* is a general name for everything included in the Eng. *sweets* (exc. in the sense of the sweet course at dinner) or for any confection having sugar as its basis. It is as commonly used in the plur. as in the sing. 'An arrangement by which they shall pay in to their teachers the pennies they ordinarily spend for candy.' 'The digestion must not be impaired by eating be-tween meals, nibbling candy, eating pastry or drinking soda-water.' 'An old lady sat near the gate offering candies for sale' (Prof. M. PUPIN, From Immigrant to Inventor, 43). 'The simple candies of yore—pepper-mint sticks, gum drops, candy hearts inscribed with sentimental mottoes—were supplemented by boxed con-fections' (Prof. A. M. SCHLESINGER, The Rise of the City, 135).

The Am. *candy store* thus = Eng. *sweet shop.*

cane. In Eng. only a slender stick is ordinarily called a *cane*; e.g. that used as an instrument of punishment, or the *swagger-cane* carried by soldiers when walking out. In Am. a *cane* may be of any size and thickness. In his Retrospections (i. 163) John Bigelow, referring to the notorious attack made on Charles Sumner in the Senate Chamber, says that he was 'assaulted and brutally beaten with a cane'. A few pages later he describes the assault as having been made with a bludgeon. One of the characters sketched by Dr. Harold Zink in City Bosses in the U.S. (p. 308) carries 'a blackthorn cane'. H. Justin Smith (Chicago, 139) refers to 'the canes stockmen punch steers with'. An Am. paper, reporting Viscount Snowden's introduction to the House of Lords, describes him as 'leaning heavily upon his two canes'. See RUSH and SWITCH.

can not.
'Forever!' 'tis a single word.
Our rude forefathers deemed it two.'
So wrote C. S. Calverley. He might have made the same comment on *cannot*, but in this case the preference for two words is a characteristic not only of our rude forefathers but of our cultivated Am. contemporaries. For example: 'That can not be the President's view' (Dr. J. M. BECK, May it Please the Court, 427). Dr. Krapp thinks the Am. custom more consistent than the Eng., inasmuch as similar combinations—such as *will not, shall not, may not, might not*—are always written as two words. The difference between Eng. and Am. practice in writing has probably arisen from a difference in speaking. An Englishman actually says *cannot*, not *can not*, whereas an Am., with his more deliberate enunciation, distinctly separates the *can* from the *not*.

canopy. In Am. *the canopy* sometimes = *the canopy of heaven*. 'What under the canopy does little poverty-stricken Greece want with an outfit of warships?' Here *under the canopy* = *in the wide world.* Cf. Shakespeare, *Coriolanus*, IV. v.

canton is unknown in Eng. exc. as a technical term of heraldry or as denoting a political division of Switzerland. In Am. it has a special use, illustrated in the following quotation: 'Lt. Col. E. E. Gilson, of Canton Athol, has been elected colonel of the 5th regiment of Odd Fellows, department of Massachusetts. This regiment includes a number of cantons in the middle and western part of the state.'

canvas(s). At an Eng. election *canvassing* is house-to-house visitation for the solicitation of votes. In Am. it is also the official counting or scrutinizing of the votes after the polling. Accordingly, *canvasser*,which in Eng. denotes only a person who solicits votes, is in Am. also equivalent to the Eng. *scrutineer*. 'The canvass of the vote in Illinois has been completed, and the totals give the Rep. candidate's vote as 632,745 as against 328,006 for the Dem. candidate.' 'Governor Murphy has appointed the State Board of Canvassers . . . The board will meet in the State House next Tuesday, and officially determine the number of votes which were cast for the different candidates for State offices at the recent election.' 'Application was made for a mandamus compelling the recanvassing of 43 alleged void ballots.' 'The election boards canvassed the returns' (Prof. A. E. MARTIN, Hist. of U.S. ii. 147).
The *canvas-back* (*duck*), a much-prized table delicacy in Am., is a variety of duck (*Fuligula valisneriana*) which owes its name to the colour of its back feathers. 'These are the hasty conclusions of a man who has eaten his canvas-back and drunken his claret' (W. D. HOWELLS, Letters Home, 46). '"No, I didn't starve," I answered, "but I haven't lived on canvas-back duck nor lobsters and things"' (E. L. BANKS, Autobiog. of a Newspaper Girl, 93).

††capacity. Am. *to capacity* = Eng. *to its utmost capacity.* 'A large

mass meeting was held with the large auditorium filled to capacity' (D. L. COLVIN, Prohibition in the U.S. 307). Other ellipses of a similar kind may often be met with. 'The closing years of the century found Columbia and N.Y. University crowded beyond capacity' (Prof. A. M. SCHLESINGER, The Rise of the City, 215). 'The village that once counted its houses by the dozen was built up towards capacity' (H. JUSTIN SMITH, Chicago, 114).

One may even find *capacity* used as an adj. '*The Moth* drew capacity audiences at one theatre' (Dict. Am. Biog. vi. 430).

captain is in Am. not only a military but a police rank and title. 'When the leaders gave the command to march, the mounted police captain swung his men across the formation.' 'I was strolling on the East Side with an elderly police captain' (UPTON SINCLAIR, Candid Reminiscences, 38). 'The city is usually divided into a number of precincts or districts for police administration, with a captain as chief commanding officer in each' (C. C. MAXEY, An Outline of Municipal Government, 162).

The title of *captain*, like that of COLONEL (q.v.), may also be acquired in Am. by appointment as a member of the pseudo-military staff which escorts a State Governor on certain formal occasions. 'While Theodore Roosevelt was governor he appointed Mr. Goddard a staff aide, and it was from this commission that Mr. Goddard acquired the rank of a captain. Although Captain Goddard was not really a military man, and the title which clung to him was somewhat misleading, he was an organizer and a believer in discipline.'

†**caption.** In Eng. the technical term for part of a certain legal instrument. In Am. the heading of a newspaper article or of a chapter in a book; hence extended to mean almost any kind of title. Accordingly, when the film was invented, it was immediately adopted into the vocab. of the cinema. 'Atlanta University has recently published an important study under the caption of "The Negro Church".' 'Residents should carefully state in their entries under the captions "Descriptions of Articles" and "Foreign Cost or Value" the articles obtained abroad, with the cost price of each article' (U.S. Treasury notice). 'In the *Arena*, I reviewed a novel by Bourget under the caption etc.' (HAMLIN GARLAND, Roadside Meetings, 199). 'Under the head of business promotion may be placed the activities of the Federal Government in . . . Under this caption likewise belongs etc.' (C. A. and W. BEARD, The Am. Leviathan, 468). 'One marvels at the zeal for machines which inspires the caption sometimes seen in Russia: "The true God—the Machine"' (NORMAN THOMAS, America's Way Out, 294).

car. In the vocab. of Am. railways, *car* corresponds to the Eng. *carriage* or *coach*, and *the cars* is a common synonym for *the train*. 'Were the type only more generous, so as to invite reading in the cars, this would be almost an ideal publication.' 'I took the train for Gordon. I arrived there on Christmas Eve. I was the only passenger to leave the cars' (C. H. STERNBERG, Life of a Fossil Hunter, 207). Such compound terms as *baggage-car, freight-car,* and *mail-car* are also peculiar to Am. Am. *street car* = Eng. *tram car,* and Am. *car fare* = Eng. *tram fare.* 'For the cost of a car fare up and down town a man can now buy one of the greatest books which the world has ever produced.' 'In Knoxville the street cars went like sleepy tortoises; they were pulled by mules' (W. G. McADOO, Crowded Years, 44).

The *cage* of a lift is also called a *car* in Am. 'The elevator man seemed to lose control of the elevator at the 5th floor. The car made a sheer drop from the 4th story to the basement.'

card may be used in Am. to denote

a printed announcement on a personal matter, not necessarily printed on pasteboard. 'Hon. W. W. Osborne gave out the following card to-day' says an Atlanta newspaper, and there follows a statement of Mr. Osborne's political views occupying a column and a half. 'Mr. Walter of the London *Times* has found it necessary to publish a card reminding his readers that the control of that newspaper etc.' 'Those gentlemen promptly published cards in the oil region papers repudiating the Chamber's action' (J. T. FLYNN, God's Gold, 209). An advt. inserted by Walter Hines Page in a newspaper when seeking a job is described by his biographer as a card (Earlier Life and Letters of Walter H. Page, 129). For *calling card*, see VISIT.

cardinal is the name of a North Am. bird with fine red plumage and a crest on its head. Its scientific name is *Cardinalis virginianus*, and it is described as an oscine passerine bird of the family Fringillidae. James Lane Allen derived the title of his novel, *A Kentucky Cardinal*, from this bird, and not from a Prince of the Church. 'High on a branch a gorgeous cardinal sat triumphant.' 'The jays and cardinals that came in the noon quiet.'

care. In Am. the expression *take care of* is used euphemistically in two senses. It may mean *keep under*, or even *get rid of*, remove. 'Take all these elements of discontent and mould them into one, and put over them a daring leader, and you have a formidable foe which will give the conservative forces of the nation a big job to take care of it.' 'Elaborate and ingenious devices were proposed to take care of every conceivable obstacle to a final peaceful settlement' (IDA M. TARBELL, Owen D. Young, 145).

It may also mean *provide for, look after the interests of.* 'The needless multiplication of offices to "take care of" political henchmen.' 'He found himself besieged with petitions for jobs by veterans who "looked upon the Governor as their only friend" . . . It was impossible to take care of all of them, but he did his best as long as he held office' (H. F. PRINGLE, Theodore Roosevelt, 198). 'The older boys who are openly "bold and bad" are almost always secure in the conviction that, if one of them should get caught, he will not be severely dealt with, that local politicians to whom he and his family are attached will take care of him' (JANE ADDAMS, The Second 20 Years at Hull House, 314). 'The financing of hog production has been taken care of by local banking institutions' (Prof. E. S. SPARKS, Agricultural Credit in U.S. 377).

career. The Am. term *career man* means something entirely different from *careerist*. For a long period the U.S. was accustomed to appoint as its representatives abroad men who had hitherto spent their lives in Am. politics, business, legal practice, education, &c. After serving for a few years as ambassadors or ministers they returned to their previous occupations. An attempt, however, is being made to create a professional diplomatic service, whose members shall make of it a lifelong career. These are accordingly known as *career men*. One may compare the French term, *diplomate de carrière*. Thus, in the introductory chapter of his memoir of Henry White, Allan Nevins says of him: 'He illustrated better than any other Am. of the time the possibilities of skilled service by a diplomatist of career. Indeed, he was our first eminent "career man" in the field, rising from the humblest posts in the profession to some of the highest.' 'Our greatest diplomatists have been, not "career" men, but Franklin in the Revolution, Jay at its end, Washburn and Charles Francis Adams in the Civil War, Page and Gerard, Whitlock and Morgenthau in the last—all men of action with no department training' (F. J. STIMSON, My U.S. 375).

Similarly *career = professional* in 'I think the career professors look somewhat askance at one who comes in from the outside world—just as career secretaries in diplomacy do upon a chief who has not gone through all the grades, but who comes in fresh from big business or big politics' (F. J. STIMSON, My U.S. 190).

carom. This billiards term, an abbrev. of *carambole,* is now obs. in Eng., having been superseded by *cannon,* but is still current in Am., both as a noun and as a verb. As in the case of *cannon* in Eng., its application is not restricted to the game in connexion with which it originated. 'A well-dressed man caromed against me on his way to the elevator.'

carousal. 'For the children there is a Ferris wheel, a carousal, a scenic railway, and a most wonderful shooting gallery.' In this example, *carousal* is far from denoting an orgy. It is, in fact, a quite different word from the Eng. *carousal,* which is of German origin and means a *drinking bout.* This is the French *carrousel,* which means a *merry-go-round.* Sometimes the confusion is avoided by the retention of the French spelling. 'The shrill blasts of the steam-organs of the carrousels' (K. BERCOVICI, Manhattan Side-Show, 258).

carpet-bagger. In Eng. politics this is a somewhat contemptuous term for a Parliamentary candidate who is unknown to the electors before his candidature. The suggestion is that his only stake in the constituency is the carpet-bag—a form of luggage, by the way, which has become practically obsolete of late years—which he brings with him to his hotel. Being so lightly equipped, he may be sent by the party organizers to contest this seat or that as occasion may require. In Am. this type of politician is unknown, owing to the custom which forbids the candidature, either

for Congress or for a State Legislature, of any person not previously resident in the constituency. The term is applied, however, to those Republicans who went down from the North to seek office or political influence in the Southern States during the Reconstruction period, and the administrations dominated by these men are known as *carpetbag governments.* 'With the overthrow of the carpet-bag governments, the South began to shoot up into a new prosperity.' 'In the South conditions [after the Civil War] developed as might have been expected. A disgraceful horde of office and spoils seekers from the North, known as "carpet-baggers" swarmed over it. Combining with the riffraff of Southern whites, known as "scalawags", and the utterly ignorant negroes, they formed parties, elected the legislatures, and stole with the complete abandon of Boss Tweed and his gang in N.Y.' (J. TRUSLOW ADAMS, The Epic of Am. 286).

Acc. to the dates of quotations in the *O.E.D.,* the Am. use of the term preceded the Eng.

carry, carrier. †An Eng. shopper asks a tradesman if he *keeps* or *sells* such-and-such an article. An Am. shopper often asks if he *carries it.* 'The greengrocery is a sidewalk stand and very little else, and rarely does the vegetable dealer carry fruit also.' 'One house in this city carries 1,200 designs in picture post cards.' 'All sizes from 32 to 42 inches are carried in stock.' Cf. HANDLE.

So, too, the contents of a newspaper or magazine are *carried* by it. 'This number will be followed by a fiction issue for July. Each of the other summer and autumn numbers will also carry a special plan.' 'Our readers must have noticed that we are carrying a large amount of advertising for a magazine in its first year.' 'The *Times* carried frantic editorials' (L. ADAMIC, Dynamite, 209). 'Religious journals of all kinds carried an abundance of material showing this concern' (Prof. L. J. SHERRILL, Presbyterian Parochial Schools, 10). The term may even be applied to a book; e.g. 'The New Testament, carrying the story of the life of Christ, naturally relates many of the instances' (W. F. DEXTER, Herbert Hoover and Am. Individualism, 31). In Eng. a *carrier* is a person or firm engaged in the conveyance of parcels, and thus corresponding to the Am. *expressman* or *express agency*. The Am. *carrier* is a *postman*. 'He was a daily reader of the paper, and always welcomed its delivery by the rural carrier.'

carryall. In Eng. a sort of haversack, also known as a *holdall*, in which a traveller may carry articles of an unwieldy shape that would make them inconvenient for packing in a bag. In Am., a carriage of a rather primitive type, used mainly in rural districts. 'Once the Massachusetts Highway Commissioners chose to make their inspection tours about the State by means of a horse and carryall.' 'An old carryall came shambling along the road; there were two people in it' (MARGARET DELAND, Dr. Lavendar's People, 43). 'A rough and dusty, rather hilly, road, two horses, and a huge, heavy, dignified "carryall" holding four people' (K. D. WIGGIN, My Garden of Memory, 5). The word in its Am. use is a corruption of *carriole*.

casket. An Am. schoolgirl once wrote of the 'funereal effect' of the scene in *The Merchant of Venice* in which the suitors make their choice. So lugubrious an association would never have occurred to an Eng. girl, for she would have known *caskets* only as small boxes, used to contain jewels or other precious articles. In Am. the term commonly denotes *coffins*. 'When we stand by the side of the casket, and our thoughts go roaming out searchingly after the loved one that is gone' (Dr. C. H. PARKHURST, A Little Lower than the Angels, 264).

'When one of the gangsters is shot, they give him a funeral costing tens of thousands of dollars, burying him in a silver casket' (L. ADAMIC, Dynamite, 359). 'In the U.S. the old wedge shaped coffin has become obsolete; different styles and grades of caskets are available, ranging from a cheap cloth covered pine box to an expensive cast bronze sarcophagus' (Encycl. Social Sci. vi. 527).

Accordingly, Shakespeare provides for Americans a casket scene not only in *The Merchant of Venice* but also in *Richard the Third*. 'Flavia played Lady Anne in the casket scene in "Richard the Third". Dressed in the royal robes of that period, she stood on the stage before a real casket, an antique loaned by a local undertaker' (L. N. WRIGHT, Limbs of an Old Family Tree, 114).

catalogue, in the terminology of Am. colleges and universities = Eng. *calendar*. 'The year when Lowell's name first appears as a professor in the Harvard catalogue' (Dr. E. E. HALE, Lowell and his Friends, 170). 'The catalogues of many of our leading universities now offer special courses in Dante' (W. M. PAYNE, Editorial Echoes, 21).

Hence the term is sometimes applied to a school *prospectus* or *curriculum*. 'Consider the disconsolate father as he sits before the fire with the catalogues of 30 boys' schools piled high before him.' 'Our schools are sadly lacking in that they have excluded from their catalogues the study of Imagination' (Dr. R. B. H. BELL, The Life Abundant, 169).

cattleman. In Eng. a workman who attends to cattle, a drover. In Am. an owner of cattle. 'I once went to interview a large landowner and wealthy cattleman from the far West' (E. L. BANKS, Autobiog. of a Newspaper Girl, 267). 'Cattlemen, who were permitted to lease grazing rights from the tribes who owned them, occupied vast stretches of country' (Prof. A. E. MARTIN, Hist. of

U.S. ii. 283). Cf. COWMAN and SHEEP-MAN.

caucus. This word has been borrowed by Eng. politicians from Am., but has suffered a radical change of meaning in the process. The main difference is that in Am. it denotes a specific type of *meeting*, but in Eng. a specific type of *organization*. 'In the U.S. a caucus is a meeting by members of a party or faction for the purpose of choosing party leaders, formulating policy, or naming candidates for public office. It is a meeting of a small group within a larger group: of voters in local districts, of representatives in municipal, county and state legislatures or in Congress, or of a corresponding group in a non-political organization. "Caucus" in Great Britain refers to the standing organization of a political party. It came into general use in 1878 when misapplied by Lord Beaconsfield to the Liberal Association of Birmingham, but is now applied to controlling organizations of all parties' (Encycl. Social Sci. iii. 277). Accordingly, Eng. *caucus* = Am. *machine*.

The Eng. use is illustrated in this extract from a London paper: 'If we may credit the N.Y. correspondent of the *Times*, that city is not governed by the elected municipality, but by Tammany Hall, a political caucus.' Examples of the Am. use are: 'The Dem. leaders in the Senate announce that they shall hold a caucus on the Wood case, and they expect to secure a two-thirds vote to stand solidly against confirmation.' 'Senators Lodge and Crane were unanimously nominated to represent Massachusetts again, at a caucus of Rep. members of the Legislature to-day.'

The distinction between a *caucus* and a *conference* is thus expressed by a former Senator, G. W. Pepper (In the Senate, 26). 'Such meetings [of members of a party in the Senate] are either caucuses or mere conferences. If a caucus, it is understood that all who participate will subse-quently act on the floor of the Senate in accordance with the majority vote in the caucus. By the action of a conference nobody is bound.' Hence Lincoln Steffens refers to 'the caucus-bound members of a legislature' (The Shame of the Cities, 10). 'He said to the delegates that the meeting was not a caucus, but merely a conference for the exchange of views' (W. G. McADOO, Crowded Years, 145).

centennial. In Am. *centennial, bicentennial*, &c., are preferred to *centenary, bicentenary*, &c., which are more usual in Eng. 'London celebrated on the 1st. of August the centennial of the opening for traffic of the present London Bridge.' 'Many particulars respecting his life and character have been brought out by the bicentennial of his death' (S. W. DUFFIELD, Eng. Hymns, 24). 'The celebration, in 1930, of the fourth centennial of the adoption of the Augsburg Confession' (H. P. DOUGLASS, Church Unity Movements in the U.S. 218).

The name of *the Centennial State* is sometimes given to Colorado because it became a State in 1876, i.e. 100 years after the Declaration of Independence.

central. In the vocab. of the Am. telephone system, *Central* takes the place of the Eng. *Exchange.* 'The telephone company was planning to install a "Central" in our village.' 'In a moment the bell rang, signifying that connection had been made with central.'

†**cereal** has been in Eng. a book-word, rarely to be found exc. in statistical articles in which various agricultural products are classified. In Am. it is in everyday use to denote porridge or similar fare served as part of a meal, esp. breakfast. 'Patent cereals, competitive substitutes for the oatmeal of sturdy Scots, were only a little while ago inevitable on any well-regulated breakfast table.' Mrs. Rorer, in her Cook Book, advises

that fruits should be served 'with cereals or breads'. 'To breakfast all alone was delicious; to stroll, unhurried, to the sideboard and leisurely choose among the fresh cool fruits; to loiter over cream-jug and cereal' (R. W. CHAMBERS, The Fighting Chance, 145).

certificate. In the vocab. of Am. education, the technical term for a document accepted by colleges from school authorities as qualifying a candidate for admission without further examination. 'The lax enforcement of published requirements for admission, together with the very general acceptance of certificates from uninspected and unvisited schools, has demoralized college standards very generally.' 'Certificates accepted by leading colleges and West Point' (School advt. in Who's Who in Am.).

A *silver certificate* is a piece of paper money issued by the Government and used as currency. 'The Act of 1886 had authorized the issue of silver certificates in smaller denominations than $10' (Prof. T. J. GRAYSON, Leaders and Periods in Am. Finance, 380). 'How much money there is in any society depends not upon how many certificates called dollars are in existence, but upon how efficiently those dollars are serving human needs' (E. A. FILENE, Successful Living in This Machine Age, 46).

†**chafing-dish** once denoted in Eng. a kind of portable grate, or a vessel to hold fuel—esp. burning charcoal—for heating anything set on it. The *O.E.D.* gives quotations ranging from 1483 to 1825, the latest being from Scott's *Talisman*, where we read of 'a chaffing-dish filled with charcoal'. The modern meaning of the word is an importation from Am., where it came to be used of a dish in which food can be cooked, or kept hot, after it is brought to table. A lamp fitted to the dish underneath, or an electric current, supplies the heat. 'The chafing-dish in the hands of a highly

trained cook is a practical toy, capable, within limitations, of contributing to the gayety of life; but in the hands of an amateur it merely puts another burden of responsibility on the overtaxed digestive organs.' 'There was not a caterer, as at the first reception, but Ida herself cooked dainty messes in a silver chafing-dish, and the white-capped little maid passed things' (MARY E. WILKINS FREEMAN, By the Light of the Soul, 93).

chain. The *chain-gang* is part of the penal system of some of the Southern States. The term denotes a group of prisoners who are set to work on the roads and are secured against escape by being chained. See BALL. 'Under this law, domestic servants have repeatedly been sent to the chain-gang for alleged violation of contract.' 'Cities are permitted to establish chain-gangs for the purpose of working on streets, roads, and other public works, using therein any male person over 18 years of age serving a jail sentence or subject to imprisonment for failure to pay a fine for violation of city ordinances' (F. W. HOFFER, D. M. MANN, and F. N. HOUSE, The Jails of Virginia, 138). 'Even the chain gang sings to the clink of leg shackles as picks are swung deep into roadside ditches' (J. PETERKIN, Roll, Jordan, Roll, 116).

For *chain stores*, see STORE.

chair is often personified in Am. to mean *chairman*. 'The chair was pounding and calling for order.' 'No one could be heard, nor any one listened to; so the chair sat down and lit a cigar' (F. J. STIMSON, My U.S. 133). 'The presiding officer, Senator Keen, replied: "The Chair is not aware that there is any Senate Committee of that name"' (Prof. N. W. STEPHENSON, Life of N. W. Aldrich, 187). The word is obs. in this sense in Eng. exc. in appeals of 'Chair!' and in such phrases as 'address the chair' and 'support the chair'.

The word is also technically used

of the seat occupied by a witness = Eng. *box*. Looking in one day at a meeting of a Senate Committee, I wished to know who was presiding, and accordingly asked my neighbour if he knew who was in the chair. In reply I was given the name of the witness then under examination. 'Hadley replied there was one place to answer questions and that was in the witness chair' (J. T. FLYNN, God's Gold, 413). See STAND.

It may further be used, without qualification, of the *electric chair* in which criminals are placed for execution. 'The Batchelor-Leonard murder case, where the quite evident effort to save the white principal by railroading the Negro agent to the chair was defeated' (C. S. JOHNSON, The Negro in Am. Civilization, 371). How the last two senses may be confused is illustrated by an incident reported in the N.Y. *Times* of May 12, 1904: 'Vincenzo Calido came into the Court of General Sessions yesterday morning, pale and trembling with fear, because he had understood his counsel, Stephen J. O'Hare, to say that he must die in the electric chair. Lawyer O'Hare had said just before the adjournment of the court on the previous day: "You must take the chair." The lawyer meant that Candido would have to go on the witness stand, but the Italian understood that he was to be executed immediately.'

A *chair car* in an Am. railway train is a car (for which higher fares are charged) in which passengers are accommodated in separate arm-chairs instead of the usual seats. 'He had slunk into a day coach, fearing to go into the chair car lest he should meet some one he knew.'

chambermaid. In Shakespeare's *Twelfth Night* Olivia's woman, Maria, is introduced as her chambermaid. Modern Eng. usage, however, distinguishes between a *chambermaid*, who serves in an inn or hotel, and a *housemaid*, who performs similar

duties in a private house. In Am. *chambermaid* is used indiscriminately for both these servants. Hence such advertisements as 'Lady going to Europe wishes to place second man and chambermaid'. 'Wanted: a neat young girl as chambermaid and waitress in small private family.' 'Rose was chambermaid as well as nurse' (GERTRUDE ATHERTON, Adventures of a Novelist, 32). See also WAITRESS.

†**chance.** In Eng. (1) a *fortuitous event* or (2) a *probability*, as distinct from a certainty. In Am. also a *risk* or *hazard*. Hence to *take a chance* (or *chances*), a common expression in Am., means something rather different from the Eng. expression *take one's chance*. The Am. expression emphasizes the element of risk or danger, whereas the Eng. suggests nothing more than the uncertainty of the result. Thus, in a discussion of trolley accidents, one reads that 'the companies connive at the taking of chances by their employees'. 'A man takes chances on a parachute.' 'The stockholder can afford to take the chances because he is looking for large and dazzling returns.' 'The industrial pioneer—the man who starts enterprises, takes whatever chance they involve, and builds them up with his own brains and hands' (H. CROLY, Marcus Alonzo Hanna, 79). 'Lee took chances which a general would not dare to consider unless forced by dire necessity' (Prof. A. E. MARTIN, Hist. of U.S. i. 712). 'Of course the President knew that he was taking a chance. Everything depended on the relative numbers of the two sorts of Democrats' (Prof. N. W. STEPHENSON, Nelson W. Aldrich, 303).

chancellor. In some Am. universities, e.g. the University of N.Y., the active head bears this title, which accordingly does not denote the ceremonial head, as in Eng.

In certain States, the term denotes a judge of the Court of Chancery. 'On

Feb. 24, 1814, he [James Kent] was appointed chancellor of the N.Y. court of Chancery' (Dict. Am. Biog. x. 345). In New Jersey the chancellorship is virtually a chief justiceship. 'The judges of the State immediately combined to have one of their own number made chancellor—the highest judicial officer in New Jersey' (J. KERNEY, Political Education of Woodrow Wilson, 194).

chaps. 'Where are the cowboys in chaps who used to tend this corral?' In this quotation *chaps* has no connexion whatever, in either derivation or meaning, with the Eng. *chaps*. It is an abbreviation of a Mexican-Spanish word *chaparajos*, denoting overalls of sheepskin or leather worn by cowboys to protect them from the thorns of the *chaparral*, a thick entanglement of bushes. 'His striking appearance in chaps and sombrero, which he wore indoors and out, made him the sensation of the season' (Dict. Am. Biog. xii. 622). 'They waved their hats and rode off, their heavy chaps flapping in the wind like clipped wings' (H. CAHILL, in Life in the U.S. 91).

chapter is the technical term for a local branch of a college Greek letter society. (See 'The Universities' in Bryce's *Am. Commonwealth.*) 'To this little circle somebody addressed himself who wanted to establish a chapter of Alpha Delta Phi in Cambridge' (Dr. E. E. HALE, Lowell and his Friends, 26). 'These friends gathered to form the first chapter of a Greek letter fraternity at our college' (L. LEWISOHN, Up Stream, 89).

charge. To *charge that* is a locution rare in Eng. but common in Am. In Eng. the verb requires a direct accusative of the person or thing; e.g. one charges a man with an offence or charges an offence on a man. One would say 'he brought the charge that . . .' rather than 'he charged that . . .' 'The other side charges

that scores of its votes were thrown out by the election inspectors.' 'The Chicago grand jury returned an indictment which charged that the Chicago and Alton had given rebates' (H. F. PRINGLE, Theodore Roosevelt, 420). 'He charged that secret spies had gained admission' (MARK SULLIVAN, Our Times, iii. 493). In Eng. this would be *alleged*.

In Am. a customer who secures the privilege of purchasing goods on credit with the understanding that he will pay for them at the end of the month is said to have a *charge account*. 'The proportion of returns on charge accounts is much greater than on cash or C.O.D. sales.'

charter. In Am. the term *charter member* denotes an original or foundation member of an institution or society, whether it was formed by the grant of a charter or not. 'The Amateur Dramatic Association, formed for acting Shakespearian plays, enrolled Kelly as charter member' (Dr. H. ZINK, City Bosses in U.S. 115). 'He was a charter member of the Am. Association of Economic Entomologists' (Dict. Am. Biog. vi. 510). See also SLEEP.

check. Am. *check* = Eng. *cheque*. A *certified check* is defined by the *Century Dict.* as 'a check which has been recognized by a competent officer of a bank as a valid appropriation of the amount of money specified therein to the payee, and bearing the evidence of such recognition'. According to *Webster's Dict.*, it is 'a check certified to be good by the bank upon which it is drawn by the signature of (usually) the cashier or paying teller with the word "good" or its equivalent across the face of the check'. 'The certification', adds Webster, 'operates as a guarantee that the signature is genuine, that the bank has in its possession sufficient funds of the drawer to meet the check, and that it will hold enough thereof in readiness to meet the check; it also operates to release the drawer and the indorsers, if any. It does not guarantee the body of the check to be genuine.' It must be remembered that the system of crossing cheques is unknown in Am., and that an Am. bank teller will only cash cheques when the payee is personally known to him or is satisfactorily identified. 'A certified check on a National Bank payable to the order of the City Controller of the City of Pittsburgh, for 5 per cent. of the bonds bid for, must accompany each proposal' (Advt.). 'When the trial was over, the superintendent of the detectives handed the young fellow a certified check for $500, his share of the reward offered for the arrest and conviction of the safe-breakers.'

The term *checking account* is sometimes used in Am. for *banking account*. 'She preferred the more generous way, and they had a joint checking account.' 'Checking accounts had been opened in a Philadelphia bank for Chandler' (C. G. BOWERS, The Tragic Era, 524).

The use of *check* to denote a *counter-foil* or *tally*, as well as that of the corresponding verb, is no longer peculiar to Am., but the compounds *check-room* and *checking-room*, denoting a cloak-room or depository for left luggage, have not yet crossed the Atlantic. 'The operator of check-rooms pays the highest sums for the privileges in those establishments where the greatest numbers of banquets and balls are held.' 'He arrived at the station carrying a small grip, and asked Charles where the checking-room was.' 'The checking-room for 3,000 wraps' (E. F. DAKIN, Mrs. Eddy, 378).

When an Am. who has been staying at an hotel has settled his account and handed to the hotel clerk the key of his room, he is said to *check out*. 'Paid my bills and checked out of the Grand hotel' (Dr. FRANKLIN H. MARTIN, The Joy of Living, ii. 457). The expression has also a fig. use. 'President Coolidge might well have appointed him Governor of the Federal Reserve Board when Crissinger checked out' (The Mirrors of Wall Street, 226). Here *checked out = resigned*.

The verb *check* has also in Am. certain uses that have nothing to do with travelling by rail or sojourning at a hotel. It is a trans. verb, meaning *keep check on*, and an intrans., meaning *tally*. 'The organization checks the ward and precinct of the official and keeps close track of who is back of him' (Prof. C. E. MERRIAM, Chicago, 29). 'My figures check generally with those of other agencies' (L. F. CARR, Am. Challenged, 21). Similarly *check up* is both trans. and intrans. 'Mr. Schaffner said he would check up some of the alleged grievances that we transmitted to him, and on examination found conditions of which he had not been aware and of which he did not approve' (Prof. C. E. MERRIAM, Chicago, 117). 'What better criterion does the man at the breakfast table possess than that the newspaper version checks up with his own opinion?' (W. LIPPMANN, Public Opinion, 329). This verb is often followed by *on*. 'The grower did not relish a long and expensive trip to headquarters to check up on reports' (C. A. and W. BEARD, The Am. Leviathan, 542). 'An inspector was usually sent out to check up on all the information, and, if everything was found satisfactory, the loan was made' (Prof. E. S. SPARKS, Agricultural Credit in U.S. 373).

Hence the noun *check-up*. 'A check-up on sermons taken on a random Sunday showed that 70 per cent. of them consisted merely of criticism and that only 30 per cent. attempted to lead constructively.' 'A check-up of the most important steel companies showed 4,164 Negroes' (S. D. SPERO and A. L. HARRIS, The Black Worker, 154). Am. *check-up committee = Eng. auditing committee*.

A *check list* is a list used for reference or verification. 'When the catalogue was announced it was hoped that it would be a distinctive contribution to bibliographical literature and a kind of monument to its subject. But this is a merely utilitarian production—little more than a check list.'

checker. In an Eng. village one may come across an inn called The *Chequers*, or *Checkers*, sometimes with a sign reproducing the alternate black and white squares of a chessboard. This is a reminder of the time when the game of chess was called *checkers*, and a *chessboard* was known as a *checker-board*. *Checker-board* is still a common name for such a board in Am., and one of the games played on it is called *checkers*—not chess, however, but draughts. 'Checkers, another popular game, is played without any scientific pretence, and chess is not attempted at all.' 'Crossroad stores, where discussion is as constant a pastime as checkers' (Prof. H. J. FORD, Woodrow Wilson, 85). 'A vast checkerboard of cultivated fields.' 'Fleets of barges lay upon the river like the black squares of some huge checkerboard.'

Hence *checker-paned*. 'How those checker-paned windows bring back the picture of that village green! The meeting-house has them, lantern-like, wide and high, in three sashes' (WINSTON CHURCHILL, Coniston, 3).

The compound *checkerberry* denotes an Am. plant of the wintergreen class and also its fruit. 'The introduction of peppermint and checkerberry essences has almost resulted in driving carraway seeds out of the pharmacopoeia of the family.' 'Picking checkerberries in his pasture.'

cheer. In Am. the compound *cheer-leader* is the recognized—one might almost say, official—term for a person who leads the organized cheering at an athletic contest. 'The group on the dust-bin begins rousing the crowd with methods like those of a college cheer-leader' (E. WILSON, The Am. Jitters, 39). The term is sometimes used fig. 'On March 16th the inde-

fatigable cheer-leader of the Presidential optimists, Julius H. Barnes, the head of Mr. Hoover's new National Business Survey Conference, spoke as if trouble were already a thing of the past' (F. L. ALLEN, Only Yesterday, 340).

cherry. In Am. a *cherrystone* may be a wholesome and agreeable article of diet. 'The clam which we know on the menu as cherrystone is a round, hard-shelled mollusk, technically a quohog. The cherrystone is a Southern variety, and its name is a corruption of Cheritan, in Virginia' (H. RIPPERGER, in N.Y. Times Mag., July 22, 1934).

chicken. The Eng. visitor to the U.S. needs to be warned, when he studies the menu at a restaurant, that in Am. *chicken* is sometimes loosely used in the sense of *fowl*. 'Chickens, ducks, and turkeys have the run of the kitchen.' 'On a much larger number of estates slaves cultivated their own vegetable gardens or kept their own chickens' (Prof. C. S. SYDNOR, Slavery in Mississippi, 98). Hence Am. *chicken-yard* = Eng. *fowl-run*.

chicory. Though the dictionaries give no indication of any difference, one finds, in buying vegetables in an Am. market, that Eng. *chicory* = Am. *endive* and Am. *chicory* = Eng. *endive*. The French *chicorée* similarly denotes the Eng. *endive* and the French *endive* the Eng. *chicory*.

choice. The expression *choice of*, meaning *making much of, setting great store by*, is now heard in Eng. only in certain dialects. An Am. example is found in Kate Douglas Wiggins' novel, *Rebecca*, where the heroine, fearing she has lost her trunk, says: 'It's my mother's trunk, and she's very choice of it;' i.e. she sets great store by it.

chopper. In Am. the railway servant who stands, as an inspector, by the receptacle into which passengers throw their tickets at the beginning or end of their journey by an elevated or underground railway. The term is also applied to the attendant who receives the tickets of patrons of theatres, ball parks, &c. 'I asked policemen, ticket-sellers, and choppers if they had seen a lady in a gray dress with two valises pass through.' 'Mr. Dooley' speaks of handing one's ticket 'to th' chopper at th' big gate'. 'In those days, as he tells us, it was his one particular and engrossing employment to do right, just as it is the one particular and engrossing employment of an elevated railway ticket-chopper to chop tickets, and Paul went about it in very much the same way that the chopper goes about it' (Dr. C. H. Parkhurst, A Little Lower Than the Angels, 205).

chorister is sometimes used in Am. in the sense not of *member of a choir* but of *precentor*. 'Moody had engaged a young man, Ira D. Sankey, to be chorister in his church and Sunday school' (W. R. Moody, Life of D. L. Moody, 141).

chuck. The term *chuck steak* is used in Am., as in certain Eng. dial., to denote a cut of beef lying between the neck and the shoulder-blade. It is usually the cheapest meat in the market. 'Chuck steaks 8 cents per pound at the Capital Meat Market' (Advt.). 'A bad cook will spoil a four-pound porterhouse, where a good one will take a chuck steak, make a few passes over it with seasoning and fixings, and serve something that will line your insides with happiness' (G. H. Lorimer, Old Gorgon Graham, 257).

The compound *chuck-box* denotes a box containing food supplies for cowboys, pioneers, &c. 'A carpenter was then at work building chuck-boxes for each of the six commissaries' (Andy Adams, The Outlet, 16). Such supplies are carried from place to place in *chuck-wagons*. 'On reaching the supply point, there was a question if we could secure the simple staples needed. The drive that year had out-stripped all calculations, some half-dozen chuck-wagons being in waiting for the arrival of a freight outfit which was due that morning' (op. cit. 56).

church. The derivative adj. *churchly* is rare in Eng. but frequent in Am. 'A lady who, being the parishioner of one of the brainiest preachers in the whole country, has had interesting churchly experiences.' 'The Calvary Church choir may be accepted as representative of the worldly as well as the churchly side of the choir boy's life.' 'He was an ecclesiastic who looked upon human life wholly from the restricted churchly point of view' (Prof. L. O. Brastow, Representative Modern Preachers, 252). 'Indifferent to ecclesiastical forms or even churchly control' (Prof. Barrett Wendell, The Temper of the 17th Century, 222). In these examples an Eng. writer would have used either *church* or *ecclesiastical*.

circuit. Methodists all the world over use this word in the same spec. sense, but *circuit rider* is a term peculiar to Am. The name is given to a minister who, in the early days of Am. settlement, had charge of so large a circuit that he was constantly in the saddle. 'Stout-hearted, downright, muscular, practical, the circuit-rider faced the actual world of the frontier, and saw it clearly.' 'In 1846 the Democrats gave him for a competitor the famous Methodist circuit-rider, Peter Cartwright, one of the best-known and beloved men of that period on the frontier. He was the highest type of itinerant preacher. For 60 years he travelled on horseback throughout the Western country, marrying the young people, baptizing their children, burying their dead, preaching by the wayside and in the forests' (W. E. Curtis, The True Abraham Lincoln, 138). 'There was no service sung or spoken over the dead, for the circuit-rider was then three months away' (John Fox, Jr., Little Shepherd of Kingdom Come, 2).

For *circuit attorney*, see ATTORNEY.

circulate. In Am. *circulate* sometimes = Eng. *circularize.* 'Rhodes and Co. issued leaflets and pamphlets which circulated the offices of railroads and factories' (T. BEER, Hanna, 78).

In its intrans. use the word may be applied to the movement of persons as well as of things. Cf. French *circuler.* 'In order to counteract any unfavourable idea, I was advised to circulate as much as possible among the voters' (Prof. C. E. MERRIAM, Chicago, 271). 'I started off on foot with friends but soon lost them and circulated in the crowd by myself' (ALICE ROOSEVELT LONGWORTH, Crowded Hours, 225). 'When the club met we children were allowed to be present, and to circulate among the grown-ups' (EDITH WHARTON, A Backward Glance, 46).

circumstance. Am. *not a circumstance to* = Eng. *nothing in comparison with.* 'Undigested securities are not a circumstance to undigested political principles.' 'Hamlet without the ghost would not be a circumstance to it' (UPTON SINCLAIR, Money Writes, 37). 'Zwingli's troubles because of the peasants were, however, not a circumstance to those caused by the Baptist party in Zurich' (Prof. S. M. JACKSON, Life of Zwingli, 240).

citizen. 'When he speaks not like a citizen,' says Menenius of Coriolanus, 'you find him like a soldier.' In this sense, *citizen* has long been superseded in Eng. by *civilian,* but the Shakespearian usage survives in Am., where the word is commonly employed, without any suggestion of the possession of the rights of citizenship, to denote a private person as distinct from a member of a uniformed force. 'Happily, in this city the situation has improved as between the citizen and the policeman.' 'Several school teachers were cut off by the smoke and flame, but all were taken out in safety by citizens, policemen, and firemen.' 'At Browns-

ville, negro soldiers rioted, killing and wounding several citizens' (MARK SULLIVAN, Our Times, iii. 453). The difference of idiom is illustrated further in the colloq. term denoting the dress of an officer off duty. In Eng. this is *civvies,* i.e. civilians' dress, but in Am. *cits,* i.e. citizens' dress. 'Later, they were joined by Major W. V. Judson, of the engineers, in "cits".'

Am. citizen is the term corresponding to *British subject.* Americans are naturally annoyed when they see in an Eng. paper, as they frequently may, a reference to one of their compatriots as 'an Am. subject'.

citizen is also used in Am. as a synonym for *resident, inhabitant.* 'The citizens of Nutley held a meeting last night for the purpose of discovering some means whereby the train service may be improved.' This, too, is a survival of a sense now obs. in Eng.; e.g. 'He joined himself to a citizen of that country' (Luke xv. 15, A.V.).

citizens' committee is an alternative name for the *vigilance committee* which maintains order after a fashion in a new and imperfectly organized community. 'The British labor movement has no parallel in recent years to the mob violence of W. Virginia, Bisbee, Ariz., or Ludlow, Colorado. Lynch law and "citizens' committees" are practically unknown' (P. BLANSHARD, Outline of British Labor Movement, 83).

city. In Eng. a large and important town, or one that contains a cathedral. 'In the statistical publications of the U.S. government, a city is defined as an aggregation of 8,000 persons living in one territorial unit and under one local government' (Prof. A. B. HART, Actual Government, 181). Thus, H. N. Casson (Life of C. H. McCormick, 212) refers to 'a sixty-car train travelling eastward with enough wheat in its rolling bins to give bread to a city of 10,000 for a year.' Accordingly, as the Am. *city* corresponds very nearly to the Eng. *town*, Am. *city hall* = Eng. *town hall*. 'Desperate men out of work have stormed city halls from coast to coast.' 'Much moral turpitude prevailed in a surprisingly large number of state capitals and city halls' (Prof. A. E. MARTIN, Hist. of U.S. ii. 96). In N.Y. there is not only a *city hall* but a *town hall*. The latter is not, however, a municipal building, but a privately owned hall used for lectures, &c.

claim. 'A citizen of a foreign country claiming to be imprisoned for some act committed with the sanction of his government' (C. A. and W. BEARD, The Am. Leviathan, 121). What does this mean? Acc. to Eng. usage, its only possible meaning, though an incredible one, would be that the person mentioned demands imprisonment as his due. The context, however, shows that nothing of the kind is intended. The writers are speaking of occasions on which a Federal judge may issue a writ of habeas corpus. Among the occasions specified is when the prisoner on whose behalf the writ is desired is such a person as is described in the above quotation. That is to say, 'claiming to be imprisoned' = 'asserting that he is imprisoned'. In Am. the verb *claim* has lost its distinctive meaning of *demand as one's due*, having become a mere synonym for *assert, state*. 'Buckle, in his History of Civilization, claims that men and women are divided into three classes.' 'Plato claimed that, before his Republic could be established, the adult population must be killed off' (Prof. H. W. SCHNEIDER, The Puritan Mind, 36). 'The Apache did not eat turkeys, claiming that they were not good to eat as turkeys ate snakes' (B. DAVIES, The Truth About Geronimo, 108). 'All who were connected with these industries claimed that they would be ruined by any decrease in duties' (Dr. J. H. FREDERICK, The Development of Am. Commerce, 178).

Similarly the noun *claim* means, in Am., nothing more than *assertion* or *contention*. 'Some difference of claims continues between the merchants and the functionaries in charge at the appraiser's warehouse as to where the blame lies for such delays as have occurred.' 'Koepping killed Martini and afterwards made affidavit that Martini's wife killed him and that he had assumed the homicide to save her. She failed to substantiate his claim.' 'The claim that Am. will never have a merchant marine unless it is privately owned and managed' (W. LIPPMANN, Public Opinion, 122).

A *claim agent* or *claims agent* is a person who undertakes professionally the cases of clients seeking compensation or relief from Congress. 'Claim agents and pension agents subscribe [to the *Congressional Record*] in order to follow the course of private bills in which they are interested.'

class. 'George von L. Meyer had been a class ahead of him at Harvard' (H. F. PRINGLE, Theodore Roosevelt, 381). This does not mean, as an Eng. reader would suppose, that Meyer took higher honours than Roosevelt, but that he entered Harvard a year in advance of him. The word *class* is a technical term at both Eng. and Am. universities, but with widely different meanings. In Eng. it denotes one of the divisions in which successful candidates are grouped at an examination, esp. an examination for honours. In Am. the name is given to the whole body of students of any particular year in the normal four years' course. (In his first year, a student is a member of the freshman class; in his second, of the sophomore class; in his third, of the junior class; and in his fourth, of the senior class). It bears the label of the year in which these students have completed (or will complete) their course. Thus the class of 1935 at Harvard consists of the students who entered that university in 1931 and will graduate in 1935. When it is said that A and **B**

were in the same class at Oxford, what is meant is that they were placed in the same class (1st, 2nd, or 3rd) in the same honours examination (Lit. Hum., Mathematics, or whatever it may have been) in the same year. To say that A and B were in the same class at Harvard means simply that they entered in the same year and accordingly graduated in the same year. 'Brown University began its 140th year this week with an entering class of about 180.' 'Loyalty to class and to Yale are the first lessons of a freshman.' 'The class of youngsters who entered Harvard College in 1856, when Lowell began his work there, graduated in 1860' (Dr. E. E. HALE, Lowell and his Friends, 180). 'In Yale (class of 1896) he had played better than average football' (SINCLAIR LEWIS, Dodsworth, 9).

†A common Am. locution is *in the same class = of the same type, of the same rank*. 'That township school which hopes to pay its expenses with the product of an oil well in its front yard is merely endeavoring to get in the same class with the University of Chicago.' 'He would now and then select some one word or expression to bear the opprobrium of corrupting the speech, while he employed without hesitation scores of others which were exactly in the same class, and therefore justly exposed to the same exception.'

The mail sent through the U.S. Post Office is divided into *classes*. First-class matter consists of letters; second-class, of registered newspapers and periodicals; third-class, of miscellaneous printed matter and merchandise not exceeding 8 oz. in weight; and fourth-class, of all other matter allowed to be sent by post. 'In Christmas packages there are often inclosed brief notes, and the presence of such messages makes the matter first class.' 'There is something anomalous in the power of life and death over periodical publications which is conferred upon the Third Assistant Postmaster-General in the decision of questions relating to second-class postage.' 'First-class mail is commonly supposed to afford a handsome surplus, while second-class rates eat up this surplus.'

The word *class* is not used in Am., as it is in Eng., to denote the different types of accommodation provided on the railways. These differences are indicated by other terms, which do not conflict with the popular theory that there are no class distinctions in Am.

classify, classification. *classified service.* See first quotation. 'The act of January 16, 1883, is the basis of the present Federal civil service . . . The act provides for the classification of clerks and other officers into four groups, according to their compensation; and hence all the persons subject to competitive examination are said to be in the classified service' (Prof. A. B. HART, Actual Government, 290). 'Country post offices are not embraced in the classified service.' 'In the Senate, as in the House, I have done everything in my power for the reform of the civil service. In the present Congress I took part in bringing the census force within the classified service.'

For *classification yard*, see first quotation. 'Into the classification yards long trains of freight cars are run; there they are broken up into smaller trains destined for the various termini of the road, a work requiring large forces of experienced trainmen and a highly perfected system in order to insure accuracy and promptness.' 'The grading has about been completed for the great classification yards of the Pennsylvania [Railroad].'

For *classification club*, see CLUB.

cleanse is often preferred in Am. where *clean* would be used in Eng. Thus, the department of a municipality that is responsible for the care of the streets is commonly known as a street-cleansing department. 'Carpet cleansing for 40 years' (Advt.). 'Washwoman Demands Extra Dollar for Cleansing 344 Pieces in One Week' (Newspaper headline).

clear is often used in Am., but rarely in Eng. (exc. in dial.), in the sense of *all the way, all the time.* 'One might chase coyotes from there clear into Texas.' 'Mr. Taft's greeting to the man he was so soon to succeed was: "Mr. President, even the elements protest." "Mr. President-elect," quickly rejoined Mr. Roosevelt, "I knew there would be a blizzard clear up to the minute I went out of office."' 'We went clear on to the end' (W. G. McADOO, Crowded Years, 72). 'He wrote one hymn which has been sung clear around the globe' (Dr. C. R. BROWN, They Were Giants, 220).

clergyman. In Eng. usually a *priest or deacon of the Church of Eng.* In Am. a *minister of any religious body.* In *Who's Who in Am.*, the profession of Baptist, Congregationalist, Methodist, and other ministers is ordinarily given as *clergyman.* So, too, in the *Dict. of Am. Biog.* one finds many such entries as 'Field, David Dudley, Congregational clergyman' and 'Foster, George Burman, Baptist clergyman'. In his account of his own education Henry Adams refers everywhere to the Unitarian ministers of Boston as the Unitarian clergy. The Bishop of the diocese of Western Massachusetts in the Protestant Episcopal Church is quoted (Churchman, Mar. 11, 1905) as speaking of 'clergymen of your denomination' in an address to Congregationalists. 'He was ordained a clergyman of the Congregational Church' (MARK SULLIVAN, Our Times, iii. 476).

clerk. In Am. *clerk* denotes a *shop assistant* quite as often as a *secretary* or a *person who keeps records or accounts.* 'Many good books fail to sell because people are afraid the clerks will laugh at them for mispronouncing names.' 'Wanted, grocery clerk to drive order team' (Advt.). 'These very features are to be found in the faces of bar-maids and ribbon clerks.' 'He walked across the country to New Salem and became a clerk in the store of Denton Offutt, measuring calico, weighing out sugar and nails, tending a grist-mill, and making himself useful to his employer' (W. E. CURTIS, The True Abraham Lincoln, 33). Hence the verb *clerk* in a corresponding sense. The late J. G. Cannon, Speaker of the House of Representatives, once said, referring to the days of his youth: 'I clerked in a country store for 5 years. I had to get up, make the fire, sweep out, eat breakfast, and be ready for business by 6 o'clock.' In Am. *clerk* is pronounced *clurk*, not *clark*, as in Eng.
'He praised the village pavements,
    and he asked Tom Jones, the clerk,
About the cost of doing them, and
    who had done the work.'
One day, the compiler of this dictionary, entering a Philadelphia hotel and wishing to engage a room, but not knowing at which of several desks the register was kept, went up to one of them and inquired whether it was the desk of the hotel clerk. 'No,' was the reply; 'this is the Hotel Lafayette.' Having, in a thoughtless moment, pronounced the work *clerk* in the Eng. fashion, he had been supposed to be asking whether the hotel in which he found himself bore the name of the Hotel Clark.

clip. In Am., as in some Eng. dial., the noun *clip* may mean *rate of movement, pace, speed.* 'A northwest gale was blowing at a 40-mile clip.' 'Marer started up the drive at a fast clip.' 'He steps along at a pretty lively clip.'
The verb *clip* is commonly preferred to *cut* when one is referring to the use of scissors in taking an extract from a newspaper. Thus, Am. *clipping bureau* = Eng. *press-cutting agency.* 'A suggestion that should be clipped and pasted for reference.' 'He produced a clipping from a morning paper.' 'Col. Roosevelt sent me a number of these newspaper

clippings' (JANE ADDAMS, The Second 20 Years at Hull-House, 44). 'A library where 800 newspapers are clipped and filed' (Dr. A. FLEXNER, Universities, 333). 'She shunned publicity and was said never to have subscribed to a clipping bureau nor preserved a press notice' (Dict. Am. Biog. vi. 276).

cloak-room. In the British Parliament, the lobbies are the centres of gossip for members. In Congress, the *cloak-rooms* serve that purpose, LOBBY (q.v.) being used in Am. in a special sense. 'This story, which has now got into circulation in the Senate cloak-rooms, is variously interpreted.' 'Colleagues stop as they pass one's chair to drop a summons to the cloak-room for consultation' (G. W. PEPPER, In the Senate, 26). 'It was discussed in the Senate cloak-rooms' (D. LAWRENCE, The True Story of Woodrow Wilson, 289). 'Their speakers for independence before the House and Senate committees were commended in the Congressional cloak-rooms' (Sen. H. B. HAWES, Philippine Uncertainty, 39).

close. In Eng. an election which is won by a narrow majority is described as a *close* contest. In Am. the adj. is transferred to a State or district (= Eng. constituency) where the rival parties are almost equally matched. 'What that candidate's record and opinions may be matters little, so long as he can demonstrate his capacity as a vote getter in the closer Northern States.' 'In the last Congressional election there were comparatively few close districts; and, indeed, out of the 386 districts in the U.S., there were only 27 wherein a member was returned with a majority of less than 1,000.' A *close district* in Am. is thus something entirely different from the *close borough* which was one of the scandals of the Eng. Parliamentary system before the Reform Act of 1832.

†Am. *close call* = Eng. *close shave* (fig.), *narrow escape, near thing*. The brevity of the term makes it esp. convenient for headlines. 'Close Call for French Ministry. Government Escapes Defeat by Four Votes.' 'Close Call of Crowded Train. Lackawanna Locomotive Tank Derailed on Verge of Twenty-foot Embankment.' 'Harvard had a mighty close call on the gridiron this afternoon. The Carlisle Indians scored 11 points, while the Crimson scored 12.'

†The verb *close* (trans. and intrans.) is often intensified in Am. by *down, up,* or *out,* all three of which have the same meaning in this connexion, in spite of the apparent contradiction between the first two. 'He has issued orders to temporarily close down all of the operations of the company.' 'The works would close down on June 30th; all employees were to consider themselves discharged' (B. J. HENDRICK, Life of Andrew Carnegie, 339). 'The poolrooms are unlawful, and the District Attorney is bent on closing them up.' 'To close up the business of the Bank in 1836 would mean the calling in of a great mass of loans' (Prof. A. E. MARTIN, Hist. of U.S. i. 407). 'Two of the native papers were being threatened with being closed out.' 'The next month was spent in finally closing out the affairs of the Pacific Fur Co.' (K. W. PORTER, John Jacob Astor, 232).

Am. *closed season* = Eng. *close season.* 'It was the closed season for grouse.'

†There has been coined in Am.—probably at Hollywood—the noun *close-up*, which denotes a view taken at close quarters, an intimate view. 'We have the spectacle of at least one great industry which affords us a close-up of the ruthless sabotage of invention hurling its wooden shoe into the machinery of production.' 'As editor of the *Trenton Times* I saw him start, and through all the years of his public life I got frequent close-ups' (J. KERNEY, Political Education of Woodrow Wilson, xvi). 'Pershing got [at Paris] a close-up of the intimate part European statesmen play in

actually directing wars, as well as bringing them on' (J. KERNEY, op. cit. 424).

club. The Am. term *classification club* denotes a club whose members are classified acc. to their occupations and derive their qualification for membership from the fact that they follow the occupation which they represent. 'The Rotary Club of Chicago is the progenitor of all classification clubs and organizations of its type, including Exchange, Kiwanis, Lions, Gyro, Zonta (Women's), Co-operative, Civitan, etc.' (Rotary? 49). The Am. *country club* is far from being an expression of the social activities of a rural community. It provides for city residents an opportunity for outdoor sports and other relaxations within easy motoring distance of their homes. 'As house and apartments became smaller, the country club became the social center of the small city, the suburb, and the summer resort, and to its pretentious clubhouse, every Saturday night, drove men and women for the weekly dinner dance' (F. L. ALLEN, Only Yesterday, 110). 'The wealthy fostered the growth of country clubs where, amidst the lovely verdure of hill and dale, such pleasures as polo and golf might be pursued under the best obtainable conditions. In the nineties country clubs could be found in well-to-do communities from Palm Beach to Puget Sound' (Prof. A. M. SCHLESINGER, The Rise of the City, 316). Acc. to Prof. Schlesinger, the Brookline Country Club, founded in 1882 near Boston, was apparently the first of these clubs.

Acc. to the *Concise Oxford Dict.*, a *sandwich* consists of 'two slices of bread with meat or other relish between'. That definition would have to be modified to apply to the Am. *club sandwich*, which consists of several layers of bread and filling, so that it may constitute the greater portion of a substantial meal. It is eaten with a knife and fork.

The term *clubman* is defined by the *O.E.D.* as *a member of a club*. The *Century Dict.* adds to this definition a second : *one who prefers the life of clubs.* The addition is significant. 'He was not a professional reformer; he was ostensibly a club-man and man about town like another' (A. HODDER, A Fight for the City, 12). That is to say, the Am. *clubman* is the male analogue of the *Society woman.*

See CAMPAIGN, DUES, and INITIATION.

coach. 'The coachers go to the halls where the shows are rehearsing, and instruct the singer and chorus in the necessary business.' 'You may walk the towpath [at Oxford] on a January afternoon, and you shall find coachers splashing through the mire and shouting their orders to the crews.' These examples are taken from Am. newspapers dated 1904. Since then, *coacher* has been superseded by the Eng. *coach.* According, however, to the baseball glossary in the 14th edition of the *Encycl. Britann.*, *coacher* is still the technical term in Am. for a 'man who may or may not be actively in game and, standing at corner of diamond, encourages team at bat.'

coal. In Am. bituminous coal is commonly known as *soft coal* and anthracite as *hard coal.* 'Hard Coal Back at $6.25. The last monthly advance in the price of domestic sizes of anthracite coal goes into effect tomorrow, making the retail price $6.25.' 'A force always working against public cleanliness is the soft-coal smoke which defaces nearly all Western cities' (Prof. A. B. HART, Actual Government, 572).

cockney. Acc. to the *O.E.D.*, before this word was used spec. of one born in the city of London, it was 'a derisive appellation for a townsman, as the type of effeminacy, in contrast to the hardier inhabitants of the country'. In this sense it is now obs. in Eng., but may occasionally be met with in Am. 'Americans to-day are more interdependent than ever before in the history of the nation. The artificial life of the cities is proverbial. But now even many rural districts are as dependent on the beef packer, the vegetable canner, the milk condenser, and the anthracite mining company as the veriest cockney.'

co-education. This term is common to Eng. and Am. Peculiar to Am., however, is the abbreviation *co-ed* (or, more commonly, *coed*) meaning a girl student or girl pupil at a co-educational institution. The term is seldom used of a boy or young man attending such an institution, though logically it would be equally applicable to him. 'Evidently the Oxford man does not have that yearning to go to class in a sweater which, in Am. colleges, is the cause of many a bitter petition to have the irksome presence of the coed done away with.' 'The Tufts College coeds proclaimed their independence to-night by giving a big dance and shutting the men out completely.'

collect. In Am. a boy may call periodically at your house, saying that he has come to collect for *The Times*. He is not seeking charitable donations, but has been sent by the newsagent who supplies you with your daily paper, in order to ask for what you owe him. Similarly, a telegram that is paid for when received instead of when sent is marked *Collect*. 'As far as practicable, the forecast messages will be telegraphed at the expense of the Weather Bureau; but, if this is impracticable, they will be furnished at the regular commercial rates and sent "collect"' (World Almanac). Thus, *C.O.D.*, which in Eng. is understood to mean *Cash on Delivery*, means in Am. *Collect on Delivery*.
In Eng. a *collector* is usually an official who collects taxes or rates. In Am. the name is given not only to an official of the Internal Revenue Department but to a Customs official.

'In his earlier life he was District Attorney and later Collector of the Port of N.Y.' (M. GOUVERNEUR, As I Remember, 44). Such an official is in charge of a *collection district*. 'The coast of the ocean fronts and the Great Lakes is divided into 120 tariff collection districts; the interior and the coast together are divided into 63 internal-revenue collection districts' (Prof. A. B. HART, Actual Government, 7). It may be noted that in certain provinces of India a *collector* is the chief administrative official of a district, where, although his spec. duty is the collection of revenue, he also exercises certain magisterial authority.

colloquy is a technical term in the Am. Congress to denote the dialogue, or interchange of opinions, that takes place when a member, in the course of a speech, is interrupted by a fellow-member, and the two of them spend a few minutes in arguing with, and replying to, one another. 'Near the close of the controversy, Senator Clarke rashly involved himself in a "colloquy"—the pompous senatorial term for informal discussion—which he opened by the rash device of quoting Aldrich not quite fairly' (Prof. N. W. STEPHENSON, Nelson W. Aldrich, 299). 'In the colloquy which followed, Senator Smoot drew from Mr. Newlands the statement that he would apply such a leasing law to all other mineral deposits as well as coal' (A. B. DARLING, Public Papers of Francis G. Newlands, i. 101). 'He spoke extemporaneously, and at times engaged in colloquy, so that the affair was rather more of a free conference than a formal address' (Prof. H. J. FORD, Woodrow Wilson, 44).

colonel. This title may be acquired in Am. by appointment as a member of the staff of a State Governor. The main duty it involves is that of riding in uniform in the procession at his inauguration and at other official functions. 'He was appointed an aide-de-camp on the staff of Governor David B. Hill, and thus acquired the title of Colonel by which he still is popularly known.' 'A few weeks before his retirement from Trenton, Wilson, as a matter of compliment, had named the younger Birch as personal aide-de-camp on the governor's staff, giving him the title of colonel' (J. KERNEY, Political Education of Woodrow Wilson, 314). 'It was Governor Hogg who provided House with the title of "Colonel", by appointing him, entirely without the recipient's suspicion, to his staff' (Prof. C. SEYMOUR, Intimate Papers of Col. House, i. 39). The mere offer of such a post appears to be considered an adequate justification for the use of the title. In its biography of Milton McRae, a prominent figure in the Am. newspaper world, the *Dict. Am. Biog.* says: 'He refused a commission on the military staff of McKinley, when he was governor of Ohio, and was promptly dubbed "Colonel" by his newspaper colleagues. The title thus bestowed clung to him and was proudly borne.' Acc. to the same authority, W. C. Goodloe, a Kentucky politician, 'never rose above the rank of captain, his title of "Colonel" being the honorary title quite commonly bestowed upon Kentuckians with and without military experience'. See also CAPTAIN.

Col. House tells an amusing story of the embarrassment this title caused him when he was invited to Potsdam in June 1914. 'I had cautioned Gerard [the U.S. Ambassador to Berlin] before coming to Berlin not to use the title of "Colonel" when referring to me or when introducing me after I arrived. This did not serve my purpose, for Bernstorff [the German Ambassador to Washington] had cabled of my coming, so I became "Colonel" immediately. Most of my time at luncheon was used in explaining to my neighbors the kind of Colonel I was—not a real one in the European sense, but, as we would say in Am., a geographical one. My explanation finally reached Falkenhayn's consciousness, but my neighbor from Saxony was hopelessly befuddled and continued until the last to discuss army technique' (Intimate Papers of Col. House, i. 260).

colony, colonial, &c. The word *colonial* has quite different associations in Eng. and Am. In Am. it refers specifically to the period of Am. hist. before the Revolution, and is often spelt with a capital initial. 'Tallow candles will never be heard of again, except as a historic bit of Colonial economy.' 'On the front of the lot there will be erected a brick building of Colonial architecture.' 'The atmosphere of education in which he lived was colonial, revolutionary, almost Cromwellian' (The Education of Henry Adams, 7). 'A carpenter may be able to make a splendid Colonial window or a beautiful Renaissance door' (W. D. ORCUTT, The Kingdom of Books, 59). 'The seats of chairs showed signs of wear. Some of them were of Colonial respectability' (Dr. S. WEIR MITCHELL, Constance Trescot, 55). The word thus comes sometimes to be almost a synonym for *antique*. 'Sometimes we wonder whether personal reminiscences will ever become colonial. Will people some day search for them as they do for old china and old books and old mahogany?'

The term *Colonial Dames*, however, does not denote the Pilgrim Mothers, but a society whose members trace their ancestry back to colonial days. 'The bill empowering the park commissioner to grant to the Colonial Dames the custody of the Jumel mansion.' 'Your German doctor who has compassed sea and land with the zeal of a Pharisee for a proselyte or a Colonial Dame for a pedigree, to add some new fact to the mass of human knowledge.'

Colonialism sometimes refers to this early period. 'Through the southern part of Maryland to the Potomac, a region of old families, old prejudices, sleepy Colonialism, and the colored brother.' More frequently it denotes the political doctrine which in Eng. goes by the name of *Imperialism*. 'Colonialism has never really become a part of the Am. national scheme, despite all the talk of Mahan, Whitelaw Reid, Theodore Roosevelt, Henry Cabot Lodge, and the rest of that noble company.' 'McKinley, Root, Roosevelt and Taft have all at one time or another declared for eventual independence of the Philippines. Probably few Americans hope to see colonialism perpetuated.'

The word *colony* is sometimes used in Eng. to denote a group of foreign residents in a city; e.g. the French colony in Soho. In Am. this use of the word is considerably extended, as in the following examples: 'The Reno divorce "colony" is highly lucrative to the hotel-keepers.' 'The diplomatic colony will be well represented in Washington by the middle of October.' 'Disapproval and even indignation were expressed yesterday by members of the Ohio delegation in Congress . . . The news from Columbus created a profound stir in the Ohio colony, and not a single member of the House or Senate showed any sympathy with the movement.' 'Before the [civil] war, many wealthy Southerners frequently spent their summers in the North. There was a considerable Charlestonian summer colony in Rhode Island at times' (J. TRUSLOW ADAMS, America's Tragedy, 145).

A mention of the votes cast by *colonizers* at an Am. election has nothing whatever to do with the political choices made by immigrants. The persons referred to are men who —having possibly voted already in their own district—are imported into another district, where they make a false declaration of residence, in order to cast a fraudulent vote there. 'The attempt to colonize in the Third Ward by a faction of the Dem. party was frustrated to-day by the decision of Justice Howard to the effect that 25 names were illegally enrolled.' 'The superintendent of elections is authority for the statement that there are gangs of colonizers and repeaters in the city.' 'Indianapolis, owing to its geographical position and transportation facilities, is an easy city to colonize from Kentucky—not quite so easy as Cincinnati, but sufficiently inviting to the professional colonizer to make its reputable citizens uncomfortable as each successive election approaches.'

column. In the political vocab. of Am., *column* is used to denote the whole body of supporters of a certain party or candidate. In this sense it is probably an adaptation of the military use of the word. 'If the Philippine bill should eventually become a law, and importations should interfere with the manufacture and sale of beet sugar, the resulting dissatisfaction would be sufficient to throw Michigan into the Dem. column.' 'On Nov. 8 Roosevelt won overwhelmingly. Even Missouri went into the Rep. column' (H. F. PRINGLE Theodore Roosevelt, 356). In Eng. *ranks* would be used in this sense.

Am. has coined the word *columnist* to denote a journalist who contributes regularly to a newspaper a column of miscellaneous comment on men and things—the kind of contribution that in the Eng. press used to be called a *causerie*. 'The cartoonists, the columnists, and the paragraphers, who strike out flashes of wholesome humor' (Prof. E. MIMS, Adventurous Am. 139). 'Since 1891 he has been connected as reviewer, editorial writer and columnist with Philadelphia newspapers' (Prof. J. M. MANLY and E. RICKERT, Contemporary Am. Lit. 153).

come. In reply to a knock at the door, Am. *Come!* = Eng. *Come in!* Am. *come by* = Eng. *call, look in.* 'It was delightful to have him come by after church and take me off to his parsonage for Sunday dinner.'

†The Am. expression *come to stay* = Eng. *become a regular thing, attain a permanent standing.* 'The national convention came to stay in Am. politics 72 years ago.' 'It was evident that Am. had at last produced a novelist who had come to stay' (W. M. PAYNE, Editorial Echoes, 107).

Am. *come out* = Eng. *turn out, come off.* 'They avoid those controversies over exact facts in which he has invariably come out second-best.' 'The five editors had the further privilege of assuming the whole pecuniary responsibility for the undertaking. How this came out I do not know' (Dr. E. E. HALE, Lowell and his Friends, 30).

In Am. the compound *come-outer* has been invented to denote a reformer who is so dissatisfied with the slow pace of the body—whether religious, political, or what not—to which he belongs that he comes out of it to form a more progressive group. 'Dr. Holmes was rather a believer in existing institutions than a come-outer.' 'The Rep. party was all the while stolidly implacable towards its come-outers for conscience' sake.' 'Storey's family associations were neither with the fashionable world nor with the more extreme "come-outers", though there were contacts with both' (M. A. de W. HOWE, Portrait of an Independent, 30). Hence also *come-outism.* 'He was also opposed to the extreme reformers such as Garrison who advocated "Come-Outism" to church members' (Dict. Am. Biog. xiii. 22).

††The Am. term *come-back* denotes a *return* to a position once lost, esp. in politics. 'The spectacular comeback which placed "Big Bill" for a third term in the office of mayor of Chicago' (Dr. H. ZINK, City Bosses in U.S., 289). 'Bryan, after two defeats at the polls and a merciless snubbing in the party convention at St. Louis, was making his comeback' (WILLIS J. ABBOT, Watching the World Go By, 261). 'The same sort of strain breaks down practically every man who goes into public life and attempts to meet its impossible demands. Yet men like that have a come-back like cork' (JULIA B. FORAKER, I Would Live it Again, 98).

†Am. *come-down* = Eng. *descent.* 'The General Board plan is a gradual come-down from the programme which Congress indicated' (C. P. HOWLAND, Survey of Am. Foreign Relations, 1931, 400).

comfort, comfortable, comforter. Am. *public comfort station* = Eng. *public convenience.* Similarly, *comfort room.* 'The excavation for the public comfort station in Chatham Square.' 'He continued his progress through the park. He passed comfort stations, hothouses, reservoirs, playgrounds, etc.' (R. NATHAN, One More Spring, 44). 'The rear houses seem unfit for human habitation, with their peeling walls and rickety stairs, and none of the modern accommodations. Even the comfort rooms are downstairs, as well as the water' (K. BERCOVICI, Around the World in N.Y. 53).

The Eng. *comforter* is a long woollen scarf. The Am. *comforter* or *comfortable* is a wadded quilt. 'This handmade wool-filled chintz comforter was esp. designed for a summer bedroom, as there are always occasional nights during the summer months when additional covering is needed, and such a comforter, covered with brightly colored small-patterned chintz, is vastly more decorative than an extra blanket' (Advt.). 'He swung his thick legs over the edge of his lilac satin comforter' (SINCLAIR LEWIS, Dodsworth, 16). 'She did not get into bed, but took a silk comfortable off and wrapped it around her' (M. E. WILKINS FREEMAN, By the Light of the Soul, 437). 'A big bed is piled high with patchwork comfortables' (E. HILTS, in Life in the U.S. 118).

commencement. At Cambridge and Dublin the annual ceremony at which honorary degrees are conferred is called the *commencement.* The term is used in Am. to denote the annual degree day at a college or university, and also the school ceremony which corresponds to the Eng. *speech-day*. 'June, the month of brides and commencements, is here. Preparations for the approaching commencement season are being made by the schools and colleges.' 'For the younger girls, commencement frocks are made short.' 'He got away to the Harvard commencement, where a gold medal was presented to President Eliot by the alumni' (E. S. MARTIN, Life of J. H. Choate, i. 460).

commissary is a term used in Am. to-day, as formerly in Eng., to denote an officer responsible for the supply of food to a number of persons, esp. soldiers. In Am. it may also be applied to the provisions themselves and to the office from which they are distributed. 'I argued that a wagon-way could be easily cut in the bank and the commissaries lowered to the river's edge with a rope to the rear axle' (ANDY ADAMS, The Outlet, 245). 'Vacated garages, stores and halls have been utilized as local relief headquarters and commissaries . . . The erstwhile showroom is a commissary.' 'Sales at the plantation commissary are interesting' (G. M. NEELY, in Life in the U.S. 224).

common. The use of this word in the sense of *generally accessible, affable, sympathetic* is now obs. in Eng. The quotations given in the *O.E.D.* range from 1382 to 1609. The latest is from the Douay Bible: 'I trust that he wil deale modestly and gently . . . and that he wil be common unto you.' This meaning is still retained in some parts of the U.S. Cecil Sharp, as reported in his biog. (p. 175), considered that the greatest compliment ever paid him was the farewell remark of a singer in the Appalachians to himself and his companion: 'My husband and I are sorry you are going. We like you both—you are so nice and common.' For *common stock*, see STOCK.

commonwealth. We speak of 'the Commonwealth of Australia'. It was in this sense that Lord Bryce used the word when he entitled his great book *The American Commonwealth*. But this is not the Am. sense. In Am. the term is applied to any of the several States individually, not to the whole country as a federated unit. Officially, its use is restricted to the States of Massachusetts, Pennsylvania, Virginia, and Kentucky. 'The ancient, elaborate and impressive ceremony which culminates in Col. Olin's sonorous and solemn appeal: "God save the commonwealth of Massachusetts".' 'Such freedom as exists to-day among the 48 separate commonwealths of the Am. Union.' 'There may be some ground to apprehend that in the U.S. the cities and federal government are increasing in importance more rapidly than our commonwealths' (Prof. R. T. ELY, Evolution of Industrial Society, 328). 'An Act was passed for the purpose of "increasing the banking capital of this Commonwealth". This Act established at Norfolk the Exchange Bank of Virginia' (G. T. STARNER, 60 Years of Branch Banking in Virginia, 84).

community. In Am. this word, in the sense of a body of persons living in the same locality, goes to form several spec. terms. A *community center* 'may be defined as a meeting place where people living near by come together to participate in social, recreational and cultural activities and build up a democratic organization that will minister to the needs of the community' (Encycl. Soc. Sci. iv. 105). A *community chest* is a fund in which the charitable donations of a community are co-ordinated. 'Financial federations known as community chests have become a widely accepted means of unifying the social service activities of a city. The community chest was at first looked upon as a dangerous innovation that might centralize control in the hands of a few people or enable financial interests to dominate social service policies. Present experience indicates that these fears were unfounded' (op. cit. 107). A *community church* is a church composed of members of various denominations who unite in a single organization instead of grouping themselves in several separate churches. The charitable and philanthropic activities of a club or similar organization are described as its *community service*. The term *community singing*, which originated in Am., is now familiar in Eng.

commute. In Eng. *commuting* or *commutation* may mean (1) the changing of a penal sentence for one that is less severe, (2) the buying off of a recurrent obligation by the payment of a lump sum, as in the case of annuities, or (3) the changing of an obligation in kind into an obligation in money, as in the case of tithes. In Am. the term is most frequently applied to the *commuting* of one's railway fares by taking a *commutation ticket* = Eng. *season ticket. Commuting* thus comes to mean travelling regularly by train, ferry, bus, &c., between home and office. 'A large number of Wall Street folk commute by the Erie.' 'The maids of Montclair presented their claims for consideration in the matter of the dinner hour. Commuting has made 7 o'clock dinner the custom in suburban districts.' 'Mr. Wilson continued to live in Princeton, commuting every morning the twelve miles between his home and his office' (D. LAWRENCE, True Story of Woodrow Wilson, 88). The word has been extended to mean frequent travel to and fro, over distances so great that the issue of a season ticket would be out of the question. Thus Lincoln Steffens (Autobiog. 702 and 741) says: 'Between trips to the Pacific coast I was commuting to and from Europe' and 'I spent the first two years of the war commuting between Washington and Mexico, Cuba, and Porto Rico.'

commuter is naturally used in a corresponding sense. 'There were several fights between the railroad men and angry commuters.' In *The Light of the Soul* Mary E. Wilkins Freeman says of one of her characters that 'he was so tired of seeing the same train, the same commuters, taking the same path across the station to the ferry-boat'. 'Running with the ungainly fierceness of a commuter slogging for a train' (CHRISTOPHER MORLEY, John Mistletoe, 62).

company. In Am. the term *company union* denotes a union 'instigated and practically dominated by the employers, organized and conducted for the purpose of combating or displacing independent unionism' (R. F. HOXIE, Trade Unionism in U.S. 51). 'British employers do not use the term collective bargaining to mean dealing with "company unions" or employees' organizations set up by the employers themselves. There are virtually no "company unions" in Great Britain exc. the organizations of foremen and supervisors' (P. BLANSHARD, Outline of British Labor Movement, 49). 'The employers sought to organize the workers into harmless company unions controlled from the main office' (L. ADAMIC, Dynamite, 326). 'The terms company union and employee representation are often used interchangeably, esp. in the U.S., where trade unionists commonly refer to any shop committee, works council or industrial assembly established without the assistance of trade unions as a company union. In recent literature, however, company union has come to designate a special form of employee representation which not only seeks to become a substitute for the trade union but also uses the methods and the forms of organization of the trade unions. It is usually an employers' association within a plant making collective bargaining contracts with the employer' (Encycl. Soc. Sci. iv. 123).

compensation, compensate. In Am. *compensation* sometimes = *salary, payment for services rendered*, without any suggestion of making amends for loss or damage. This sense of the word goes back at least to 1787, when the Constitution of the U.S. provided that Senators and Representatives should receive 'a compensation for their services, to be ascertained by law, and paid out of the Treasury'. Senator William Maclay, in an entry in his journal dated Aug. 25, 1789, speaks of moving a 'compensation bill' fixing the 'wages' to be paid members of Congress. The following are modern examples: 'The Filipino teachers will naturally be able to accept a much less compensation than the Am. teachers.' 'The compensation of judges is commonly much less than the ordinary professional income of good lawyers' (Prof. A. B. HART, Actual Government, 153). 'In 1860 the compensation of the former [the skilled labourer] ranged from $1 to $2 a day and that of the latter [the unskilled] was about half as much' (Prof. A. E. MARTIN, Hist. of U.S. i. 517).

Similarly to *compensate* = to *pay for services*. 'A campaign against the fee system in compensating public officers.' 'Members of city councils are almost invariably compensated for their services' (C. C. MAXEY, Outline of Municipal Government, 293).

In its normal sense *compensate* is often used in Am. without the *for* with which it would usually be followed in Eng. 'The increased cost of living could be compensated by protective duties.' 'It is only a few of these words which have excited much feeling, but the smallness of the number has been compensated by the acrimony displayed' (Prof. T. R. LOUNSBURY, Standard of Pronunciation in English, 129).

complected is a term affected by Carlyle, who used it in the sense of *interwoven, complicated*. In Am., as a colloq. term, it = Eng. *complexioned*. A character in K. D. Wiggin's *Rebecca* is represented as saying: 'Lorenzo was dark complected, you remember.' 'The general manager remarked to his superintendent of machinery: "Joe, did you notice that dark-complected man with glasses?"' (J. K. WINKLER, Life of J. Pierpont Morgan, 198).

composition. What is called an *exercise book* in Eng. schools is known as a *composition book* in Am.

concede is often used in Am. where *admit* or *recognize* would be preferred in Eng. 'The conceded desirability of having Presidential inaugurations take place in warmer weather.' 'It will readily be conceded that private contract must not stand above public policy' (Prof. R. T. ELY, Evolution of Industrial Society, 419). 'The project did not look attractive to private capital, and it was generally conceded that such a road could be built only with government aid' (G. T. CLARK, Leland Stanford, 164). 'Most well-informed observers, while they conceded the personal popularity of Roosevelt, believed that the lack of an established organization would prevent his election' (Prof. C. SEYMOUR, Intimate Papers of Col. House, i. 70).

Hence Am. *concededly* = Eng. *admittedly*. 'The Rollin sisters were concededly pretty' (C. G. BOWERS, The Tragic Era, 351).

conclude, in the sense of *decide finally*, has a classical Eng. example in the A.V. of Acts, xxi. 25: 'As touching the Gentiles which believe, we have written and concluded that they observe no such thing.' Nowadays it is rare in Eng., but not unusual in Am. E. S. Martin's biog. of J. H. Choate gives three examples, at least, from his letters: 'I see that the Senate Foreign Relations Committee has concluded to drop the Hay-Pauncefote Treaty' (ii. 126); 'I am very sorry that you and Mary did not conclude to cross the ocean this summer' (ii. 146); 'I am beset by an overwhelming number of invitations, but I have concluded to make only two "positively last appearances"' (ii. 273). 'We knew that they must have seen us, and concluded to stay where we were until we could make them out' (C. H. STERNBERG, Life of a Fossil Hunter, 197). 'I concluded to take his advice' (G. ATHERTON, Adventures of a Novelist, 398).

concourse is a spec. term in the vocab. of Am. railways. It denotes the large open space, or main hall, in the centre of a station of the modern type. Around it, or around its approaches, may be found the ticket offices, refreshment rooms, shops, &c. In a newspaper description of a new terminus in N.Y. we read that 'parallel to and connecting with the main waiting room by a wide passageway between the subsidiary waiting rooms is the concourse, a covered assembling place over 100 feet wide, extending the entire width of the station and under the adjoining streets. Two sets of stairs descend from it to each of the train platforms on the track level.'

condition. In Am. a student who fails to pass an examination in all the necessary subjects is sometimes allowed to proceed to the next academic stage on condition that he makes up these deficiencies within a certain time. The omitted subjects are then technically called *conditions*, which the student has to *work off*. 'Examinations interfered materially with the progress of Columbia's football practice yesterday. Many of the new candidates are taking examinations for entrance to the university, and several of the older students are working off conditions.' 'Through the intervention of a faculty member he was permitted to enter with an unorthodox number of conditions.' 'She passed in only two subjects, but went cheerfully into the preparatory department with her five conditions' (K. D. WIGGIN, Rebecca, 213).

Hence the verb *condition.* 'I went to Baltimore in 1884, conditioned in Greek and mathematics and weak in Latin.' 'Their author had no intention of making a literary career when, a conditioned sub-freshman, he entered Bowdoin College with the class of 1871' (Dict. Am. Biog. xiii. 43).

conductor is the common term in Eng. for an official who looks after passengers in a bus or tram-car. In Am. it is also used of the railway official who in an Eng. passenger train is called a *guard*. In the case of a freight train, the Am. *brakeman* or *trainsman* corresponds to the Eng. *guard*.

confederacy, confederate. In Am. these terms are rarely used in their general sense, being restricted to a specific meaning arising from the Civil War. The word *Confederacy* denotes the league of eleven States— S. Carolina, Mississippi, Florida, Alabama, Georgia, Louisiana, Texas, Virginia, Arkansas, Tennessee, and N. Carolina—which seceded from the Union. The adj. *Confederate* is applied to the States which were members of that league, the troops which fought on their side, &c. 'These rivers were natural roadways into the Confederacy, and it was an important step when Grant captured the forts.' 'A tall, erect, slight, courtly man with the slouched hat that spoke the Confederate veteran.' 'A superior court had reversed the conviction of a man who had passed Confederate money' (H. F. PRINGLE, Theodore Roosevelt, 56).

confidence. Am. *confidence game* = Eng. *confidence trick*. 'S. A. Potter was arrested to-day on a charge of operating a confidence game. Potter and two companions are said to have netted $1,500,000 in the past few years by the operation of their schemes.' The term is sometimes abbreviated to *con game*, and a practitioner of the trick may be called a *con man*. 'Two sailors said he worked the con game on them Saturday morning. They gave him $23 in good money for a $50 counterfeit bill.' 'He has a police record and is said to be a con man.'

consent. The Am. *consent decree* somewhat resembles the Eng. *agreed verdict*. 'A suit was brought in one of the U.S. courts which ended in what is known as a "consent decree", by which is meant a decree to which both sides assented' (Prof. T. J. GRAYSON, Leaders and Periods of Am. Finance, 395). 'A consent decree signed in the U.S. District Court at Wilmington provides for the distribution over certain specified periods of all Radio Corporation of Am. stocks owned by the General Electric and Westinghouse Electric and Manufacturing Companies' (World Alm. for 1933, 122).

††**conservative.** In his *Dict. of Modern Eng. Usage*, H. W. Fowler describes as 'perhaps the most ridiculous of Slipshod Extensions' the 'rapidly spreading use of this word as an epithet, in the sense of *moderate, safe*, or *low*, with *estimates, figure*, etc.'. A similar protest was made by the late Sir E. T. Cook (More Literary Recreations, 248), who speculated as to the origin of this misuse of the word, and wondered whether it was 'the subtle invention of some politician, designed to wipe out the Gladstonian charges against the Conservatives, and connected with the term "Moderate" by which Conservatives called themselves in London politics'. Actually it is an importation from Am., where it became current long ago. Thus, in his Evolution of Industrial Society, published in 1903, Prof. R. T. Ely says (p. 204) that 'Lecky's History of European Morals gives a conservative statement of the ethical consequences of luxury'. 'The visitors were spending on the island the enormous total of $1,500,000 a day, and this is a conservative estimate' (N.Y. Tri-

bune, Sept. 6, 1903). When the *N.Y. Sun* of Sept. 5, 1904, says that 'this and the 15th are the only two Congress districts which conservative minded Republicans think their party will be able to carry next November', it does not mean Republicans of conservative views but Republicans who do not hold extravagant expectations of the electoral chances of their party. 'Wearing a diamond pin, conservatively valued at $75' (San Francisco Chronicle, July 12, 1904).

conservator. In Am. the technical term for a person appointed to care for idiots or lunatics and look after their property. 'Conservators are daily appointed over men who hold less crazy notions.'

The term has also been adopted in connexion with President Franklin D. Roosevelt's National Recovery programme. 'Title II [of the Emergency Banking Act of 1933] authorized the Comptroller of the Currency to appoint conservators for national banking associations. . . . The office of a conservator is practically the same as that of a receiver, but the manner of the appointment of conservators, the powers they possess, and the procedure under which they operate, are all designed to provide more flexible and speedier administration of the institutions committed to their care than is customary in the usual receivership process. The conservator's primary purpose, as the name implies, is to conserve the assets of a bank for the benefit of the depositors, the creditors, and the stockholders. To that end he has complete charge of the assets and business affairs of the bank' (C. A. BEARD and G. H. E. SMITH, The Future Comes, 20).

conservatory. In Eng. *conservatory* commonly denotes a *greenhouse*. The French form *conservatoire* is preferred in the sense of *school of music*. In Am. *conservatory* is ordinarily used in the latter sense. 'A list of conservatories and university and college music departments in the South' (U. M. GREGORY in Culture in the South, 289).

considerable. In Am. *considerable* often = Eng. *a considerable amount, a good deal, much.* 'It takes considerable to surprise a professional gambler.' 'Their only fault was an over-plenty of grass, which was considerable of a handicap to the Eng. golfers.' 'When the engineers now say that the estimate of three years ago was too low by only $143,000,000, they fail to cover the ground by considerable.' 'Considerable of his time was spent measuring the angles between the different stars' (F. S. HARRIS, Scientific Research and Human Welfare, 207).

consolidated. For the Am. term *consolidated ticket office* see the first quotation. 'Instead of a separate ticket office in cities for each railroad, consolidated ticket offices, where a ticket for any train on any road could be purchased, were established' (F. J. HASKIN, The Am. Government, 393). 'There are four consolidated ticket offices in N.Y. city.' In Eng. such an office would be called a *joint booking office.*

construction. This word forms part of several technical terms in the vocab. of Am. railways; e.g. *construction laborer* = Eng. *navvy,* †*construction train, construction crew, construction gang* = Eng. *gang of navvies.* 'Where serving as construction laborers on the railroads, they have received less than other races' (J. W. JENKS and W. J. LAUCK, Immigration Problem, 4). 'Here the construction train rumbles up to the end of the completed track, the rails for the next section are taken from the storage cars, dumped upon the ground with a clang, then carried to their place and slowly lowered upon the ties.' 'The bulk of the names on construction crew pay-rolls began with "O" or "Mc"' (MARK SULLIVAN, Our Times, iii. 395). 'For years his

construction gangs were busy at widely separated points [on the Union Pacific]' (Prof. T. J. GRAYSON, Leaders and Periods of Am. Finance, 436).

The terms *strict construction(ist)* and *broad construction(ist)* or *liberal construction(ist)* denote two opposing schools of political thought with regard to the interpretation of the U.S. Constitution. The nature of their difference is sufficiently indicated in the following quotations. 'He was a "strict constructionist", and, as the Constitution did not say in so many words that the U.S. might acquire new territory, he denied the ability of the U.S. to do so' (W. F. JOHNSON, A Century of Expansion, 101). 'Here, too, he [Hamilton] rendered a still more broad and signal service, in first setting forth in clear and convincing terms the theory of implied powers and resulting powers vested in the National Government under the Constitution—the theory that every power clearly given involves necessarily the right in Congress to use every necessary and proper means to carry that power into execution. In other words, he was the author of the doctrine of liberal construction, which has enabled the Supreme Court from time to time to adopt and apply the general provisions of the Constitution, as its framers intended, to successive national exigencies as they arose, whereby that venerated instrument has grown with the growth of the nation, instead of being left behind and discarded as an outworn garment rent asunder at every seam' (J. H. CHOATE, Address on Hamilton, 61).

†**contact** is a familiar word in Eng., esp. in the expressions *be in contact with, come into contact with.* It is in much more general use, however, in Am., notably in the plur. form *contacts,* which = Eng. *associations* or *acquaintanceships.* 'My contacts with Governor Sproul have been many and friendly' (G. W. PEPPER, In the

Senate, 3). 'Years ago it was customary for the head of the police
force in any large city to maintain
certain useful contacts with the
underworld' (JANE ADDAMS, The
Second 20 Years at Hull-House, 249).
'Intellectual concentration would
take too much time; it would restrict
the student's social contacts' (Dr. A.
FLEXNER, Universities, 69). 'He was
at his post in the legation, gaining
experience steadily, enjoying his
contacts with Lowell' (A. NEVINS,
Henry White, 55). 'All contacts between the editor and the President
kept on a formal plane' (F. F. BOND,
Mr. Miller of The Times, 113).
The word is also used as a trans.
verb in a corresponding sense. 'The
new secretary of the club has been
spending the past few days in the
Berkshire contacting new members
and meeting old members of the
club.' 'Mr. Dickey contacted every
family in three representative agricultural counties and found the
economic facts of their existence'
(L. F. CARR, Am. Challenged, 61).

contest. In Eng. a *contested election*
is one at which there is more than one
candidate for a vacancy; i.e. where
there is a contest, and not an un-
opposed return. In Am. it is also an
election whose result is challenged as
invalid. 'The House of Representatives and the Senate are the judges of
the election, returns, and qualifications of their own members, and
therefore contested elections are not
determined by a judicial tribunal, as
in Eng.' (C. A. BEARD, Am. Government and Politics, 229). A quotation
in the *O.E.D.* from the Letters of
Junius shows that this Am. use of the
term was once the Eng. use also.
†The derivative *contestant* is recognized by the *O.E.D.* as of Eng. origin,
but until recent years it has been
seldom used in Eng. In Am., on the
other hand, it has long occupied the
place of the Eng. *competitor*. 'The
friends of the various contestants
make up a far larger audience than

one finds at similar sports in Am.'
(J. CORBIN, An Am. at Oxford, 135).
'The designs being submitted to a
jury of architects who voted on them
without knowing the names of the
contestants' (E. WHARTON, Sanc-
tuary, 89).

continent. In Eng. *the continent*
means the continent of Europe, but
in Am. the continent of N. Am.
'Louisville is now the Mecca of
Pythians from every quarter of the
continent.'
The continental U.S. is a term used
to denote the U.S. of the mainland,
in distinction from the nation's overseas possessions. 'The census of
1870 showed that in the continental
U.S. there were living 38,558,000
persons' (L. M. HACKER and B. B.
KENDRICK, The U.S. since 1868,
128).
Continental Congress was the name
of an assembly of delegates from
twelve colonies meeting at Philadelphia in 1774 and of a similar assembly which first met in 1775 and
continued to exercise certain powers
of government until the Federal
Constitution came into force. This
Congress issued currency notes, popularly known as *continentals*, whose
subsequent depreciation gave rise to
a proverbial term. 'The paper money
of the U.S. declined to zero, and the
phrase "not worth a continental"
was so impressed upon the people
that, unlike the money to which it
referred, it gained a lasting circulation' (J. TRUSLOW ADAMS, The Epic
of Am. 97). 'He talks like a man who
has laid in a supply of lightning
rods and doesn't care a continental
how soon the storm comes.' '"Look
here, Jethro," said Mr. Balch, "I'm
beginning to think you don't care a
continental about this business"'
(W. CHURCHILL, Coniston, 498).

contour has sometimes in Am. a fig.
sense unknown in Eng. 'Mr. Black-
burn is jubilant over the contour of
things, and says he is confident of
election.' 'The contours of the dis-

cussion confirm in a general way the diagnosis of the report' (C. M. Clay, The Mainstay of Am. Individualism, 3).

contraband. 'In 1862 Gen. Grant appointed him superintendent of contrabands. At one time he had under his charge 150,000 contrabands; many of these he placed on abandoned plantations, and 70,000 of these able-bodied men were enlisted as soldiers.' This peculiar use of *contraband* is explained in the following quotation, relating to the Civil War: 'When fugitive slaves had come within the lines of Gen. B. F. Butler's command at Fortress Monroe, he refused to give them up to their masters and set them to work on his own fortifications. He called them "contraband of war", and "contraband" continued to be the nickname of the confiscated negroes throughout the war' (Prof. D. S. Muzzey, The Am. Adventure, i. 554 n.).

convention. In Eng. the regular annual meeting of a religious, educational, social, commercial, or other organization is usually called a *conference*. In Am. it is a *convention*. (When this term is used in Eng., it applies to an informal assembly only; e.g. we have the Keswick Convention but the Methodist Conference.) Thus, the annual convention of the National Education Association corresponds to the annual conference of the National Union of Teachers. 'The discussions which one hears at business meetings and conventions.' 'The delegates to the annual convention of the National Piano Manufacturers' Association of Am.'

In Am. politics this term has certain spec. meanings. The official meetings which decide the affairs of the political parties are known as *county, city, district, state,* and *national conventions*. Each such assembly is composed of delegates appointed by conventions of next rank or by the primaries. The national convention, held every fourth year, is sometimes called a *nominating convention,* as its principal function is to nominate the party's candidate for the Presidency.

The word *convention* is also the name for a representative body called to frame or revise a political constitution. The Constitution of the U.S. was drawn up by the Federal Convention which met in 1787. So, too, most of the constitutions of the various States are the product of conventions elected for the purpose, and many such constitutions include a proviso requiring the calling of further conventions, at fixed intervals, for the consideration of constitutional amendments. Accordingly, the Am. meaning of the term *constitutional convention* is entirely different from its Eng. meaning. In Eng. it denotes one of those constitutional customs or maxims which, though not embodied in any legal enactment and not enforceable by the courts, are nevertheless, in Freeman's words, 'in practice held hardly less sacred than any principle embodied in the Great Charter or in the Petition of Right'. As examples of these conventions Dicey gives such maxims as: 'The King must assent to any bill passed by the two Houses of Parliament' and 'When the House of Lords acts as a Court of Appeal, no peer who is not a law lord takes part in the decisions of the House'. In the Am. political system also there are many such conventions; notably, that which requires that the Presidential Electors appointed in a State shall support the candidate to whom the popular vote has given a majority, and shall not exercise their independent judgement. The term *constitutional convention,* however, cannot be applied to such a practice, as it has already been pre-empted for something altogether different. Hence, when the compiler of this dictionary published a few years ago a study of the subject, he was reluctantly compelled to adopt for it the title 'The Usages of the Am. Constitution'— reluctantly, because the word *usage* does not express the leading idea as precisely as *convention*. A *usage* is merely a customary or habitual practice, whereas a *convention* is a practice that is established by general tacit consent.

cook. In Am. *cook* takes the place of Eng. *cookery* or *cooking* in compound words. Thus Am. *cookbook* = Eng. *cookery book*. (Cf. German *Kochbuch*.) 'It is a medium-sized book, on the back of which is stamped "General Mess Manual and Cookbook, U.S. Navy".' 'Chemistry can thus be reduced to a series of cookbook receipts' (SMITH and HALL, Teaching of Chemistry, 34). 'Specialized, or partly specialized, cookbooks are many' (G. OVERTON, Cargoes for Crusoes, 116).

So, too, Am. *cookstove* = Eng. *cooking stove*. 'The cabin could barely hold cookstove and dining-table' (C. MOFFETT, Careers of Danger, 64).

copy. In Eng. a book in which a writer of letters or other documents keeps copies of them is now called a *copying-book*. It was once called a *copy-book*, but that word is now restricted to a book in which models of handwriting are set for learners to imitate. The earlier use survives in Am. 'Years later, when his original copy-books were discovered, the world was startled to find how many hundreds of letters this persistent man had written in a vain effort to collect the taxes' (Prof. T. J. GRAYSON, Leaders and Periods of Am. Finance, 30). 'This collection includes a copy book of letters from Buchanan to Marcy' (A. A. ETTINGER, The Mission to Spain of Pierre Soulé, 506).

The functions of a *copy-reader* in an Am. newspaper office correspond largely to those of a sub-editor in an Eng. office. 'Each of these departments has a force of copy-readers, whose duty it is to edit the matter written by the reporters and correspondents' (E. L. SHUMAN, Practical Journalism, 18). 'Everything which the young reporters wrote received the closest editing. Their stuff passed not to a copy-reader as now, but to an editor direct' (F. F. BOND. Mr. Miller of *The Times*, 39). 'With this paper for 22 years, he worked variously as reporter, copyreader, telegraphic editor, city editor, and special correspondent' (Dict. Am. Biog. xii. 413).

cordially serves in Am. as an alternative to *faithfully* or *sincerely* in the formula for closing a letter. For published examples, see The Letters of Franklin K. Lane, 33, 115, 116, 118, &c.; The Intimate Papers of Col. House, i. 50, 173, 232; iii. 400; Letters and Memorials of Wendell Phillips Garrison, 15, 112; Life and Letters of Edwin Lawrence Godkin, ii. 128, 181; and The Letters and Friendships of Sir Cecil Spring Rice, ii. 197, 314, 324 (Letters of Pres. Wilson).

corduroy. The ribbing of corduroy has suggested in Am. the term *corduroy road* to denote a primitive road of tree-trunks laid across swampy ground. 'During the rainy season the ground is too soft to permit the use of trucks, and the logs are loaded on rude sleds, while the roads are roughly corduroyed by placing hardwood poles, about three inches in diameter, across the track, two or three feet apart.' 'While you are crossing that bridge you are an active imitation of popcorn being popped, for the bridge is built like an old corduroy road, and you bump and shake like a man with a combination of the ague and St. Vitus dance.' Dr. Lavendar, in one of Margaret Deland's stories, says he feels as if he had been driven ten miles on a corduroy road. 'The coach was forever thumping over corduroy roads' (U. SINCLAIR, Manassas, 42). See also Dickens's *Am. Notes*, c. 14.

corn. Oliver Wendell Holmes (One Hundred Days in Europe, 220) pictures an average American and an average Englishman talking together. One of them speaks of the beauty of a field of corn. 'They are thinking', he remarks, 'of two entirely different objects; one of a billowy level of soft waving wheat, or rye, or barley; the other of a rustling forest of tall, jointed stalks, tossing their plumes and showing their silken epaulettes, as if every stem in the ordered ranks were a soldier in full regimentals.' For *corn*, in Am., always denotes what in Eng. is called *maize*, or *Indian corn*. In the British Isles, 'as a general term, the word includes all the cereals—wheat, rye, barley, oats, maize, rice, &c. Locally, the word, when not otherwise qualified, is often understood to denote that kind of cereal which is the leading crop of the district; hence in the greater part of Eng. *corn = wheat*, in North Britain and Ireland = *oats*' (O.E.D.). Prof. Freeman points out (Impressions of the U.S.) that the Am. restriction of *corn* to Indian corn is analogous to the narrower use of *beast* among Eng. graziers and of *bird* among Eng. sportsmen. See also POP.

The following quotations illustrate the Am. use of the word. 'The corn was in tassel now, and rustled softly in the fields.' 'The corn crop promises the largest yield in the country's history. But the wheat crop has not fared well.' 'What was formerly a great wheat-growing region has turned to corn.'

Corn has, of course, the same meaning in its various Am. compounds, such as *corn bread*, *corn cob*, *corn dodger*, *cornfield*, *corn fritter*, *corn husk*, *corn mush*, *corn pone*, *corn shucking*, *corn starch*. The one example of the Eng. adoption of the Am. meaning seems to be *corn flour*, which in Am. is called *corn starch*.

Eng. *corn = Am. grain*. Thus Eng. *corn harvest = Am. grain harvest* and Eng. *corn factor = Am. grain broker*.

corporation. At the time of the Hatry sensation a N.Y. paper came out with the headline, 'London Stock Exchange Suspends Dealings In British Corporation Stocks', and for a quarter of an hour Wall Street was staggered. The suspension was actually of dealings in the stocks of certain municipal corporations. In Am. all business companies are commonly spoken of as *corporations*, and the headline accordingly read as if it meant that the London Stock Exchange had suspended dealings in the shares of all British companies. This use of the word goes back as far as the time of Dickens, for the *O.E.D.* quotes a passage from his *American Notes* in which he speaks of 'what we should term a Company of Proprietors, but what they call in Am. a Corporation'.

Thus, the statement that 'down to 1901 Massachusetts corporations were not permitted to issue preferred stock' does not refer, as the Eng. reader might suppose, to municipalities but to business companies. 'Joint stock companies, as corporations were still called [in 1819], had been organized in great numbers' (A. M. SIMONS, Social Forces in Am. Hist. 161). 'The profits of big corporations are more public than those of small firms' (W. LIPPMANN, Public Opinion, 44). 'In the states of this country the principal duty of the state government is to maintain the system of the courts, to care for prisons and asylums, and to have general charge of the corporations which do business within its limits, such as the railways, manufacturing companies, etc.' (Prof. N. S. SHALER, The Citizen, 76).

Writing in *Harper's Monthly*, W. D. Howells says of some Am. visitors to Chester that 'they rode on the tops of the municipal tram-cars with apparently no apprehension for their violation of the sacred Am. principle of corporational enterprise in transportation'. Here *corporational* is in direct contrast with *municipal*.

Hence Am. *corporation law* = Eng. *company law*, and the Am. *corporation lawyer* or *corporation attorney* is not the legal adviser of a municipality, but a lawyer whose services are retained by business interests. When Theodore Dreiser declares (Tragic America, 10) that 'corporation police have perpetrated lawless terror upon strikers', he means by *corporation police* not a municipal police force but a body of police maintained and controlled by a mining company.

corresponding member. In Eng. this term is used in its literal sense, denoting a foreign member of a society who communicates with it by letter. In Am., election as a *corresponding member* is a compliment paid to a visitor actually present at a meeting of the society. It confers on him the right of taking part in the proceedings, without the power to vote.

Cossack. The special Am. use of this word is sufficiently indicated by the following quotations. 'In the Standard Steel Car Co. strike at Butler, Pennsylvania, state police were called in and those workers born in Tsarist Russia were not surprised to see mounted troopers riding into their very homes, scattering curses and terror among women and children. In fact, the state troopers were dubbed "Cossacks" by strikers who had felt the impact of mace on skull' (H. O'CONNOR, Mellon's Millions, 208). 'The operators had already formed the Coal and Iron Police, that private army, clothed with the police power of the state, which has long been infamous in labor history as the Pennsylvania Cossacks' (A. BIMBA, The Molly Maguires, 55). 'No other ostensible democracy in the world in recent years has seen the police machinery used against labor as state troopers or "Cossacks" are used in our states North and South' (NORMAN THOMAS, America's Way Out, 270).

cottage. In *Words and Their Ways in Eng. Speech* Greenough and Kittredge devote more than a page to the history of this word in Am. 'We have never', they say, 'really had the *thing* in Am.', as the conditions of rustic life have, from the very first, differed essentially from those in Eng. Hence *cottage* has always had literary and sentimental connotations in Am. The word seemed to meet the demand for a name for the dwellings in the country or at the sea in which Americans nowadays spend a part of the summer. 'It had precisely the rural and sentimental associations required, and it served to distinguish these temporary shelters from the larger and more substantial "houses" in the neighborhood. Hence, *cottage* came to mean a "summer residence", however splendid, like the cottages at Newport, which are really villas on a very grand scale.'

This use of the word is illustrated in the following passages. 'The scope of daily necessities has expanded almost as greatly in the laborer's cottage as in the Newport cottage of the millionaire.' 'The French critic Geoffroy has warned us against being taken in by the "false naïve", and certainly that warning would be necessary for an intelligent foreigner who should adjust his wardrobe and expectations to a "cottage" on the cliff walk.'

'In the country farmhouse,' Mrs. Rorer tells us, 'schmierkase, or cottage cheese, is made from sour milk' (Mrs. RORER's New Cook Book, 270). Its rural origin is presumably responsible for the name *cottage cheese.* It seems to be very much the same as the Eng. *curd cheese* or *cream cheese.* Dr. R. L. Alsaker (Eating for Health and Efficiency, 155) gives the following recipe for it: 'Pour clabbered milk in muslin bag and let it drain in cool place. Do not drain entirely dry, but leave some whey in the mass. After draining, beat well, adding some rich milk, either sour or sweet; or add cream. Do not beat enough to remove the little lumps entirely.' More elaborate instructions and warnings will be found in an article on 'The Arcadian School of Cookery' in the *Atlantic Monthly* of Dec. 1933. Its author, Mr. Wendell Brooks Phillips, assures us that cottage cheese at its best surpasses every other dairy product, but complains that 'nine tenths of the cottage cheese that one encounters has been grossly, palpably mishandled'.

councilman. Exc. that it is retained in connexion with the Common Council of the City of London, *councilman*, as a designation for a member of a municipal council, is now obs. in Eng., having been superseded by *councillor*. It is still the normal term in Am. 'There was [at Philadelphia] the same old arrangement of a mayor, councilmen, and the usual elected officials' (L. STEFFENS, Autobiog. i. 408).
There has been formed from this word the adj. *councilmanic*, probably on the analogy of *aldermanic*. 'Yesterday's voting was comparatively light, as there was not much interest in the contest, aside from councilmanic fights in a few wards.' 'The Municipal League elected ten of the councilmanic candidates whom it had endorsed' (Dr. H. ZINK, City Bosses in U.S. 242).

count. If Am. election officials make a fraudulent return by ignoring some of the votes cast for a certain candidate, they may be said to *count out* (1) the votes thus ignored and (2) the candidate who suffers thereby. (1) 'It is well known that votes have been habitually counted out by the reactionary groups in Spanish politics. This, plus the local boss and the use of money to buy votes wholesale, used to be effective.' (2) 'In the course of his speech, he referred to his candidacy for mayor and his defeat. "And counted out" spoke up some one in the audience.' 'Henry George [when a candidate for the mayoralty of N.Y.] lacked party machinery, particularly watchers at the polls, and he believed he was

counted out' (Dict. Am. Biog. vii. 215). 'In 1838 he ran for Congress but was "counted out" by 5 votes after 50 ballots had been thrown out because the voters had spelled his name "Duglas" and not "Douglas"' (E. D. ADAMS and J. C. ALMACK, Hist. of U.S. 494).
In Am. *counting room* is generally preferred to *counting house*. 'Criticism of the theatre is subject to many limitations, not the least of which is the overshadowing whiphand of the counting room.' 'He disabused the Am. business man of his conviction that divine right had passed from the throne to the counting room' (H. F. PRINGLE, Theodore Roosevelt, 370). 'To go back East was to get into another life, a life of crowded population, of drawing-rooms and counting-rooms' (J. TRUSLOW ADAMS, Epic of Am. 154).

county. For the place of the county in the local government of the U.S., see Bryce's *Am. Commonwealth*, chapters xlviii and xlix. In Am. the name of a county is always followed by the word *county*, usually with a capital initial. Thus, one would say that such-and-such a place is in *Suffolk County*. In Eng. it would be said to be in *Suffolk*, or in *the county of Suffolk*—never in *Suffolk County*. (In Ireland, *County*, often abbrev. to *Co.*, is prefixed to the name; e.g. *Co. Dublin*.) This difference in usage sometimes gives rise to misunderstandings. Thus, a famous Am. author once inquired in his London hotel for a schedule of the trains to Surrey, where, as he explained, a friend of his lived whom he wished to visit. He naturally assumed that, if Surrey were a county and not a town, it would appear in his friend's address as *Surrey County*.
Am. *county seat* = Eng. *county town*. 'The country has changed greatly since then; the schoolhouses are no longer built of logs, and the county seat has a stone court-house.' 'In all probability the county seat of

Richmond County will be removed as soon as possible from Richmond Village to New Brighton. All Staten Islanders are unanimous in the opinion that New Brighton would make a much more convenient seat for the county administration.' 'He was in mortal terror of being arrested and taken to the county seat at Newholm for violation of the liquor law' (M. E. WILKINS FREEMAN, Shoulders of Atlas, 48).

In Am. a *county court* has jurisdiction in criminal as well as civil cases. In some parts of the U.S. the name is given to a body of men which has no judicial functions at all but is a board of supervisors chosen to attend to certain important branches of the county business.

course. In Am. colleges and universities a degree conferred after the applicant's fulfilment of the normal requirements as to studies, examinations, &c., is said to be conferred *in course*. 'After the degrees in course had been given, honorary degrees were conferred on etc.' 'Degrees, on the whole, have an uncertain significance, though a degree "in course" at an institution where the highest standards are maintained still possesses an honorable usefulness.'

court. In Am., *court* may be personified and used as a synonym for *judge*. 'The Court himself, possessed of a countenance and bearing elsewhere commanding, appeared little more than a pygmy here, in spite of his elevation on the bench.' The word may be so employed even officially. Thus, Judge Caverly, in his judgement in the Leopold-Loeb murder trial in Chicago in Sept. 1923, made the following statement: 'It is not for the Court to say that he will not in any case enforce capital punishment as an alternative, but the Court believes that it is within his province to decline to impose the sentence of death on persons who are not of full age.'

The *Great and General Court* of Massachusetts is not a judicial tribunal but the State legislature. 'The Great and General Court of the commonwealth began work yesterday, when both legislative houses convened.' Cf. the Eng. *High Court of Parliament.*

Am. *court house* does not always = Eng. *law court.* It is sometimes part of the name of a town in which a law court is held. 'Twenty-one buildings in the heart of Cape May Court House, the county seat of Cape May County, were burned early to-day.' 'Her scholars were equally well cared for, whether they hailed from Washington Square or Washington Court House' [i.e. whether from an aristocratic neighbourhood or from a rural district] (WINSTON CHURCHILL, Coniston, 323).

courtesy. When an Am. newspaper or magazine prints an illustration by permission of the owner of the copyright in such picture, acknowledgement is usually made in the terms, *(By) courtesy of,* &c. In a similar case in Eng. the conventional acknowledgement is *By favour of,* &c.

To be granted *the courtesies* (or *courtesy) of the port* is to be exempted from the usual Customs examination. 'He requested that the courtesies of the port be extended to the treaty commissioners from the new republic.' 'That Senators and Representatives mind the rigors of customs inspections when they have to endure them was made evident by the roar they sent up when the State Department threatened to deprive them of the courtesy of the port, so that they might no longer railroad in their own purchases scot-free.' 'The Secretary issued to-day a circular defining more closely "the courtesies of the port". The distinction between facilitation and courtesies is emphasized, and it is the former only that goes to invalids, persons arriving in charge of their dead, etc.'

For *Senatorial courtesy,* see the following quotation. 'A Senator objecting to a candidate nominated from his State [by the President] can count upon abundant support from his fellow Senators, every one of whom realizes that it may be his turn next to need support in a similar contingency. This is what is called "Senatorial courtesy"' (F. E. LEUPP, Walks about Washington, 87).

†cover. In the vocab. of Am. journalism *cover* = Eng. *report*. 'A reporter of long and varied experience, esp. in covering accidents, fires, crimes and the like.' 'The special correspondent of that paper has performed a notable service by the calm and judicial manner in which he covers the annual congress of the National Negro Business League.' 'The Russians were far more adroit in handling the newspaper correspondents who covered the deliberations' (H. F. PRINGLE, Theodore Roosevelt, 387).

cow. Esp. in the Western States, *cow* is found in many compounds with the meaning of *cattle*. Thus a *cowboy* or *cow-puncher* is a man in charge of the live stock on a ranch. 'He is considered a poor makeshift for a cowboy who cannot subdue and ride a wild pony in these efforts.' 'The rancher with his force of cowboys, cooks, etc., formed a self-supporting unit' (A. M. SIMONS, Social Forces in Am. Hist. 138). 'In 1871 more than 600,000 cattle, each herd in charge of its cowboys, followed the long trail up from Texas' (J. TRUSLOW ADAMS, The Epic of Am. 292). 'A band of genuine Western "cow-punchers"—men who have "rounded up" the herd, "hog-tied" and "cut out" big steers, "busted" broncos, ridden and conquered outlaws and braved many a storm.' 'A volunteer regiment of cavalry, in which the dare-devil cow-punchers of the prairie rode side by side with the adventurous scions of the most distinguished families' (E. B. HOLT's translation of Dr. H. MÜNSTERBERG, The Americans, 75). The Am. cowboy rides about the ranch on a *cow pony*. 'Ben got aboard the cow pony he had used in his cattle punching days.' 'The Rough Riders were cantering up and down Pennsylvania Avenue, tethering their cow ponies to lamp-posts in front of hospitable saloons' (H. F. PRINGLE, Theodore Roosevelt, 362).

The word *cowman*, in its Am. use, is esp. likely to be misunderstood in Eng. At the Eng. census of 1931, a specimen census-paper officially circulated mentioned a cowman as an employee of a farmer. That would have been impossible in Am., where a cowman is not a farm hand who attends to cows, but an owner of cows (or, rather, of cattle), usually on a very large scale. 'According to his story, he was a Northern cowman, and had purchased the cattle a few days before in Dodge' (ANDY ADAMS, The Outlet, 164). 'All the people who had settled this valley had gone never to return; the cowman had bought up all the homesteads' (C. H. STERNBERG, Life of a Fossil Hunter, 245). See also CATTLEMAN and SHEEPMAN.

Other Am. compounds are *cow-camp*, *cow-country*, and *cow-town*. 'In cow-camps a soldier's introduction is usually sufficient' (ANDY ADAMS, The Outlet, 40). 'How many communities, even in mining camp and cow-country, elect men to office while out on bail for a prison offence?' 'The cow country of the Far West provided another chapter in the later history of the Am. frontier' (L. M. HACKER and B. B. KENDRICK, The U.S. since 1865, 133). 'We pay a brief visit to the cow-towns, where the cowboys dance and drink and gamble through the night.' 'The "cattle kings" began to appear in the "cow towns", where they met their herds driven in by the cowboys' (J. TRUSLOW ADAMS, The Epic of Am. 292).

A *cowcatcher* is a frame fixed in front of a railway engine to remove cattle or other obstructions. 'When the locomotive stopped, the child was sitting on the rail less than two feet in front of the cowcatcher.' Cf. PILOT.

The Eng. *cowslip* is the *Primula veris*. The Am. is the *Caltha palustris*, or marsh marigold.

A compound peculiar to Am. is *cowbird*, denoting several species of Molothrus. The bird is so named, acc. to the *Century Dict.*, from its accompanying cattle. It is sometimes called *cow bunting*.

The *cow-pea* is largely grown for fodder in the Southern States. Its botanical name is *Vigna sinensis*.

cracker. See BISCUIT. 'Subsisting part of the time on cheese and crackers.' 'The soft-wheat flours have high starch content, and are particularly suited for cake and pastry, soda biscuit, and crackers' (T. C. BLAISDELL, The Federal Trade Commission, 138).

At the CROSS-ROAD (q.v.) stores, the local wiseacres are commonly pictured as seated on *cracker-boxes* or *cracker-barrels* while they discuss public affairs. 'He was at home among "the boys" in mining camps, railroad yards, and around the cracker barrels of country stores' (L. SYMES and T. CLEMENT, Rebel Am. 230). 'Politics, rum, riches, and religion—these were the favorite topics of Am. cracker-barrel debaters' (J. T. FLYNN, God's Gold, 37). 'His sudden alternations between inspiring religious eloquence and the cracker-barrel vernacular of the backwoods' (E. WILSON, The Am. Jitters, 231). 'He was one of the horde of cracker-box politicians who were swept into the General Court' (Dict. Am. Biog. vi. 6). 'Crackerbox Philosophers in Am. Humor and Satire' is the title of a study of Am. folk humour published by the Columbia University Press.

The word *cracker* also denotes a member of 'an inferior class of white hill-dwellers in some of the southern U.S., esp. in Georgia and Florida' (Century Dict.). Acc. to the same dict., this name is said to have been applied to them because cracked corn is their chief article of diet. 'There is something pathetic in the way the cultivated and high-class Southern people, who formerly were represented in public life by scholarly gentlemen, are now overridden by the "cracker" element.'

cramp is more usual in Am. in the plur. than in the sing. 'He had been swimming for over an hour, when he suddenly sank, presumably from cramps.' 'One should never go swimming right after eating, for so doing tends to bring on cramps.' 'He went bathing in the sea, was seized with cramps, and drowned before help could reach him' (Dict. Am. Biog. ix. 228).

cranberry. Acc. to Prof. G. H. McKnight (Eng. Words and Their Background, 28) this term applies in Am. to a different species from the one so called in Eng. This distinction is confirmed by the *O.E.D.*, which says that the Eng. cranberry is *Vaccinium oxycoccos*, but the Am. is the larger fruit, *Vaccinium macrocarpon*.

credit, in the vocab. of Am. education, denotes a certificate attesting the completion of a certain course of study. The *credits* given in Eng. School Certificate examinations attest the attainment of a higher standard than is required for an ordinary certificate. '"Count" and "credit" are Americanisms: the words mean that a given subject has been studied in class so many hours a week for so many weeks or months; at the end of the period a written examination is held. Students who pass have finished with the subject' (Dr. A. FLEXNER, Universities, 46). 'Getting an education is, externally at least, a process of passing courses, and rolling up a score of credits which at the end of a specified time can be cashed in for a degree' (Prof. M. A. MAY, The Education of Am. Ministers, iii. 59).

The National Association of Credit

Men and the N.Y. Credit Men's Association are among the entries appearing annually in the World Almanac's list of Am. Associations and Societies. A *credit man,* acc. to Webster, is an employee of a business house who fixes the amount of credit to be allowed to customers.

In Am. a sale of a bankrupt's stock is sometimes called a *creditors' sale.*

creek. 'West of New York everything that runs is a "creek". Brook, as a spoken word, is gone—the most regrettable loss the English language has suffered in Am. With us a creek does not run, but is a crack or inlet of the sea' (Prof. G. H. PALMER, Life of Alice Freeman Palmer, 277). The claim Prof. Palmer thus makes for New Eng., as retaining the Eng. use of the word creek, needs to be discounted by the fact that M. M. Mathews (The Beginnings of Am. Eng. 7) notes an example in New Eng. official records, as early as 1638, of its use in the sense of a stream. However that may be, in most of the U.S. to-day a *creek* is a *small stream.* 'The soft rustling of many pines modifies the noisier clamor of the creek.' 'The Assanpink Creek is ordinarily a quiet little creek that wends its way harmlessly through the city.' 'The local chronicle of this district was particularly interesting because of the famous River Wharfe (we should call it a creek in Am.), a narrow turbulent stream with a dark history' (G. ATHERTON, Adventures of a Novelist, 240). 'The cold Cherwell stream is a clean country creek' (CHRISTOPHER MORLEY, John Mistletoe, 326). Rock Creek Park, one of the sights of Washington, is a park through which flows a stream called Rock Creek.

crematory is the form ordinarily preferred in Am. to the term *crematorium,* usual in Eng. 'There are now 109 crematories in the U.S.' (World Almanac for 1933, 799).

crescent. For the reason why New Orleans is sometimes called the *Crescent City,* see the second quotation. 'The order is signed by Secretary Meyer, but he never was in New Orleans, probably, and it must be presumed that the act is really Mr. Taft's own, for the president was in the Crescent city but about a month ago.' 'Once the great bend in the river gave to the city a rounded shape and the name of the "Crescent City"—a name without meaning to-day, save that its principal streets running north and south curve to follow the bend in the river' (Prof. E. W. PARKS, in Culture in the South, 507).

†**crew.** In Am. a body of men employed on a particular job, not necessarily nautical. 'The crew of a local freight train had accidentally failed to close the switch.' 'There were not enough tank builders in the U.S. to do the work, and crews were brought from Canada.' 'The injured girl was one of a night crew of 25 girls making electric apparatus in the building.' 'The Japanese invasion of the lumber industry has been of a supplementary character. In no instances do we find a complete Japanese crew' (E. G. MEARS, Resident Orientals on the Am. Pacific Coast, 279). 'In those days a "turpentine orchard" frequently gave a young man his start in life. A crew of negroes and several thousand trees were the necessary stock in trade' (B. J. HENDRICK, Earlier Life of Walter H. Page, 10). Dr. F. S. Harris speaks of a crew of men boring the Simplon Tunnel (Scientific Research and Human Welfare, 205) and says that, before the modern paper-making processes were evolved, 'it required a crew of three men about a day to mold and finish 4,000 small sheets of paper' (ibid. 257).

cricket has in Am. the additional meaning of a *low wooden stool.* In this sense it is now obs. in Eng. exc. in dial. 'Children up to the age of six were encouraged to sit on crickets throughout the sermon and draw or look at pictures' (Prof. MARY ELLEN CHASE, A Goodly Heritage, 142).

crimson is the Harvard colour. 'The Indians got the jump on Harvard, and time after time sent the Crimson line back for a yard or two.' 'It seemed to those who watched that Harvard's reach, with the failure to finish strongly, lost the Crimson a fraction of a foot at each stroke.'

††**crook.** The use of this term to denote a *rogue* is now familiar in Eng., but it is a modern importation from Am. 'All the most likely resorts of crooks are being carefully watched by detectives.' 'Mr. Young worked out his theory for the correct handling of crooks, of whom there was probably a more abundant crop on both the business and the political sides of utilities than now' (IDA M. TARBELL, Owen D. Young, 94).

crop. In the Southern States much land is cultivated by *croppers* or *share-croppers* under the *share crop* system, which is described in the first of the following quotations. 'The aspiring but poverty-stricken husbandman must first become a "cropper" or share tenant, obtaining tools, seed and draft animals from the landlord and usually giving him half of the crop grown' (Prof. A. M. SCHLESINGER, The Rise of the City, 6). 'The Negro share-croppers in the South are held in a state of peonage which differs little from their original state of slavery' (E. WILSON, The Am. Jitters, 192).

cross-roads. In Eng., mention of *cross-roads* evoked, in the old days, associations with the burial of suicides. Nowadays the word suggests rather a problem of the regulation of motor traffic. In Am. it commonly carries with it a provincial or rural implication. The place where highways intersect is apt to be the site near which the rudiments of a village grow up. It commonly has a general store or a blacksmith's shop where the scattered inhabitants of the countryside meet for gossip and discussion. 'There was not a cross-roads in Kansas that was not swarming with men, full of drug-store whisky, chewing sweet flat tobacco, whittling dry-goods boxes, and cussing the government'. 'The radio and the sound-pictures have made familiar to the voters at any cross-roads the voice, lineaments and physical set-up of candidates.' 'Thousands of heartening messages poured into the White House from the cross-roads. The people saw in Roosevelt the prophet of a new social creed' (J. K. WINKLER, J. Pierpont Morgan, 244). 'He would scatter his stock throughout the land and make people at every crossroads partners' (The Mirrors of Wall Street, 159).

Both *cross-road* and *cross-roads* are often used attrib. 'A personal campaign which has taken them into all the cross-roads hamlets.' 'President Cleveland was the first President with the moral courage to place an obstacle in the way of the cross-roads politicians who sought a pleasant berth abroad.' 'Around comfortable stoves in cross-road stores, where discussion is as constant a pastime as checkers' (Prof. H. J. FORD, Woodrow Wilson, 85). 'Men grown old still sit in cross-roads grocery stores, and tell of the giants who once lived' (H. F. PRINGLE, Theodore Roosevelt, 161).

crow. Am. *eat crow* = Eng. *eat humble pie.* 'There appears to be one disappointed man who can't eat his crow without making faces over it.' 'High tariff had forced the farmers to eat crow in the shape of high prices for non-agricultural products' (L. F. CARR, Am. Challenged, 90).

Am. *a crow to pick* = Eng. *a bone to pick.* 'The city of Hartford has a very black crow to pick with the President. He was riding on a train which stopped there the other day, and he actually asked where he was.' The *O.E.D.* recognizes *a crow to pluck* or *pull* (rarely *pick*), but its latest example is dated 1849.

crowd. †In Am. the noun *crowd* does not necessarily suggest a throng or large number. It is practically a synonym for *group.* Thus, one may remark of a certain family of singers, who were favourite performers 20 years ago: 'I don't believe there's one of the original crowd left.' 'He had been forced into the N.Y. Central directorate by the Standard Oil crowd.' 'It is said that his resignation was forced, the President wanting the place for one of his own crowd.' 'The man coming home from work with his own crowd would stop in a saloon and treat six or eight men' (JANE ADDAMS, The Second 20 Years at Hull-House, 230). 'On warm summer evenings we would organize a picnic crowd, a group of 10 or 12 boys and girls, and go to the summit of Lookout Mountain' (W. G. McADOO, Crowded Years, 36).

The verb *crowd* has a wider application in Am. than in Eng., both (1) literally and (2) figuratively. It has become almost a synonym for *push, compel, bring pressure to bear on.* (1) 'He died from the effects of an accident several days ago, when his horse crowded him over on to a sidewalk.' 'There is a rent in the old wine-skin under the crowding of the fresh fermentation' (Dr. C. H. PARKHURST, A Little Lower Than The Angels, 44). (2) 'It would be bad policy for the business management of the line to crowd the technical management into the abandonment of any conditions of safety.' 'In the grade schools, the specialists are crowding the grade teacher, and the latter is complaining that she has not sufficient time to teach thoroughly the three R's.' 'Holland was crowding Spain for first place in the commercial world' (A. M. SIMONS, Social Forces in Am. Hist. 50). 'A new article of faith is crowding for admission into the creed of Am.' (NORMAN THOMAS, America's Way Out, 44).

†Hence *crowd out* and *crowd up* = Eng. *drive out* and *drive up.* 'He is a very large stockholder in the Illinois Central, and was crowded out of the road's presidency by a man who is not known to have any large personal interest in the property.' 'The Rockefeller and the Morgan interests were also anxious to crowd Carnegie out' (R. I. WARSHOW, Story of Wall Street, 99). 'The price of cotton is being crowded up higher than conditions of supply and demand warrant.'

crystal is popularly used in Am. to denote the glass cover protecting the dial of a watch; commonly called in Eng. a *watch-glass.* In Eng. *crystal* is used in this sense by watchmakers only.

†**cub** is sometimes used in Am. as an adj., as a suitable epithet for an apprentice or novice. 'The recorder of the experiences and emotions of a cub pilot on the Mississippi.' 'Five months after his appearance in the office as a cub reporter, Page found himself editor-in-chief' (B. J. HENDRICK, Earlier Life of Walter H. Page, 131). In Eng. the normal term would be *junior reporter.*

cucumber. In some parts of Am. this name is given to the *magnolia.* 'There is the magnolia, which they [the people of the Appalachian Mountains] call the wild cucumber, because of the scarlet, cucumber-shaped seed it bears in autumn. It grows very freely from 20 to 40 feet in height and is thick with blossom' (CECIL SHARP, in a letter quoted in his biog., p. 161). Webster defines the *cucumber-tree* as 'any of several Am. magnolias, esp. *Magnolia acuminata,* said to be so called on account of a slight resemblance of its young fruit to a small cucumber'.

cunning. In Am. this word often lacks any idea of dexterity or slyness. It is a common term of endearment, applied esp. to children and pet animals of small size. 'What a cunning little baby!' is the Am.

equivalent of the Eng. 'What a ducky little baby!' 'The woman likes them [Shetland] ponies because they are "cunning"; she likes to pet and fondle them.' Applied to things, *cunning = dainty* or *dinky*. 'The funniest and cunningest of little jointed china dolls.' 'The students munch cunning little tea cakes while the instructor lectures.' J. H. Choate reports George Meredith as living in 'a cunning little cottage' (E. S. Martin, Life of J. H. Choate, ii. 192). See CUTE.

cup. In Am. cooking recipes *cup* is a definite measure, denoting half an Am. PINT.

curve. 'Mr. Dooley', in writing of a certain Am. Secretary of War whose policies were difficult to understand, remarks that people were unable to get on to his curves. This use of *curve* is a metaphor from baseball, where, acc. to the *Century Dict.*, it denotes 'the course of a ball so pitched that it does not pass in a straight line from the pitcher to the catcher, but makes a deflection in the air other than the ordinary one caused by the force of gravity'.

custom. In Am. *custom clothes* are *clothes made to measure*; i.e. for individual customers. Hence Am. *custom suit = Eng. bespoke suit.* 'Our custom department will make to order any special style which may be desired' (Advt.). 'As perfect-fitting as the finest custom garments' (Advt.). 'When this toiler set up his little shop over 30 years ago, custom shoemaking was a fine trade, and no man of standing would wear ready-made shoes or boots.' 'Custom tailoring requires a higher grade of skill than the manufacturing of ready-made clothing' (Dr. I. A. Hourwich, Immigration and Labor, 368). 'Custom and repairing work is still done in the little tailoring and shoemaking shops that speak a sort of defiance to the great emporiums' (W. J. Ghent, Our Benevolent Feudalism,

19). 'The straining pockets of his custom-made trousers' (Florence Converse, Efficiency Expert, 35).

cut. ††In Am. the verb *cut* = Eng. *reduce* and the noun *cut* = Eng. *reduction*. 'In 1912 there were 600 deaths and 15,000 injuries among railroad employees due to falls from cars. Ten years later these figures had been cut to 66 deaths and 5,566 injuries' (F. J. Haskin, The Am. Government, 387). 'He kept cutting his price and increasing his sales' (L. Steffens, Autobiog. 853). 'President Taft informed his Cabinet officers, after scrutinizing the final draft of estimates, that there must be a further and deeper cut in them.' 'Cut in Courses at Harvard' is the heading of a newspaper article giving particulars of a reduction in the number of college courses.

In the vocab. of Am. railways, *cut* = Eng. *cutting*. 'The high winds blow the snow back into the cuts.' 'Although the new four-track system through Bergen Hill has been spoken of as an open cut, it is not strictly such, as it contains four short tunnels.'

In Eng. one may speak of a *cut from the joint*. In Am. *cut* may denote the joint itself. 'Our bill at the butcher-shop in town dropped as Lenore learned how to make cheap cuts of meat palatable and tender.'

In politics, to *cut* a TICKET (q.v.) is to vote for some candidates on the ticket and reject others. The candidates thus rejected are also said to be cut. 'In the country towns the Republicans are not cutting their State ticket in any particular, but are making changes on the county ticket.' 'Information received indicated that the Rep. nominee for Governor was being cut by the farmers on account of his policy while cattle commissioner.'

Am. *cut-off* = Eng. *by-pass, short cut.* 'The Chatsford Park cut-off will afford an easier and shorter route to Santa Barbara.' 'Lovell ordered me forward to notice the trail and course, as the latter was a cut-off and much nearer than by road' (ANDY ADAMS, The Outlet, 332).

In Am., land from which timber has been cleared is described as *cut-over*. 'Expansion of the agricultural area has been promoted by encouraging the settlement of cut-over farm lands' (C. M. CLAY, The Mainstay of Am. Individualism, 210). 'He had a plan for getting the soldiers back to the soil by assisting them to procure tracts of cut-over land' (Dict. Am. Biog. xiv. 536).

In Am. *cutter* may denote not only a vessel but a light sleigh, usually drawn by a single horse. 'Jack Finch was awakened by his stableman at 5 o'clock, and informed that there was enough snow on the ground to carry a cutter.' 'The snow was still falling thickly when Orrin Bosworth drove up in his cutter to Saul Routledge's gate' (E. WHARTON, Here and Beyond, 79).

cute, an abbreviation of *acute*, is used in Am. not only with the normal meaning of that word but as a synonym of the Am. CUNNING (q.v.). 'The cutest thing of human kind is the papoose'. Babies' cute little black, white or red slippers.' When the heroine of 'Gentlemen Prefer Blondes' lunches at the Ritz, she sees 'a quite cute little girl' at the next table, and when she goes shopping she buys 'some quite cute hats'.

cycler. In Am. the form *cycler* is preferred to *cyclist*, and, accordingly, *bicycler* to *bicyclist* and *tricycler* to *tricyclist*. 'Cyclers Started in Six Days' Contest' (newspaper headline). 'The appearance of bicyclers for the first act' (H. A. FRANCK, Vagabond Journey, 283). 'The small boys of the city are wont to call out to a stray bicycler' (R. S. and H. M. LYND, Middletown, 283). The late Joseph Pennell once wrote to the N.Y. *Nation* (vol. 48, p. 97) to protest against its use of *cyclist*, 'an almost unpronounceable and certainly point-

less term', instead of the Am. word *cycler*. An editorial note referred him to κυκλίζω, on the analogy of *botanist* from βοτανίζω, and added: 'Patriotism has nothing to do with building words correctly from the Greek.'

cyclone. The Am. *cyclone cellar*—a cave or hole in the ground which affords a place of refuge from a cyclone—lends itself easily to fig. uses. 'The Senate is the stronghold of wealth, the trusts, the railroads, the tariff, and privilege generally. It is important that these interests should have a stronghold somewhere, these windy days. The Senate is their cyclone cellar; they are safe there.' 'Prices boomeranged [at the outbreak of war in 1914] while gold, the international common denominator, fled to the cyclone cellars, leaving foreign exchange to ricochet around the globe' (The Mirrors of Wall Street, 43). An alternative, in less frequent use, is *tornado cellar*.

D

dandy. In Am. the equivalent of the Eng. vulgarism, *treat*. 'That freshman race yesterday was a "dandy". Everybody who saw it says it was one of the liveliest struggles New London ever saw.'

Also used as an adj. = Eng. *tip-top*, *first-rate*. 'A few days ago I overheard one man telling another that he had just given his mother-in-law "a dandy funeral".' 'The special agent is chosen because he has proved himself to be a "dandy salesman".' Cleveland Moffett (Careers of Danger and Daring, 235) quotes one fireman as saying of another: 'He's a wonder, sir; he's the dandiest man. Say, did ye ever hear how he crawled under that blazing naphtha tank and got a man out who was in there unconscious?' 'Most farmers have a much wider choice of food than we have mentioned, but even those who are limited in their selection can have dandy food' (Dr. R. L. ALSAKER, Eating for Health and Efficiency, 425). A somewhat similar use of the word is reported by Wright's *Dial. Dict.* from Scotland, where it means *fine, gay, showy, flashy.*

dark horse. In the vocab. of Am. politics this term, borrowed from the race-course, has a spec. meaning. It denotes a candidate for the Presidential nomination, at a national party convention, who is not widely known throughout the country and has little chance of being nominated except to settle a deadlock when no FAVOURITE (q.v.) can secure a majority. Garfield in 1880 and Harrison in 1888 were examples. Garfield's name was not brought forward until the 31st BALLOT (q.v.), when he received one vote. He was nominated on the 36th with 399 votes. Harrison was fifth in order on the first ballot, with only 80 votes to Sherman's 229. He was nominated on the eighth with 544.

data. In Am. this plural is often treated even by educated writers and speakers as a singular. In Eng. such misuse of the word is considered a solecism. 'No provision was made for the publication of this data' (F. J. HASKIN, The Am. Government, 159). 'The classification of this data is a great task' (Prof. C. MCCARTHY, The Wisconsin Idea, 245). 'I went over the data which Houston had prepared, and added to it and eliminated from it whatever seemed necessary. This data was afterwards given to Governor Wilson, who based his tariff speeches largely on it' (Intimate Papers of Col. House, i. 49).

The word sometimes = *facts* or *news,* without any suggestion that this information is to be the basis of an argument or calculation. 'Sun Square Apparatus Ready to Announce Convention Data' (Newspaper headline). 'He also collected all data relating to the early Swedish settlers of Pennsylvania, as well as any material concerning the development of the state' (Dr. A. S. W. ROSENBACH, Books and Bidders, 8).

date. †In Am. *date* is frequently used to denote an *appointment* or *engagement* for a certain time. 'Mr. Bryan is going to Europe partly on business and partly for pleasure. He denied that he has any "dates" with any of the crowned heads of Europe.' 'The cruiser Minneapolis made three "dates" to sail before she got away.' 'So little suspicious were we still that we even made a date to meet our Hamburg friends late that August of 1914' (F. J. STIMSON, My U.S. 222).

Hence *dateless = without social engagements.* 'The young men at Northwestern University have agreed to join the young women of that institution in observing three dateless nights each week. The action was taken by representatives of fraternities and various other groups, mainly in the interest of men students working their way through college who are not able financially to engage in intensive social life.'

The Am. expression *without date = sine die.* 'The World Economic Conference, at London, recessed without date' (N.Y. World Almanac for 1934, 108).

davenport. In Eng. a kind of desk or escritoire; in Am. also a kind of couch or divan.

day. An Am. idiom is the omission of *the* before *day after, day before.* 'Day after election, people will want to know etc.' 'Day before yesterday the President was again in a state of terrific determination.' 'I am to take up what we need day after to-morrow' (RUTH HALL, The Pine Grove House, 91).

daylight. What is called *summer time* in Eng. is known in Am. as *daylight saving time.* The originator of the scheme, the late William Willett, used the term *daylight saving time,* but the law adopting his plan was called a *Summer Time Act*, and *summer time* thus came to be the term in general use in Eng. The Am. term is obviously preferable, as it indicates more precisely the purpose of the change of reckoning. It also avoids the absurdity of applying the name of *summer time* to a bitterly cold April morning.

deacon has a peculiar use in Am., where the name is given to the skin of a newly-born calf. It must weigh less than 8 lb. 'Last year I sold deacon hides for 35 cents.'

dead. The Am. compound *deadfall* denotes a trap for large game, so contrived that a heavy weight falls upon the prey. The term is often used fig. 'He might be on the lecture platform in Am.—that deadfall for more than one great doer.' '"There's a deadfall down here on the river", said he, "that robs a man going and coming. They've got booze to sell you that would make a pet rabbit fight a wolf"' (ANDY ADAMS, Log of a Cowboy, 251).

deal has a spec. meaning in Am. politics. 'In very highly organized political parties, the stock voter will accept the orders of his suzerain to vote against his party. This makes possible the political deal, which means that the heads of rival parties agree each to support some of the candidates of the other's ticket, thus rendering the election of the least desirable men almost a certainty' (Prof. A. B. HART, Actual Government, 100). 'There had been deals and counterdeals between Tammany and anti-Tammany Democrats' (H. F. PRINGLE, Theodore Roosevelt, 66).

It is, of course, by no means in this sense that the term *New Deal* is applied to Pres. Franklin Roosevelt's policies. He has himself endorsed the suggestion that it 'expresses a satisfactory combination of the Square Deal and the New Freedom' (On our Way, x).

dear. The observant Prof. Félix
Boillot has noted (Le Vrai Ami du Traducteur, 97) that in Am. the formula 'My dear Mr. So-and-so' is less familiar than 'Dear Mr. So-and-so', while in Eng. it is quite the contrary.

debenture. The difference between the Eng. and the Am. use of this term may be understood from the following quotations. 'In general, the term *debenture* in British usage designates any security issued by companies other than their shares, including therefore what are in the U.S. commonly called *bonds*. When used in the U.S., *debenture* generally designates an instrument secured by a floating charge junior to other charges secured by fixed mortgages, or, specifically, one of a series of securities secured by a group of securities held in trust for the benefit of the debenture holders' (Webster's Dict.). 'The term *debenture* is commonly used in Great Britain to designate all classes of certificates or written instruments issued under seal and evidencing indebtedness of companies (i.e. corporations). Its Eng. use is thus largely equivalent to the word *bond* in the U.S., where *debenture* is ordinarily restricted to certificates of corporate obligations having no special security such as mortgage, lien, or assignment of property. The common British expression, *debenture stock*, designates "borrowed capital consolidated into one mass for the sake of convenience", and partakes somewhat of the nature of preferred stock' (Encycl. of the Social Sciences, v. 29). The same authority adds that it is only since 1900 that *debenture* has come into general use in Am. to designate unsecured corporate obligations.

decedent. In Am. this term, now obs. in Eng., is commonly preferred to *deceased*. 'The Mercantile Trust Co. is to act as executor and trustee, and is to hold all the estate in trust for the decedent's daughter.' 'The taxation of the estates of decedents' (Prof. R. T. ELY, Evolution of Industrial Society, 273).

deck. In Shakespeare's day, a *pack* of cards was called a *deck*.
'But, whiles he thought to steal the single ten,
The king was slily fingered from the deck' (3 Henry VI, v. 1).
This use of the word, long obs. in Eng., survives in Am. 'The doctor prescribes a sea voyage, a pipe of tobacco, a flask of whisky, a deck of cards, and a few assorted detective stories.'

declination. In Eng. this term is obs. exc. in the scientific sense. In Am. it = *non-acceptance* or *refusal*. 'One of the most remarkable situations in the political history of the city has been precipitated by the declination of every one of the eight candidates placed in nomination for the city offices at the recent Dem. city convention.' 'The letter contains a respectful but firm declination to attempt to make good in the office in which George III had so recently failed' (Prof. D. S. MUZZEY, The Am. Adventure, i. 129). 'More than one Scottish constituency requested Carnegie to stand for Parliament—all of which advances he met with the usual declination' (B. J. HENDRICK, The Life of Andrew Carnegie, 280).

decoration. *Decoration Day* is an alternative term for *Memorial Day*, an annual commemoration of the soldiers who fell in the Am. Civil War. It derives its name from the practice, on this day, of placing flowers on their graves. Acc. to the *World Alm.*, it is observed on March 30 in all States and possessions exc. five of the Southern States. 'Although Decoration Day is a legal holiday throughout the country, it is becoming a day more and more of baseball games and less of memorial observance.' 'Each year I spent six weeks with my grandparents, three in the spring taking in Decoration Day' (ALICE ROOSEVELT LONGWORTH, Crowded Hours, 9).

dedicate. In Am. the use of this word, in connexion with the formal opening of buildings, &c., is not restricted, as in Eng., to religious ceremonies. 'The beautiful Goodwin Memorial Library building was dedicated yesterday by appropriate and inspiring exercises.' 'The Massachusetts Talc Company's new mill was dedicated Friday evening with a concert and ball.' 'On Tuesday afternoon the great Wanamaker store was formally dedicated, and the Secretary of the Treasury made the opening address.' 'The Chicago Board of Trade had recently dedicated its new $2,000,000 building' (L. ADAMIC, Dynamite, 65). If Eng. publications had been reporting such events, they would have used *opened* instead of *dedicated*.

degree. In Am. murders are classified in two degrees. Murder in the *first degree* is an unlawful, intentional, and premeditated homicide, or homicide resulting from the commission, or attempted commission, of one of the graver crimes, such as arson, burglary, or rape. Murder in the *second degree* is such a homicide without premeditation, or resulting from the attempt to commit some lesser crime. 'It is the general opinion among those who have followed the case closely that a verdict of murder in either the first or second degree will be returned.'
Degrees are similarly recognized officially in certain other crimes. 'He pleaded guilty to burglary in the third degree in stealing several articles from the home of his father and brother. He previously pleaded guilty to forgery in the second degree.'
The *third degree* is a system of pressure applied by the police in order to extract confessions from persons in custody. 'He was at first arrested merely as a suspicious person, but when put through the "third degree" at the station, the detectives say, admitted that he entered the house last night.' 'After being taken to Police Headquarters last night the

"third degree" was given the prisoner, and under this strain Hunt broke down and made a confession.' This third degree, apparently, itself permits of gradations. Writing in the *Atlantic Monthly* of Sept. 1931, E. J. Hopkins, who had just been investigating Am. police methods for the Wickersham Commission, said: 'If the term "third degree" be applied only to cruel and abnormal forms and grades of torture, plenty of cases can be cited, but still they are exceptional. If it be taken to include any use of physical violence to make a man confess—slaps, shoves, blows, kicks, beatings with soft weapons or with hard,—it is absent from a few cities, occasional in many, and current custom in the two largest. If it be taken also to cover threats, lies, display of weapons, exhausting grilling, and the like, it is the exceptional Am. city where it does not exist. If it be interpreted to refer —as I think it should—to the secret police inquisition of whatever type where the demand is made that the arrested person incriminate himself, and the 5th Amendment is thereby breached, then the third degree is all but universal.' It has been suggested that the use of this term derives from the *degrees* in the initiation of Freemasons.

delegation, in the sense of *body of delegates*, is spec. used of a group of members of Congress representing a particular State. 'The entire delegation from Texas, including the newly elected representative from the 5th District, were behind Mills' candidacy [for the Speakership of the House]' (S. H. ACHESON, Joe Bailey, 45).

This word also takes the place of the Eng. *deputation*. 'Near the end of the month a delegation was sent to Washington [from N.Y. bankers] to ask the secretary for a more effective form of relief' (Dr. M. G. MYERS, The N.Y. Money Market, i. 189).

delinquent may be applied in Am. not only to the person who offends

but to the matter in regard to which he is delinquent. 'An examination of the public records discloses the fact that in the city of O'Neill there is delinquent real estate taxes to the amount of more than $80,000. In many cases the property is not worth as much as the delinquent taxes against it.' 'The number of forced sales resulting from the foreclosure of mortgages, bankruptcies, and delinquent taxes showed an increase of 25 per cent.' (W. LIPPMANN, The U.S. in World Affairs in 1932, 6).

democracy, democrat. In Am. *the Democracy* (with a capital initial) is often used as a synonym for *the Democratic party*. 'Reports of dissensions in the Nebraska Democracy are incorrect.' 'The answer of Missouri will be national, almost racial, in importance. Both the Democracy and the democracy are being put to the test out there.' 'The main feud within the Democracy itself raged between the Carter H. Harrison forces and the Sullivanites' (Dr. H. ZINK, City Bosses in U.S. 296). 'The Democratic resolutions committee had written a straightforward revenue-tariff plank into the Democracy's platform in 1892' (L. M. HACKER and B. B. KENDRICK, The U.S. since 1865, 95).

Eng. papers sometimes refer to 'the Democrat party', 'the Democrat candidate', &c. In Am. the word *Democrat* is never an adj. but always a noun. The adj. applied to the party, its candidates, its tickets, &c., is invariably *Democratic*.

A *democrat wagon* has nothing to do with politics. The *Century Dict.* defines it as 'a light wagon without a top, containing several seats and usually drawn by two horses', and adds that it was originally called a *democratic wagon*. 'This morning, going for a walk before breakfast, one met a democrat wagon coming in. On the driving seat were the prosperous farmer and his young lady daughter; and in place of the rear seat there was a tethered calf.' 'In the course of my boyhood the buggy and the very convenient democrat wagon, turned out by factories, came into general use' (W. W. FOLWELL, Autobiog. 23). Sometimes the word *wagon* is omitted. 'On one such occasion he drove a covered three-seated democrat' (W. R. MOODY, D. L. Moody, 474).

denominational is often used by members of the Protestant Episcopal Church as a collective term for other Protestant Churches—i.e. those corresponding to the Free or Nonconformist Churches in Eng. 'The results which have been obtained by many of the denominational churches in this country.' 'The apparent ignorance of our clergy concerning general religious conditions and movements upon which their denominational brethren were well-informed.' Both these extracts are from the N.Y. *Churchman*, an organ of the P.E. Church.

department. In Am. this term denotes not, as in Eng., a subdivision of one of the great offices of state (e.g. the Bankruptcy Department of the Board of Trade or the Factory Department of the Home Office) but one of the main divisions of the Federal Administration, whose heads constitute the President's Cabinet. Thus, the Constitution of 1789 authorizes the President to 'require the opinion, in writing, of the principal officer in each of the executive departments' and authorizes Congress to vest the appointment of inferior officers 'in the heads of departments'. At present these departments consist of the Department of State, the Treasury Department, the War Department, the Department of Justice, the Post Office Department, the Navy Department, the Department of the Interior, the Department of Agriculture, the Department of Commerce, and the Department of Labor. See BUREAU.

The term *department store*, now familiar in Eng., is of Am. origin.

depositary, depository. This word has a spec. meaning in the Am. banking system. 'The National Bank Act provided that public revenue, exc. customs dues, might be deposited in national banks. For 30 years such deposits were considered as an exceptional expedient to be used only in emergencies. But as its business grew, it became more and more necessary for the Government to avail itself of them, and the result was a fully developed system of regular and special national bank depositaries for all Government revenue' (B. H. BECKHART, The N.Y. Money Market, iv. 186). 'Under this scheme, the Government was to discontinue using banks as depositories and was to establish subtreasury offices in connection with the warehouses' (Prof. E. S. SPARKS, Agricultural Credit in U.S. 143).

Another kind of Government *depository* is described as follows. 'The publications of the Government Printing Office are regularly sent to many libraries where the general public reads. By special act members of Congress are empowered to designate certain institutions in their respective districts as "depositories". Such libraries are entitled to receive automatically all issues from the federal press without charge other than transportation costs' (C. A. and W. BEARD, The Am. Leviathan, 636).

depot was once the ordinary term for a railway station in Am., but this usage is now becoming obs. William Dean Howells, writing in *Harper's Monthly*, Nov. 1906, of a visit to Eng., says: 'Even the wood-built stations we whisked by had a charm because they were like the clap-boarded depots, freight and passenger, at our rustic junctions.' The *Depot Street* of some small Am. towns corresponds to the Eng. *Station Road*. See TERMINAL.

deputy is often to be understood in Am. as an abbrev. of *deputy sheriff*. (See SHERIFF.) 'Then the superintendent of Smuggler-Union mines opened a mine with scabs, most of whom were armed and sworn in as deputies' (L. ADAMIC, Dynamite, 138). 'The sheriff of Allegheny County appeared at the works with 120 deputies, and was met by a mob of strikers' (B. J. HENDRICK, Life of Andrew Carnegie, 827).

derby. For some unknown reason the town of Derby has given its name to *derby hat* or *derby*, the Am. term for a *bowler*. The word is pronounced as spelt, not *darby*. 'Our derbies are as comfortable as the soft hats' (Advt.). 'The earliest arrival was John Burns, who was dressed in his customary reefer jacket and derby hat.' 'The stiff derby hat always stands on the top of their large egg-shaped heads' (K. BERCOVICI, Around the World in N.Y. 29). 'He looks very compact, decent and well satisfied in his dark coat and black derby' (E. WILSON, The Am. Jitters, 134).

derelict. The Am. use of this word is a linguistic curiosity. It is properly a passive participle, and is invariably so used in Eng. Somehow or other it has become active in Am., where it is applied not to a person who has been abandoned but one who has abandoned; i.e. not a *derelict*, correctly speaking, but a *delinquent*. Thus, in a letter of Sept. 12, 1904, formally accepting nomination to the Presidency, Theodore Roosevelt wrote: 'I should be derelict in my duty if I used a false construction of the Constitution as a shield for weakness or timidity.' Properly, of course, it would be the duty itself, not Mr. Roosevelt, that would be derelict in such a case. In a letter quoted in Thayer's biography of him (ii. 225) John Hay writes: 'Various other gentlemen think that we are derelict in our duty in having got a whole loaf and not having demanded two.' When the word is thus used by writers like Roosevelt and Hay, it is not surprising to find the same solecism in the newspapers. 'The

police authorities may have seemed to be derelict because of their apparent inactivity.' 'General Stakelberg was therefore justified in making the fight—he would have been derelict in not doing so.' 'It is clear that the Rapid Transit Commission was derelict when it approved the clauses in question.'

It is true that in Eng. *dereliction* is used as a synonym of *delinquency*, but that is quite a different matter. For *dereliction* is not a passive participle, as *derelict* is, but a verbal noun with an active signification. Accordingly, *guilty of dereliction* is as legitimate as *guilty of assassination* or *defamation* or *malefaction* or *seduction*. Thus *dereliction = delinquency*, just as *abstention = abstinence*.

desk. For a specialized Am. use of this word, see the first of the following quotations. 'Now, "desk" in a newspaper office is a generic name for a department that edits copy. It does not imply that the rest of the staff write on their knees.' 'The reporters who write up the sensational event—each one is hoping to attract the attention of the "desk"' (UPTON SINCLAIR, Money Writes, 18). 'For a time he was in complete editorial charge, but in 1857 he sold out his financial interest and ceased to hold a regular desk position, though he continued as a contributor' (Dict. Am. Biog. ix. 147). An Am. book entitled *Newspaper Desk Work* is a manual for the sub-editor. What in Eng. is called the *office copy* of a book is in Am. the *desk copy*.

In Am. *desk secretary* denotes a secretary whose duties lie wholly within the office, as distinct from a FIELD SECRETARY (q.v.).

dessert denotes in Eng. the uncooked fruit, nuts, &c., served at the end of a dinner. In Am. it includes the course of pies, puddings, &c., corresponding to what in Eng. is known as the sweet course. Senator William Maclay, in an entry in his *Journal* dated Aug. 27, 1789, describes a dinner given by

George Washington during his Presidency, at which 'the dessert was, first apple-pies, pudding, etc.; then iced creams, jellies, etc.; then water-melons, musk-melons, apples, peaches, nuts'. 'Sweet-potato pie is a favorite Southern dessert.' 'The dessert which he preferred was a plain rice pudding' (H. CROLY, Life of Senator Hanna, 447). The word may be used in Am. in the plur. 'Desserts should not be eaten every day, but when they are taken they should be rather plain, such as gelatine, fruit gelatine, custard, fruit either cooked or raw, fruit whip, plain cake like sponge cake, and ice cream' (Dr. R. L. ALSAKER, Eating for Health and Efficiency, 61). 'The average cook spends her time in making cakes and desserts' (A. C. ARNOLD, The Triangle of Health, 120).

The discrepancy between the Eng. and the Am. idiom seems to depend upon a difference in point of view as to what should be considered the final course of the dinner. The word is derived from the French *desservir* = *to remove what has been served, to clear the table*. Hence if you regard the sweets as the last course, you will call this course the *dessert*, as they do in Am.

Oddly enough, *dessert spoon* is the name given in Eng., as well as in Am., to an implement which is of service in dealing with dessert in the Am. sense only.

detail. In the sense of a small body of men detached for a particular service, the use of *detail* is in Eng. confined to the army. In Am. it may also be used of police, or even of the staff of a newspaper. 'A detail of police managed to break openings for the slow passage of the cars.' 'The *Tribune* had four details of men at North Brother Island the day of the disaster.'

develop. A peculiar Am. use of *develop*—which may be found in Jane Austen but is now obs. in Eng.—is in the senses of (1) *bring to light*

and (2) *come to light, transpire.* (1) 'Day in and day out he bombarded Hamilton and Wolcott with demands for accounting after accounting, explanation after explanation. He did develop the fact that enormous lump sum appropriations had been made' (Prof. T. J. GRAYSON, Leaders and Periods of Am. Finance, 95). (2) 'It developed to-day that the commercial vehicle show is to be a complimentary event.' 'Through a further exchange of notes, it developed that the minister's notification was based on an assumption rather than on information' (L. F. HILL, Diplomatic Relations between U.S. and Brazil, 22).

devil(t)ry. In Am., as in Scottish dial., *devilry* has acquired an unnecessary *t*, so that it appears as *deviltry*. 'She was abetted in all her deviltry by her mother.' 'Moved by a spirit of pure deviltry' (K. W. PORTER, John Jacob Astor, 1056). 'Indulging in wilful deviltry of all sorts' (Dr. L. N. RICHARDSON, Hist. of Early Am. Magazines, 138).

Similarly *daredevilry* has become *daredeviltry*. 'The automobile will have to be rescued from the daredeviltry and carelessness which too often sit in control of the machine's operations.' 'The boats were wood burners, and they were operated with the utmost daredeviltry' (Prof. T. J. GRAYSON, Leaders and Periods of Am. Finance, 313).

diamond is used in Am. to denote a *baseball field*, corresponding to the football GRIDIRON. Acc. to the baseball glossary in the 14th edition of the *Encycl. Britann.*, it may mean 'either all the field or the field between bases, more generally the latter'. 'The ideal of the growing lad is often found in the hero of the gridiron or the diamond.' 'Their baseball teams battle on its diamonds' (H. JUSTIN SMITH, Chicago 89). 'Though he became one of the famous ball players of his time, Miller Huggins was very small in comparison with his rivals on the diamond' (Dict. Am. Biog. ix. 346).

The State of Delaware is sometimes called *the Diamond State*.

diction. In 1930 the Am. Academy of Arts and Letters awarded a gold medal for diction. To an author or orator? No; to an actor. For in Am. *diction* has somehow or other— possibly through French influence— come to be a matter of utterance rather than of literary or oratorical style. The *Atlantic Monthly* of Feb. 1931 publishes the speech given by George Arliss when this medal was presented to him. 'There is no doubt', he says, 'that good diction is far too rare. By "diction" I mean the speaking of words correctly and easily. . . . The value of the talking screen in the improvement of the diction of the masses cannot be overestimated. Not that the masses would go to the movies to learn how to speak; but young people are inclined to be very imitative, particularly of those actors and actresses whom they especially admire.' In Eng. *enunciation* or *elocution* would be used in this sense. The word is also used in Am. in the normal Eng. sense. 'Fineness of style, esp. in the choice and disposition of words and in the harmonies of diction' (H. S. CANBY, Better Writing, 66). Possibly the two senses are combined in the following: 'Two seminaries have stretched their department of practical theology to include courses in microphone diction' (Prof. M. A. MAY, The Education of Am. Ministers, iii. 41).

different. †M. Félix Boillot (Le Vrai Ami du Traducteur, 103) mentions that in a London 'Tube' he has seen an advt.: 'The wall papers that are different.' This, he explains, does not mean that no two of these papers are alike, but that these wall papers are not like other wall papers. As yet this peculiar use of *different* is not frequent in Eng., but it may often be met with in an Am. advt., as an alternative to EXCLUSIVE (q.v.), or to *distinctive*.

In Am. *different than* sometimes

takes the place of *different from*. 'I can't see why a Negro should be any different than any other man about all that.' 'The problems affecting the Am. resident Chinese and Japanese are much different than those existing in 1900' (Prof. E. G. MEARS, Resident Orientals on the Am. Pacific Coast, iii). 'A sample of preëlection sentiment derived from tabloid readers would doubtless give very different results than a sample taken from the readers of the *N.Y.Times*' (C. E. ROBINSON, Straw Votes, 90). The *O.E.D.* quotes examples of *different than* from Goldsmith, J. H. Newman, and other Eng. writers, but says that the usual construction in Eng. is now *different from*.

dipper is rarely used in Eng. in its common Am. sense of a sort of ladle, mainly used, as its name implies, for dipping up liquids. It has a larger bowl than the ordinary ladle. 'I lean forward in the saddle to take the proffered dipper of cool spring water.' 'She left the dipper on the kitchen shelf instead of hanging it up over the pail' (K. D. WIGGIN, Rebecca, 64). 'The quiet life of the town drowsing about its courthouse square with its wooden pump and iron dippers' (R. S. and H. M. LYND, Middletown, 13).

The *Dipper, Big Dipper,* or *Great Dipper* is the Am. name for the *Great Bear.* 'A child was asked if she had ever seen the Great Dipper. "Oh, yes," she replied, "I saw it in my geography." This is better than not to have seen it at all; but the proper place to have seen it is in the heavens.' 'The deep northern sky where the Dipper gleamed faintly through the haze of heat that rose from the city' (W. P. EATON and E. M. UNDERHILL, Runaway Place, 235). 'In 1889 you could still discern the Big Dipper in the N.Y. sky' (JULIA B. FORAKER, I Would Live it Again, 168).

directory. In Eng. = *a list of residents.* In Am. used also in the sense of the Eng. *directorate,* i.e. board of directors. 'Much significance is attached to the change made last week in the directory of the Michigan Central Railroad Co.' (There follows a list of newly-elected directors.) 'The Methodist Protestant Conference to-day elected W. B. Usleton to the Baltimore Book Directory, in place of Daniel Baker, who resigned after being elected yesterday, because other members of the directory were not re-elected.' 'The Senator from N.Y. was a member of 70 directories, which brought him more than $50,000 a year in attendance fees alone' (Dr. C. C. REGIER, The Era of the Muckrakers, 111).

dirt is used in Am. in several special senses. A *dirt farmer* is one who is not afraid to tackle the disagreeable jobs of agriculture, as contrasted with one who will not soil his own hands with manual labour. 'The old fellow was dressed as a dirt farmer or homesteader would be in Nebraska.' 'These men bear about the same relation to the rank and file of the profession that the registrar of an agricultural college does to a real dirt farmer.' 'Old Brack was a practical dirt farmer, extracting his living from the soil with his own hands' (B. J. HENDRICK, Earlier Life of Walter H. Page, 46). Less frequently *dirt farmer* denotes an agriculturalist as distinct from a cattle-breeder. 'The advance of the dirt farmer into the cow country was accomplished with much friction. The economic systems of the farmer on the one hand and the cattleman on the other were diametrically opposite' (Prof. A. E. MARTIN, Hist. of U.S. ii. 124).

Am. *dirt floor* = Eng. *earth floor, unpaved floor.* 'Three good-sized native houses, with thatched roof and dirt floor.'

A *dirt roof* is a roof made of turf. 'A log cabin of two rooms, with a dirt roof.'

A *dirt road* is one that is not macadamized or otherwise paved. 'The use of tar or oil upon the roads would not be possible, most of the highways being soft "dirt" roads. To be of any practical benefit the road to which the oil or tar is applied must be well built, smooth, and hard.' 'Urban progress crept toward the town. The dirt roads leading to it were graveled, and finally hard-surfaced' (H. JUSTIN SMITH, Chicago, 114). In Eng. the term *dirt road* is unknown, though *dirt track* is familiar in connexion with motor-cycle racing.

Am. *dirt wagon* = Eng. *dust-cart.* 'A team of horses attached to a dirt wagon became unmanageable on Third Avenue.'

discard. In Eng. *discard* is seldom used as a noun, except as a technical term in card-playing. In Am. the noun *discard* may often be met with, apart from that game. 'The old high wheel was relegated to the pile of discards at the back of the bicycle repairman's shop.' It is most common in the phrase *throw into the discard* and in similar expressions. 'A candidate defeated in a state-wide primary is popularly regarded as having been thrown into the political discard' (G. W. PEPPER, In the Senate, 56). 'Miss Finley's books are among those which changing standards have thrown into the discard' (Dict. Am. Biog. vi. 390). 'Congress swept his whole ambitious plan into the discard' (Prof. T. J. GRAYSON, Leaders and Periods of Am. Finance, 250).

dispensary denotes in Eng. either an apothecary's shop or a charitable institution where the poor may obtain medicine and medical advice for little or nothing. A special Am. use is thus described: 'The dispensary system, or system of state monopoly, was to a large degree an Am. adaptation of the Gothenburg system of private monopoly.... The Gothenburg system and the dispensary system were alike in that the intention of each was to eliminate the element of private profit from the sale of liquor. . . . Although there had been local dispensaries at Athens, Georgia, and a few other places, the dispensary system as a state measure was first put into operation in S. Carolina. . . . There was a central state dispensary for the wholesale distribution to the local dispensaries. The profits of the central dispensary were devoted to the school fund and those of the local dispensaries were divided between the municipality and the county. Purchasers were required to make written application for what they bought and the liquor was not to be drunk on the premises' (D. LEIGH COLVIN, Prohibition in U.S. 293).

dissenter. In Eng. this word is used spec. of one who dissents from the Church of Eng., esp. a Protestant Nonconformist. In Am., where there is no established church to dissent from, it has the more general meaning of the Eng. *dissentient.* 'With two dissenters, the committee reported against the petition.' 'The story is told of Justice Holmes that, when an admirer brought him a copy of his collected dissents to be autographed, he picked up his pen somewhat reluctantly and murmured under his breath, "I don't seek my reputation as a dissenter".' 'The majority of the Democrats were for the use of both gold and silver, and the dissenters favored gold' (M. R. WERNER, Life of W. J. Bryan, 65). 'These incidents shook the faith of some of the Boston Scientists, and 36 dissenters withdrew from the organization' (Dict. Am. Biog. vi. 12).

district. In Am. the area represented by a member of the House of Representatives at Washington is a *district,* or *Congressional district.* The Eng. analogue is a Parliamentary *division,* or, more popularly, a *constituency.* An Eng. *district (rural district* or *urban district)* has nothing to do with representation in Parliament. It is a division of a county, and its local affairs are administered by a district council. 'If the Democrats can carry 17 districts now represented by Republicans, while the latter make no inroads into the Dem. column, the next House will be Dem.' 'Acc. to the British law, the Labor Party or any other party may nominate a candidate from outside the district in which he seeks election. This makes it possible for the Labor Party to elect most of its national leaders to Parliament even if they live in London' (P. BLANSHARD, Outline of the British Labor Movement, 26). 'In spite of his cold exterior and lack of personal magnetism, he seldom had real difficulty in securing his district's vote for election to the House' (Prof. D. C. BARRETT, Greenbacks and Specie Payments, 196).

Hence the verb *district = divide into constituencies.* 'Before votes can be cast, two preliminaries are common— districting and registration' (Prof. A. B. HART, Actual Government, 71). Accordingly, the process of *redistricting* corresponds to the Eng. *redistribution of seats.* 'The rural elements tried to postpone the redistricting that would give the rapidly growing city its fair representation' (T. C. PEASE, The U.S. 581).

The constituencies which send members to a State Legislature are also called *districts.* An *election district* (not to be confounded with a Congressional district) is a smaller division still. 'No man can become the big political man of his newspaper unless he begins at the very lowest rung of the latter. He must know the facts of the election district before he can correctly grasp the situation in the assembly district.' A *district leader* is the party head in an assembly or election district. 'One of the characteristics of the Tammany organization is that the district leader takes an interest in his people all the year round.' See also SECTION.

For the meaning of *school district* see the following quotation. 'The smallest unit of school administration is the school district, which in many states has its own board, raises its own taxes, and appoints its own teachers'

(Prof. A. B. HART, Actual Government, 542). See also SCHOOL.

The Am. judicial system includes a number of Federal *district courts*—at least one in each State, and nearly 20 in a large State like N.Y.—presided over by *district judges*. It is in these courts that most Federal cases are tried in the first instance.

For *district attorney* see ATTORNEY.

†**ditch.** In Eng. the verb *ditch* means *provide with ditches*. In Am. it also means *throw into the ditch*, and hence, of railway trains, *throw off the line*, *derail*. 'Seven passengers were injured by the ditching of a passenger train near Perry. The train ran into a washout while going 40 miles an hour.' The word is also used in a fig. sense. 'The Canadian Liberals felt much relieved over the President's veto of the Farmers' Free List Bill, inasmuch as its enactment into law would have ditched them in their reciprocity campaign.' 'Stonewall Jackson's failure to come to Lee's aid on June 26, 1862, nearly ditched Lee's victory.'

divide is in Am. sometimes a noun, in the sense of *watershed*. 'As fair as a green valley before the pioneer struggling over a divide from a desert.' 'Upon reaching the divide between Beaver Creek and Red River, I saw a lot of tents' (C. H. STERNBERG, Life of a Fossil Hunter, 221). 'The great flood disaster, when the Des Plaines River, rising in the swell of spring, spilled over the divide separating it from the Chicago south branch' (H. JUSTIN SMITH, Chicago, 38).

division is in Am. the technical term for a section of a railway. 'After having tried a plan for having engines haul freight trains through from Philadelphia to Pittsburgh, the Pennsylvania has decided that the old way of changing locomotives at each division was the most economical.' 'When the wrecking train is off duty you find it standing on a side track at the end of the railroad, if the road

is a short one; or at some division headquarters, if an extensive system.' 'When his friend and patron became vice-president of the Pennsylvania Railroad in 1859, Andrew succeeded him as superintendent of the western division' (Prof. T. J. GRAYSON, Leaders and Periods of Am. Finance, 409).

For the spec. meaning of a *division* in Congress, where it denotes something quite different from a *division* in Parliament, see YEA.

do. On *do*, as an auxiliary with *have*, Dr. H. Bradley says: 'The use of the auxiliary *do* is correct Eng. only when *have* expresses something occasional or habitual, not when the object is a permanent possession or attribute. It is permissible to say, "Do you have breakfast at eight?" or "We do not have many visitors"; but not, "Does she have blue eyes?" or "He did not have a good character"' (The Making of English, 71). Dr. Bradley adds that this convenient distinction in usage seems to be in danger of being lost, largely through Am. example. Of Am. example there is certainly no lack. 'The business of writing and editing does not have such well-defined methods of approach.' 'It [Chicago] does not have the custody of the nation's governing equipment and personnel, nor the responsibilities that go with them' (Prof. C. E. MERRIAM, Chicago, 304). 'The groupings of the studies in these institutions are entirely different from those which prevail in Germany, esp. owing to the fact that emphasis is laid on the college, which Germany does not have' (Dr. E. B. HOLT's trans. of Münsterberg's The Americans, 397). 'Her later works do not have the charming spontaneity of her romances of the Tennessee mountains' (Dict Am. Biog. xiii. 345).

Am. *do up* = Eng. *do for*. 'Canadian interests were seeking to acquire control of the Boston & Maine when his foresight and nerve did them up.'

docket. In Eng., as a legal term, a

docket is a register of the judgements pronounced by a Court. In Am. it is a list of causes for trial or of the names of persons whose causes are pending. It thus corresponds to the Eng. *cause list.* 'It had been argued before the Supreme Court and restored to the docket for re-argument.' 'The over-crowded docket, and the large number of cases which must be heard daily, make it virtually impossible for the judge to render an intelligent decision' (M. A. ELLIOTT and F. E. MERRILL, Social Disorganization, 698). The verb *docket* is used in a corresponding sense. 'Some cases dragged on for years. The average pendency of cases resulting in cease and desist orders was seven months after docketing' (T. C. BLAISDELL, The Federal Trade Commission, 282).

doctor. In Am. this honorific title is commonly given not only to physicians, as in Eng., but to dentists, and sometimes even to druggists. 'Dr. . . ., a dentist, has his home and office in the rear of the burned building.' 'Prince Louis of Battenberg had an expensive experience with Am. dentistry. For work on four teeth, extending altogether over about twelve hours, Dr. . . . of N.Y. charged him $1,000.' 'Dr. . . ., one of the oldest druggists of the District of Columbia, died yesterday.' 'I secured a situation with Dr. . . ., who owned two drug-stores.' See also PHYSICIAN.

dodger. In Eng., a person who practises dodges. In Am. also a small advertising leaflet. 'Banners do not influence these men; dodgers they never read; and they make no part of cart-tail audiences.' When a N.Y. theatre hung at the foot of its stairs a big sign, 'Positively No Throw-aways Allowed', a newspaper explained that a throwaway was 'a card or dodger announcing some future event, which the promoters are anxious to distribute and the management equally anxious not to have strewn about the premises'.

A *corn dodger* is defined by the *Century Dict.* as 'a kind of cake made of the meal of Indian corn and baked very hard'.

doggerel is sometimes used in Am. in the plur. 'Doggerels had been written about her' (The End of *The World*, 126).

†**doll.** The noun *doll* has given rise in Am. to the verb *doll up* = Eng. *dress up to the nines.* 'A dolled-up blonde had called at his office' (E. WILSON, The Am. Jitters, 234). 'When Juan Schmidt saw the old man dolled up with bracelets and rings and a red bandanna around his neck, he laughed hard' (H. CAHILL, in Life in the U.S., 85).

dollar. The meaning of *dollar diplomacy* will be clear from the following quotations. 'With Philander C. Knox, secretary of state under Taft, was associated the phrase "dollar diplomacy"—the support by diplomatic means of concessions to Am. capital of rights to exploit natural resources' (T. C. PEASE, The U.S. 570). 'In the conduct of foreign relations one of Knox's chief policies was the encouragement and protection of Am. investments abroad, or as it is popularly and somewhat opprobriously termed, "dollar diplomacy"' (Dict. Am. Biog. x. 479). 'Coupled with the practice of "dollar diplomacy", that is of using our diplomatic service for the purpose of promoting loans and other economic interests in foreign, and mostly back-ward, countries, the theory of protectorates quickly took further tangible form' (J. TRUSLOW ADAMS, Hist. of the Am. People, ii. 308).

For *dollars to doughnuts,* see DOUGH.

dome. One of the most sensational events of President Harding's administration was what is known as the Teapot Dome scandal—the secret and corrupt leasing to a private owner of certain oil reserves of the U.S. Navy which were situated at Teapot Dome, Wyoming. How came the word *dome* to be used of an oil reserve? An explanation will be found in the following passage: 'In the dreary, rainy winter of 1900, the prospector was drilling with dogged persistence into a "salt dome" on the Texas gulf plain. . . . The Lucas gusher spewed its black gold to a crest 200 feet above the dome. . . . Men bought and sold land within 20 miles of the ten-foot hump on the coastal plain known ironically as a "dome". . . . After the Yugoslav prospector's lucky strike of 1900, every salt dome on the Gulf Coast was seized upon by avid wildcatters and company agents' (H. O'CONNOR, Mellon's Millions, 93, 94, 95, 101). First of all, that is to say, the humps of salt on the Texas plain were facetiously called *domes*. Next, it was beneath one of these domes that an extraordinarily rich supply of oil was discovered. Then the word came to be used of any oil well, even as far away as Wyoming.

domestic is much more commonly used in Am. than in Eng. in the sense of *not foreign*. Thus Am. *domestic postage, domestic mails* = Eng. *inland postage, inland mails*. The story is told of a newly arrived Irishman who was standing in front of the letter-boxes at the N.Y. Post Office, much puzzled as to the box into which he should drop a letter to his sweetheart. He found three boxes, labelled City, Domestic, Foreign. 'Faith,' he said, 'this is a problem. Maggie's a domestic, she lives in the city, and she's a foreigner. What beats me is how I'm to get the letter in the three holes at wanst.' Similarly the contents of a newspaper may be summarized under the headings Domestic (news from all over the U.S.), Local (news from the immediate neighbourhood) and Foreign (news from abroad). Am. *domestic missions* = Eng. *home missions*; e.g. 'Most of the last graduating class had decided to go to the mission fields, both foreign and domestic.'
The word often means *home-grown*,

home-made. One may even be offered 'roast domestic duck'. 'Some of the bags are domestic, many are imported.' 'Good domestic corsets' (Advt.). 'The ammonia process was used in its early days at Syracuse, N.Y., and for many years furnished the only domestic soda, the larger part of that used being imported' (Prof. J. L. HOWE, Inorganic Chemistry, 213).
A notice in a department store announcing *domestics* in the basement does not indicate a servants' registry but the department of house linen and other household equipment.

donate, an example of back-formation from *donation*, is a word which in Eng. is eschewed by good writers as a pretentious and magniloquent vulgarism. In Am. on the other hand, it has acquired a place in the vocab. of quite reputable terms. 'Thomas Hollis donated a large collection of recent authors' (Prof. H. W. SCHNEIDER, The Puritan Mind, 193). 'Through the generosity of owners many of them were donated to the public' (Prof. A. E. MARTIN, Hist. of U.S. ii. 776). 'Altogether Congress donated some 20,000,000 acres in the decade' (Prof. D. S. MUZZEY, The Am. Adventure, i. 479). 'He donated land to all creeds for churches, school-houses and burial grounds' (R. L. HAWKINS, Mme de Staël and the U.S. 18).
For *donation party*, see the first quotation. 'As the minister's salary was only a meager support, it was the custom to add to his comfort by a donation party early in the winter. This was a much-prized social opportunity and the gifts of good things to eat and to wear added much to the comfort of the minister and his family' (W. W. FOLWELL, Autobiog. 17). 'There are in Am. to-day thousands of worthy people who have grown too fashionable to attend the weekly prayer-meetings, the monthly church sociables, and the yearly donation party.'

door. The compound *dooryard* is peculiar to Am. It is the name for a small patch of ground adjacent to the door of a house, and thus generally corresponds to the Eng. *back yard* or *back garden.* 'When Lilacs Last in the Dooryard Bloomed' is the title of one of the best known of Walt Whitman's poems. 'The great pile of spruce cordwood which he regularly hauled to his sister's dooryard during the winter.' 'Until every citizen sees to it that his own home, however simple, and his own dooryard, however small, is not a blemish in what otherwise is growing to be a beautiful village' (Dr. LYMAN ABBOTT, Am. in the Making, 150). 'In a few minutes Bill was driving a handsome rig into his dooryard' (J. T. FLYNN, God's Gold, 31).

See also TRIM.

dormitory. Eng. readers will be puzzled by some reports from Am. colleges if they are not aware that a *dormitory,* which with them means a sleeping-room containing several beds, is in Am. a hostel or hall of residence for students. There is accordingly no tautology in a reference to 'a dormitory bedroom'. 'Hogan entered college poor. He now lives in the best dormitory.' 'The men [at Oxford] room in the college dormitories forming part of a quadrangle.' 'Not only has the absence of dormitories kept away students living at a distance, but it has served to drive away many residents of the city, who desired the college life which only dormitories can give.' 'The physical training of girls receives special attention in Am. —Radcliffe College, for example, having had a gymnasium before a dormitory' (Prof. H. H. HORNE, Philosophy of Education, 94). 'New dormitories grouped about a main quadrangle were to be built in which preceptors and unmarried instructors of the faculty were to live' (D. LAWRENCE, True Story of Woodrow Wilson, 23).

dough is in Am. a colloquial term for *money,* esp. when spent in political activities. 'Governor Odell's dough bag soon will be filled with more than enough money to pay the legitimate expenses of this campaign.' 'This is Tammany's regular annual "dough-day"—that is, the day on which the district leaders come to Tammany Hall for election day funds.' There is a story of an ardent lover, but poor speller, who wrote to a girl's father asking for her hand. His note ran: 'I want your daughter, the flour of your family.' 'Are you sure it isn't my dough you're after?' replied the father.

The Am. *doughbird* is the Eskimo curlew, or *Numenius borealis.*

A boiled dumpling is sometimes called in Am. a *doughboy.* This name is also facetiously given to an infantry soldier, who, acc. to the *Standard Dict.,* is so called by cavalrymen because of the globular buttons on his uniform. 'Lord Roberts speaks as if, to the mass of British cavalry officers, "cold steel", whether in the form of lance or sabre, was still the only weapon suitable for a mounted force, and shooting dismounted a disgusting practice which reduced a bold cavalier to the level of a "doughboy" at once.' 'The doughboy learned to use garlic in France.'

The compound *doughface* denotes a flabby or pliable person, whose character, so to speak, is made of dough. During the abolitionist agitation it spec. indicated a Northerner who showed a tendency to undue compliance with the demands of the South. 'The same arguments are employed that Northern doughfaces used to be plied with in slavery days.' 'Cass was reputed "a northern man with southern principles"—popularly known as a "doughface"' (Prof. D. S. MUZZEY, The Am. Adventure, i. 441).

The Am. *doughnut* presents a mysterious problem to Eng. readers of an article in the *Atlantic Monthly* of May 1934. A contributor, describing his experiences in a shipwreck, says that he seized a life preserver, 'which looked like a large white doughnut'. Such a comparison is utterly unintelligible unless one is aware that the Am. doughnut is not a ball, like the Eng., but has the shape of a ring. This difference was evidently unknown to the Am. artist whom a N.Y. magazine commissioned a few years ago to illustrate an article by an Eng. writer on the spec. culinary products of various districts of Eng. In his 'gastronomic map' the Isle of Wight's speciality was represented by something that no native of the island would ever have recognized as a doughnut, for it pictured a doughnut of the annular Am. type.

The expression *dollars to doughnuts* takes in Am. the place of the Eng. *all Lombard Street to a China orange*. 'Your murderer stands in the corner behind you to deliver the fatal blow, but it is dollars to doughnuts not a soul will see him.'

dove. In Am., as in certain Eng. dial., *dove* is not only a noun but a verb, being the past tense of *dive*, so formed on the analogy of *drive* and *drove* (and, of course, with the same *o* sound as in *drove*). 'In a spirit of daring he dove into what proved to be a sandhole, and never regained the surface.' 'I was standing up at the time and the shock pitched me forward, so that I dove right through the window' (THEODORE ROOSEVELT, in the published letters to his children). 'He rushed to the water's edge and dove toward the place where the two had disappeared from view' (L. F. STRYKER, Andrew Johnson, 2).

draft. In Am. *draft* is spec. used of *conscription* for the army. 'They didn't believe in war, and went to Mexico to avoid the draft' (A. G. HAYS, Let Freedom Ring, 280). 'The imposition of a draft system when voluntary enlistment failed' (Dr. W. MacDONALD, Three Centuries of Am. Democracy, 210). 'There have been draft and other riots in N.Y. City.' These draft riots were an outbreak in

1863, in protest against conscription for service in the Civil War.

It should be noted that *draft* is the Am. spelling of the Eng. *draught*, while the Eng. *draft* appears in Am. as *draught*. 'The noon sun and the chilling draft are his enemies' (Dr. A. J. BROWN, The New Era in the Philippines, 49). 'Though the brim be touched by a bitter draft' (WILBUR D. NESBIT, The Trail to Boyland, 129). 'The landed people in Wisconsin raise draft horses rather than the racing or saddle breed' (Prof. C. E. CASON, in Culture in the South, 490). 'She had already made a draught of an opening paragraph incorporating her suggestion' (E. WILSON, The Am. Jitters, 147). 'It is Witte who has draughted the most comprehensive employers' liability law in Europe' (SEN. A. J. BEVERIDGE, The Russian Advance, 439).

Am. *drafter* = Eng. *draught-horse*. 'A nice lot of well-broken useful horses, from the nice pleasant driver to the large, strong, rugged drafter' (Advt.).

drawing-room may denote in Am. a section of a railway train in which more luxurious and more private accommodation is provided than in the ordinary cars. An announcement issued by the N.Y. Central runs as follows: 'For uniformity in designating rooms in Parlor and Sleeping Cars, rooms having three berths will be termed Drawing-Rooms; rooms known heretofore as Compartments and other rooms having only two berths will be termed Staterooms; cars that have been termed Drawing-Room Cars are hereafter to be called Parlor Cars, and rooms in these cars are termed Drawing-Rooms.' 'I sat in my drawing-room on the train' (ANITA LOOS, Gentlemen Prefer Blondes, 197).

dresser. In Eng. a *kitchen sideboard*, with shelves for plates, dishes, &c. In Am. a *chest of drawers*, or *dressing-table*, for the bedroom. 'A clever woman, whose hotel bedroom had also to serve as a sitting-room, solved the problem of the dresser ingeniously. The piece was a very good mahogany, inlaid, and had a handsome round mirror. The upper drawer was used for the brushes and toilet articles usually kept on the dresser.' 'In the bedroom a large closet left space for nothing save the bed, dresser, and standing room for one' (I. G. MORTON, in Life in the U.S. 134).

drive is frequently used in Am. to denote an energetic, organized campaign, esp. for the raising of money. 'The drive for $100,000 to buy a site for the Lutheran College will get under way tomorrow.' 'No precise calculation can be made of the drives and counterdrives to which the President is subjected' (C. A. and W. BEARD, The Am. Leviathan, 253). 'In 1904–5 the alumni raised $2,300,000 in response to Eliot's appeal for a general increase of faculty salaries. This step was one of the early examples of "drives" which afterwards came into force' (Dict. Am. Biog. vi. 73). 'From Liberty-loan campaigns he turned to community-chest drives and college-endowment-fund drives and church-membership drives and town-boosting drives and a multitude of other public campaigns' (F. L. ALLEN, Only Yesterday, 227). A detailed account of the history and methods of money-raising drives in Am. will be found in the *Encycl. Soc. Sci.* v. 238.

In Eng. a private road leading from the highway to a house is called a *drive*. In Am. it is a *driveway*. 'Several mounted officers dashed up our driveway' (M. GOUVERNEUR, As I Remember, 322). 'Back from the main road, on a curving driveway, connected with it, was a two-story colonial structure' (Dr. FRANKLIN H. MARTIN, The Joy of Living, i. 161). 'Harding's first official act was . . . to permit flivvers and trucks to detour from Pennsylvania Avenue up the driveway and chortle right past the presidential front door' (F. L. ALLEN, Only Yesterday, 125).

The term *driveway* is also occasionally used to denote a public road. 'The Paseo [of the city of Mexico] is one of the most noble driveways to be found in any land.' 'A chain of parks connected with splendid driveways is desirable' (H. M. POLLOCK and W. S. MORGAN, Modern Cities, 109).

See also RIDE.

drop. Am. *get the drop on* = Eng. *take at a disadvantage*. Its original meaning is 'have the chance to shoot before the antagonist can use his weapon' (O.E.D. Suppl.). 'His conspicuous virtue is the agility of the man who never lets the other folks get the drop on him, rather than that of the executive who picks his way cautiously through the maze of international complications.'

The Am. term *drop letter* denotes a letter addressed to a place within the delivery area of the office where it is posted.

drouth, a form now archaic or poetic in Eng., though still in use in Scotland, is often preferred in Am. to *drought*. 'The record-breaking drouth in Kentucky is beginning to decrease the mill supply in Louisville.' 'In 1887 the drouths came, and the reaction set in' (V. F. CALVERTON, The Liberation of Am. Lit. 336). 'It was a famine caused primarily by great drouth' (NORMAN THOMAS, America's Way Out, 74). 'Excessive rain followed by drouth' (Prof. IRVING FISHER, Mastering the Crisis, 32).

drug. The Am. *drug-store* corresponds to the Eng. *chemist's shop*, but it is not limited to the functions suggested by its name. The sale of 'soft' drinks is usually one of its chief activities. 'There were four clerks in the drug-store when the telephone bell rang. Two were at the prescription counter, one was serving ice-cream soda, the fourth was arranging packages of cough drops in a wicker basket.' 'He suggested that they should go out to the drug-store and get some soda-water' (ALICE HEGAN RICE, Sandy, 138). 'The driver of the street car would obligingly halt and let one run into a drug store for an ice cream soda' (GERTRUDE ATHERTON, Adventures of a Novelist, 198). In Am. *druggist* is not an antiquated term, as it is nowadays in Eng.

drummer is used fig. in Am. of a *commercial traveller*, who (metaphorically) goes about beating a drum to secure custom. 'Drummers using the automobile are able to make 50 per cent. more calls on customers than could be achieved under the old system of traveling by railroad trains.' 'The drummer is the hotels' best regular patron. He supports them when the traveler for pleasure cannot be counted upon' (H. RHODES, Am. Towns and People, 189). 'The increase of advertising was attended by a decline in the number of drummers or traveling salesmen' (Prof. A. M. SCHLESINGER, The Rise of the City, 196).

dry. Both as adj. and noun, *dry* is in Am. a common synonym for *prohibitionist*. 'Town after town went dry under the Adams law.' 'The convention hall is to be absolutely "dry" during the sessions. Plenty of good clear water will be on tap, but there is to be neither a bar nor a buffet in the building.' 'Personally a dry, but politically a wet, he has refused political nominations because of his stand against the 18th Amendment.' 'Almost any dry could tell you that prohibition was the basis of Am. prosperity' (F. L. ALLEN, Only Yesterday, 254). Cf WET.

Am. *dry out* = Eng. *dry off.* 'Another good feature is that it [a raincoat] dries out in good shape' (Advt.). 'The farmers have torn the stacks apart, and the bundles are drying out quite rapidly.'

Dry farming. See quotations. 'A system of agriculture known as "dry farming" is being successfully used in the semi-arid districts of Colorado and other Western States in place of extensive schemes of irrigation. . . . It consists in so preparing the soil in semi-arid regions that it will catch what little annual rainfall there is, and store it within reach of the roots of plants to be grown.' 'Dry farming may be defined as the production of crops under such climatic conditions that the yield is usually and primarily limited by low rainfall' (Encycl. Soc. Sci. v. 252).

Dry goods is the name given in the vocab. of Am. stores to articles of drapery, mercery, and haberdashery, in distinction from groceries, hardware, &c. Prof. E. A. Freeman (Impressions of U.S. 63) remarks that he can see no reason for this use of the word, as other articles seem to the untechnical mind to be equally dry. But the phrase, he points out, is just like the Eng. *hardware*, which does not take in all things that are in themselves hard. 'If a dealer in dry-goods were to put upon his counter a "beautiful line of alpacas".' '"Too much dry goods for the women; too much wet goods for the men" is the epigrammatic explanation of the divorce evil offered from the bench by a southern judge.'

duck. 'In Jan., 1875, a lame-duck Congress passed the Resumption Act' (L. M. HACKER and B. B. KENDRICK, The U.S. since 1865, 204). This metaph. use of *lame duck* recalls a curious feature of the Am. political system. A new House of Representatives is elected in Nov. of every second year. A section of the original Constitution of the U.S. required the House to meet on the first Monday in Dec., unless a different day should be appointed by law. Until 1933, it was the practice for the House that thus assembled in Dec. to consist, not of the members elected in the previous month, but of those elected in Nov. two years before. Accordingly, this body included many persons who had recently failed to secure re-election, and who, in spite of this rejection by their constituents, continued to serve in Congress until the session came to an end in the following March. Such members were popularly known as *lame ducks*, and the Congress or session in which they sat was called a *lame-duck Congress* or *lame-duck session*.

The 20th Amendment to the Constitution, ratified in Jan. 1933, brought this anomaly to an end. It provided that a new session of Congress should begin on Jan. 3, instead of Dec., and that the term of office of previous members should expire on that date. Accordingly, the House assembling in Jan. will henceforth consist of members elected in the previous Nov., and there will no longer be any lame ducks in this sense.

The term is also occasionally applied to a politician, whether an ex-Congressman or not, who, on failing to be re-elected, is consoled by appointment to some office other than that which he has just held. 'A nice old Ohio politician who after having been governor of the State became a lame duck and was appointed to preside for four years over the U.S. Industrial Commission' (F. J. STIMSON, My U.S. 137). 'Former Senator William E. Chandler, holding a lame-duck appointive post at the capital' (H. F. PRINGLE, Theodore Roosevelt, 366).

The material known in Eng. as *duck* is sometimes called *ducking* in Am. 'Splendid selection of duckings from which to make awnings' (Advt.).

dues. This word is specialized in Am. as the normal term for a club *subscription*. 'The annual dues of resident members shall be $50' (By-laws of a Washington club). 'The dues of the club had to be increased, and the membership began to falter.' 'The kind of millionaire's club whose entrance fee and annual dues are payable in the golden coin of happiness' (W. E. SMYTHE, City Homes on Country Lanes, 95). 'He said the Century Club was a fine club. He had tried to resign twice or so as the dues were too high for him, using it as little as he did' (Prof. A. G. KELLER, Reminiscences of William Graham Sumner, 97).

dumb. 'I was once immensely surprised', says Edward Shanks (Evening Standard, Feb. 14, 1931) 'by an Am. girl who passionately observed to me of her sister, "Amabel is too dumb; she never stops talking".' Hilaire Belloc, in *The Contrast*, mentions that an Am. once said to him: 'The trouble with you English is that you are dumb,' and protests that in the modern world there are no men with a greater command of expression than the English. Whereupon the *N.Y.Times* (May 11, 1924) comments: 'Taking "dumb" in the ordinary meaning of the word, the old Parliamentarian was right; but what the Am. meant by "dumb", using the vulgar speech here, was "stupid", being nothing more nor less than German *dumm*, foolish, stupid—which, of course, on the part of that Am. was slang, likewise a childish and stupid bit of rudeness.' Most Eng. readers would miss the point of the play upon the two meanings of the word when an Am. paper remarks that 'it often happens that a man is not suspected of being dumb until he begins to talk'. This special Am. use of the word is too common to be set down as mere slang. 'If he knew where the money went, and he would have been dumb if he did not know, it did not excite him' (W. A. WHITE, Masks in a Pageant, 488). 'Surely he was not so dumb that he could not have known that' (T. DREISER, Tragic Am. 350). Cf. FRESH.

Hence the application of the term *dumb-bell* to a stupid person. 'The quarterback who calls for the wrong play will be known to the surrounding countryside as a dumb-bell for the rest of his days.'

The compound *dumb-waiter* denotes

in Eng. a revolving table used in a dining-room in order to dispense with the services of a waiter. In Am. it means a lift used to carry food from the kitchen to the dining-room. 'The fire started on the third floor, near the dumb-waiter shaft.' 'When I assisted the parlor maid in carrying food and dishes from the kitchen to the dining-room I sighed for the "dumb-waiter" or lift, of which we make use in our modern-built Am. houses' (E. L. BANKS, Autobiog. of a Newspaper Girl, 85).

duster. In Eng. a cloth for removing dust, esp. from furniture. In Am. also a light overcoat or wrap to protect one's clothes from dust. Cf. the Eng. *dust-cloak* and *dust-coat*. 'The newcomer wore a linen duster.' 'The Judge's coat was just a light duster.' 'He had forgotten to bring along any winter wearing apparel, so, although the nights were quite cold, he emerged from the tent in a summer suit and linen duster' (C. H. STERNBERG, Life of a Fossil Hunter, 94). 'Aristocratic drivers in linen dusters and lemon-colored gloves to hold the reins' (Dr. G. D. LYMAN, The Saga of the Comstock Lode, 220).

Dutch in Am. often = *German*, as it did in Eng. up to the 17th century. In *The Earlier Life of Walter H. Page* there is printed a letter, written by him when studying in Berlin in 1877, in which he says to his mother: 'You must not ever feel ashamed of your Dutch blood.' The editor comments in a footnote: 'Page, of course, means German; in his day—and sometimes now—it was common in the U.S. to call Germans Dutchmen.' 'Mr. Buchman was born and lived through youth and young manhood near the heart of the "Pennsylvania Dutch" district in Eastern Pennsylvania. It is from that simple, stolid, deeply religious German Lutheran stock that Mr. Buchman comes.' A *Dutch lunch* or *Dutch supper* is one at which each person pays for his own share of the meal or brings his own provisions. 'Dancing was enjoyed by all, as was the Dutch lunch which was partaken of at intervals during the evening.' 'It is too bad that our young hopefuls at college have to buy their own golf caps and sweaters, thus depriving themselves of money they need to buy plug-cut and Dutch suppers with.'

To *beat the Dutch* is to do something that causes intense surprise, that takes away one's breath, that flabbergasts one. '"Well, you women do beat the Dutch", said her brother, with a tenderly indulgent air, as if he were addressing children' (M. E. WILKINS FREEMAN, By the Light of the Soul, 277).

†dyed. In its fig. use the Eng. expression *dyed in grain* appears in Am. as *dyed in the wool*. 'Senators are no longer elected by dyed-in-the-wool party men, but by voters in the mass.' 'She was in some respects a remarkable character, a "dyed-in-the-wool" Southerner, and a woman of unusual personal charm' (M. GOUVERNEUR, As I Remember, 273). 'In 1828 a real dyed-in-the-wool Dem. was elected President of the U.S. for the first time in its history' (Prof. T. J. GRAYSON, Leaders and Periods of Am. Finance, 182). 'I have never been a free trader nor a dyed-in-the-wool protectionist' (E. A. FILENE, Successful Living in this Machine Age, 163).

E

East. 'I asked a well-known professor at one of the largest and best-known universities in the East what, in his candid opinion, his university did for the many thousands of students who annually attended it' (J. TRUSLOW ADAMS, A Searchlight on Am. 125). If this sentence had occurred in a book by an Eng. writer, the reference would have been to a university in India or China or Japan. Mr. Adams, however, was referring to a university in the Eastern part of the U.S., which is what an Am. always means by *the East*. The term is vaguely used. 'The East', according to the *Republican*, of Springfield, Mass., 'is a relative term as one traverses the Am. continent. Thus, when the California newspapers report that settlers from the East are locating in Glynn county, the far easterner is surprised to read that the reference is to people coming from Dakota.'

When an Am. has Asia in mind, he speaks of *the Orient*, which, accordingly, is not in Am. a poetical or affected term as it is in Eng. 'That peace in the Orient will lead to a great industrial and commercial development in China admits of no question.' Mrs. Rorer tells us in her Cook Book that 'in the Orient the young fronds of the common brake are used as a green vegetable'. 'Between times he visited Greece, Turkey, Africa, Australia, and the Orient' (Dict. Am. Biog. vi. 526). 'In the western world, as distinguished from the Orient, this tendency was supported by the religious beliefs of the people' (Dr. N. M. BUTLER, Looking Forward, 98).

See also SIDE.

eat. There are many passages in the A.V. of the Bible where *eat* = *take one's meals*. This meaning, now obs. in Eng., persists in Am. (One may compare the use of the German *essen*.) 'The working woman must not eat irregularly, if she be inclined to be nervous. If the working woman eats at 12, let her observe the hour with fidelity.' A character in one of David Graham Phillips's novels—strange to say, an Eng. nobleman—remarks: 'The Longviews invited me to feed with them. They eat in their sitting-room.' 'In Princeton, all freshmen eat in the college commons' (W. A. WHITE, Woodrow Wilson, 145).

Hence the *eating club* and *eating hall* at an Am. college correspond to the Eng. *dining club* and *dining hall*. 'His eating club was "The Alligators", which he joined in his sophomore year' (Prof. H. J. FORD, Woodrow Wilson, 9). 'By a college I mean not merely a group of dormitories, but an eating hall as well where all the residents of the college shall take their meals together' (WOODROW WILSON, quoted in his biog. by Edith Gittings Reid, 102).

As a noun, *eat* is, as yet, a vulgarism, mostly to be found in such advts. as 'Big Eats Café'. In *Dodsworth* (p. 22) Sinclair Lewis describes his hero as driving along Conklin Avenue past 'lunch-rooms with the blatant sign "Eats".' The word may sometimes be used by the writer of a book; e.g. 'Tickets, selling at 5 dollars each, provided some eats, an average of 25 drinks of liquor apiece, and left a substantial balance in the political treasury' (Dr. H. ZINK, City Bosses in U.S. 89). Dr. Zink, however, is describing a Tammany outing, and is presumably suiting his vocabulary to his theme.

The Am. compound *eating-apron* denotes a kind of bib. 'Ever since he and she wore eating-aprons at Franklin's little table in the Hyde Park nursery where they used to have their bread and milk supper together' (B. MOSES, Franklin Delano Roosevelt, 53).

editor. †An Am. newspaper has many editors, for almost every member of the staff who is in charge of a department is dignified by that title. 'Under the managing editor are the city editor, who collects the local news; the telegraph or news editor, who collects the matter that comes by wire; and the various department editors—dramatic, literary, sporting, commercial, real estate, and others' (E. L. SHUMAN, Practical Journalism, 18).

The spec. meaning given in London to *the city*, i.e. the financial district, has led to the use of *city editor* in the London press to denote the person in charge of the financial department. The corresponding member of the staff of an Am. paper is called the *financial editor*, while the *city editor*, as mentioned in the above quotation, is responsible for the collection of local news. 'To-day the Supreme Court is no longer an asset for the all-important city editor. Public interest in its deliberations is moribund' (Dr. J. M. BECK, May it Please the Court, 26). 'Sitting as city editor for the occasion, I have covered every angle of the story by assigning a brilliant man to write it up' (The End of the *World*, 4). 'Rough-and-ready writers never suffer from beauty rash. Journalists soon learn to escape it, for the city editor keeps drastic medicines for this disease' (H. S. CANBY, Better Writing, 113).

†Am. *editorial* = Eng. *leading article* or *leader*. 'Recently our newspapers have been filled with editorials on our diplomacy as it affects Manchuria' (Sen. A. J. BEVERIDGE, The Russian Advance, 5). 'His wider reputation rested on his political reporting and on his editorials' (Dict. Am. Biog. vii. 622).

Hence Am. *editorial writer* = Eng. *leader-writer*. 'He has lately become an editorial writer on the *Boston Advertiser* and *Record*, after serving a considerable apprenticeship on those and other Boston papers as a reporter.' 'A newspaper editorial writer from the West, author of countless editorials and many magazine articles' (L. F. CARR, Am. Challenged, 282). 'The young reviewer or editorial writer will be smart rather than sound' (H. S. CANBY, Better Writing, 121).

educational. The various acts of Parliament dealing with education are called in Eng. *education* acts. In Am. *educational* is used in such a connexion. 'The educational act passed by the British Parliament.' 'There was before the Senate a measure known as the Blair Educa-tional Bill, the purport of which was to extend federal aid in an effort to overcome illiteracy' (G. T. CLARK, Leland Stanford, 456).

effective. It is necessary to beware of misunderstanding this word in a peculiar use it often has in Am. Thus, when Pres. Taft said, of certain prospective changes in tariff schedules, that he looked forward to June 1 as the date 'when most of these changes will become effective', he did not predict that on that date they would accomplish their purpose. Again, when F. J. Haskin (The Am. Government, 429) says that 'nation-wide prohibition became effective in the U.S., Jan. 16, 1920' he by no means intends us to understand that on that date the drink traffic ceased. In Am. a law or order or railway time-table is said to be *effective* on the day that it comes into operation. 'An order was made, effective Aug. 1, 1923, which reduced gas rates' (Dr. J. M. BECK, May it Please the Court, 273). 'Congress enacted a law, effective Sept. 30, 1818, closing the ports of the U.S. to British vessels' (Dr. J. H. FREDERICK, The Development of Am. Commerce, 115).

election. Am. *special election* = Eng. *by-election*. 'The special election in the 14th congressional district to fill the vacancy caused by the death of William C. Lovering will be held on March 22.' 'When the council confers aldermanic rank upon its own members, special elections in the wards fill the vacant councillorships' (ALBERT SHAW, Municipal Government in Great Britain, 31). See also CONTEST.

elective. In the terminology of Am. education, *elective* = Eng. *optional*. 'In all these institutions until recently religious instruction has been required; those that have registered with the Chinese government, however, have been compelled to make such instruction elective' (Survey of Am. Foreign Relations, 1930, 83). In

Am. schools and colleges *the elective system* is a system acc. to which the student is free, within limits, to choose his own subjects for study, instead of having to follow a prescribed curriculum. 'Practically the elective system is something like restaurants à la carte, and one is most apt to order what he sees his neighbors enjoying.' 'He had been educated before the elective system came in, and he had a pathetic veneration for the old curriculum' (Dr. S. McC. CROTHERS, The Pardoner's Wallet, 82).

As a noun, *elective = optional subject.* 'The idea of grouping electives is the fundamental difference between Eng. and Am. education' (J. CORBIN, An Am. at Oxford, 167). See also REQUIRE.

elector. In Eng. *elector* and *voter* are synonyms. In Am. there is a distinction between them, *electors* being the technical term for the persons—themselves chosen by popular vote in the various States—on whom falls the duty, now purely formal, of electing the President of the U.S. (One may cf. the use of the term to denote those Princes of Germany who were formerly entitled to take part in the election of the Emperor.) These electors are sometimes spoken of as constituting an *electoral college*, but this use of the term is not strictly accurate, as they meet and vote in separate State groups and not as a single national body.

The *electoral vote*, cast by these electors in Jan. of every fourth year, is thus distinguished from the *popular vote*, which is cast in the general election of the previous Nov., and which formally results in no more than the choice of electors though it actually decides between the various candidates for the Presidency. 'Though it [the Prohibition party] has never cast an electoral vote, its candidates have been in the field in every presidential compaign since 1870' (Prof. A. E. MARTIN, Hist. of U.S. ii. 765). That is to say, this party

has never obtained sufficient popular support to place one of its members among the persons chosen by any State as its electors. 'The election resulted in Wilson's receiving 435 electoral votes, while Roosevelt got 81 and Taft but 15. In the popular vote Roosevelt ran more than 600,000 ahead of Taft' (J. KERNEY, Political Education of Woodrow Wilson, 247).

elegant. In Am. *elegant* does not necessarily imply refinement or good taste, but is colloq. sometimes almost a synonym for *excellent, first-rate.* 'For sale—80 acres well improved, near Midlothian Golf Club; elegantly situated' (Advt.). 'Lecture by Dr. Fox. Students of Elizabeth College Enjoy an Elegant Discussion of "The Perfect Life"' (Newspaper headline). It is also more freely used than in Eng. in the sense of *fashionable, stylish.* 'Altogether it was a social function which would have been considered elegant in N.Y.' (Dr. A. J. BROWN, The New Era in the Philippines, 56). 'The most elegant of these homes were occupied by officers' (Dr. O. T. BARCK, N.Y. City During the War for Independence, 83). 'This is one of the most elegant of all the thick soups' (Mrs. RORER'S New Cook Book, 81).

elevated. The term *elevated train* denotes a train which in certain Am. cities runs on an *elevated railroad*; i.e. a railway whose track is constructed, high above the street level, on strong latticed iron columns. 'When I first rode in a first-class car in Japan and saw several dainty Japanese women in pretty silks standing, while Japanese men remained resolutely seated, I could almost fancy I was on an elevated train bound for Harlem.' 'The cars were drawn by little steam locomotives, as the elevated trains were at first in N.Y.' (E. L. MASTERS, The Tale of Chicago, 241).

The word *elevated* in this sense is sometimes abbreviated to *L* or *El.*

'The L. rumbles overhead.' 'Irma lives under the El. in the first of a small solid row of tarnished pink brick houses' (E. WILSON, The Am. Jitters, 126).

elevator is used in Am. in two spec. senses: (1) a building for the storage and distribution of grain, which is loaded and unloaded by an endless carrier studded with metal cups or buckets; and (2) a lift.
(1) 'The elevators now in progress of construction will give a total storage capacity of nearly 7,000,000 bushels.' 'Country elevators are full and central elevators overflowing. Wheat—wheat everywhere.' 'The general movement of the grain is from the farmers to the country grain elevators, and thence to the terminal markets' (T. C. BLAISDELL, The Federal Trade Commission, 131).
(2) 'The people should be as free to step on a street car without charge as to ride in an elevator in a down-town building.' 'Maria began climbing the stairs. There was no elevator' (M. E. WILKINS FREEMAN, By the Light of the Soul, 161). See CAR.
Am. *freight elevator* = Eng. *hoist*.

ell. In Am. an *ell* is not always a measure of length. It is sometimes a wing of a building, joined to it in such a way that the two together are in the shape of the letter L. 'A large room, with an ell of smaller size, and a wide square doorway between, formed the dance-hall of the evening.' 'She had built an ell to the house in order to provide a dwelling for the man who managed her farm' (K. D. WIGGIN, My Garden of Memory, 361). Sometimes it is written L. 'In the rear of the building was an L section.' 'Her room was in the L' (K. D. WIGGIN, Rebecca, 97).
This word must be distinguished from *El.*, an abbrev. of ELEVATED (q.v.).

emigrate is used in Am. not only of removal from one country to another but also of removal from one

State in the Union to another. 'Vanderbilt May Emigrate' is the heading of a newspaper report that Vanderbilt is likely to remove from N.Y. to Philadelphia. 'John T. Morgan was born at Athens, Tenn., 1824; received an academic education, chiefly in Ala., to which State he emigrated when nine years old' (Congressional Directory for 1903, 1). 'Albert Alonzo's father emigrated to the Middle West from New England as a pioneer physician' (Dr. H. ZINK, City Bosses of U.S. 334).

eminent domain. In Eng. this term is rarely used exc. in connexion with matters of international law. In Am. it is commonly employed to denote the power of expropriation exercised within its own borders by the Federal Government or an individual State. 'The shores of all these reservoir lakes belong to the State, sufficient land around each for the establishment of a "flow line" having been given by right of eminent domain.' 'The Federal Government also enjoys the power of eminent domain; in other words, it may take private property for public use; but it must make just compensation to the owner' (C. A. and W. BEARD, The Am. Leviathan, 64). 'Private property cannot be taken by the power of eminent domain for a private purpose even though compensation be made. The use must be a public one. . . . The national government may, for instance, exert this power in order to obtain sites for public buildings, in order to construct highways for interstate commerce, and for the purpose of establishing parks and national memorials' (Prof. C. K. BURDICK, The Law of the Am. Constitution, 419).

endive. See CHICORY.

†**engineer.** In Am. this word may denote not only one who follows the profession of engineering but also an *engine-driver*. This use has hitherto been rare in Eng. except with regard

to marine engines. 'As engineer he traveled over 2,000,000 miles, carrying 500,000 passengers without a single accident.' 'The engineer of a fast-moving train must accept the instructions of the signal' (F. J. HASKIN, The Am. Government, 230).

enjoin, as commonly used, has precisely opposite meanings in Eng. and Am. In Eng. it means *prescribe*, but in Am. *prohibit* (by the issue of an injunction). Thus we find an Eng. judge quoted by a London paper as saying that it was ridiculous to grant licences expressly enjoining Sunday closing of public-houses and at the same time to frame elaborate rules for Sunday opening. The following examples illustrate the Am. use. 'It will, of course, be impossible to enjoin the collection of the tax, and presumably the attacks on the law will come in the form of suits for recovery of taxes which have been paid.' 'No political democracy but ours permits courts to enjoin acts in themselves peaceful and not illegal during times of strike. . . . Even church-going has been enjoined in one famous case in Pennsylvania, and only private prayer for success has been left as a legal weapon' (NORMAN THOMAS, America's Way Out, 270).

enlarge may still be used in Am. in the sense, now archaic in Eng., of *set free, release.* 'Mrs. Maybrick would have been enlarged on parole, in the year she was, under the prison policy of Eng., had no person in the world ever asked for her enlargement.'

enlisted men is a common term in Am. for the *rank and file* of an army. 'No major battle displayed less generalship, and none more courage on the part of the enlisted men' (Dict. Am. Biog. vii. 495). 'Gen. Pershing with a staff of 53 officers and 146 enlisted men sailed for Liverpool' (Prof. A. E. MARTIN, Hist. of U.S. ii. 638).

Hence *enlisted grade*, denoting a rank below that of commissioned

officer. 'He enlisted in Company L of the 16th Illinois Cavalry and served through the various enlisted grades in that organization' (Dict. Am. Biog. xii. 37).

entry. In Am. *entry* may denote the door, lobby, or hall by which one enters a building. This would now be called in Eng. an *entrance.* 'Every farmer who had a spare room or a cot in a back entry.' ' "Put the trunk in the entry, and we'll get it carried upstairs this afternoon," she said' (K. D. WIGGIN, Rebecca, 36).

In Am. *entry* may also be used in the sense of *beginning* (of a period of time). 'We print upon another page an act of the Legislature which became operative with the entry of the month.'

equalization. In many Am. States and counties there is a *board of equalization*, appointed to compare and revise the valuations of taxable property made by the various local assessors, so that the incidence of taxation may be the same in all localities.

equity may denote in Am. not only a principle of justice or a system of law but a spec. asset, which is defined by the *Century Dict.* as 'the remaining interest belonging to one who has pledged or mortgaged his property, or the surplus of value which may remain after the property has been disposed of for the satisfaction of liens'. 'His equity is in his wife's name now; when did he put it there, and was it to defraud creditors?' 'With only a preëmption title to my land, I now planned to "prove up" on it, sell my equity in it, and use the money toward my education' (HAMLIN GARLAND, Roadside Meetings, 3). 'Homes and farms in process of purchase were left in the hands of the original owners without any attempt to recover any equity the purchaser may have had in them' (R. R. MOTON, What the Negro Thinks, 59).

In the following passage from a newspaper article the word has come to be used fig. 'It is by no means certain that the issue may not prove ultimately an asset of some importance to the Democrats. At least, there is no doubt that they intend to retain their equity in it.'

A *bill in equity* is defined by the *Century Dict.* as 'in an equity suit, the pleading in which the plaintiff sets forth the circumstances on which he bases his claim for relief'. 'The Indian Bureau and the Department of Justice have joined forces to oppose the alleged misuse of lands awarded by treaty to the White Earth tribe of Chippewa Indians. Nearly 600 bills in equity have been filed in the U.S. Circuit Court for the district of Minnesota against persons alleged to have obtained tracts of lands otherwise than under the provisions of the treaty.' 'This combination was dissolved by a bill in equity filed by the Department of Justice alleging violation of the anti-trust laws' (T. C. BLAISDELL, The Federal Trade Commission, 140).

European. For *European plan*, see quotation. 'Some of the hotels are operated on the European plan exclusively, that is to say, the patron merely rents a room and is privileged to get his meals wherever he sees fit, his hotel expense being proportionately reduced. The American plan provides dining room privileges, the boarders being entitled to the regular course of meals each day without extra charge. Each plan has its advantages, the European plan recommending itself to those whose movements are likely to be uncertain while in the city, as it would be a decided inconvenience and waste of time to journey back to the hotel for meals. The tendency of recent years has been to operate on both plans' (MORRIS's Dict. of Chicago).

evacuation. The term *Evacuation Day* denotes the anniversary of the day on which N.Y., Boston, or other Am. city was evacuated by the British troops after the Revolution. In N.Y. it is celebrated by the raising of the Am. flag at the Battery and at the old blockhouse in Central Park.

evil. In Am. the derivative *evilly*, now little used in Eng., sometimes takes the place of *ill*. 'They did not despise him. Rather did they tolerate him in a broad human way, as one tolerates any creature evilly treated in the making' (JACK LONDON, White Fang, 189). 'Neither of them could conceive of anything being wrong with any of their friends—an excellent trait, if one's friends are not evilly disposed' (W. G. McADOO, Crowded Years, 144).

examiner. A variety of examiner peculiar to Am. is the *bank examiner*. He is a public official, appointed to visit the banks and audit their accounts. 'The bank examiner came to his town and told the bank it had to get rid of its frozen assets.' 'The Banking Department and its bank examiners occupy a well-defined position towards the public. The opening of an institution's books and vaults to the frequent supervision of the experts appointed by the State is a condition of granting the bank its charter.' 'The Federal Farm Loan Board has general supervisory power over these banks. In addition to granting charters, it appoints the examiners who examine the banks at least twice a year' (Prof. E. S. SPARKS, Agricultural Credit in the U.S. 398). 'It appears that national bank examiners have not under the present laws the right to examine affiliates of banks' (Upton Sinclair Presents William Fox, 364).

excellency. The title of *His Excellency* is given in the British Empire to ambassadors, colonial governors, and the commander-in-chief in India. In Am. it is given, by the constitutions of those States, to the governors of Massachusetts and New Hampshire, and is popularly applied also to governors of other States and ambassadors from foreign powers. 'It was to have been expected that the decision of the governor not to be a candidate for re-election would enliven the field of political gossip. . . . His excellency is in receipt of protesting letters from all over the state.' 'The second factor on which victory hung was none other than his Excellency, Alva Hopkins, governor of the state' (W. CHURCHILL, Coniston, 502).

excelsior. Longfellow's poem is not the only association an Am. has with this word. He uses it to denote soft wood shavings used for stuffing. 'Start a fresh fire with an abundance of light material, such as shavings or excelsior' (Mrs. RORER'S New Cook Book, 36). 'The voter in an election who likened his plight to that of a donkey between two bales of excelsior' (M. A. DE W. HOWE, Portrait of an Independent, 312). 'Grass dried into a sort of pale excelsior' (CHRISTOPHER MORLEY, John Mistletoe, 219). 'The country was as dry as excelsior' (H. CAHILL, in Life in the U.S. 86).

excise. In Eng. an *excise law* deals with the manufacture of liquors. In Am. it deals also with their sale, and is thus generally equivalent to the Eng. *licensing law*. 'In many places the back doors of the saloons have stood wide open all night and no attempt has been made to conceal the open violation of the excise law.' 'The matter of closing the Chicago saloons on Sundays and enforcing the excise laws' (Dr. H. ZINK, City Bosses in U.S. 286). 'Fundamentally, Roosevelt was not a prohibitionist, nor did he really care whether beer or anything else was sold on Sunday. He started with the sound position that violations of the excise law led to extortion by the police' (H. F. PRINGLE, Theodore Roosevelt, 140).

exclusive. In Am. the meaning of this term has so far departed from its etymological signification that it has virtually become a synonym for *first-rate, high-class*. The proprietor of a hotel advertises it as 'distinctive for its elegance, exclusiveness, high-class patronage and liberal management'. The principal street of a foreign city is described as notable for its 'sumptuous clubs, glittering shops, exclusive tea-rooms'. A news item is headed: 'Society Woman a Housemaid. Member of an Exclusive Family Becomes a Servant Girl.' 'The most exclusive stores', 'our new and exclusive models for winter wear', 'exclusive scarfs for men', 'the largest and most exclusive line of imported wash materials' are typical examples from advertisements. Those who sell these goods sometimes appropriate this epithet to themselves; as 'exclusive haberdashers', 'exclusive stationers'. A *N.Y. Times* advertisement describes Bond Street, London, as 'perhaps the most exclusive shopping avenue in all of Europe'. Dr. Harold Zink (City Bosses in U.S. 85) refers to 'bosses who have established homes in exclusive sections' of N.Y.; i.e. who live in fashionable districts. 'She went to Lake Forest, to teach in an exclusive boarding school' (R. W. BABSON, Washington and the Revolutionists, 88). A school of that kind would call itself in Eng. a *select* school. It is said that, in a pamphlet once issued to boost the attractions of a certain Am. city, one of the points was that it had 'the largest exclusive club in the world'.

executive is in Eng. much more frequently an adj. than a noun. In Am. it is quite as often a noun.
When used as a noun, it commonly denotes in Eng. a body of persons (e.g. a committee or board), but in Am. a single person. The name, sometimes qualified by *chief*, is applied to (1) the President of the U.S., (2) the Governor of a state, or (3) the Mayor of a city. (1) 'The ease with which the Executive can exercise war powers without the express sanction

of Congress.' 'Notwithstanding that midnight was the published time of arrival of the train bearing the President, a large number of people assembled at Union Station and gave the Chief Executive an enthusiastic greeting.' 'If something happened that required the attention of the President immediately, he did not hesitate to communicate promptly with the Chief Executive' (D. LAW-RENCE, True Story of Woodrow Wilson, 227). (2) 'The practice of members of the Legislature running to the Governor with every rough draft of a bill in order to get his advance approval, has come to be a fearful devastation of the Executive's day.' 'The occasion was rendered notable by the presence of Governor Murphy, the Chief Executive of the State.' (3) 'No doubt the present Executive has not pleased everybody. No Mayor ever does.'

In the vocab. of Am. business an *executive* is an official of a firm or company who possesses power to act in matters within his department. Prof. F. W. Taussig and C. S. Joslyn (Am. Business Leaders, 36) divide such officials into *chief executives*, including the president of a business corporation and the chairman of its board, and *subordinate executives*, including the vice-presidents, treasurer, secretary, and general manager. 'A plan was evolved by National Chairman Raskob, himself new to politics but experienced as one of the notable executives of the country, to apply business principles to a national political party.' 'Each of us should learn young whether he is, roughly speaking, an executive or a thinker, artist, talker, worker, scholar, or scientist' (L. STEFFENS, Autobiog. 621). 'Young Morgan had withdrawn from his father's old firm, and had, together with another young executive, formed his own banking house' (R. I. WARSHOW, Story of Wall Street, 289). 'Certain qualities possessed by Gary made him an ideal executive—perfect self-control, un-

failing tact, and extraordinary patience in dealing with conflicting points of view' (Dict. Am. Biog. vii. 176). 'You noted him as a man of importance, as an executive' (SIN-CLAIR LEWIS, Dodsworth, 18). 'Franklin taught the lesson that the province of the executive is to do the big things and to leave to others the routine of carrying on' (Prof. A. H. QUINN, The Soul of Am. 32).

As an adj. the Am. *executive* would often be represented in Eng. by *administrative* or *managing*; e.g. an executive position = an administrative post, a post as manager.

An *executive agreement* is an arrangement made by the President of the U.S. with a foreign Power which is to all intents and purposes a treaty, but which, by being formally a mere agreement, escapes the necessity of being sent to the Senate for confirmation. For examples, see C. A. Beard, *Am. Government and Politics*, 204, and Senator S. M. Cullom, *Fifty Years of Public Service*, 393.

The Executive Mansion was formerly the official designation of the President's residence. Under President Theodore Roosevelt it was superseded by *The White House*, already the popular name for it. It is still the usual official name for the residence of a State Governor. See WHITE.

An *executive order* is an order issued by the President in some matter of administration that can be dealt with apart from legislation by Congress. It corresponds in some measure to the Eng. *order in council*. 'The senator arraigned the President for overriding the Constitution, violating the obligations of a solemn treaty, and resorting to the device of an executive order to accomplish what Congress had failed to enact into law.' 'The act also provided that the President could suspend, by executive order, whenever in his discretion the needs of foreign commerce so required, the laws relating to survey, inspection and measurement of vessels under the Am. flag' (Dr. J. H. FREDERICK,

Development of Am. Commerce, 263).

One of the most curious examples of the acquisition of a new meaning by usage has occurred in connexion with the term *executive session*. Whenever the U.S. Senate proceeds to deal with executive as distinct from legislative business—i.e. when it considers communications from the President respecting nominations to office or the conclusion of treaties—it is said to go into executive session. Such sessions are ordinarily held with closed doors, the galleries being cleared of newspaper representatives and of the general public. Accordingly, to *go into executive session* has come to mean to *meet in private*, or *in camera*. Thus, when in a report of a Methodist conference or of a political or educational convention one reads that at a certain stage of the proceedings it 'went into executive session', the use of this phrase is not intended to suggest anything as to the nature of the business thereafter transacted. It simply means that at this point reporters and other outsiders were excluded. 'The committee of the policy-holders [of an insurance society] went into executive session at 2 o'clock, and the deliberations of the afternoon session will not be made public until 5 o'clock, when a statement will be issued.' 'Almost as soon as we arrived, the President and I went into executive session. The President closed his study door so as not to be interrupted' (Intimate Papers of Col. House, ii. 419). 'If he carries his shrewd business sense into his political career, he will be very sceptical regarding flattering remarks of this sort. When they become too numerous it might pay him to go into executive session with himself for the purpose of asking how many such compliments he would have received if he had been a poor man.' How completely the acquired sense of the term has ousted its proper meaning may be seen from the following passage: 'Senate precedent was broken in the decision to receive and consider the [Versailles] Treaty in open instead of executive session' (Am. Year-book for 1919, 9). Nothing could be more precisely called an executive session than a session occupied in discussing the confirmation of a treaty, but by 1919 the original use of the term had completely disappeared.

exercises. In the sense of *ceremonies*, this word is found in Eng. only in the term *religious exercises*, and even so it sounds rather old-fashioned nowadays. In Am. there is no such limitation. In describing the proceedings when Mr. Hoover was formally notified of his first nomination to the Presidency, the *N.Y. Times* says: 'The exercises in the stadium began nearly two hours before Mr. Hoover was scheduled to appear. Four brass bands had a part in the preliminary program.' The Springfield *Republican*, a few years ago, mentioned a pageant and tableau as 'the chief feature of the inauguration exercises' of the Lord Mayor of London. 'The new building of the High School of Commerce was dedicated this morning with elaborate exercises.' 'The opening exercises of the Iron and Steel Institute.' 'More than 1,500 members of the Order of Eagles were in attendance at the initiation exercises.' 'Nassau Hall, where the formal exercises opening the University for the year were to be held' (D. Lawrence, True Story of Woodrow Wilson, 24). See also GRADUATE.

exhibition. In the vocab. of Am. education, *exhibition* is used in a different sense from its meaning in Eng., where it denotes a sum of money given to a student annually, for a fixed term of years, to assist in defraying his school or college expenses. 'The place of the "commencement", as we now know it, seems to have been taken during the days of parochial schools by the use of "exhibitions" and "public examinations".

It was the custom to end the year's work with a public "exhibition". These were programs consisting of such items as music, recitations, essays, orations, debates, dialogues, tableaux, charades, colloquies, and so forth; giving the students an occasion for public appearance in several capacities' (Prof. L. J. SHERRILL, Presbyterian Parochial Schools, 117). 'They were within the number of 24 students [at Harvard] who had had honors at the several exhibitions up to that time' (Dr. E. E. HALE, Lowell and his Friends, 29). 'There were three great days in the college year [at Hobart]. First was the Sophomore Exhibition at the end of the first term, in which the sophomores competed for a small prize for declamation.... At the end of the second term came the Junior Exhibition, and a competition for original orations' (Dr. W. W. FOLWELL, Autobiog. 58).

expansion. The term *expansion* and its derivative *expansionist* have a spec. reference in Am. to the increase of the territory of the U.S. 'From the beginning the U.S. has been an expansionist nation, and its area has been increased from 828,000 square miles in 1789 to 3,692,000 square miles in 1902' (Prof. A. B. HART, Actual Government, 342). 'The Louisiana purchase nearly doubled the area of the U.S., and the nation was committed to a policy of expansion which thereafter was steadily pursued' (Dr. W. MACDONALD, Three Centuries of Am. Democracy, 110).

express. In Eng. this word suggests speed—an accelerated service of some sort. To an Am. it suggests primarily the carriage of goods or parcels by other than a Government agency. Thus in Eng. *express delivery* means the delivery of letters or packets by the Post Office in advance of the normal delivery, but in Am. a similar service is called *special delivery*. A book by James Branch Cabell, incorporating letters he received through the post, has 'Special Delivery' as its title. *Express delivery* would be understood in Am. to mean delivery by a firm of carriers.

In Am. a business firm of this kind is called an *express company*. 'The very slight effort on the part of express companies to find persons, and their frequent indifference about addresses' (Prof. R. T. ELY, Evolution of Industrial Society, 244). 'The post office is no model for government-run enterprises, yet no one would dream of turning it over to the express companies which for years blocked the enormous boon of parcel post' (NORMAN THOMAS, America's Way Out, 158). The service rendered by such a company, or the company itself, may be called simply *express*. 'Stowe received a telegram saying that $300 had been sent to him by express.' 'She shipped her trunks by express, packed her jewelcase and valise, and met Desmond at the station' (R. W. CHAMBERS, The Fighting Chance, 405). 'The edition will be limited, and the price will be $3. This will include express charges, packing in boxes, etc.' (Advt.).

Goods consigned to an express company are carried on the railways in *express cars*, and collected and delivered by *expressmen* in *express carts* or *express wagons*. 'Two men, said to be Baker's companions, became frightened at the large number of armed officers entering the express car, and made their escape.' 'While helping an expressman carry her trunks to her room, she fell through the open trap with the trunk.' 'Every side-street rang with the hideous clatter of drays and express carts' (HAMLIN GARLAND, The Tyranny of the Dark, 245). 'My trunk is packed and already trundled out to the express wagon.'

Hence the verb *express* = *send by an express company*. 'The trunks were expressed to Sullivan County, where the honeymoon was to be.'

extend. †This term is commonly used

in Am. where Eng. usage would prefer *offer* or *present*. 'The messages of welcome extended through this journal.' 'President McKinley extended to Dewey the thanks of the Am. people for "his splendid achievement of overwhelming victory"' (Prof. A. E. MARTIN, Hist. of U.S. ii. 367).

The Am. use of *extended* does not carry with it any suggestion of continuation or prolongation, but is simply a synonym for *long*. It thus corresponds largely to the Eng. *extensive, full-length*. 'We present herewith extended lists of books recently published.' 'To familiarize himself with the wishes and the economic conditions of the country, Washington made an extended tour through New Eng.' (Prof. A. E. MARTIN, Hist. of U.S. i. 96). 'In 1889 he took an extended trip to Europe' (Dict. Am. Biog. vi. 363). 'There must naturally arise many issues requiring not only consideration but sometimes an extended discussion' (C. A. and W. BEARD, The Am. Leviathan, 723).

In Am. *extension* may denote an addition to a house, usually of lower elevation than the main building. 'The tin roof blew off the extension one windy night' (RUTH HALL, The Pine Grove House, 12). An *extension bag* is a bag that may be expanded to hold more articles than it normally contains. 'Spring came at last, and with the general season arrived, as usual, every variety of drummer. They came with extension bags filled with samples.' An *extension table* is a table in which a leaf may be inserted.

F

faculty. In an Eng. university a *faculty* is one of the departments of its teaching. Traditionally there are four faculties—Theology, Law, Medicine, and Arts. In Am. the word denotes the whole of the teaching staff at a university, college, or school.

'Several members of the faculty complained that they were having trouble with students who "asked questions out of season"' (L. STEFFENS, Autobiog. 647). 'The producing forces in the college are its faculty, its administrative officers, and its trustees' (Prof. A. H. QUINN, The Soul of Am. 184). 'In 1891 President Jordan chose him to be one of the 15 professors who formed the original faculty of Stanford University. . . . In 1901 he resigned from the faculty in protest against the dismissal of Prof. Edward A. Ross' (Dict. Am. Biog. ix. 277). 'In order to get the class of teachers that he wanted for the faculty of the Van Hornesville District School it was necessary to provide living quarters' (IDA M. TARBELL, Owen D. Young, 285).

fail. In Eng. and Am. alike, a person or enterprise is said to fail when he or it comes to grief. In Am. *failed* may be applied as an adj. in such a case, as though *fail* were used trans. Thus *failed = who* (or *which*) *has failed*. 'The work of examining the books of the failed firm will be begun to-morrow by the accountants.' 'It does not follow that the failed author is a bad critic.' 'The liabilities of the failed banks reached greater totals than were recorded for any other State in the Union' (F. L. ALLEN, Only Yesterday, 281). 'The liabilities in 1932 amounted to less than twice the liabilities of failed enterprises in 1928 and 1929' (EVANS CLARK, Internal Debts of U.S. 197). One may compare the Babu 'failed B.A.', which is not, however, a precisely similar use, as it does not denote a B.A. who has failed but a candidate who has failed to become a B.A.

fair. In the sense of *completely, fully*, or *clearly, distinctly*, this word is now obs. in Eng., exc. in certain dial., but is still current in Am. 'She threw a stone fair at the motorman' (i.e. straight at). The expression *for fair = in reality, seriously, right enough*. '"I seem to be putting my foot in it for fair," said the marine, looking discouraged.'

†In Am. *fairly* is current in the sense of *positively, actually, quite.* 'An impatient spectator began a stamping of feet, and this was taken up by the rest, fairly shaking the building.' 'The pigeons which at times fairly darkened the sky in flocks which extended from horizon to horizon' (J. TRUSLOW ADAMS, The Epic of Am. 6). 'Wherever Taft ran ahead of Father's figures, they fairly gloated' (ALICE ROOSEVELT LONG-WORTH, Crowded Hours, 156).

fakir. In Am. this word does not always mean an *Indian devotee.* Sometimes it = *faker.* 'There are fakirs as well as real scientists, cranks as well as inventors' (Prof. E. MIMS, Adventurous Am. 21). The word is applied esp. to a street pedlar, who goes about selling *fakes,* or odds and ends, largely sham or worthless. 'One may see at almost any of the downtown corners a street fakir selling shoestrings of all colors.' 'They find the patent-medicine fakir on his motor-truck still holding a considerable crowd' (E. WILSON, The Am. Jitters, 95).

fall. In Eng. *fall* sometimes = *autumn,* but only in some connexion where a suggestion of the falling of the leaves makes its use appropriate; e.g. it might be found in a description of a country walk taken in October. In Am. it is the ordinary term for *autumn* as a chronological period, without any thought of what may be seen in the woods. 'With an eye to the fall elections.' 'The fall term of the public schools opened Tuesday morning.' 'The Union Pacific interests quietly commenced in the fall of 1900 to purchase the Burlington system' (J. M. BECK, May it Please the Court, 335).

†Am. *fall down* = Eng. *come to grief, fail.* 'The architects who are rebuilding N.Y. must face that problem or fall down on the job to which they set themselves.' 'San Francisco

was falling down esp. in shipbuilding; even repair work went elsewhere' (L. ADAMIC, Dynamite, 202). 'I saw France, making trading consuls into diplomats, fall down completely in its diplomacy at Buenos Aires for that very reason' (F. J. STIMSON, My U.S. 375).

†Am. *fall for* = Eng. *be captivated by.* 'The Am. Magazine fell violently for the idea, and promised to make a serial out of our adventures' (UPTON SINCLAIR, Candid Reminiscences, 173). 'The Am. liberals, who so easily fall for every new political scheme, went over to Bryan on free silver almost to a man' (E. GOLDMAN, Living My Life, 179).

Am. *fall over one another* = Eng. *tumble over one another, compete with one another.* 'They hand over their "good money" in abundance to the party of the President, who explicitly fall over one another in their anxiety to advertise said promise of immunity.'

Am. *fall over oneself* = Eng. *be in a tremendous hurry.* 'The independent element is not falling over itself to come to his assistance.' 'Other publishers were falling over themselves to get out books which would reap an advantage from the craze' (F. L. ALLEN, Only Yesterday, 191).

family. When Taft succeeded Theodore Roosevelt in the Presidency, they 'had conferred together on the matter of the Cabinet, and Roosevelt had not asked for the retention of a single member of his family' (H. F. PRINGLE, Theodore Roosevelt, 507). The inevitable inference is that the Roosevelt Cabinet was a glaring example of nepotism—inevitable, unless one happens to know that in Am. the members of a Cabinet are often spoken of as the President's *official family.* 'Sherman's appointment as the finance minister was in conformity with the usual desire and practice of the chief executive to have at least one intimate and trusted friend in his official family' (Prof. D. C. BARRETT,

Greenbacks and Specie Payments, 194). 'As for the rest of the Cabinet there were many possible choices; so many, indeed, that Mr. Wilson did not decide on the last one of his official family until his inauguration day was close at hand' (W. G. McADOO, Crowded Years, 180). The term is also sometimes applied to members of the Cabinet of a foreign Prime Minister. 'Clemenceau left the heavy feasting to others in his official family' (J. KERNEY, Political Education of Woodrow Wilson, 421).

In Mr. McAdoo's book there is one instance (p. 63) of the inclusion in this term of a subordinate Federal official outside the Cabinet. 'In the official family of Grover Cleveland there was an Assistant Secretary of the Navy named William McAdoo.' This extension of the normal use of the term, however, is rare.

††fan. In Am. a *fan* is not only a contrivance for providing a current of air, but an enthusiastic devotee, esp. of games or athletic sports. 'The veteran was in splendid form, and when he is that, every baseball fan knows that the opposing team has little chance to win.' 'Senator Harrison and I were both baseball fans' (G. W. PEPPER, In the Senate, 34). 'None of these men and women [rescued from a burning ship through a radio message] need again be told the value of wireless. They are life fans of the art' (Dr. F. S. HARRIS, Scientific Research and Human Welfare, 81). 'Secretary Ickes is a dahlia fan! For years his hobby has been gardening and his speciality has been the petaled curls of dahlias' (R. W. BABSON, Washington and the Revolutionists, 127). The word, in this sense, is commonly said to be an abbreviation of *fanatic*. It is at least possible, however, that it may be an extension of one of the ordinary meanings of *fan*; i.e. 'fig., any agency which excites to action or which stimulates the activity of a person or an emotion, producing effects analogous to those of a fan in exciting flame' (Century Dict.).

farm is sometimes modestly used in Am. to denote a *country house*. 'When one of George William Curtis's heroes was invited to spend the Sabbath out of town, he arrived some time on Saturday at a country "place"; his grandson passes the week's end at a "farm".' See COTTAGE.

Another special sense of the word is illustrated in the following quotation. 'There are many "farms" on the waterfront, for a "farm" is simply the open shore space in front of a dock' (ERNEST POOLE, The Harbor, 322). See also SUBSISTENCE and TOWN.

fast is an epithet we apply to a clock which indicates a time in advance of the correct time. By analogy, the same word is applied by Eng. engineers to any instrument having a dial—e.g. an ammeter may be said to read fast—and in Am. is commonly used of scales indicating a weight which is more than the actual weight. 'Most of the dishonest tradesmen are to be found among those who do business with poor customers who buy in small quantities. Such people lose heavily if the scales on which their purchases are weighed daily are fast only half an ounce, and the dealer's gains are correspondingly large at the end of a year.'

faucet is in Eng. an unusual word exc. among engineers. In Am. it is the everyday term to denote what in Eng. is called a *tap*. 'Many of the practical details of kitchen equipment, such as sinks and faucets.' 'The question as to who left the faucet running in the bath room' (L. N. WRIGHT, Limbs of an Old Family Tree, 148). 'He was granted patents for a sewing machine, a water faucet, and a window sash' (Dict. Am. Biog. x. 611). 'He could turn on again instantaneously, as one would turn on a faucet, all the energies which had been arrested' (Prof. N. W. STEPHENSON, Nelson W. Aldrich, 362).

favo(u)rite. If one is reading an account of the proceedings at an Am. national party convention, it is important to keep in mind the distinction between a *favorite* and a *favorite son*. A *favorite*, as defined by Bryce (The Am. Commonwealth, ii. 188), is 'a politician well known over the Union, and drawing support from all or most of its sections', whereas a *favorite son* is 'a politician respected or admired in his own State, but little regarded beyond it'. 'The demand made of every proposed favorite son, or suddenly unblanketed dark horse, will be, "Can he carry N.Y., New Jersey, Connecticut, or Indiana?"' 'Massachusetts has a favorite son who may be heard from more or less before the convention meets.' 'Long before the expiration of his term of office different parts of the country were recommending their "favorite sons" for the succession' (Prof. D. S. MUZZEY, The Am. Adventure, i. 330).

††feature is used in Am. as a verb in the sense of *give special prominence to*. 'A few schools for girls feature domestic training.' 'All the papers this morning feature the case.' 'Dick Croker rather liked to see his grizzled face in the papers, and published a large collection of cartoons that featured himself' (Dr. H. ZINK, City Bosses in U.S. 33). 'A landlady who features cornbread and hot biscuits will have a Southern clientele' (F. J. HASKIN, The Am. Government, 479). It may also mean *be a prominent feature of.* 'Evening chapel services, at which historical talks were given, featured the opening of Tuskegee Institute's 50th anniversary celebration' (World Almanac, 1932, 104).

The word is also used as an attrib. noun. 'An artist who can sketch a suitable illustration for every feature advertisement' (E. L. SHUMAN, Practical Journalism, 193). 'Hearn soon gave this up to do feature articles for

the *Cincinnati Enquirer*' (Dict. Am. Biog. viii. 485).

†feed. In Eng. a farmer feeds horses on oats. In Am. he feeds oats to horses. 'It is cheaper to feed slop to a dear, unselfish and modest neighbor's hogs than it is to feed lawn grass and flowers to his cows.' 'If mince pie makes the Mount Holyoke girls drowsy after luncheon it ought to be fed them at night.' 'McCann had a hunk of dried buffalo meat, and was feeding it to some Indian children' (ANDY ADAMS, Log of a Cowboy, 336). 'Horse chestnuts are so called from being fed to horses' (J. B. GREENOUGH and G. L. KITTREDGE, Words and their Ways, 365).

feel, in the sense of *examine by touching*, is in Am. often followed by *of.* 'The calm camera man, feeling of the bulb of his instrument and taking sight.' 'Feel of their ears now and then, for the ear is the horse's thermometer.' 'Those of the public who begin to feel of their pocketbooks' (Prof. C. E. MERRIAM, Chicago, 277). 'There was a little red hole in his side, from which the blood trickled; and he felt of it, and poked his finger into it, to see where it went to' (U. SINCLAIR, Manassas, 392). Cf. SMELL.

fence. Except in the term *barbed-wire fence*, this word is ordinarily used in Eng. of wooden barriers only. In Am. it may also denote an iron railing, or a wall of brick or stone. 'Why not protect your lawn with a good iron fence?' (Advt.). 'A high iron fence divides the playground' (C. S. JOHNSON, The Negro in Am. Civilization, 268). 'The tiny yards were separated from the street with a brick fence' (L. N. WRIGHT, Limbs of an Old Family Tree, 166). 'Out of N.Y. and New England come reports that stone fences are disappearing from many farms' (G. A. HASTINGS, Happy Journeys to Yesterday, 34). See SNAKE and SPITE.

As a farmer looks after his fences to keep his cattle from straying, so a Congressman or other official politician in Am. **is** said to *look after his fences* when he spends time in conciliating or canvassing voters in his district (= Eng. *nursing his constituency*). 'While engaged in securing his position in Ohio, he [Sherman] had incidentally given utterance to a political phrase that has become idiomatic. When visiting the State in 1879, ostensibly to look after his farms, he had protested that he came only "to repair my fences", a term to which the newspapers promptly gave its present political meaning' (T. C. PEASE, The U.S. i. 527). 'As election approaches, members are very impatient to get home and look after their fences—that is, to make preparations for a renomination' (Prof. A. B. HART, Actual Government, 229). This use of the term may be extended to apply to the precautionary tactics of leaders outside Congress. 'For the second time in its history, the most conservative labor body in the world [the Am. Federation of Labor] came near to "capture" by the radicals. Thereafter Gompers looked to his fences, and a battle was on that was not to slacken until after 1915' (L. SYMES and T. CLEMENT, Rebel Am. 224).

fender has a spec. use in the Am. automobile vocab., being used to denote that part of a car which in Eng. is known as the *wing*. 'The fender at present used by automobiles is intended only to preserve the car itself from injury.' 'A thousand-ton electric shear reduces chassis, springs, wheels, fenders and all to a junk fodder' (E. WILSON, The Am. Jitters, 87). 'He couldn't, just now, be very excited about the new fenders for the Revelation car' (SINCLAIR LEWIS, Dodsworth, 184). 'The Buick roared forward, kissing Ellery's right fender none too gently' (ELLERY QUEEN, The Siamese Twin Mystery, 25).

†**fetch.** In Am. *fetch up* (intrans.) = Eng. *end up*, *finish*. 'He tried again and again for the governorship before

attaining it, and if he tries often enough he may fetch up in Congress.' '"Lord!" he murmured. "I wonder where this thing is going to fetch up"' (F. NORRIS, A Deal in Wheat, 48).

fiat is best known in Am. in the compound *fiat money*, denoting, acc. to the *Century Dict.*, 'paper currency issued by a government as money, but not based on coin or bullion'. *Greenbacks* is a popular term for the same thing. A *fiatist* is an advocate of the substitution of such currency for bank-notes as a circulating medium. 'When the first battle was fought against greenback or fiat money, back in the seventies, whatever they were on the Atlantic Coast, they were fiatists in the West.' 'The Continental Congress went gaily down the primrose path of fiat money' (Prof. T. J. GRAYSON, Leaders and Periods of Am. Finance, 16).

field is used in Am. in certain combinations unknown in Eng. A *field secretary* is an officer of a society whose sphere lies in the country—in visiting branches, in general propaganda, and so on. He is thus a sort of organizing or travelling secretary, in distinction from the *desk secretary*, whose duties lie in the office. 'The labors of the field secretary during the year have been put forth in increasing the membership of the society, in visiting and addressing important conventions, in the investigation of opportunities for founding branch societies, and in the work of organizing the second National Peace Congress.'

Similarly, a newspaper may have a *field editor*, who is not, as one might suppose, the editor of its agricultural columns. 'On a paper covering a wide territory there may be an assistant editor (sometimes called field editor) stationed at each important center throughout the country' (H. M. SWETLAND, Industrial Publishing, 54).

A *field study* or *field survey* means a study or survey of concrete facts as discovered by investigation on the spot. 'We have as yet no method for summing up individual incomes into a family income, exc. that of direct field studies' (E. E. HUNT, An Audit of Am. 8). 'There is need of a thorough field survey to determine how accurate are the homicide reports now being made to state and federal bureaus of vital statistics' (Prof. H. C. BREARLEY, Homicide in U.S. 10).

Am. *field strawberry* = Eng. *wild strawberry.* 'It is said ripe field strawberries have never been picked at this time of year before.'

fierce is a colloq. term in Am. to describe something that is painful, unpleasant, or troublesome. 'At any conversational melee you may learn that the weather has been fierce, that the last play was fierce, that the cradle song at yesterday's recital was fierce, that the servant problem is fierce, and that the dinner to-morrow night is likely to be fierce.' 'To use a Briticism, it was "cruel"; the corresponding Americanism was more appropriate—it was "fierce"' (JACK LONDON, People of the Abyss, 150). The word is also used as an adv., in corresponding senses. 'I broke a finger on my right hand and sprained the joint on it too. It ached fierce.'

figure. In addition to its Eng. senses the verb *figure* has commonly in Am. the meaning of *calculate, compute, reckon, estimate,* even when no numerical consideration is involved. 'Railroad statisticians have figured that the grain traffic for this crop year will aggregate 1,500,000 carloads.' 'Men in small fishing boats, venturing out of sight of land, figure how far they are out by tasting the water.' 'We figured that the entire job, as we had planned it, would cost $4,000,000' (W. G. McADOO, Crowded Years, 73). 'Haywood figured that without the cries of hungry children the strikers would be able to hold out longer' (L. ADAMIC, Dynamite, 170).

This meaning of the verb is often intensified by the addition of *out* or *up.* 'The assessors have figured out the tax rate and have found that it will be $17 on $1,000.' 'At first I could not figure out a way, in that level country, to approach them near enough to give my horse a fair chance in a run.' 'Have we figured out how the National Government would proceed if it undertook such an enterprise?' (C. NAGEL, Speeches and Writings, i. 240). 'If Ford wants a new suit, he gets it, without stopping to figure up whether he has had a good year or not' (E. A. FILENE, Successful Living in this Machine Age, 52).

To *figure on* may mean either (1) to *make calculations respecting,* or (2) to *count on, rely on.* (1) 'The date of opening bids was postponed in order to give the various steel companies time to figure on the contract.' (2) 'This would be an important item to a State leader, figuring on controlling the State delegation.'

In Eng. one may speak of cutting a brilliant figure or cutting a poor figure, but scarcely of *cutting no figure* at all. In Am. this is possible. 'Grain speculation is now reviving. The price cuts no figure. It is a case of shut your eyes and buy.' 'Eligibility is merely a question of scholarship. Previous deportment cuts no figure.' 'Religion practically cuts no figure as a motive for emigration' (Dr. H. P. FAIRCHILD, Greek Immigration to the U.S. 60). Accordingly, Am. *cuts no figure* = Eng. *counts for nothing.*

file. The verb *file* is worked very much harder in Am. than in Eng. In Eng. a business man files his papers by putting them away for reference in their proper pigeon-hole or cabinet, and a lawyer files an information or a bill in Chancery. In Am. almost any kind of official report or statement is said to be filed, and the word is often loosely used of the formal presentation of a document to the official whose duty it will then be to place it on his file. 'The will of A. P. Fitch was filed for probate in the Surrogate's office yesterday.' 'Plans were filed to-day, at the Bureau of Buildings, for an eight-story addition to the Tribune building.' 'It was announced at the District Attorney's office to-day that the Assistant District Attorney had filed his resignation.' 'The annual report of the police department was filed to-day with the mayor.' 'The more liberal civil service laws permit removal upon the filing of written charges against the employee with an opportunity for him to reply' (C. C. MAXEY, Outline of Municipal Government, 108). 'It is the practice for the judges who are not in accord with the ruling of the majority to file a "dissenting opinion"' (C. A. and W. BEARD, The Am. Leviathan, 116). 'The circulars request the members who desire tickets for the game to file their applications with the secretary of the Athletic Association not later than Nov. 1.' 'Requesting them to file their bids in 48 hours' (Prof. M. PUPIN, From Immigrant to Inventor, 344). In his criticisms of the Am. State Department (My U.S. 298) F. J. Stimson complains that it does not read an ambassador's dispatches but 'files them away'. An Eng. writer would have been more likely to say that it pigeon-holes them.

filibuster. The word *filibustering*, not used in Eng. exc. in its original sense of *buccaneering*, has been adopted in Am. politics as a technical term for obstructive tactics in a legislative assembly. 'In ordinary use, the word "filibuster" means to act as a freebooter or buccaneer, but in parliamentary practice it means "to obstruct legislation by undue use of the technicalities of parliamentary law or privileges, as when a minority, in order to prevent the passage of some measure obnoxious to them, endeavor to tire out their opponents by useless motions, speeches and objections". Frequently, the purpose of a filibuster is to call the attention of the country in an emphatic way to the policy of the majority' (C. A. BEARD, Am. Government and Politics, 273). Acc. to Prof. A. B. Hart (Actual Government, 250) 'filibustering differs from obstruction only in being more systematic and longer continued'. 'The Penal Code Bill was before the Senate during almost the entire session Tuesday and was subjected to filibustering tactics on the part of the minority that resulted in almost no progress being made upon it.' 'The bill passed the House, but the opposition in the Senate, by the use of the most extraordinary filibustering tactics, prevented it from coming to a vote at that session of Congress' (W. G. McADOO, Crowded Years, 297).

fill. This verb is much more widely used in Am. than in Eng. It often has the sense, now obs. in Eng., of *fulfil*. 'It fills every requirement of the most advanced ideas in underwear making' (Advt.). 'During the campaign he filled 125 speaking engagements' (D. L. COLVIN, Prohibition in U.S. 171). It also = Eng. *make up*, in relation to medical prescriptions. 'My business was devoted almost exclusively to the filling of prescriptions written by physicians.' 'A prescription which the nearest pharmacist might fill easily enough' (Prof. C. E. MERRIAM, Chicago, 84). An Am. dentist *fills*, not *stops*, a tooth that has a cavity in it. (In Eng. also *fill* is the technical professional term, but it is not in popular use.) †In Am. to *fill* an order is to *execute* it. 'His cars almost sold themselves, and he had more orders than he could fill' (E. A. FILENE, Successful Living in this Machine Age, 142). See also BILL.
Am. *fill out* = Eng. *fill up*. 'If the editor needs it to fill out the page.' 'The law requires every applicant for a license to fill out a blank.' 'A lady

living in a quite inaccessible village filled out a coupon' (Prof. A. FLEXNER, Universities, 139).

Am. *fill up* = Eng. *stuff up*, in a colloquial fig. sense. 'Filling him up with large tales about dissatisfaction in the Citizens' Union.'

In Am. the *stuffing* of a fowl, turkey, &c., is often called its *filling*.

††The term *filling station* denotes a place where a motorist may obtain a fresh supply of GAS (q.v.). 'There are nearly as many filling stations as grocery stores; there is one station for every 80 cars.' 'Filling stations, the wayside temples of Am. life' (C. MORLEY, John Mistletoe, 220). 'In that same city a Negro cannot get gas at a filling station patronized by whites' (R. R. MOTON, What the Negro Thinks, 213).

finding. In an Am. department store one may come across a notice, 'Shoe Findings'. An inspection will show that the term *findings* includes shoe laces, shoe polish, and similar accessories. The *Century Dict.* defines the word as meaning 'the tools, appliances, and materials which some workmen have to furnish in their employment, particularly those used by shoemakers; hence shoemakers' supplies in general, except leather'. Webster mentions also dressmakers' findings (buttons, linings, &c.) and jewellers' findings (small parts for repairing). 'He began peddling merchandise, principally watches and watch findings, throughout the Southern States' (Dict. Am. Biog. ix. 408). 'The time had passed when the farmer had his leather worked up into shoes by an itinerant artisan. In such case the farmer had to provide the findings' (Dr. W. W. FOLWELL, Autobiog. 25).

fire. The technical terms relating to conflagrations differ considerably in Eng. and Am. In Eng. a *fire department* is that department of an insurance office which deals with insurances against fire; in Am. it is a fire brigade. The members of a fire

brigade are called in Eng. *firemen*, but in Am. also *fire fighters*. 'The most modern equipment of all kinds should be at the command of the fire fighters at a moment's notice.' A *fire marshal* is an official who investigates the origin of fires. 'The fire marshal is investigating a blaze which was discovered this morning in an apartment house.' The name *fire lines* is given to the cordon drawn by a fire brigade around an area within which spectators are not allowed. 'During the fire a Columbus Avenue open car became stalled in the fire lines.' See also BUG.

In Am. an incendiary fire is said to be *set*. In Eng. one may say of an incendiary that he *sets fire to* a building or that he *sets* a building *on fire*, but not that he *sets a fire*. 'His employees believe that the fire was set by hoboes who had been driven out of the stable by the night watchman.' 'Two fires in tenement house letter boxes were set to-day at an early hour.'

†As a verb, Am. *fire* = Eng. *sack*, *dismiss peremptorily*. 'The Office-Boy's Record. Monday, hired; Tuesday, tired; Wednesday, fired!' 'The superintendent declared that he would fire any man who joined the organization' (S. D. SPERO and A. L. HARRIS, The Black Worker, 434). 'Psychiatrists were installed in business houses to hire and fire employees' (F. L. ALLEN, Only Yesterday, 198).

first. The *first floor* of an Am. building is what would be called the *ground floor* in Eng., and the numbering of the higher floors follows acc. to the same reckoning.

In Eng. one may speak of *the first* of the month, meaning the first day of it. In Am. one may speak also of *the first* of the year, or of the week; not, however, meaning the first day of this period but the first part of it. 'I once heard Chief Justice White say, about the first of the year, that if he did not hear another argument he could not possibly before summer read all the records and briefs which had been filed from Oct. to Jan.' (Dr. J. M. BECK, May it Please the Court, 27). See also LAST.

Am. *first name* = Eng. *Christian name.* 'The fact that few men, even his most intimate friends, ever addressed Harrison by his first name showed his aloofness' (Prof. A. E. MARTIN, Hist. of U.S. ii. 230). 'There was always between them a formality even when they used each other's first names' (SINCLAIR LEWIS, Dodsworth, 371). 'Another device to promote fellowship was the imposition of a ten-cent fine on any member calling another "Mister" instead of by his first name' (Rotary? 26). See also GIVE.

First, last, and all the time is originally a formula used by the spokesman of a State delegation at a national party convention in putting forward a candidate for the Presidential nomination. It pledges (or seems to pledge) these delegates not to 'trade' their vote to any other candidate while the struggle for the nomination is in process. This slogan has also come into use as an expression of unwavering opinion or policy. 'Laurier has stood first, last, and all the time for Canada.' 'Mr. George Meredith, of Eng., foreshadows a state of society permitting marriage for certain limited periods. If this is a movement to render it legal for Eng. noblemen to marry a new Am. heiress every little while, we are against it first, last, and all the time.'

The wife of the President of the U.S. is sometimes distinguished by the honorific, *first lady of the land,* or *first lady.* 'Mrs. Roosevelt observed Sunday quietly. In the morning the first lady of the land attended church.' 'Mrs. Pierce could never be diverted from her all-absorbing sorrow, and I shall always remember the grief-stricken expression of this First Lady of the Land' (M. GOUVERNEUR, As I Remember, 255). 'Colonel Harts, the President's aid, entered and announced the President and Mrs. Wilson. The President, with the first lady, entered' (Dr. FRANKLIN H. MARTIN, The Joy of Living, ii. 155). 'She became a social figure of the first importance when her husband assumed the secretaryship of state in 1801. Jefferson was a widower and Dolly Madison was in effect the "first lady"' (Dict. Am. Biog. xii. 181).

fit is spec. used in Am., both trans. and intrans., in the sense of *prepare (for college).* 'Mrs. Roosevelt will attend the prizeday exercises at Groton School, where her eldest son is fitting for college.' 'In his 12th year Emmons entered the Dixwell Latin School. He was fitted for Harvard' (Dict. Am. Biog. vi. 151). A school which prepares its pupils for college may accordingly be called a *fitting-school.* 'In fitting-school and in college he had gone deeply into sports.' 'The Latin grammar schools were essentially fitting-schools for the colleges' (P. E. SARGENT, Handbook of Am. Private Schools, 11).

five. The alternative terms *Five Nations, Five Tribes,* and *Five Civilized Tribes* denote a certain group of Indian tribes whose composition, as the following quotations show, is variously given. 'The N.Y. Iroquois tribes—the Senecas, Cayugas, Onondagas, Oneidas, and Mohawks—formed, probably about the beginning of the 17th century, a very powerful confederacy, known to the Eng. as "The Five Nations". The descendants of these tribes still hold large tracts in central N.Y.' (The Tuscaroras were subsequently added to the original Iroquois confederacy, and the term *Six Nations* then came into use.) 'There are in the five tribes—Cherokees, Creeks, Choctaws, Chickasaws and Seminoles—between 80,000 and 100,000 homesteads represented.' 'The latest Indian budget bill authorized the removal of all restrictions upon the alienation of their lands by any of the members of the Five Civilized Tribes who desired it.'

In N.Y. the spot where Worth, Baxter, and Park Streets intersect is popularly called *Five Points*. The number is five, not six, because originally Worth Street only met the other two streets and did not run across them. At one time the Five Points district was proverbial for rowdyism and vice, but the character of the neighbourhood, like that of *Seven Dials* in London, has since been changed.

fix. In Eng. the verb *fix* is commonly restricted to the meaning of *establish, make stable, place in a permanent position*. In Am. it is a serviceable word-of-all-work which saves the trouble of finding the spec. term to describe almost any kind of adjustment or repair. As long ago as 1837–8 Capt. Frederick Marryat, when travelling in Am., noted this convenient use of the word. He was asked, 'Shall I fix your coat or your breakfast first?' meaning 'Shall I brush your coat or get ready your breakfast first?' 'He has one tooth that has been bothering him for some time, and he concluded that he couldn't find a better day to have it fixed than on his 88th birthday.' '"I wish you would ask Irene to fix the hearth fire" Evelyn had said to Maria when they entered the room, which did seem somewhat chilly. Maria asked the girl to do so, and when she had gone and the fire was blazing Evelyn said &c.' (M. E. WILKINS FREEMAN, By the Light of the Soul, 356). *Fix up* has the same extensive meaning. 'The mending of fences, the painting of buildings and the general fixing up and beautifying of barns and sheds.' 'Illinois is having a hard time obtaining a satisfactory primary election law. The first one enacted was set aside by the State Supreme Court as unconstitutional. It was then fixed up to meet the objections of the Court.'

Well fixed = well-to-do, well off. 'He has never since he has been in college made any display of his wealth, but it is generally known that he is as well fixed as any man in the university.' 'Most of the men on the paper envied him his fame and money. Oh, he was well fixed now!' (R. MONTAGUE, in The End of the World, 50).

Another Am. colloquialism is *fix to* in the sense of *get ready to*. 'As they started home, one of the men remarked: "What a pretty night! The moon is fixing to shine!"'

The *fixings* of a meal are the adjuncts to, or garnishings of, its main ingredient. 'The clambake, with the fixings which accompanied it, was pronounced excellent.' 'The cranberry season on the Cape Cod bogs is reported to have been the poorest ever known. Apparently some of the fixings for the Thanksgiving turkey will come high this year.' The same word may denote trimmings or minor articles of clothing. 'Fall Fixings for Men' (Advt.). 'Of stocks and collars and fixings generally for the neck and shoulders there is no end.'

flag. The verb *flag*, in the sense of *signal*, is rarely used in Eng. exc. with regard to nautical signalling. In Am. it is often applied to the stopping of a railway train by means of a flag or other signal. 'With a red tablecloth she flagged the westbound passenger train when it was within a few yards of the bridge.' 'Harriman knew that the express could be flagged at Goshen if there were any passengers for points west of Buffalo' (J. K. WINKLER, J. Pierpont Morgan, 193).

A *flag station* is a station at which trains stop only when signalled. 'In 30 years it has risen from a railroad flag station to a place of 100,000 inhabitants.' 'He lifted him on a horse, galloped to the flag station two miles out of town, and put him on the north-bound train' (T. DIXON, The Clansman, 356).

For the meaning of *flagman*, see the first quotation. 'The flagman is the rear brakeman on the train. He runs back with the flag when the train is stopped for any reasons between stations, and when there is heavy traffic he aids in collecting the tickets and fares.' 'A train had stopped to put off a car, and had just sent back a flagman to warn the approaching stock train.'

On June 14, 1777, Congress adopted the Stars and Stripes as the national flag. The anniversary of that date is accordingly observed as *Flag Day.* 'The Mayor has issued orders that flags shall fly from the City Hall on June 14 in observance of Flag Day, the anniversary of the adoption of the flag of the U.S. The Superintendent of Schools has requested of all public schools that part of the opening exercises on that day shall be devoted to the flag and the honor due to it.' See TAG.

flannel. The Am. *flannel cake* is by no means as indigestible as it sounds, for no woollen ingredient actually enters into its composition. It is defined by Dr. R. H. Thornton as 'a soft thin cake usually eaten with molasses'. 'Your cakes of the buckwheat and "flannel" variety' (E. L. BANKS, Autobiog. of a Newspaper Girl, 166).

flash. A technical term of the Am. newspaper world, denoting a very brief item, sent over the telegraph or telephone wires as a preliminary to a fuller report. 'City editors looking for a noon-edition flash' (H. JUSTIN SMITH, Chicago, 133). 'It became known that the national chairman had typhoid fever, and the obituaries were rushed into type to be used when the flash came' (H. F. PRINGLE, Theodore Roosevelt, 349). See also BULLETIN.

flat. The table utensils with which one eats one's meals are called in Am. *flat silver* or *flat ware*, presumably because they lie on the table horizontally instead of standing up perpendicularly. Thus an advt. of 'silver-plated flatware' specifies the articles offered as including dessert forks and spoons, dinner knives, gravy ladles, tea spoons, &c. 'The parson's wife recalls with a thrill the gift of flat silver from the vestry on an anniversary.'

In the vocab. of Am. railways a *flat-car* is a car that has neither sides nor top. 'A string of flat-cars on a siding loaded with iron beams and pillars.' 'The bronzed Korean, the queued Chinaman, and the blue-eyed yellow-haired Russian soldier arrange themselves on an open flat-car in a human mosaic of mutual agreeableness' (Sen. A. J. BEVERIDGE, The Russian Advance, 16).

Flat-footed is often used in Am. in a fig. sense which has nothing to do with the literal sense of the term but is apparently suggested by the metaphor of 'putting one's foot down'. Accordingly, it = *downright, thoroughgoing, pronounced.* 'His withdrawal this morning is not forcible and flat-footed, but of the same halting character as his political movements.' 'I had over 40 dollars, but I only promised to loan mine if it was needed, while Priest refused flat-footed either to lend or bet his' (ANDY ADAMS, Log of a Cowboy, 250). 'Germany came out flat-footed with the belligerent warning that she would engage in unrestricted submarine warfare' (W. G. McADOO, Crowded Years, 367).

As a noun, *flat* may mean (1) an expanse of level country, or (2) a flatboat. (1) 'The hitherto neglected pine hills and pine flats along the Gulf.' (2) 'An observer counted 197 flats and 14 keel boats that passed the falls of Ohio in 2 months' (Prof. A. E. MARTIN, Hist. of U.S. i. 287).

flaunt may sometimes be found in Am. in the sense of *flout.* 'Though a temperate discussion of the desirability of birth control, the treatise, flaunting many accepted conceptions and values of the period, did not escape court action' (Dict. Am. Biog. x. 472). 'Young men and women who are tasting the first heady joys of earning their own living are not readily amenable to parental discipline. When self-support appears easy, the temptation to flaunt family control is very great' (M. A. ELLIOTT and F. E. MERRILL, Social Disorganization, 573).

††fleet. The *O.E.D.* describes as 'now rare or dial.' the use of this word to denote 'a number of persons, birds or other objects moving or employed in company'. In its Suppl., however, it notes the revival of this usage in the sense of 'a number of vehicles or aircraft forming a definite group or unit'. This revival originated in Am. 'Large fleets of trucks and automobiles' (F. J. HASKIN, The Am. Government, 433).

flicker. In addition to its Eng. meaning, *flicker* is in Am. the popular name for a sort of woodpecker. 'The flicker is yarruping from the cottonwood. He is full of the spring and noisy as a whole congress of blackbirds, though his note is not mere noise, for he has on occasion some sense of tune.' 'When there was a gap in the mountains, he could hear the querulous, senseless, love-quarrel of flickers going on below him' (J. Fox, jr., The Little Shepherd of Kingdom Come, 17).

float. ††There has originated in Am. a spec. use of *float* to denote a tableau or show on a moving platform as part of a procession or parade. 'A procession of 50 beautiful floats was the first on the program. These floats represented the prominent business houses of the city and some of the fraternal insurance orders.'
In the vocab. of Am. politics *floater* is a spec. term for a man who, at an election, casts a vote to which he is not entitled; so-called because such men often float from one election district to another on election day in order to cast several votes. 'The chief difficulty the authorities have to contend with now is the gangs of "floaters". These consist chiefly of men brought from near-by cities, "loaned" by brother bosses (for a

consideration, of course), who vote early under the names of legal voters, before the latter get to the polls.' 'There have been cases in which, on the day of an election, the party heelers on both sides have agreed to divide their campaign funds, and let the floaters cast their ballots uninfluenced' (Prof. A. B. HART, Actual Government, 106). 'The Conservatives were powerless before the importation of "floaters" from a neighboring State' (P. LEWINSON, Race, Class and Party, 47). Cf. REPEATER.

floor. In Am. a speaker who takes part in a debate is said to be *on the floor*, or to *get*, *have*, or *take the floor*. 'After Bailey had spoken, Tillman got the floor and poured into the Congressional Record a carefully written account' (S. H. ACHESON, Joe Bailey, 30). 'He [Congressman Keith] was not frequently on the floor, but was ready with objection and effective reply' (Dict. Am. Biog. x. 294). 'Some diners jumped to their feet and demanded the floor' (E. GOLDMAN, Living my Life, 965).
In an Am. legislative assembly, the member who directs the tactics of his own party on the floor of the house is called its *floor leader*. In the case of the majority party in Congress the limiting word *floor* is important, because the chief leader of that party is the Speaker. 'The seniority rule of the Senate made him the Rep. floor leader in 1929.' 'Mr. Hitchcock, who had charge of the Treaty on behalf of the President, was for the most part the Dem. floor leader' (Am. Year-book for 1919, 3). 'In considering leadership in the House we must take account of the floor leader chosen by the party caucus. Each party has such an agent. It is his duty to keep in close touch with the rank and file of his party colleagues, to learn their opinions, to understand their prejudices and ambitions, and whenever necessary to "line them all up" in support of some measure on which the party leaders have

reached a decision' (C. A. BEARD, Am. Government and Politics, 265). His duties, accordingly, seem to correspond largely to those of the Eng. *whip*.

Am. *floorwalker* = Eng. *shopwalker*. 'When a customer asked for "Nicholas Nickleby", she hurried off to the floorwalker to learn whether he was employed there.' 'If you want silk goods and you arrive in lingerie, the thing to do, of course, is to consult the floorwalker.' 'He had some 15 minutes before gone in at the same doorway, questioned the same floorwalker, and he found himself in due time walking amongst a bewildering lot of models on the third floor' (W. CHURCHILL, Coniston, 310).

See also FIRST and GROUND.

flop. In the vocab. of Am. politics the verb *flop* is used fig., in the sense of the Eng. *rat*, *'vert*. 'Much has been made of the manner in which a number of N.Y. newspapers have flopped to his support.' It may also be used trans. 'The way in which he flopped that paper to the most ardent support of the Rep. candidate was one of the sensations of the last national campaign.'

Hence, *flopper*. 'There are always floppers. The mere circumstance that somebody deserts his party and goes over to the other proves nothing.'

Am. *flophouse* = Eng. *doss-house*, *common lodging-house*. 'The flophouses are overcrowded with strong jobless men' (L. ADAMIC, Dynamite, 422). 'Passing from bad to worse, he sleeps in the flop-house when he has a dime' (M. A. ELLIOTT and F. E. MERRILL, Social Disorganization, 509).

flour. The compound *flouring-mill* is peculiar to Am. It denotes a mill for making flour, as distinct from a *grist-mill*. See GRIST. 'Fire destroyed the large elevator and flouring-mill of E. M. Baker and Co. last night.' 'Two considerable flouring-mills have been built in Harbin since the author was there, one of them, it is said, with a daily capacity of several hundred

barrels' (Sen. A. J. BEVERIDGE, The Russian Advance, 67).

flunkey. For a special Am. use, see quotation. '"Flunkeys" in the North-west do not wear uniforms; their work is to act as assistant cooks in mining and lumber camps.'

flurry. In addition to its ordinary Eng. meanings, *flurry* denotes in Am. a *sudden shower*, usually of snow. 'Saturday's was a real snowstorm and not a flurry. It demoralized the street railway company and served to tie up the Boston and Albany all day.' 'There were several brisk flurries during the afternoon, but the snow was wet and melted as soon as it reached the ground.' 'The snow, which had begun as an insignificant flurry in the morning, developed into a storm by afternoon' (ALICE HEGAN RICE, Sandy, 190).

flyer. In Am. an express train or steamer is sometimes called a *flyer*. 'The day coach on the accommodation train was telescoped, as was the mail car on the flyer.' 'Mr. Northbrook was coming on the two o'clock flyer' (E. O. WHITE, Lesley Chilton, 334).

†folder. In Eng. an instrument for folding paper, or a folding case for loose papers. In Am. also a small pamphlet, usually for advertising purposes, which is not stitched or wired but folds up like a map. 'An official exposition folder, containing much valuable information about the resources of that region, is on file at the Interior Department.' 'The Am. federation began the publication of a monthly folder, "The Brotherhood", in Oct., 1905. The publication was successful at once, and has now grown to magazine size, issued 5 times a year.' 'As full of extravagant descriptions as a travel folder.'

font, in Am., sometimes = a *fount* of type, a sense in which it is now obs. in Eng. 'When this uneven spacing has been made, the letters in some lines seem to belong to different fonts' (T. L. DE VINNE, Correct Composition, 194). 'Foster became the pioneer printer of Boston. He produced his best work after 1678, having in that year acquired a new font of long primer' (Dict. Am. Biog. vi. 549).

fool. Am. retains the practice, now obs. in Eng., though still to be found in Scottish dial., of considering *fool* an adj. as well as a noun. Walter Hines Page is quoted in the *Booklovers' Magazine*, Aug. 1904, as saying that 'we have fool politicians and fool newspapers'. 'Some of Marischal's fool friends have been pestering him to come forward as a candidate for the vice-presidency.' 'Of course, the way I put it, it seems like a fool notion.' 'We have one city after another trying a commission form or some other fool idea of government' (L. STEFFENS, Autobiog. 851). 'The local banks have failed through the speculations of some fool gambler in Louisville' (E. WILSON, The Am. Jitters, 104).

foot. In Eng. to *foot* a bill is to *pay* it. In Am. there is also current the term *foot up = add up, tot up*, both (1) trans. and (2) intrans. (1) 'He is not indulging in glittering generalities; he puts the items all down and foots them up.' 'His expenditure reached figures which surprised him when he found leisure to foot up his debit page' (F. E. LEUPP, Walks about Washington, 48). (2) 'Other articles figuring on the debit side of the ledger and footing up generous totals.' 'The receipts for the sale of public land now foot up to about $3,000,000 a year' (Prof. A. B. HART, Actual Government, 337).
In Eng. *footless* has only its natural meaning of *having no feet*, lit. or fig. Thus Tennyson's 'footless fancies' (Maud, xviii. 8) means 'fancies without footing or basis'. In Am.—possibly through confusion with *bootless*—the word has also come to mean *futile*. 'To seize the mines would be about as footless as the

French attempt to get coal by sending soldiers into the Ruhr.' 'These footless errands done, I went up into the Senate press gallery' (L. STEFFENS, Autobiog. 738). 'I have always thought that it was best for the President to go to Paris. It is footless to speculate now as to what might have happened if he had not gone' (Attorney-General T. W. GREGORY, quoted in The Intimate Papers of Col. House, iv. 233).
'Thus saith the Lord, The heaven is my throne, and the earth is my footstool' (Isa. lxvi. 1). This passage has suggested a metaphor in common use in Am. as a synonym for *the earth*. Sometimes it appears as *God's footstool*, sometimes as *the footstool of the Almighty*, and sometimes as *the footstool* simply. 'To-day we are the greatest manufacturing country on God's footstool' (i.e. under the sun). 'If I were sure of living three or four hundred years on this footstool of the Almighty' (L. MEAD, Word-Coinage, vii). 'The age-old desire of the land worker to own that part of the footstool which he tills.'

force. In Am. the term *force bill* is popularly used to denote a measure of a coercive nature, esp. one which authorizes the President to employ troops to secure its enforcement. 'There is in the Am. nation a fixed hostility to the employment of troops at polling-places. Every administration which has ever passed a force bill, or even made a serious endeavor to do so, has lost the House of Representatives at the next election.' 'All the congressional districts of the South exc. four sent [in 1878] Democrats up to Washington. These men were determined to repeal the Federal election laws, or "Force Bills", which provided for the supervision of elections by appointees of the Federal courts and empowered the Federal marshals and deputy marshals to use soldiers to keep order at the polls' (Prof. D. S. MUZZEY, The Am. Adventure, ii. 119).

fore. The word *forehanded,* now obs. in Eng., is still current in Am. in the sense of *well-to-do, prosperous.* 'He became a very forehanded man at one time; travelled about in private cars and gave other evidences of opulence.' Another compound, also obs. in Eng. but surviving in Am., is *fore-room,* meaning *front room.* 'Low, white cottages, of which the fore-rooms, at least, were as if sealed in perpetual slumber.'

foreign. In Am. not only *belonging to another country,* but, in one connexion, *belonging to another State.* 'A favorite device is to lay a lower tax on corporations chartered by a state than on "foreign corporations", a legal term which includes all corporations chartered by other states but doing business in the state concerned' (Prof. A. B. HART, Actual Government, 387). 'As each state of the U.S. has plenary incorporating power, a corporation incorporated in one state was early and still is held to be foreign with respect to all others' (Encycl. Soc. Sci. vi. 354). This use of the term seems to be confined to the particular instance mentioned. In some Eng. dial. the word *foreigner* may be applied to a person not living in the immediate neighbourhood.

former is often used in Am., in place of *Ex-,* as a prefix to a title. 'Former President Grant, as Special Commissioner, negotiated such a treaty with the Mexican representative' (C. P. HOWLAND, Survey of Am. Foreign Relations, 1931, 57). 'Former Ambassador White was not a partisan' (D. LAWRENCE, True Story of Woodrow Wilson, 245). 'The opposition to the idea of a league of nations expressed by former Senator Beveridge' (W. S. HOLT, Treaties Defeated by the Senate, 251).

four hundred. See first quotation. 'A chance remark of McAllister in 1890 that about four hundred people

in N.Y. comprised the inner circle gave coinage to an expression which became synonymous the country over for the smart set. Every considerable city soon had its "Four Hundred", and local newspapers vied with their N.Y. contemporaries in giving prominence to society news' (Prof. A. M. SCHLESINGER, The Rise of the City, 153). 'Indulgent acceptance of European snobbishness becomes the easier in view of the wide interest bestowed on our own mushroom "four hundred", and, indeed, on any person who offers the slightest pretext for notoriety.' 'People in Edgham aped society, they even talked about the "four hundred"' (M. E. WILKINS FREEMAN, By the Light of the Soul, 93). 'Who are the four hundred in N.Y.'s colored society? An outsider would be very bold who should attempt to answer. Twenty-five years ago the New Yorker born, esp. the descendant of some prominent anti-slavery worker, would have held foremost social position' (MARY W. OVINGTON, Half a Man, 176).

frame. This word is found in Am. in various compounds such as *frame building, frame cottage, frame dwelling,* and *frame house,* which denote a rustic building constructed with a skeleton frame of timber and usually covered in also with wood, often in the form of shingles. 'Our [college] chapel was a small frame building with a bell in the tower' (JULIA B. FORAKER, I Would Live it Again, 63). 'It was a small, plain, frame cottage, such as a village carpenter might build' (HAMLIN GARLAND, Roadside Meetings, 69). 'Walter's father built, in front of this, a two-story frame dwelling' (B. J. HENDRICK, Earlier Life of Walter H. Page, 13). 'The growing popularity of brick and the popular interest taken in concrete construction go to indicate that the era of frame houses in the U.S. is beginning to pass.' 'No sooner had the people of each colony overcome the initial difficulties of settlement than they began building substantial frame houses' (T. J. WERTENBAKER, The First Americans, 286). 'With the fee received from one of his earliest important cases he purchased a modest frame house in an unfashionable part of Springfield' (W. E. CURTIS, The True Abraham Lincoln, 45).

†Am. *frame-up* = Eng. *trumped-up charge*. 'They were taking the view that the McNamaras were innocent and the case against them a frameup' (LINCOLN STEFFENS, Autobiography, 659). 'From the beginning there could be no doubt that it was a frame-up. The crime and the alleged criminals simply did not fit' (L. ADAMIC, Dynamite, 312). A person who becomes the victim of such a charge is said to be *framed*. 'Governor Roosevelt pardoned 6 N.Y. City women who had been "framed" by the police vice squad' (World Almanac for 1932, 94).

franchise. In G. A. Birmingham's novel, *The Lost Tribes*, Mr. Mervyn, an Irish Protestant clergyman, misunderstands a reference made to 'the franchise' by Bobby Sebright, an Am. journalist. To Mr. Mervyn the word means the power of voting. Bobby explains that 'on our side franchise means sole right of running street cars, electric light, telephones and general public conveniences granted by State Congress (*sic*) or other representative authority in return for considerations of value given by applicant financiers to ward bosses'. It is thus equivalent to what in Eng. would be called a *commercial privilege* or *concession*. In Eng. the word is sometimes used in a sense akin to the Am., but only in legal documents. If we hear of a debate in Eng. on *the franchise question*, we may infer that the topic of discussion has been a matter connected with the suffrage. In Am. it would mean a discussion of the granting of privileges by public bodies to private companies. 'There had been political

corruption in the granting of franchises in Eng. as well as in our own country, in the early days of railroad development.' 'To release itself from dependence upon private water companies has taken the City of London a great many years and cost it a great deal of money. The franchises of the water companies supplying London had become very valuable.' 'Franchises of one kind and another won over the street railways and many of the public service corporations to the support of the Magee-Flinn organization' (Dr. H. ZINK, City Bosses in U.S. 126).

The word also denotes membership of the organization of newspapers known as the Associated Press. 'Every newspaper having an Associated Press franchise contributes its share toward the expense of employing agents in the various cities.' 'He was sent to N.Y. in order to secure a press association franchise for the new journal' (Prof. G. R. GEIGER, The Philosophy of Henry George, 38).

fraternity. In Eng., except in its abstract sense, this word denotes a *religious brotherhood*. The Am. *fraternity* is an organization of students, usually designated by two or more Greek letters (e.g. the Phi Beta Kappa) and existing in the form of separate CHAPTERS in many colleges. There are in all about 250 fraternities and sororities (the similar organizations of women students) with 5,910 chapters. 'In Balliol there are three debating clubs, and they are of course in some sense rivals. Like the fraternities in an Am. college, they look over the freshmen each year pretty closely' (J. CORBIN, An Am. at Oxford, 54). Mr. Corbin tells us that 'the fraternity houses so widely diffused in Am. offer almost a counterpart of the halls of the golden age of the mediaeval university' (op. cit. 269). 'These very friends gathered to form the first chapter of a Greek letter fraternity at our college and— left me out. I did not know then that the fraternities do not admit Jews' (L. LEWISOHN, Up Stream, 89). 'Harvard had never wholeheartedly adopted the fraternity system which filled the social wants of under-graduates in most of the colleges' (H. J. COOLIDGE and R. H. LORD, Archibald Cary Coolidge, 61). The word is popularly abbreviated to *frat*. See also KEY.

A *fraternity* must be distinguished from a *fraternal order*, the Am. equiva-lent of the Eng. *friendly society*.

fraud. A term peculiar to Am. is *fraud order*, whose meaning is suffi-ciently indicated in the following quotations. 'Congress has enacted that any person or company which is obtaining money or property through the mails by means of false or fraudulent pretenses or promises, may be barred from the use of the mail entirely. Under a "fraud order" all mail directed to such person or company is stamped "Fraudulent" on the outside and returned to the sender' (C. KELLY, U.S. Postal Policy, 150). 'It is often impossible to prosecute the advertisers, and the most the post-office department can do is to issue what is known as a fraud order. Such an order peremp-torily and without redress stops the mail of the advertiser' (E. E. CALKINS and R. HOLDEN, The Art of Modern Advertising, 258).

freight. In Eng. this term is ap-plied to goods transported by water only. In Am. it includes land trans-port also. 'Much of the traffic on state highways consists of heavy trucks conveying freight for profit' (CASSIUS M. CLAY, The Mainstay of Am. Individualism, 208). Thus *freight train = goods train*; *freight car = goods wagon*; *freight depot = goods station*; and *freight yard = goods yard*. 'Two freight trains on the Pennsylvania Railroad crashed to-gether early to-day.' 'It would re-quire a railway caravan of 14,000 freight cars to carry the machines from the factory to the farmers'

(H. N. CASSON, Life of C. H. McCormick, 196). 'Two youths were seen prowling about the freight yards of the N.Y. Central.' The verb *freight* has a similar extension of meaning. 'Wagon teams met the steamer, and freighted goods far across the deserts to mines in Arizona.'

Accordingly the occupation of a *freighter* may be a landsman's job. A member of Congress, in an auto-biographical notice supplied to the 1903 Congressional Directory, says that he 'worked on his father's farm until the age of 14, when he took up the business of freighter, and for several years carried goods and miners from the end of the railroad in Nebraska to the mining and cattle camps in the Black Hills.' And Andy Adams (The Log of a Cowboy, 334) describes certain men as 'fine types of pioneer—buffalo hunters, freigh-ters, and other plainsmen'.

Freight train is often abbrev. to *freight*. 'He saw the fast freight approach at high speed.' 'He roused irate travelling-men for the 4.14 freight to Waterbury' (SINCLAIR LEWIS, Work of Art, 41).

See also ELEVATOR and SHIP.

fresh. Sir J. Foster Fraser has con-fessed to his embarrassment when one morning in N.Y. he told a young woman that she was looking very fresh, and found that he had to apologize for a remark that he had intended as a compliment (*Evening Standard*, July 12, 1926). In Am. *fresh = forward, saucy, presumptuous*. This use seems to be an appropriation of the German *frech*, assimilated to Eng. pronunciation. Cf. DUMB. In colloq. Eng. *fresh* has the quite different meaning of *exhilarated by drink*.

In Am. the term *freshman* may be applied to school pupils as well as college students. 'He would have given the tests to the second-year pupils or at least the freshmen of the high school.'

The term *freshwater college* is often used in Am. to denote a comparatively small college. It is so called, acc. to Webster, because the first large Am. colleges were situated on the seaboard. 'We seldom read of magnificent gifts to the smaller "freshwater" colleges in the U.S.; but graduates of these institutions hold their own in competition.' 'Greeneville College, a little "freshwater" institution near the banks of the Nolichucky River' (L. P. STRYKER, Andrew Johnson, 4). 'Just as, in Great Britain, he could not be persuaded to increase the emoluments of Oxford and Cambridge, but concentrated on the four Scottish universities that drew their students from the cottage and the city, so, in the United States, it was the "freshwater" college, engaged, for the large part, in training the sons and daughters of farmers and the proletariat, which received the most friendly consideration' (B. J. HENDRICK, Life of Andrew Carnegie, 602).

frills is not unknown in Eng. in the sense of *affectations* (e.g. putting on frills), but its fig. use is wider in Am., where it may denote *showy accomplishments* or *unnecessary adornments*. 'The quiet village street pleased him. So did the house, massive but with no undemocratic frills about it.' 'No Frills on Trains' is the headline of a newspaper paragraph reporting the decision of a railway company not to use gold leaf any longer in numbering its engines. 'There were no frills then, such as physical culture, manual training and the like' (M. GOUVERNEUR, As I Remember, 24).

frontier. 'By 1860 the frontier had advanced to a line running coincident with the western borders of Minnesota and Iowa, across the center of Nebraska and Kansas, and thence southward through approximately the middle of Texas' (Prof. A. E. MARTIN, Hist. of U.S. ii. 105). This passage is likely to bewilder any Eng. reader who is not aware of the

peculiar Am. meaning of *frontier*. What foreign country, he will ask, abutted on Minnesota as recently as 1860? The explanation is that, while in Eng. *frontier* means a boundary between two countries, or the territory adjacent to the boundary line on either side, in Am. it is used to denote the limit of settlement within the U.S., as defined by a certain density of population. Thus, in his *Oxford Hist. of the U.S.* (i. 3, footnote) Prof. S. E. Morison warns his readers: '*Frontier*, wherever found in this book, will be understood as having exclusively the Am. connotation. For the international frontier the word *boundary* is used.' Those who are interested in the subject will find in *The Frontier in Am. Hist.*, by Prof. F. J. Turner, an illuminating study of the movement of this imaginary line from generation to generation. A briefer account is F. L. Paxson's article in the *Encycl. Soc. Sci.*, vol. vi. The following examples illustrate the Am. usage. 'Northampton, though a frontier town, was [in 1727] one of the most aristocratic and prosperous communities outside of Boston' (Prof. H. W. SCHNEIDER, The Puritan Mind, 102). Walter Hines Page, returning in 1883 to his native State, N. Carolina, after nearly five years' absence, writes: 'It occurred to me for the first time that this region is yet a frontier—a new land untouched except by pioneers, pioneers who had merely lingered until they had thought the land worn out' (B. J. HENDRICK, Earlier Life of Walter H. Page, 161). 'The life was a mixture of frontier and civilization' (F. J. STIMSON, My U.S. 14). 'The penalty of the frontier, which exalts the hardier virtues, lies in its depreciation of qualities which are not immediately serviceable' (L. EINSTEIN, Roosevelt, 99).

Hence *frontiersman*. 'He was a typical frontiersman of the older sort. Standing 6 feet, broad-shouldered, ruddy-faced, with abundant curling hair worn long at the back, he was of the truculent, animal tribe.' 'Because of their isolation, the frontiersmen developed self-confidence and practical economic, social, and political equality' (Prof. A. E. MARTIN, Hist. of U.S. i. 23).

fry. For *fry the fat*, a term of the Am. political vocab., see quotations. '"Fat-frying" is a figure of speech—in politics. It is a fact in hog-killing. It owes its use or vogue to the cartoonists. They made it form an idea to the mind by flashing it on view as a picture to the eye. As the "fat" is "fried" out of hogs for a distinct use, so were, so are, campaign contributions "fried out" of big business men who feel dependent on "government" for favors.' 'It is reported that the chairman of the Rep. national committee is disheartened because his new frying pan won't work. It is stated that the trusts and corporations and capitalists refuse to have the fat fried out of them, and that the Rep. campaign is already on the point of collapse.' 'All the "frying of fat" out of protected manufacturers has gone upon the understanding that large subscriptions to a party fund carry with them the right to dictate the laws affecting the business of the subscribers.'

††**fudge.** In addition to the Eng. meaning of *fabrication* or *nonsense*, this word denotes in Am. a sweetmeat made of sugar in many varieties. 'Apple butter, chocolate fudge— dainties that usually require careful watching and constant stirring.' 'The student's college work is better done without a running accompaniment of fudge and other between time things to eat.'

fundamental. For the Am. derivative *Fundamentalist* see the first quotation. 'Those who believed in the letter of the Bible and refused to accept any teaching, even of science, which seemed to conflict with it, began in 1921 to call themselves Fundamentalists' (F. L. ALLEN, Only

Yesterday, 199). 'They make selective appeals; one, for example, to fundamentalist constituents, another to people of advanced theological position' (H. PAUL DOUGLASS, Church Comity, 149).

†**funeral.** In Eng., restricted to the actual interment, together with the ceremonies at the graveside. In Am., applied also to ceremonies that may take place at a different time and place. Thus, on the death of a Senator, a newspaper announces: 'An official funeral will be held in the Senate chamber to-morrow at two o'clock, and the body will be taken to Tennessee to-morrow evening.' In connexion with the death of another Senator, it is announced that 'as the weather was cold and cloudy to-day, it was decided to hold the funeral in the armory, instead of on the lawn of his home, as had been intended.' Another paper reports that the funeral of a young Springfield woman, who had died in a N.Y. hospital, was 'held Sunday afternoon at the home of her mother'. On the death of President McKinley the Mayor of N.Y. appealed to the Secretary of State that the arrangements for the obsequies might 'include a public funeral in this city'. The *Dict. of Am. Biog.* tells us that on the death of C. W. Eliot, ex-President of Harvard, 'his body was brought to Cambridge, and after a funeral in Appleton Chapel was interred in Mt. Auburn Cemetery'. 'The funeral was held in the room where Mrs. Rockfeller died' (J. T. FLYNN, God's Gold, 464).

Am. *funeral director* or *mortician* = Eng. *undertaker.*

furnishings. This word, in common use in Am., does not precisely correspond to the Eng. *furniture.* It includes a great many articles of household equipment that would not come under that term. 'The police have found the robbers who have been stripping partly completed houses of lead pipes, telephone wires, gas and water fixtures, and other furnishings.' 'To none of his furnishings had he given more careful thought than to the rugs' (Prof. N. W. STEPHENSON, Nelson W. Aldrich, 407). 'The case had its origin in an investigation of the Commission into the house-furnishings industry. One section of the report was devoted to aluminum kitchen utensils' (T. C. BLAISDELL, The Federal Trade Commission, 240). There is an Eng. approximation to this use in the term *soft furnishings*, sometimes used in shops to denote curtains, &c.

fuse, fusion. In Am. these terms are used not only in the lit. sense, as in Eng., but fig. of a political combination between different parties. What in Eng. is called *a coalition government* would become in Am. *a fusion administration*. 'The next year the factions fused and elected a compromise ticket with Smith Ely as mayor' (Dr. H. ZINK, City Bosses in U.S. 122). 'There is actual fusion in one State only, Nebraska, where the Democrats and Populists agreed upon a common ticket.' 'In Texas, a Rep.-Populist fusion elected two Congressmen' (L. M. HACKER and B. B. KENDRICK, The U.S. since 1865, 308).

G

†**gainful.** In Eng., where the use of *gainful* is rare, the idea expressed in -*ful* is prominent. It is thus a synonym for *lucrative* or *highly remunerative*. In Am., on the other hand, it does not suggest more than the receipt of payment for services rendered—payment, indeed, which may not supply more than a bare livelihood. Hence Am. *a gainful occupation* = Eng. *a paid occupation*. 'In Iowa the proportion of women engaged in gainful occupations is increasing at a rapid rate.' 'Not forced by circumstances to enter a gainful occupation, he followed his

scholarly bent' (Dict. Am. Biog. ix. 191). 'There are nearly 30 million human beings in Europe and Am. who are able and willing to work but who are not able to find gainful occupation' (Dr. N. M. BUTLER, Looking Forward, 115). There are signs that this term is coming into use in Eng. in the Am. sense. Though not recognized by the *O.E.D.* or its Suppl., the expression appears in an official volume of statistics, published in 1934, concerning the census of 1931.

gait. In Eng., *manner of walking* or *stepping*. In Am. *pace* also. 'Sometimes Schwartz [a motorist] was passed by faster travelers; occasionally he passed machines not maintaining his gait.' 'The horses were capable of a faster gait without tiring' (ANDY ADAMS, The Outlet, 311). 'Driving the horse at his utmost speed for short distances, instead of the usual practice of driving longer distances at a slower gait' (G. T. CLARK, Leland Stanford, 354).

gall, when used fig., denotes in Eng. *rancour*, but in Am. *presumption*, *impudence*. Thus, Lincoln Steffens (in McClure's Mag., Oct. 1903) records that a certain leader of a reform movement in municipal politics sent to the ward leaders on both sides for their lists of captains, lieutenants, and heelers. 'They refused, with expressions of astonishment at his "gall".'

gallon. When Am. motorists cross the border into Canada for the first time, they are annoyed at being charged more per gallon for their GAS. They soon discover, however, that its price is not really higher, for the Canadian gallon is identical with the British imperial gallon, with a content of 277¼ cubic inches. The standard Am. gallon is the old Winchester gallon, or wine-gallon, containing 231 cubic inches.

See PINT and QUART.

game. The charge is sometimes brought against Am. sport that it is obsessed by the competitive spirit, so that sheer enjoyment of the fun of the thing is almost driven out by an inordinate desire to win. If one were to take their vocabularies as evidence, however, one would infer that the competitive element was more prominent in Eng. than in Am. In football, for instance, an Englishman speaks of the Oxford and Cambridge *match*. An Am. would speak of the Oxford and Cambridge *game*. Thus a newspaper refers to 'the place from which the midshipmen's football squad comes to the annual Army and Navy game.' 'One day in Nov., 1908, I went to Princeton to see the Princeton-Yale football game' (W. G. McAdoo, Crowded Years, 115). 'The homecoming of the victors of the World Series of baseball games' (Sen. H. B. Hawes, Philippine Uncertainty, 26).

See also CONFIDENCE and SHELL.

gang by no means invariably denotes in Am. a number of men associated for a criminal purpose. It is the common term for a group of boys who habitually play together and otherwise take pleasure in each other's society. 'Nothing is more forlorn than the boy who has no gang at whose fire of friendship he may warm himself' (JANE ADDAMS, The Second 20 Years at Hull-House, 364). 'An Eastern family of boys came to Sacramento, and they fascinated me and my gang' (L. STEFFENS, Autobiog. 99). 'It is essential to distinguish between the juvenile or adolescent gangs, which, although under the sorry auspices of modern slum life, must be considered as recreation groups, and the adult criminal groups' (Encycl. Soc. Sci. vi. 565).

Hence the verb *gang* in a corresponding sense. 'He [Woodrow Wilson when a boy] was frail and never ganged with his fellows' (W. A. WHITE, Masks in a Pageant, 348).

The derivative *gangster*, on the other hand, always denotes a member of a company of violent criminals. 'As a trolley-car was passing along First Avenue, it found itself between two crowds of fighting gangsters on opposite sides of the street.' 'Chicago has never rested lightly whether under the yoke of its gangsters, its public utilities, or its reformers' (Prof. C. E. MERRIAM, Chicago, 303).

garbage. In Am. this word is spec. used to denote a certain variety of house refuse, as thus defined: 'Refuse generally is of three types: garbage, ashes, and rubbish. The term *garbage* is properly employed to mean kitchen wastes, such as the meat, fruit, and vegetable matter left over in the preparation of food; it is always in some state of decomposition, and the odors which arise from it are disagreeable. *Rubbish* includes papers, bottles, metals, rags, crates, cartons, bits of wood and similar objects; it is, as a mass, readily burned. The term *ashes* is, of course, confined to the products of combustion of coal and other fuel. . . . The city [of N.Y.] requires that the three classes of refuse be kept separate at the households, so that they may be collected separately and their disposition facilitated' (N.Y. Times, May 24, 1931). 'Some municipalities have a separate collection for ashes, garbage and other rubbish, while others have all put together and taken up at one collection' (H. M. POLLOCK and W. S. MORGAN, Modern Cities, 145).

Hence *garbage barrel, garbage can,* and *garbage wagon.* 'When I described the wretched condition of the prodigal son, a girl wondered why he didn't search the garbage barrel for something to eat.' 'One prime fundamental of every restaurant business is the garbage can.' 'An old billy-goat prospecting in garbage cans along the alleys' (MARK SULLIVAN, Our Times, iii. 384). 'It does look like a shame to let Park Avenue remain a roadway for store trucks, garbage wagons, and other disagreeable things on wheels.'

gas. 'British Gas Will Invade New England' was the heading of a news item in the Springfield *Weekly Republican* of July 12, 1928. This would leave an Eng. reader completely mystified as well as startled until he recalled that in Am. *gas* is used, in addition to its other meanings, as an abbrev. of *gasoline*, the Am. term for *petrol*. The headline in question prefaced a report that the Royal Dutch Shell combine was about to invade the New Eng. territory, for years one of the Standard Oil strongholds. 'The old Ford rocked and rattled as I gave it gas.' 'Apartment houses, office buildings, traffic lights and gas stations are doing all they can to modernize it' (Prof. V. L. COLLINS, Princeton Past and Present, 8). R. R. Moton (What the Negro Thinks, 213) mentions a city where 'a Negro cannot get gas at a filling station patronized by whites'.

†Hence *step on the gas = apply the accelerator*, and hence, fig., *quicken one's pace, hurry up*. 'Many of the critics who protest against deliberate action on the part of the Senate are not interested in brakes. They want to step on the gas' (G. W. PEPPER, In the Senate, 20).

In Am. *gas tank* is the usual name for the reservoir of gas known in Eng. as a *gasometer*. 'A desolate seductive scenery was evolving out of factories and railroad yards—out of lonely wooden viaducts, drums of gas tanks, &c.' (D. DUDLEY, Dreiser and the Land of the Free, 58).

gate. Am. *get the gate* = Eng. *be shown the door, get the sack*. 'There are only two choices: either to give in and allow one's self to become stereotyped and vapid, or to stand out against it and get the gate' (E. WILSON, The Am. Jitters, 245).

gem. An Am. *gem* is not always a precious stone. It is sometimes a kind of light muffin. 'Muffins, gems, sally lunns, and other light breads' (Mrs. RORER's New Cook Book, 19). 'Maria took her place at the table. "Those gems look delicious" she observed. . . . Maria laughed, and buttered a gem' (MARY E. WILKINS FREEMAN, By the Light of the Soul, 442).

general is not a normal rank in the Am. army, but is held only, when specially conferred upon him by Congress, by the officer who is at the time chief of the staff. The list of 'highest ranking officers in the U.S. army' given in the 1934 *World Almanac* consists of one general, 35 major-generals, and 59 brigadier-generals. Acc. to the same authority there have been only nine holders of this rank since 1775. See LIEUTENANT.

The title, however, is freely claimed and used by men outside the army altogether. 'Gen. Bristow Has Resigned' is the headline of a newspaper paragraph which reports that 'Fourth Assistant Postmaster General Joseph L. Bristow has resigned'. 'In 1875 he was judge-advocate-general on the staff of Governor Gaston, from which his title of "general" was acquired.' 'Following the local custom, the Communist papers give Mr. Chamlee the title of "General"; but this means merely that he was at one time attorney general of Hamilton County' (E. WILSON, The Am. Jitters, 184).

Gentile. In Eng. a *non-Jew*. In Am., in some cases, a *non-Mormon*. 'Representative Gentiles of Salt Lake City have held a meeting and taken preliminary steps toward the organization of a non-Mormon party.' 'This stubborn contention hindered the growing friendliness between Mormon and Gentile and for many years kept Utah from statehood' (Prof. A. M. SCHLESINGER, The Rise of the City, 46).

gentleman. In the House of Commons, one M.P. refers to another not by name but as *the honourable member*. The Congressional equivalent is *the gentleman*. 'Reply to Mr. Mondell was made by Mr. Grosvenor (Rep.,

Ohio) "I should like to know", he said, "what light the gentleman has seen. The event that St. Paul figured in on his way to Damascus was not a circumstance to the light the gentleman has seen".'

When a more precise indication of identity is required, the Parliamentary expression is *the honourable member for* such-and-such a constituency. In the Am. House of Representatives reference is made to *the gentleman from* such-and-such a State. It is significant, by the way, that it is not the DISTRICT (q.v.) but the State from which a member comes that is thus mentioned. Acc. to the theory of the Am. Constitution, a member of the House of Representatives is regarded as representing, like a Senator, the whole State and not a mere division of it. Thus, a member will be referred to as 'the gentleman from Alabama', not as 'the gentleman from the Fifth District of Alabama'. 'The presiding officer recognized the young Dem. with a nod of answering humor, and responded: "The gentleman from N.Y."' (T. DIXON, The Clansman, 138). A novel of Booth Tarkington's, with a Congressman as its principal character, is entitled *The Gentleman from Indiana*.

get has a few idiomatic uses peculiar to Am. Sometimes it would be represented in Eng. by *make*. 'I love to work, but this God-forsaken country gets me discouraged.' Sometimes it means *lay hold of*, *attract*, as when a traveller says: 'Cairo doesn't get me, altogether.' †It may signify *understand*. Thus the question 'Do you get me?' is equivalent to 'Do you take my meaning?' or 'Do you see my point?'

Except in a few locutions, such as *ill-gotten gains* and in the derivative *forgotten*, the past participle *gotten* is now archaic in Eng. It is still in everyday use in Am. 'The fire was gotten under control in about an hour.' 'The courts in their decisions have not gotten so far away from the correct use of language' (Prof. R. T. ELY, Evolution of Industrial Society, 190). 'An even more beautiful and splendidly gotten up memorial volume' (F. J. STIMSON, My U.S. 442). 'Correspondence has gotten into public print' (Prof. H. J. FORD, Woodrow Wilson, 191). 'Even a kitchen fire is gotten at some sacrifice of human life' (H. M. POLLOCK and W. S. MORGAN, Modern Cities, 126).

††Am. *get away with* = Eng. *bring off*, *secure the acceptance of*, *succeed in accomplishing*. 'A stewardess hoping to get away with any of these trite excuses before a Board of Inquiry might just as well have jumped overboard.' 'What amazes me is that these bankers and their railroads can get away with one valuation for taxes and another upon which railroad earnings are figured in percentage' (T. DREISER, Tragic Am. 101). 'The boys find that stealing is an easy way of supporting themselves. Many of them are getting away with it' (J. ADDAMS, The Second 20 Years at Hull-House, 315). 'London wondered how I could meet all the correspondents in town, tell them nothing, and get away with it' (Intimate Papers of Col. House, ii. 188). The Am. noun *getaway* = Eng. *escape*. 'The thieves opened each window catch, presumably to assure a quick getaway.' 'His confederates were blowing up the safety-box in the boot of the coach and making a getaway with the loot' (Dr. G. D. LYMAN, Saga of the Comstock Lode, 221).

Am. *get back at* = Eng. *turn the tables on*. 'If the President had not been vindictively anxious to get back at the packers for having eluded the administration in the beef trust cases, he could have accomplished his end effectively.' 'There is in Manila no power of the people or the press to get back at the government.'

Am. *get behind* = Eng. *support*, *back*. 'Good citizens should get behind candidates for aldermen who are clean and honest.'

Am. *get by* = Eng. *get through, pass muster*. 'Man is ever ready to go the easy way. He feels that there is plenty in the world so that he can get by without trying hard.' 'The post office authorities refused entry to my magazine, and I only got by through a series of accidents' (UPTON SIN-CLAIR, Money Writes, 52). 'If he works three days a week he manages to get by' (BRUCE CRAWFORD, in Culture in the South, 362).

†Am. *get on to* = Eng. *begin to realize, begin to understand.* 'Wise people are getting on to the fact that Eastwood is no ordinary real estate development.' 'The Porto Rico school teachers have been accumulating knowledge of English, and, incidentally, getting on to the manners and customs of folks of this and neighboring cities.'

†Am. *get there* = Eng. *succeed, achieve one's object.* 'Uncle Sam is a large body, moving slowly, but he has a way of "arriving", as the Frenchman says, or "getting there", in the Am. vernacular.' 'The modest candidate, who sits in his white toga in the far corner of the forum, waiting for the multitude to come and crown him aedile, is sympathetic and dramatic, but he rarely gets there.' 'He [Ibsen] seems an author very little dependent on his native vehicle in his prose dramas; he gets there, as far as concerns the effect with the reader or spectator, as well in Eng. as in his mother-speech' (W. D. HOWELLS, in North Am. Rev., July 1906).

Am. *get together* means more than *assemble*. It = Eng. *put (their) heads together, confer.* 'The strike has gone on long enough. The representatives of the unions and of the employers should get together and talk it over.' The expression often means *agree, unite.* 'The jury was unable to get together, and the presiding justice ordered them locked up for the night.' 'There is a strong disposition among the Citizens Union men and the Republicans to get together in the districts so as to make a more effective fight for the city ticket.' 'The present episode was a case of the Republicans composing their party differences and getting together' (MARK SULLIVAN, Our Times, iii. 263).

This expression may also be (1) an adj. or (2) a noun. (1) 'When finally the giant liner had been made fast, the passengers and those ashore forgot all about the delay in the get-together fun of the greeting.' 'Here was an invitation from Mr. Julius Rosenwald, inviting the members of the Advisory Commission to a get-together dinner' (Dr. FRANKLIN H. MARTIN, The Joy of Living, ii. 61). (2) 'It was the annual meeting and banquet of the alumni, and it was the biggest and most enthusiastic get-together the organization has ever held.' 'I returned for a get-together of my men to discuss their itinerary' (Dr. FRANKLIN H. MARTIN, op. cit. ii. 397).

The adj. *get-rich-quick* is applied in Am. to a fraudulent concern—such as might be called in Eng., as well as in Am., a wild-cat scheme—which exploits the desire of its victims to make money easily. 'The flaming get-rich-quick advts. of this plantation company were of a very seductive character.' 'There had been enormous increase in Am. railroad mileage. Get-rich-quick promoters were largely responsible' (J. K. WINKLER, J. Pierpont Morgan, 106).

See also ACROSS, GO, LEFT, NEXT.

Gideon. The guest at an Am. hotel may sometimes find in his room a copy of the Bible, which, he learns, has been placed there as a gift from the Gideons. The following newspaper extract will throw light upon the organization that bears this name. 'The religiously-minded commercial travellers, known as Gideons, have four prosperous camps in cities of N.Y. state.' The name is presumably derived from the story re-lated in Judges vii.

gift. 'It is time for me to see about my list of Christmas presents' is a remark heard in many an Eng. household at the beginning of Dec. In Am. the word *gifts* would take the place of *presents*, as, perhaps, it may soon do in Eng., for the advts. of Eng. shops at this season are introducing the Am. usage. 'A large part of the 64½ cents was merely a Christmas gift to the Am. silver producers' (Prof. IRVING FISHER, Mastering the Crisis, 62). 'On Christmas Gifts' is the title of a chapter in which 'Mr. Dooley' discourses on the subject.

The Southern expression, '*Christmas Gift!*' has now largely lost its original meaning and is simply a greeting, equivalent to '*Merry Christmas!*'

give. In Am. one sometimes finds *give way* appearing in the form *give away*. 'While attending to his locomotive he was hurled to death by the giving away of a bridge.' 'The epergne has given away to a hollow football filled with flowers.' 'He said that if the Democrats could not be united on a question like this they could not be united on anything, and he preferred to give away to some other leader.'

In Eng. a public man *gives* an interview. In Am. he *gives* it *out*. 'The interview given out by the Speaker yesterday.' 'The most important interview which William Howard Taft gave out while president' (Dict. Am. Biog. xi. 195).

Am. *given name* = Eng. *Christian name*. 'Are there regions in which the prevailing masculine given name is, for instance, William?' 'Senator Magee, whose given names were Christopher and Lyman' (Dr. H. ZINK, City Bosses in U.S. 230). 'An Eng. visitor in the middle eighties notes with grave consternation the difficulty Am. parents have in keeping children from swearing and from calling parents by their given names' (H. RHODES, Am. Towns and People, 233). See also FIRST.

go. Am. *go out* = Eng. *come to grief, collapse*. 'The middle span of the big railroad bridge went out as the result of floods, and it was impossible to send trains to the place of the wreck.'

The Am. compound *go-getter* denotes a person who, in Eng. idiom, has an eye to the main chance and is active in pursuit of it—a *pushing fellow*. 'The type that comes up now out of the depths of our cities as bandits, or politicians, or go-getters in business' (L. STEFFENS, Autobiog. 249). 'The young man who delivered milk for a rival company was a go-getter and soon took most of Lenard's customers' (L. ADAMIC, Laughing in the Jungle, 282). 'In the course of years Franklin has learned that the thing which is impossible to the go-getter frequently comes round of its own motion to him who waits' (P. RUSSELL, Benjamin Franklin, 238).

From this word a verb *go-get* has been coined by back-formation. 'The students herded to hear breezy young instructors exhale the new gospel of go-getting' (F. F. BOND, Mr. Miller of the *Times*, 170).

gold. At the time when gold was being transferred in large amounts from Eng. to the U.S., one could read in the newspapers of bullion being shipped from Southampton in the form of what were variously called gold bars or gold bricks. †In Am. *gold brick* denotes something entirely different—not a block of precious metal but a counterfeit that is deceptively made to look like it. It thus comes to be used fig. to mean a *fraud* or *sham*. 'Direct nomination, as we have seen it, is the greatest gold brick that was ever handed to a confiding people.' 'In many cases the diploma that the student carries home with him at the conclusion of his course is nothing less than a gold brick. It has made him believe that he has gotten an education, when he actually never had an opportunity to find out what an education is' (BOOKER T. WASHINGTON, My Larger Education, 292).

'The first-generation Jewish immigrant, who has prospered among his confrères in the Ghetto, may move to the Gold Coast in a vain attempt to forget his Old World heritage' (M. A. ELLIOTT and F. E. MERRILL, Social Disorganization, 218). 'The energetic and shrewd [immigrant inhabitants of the slums] soon seek greener pastures on the gold coast, where they hope to rear their children in luxurious oblivion of the sordid world of the slum' (op. cit. 597). Obviously the *Gold Coast* of these passages cannot be the British colony of that name in W. Africa. The term is employed in Am. to denote a district mainly occupied by wealthy and fashionable residents. It seems to have been first spec. used at Harvard. 'This policy resulted in a rapid development of what was known as the "Gold Coast", a group of dormitories to which the well-to-do students flocked.' 'The "Gold Coast", that group of lavish dormitories which will not even rent a room to an applicant until the youngster's social status has been carefully investigated.' In Chicago the term is applied to a district which stretches along the Lake Shore Drive. It is so well known in this sense that a sociological study of contrasted areas, published by the University of Chicago Press, appears under the title, *The Gold Coast and the Slum*. In a N.Y. paper, a column of news from Hollywood is headed 'From the Gold Coast.'

gondola. 'A car on the Lake Shore electric road was wrecked last night. It ran into an open switch and crashed into a gondola loaded with coal.' The kind of gondola that is exposed to such accidents has nothing Venetian about it except the name. It is a railway wagon, either with no sides at all or with very low sides, and is used to carry goods that are not liable to be injured by bad weather. 'Ships must give way to freight-cars, bottoms to gondolas' (F. J. STIMSON, My U.S. 72). 'They

left the next morning on a freight-train, travelling in a low roofless car known as a "gondola": the gondola was about two-thirds full of gravel' (E. WILSON, The Am. Jitters, 176). 'The heaped-up gondolas continued their progress from Connellsville to the several Carnegie furnaces' (B. J. HENDRICK, The Life of Andrew Carnegie, 457).

good. Am. *good* often = Eng. *well*, without any ethical implications. 'The commissioner said it was a purely social call, and that the President was looking good.' 'To feel good you must be comfortable, and to be comfortable you must have a light, thin, cool suit' (Advt.). 'The western counties have been in the habit of turning in large assessments because they want to show up good.' 'Is it not our duty "to do the backward nations good", especially if they have oil wells? To be sure, in colloquial Am. the phrase "to do them good" acquires according to accent and intonation rather different meanings' (NORMAN THOMAS, America's Way Out, 40).

†Am. *good and* = Eng. *thoroughly, quite*. 'Oh! for a reviewer who will occasionally sit down good and hard on the book written only for commercial purposes!' 'The landslide or earthquake, whichever it was, struck Massachusetts good and hard.' 'Just say to yourself, "Oh, but this will make my family and guests good and warm".'

†Am. *good for* = Eng. *valid for, admitting to*. 'A 50-cent combination ticket good for every amusement on the island.' 'Mileage books, good for 1,000 miles' travel.' 'Each received a ticket good for a night's lodging' (Dr. H. ZINK, City Bosses in the U.S. 114). 'Paid-up accident and sickness insurance policies good for the rest of their days on earth' (KATHERINE MAYO, Soldiers What Next! 19). Cf. the French *bon pour*. The expression *Good for you!* = *Bravo!* or *Well done!* 'During his

speech there were many shouts of "Good for you!" and similar expressions of approbation.'

††The Eng. use of *make good* is normally trans. only. In Am. it may be intrans. also, meaning *acquit oneself satisfactorily, fulfil expectations, achieve success*. 'With no financial experience whatever, he was put into the Treasury in true Am. style, and there he made good.' 'In the heart of every young person lies a certain fear that he may not make good, for he is conscious of a weakness in himself that he is not sure of in anyone else' (JANE ADDAMS, The Second 20 Years at Hull-House, 190). 'The President said: "When I appoint a man to office I don't want him to thank me. I want him to make good"' (G. W. PEPPER, In the Senate, 76). 'What interested me on that fascinating trip was to see that the Bolshevik government was making good, and without compromise, too' (L. STEFFENS, Autobiog. 806).

The Am. colloquialism *the goods* denotes *the real thing, the genuine article*. Thus, an editor, arranging for the salary of a new reporter, is represented as telling him that it will be increased at the end of a term if he is the goods.

†The expression *deliver the goods* means much the same as *make good*, but implies that the satisfaction is given by an actual transfer of something (e.g. votes). It is a familiar word in the vocab. of Am. politics. 'Jones is said to have promised Lucas County to Johnson. If he is able to deliver the goods, he will add five votes to the Dem.-Independent combination.' 'The delegates to the various conventions are to be chosen on Tuesday; and, as it is good politics to make them deliver the goods as soon as possible, they will be expected to assemble in their several conventions soon after their election.'

The Eng. noun *goods* in such terms as *goods depot, goods train*, is represented in Am. by FREIGHT (q.v.).

goody, a contraction of *goodwife*, is now obs. in Eng., exc. in dial. It once denoted an elderly woman in humble life. It is still in use at Harvard (and possibly some other Am. colleges) as the name for a woman who looks after the rooms of students. 'The only service we had or thought of [at Harvard] was that of the "goody", so-called, who came every day to make the beds and clean up the rooms' (J. H. Choate, in his Life by E. S. MARTIN, i. 62).

gore is now obs. in Eng., exc. in dial., but still current in Am., in the sense of a wedge-shaped piece of land. 'There are many and various size vacant gores throughout the widened part of Elm Street. These gores are of little use by themselves, and their only real utility is to extend over them the buildings adjoining them.'

gouge is sometimes used in Am. as a somewhat gruesome metaphor to describe the extraction of money under more or less pressure. 'Every day hundreds of persons are gouged for the extra nickel on riding back to the various express stations.' 'We stood to lose a little over a million apiece right there, and no knowing what the crowd that was under the market would gouge us for in the end' (G. H. LORIMER, Old Gorgon Graham, 120). The milder metaphor *squeeze* would generally represent the same idea in Eng.

grab. The Am. compound *grab-bag* = Eng. *lucky dip*. 'To read one of Mr. Chesterton's columns is like putting your hand into a penny grab-bag; there is no possible telling what you will draw out.' 'A further examination gives the impression that we are plunging into a sort of literary grab-bag, and curiosity as to what will come out next becomes the predominant element in the consciousness' (W. M. PAYNE, Editorial Echoes, 156). 'Roosevelt abruptly reached into the Dem. grab-bag of political promises, and demanded that railroad-rate making powers be conferred upon the Interstate Commerce Commission' (S. H. ACHESON, Joe Bailey, 173).

grade is a word in much more frequent use in Am. than in Eng. Sometimes it = Eng. *gradient*. 'All vehicles have to ascend South Street, which has a grade of 12 per cent.' 'Alterations of street grades left little houses perched on bluffs or sunk in dingy pits' (F. E. LEUPP, Walks about Washington, 46).

Am. *grade crossing* or *crossing at grade* = Eng. *level crossing*. 'This party of several people, filling a car operated by one of themselves, were actually engaged in racing with a railroad train for a grade crossing in the distance.' 'The menace to human life caused by the great number of railroad grade crossings' (W. G. McADOO, Crowded Years, 133).

Grade is also a term of classification in Am. elementary schools, which are accordingly sometimes called *grade schools*, or *the grades*, and their teachers *grade teachers*. 'In the British isles the classes are designated by standards, and these are supposed to correspond to our grades.' 'The next division [above the kindergarten] is usually the primary, extending over 3 to 6 years, followed by about 4 years of the grammar school; these two systems taken together are often called simply the grades' (Prof. A. B. HART, Actual Government, 543). 'He escaped the Yale for which his father planned and an education other than that of the grades' (Prof. C. E. MERRIAM, Chicago, 185). 'In all its camps in Colorado this company has established kindergartens, libraries, and, in remote places, grade schools for the children of its employees' (W. J. GHENT, Our Benevolent Feudalism, 61). 'The theory of public school music has been to have a special teacher of music to visit all the schools in town, the grade teachers attempt-

ing little between his visits exc. setting the class to sing music already familiar.' A school which is too small to permit of such classification is called an *ungraded school*. 'A public-school teacher was elected to teach at an ungraded country school having 34 pupils.' See also ENLISTED.

The verb *grade* is naturally used to denote the process of classification. 'The number of children is great enough to allow complete grading.' It also = Eng. *mark* in connexion with examinations. 'They are now teaching or grading papers.' 'Lodge demanded too much of his students and graded their papers with undue severity' (H. F. PRINGLE, Theodore Roosevelt, 37). (In Eng. one may grade eggs and other marketable commodities, but not examination papers.) It frequently = Eng. *graduate* in the sense of *apportion acc. to a scale*. 'While the grading of an inheritance tax is wise, it should not be based upon the value of the whole estate bequeathed, but upon the various bequests received.'

The intrans. use of the verb is also common in Am. It may mean either (1) *rank*, or (2) *vary by gradual stages*. (1) 'The ordinary man is not even 25 p/c efficient in telling other people what he means. What should we think of a transportation system or a postal service which graded no better than that?' 'Flavia's subjective mind graded higher than her objective mind' (L. N. WRIGHT, Limbs of an Old Family Tree, 81). (2) 'The type graded downward into the lower invertebrates.' 'Racially and culturally, the population grades without abrupt break from the native Indians to the white aristocracy' (E. B. REUTER, Race Mixture, 35).

graduate. In Am. the verb *graduate* is more commonly trans. than intrans. (the original signification of the word thus being preserved), and it is followed in the passive by *from* instead of *at*. 'Gouverneur Morris had been graduated from old King's

College with the Class of 1768' (Dr. N. M. BUTLER, Looking Forward, 344). Accordingly, Am. *whence he was graduated* = Eng. *where he graduated.* 'He has taught political economy at Oxford, whence he was graduated with high honors.'

A more important difference is that *graduate* and *graduation* are used in Am. to signify the completion of a course at any kind of educational institution. 'A loyal Harrovian, and as such an ardent admirer of Palmerston, also a Harrow graduate.' 'An unusually large number of graduates in all departments of the Young Women's Christian Association received their diplomas last evening.' 'Wanted: Bright clean boys, for office work; must be public school graduates' (Advt.). 'It is these high school graduates of June who become the college students of the following autumn' (Dr. A. FLEXNER, Universities, 52). 'I was not a graduate of an Am. seminary' (Dr. F. J. KINSMAN, Salve Mater, 56). 'She developed such an interest in cooking that her family urged her to attend the Boston Cooking School. After her graduation from that institution in 1889, she etc.' (Dict. Am. Biog. vi. 276). 'A day when a class of boys of the King's School of Canterbury was graduated' (W. WINTER, Shakespeare's England, 180). In Am. *graduate nurse* is sometimes used for *trained nurse.* 'I had seen how ill-fitted most graduate nurses were to take care of children' (E. GOLDMAN, Living My Life, 170). 'Constitutionality was again questioned on the ground that the exemption of graduate nurses from the provisions of the law was unfair discrimination' (M. C. CAHILL, Shorter Hours, 115).

Accordingly the school functions known in Eng. as *prize-days* or *speech-days* become in Am. *graduation exercises,* at which, in girls' schools, those pupils who are leaving wear *graduation* or *graduating costumes,* or *dresses,* or *frocks,* or *gowns.* 'The annual graduation exercises of the schoolship St. Mary's were held last night on board the ship.' 'This spring, girls are having their graduation frocks made so that they will be useful toilets for dressy occasions all summer.' 'She often used to go into the spare chamber and gaze at her graduating dress, which was spread out on the bed' (M. E. WILKINS FREEMAN, By the Light of the Soul, 217).

graft, used in Eng. in its horticultural and surgical senses only, is a common term in Am. to denote illegitimate profit derived by holders of political or municipal office or by persons otherwise engaged in public affairs. It is sometimes applied to the corrupt taking of money in business also. 'The public officials were once honest and efficient. To-day the whole State is honeycombed with corruption. Graft is so common as to excite no particular attention.' 'The distribution of titles by retiring British ministers is really a refined sort of social graft, and the custom easily lends itself to the paying off of political debts by a played-out and politically bankrupt premier.' 'The English call "privileges" the special interests we call grafts—franchises, special laws, &c.' (L. STEFFENS, Autobiog. 704).

Hence the verb *graft.* 'The policeman thought of Tammany days, when a police badge was license to graft.' 'In some respects the company's management made a better showing than its two big competitors. There had been much salary grafting, but less than in the Mutual or the Equitable.' 'Large business houses felt the loss from the petty grafting of stamps by office boys' (F. J. HASKIN, The Am. Government, 71).

Also *grafter.* 'The Cuban political leaders proved themselves grafters; hunters after political office and the perquisites that accompany public position.' 'The confusion and the unsettled conditions following the war presented ideal conditions for the speculator, the political manipulator, and the grafter' (Prof. A. E. MARTIN, Hist. of U.S. ii. 93).

grand stand. The *grand stand* from which spectators look on at a performance has a fig. use in Am., as illustrated in the following examples, where its employment suggests that a certain act has been performed for the sake of spectacular effect. It corresponds largely to the Eng. expression *playing to the gallery*. 'He had instigated the proceedings against the Beef Trust. He would be an excellent man to associate with the Administration in the railroad matter, for the grand stand uses the Administration intended to make of it.' 'The fact that there is a vital defect in the bill introduced into the legislature to abate the free pass evil suggests the question, Is it a grand stand play?' 'There is nothing that pleases the typical Greek more than to be the center of attraction—to be in the limelight. There is no better way of expressing this element of character than to adopt the slang phrase, and say that the Greeks are a nation of "grand stand players"' (Dr. H. P. FAIRCHILD, Greek Immigration to the U.S. 30).

grandfather. The 15th Amendment to the Federal Constitution provides that 'the right of citizens of the U.S. to vote shall not be denied or abridged by the U.S. or by any State on account of race, color, or previous condition of servitude'. In order that Negroes might nevertheless be prevented from voting, some of the Southern States wrote into their own constitutions clauses imposing educational or property qualifications for the franchise. Then, for the benefit of illiterate whites, they added a clause admitting to the suffrage any man who lacked these qualifications, provided that he had voted in or before 1867 or was the son or grandson of such person. Such a clause is popularly known as a *grandfather clause*. 'By "grandfather clauses", vesting the suffrage in classes whose grandfathers could vote, the Negro vote was made a nullity' (T. C. PEASE, The U.S. 485).

grange. It is possibly the archaic Eng. use of this term for a *barn* that suggested its adoption in Am. as the name for an *agricultural association*, first established in 1867, esp. among the farmers of the North West. 'The Farmers' Association of Ontario, which in Canada corresponds to the State granges of the U.S.' 'A modification of the immigration laws so as to permit granges and other farmer organizations to secure labor on contracts from northern Europe.' The movement which found expression in the formation of the granges is known as the *Granger movement*. The *Granger laws* were laws, passed by several States, which imposed various restrictions on the railroads in the attempt to prevent unjust discrimination and extortion in freight and passenger tariffs.

greaser is a colloq. term in Am. for a *Mexican* or *Spanish-American*. 'It describes the marvels of the desert, the Indian, the greaser, and the gold-hunter.' 'He has roughed it in Arizona, crossed the plains, and has mingled with greasers in Mexico.' 'As the Am. immigrants [in California] gained in number over the "greasers" and the yellow men they determined to hold a convention for the establishment of a civil government' (Prof. D. S. MUZZEY, The Am. Adventure, i. 445).

gridiron is used fig. in Am. to denote a *football field*. 'Let him journey to Am. League Park or to the more historic gridirons at Princeton, Cambridge, New Haven, or Philadelphia. There he will witness an Am. college football eleven in the throes of final preparation for the great annual battles.' 'The collapse of a flimsy grandstand at Des Moines is a reminder that the damage to life and limb at a football game is not all on the gridiron.' 'A close study of records would be required to show whether the fatalities are greater in polo, horse-racing, or even on the gridiron than in automobile road racing.' 'At a gridiron dinner Roosevelt shook his finger under the nose of the great J. P. Morgan' (J. T. FLYNN, God's Gold, 383). Here *gridiron dinner* has nothing to do with football. Nor does it denote, as one might suppose, a dinner cooked on a gridiron. There is in Washington an organization of newspaper correspondents, known as the Gridiron Club, at whose dinners it is customary to caricature and satirize, in their presence, some of the leading public men of the day. It is to one of these dinners that Mr. Flynn refers.

grill is used fig. in Am. with the same meaning as the Eng. *put on the rack* in its fig. sense. Witnesses or prisoners who are put through a severe examination are said to be *grilled.* 'The grilling of adverse witnesses' (H. W. TAFT, Japan and Am. 81). 'The three men were grilled about their movements on the day of the Bridgewater hold-up' (A. G. HAYS, Let Freedom Ring, 289). 'He was arrested and taken to the prosecuting attorney's office to be grilled' (A. F. RAPER, The Tragedy of Lynching, 410).

grind. In Eng. a student who toils laboriously at his books is sometimes said to grind at them. In Am. he is himself called a *grind.* 'It has not been the fashion [at college] to work anywhere near to one's capacity for fear of being a "grind".' 'A girl "grind" who has worked passionately ever since she began to win prizes in the grammar school.' 'Woodberry was a "grind", i.e. just a studious undergraduate, not a society man, nor caring for sports' (F. J. STIMSON, My U.S. 51). 'The student, Karl Marx, was a ceaseless worker. He was what college students today term a "grind"' (E. B. CHAFFEE, The Protestant Churches and the Industrial Crisis, 148).

grip. In Am. *grip* means not only a *firm hold* but a *traveller's hand-bag*—presumably because he keeps it in his own grasp instead of entrusting it to a porter. 'The succession of Eng. party leaders packing their grips for Balmoral to see the King arouses intense interest.' 'Some of them had old leather grips or canvas bags, but many had no luggage at all' (ERNEST POOLE, The Harbor, 244). 'Doc put a couple of extra shirts in a grip and started off' (G. H. LORIMER, Old Gorgon Graham, 17).

grist. In Eng. the fig. use of *grist* is confined to the expression *bring grist to the mill.* In Am. it is much more widely used, as in the following examples. 'Stored away in a back closet of the treasurer's office, Kent County has a wholesale grist of lead pencils.' 'Mr. Davis gathers together in one section a grist of tales from sea captains.' 'The fourteen cells allotted to women prisoners would be wholly inadequate to contain the daily grist if more than the smallest proportion remained in custody longer than half an hour.' 'The City's Homicide Grist' (Headline of a newspaper report of several indictments for murder). 'A good-sized grist of matters was presented in the House last week Wednesday under suspension of the rules.' 'The total grist of enrollment of medical officers at this rally was very satisfactory' (Dr. FRANKLIN H. MARTIN, The Joy of Living, ii. 327).

The compound *grist-mill*, which is only dial. in Eng., is in general use in Am. It denotes a mill to which people of the neighbourhood bring small quantities of grain to be ground for their own use. 'As a young man David carried on the farm, and for 30 years ran a saw and grist-mill on a brook that runs through the farm.' 'There was an old grist-mill by the house, and he told me his brother escaped by hiding among the rushes in the flume' (F. J. STIMSON, My U.S. 179). 'A few vegetables, with corn meal ground at a hand grist-mill seven miles away, were their chief food' (W. E. Curtis, The True Abraham Lincoln, 21).

grocery. This word is much more common in Am. than in Eng., where *grocer's shop* or *grocer's* is in more general use. In Am. *corner grocer* and *corner grocery* are esp. familiar terms. 'A bill decreeing fine and imprisonment for every corner grocer who offered for sale a sealed tin that contained adulterated food' (Prof. N. W. Stephenson, Nelson W. Aldrich, 233). 'This class sanctioned the theft of wealth in Wall Street, but threw up its hands in righteous horror at its occurrence in the corner grocery store' (V. F. Calverton, The Liberation of Am. Lit. 476). 'Whether one is running a corner grocery or the largest manufacturing plant in the world, there is only one wise rule of conduct: fix all your abilities on that single job' (B. J. Hendrick, Life of Andrew Carnegie, 173). It should be added that *grocery* and *corner grocery* are sometimes euphemisms for a drinking-place.

groom is commonly used in Am. where *bridegroom* would be used in Eng. 'The bride is a native of Adams. The groom is also a native of the town.' 'As the young couple were about to take the train for their wedding journey, the bride's brother presented the groom with an envelope' (Prof. N. W. Stephenson, Nelson W. Aldrich, 20). 'Upstairs the groom was living through rapturous throes of anticipation. For the hundredth time he made sure the ring was in the left pocket of his waistcoat' (Alice Hegan Rice, Sandy, 251). 'The announcements sent out omitted all reference to the official position of the groom' (Prof. H. J. Ford, Woodrow Wilson, 296). As the custom of providing a bridegroom with male attendants in addition to the best man has died out in Eng., the word *groomsman* is nowadays found in Am. only. 'He and Columbus Monroe were the groomsmen at the wedding' (M. Gouverneur, As I Remember, 214). 'The bride, escorted by another team containing the bridesmaids and groomsmen' (J. H. Choate, in his Life by E. S. Martin, i. 316).

The verb *groom* is used in Am. politics in the sense of preparing a person for nomination as a candidate for office. 'Grover Cleveland was being groomed for his first Presidential term' (Julian Hawthorne, Hawthorne and his Circle, 264). 'For the Rep. Presidential nomination in 1896, a candidate was once more being groomed in Ohio' (Prof. T. C. Pease, The U.S. 535). 'He permitted his friends to groom him for the presidential race' (Dict. Am. Biog. xiii. 89). The word is coming into use in connexion with the preparation of persons for non-political functions also.

†ground. In Am. an investor is said to be admitted *on the ground floor* when he is entitled to the same privileges and opportunities as the original promoters of the company or speculation. 'No attempt was made to sell stock indiscriminately, but prominent men of means were approached or invited to go in on the ground floor.' 'What was needed was that we should get in on the ground floor by acquiring treaty rights which should for ever put us on an equal footing with other nations in that locality.'

guard is the technical term in Am. for a *prison warder*. 'Hereafter, the danger of killing guards must not prevent officers from firing at escaping convicts.' 'A mutiny among 1,100 prisoners at the Joliet Penitentiary was put down after the convicts had attacked their guards' (World Almanac, 1932, 101). See life and warden.

guess. The modest Am. often says *I guess* when he really means *I feel quite sure, I am certain*. In this he is harking back to the idiom of our ancestors, for the expression was used in this sense by John Locke and Jane Austen. Thus, Am. *I guess not* = Eng. *No, indeed!* and Am. *I guess that's so* = Eng. *Certainly!* 'He removed the stud, remarking that he guessed the safest place for it was in his hotel safe.' 'When the Court moved, Chief Clerk Byrne was asked if they were going to sell the old clock or give it away. "I guess not," was his emphatic rejoinder. "We are going to take it with us."' 'The true-born Yankee has always persisted, in spite of purists, in using "I guess" as equivalent to "I think". To his shrewd good-humored curiosity, all thinking resolves itself into a kind of guesswork; and one man has as good a right to his guess as another' (Dr. S. McC. CROTHERS, The Pardoner's Wallet, 252).

In the common Am. phrase *to keep one guessing* = *to keep one on tenterhooks* or *in suspense*, the word means *conjecture*, as in Eng. 'Doubt is now thrown upon the question whether he will go to Washington at all. The governor seems determined to keep us guessing.' 'Murphy proceeded with caution, sometimes withdrawing from a position, sometimes forcing it, and altogether keeping his opponents guessing what he would do next' (Dr. H. ZINK, City Bosses in the U.S. 23).

gum is used in some parts of Am. in the plur. form *gums* to denote *goloshes*. The compound *gumshoe* seems to be employed in a fig. sense only. Its meaning will be evident from the first of the following quotations. 'Having little personal ambition, he was the "gumshoe man" of the administration. He was always around, padding softly from one committee room to another, and his job was to keep the President fully informed about what was going on in Congress' (Prof. T. J. GRAYSON, Leaders and Periods of Am. Finance, 199). 'He calls it "unostentatious labor". That is statesmanese for

"gumshoe business". Others were campaigning, speaking, seeking arguments to convince the independent voters; but the unostentatious labor was secretly arranging nominations, pledging candidates, pulling wires.' 'In Eng. divorce-seekers have to worry about the King's Proctor, whose business it is to find out whether the plaintiff has led and is leading a blameless life. He is a lawyer of standing, and he leaves the gumshoe work to his assistants, who get their clues in letters from busybodies.' 'The quiet but thorough way in which he organized the Republicans in his constituency earned him the nickname of "Gumshoe"' (Dict. Am. Biog. ix. 406).

The Am. compound *bee-gum* denotes 'a hollow gum tree in which wild bees hive or from which beehives are made; hence, a beehive, originally one made from such a tree' (Webster). The term is esp. used in the South and West. 'Along the fence on the opposite side under the sheltering branches of the apple trees are the bee gums' (J. W. HATCHER, in Culture in the South, 384).

See also MUCILAGE and RUBBER.

gun denotes in Eng. almost any kind of fire-arm exc. the pistol. In Am. it is esp. the pistol. 'Capt. Evans, Chief Engineer Brown, and the first officer clambered down the latter to the stoke-hole, with their guns ready for action. At the point of their revolvers they separated the contestants.'

Hence the *gunman* who figures so prominently in Am. police reports. 'A notorious outlaw and one of the most expert gunmen of the West.'

In Am. a fowling-piece, which fires small shot, is distinguished from the bullet-firing rifle by being called a *shotgun*. 'This section is too thickly settled to permit the use of the high-powered, small-caliber rifles which kill at a mile or more. But the shotgun loaded with slugs or buckshot is a dangerous affair.' 'The shotgun was used to keep Negroes away from the polls at election time' (R. R. MOTON, What the Negro Thinks, 130). 'A man sitting on the front seat beside the driver with a shotgun wrapped up in newspaper lying across his knee' (JANE ADDAMS, Second 20 Years at Hull-House, 241).

There is an Am. verb *gun*, used fig. in the expression *gun for* = Eng. *go in pursuit of*. 'Thus the call went out, and instantly the Republicans were out gunning for Raymond' (C. G. BOWERS, The Tragic Era, 122).

guy lacks in Am. the disparaging implications connected with it in Eng. It is a colourless term, meaning no more than *fellow, chap.* 'He is a hefty guy when it comes to Dem. conventions and the platforms and tergiversations thereof.' 'The leader looked like a guy in the financial department' (R. MONTAGUE, in The End of *The World*, 47). 'One of those real-estate guys who sell little houses to people' (H. JUSTIN SMITH, Chicago, 174). 'The literary guys are taking public matters more seriously' (E. WILSON, The Am. Jitters, 114).

Hence, *a regular guy* is a complimentary term. 'An Am. friend congratulated me on the impression I produced on a lady interviewer, observing, "She says you're a regular guy". This puzzled me a little at the time. "Her description is no doubt correct," I said, "but I confess it would never have struck me as specially complimentary." But it appears that it is one of the most graceful of compliments, in the original Am.' (G. K. CHESTERTON, What I Saw in Am. 50).

The verb *guy*, however, seems to have closer kinship to the Eng. noun, for it means *make fun of*. 'He can't help wondering if they really meant it or if they were guying him.' 'When a man buys a "gold brick" at a bargain and the thing turns out to be brass, he is guyed from Maine to Oregon.' 'There is no particular satisfaction in guying Mrs. Atherton's

books.' The use of the word in this sense in Eng. theatrical slang (as recorded in the *O.E.D.*) is probably derived from Am.

H

haberdashery denotes in Eng. various small articles pertaining to dress, such as thread, tape, ribbons, and so on. In Am. these things are called NOTIONS (q.v.), and *haberdashery* denotes articles for men's wear—such as hats, collars, cuffs, and underwear—that in Eng. would form part of the stock of a men's outfitter.

hack. In the days of Steele and Fielding *hack* might be used to denote not only a hired horse but a hired vehicle. The latter use is now confined to Am.

half. Am. *a half* = Eng. *half a* or *half an*. 'There will be a half dozen interesting contests on the Tammany side.' 'Broadway traffic was blocked for a half hour.' 'A half-dozen brands of perfumery' (Sen. A. J. BEVERIDGE, The Russian Advance, 51). 'He had enjoyed a half hour's conversation with Samuel R. Gardiner' (M. A. DE W. HOWE, James Ford Rhodes, 91).

See also STAFF.

hall is a common term in Am. to denote the chamber in which a legislative body meets. 'The legislative halls of Congress were silent today in tribute to Calvin Coolidge.' 'It does not protect acts or words, otherwise illegal, though done or spoken by a member of the legislature within the legislative halls, if not in relation to the business before it' (Prof. C. K. BURDICK, Law of the Am. Constitution, 176). 'These party facts are reflected in the halls of Congress' (Prof. H. L. McBAIN, The Living Constitution, 124). 'A great battle was fought over the admission of representatives from the new counties into the legislative halls of the

State' (Prof. C. S. SYDNOR, Slavery in Mississippi, 248).

In Am. *hall* is frequently compounded with other words to denote a place devoted to a particular kind of entertainment; e.g. †*dance hall* = Eng. *dancing saloon* and *pool hall* = Eng. *pool-room*. 'The strains of a saloon band rose to vex the girl's poetic soul with repugnant remembrances of the dance hall' (H. GARLAND, The Tyranny of the Dark, 7). 'In all of these new towns were those sinks of iniquity, the dance halls' (J. T. FLYNN, God's Gold, 119). 'A reform element wanted the pool halls removed from Main Street' (F. L. BIRD and F. M. RYAN, The Recall of Public Officers, 125). 'Pool halls seem to furnish most of the recreation for young men' (C. S. JOHNSON, The Negro in Am. Civilization, 307).

The Am. *music hall* is very different from the Eng., as the following quotation shows. 'In 1892 he built a beautiful auditorium on 57th Street, calling it the "New York Music Hall". It was found impossible to book distinguished foreign artists for a place with such a title, "music hall" in Eng. and on the Continent representing about the same thing as "variety house" in this country. Without Carnegie's knowledge and when he was absent in Scotland, the structure was transformed into "Carnegie Hall", under which denomination the greatest composers and performers for forty years have gladly made the place the musical centre of the metropolis' (B. J. HENDRICK, Life of Andrew Carnegie, 550).

The entrance hall on the ground floor of an Am. house is usually called a *hallway*, and the same name is sometimes given to corridors or passages on other floors. 'The stuffy rooms, dark hallways and inadequate sanitation arrangements of the older communities.' 'The eight-day clock in the hallway' (T. BOYD, Mad Anthony Wayne, 8). 'The umbrellas and other portable articles he had noticed in the hallway' (Dr. S. C.

McC. CROTHERS, The Pardoner's Wallet, 224). 'In the Rivington St. tenement it was the rule that each occupant had to clean and scrub the stairs and hallway of the floor he lived on' (UPTON SINCLAIR Presents William Fox, 25).

The term *hall bedroom* is applied to a bedroom over the entrance hall, on whatever floor. In a boarding-house, the hall bedrooms, being the smallest and least desirable rooms, are usually the cheapest also. 'The lonely who sit in the cheerless solitude of hall bedrooms.' 'When I was a young man I spent many of my evenings sitting in a hall bedroom—a highly moral way of life that was wholly due to a shortage of money.' 'Sleeping in a hall bedroom with the rent overdue' (U. SINCLAIR, Money Writes, 17). 'These young men were the hall-bedroom youths of that period. They lived on little and worked hard' (E. L. MASTERS, The Tale of Chicago, 196).

See also CITY and EAT.

halt. In the *O.E.D.* the latest Eng. example of *halt* as a trans. verb, exc. as a military term, is dated 1827. This usage is still common in Am. 'The special train was halted several miles outside the city.' 'Rumania was running amuck and had to be sharply halted by an ultimatum from the Allies' (A. NEVINS, Henry White, 457). 'The outbreak was delayed, not halted' (H. F. PRINGLE, Theodore Roosevelt, 397). 'The experiment was roughly halted by the outbreak of the World War' (WILLIS J. ABBOT, Watching the World Go By, 45).

hammer. The verb *hammer* is used fig. in Am. in the sense of *criticize severely*. 'The senator celebrates his acquittal in the land fraud case by hammering the federal administration for its prosecution of land and timber thieves.' 'As his hammering of the bosses took on increased speed, the enthusiasm of the audience grew in volume' (J. KERNEY, Political Education of Woodrow Wilson, 71).

hand. Am. *on hand* = Eng. *at hand, present, in attendance.* 'Men were on hand at every booth, ready to give instructions to voters.' 'Col. Roebling was close on hand at the time when Gen. Sickels lost his leg' (H. SCHUYLER, The Roeblings, 193). 'Morgan mingled freely with his guests and made them comfortable, but was always on hand when the bill was to be paid' (J. K. WINKLER, J. Pierpont Morgan, 44).

In Am. *handbook* is used in connexion with racing where *book* would be used in Eng. Hence *handbook man* = Eng. *bookmaker.* 'He had never known of a case where an officer arrested a handbook man, saw him take money, and then failed to bring the man who paid the money as a witness.' 'Mysterious wholesale wire cutting, explainable only on the grounds that the handbooking possibilities on the Derby are the bone of contention, constitutes an important development of the warfare centering about Washington Park race track.' Acc. to Webster, the bookmaker's betting book is called a *handbook* because it is carried in the hand or on the person in order to evade the laws against bookmaking.

In Am. *hand-me-down* is a colloq. term for *ready-made,* corresponding to the Eng. *reach-me-down.* 'He wears a cheap suit of "hand-me-down" clothing.' 'A colored workman ceased to be grateful for a hand-me-down suit of broadcloth' (MARK SULLIVAN, Our Times, iii. 370).

†The compound *hand-pick* is in common use in Am., in a sense that will be sufficiently clear from the following examples. 'No advocate [in Eng.] would think of hand-picking a jury, so as to eliminate all those who might be unfavorable to his client's case. In Am., on the contrary, a trial lawyer's reputation depends to a certain extent upon his ability to pick a favorable jury.' 'Napoleon then arranged for a hand-picked Assembly of Notables [in Mexico], which changed the govern-

ment into an hereditary monarchy' (L. M. HACKER and B. B. KENDRICK, The U.S. since 1865, 44). 'He had grown into the absolute dictator, and he hand-picked candidates for county and legislative offices' (J. KERNEY, Political Education of Woodrow Wilson, 38).

In Am. the compound *handscrub* is an alternative to *nailbrush.*

†The Am. compound *handspring* denotes a somersault in which the body is supported by the hands while the feet are in the air. Hence Am. *turn handsprings* = Eng. *turn cartwheels.* 'I verily believe if some portly well-dressed and venerable gentleman should take it into his head to traverse the entire length of Regent Street in a series of handsprings, not a ripple of interest or mirth would be stirred.' 'A bright little mulatto boy who turned handsprings to attract their attention' (UPTON SINCLAIR, Manassas, 108).

handle. In Eng. to *deal with.* In Am. also to *deal in.* 'Jewelry stores and other houses handling goods classed as luxuries.' 'A general merchandise mail order concern, handling clothing, groceries, carriages and machinery' (Dr. H. ZINK, City Bosses in U.S. 276). 'Many bookstores refused to handle the book at all' (V. F. CALVERTON, The Liberation of Am. Literature, 289). Cf. CARRY.

In the sense of *deal with* the word is used much more freely in Am. than in Eng. 'Sixty years ago Eng. laid the foundations of a scientific plan for handling local and private bills.' 'We shall have additional facilities for handling our growing interests.' 'The University of Chicago handles almost 30,000 students' (Dr. A. FLEXNER, Universities, 190). 'Elevated railroads could handle passengers much more quickly' (Prof. A. B. HART, Actual Government, 206). An Eng. writer might speak of handling luggage, but scarcely of handling passengers.

hang. In Am. a jury which fails

to agree on a verdict is said to be *hung*. 'Darrow was tried twice for jury-bribing. In one case the jury was hung; in the other Darrow was acquitted' (L. ADAMIC, Dynamite, 233).

For *hanger*, see the following quotation. 'Hangers are printed or lithographed cards of various shapes and sizes, to be hung up in a store' (E. E. CALKINS and R. HOLDEN, Art of Modern Advertising, 352).

†The Am. derivative *hangover* = Eng. *survival*. 'Modern realism was the product of the fat years from the mid-19th century up to the war. In these leaner times this realism is a cultural hangover, a moral superfluity.' 'He was fond of reading homilies to his subordinates, probably a hangover from the days when he taught a young ladies' Bible class' (Dict. Am. Biog. vii. 176). 'That easily inspired hatred of Germany remained as a hangover in Am. long after it had been thrown off by the British' (L. DENNY, Am. Conquers Britain, 9). 'One candidate was branded as a hangover from the corrupt aldermanic machine' (P. LEWINSON, Race, Class and Party, 23). See HOLD and LEAVE.

The term *hangout* denotes a *place of resort*, esp. in a derogatory sense. 'Whose saloon was to remain a picturesque hang-out for radicals and bohemians for the next three decades' (L. SYMES and T. CLEMENT, Rebel Am. 138). 'We once found one hundred hangouts of criminals. These resorts were not molested' (Prof. C. E. MERRIAM, Chicago, 36).

††**happening** is condemned by Mr. H. W. Fowler, in his *Dict. of Modern Eng. Usage,* as an 'unworthy literary or journalistic affectation' unknown in Eng. until about 1905. It was certainly in common use in Am. before that. 'Other happenings might temporarily switch off the gossip' (E. C. WALTZ, Pa Gladden, 123; published 1903). 'Every country paper wants a wide-awake corre-

spondent to report the local happenings in each village' (E. L. SHUMAN, Practical Journalism, 31; published 1903). Its acceptance by the leading Am. authorities on the use of language is illustrated by the following extract from an article by Prof. Brander Matthews in the *North Am. Rev.* of Nov. 1905: 'The interpretative comment with which the novelist has encompassed people and happenings commonplace enough.'

hard. In Am. *hard* is used as an epithet for spirituous liquor, to distinguish it not only from non-alcoholic beverages but from beer and light wines. 'The restoration of beer, or of beer and wine, will leave untouched the domain of the professional bootlegger, who will concentrate on hard liquor.' 'Hamilton urged that Congress should levy an excise tax on spirituous liquors. . . . He evidently regarded hard liquor as a luxury' (Prof. T. J. GRAYSON, Leaders and Periods of Am. Finance, 69). See SOFT.

In Eng. one may speak of *hard cash* but not of *hard money*. The latter term is used in Am. of coin, to distinguish it from paper money. 'Hard money disappeared from the great states of the Atlantic Seaboard at a most critical moment' (Prof. T. J. GRAYSON, Leaders and Periods of Am. Finance, 222). 'The total stock of money in the U.S. at this time was 5,400 million dollars. The Patman bill [authorizing the issue of more U.S. bonds] would have increased this amount by 45 per cent. Naturally such a proposal was viewed with alarm by the supporters of hard money' (W. LIPPMANN, The U.S. in World Affairs in 1932, 127).

In Eng. a sentence imposed on some criminals is of so many years' imprisonment *with hard labour.* A similar Am. sentence is *at hard labor.* 'He went to trial, was convicted, and sentenced to 18 years at hard labor.' 'When husband and wife both love the same person, and that person is the wife, it's usually a life sentence at hard labor for the husband' (G. H. LORIMER, Old Gorgon Graham, 146).

A sauce that is not liquid is called in Am. a *hard sauce*.

†In Eng. *hard-boiled* is an epithet for eggs only. In Am. it is used fig. as an equivalent of *hard-headed*, *sophisticated*. 'The hard-boiled individualists who have made their fortunes in business.' 'He must not have long hair or dreamy eyes. He must be hard-boiled and practical, dealing with grim, stark realities of daily life' (Prof. C. E. MERRIAM, Chicago, 265). 'Our Am. correspondents in Paris, the hardest-boiled, least sentimental of observers' (L. STEFFENS, Autobiog. 830). 'Letters from a Hard-Boiled Teacher to his Half-Baked Son' is the title of an Am. book. The term *hard-shelled* has the same meaning.

haul. In Eng. the verb *haul* carries with it a suggestion of effort and struggle. It lacks any such implication in Am., where it is commonly used in connexion with ordinary transport. 'In some parts of this State it is impossible to move thrashing machines or haul grain.' 'A second of the four engines was at once set hauling trains through the tunnel.' 'Many of the smaller railroads are extensively engaged in hauling timber and other forest products' (Dr. J. H. FREDERICK, The Development of Am. Commerce, 348). 'The wagons were hauling groceries from the neighboring steamboat landing' (Prof. C. S. SYDNOR, Slavery in Mississippi, 35).

A similar remark applies to the noun *haul*. 'Wherever trolley lines extend they ought to supersede long wagon hauls' (Prof. A. B. HART, Actual Government, 531). 'The commerce act of 1887 prohibits a greater charge for a short haul than for a long haul' (Dr. J. M. BECK, May it Please the Court, 371).

In Eng., however, the meaning of the derivatives *haulage* and *haulier* accords with the Am. sense of *haul*.

have. For *do have*, see DO.

The Am. invitation *Have a seat!* = Eng. *Take a seat!*

The compound noun *has-been*, a dial. word in Eng., is in general use in Am. It denotes a person whose days of influence or authority are now over; who, as we sometimes say, is on the shelf. 'Such occasions draw out a great number of "has beens" in the public life of the state. Men who have once held public office have a decided fancy for appearing at such times.' 'For the President to elevate over them a political novice they consider as notice to the country that either he has no confidence in their integrity or regards them as "has beens" politically.' 'The majority of the seats were occupied by homeless men, by "has beens"' (O. KILDARE, My Mamie Rose, 214).

hawk. The name *night-hawk* is applied in Am. to a bird that is not a *hawk* in the Eng. sense. Its scientific name is *Chordeiles virginianus*.

hay. In Am. the compound *hayseed* has been coined as a somewhat disparaging term for a countryman. It takes the place of the Eng. *yokel*. 'The men in the audience did not look like hayseeds, but businesslike.' 'He stood for the interests of Boston, he asserted, and asked the voters to elect strong men to the local Legislature, in order that those interests should not be over-ridden by what he termed "hayseed legislators".' The explanation commonly given of the term is that the countryman is pictured as a man who has not yet shaken the hayseed out of his hair.

In Eng. both *hayrick* and *haystack* are in use. In Am. *haystack* only is known.

haze. One of the meanings given for the verb *haze* in the *O.E.D.* is *harass with overwork*, described as a nautical term. It is perhaps from this sense that has been derived its use in Am. schools and colleges, as illustrated in the following examples.

'Ohio, in 1893, passed a law against "what is commonly called hazing". It is now replaced by a new act covering educational institutions of all kinds and defining what is meant by hazing. It is described as "any act that injures, frightens, degrades, or disgraces, or tends to injure, frighten, degrade, or disgrace any fellow-student or person attending such institution".' 'Hazing is still going on in full blast at the Naval Academy. It has driven several fourth class men to the hospital. It consists chiefly in the use of insulting and profane language to the underclassmen and compelling them by threats to undergo continuous physical exercises until exhausted.' 'The boys hazed him; he broke down and came home a wreck' (E. S. MARTIN, Life of J. H. Choate, i. 402). 'I passed into the rough and tumble of school life with a distinct shudder. There was no direct hazing, but there was a good deal of rather cruel horse-play' (L. LEWISOHN, Up Stream, 65).

head. In Am. *head for* is used not only intrans., as in Eng., but trans. also. Thus Am. *headed for* = Eng. *heading for, destined for.* 'It is believed that the three outlaws are headed for Lee's Creek.' 'It was headed for disaster and the slightest disturbance would bring it to a certain fall' (R. I. WARSHOW, Story of Wall Street, 222). 'Everett Colby was headed straight for this fate when a man got hold of him' (L. STEFFENS, Autobiog. 499). 'A young man who was two years above him in the College and was headed for the Unitarian ministry' (H. JAMES, Charles W. Eliot, i. 42). 'The newspapers reported late in 1931 that the new Coalition Government was headed in the direction of protective tariffs' (W. LIPPMANN, The U.S. in World Affairs in 1932, 86).

The Am. compound *headliner* denotes the person whose name is the most prominent attraction on a play-bill, &c. 'Miss Toby Claude, who played the role opposite Jefferson de Angeles in "Fantana" all season will be the headliner this week.' 'The Forty club will give its annual May party Thursday, May 16, at the Auditorium hotel. The "headliners" on the program will be James Whitcomb Riley and George Ade.' 'We would take ourselves to the Senate gallery to listen for hours to the speeches of those headliners among the Senators who dramatized the League of Nations fight' (ALICE ROOSEVELT LONGWORTH, Crowded Hours, 278).

hear. In Am. *hear to* is a possible alternative to *hear of*, in the sense of *entertain the idea of.* 'When I tried at last to turn our talk to herself and our affairs at home, at first she would not hear to it' (E. POOLE, The Harbor, 202).

Hebrew is frequently used in Am. where *Jew* or *Jewish* would be used in Eng. 'The races of the Roman Catholic religion have much larger numbers in the parochial schools than do the races with the Protestant religion or especially the Hebrews' (J. W. JENKS and W. J. LAUCK, The Immigrant Problem, 289).

hell. The Am. colloquialism *hell-bent* = Eng. *hell for leather, hammer and tongs.* 'Political feeling is too subdued to make it possible for the State to go hell-bent for anybody.'

help is used euphemistically in Am. as a synonym for *servant(s)* or *employee(s)*. 'Some guests will fail to leave anything for the help.' 'The large department stores are laying off help and curtailing salaries.' 'Mill help of late years have had no trouble in getting jobs.' 'In our little Kansas village, to "keep help", unless one was an invalid or lived on a big farm, was a mark of shiftlessness' (A. SURBRIDGE, Confessions of a Club Woman, 4). 'An alien engaged in the business of conducting a grocery store, meat market, or fruit stand, when the help used is alien, must keep a large card in full view showing his nationality and that of his help' (E. G. MEARS, Resident Orientals on the Am. Pacific Coast, 288).

As long ago as 1838 James Fenimore Cooper protested against this use of the word, as not always conveying the meaning intended. A man, he pointed out, does not usually hire his cook to help him cook his dinner, but to cook it herself.

See HIRE.

hemlock is in Eng. a poisonous umbelliferous plant whose botanical name is *Conium maculatum*. In Am. the name is also given to a fir or spruce, the *Tsuga Canadensis*, owing to the resemblance of its branches to the leaves of the hemlock plant. 'At last we come to that hidden glade, under the beeches, under the hemlocks.' 'He liked fishing-camps in Ontario, but never made himself believe that he preferred hemlock boughs to a mattress' (SINCLAIR LEWIS, Dodsworth, 19). 'Manufacturers of hemlock lumber in Michigan' (T. C. BLAISDELL, Federal Trade Commission, 151).

†henchman. In Eng. a *henchman* is usually 'the stalwart and trusty righthand man of the hero or villain in romantic narrative' (Prof. E. WEEKLEY, in Words Ancient and Modern). In Am. he is commonly a thick-and-thin follower and assistant of a political leader. 'Roosevelt was bitter because he knew that Platt's henchmen hoped to legislate him out of office' (H. F. PRINGLE, Theodore Roosevelt, 114). 'Sanborn was a henchman of B. F. Butler, one of the most influential members of the Rep. party in Congress' (Prof. A. E. MARTIN, Hist of U.S. ii. 135). 'Calhoun's motion not to receive antislavery petitions was echoed by his henchmen' (Prof. G. H. BARNES, The Antislavery Impulse, 110).

Hessian. In the Am. War of Independence Hessian troops were hired to fight on the British side. Hence the word *Hessian* is used in Am. to this day as a synonym for *mercenary*. Thus, a newspaper, in discussing a charge that the credentials of certain delegates to a political convention were bought, says that 'the extent to which the packing of state politics upon a Hessian basis has gone deserves to be exposed'. 'The question whether he was or was not a Hessian in that campaign is a small matter in the eye of the country at large; but the question whether the Rep. leaders were corrupting the Opposition is large and important.'

hide. Am. *hide and go seek* = Eng. *hide and seek*. 'These counsels of cowardice tend to make our public life a game of hide and go seek rather than the manly fronting of important questions.' 'One of the pleasantest and most scary of games was "Hide and Go Seek" with Father' (ALICE ROOSEVELT LONGWORTH, Crowded Hours, 7). See also PEEK.

high has several compounds which are peculiar to, or which originated in, Am.

A *highball* is a whisky and soda served with broken ice in a tall glass. 'Many of the Senators do not know what a "highball" is, and only a few Southern members have a clear notion of a mint julep.' 'A large circle of young men, seated round two tables pushed together and covered with "high balls", and bottles of carbonated water, and silver bowls of cracked ice' (D. G. PHILLIPS, Golden Fleece, 58).

The members of a secret society among Chinese living in Am. are called *Highbinders*. 'The Highbinders tracked Sam Jim to this city and murdered him.'

††The term *highbrow*, that disrespectful synonym of *intellectual*, both as noun and as adj., originated in Am. 'Where highbrows and lowbrows rub shoulders without disdain' (W. D. ORCUTT, The Kingdom of Books, 88). 'Endowed institutions think they must be useful in order that

they may not be reproached for being aristocratic or "highbrow"' (Dr. A. FLEXNER, Universities, 130).

In Eng. a person who puts on airs is pictured as riding a *high horse*. In Am. he is thought of as wearing a *high hat*. 'He gets high-hat and speaks with scorn of the Mexicans as inherently social inferiors' (E. WILSON, The Am. Jitters, 205). 'Dever's dignity was mistaken by some for "high-hatting"' (Prof. C. E. MERRIAM, Chicago, 292).

The colloquialism *high rolling* denotes *extravagant spending, cutting a dash*. 'High rolling with the spoils of their first venture at house looting led to the undoing yesterday of a pair of amateur cracksmen.'

In Am. the compound *high-toned* does not mean *high-principled*, as in Eng., but *superior, stylish*. 'The small farmer, not too high-toned to work his own farm, will succeed where the gentleman farmer who hires labor cannot.' 'The plasterers take the ground that they could remodel a broken hand, or face, or arm, as well as any "high-toned" sculptor.'

In recent years *high* has come to be used in Am. as a noun, in the sense of *high level* or *high figure*. 'He sets a new high in the use of exclamation points.' 'An analysis of annual library expenditures per enrolled student for 34 major institutions shows in dollars a high of 87, a low of 6, and an average of 22' (Prof. H. C. NIXON, in Culture in the South, 236). 'American Can, at the closing on Oct. 4th, was nearly 20 points below its high for the year' (F. L. ALLEN, Only Yesterday, 320). Cf. LOW.

hill. For a spec. Am. use of *the hill*, see quotations. 'In the ordinary conversation of Washington, one rarely hears Congress mentioned by name. In speaking of the lawmakers collectively, the familiar phrase is "the gentlemen on the hill". Washington has several hills, but "the" hill is by universal consent the one on which the Capitol stands' (F. E.

LEUPP, Walks about Washington, 54). 'Father's message in response to the House resolution was not in any way satisfactory to the irate gentlemen on the hill' (ALICE ROOSEVELT LONGWORTH, Crowded Hours, 162).

hire. 'Farmer Sprague had been discussing strikes for an hour with his hired men.' 'Occasionally, we find farmers with two or more hired men' (Prof. R. T. ELY, Evolution of Industrial Society, 379). 'The hired man came in with the milk' (JULIA B. FORAKER, I Would Live it Again, 51). 'What with the coal and the stoves and the hired woman, the monthly expenses had already doubled' (E. WHARTON, Hudson River Bracketed, 518). 'The chapters tell how the husband finds the rent and the wife the hired girls' (G. H. LORIMER, Old Gorgon Graham, 190). '"I hope she didn't go out to work as hired girl," said Sylvia. "It would have been awful for a grand-daughter of Abraham White's to do that"' (M. E. WILKINS FREEMAN, Shoulders of Atlas, 15).

This peculiarly Am. use of *hired man, hired woman*, and *hired girl* is explained by Albert Matthews in an article in the *Transactions* of the Colonial Society of Massachusetts, summarized in the *Nation* of Aug. 16, 1900. It appears that in colonial times there were three distinct classes of servants in Am.—slaves, indented servants, and hired servants. In addition there were hired freemen; i.e. ordinary free citizens, not belonging to the technical category of servants, who had temporarily 'hired themselves out'. This last class was originally meant when *hired men* were spoken of. With the growth of democratic feeling, the dislike felt for the word *servant* was shown with increasing force, and *hired man* and *hired woman* came to be used as euphemistic names for free servants. See also HELP.

In Am., generally speaking, one *hires*, rather than *engages*, a servant.

hither. Am. *hither and yon* = Eng. *hither and thither*, *to and fro*. 'He was sent hither and yon from one department of the great works to another.' 'With tremendous energy, McClure hastened hither and yon' (C. C. REGIER, The Era of the Muckrakers, 56). 'He is pulled hither and yon, to make speeches and to attend functions' (Dr. A. FLEXNER, Universities, 183). See BACK.

hoe. Acc. to the *Century Dict.* the Am. *hoe-cake* owes its name to the fact that it was originally baked on the broad, thin blade of a cotton-field hoe. It is made of Indian meal, water, and salt, and is really a kind of coarse bread. 'Muffins and rolls were enlarged into a multitude of forms of hot bread of which the hoe-cake of Indian corn meal, cooked in the ashes of the hearth, was the parent and the Indian hominy cake the grandparent.' 'The savory odor of the hoe-cakes floated over his shoulder' (ALICE HEGAN RICE, Sandy, 201). 'Sometimes this part of the programme was varied by his mixing a hoe-cake on a board, and setting it up "to do" in front of the fire' (E. ROBINS, The Magnetic North, 123).
See also ROW.

hog is rarely used in Eng. nowadays except fig., e.g. *road hog*. In Am., on the other hand, it is commonly used in its literal sense, and virtually takes the place of the Eng. PIG (q.v.). It is significant that *Whitaker's Alm.*, in its agricultural section, publishes statistics of pigs, but the *World Alm.* of hogs. Accordingly *hog-raisers' associations* correspond in Am. to the Eng. *pig-breeders' associations*, and Am. *hogpen* = Eng. *pigsty*. 'We know good land, good horses, good machinery, good grain and hogs and fruit and cotton' writes Walter H. Page in one of the letters printed in his biography. 'The hog industry is sharing with the beef-cattle industry in the readjustment following the signing of the armistice' (Am. Yearbook for 1919, 487). 'Feeding garbage to swine has been largely practiced, and a few cities have established hog farms for this purpose' (Dr. C. C. MAXEY, Outline of Municipal Government, 226). 'The most notable exception to the usual monotony was that which came late in the fall, at the hog-killing' (Dr. W. W. FOLWELL, Autobiog. 31). See also SAND.

hold. In Am. the verb *hold* is often a synonym for *keep back*, *detain*, *remand*; sometimes almost for *arrest*, *prosecute*. 'In the future trains will not be held for the purpose of taking on baggage after the regular time scheduled for stops has expired.' 'The two men were held in $1,500 bail each for trial in the Court of General Sessions.' 'In Buffalo, a girl witness was held 36 days in a gang case, then released without being used to testify.' 'If the insurance officials cannot be held for larceny, they might evidently be held for forgery or perjury.' 'Farmers frequently prefer to hold their products for better prices' (Prof. E. S. SPARKS, Agricultural Credit in U.S. 438). A decision of the Nobel Prize committee to make no award is announced in an Am. newspaper under the headline 'Nobel Committee Holds Peace Prize'.

A full account of the Am. *holding company* may be found in the *Encycl. Soc. Sci.* (vii. 403), which says: 'A holding company may be defined in the broadest sense as any company having share capital which owns securities of one or more other companies. In a more restricted but more usual sense the definition is made to turn not on ownership in but on control over another company. A holding company may thus be defined in terms of its distinguishing characteristic as any company with share capital which is in a position to control or materially to influence the management of one or more other companies by virtue, in part at least, of its ownership of securities of the latter.' 'The plan to insure stability in control took form late in 1901 in the organization of the Northern Securities Company, a holding company to act virtually as trustee of the Great Northern, Northern Pacific, Burlington, and other properties associated with Hill's name' (Dict. Am. Biog. ix. 39). 'Cases where the ownership of two or three millions in stock of the ultimate holding company carries control of hundreds of millions of capital' (NORMAN THOMAS, America's Way Out, 162).

†In Eng. *hold down* = *keep in subjection*, *oppress*. In Am. it sometimes = *keep* simply. 'It must not be said that mere strength and steadiness in holding down a job are the marks of an educated man.' 'He has proved his ability in holding down one of the most responsible positions in one of the largest railroad systems in the country.' 'For a short time I also held down a job in a picture frame factory' (MORRIS HILLQUIT, Loose Leaves from a Busy Life, 33).

†It is a common practice of bandits to compel their victims to hold up their hands at the point of the revolver. A *hold-up* accordingly denotes a robbery of this type. 'I found myself staring into the barrel of a Colt's six-shooter before I grasped the idea that it was a hold-up.' The word may also be used in a fig. sense. 'If we should go to Nicaragua now the chances of a financial hold-up there would be just as great as in Panama.' Hence *hold-up man* = *bandit*. 'Hold-up men are not as a rule organized, and often are rundown professionals who no longer are competent for the crimes requiring greater skill' (Prof. C. E. MERRIAM, Chicago, 38).

†Although it is the victims that actually hold up their hands on such occasions the expression *hold up* has curiously come to be applied to the action of the criminals. 'The gang of outlaws had planned to hold up the west-bound express.' 'It was never my fate to be held up, though frequently the stage which just pre-

ceded or followed mine was robbed.' The verb, like the noun, may be used fig. 'There were occasions when an owner [of land], seeing his opportunity to hold up the railroad, demanded an exorbitant price' (MARK SULLIVAN, Our Times, iii. 194).

†Both as noun and verb *hold up* may also be used as a synonym for *delay*, without any suggestion of intimidation. 'Out of the 900 steerage passengers, 135 failed to pass the immigration inspectors, and were held up.' 'It was not unusual for trains to be held up literally for hours by herds of buffaloes crossing the tracks' (Prof. A. E. MARTIN, Hist. of U.S. ii. 109).

The Am. compound *hold-over* has the same meaning as *hang-over* and *left-over*. It denotes a person or thing surviving from an earlier time or condition. 'There were only 40 cases on the calendar, all "hold-overs"— that is, complaints turned in during the previous administration.' 'He has himself had in charge the initial organization of his own Department. Consequently, his work has not been hampered by a horde of Tammany hold-overs.' 'Los Angeles was wailing for the staff of life and doing the best it could on crackers and cheese and hold-overs.' 'The little village of Washington in Connecticut, one of the most charming hold-overs of the past that state possesses.' 'His post-master-general, a hold-over from Monroe's cabinet' (T. C. PEASE, The U.S. 312). See HANG and LEAVE.

home. Americans often speak of Philadelphia as a 'city of homes'. To an Englishman that description is quite unmeaning. Every city is inhabited mainly by families, and all families have homes. The explanation is suggested in the following passage: 'Philadelphia is a city of homes; there is a dwelling house for every five persons of the population' (L. STEFFENS, The Shame of the Cities, 194). It thus appears that in Am. *home* denotes a house inhabited by a single family, as distinct from a flat or boarding-house. Hence the word is often used where *house* would be used in Eng. 'Building of Homes Goes On Steadily' is the heading of a news item reporting a decrease in the housing shortage. 'Experience has demonstrated that hot water or steam is the most healthful and satisfactory agent for heating homes' (Advt.). 'One new industry that seems to meet these requirements is the manufacture and assembly of machine-made homes.' 'I was asked to dinner in the finest home in the city' (A. SURBRIDGE, Confessions of a Club Woman, 90). As Greenough and Kittredge point out (Words and their Ways, 143) *home* is thus losing in Am. the 'tender connotations' which find expression in the familiar song, 'Home, sweet home', having become little more than a colourless synonym for *house* or *residence*.

Another spec. Am. use is seen in such expressions as *the Smith home* = Eng. *Mr. Smith's*. 'Mrs. Roosevelt left here yesterday for the Wilmer home.' 'Their meeting took place at the Wilcox home in Buffalo' (H. F. PRINGLE, Theodore Roosevelt, 239).

The attrib. use of *home* is much more frequent in Am. than in Eng. 'With his formal education behind him, Bailey returned to his home county' (S. H. ACHESON, Joe Bailey, 18). 'This woman was a former acquaintance of Flavia's in her home town' (L. N. WRIGHT, Limbs of an Old Family Tree, 92). 'All this in his home city, to which he was deeply attached' (E. L. MASTERS, The Tale of Chicago, 124). 'The effect may be noted in the author's home state' (CASSIUS M. CLAY, The Mainstay of Am. Individualism, 15).

The baseball glossary in the *Encycl. Britann.* defines *home plate* as 'base at first corner of diamond and that also at which batter stands to bat', and *home run*, or *homer*, as 'a hit that permits batter to make circuit of all bases without error being made in handling the ball'. These terms are sometimes used fig.

For *Old Home Day* and *Old Home Week*, see OLD.

homely. St. John Ervine has confessed (Observer, Jan. 13, 1929) that on his first visit to the U.S. he utterly disgraced himself by saying of a lady to whom he wished to be complimentary that she was *homely*. 'My meaning', he explains, 'was that she put people at their ease and made them feel at home, but in Am. *homely* means plain, if not actually ugly.' Thus: 'John Sharp Williams has got rid of two days' beard he wore, but he is still the homeliest man in St. Louis. He bitterly disappoints the swarms of admirers who eagerly ask to have the brilliant Dem. pointed out. "What, that homely man?" is the universal and disappointed query.' '"The homeliest face I have ever seen", said a painter the other day, "was that of a girl who might just as well have been pretty".' 'She had a puzzled expression. Maria's hair was diverting her from her own troubles. She could not understand why any girl should deliberately make herself homely' (MARY E. WILKINS FREEMAN, By the Light of the Soul, 442). 'As far as physical good looks are concerned, municipal bosses do not seem to be distinctive. The majority are neither dashingly handsome nor painfully homely' (Dr. H. ZINK, City Bosses in U.S. 14). 'Those who wish to live in this way, growing sick and homely and old long before their time, have a right to do so' (Dr. R. L. ALSAKER, Eating for Health and Efficiency, 167). 'The reason which sometimes impels business men to employ male stenographers or homely female stenographers: fear of domestic complications' (Rotary? 122).

homestead. 'In 1862, by the Homestead Act, Congress established the principle of giving away a quarter section of land to any head of a family, native or immigrant, after he had lived five years upon it and had paid a fee of about $40' Prof. A. B.

HART, Actual Government, 339). Accordingly the term *homestead*, which in Eng. has the general meaning of *farmstead*, is spec. applied in Am. to a piece of land thus allotted under the Homestead Act. 'One day the agent called us in and said that there was one isolated homestead away up on the eastern slope of the valley. We filed on [i.e. made formal application for] it' (M. H. HARTWICK, in Life in the U.S. 1).

Hence the verb *homestead* and the derivative *homesteader*. 'The little claim that he homesteaded was, in the beginning, like those of his neighbors.' 'He freighted across the prairie until he had made some money and then he homesteaded on a rise in the prairie where he liked the view' (M. McKERNAN, in Life in the U.S. 212). 'A solitary homesteader built him a cabin at the foot of Ceriso.' 'Homesteaders came by thousands in almost penniless estate' (A. NEVINS, The Emergence of Modern Am. 159). See also SUBSISTENCE.

hono(u)r system. In Eng. universities, this term denotes the system by which special distinction is awarded to students who pass a more advanced examination than that taken by pass-men. The Am. meaning is shown in the following quotations. 'There has of late been considerable discussion of the so-called honor system in colleges. The phrase generally applies merely to the conduct of written examinations, during which the students, being on honor to accept no aid, are released from supervision of any kind.' 'The most successful plan of combating the tendency of college students to cheat in examinations has been some form of an "honor system", by which the pupil is implicitly trusted and his statement accepted that he used no dishonest aids.' 'The men who were against the honor system said that at Columbia, under existing conditions, there was lacking that *esprit de corps* which was absolutely neces-

sary before any honor system could be made effective.'

hono(u)rable. In Am. there is no official rule determining the application of the title *Honorable* (commonly abbreviated, as in Eng., to *Hon.*). In general practice this title is applied to (1) the President and members of his Cabinet, (2) members of either House of Congress, (3) State Governors and holders of the more important State offices, (4) members of State Legislatures, and (5) almost any other politician or government official, major or minor, to whom one desires to pay a compliment. In his autobiog. W. G. McAdoo relates how, when he was an obscure country lawyer in his 21st year, he succeeded in getting himself appointed to fill a vacancy as an alternate delegate among the Tennessee representatives to the Dem. national convention. 'The secretary', he tells us, 'made out a card of credentials in the name of the "Honorable" W. G. McAdoo. I certainly felt very important' (Crowded Years, 38). It should be noted that the title is not used by the newspapers in their references to the persons to whom it is given, but only in more or less formal documents. Thus, if Mr. Hull, the Secretary of State, were speaking at a public dinner, he might be introduced as 'the Honorable Cordell Hull' and his name might so appear in the programme of the proceedings, but the title would usually be omitted in the newspaper reports of his speech.

Am. newspapers, misled by the application of the term to members of Congress, often apply the same title to members of the British Parliament. A leading New Eng. paper has even made itself responsible for the remarkable statement that 'all members of Parliament are "right honorable"' (Springfield *Weekly Republican*, Nov. 5, 1931). Actually, neither *Hon.* nor *Right Hon.* is ever given to an M.P. in virtue of his election, although one member refers to another, in the course of a debate, as 'the hon. gentleman' or 'the hon. member'. In Eng. the title of *Hon.* is given to (1) the children of peers in certain instances, (2) past and present maids of honour, (3) judges of the High Court, and (4) members of government or executive councils in India and the Dominions. *Right Hon.* is the title of privy councillors, peers below the rank of marquis, the holders of certain high judicial offices, and the lord mayors and lord provosts of certain cities.

In Eng. an unpaid secretary of a society is commonly called its *honorary secretary.* This is often abbreviated to *hon. secretary* or *hon. sec.* The *hon.* in this designation is frequently misunderstood in Am. Thus, a N.Y. literary paper reviews a book by 'the Honorable Secretary of the Royal Astronomical Society'.

hood. The *hood* of an Am. automobile is not a folding roof, but that part of the car which in Eng. is known as the *bonnet.* 'When the family goes to the automobile show the mother will be apt to stand back and say, "That's a beauty. I want that one". Dad will be likely to open the hood and say, "Seventy horsepower. That's the one I want".' 'The less spectacular horsepower hidden under the hoods of motor trucks' (G. A. HASTINGS, Happy Journeys to Yesterday, 38).

†**hook.** In the vocab. of Am. radio, the derivative *hook-up* has been coined to denote a connexion between different transmitters. 'The educational features offered by the central stations may or may not be distributed on the local or regional hookups.' 'A radio hook-up is now made so that millions of listeners throughout the country may hear the speeches' (C. A. and W. BEARD, The Am. Leviathan, 225). 'J. Pierpont Morgan spoke for the first time over the radio from his home on Madison Ave., N.Y. City, over a nation-wide N.B.C. hook-up' (World Alm. for 1933, 101).

hop. The verb *hop* may be used trans. in Am. in the sense of *jump on to.* 'An ordinary citizen may pack his bag, hop a train for Washington, and transact his own business with the Departments.' 'Hopping a freight cost Edward Monahan both feet and may cost him his life. He was with other boys at Gardner Falls to catch a ride on a west-bound freight, when he fell off a car, the wheels passing over the left leg at the knee and the right leg at the ankle.' 'Doing something that would justify me in packing my bag and hopping a train to Chicago' (ALICE ROOSEVELT LONGWORTH, Crowded Hours, 212).

†**horse.** For some unknown reason the quality known as *common sense* in Eng. is also called *horse sense* in Am. 'Dress to suit the weather. The spectacle of hundreds of men in high double-band collars, mopping their perspiring necks, is not one to inspire enthusiasm for the much-vaunted "horse sense" of the Am. people.' 'There was plenty of good, solid, horse-sense in Flood's advice' (ANDY ADAMS, Log of a Cowboy, 29). 'This was a non-scientific, horse-sense method of much value' (P. E. SARGENT, Handbook of Am. Private Schools, 47).

hostile is in Am. sometimes a noun, denoting an Indian belonging to a tribe which is unfriendly to the whites. 'The hostiles assured the General that they were tired of constant warfare' (B. DAVIS, The Truth about Geronimo, 69).

†**hot.** The Am. term *hot dog* denotes a sort of sandwich, consisting of bread or a split roll in which is enclosed a hot sausage daubed with mustard. It is a favourite edible at Coney Island and other popular resorts. 'The hot-dog stands on the motor roads sell gin' (E. WILSON, The Am. Jitters, 1). 'One five-cent glass of cider secured for me a square meal of "hot dogs" between thick

slices of rye bread' (Dr. FRANKLIN H. MARTIN, The Joy of Living, i. 158).

For *hot air*, see AIR.

house. When it forms part of the name of a building, *house* denotes in Eng. either (1) a large, and usually aristocratic, place of residence, as Hatfield House, Apsley House, or (2) an office-building, as Unilever House, Shell-Mex House.

In Am. a name of this kind, in distinction from the Eng. practice, is always preceded by the definite article. In a city it denotes an hotel. 'More serious prospectors sat around the hotel lobbies—the Am. House, the Eagle House, and dozens of others' (J. T. FLYNN, God's Gold, 95). In the case of the most recent buildings, however, the tendency is to supersede *House* by *Hotel*. In the country the word denotes a place of residence, often of a quite unpretentious type. 'The only person in the village who could remember his coming to Harpledon and opening and repairing the old Cranch house was old Miss Lucilla Selwick, who lived in the Selwick house' (E. WHARTON, Here and Beyond, 34).

The distinction between these two meanings is indicated by the use or non-use of a capital initial. Thus, *the Johnson House* would be understood to be an hotel, while *the Johnson house* would be a house occupied by a family named Johnson.

See BUILDING and HOME.

housekeeping. In Am. the term *light housekeeping* is employed to denote a *ménage* in which a person rents a room which is provided with facilities for the preparation of minor meals. 'To let, two and three furnished rooms, with bath, for light housekeeping' (Advt.). 'High-priced rooms, many with board, high-sounding accommodations that dissuaded us from asking if light housekeeping would be tolerated' (Dr. FRANKLIN H. MARTIN, The Joy of Living, i. 133). It is told of Ella Wheeler Wilcox that she once wrote

for a newspaper some verses containing the line: 'My soul is a lighthouse keeper.' To her horror it appeared in print: 'My soul is a light housekeeper.'

hundredweight. The Eng. hundredweight = 112 lb. avoirdupois, but the Am. = 100 lb.

hunt. An Englishman hunts foxes, stags, otter(s), and even hares. When he pursues grouse or partridge with a view to their slaughter, he does not go hunting but shooting. An Am., on the other hand, hunts feathered creatures and four-legged animals alike. 'The hunt is better than for years, the high tides having brought the mud hens and reed birds in countless thousands.' 'Many Americans are among the enthusiastic sportsmen who for the last three days have been hunting the grouse of Scotland.' 'The Massachusetts hunting season has been disappointing. The two months when it has been allowable to shoot ruffed grouse, woodcock and quail have been ill-suited for the sport.' In a N.Y. paper a picture of a large flock of wild ducks is entitled 'A Huntsman's Dream of Paradise'. An Eng. paper would have used the word *sportsman*.

hurry is in Am. an adj. as well as a verb and a noun. 'The Commissioner sent a hurry message to Albany, to have the bill affecting his department amended.' 'The Mayor made a hurry visit to the city.' 'I sent a hurry call to the Charity Hospital' (E. GOLDMAN, Living My Life, 142).

hurt. The past partic. *hurt* may be applied in Am. to things as well as persons. 'The eagerly awaited hurt book sale begins to-day. Every book that has suffered in the least in the Christmas rush is included' (Advt.). In Eng. such books would be described as *damaged* or *shop-soiled*.

husky is used in Eng. only in the senses of *dry as a husk*, and (of a voice) *hoarse*. In Am. it also = *sturdy*. 'The veterans are not veterans at all,

but the huskiest set of young fellows.'
'The streets and country roads are
thronged with husky, able-bodied
men.' 'The trade required little skill;
almost any husky young man with
good nerves could pick up all its
tricks in a short time' (L. Adamic,
Dynamite, 189).

As a noun, *husky* denotes an *Eskimo
dog.* 'He has lived in Alaska in the
white wilderness, with a good bunch
of huskies between him and death.'

hustings, now rare in Eng., because
the thing it once denoted was abo-
lished by the Ballot Act of 1872, survives in Am. in the sense of a platform at a meeting held during an
election campaign. 'The Dem. hustings from Esopus to Brooklyn teemed
with infamous charges, scandalous
hints and innuendoes.' 'How the
phrase rolled and boomed from
thousands of hustings that year
throughout the South and West'
(S. H. Acheson, Joe Bailey, 37).
'He proved himself one of the most
effective and convincing speakers we
ever had on the hustings' (Prof. J. L.
Laughlin, The Federal Reserve Act,
175).

†**hustle** is usually trans. in Eng. and
= *jostle.* In Am. it is most commonly
intrans., as in some Eng. dial., and =
move quickly and energetically, not to
say *fussily.* 'Some other means of
raising the needed money will be
devised, and the pastor will get out
and hustle for it.' 'Must furnish
satisfactory recommendations as to
his ability as a progressive, level-
headed, hustling man' (Advt.). 'A
man 68 years old has walked from
Philadelphia to this city in 23 hours.
Even an old man hustles when he is
getting out of Philadelphia for N.Y.'
'The southern states and the great
undeveloped western territory were
filled with hustling pioneers' (Prof.
T. J. Grayson, Leaders and Periods
of Am. Finance, 176). 'Gary and
Frick hustled by special train at midnight to Washington' (J. T. Flynn,
God's Gold, 430).

Hence the nouns *hustle* and *hustler.*
'The firemen put on a little extra
hustle in getting around.' 'He was
the sort of hustler that, when a
branch line was needed in haste,
would have his rails down before the
ordinary man could get his bid in.'

hyphenate. 'Wasn't the President's
message on the hyphenated gentlemen bully?' (Letters of Franklin K.
Lane, 188). Had Mr. Wilson, then,
been following Lord Randolph Churchill's example and castigating the
mediocrities with double-barrelled
names? Not at all. The objects of
the President's denunciation were
certain German-Americans who had
been engaged in intrigues against
the welfare of the U.S. The term
hyphenated Americans is in common
use to denote German-Americans,
Irish-Americans, and so on, esp. when
there is reason to suspect that, though
technically Am. citizens, their allegiance is really divided between the
nationalities represented on both
sides of the hyphen. They are sometimes called *hyphenates* and their
divided loyalty is described as
hyphenation. 'They [German immigrants in the Middle West] kept their
own social organization and even
went so far as to get the State laws
published in the German language
in Indiana in 1858. This tendency
toward hyphenation has made the
Germans a less valuable element in
the Am. population up to the present
time than they should have been'
(Madison Grant, Conquest of a
Continent, 181).

I

ice. †The Am. metaphor *cut ice* is
very different in meaning from *break
the ice.* It is equivalent to *count for
anything,* and is usually found with
a negative. 'He admitted that the
international strike he had called did
not cut much ice.' 'The czar is to
send an ice-breaking boat to the Far

East, realizing apparently that his forces haven't been cutting much ice over that way.' 'It took me little time to discover that belonging to the best Society in San Francisco cut no ice in N.Y.' (G. ATHERTON, Adventures of a Novelist, 143).

Am. *ice water* = Eng. *iced water.*

Ill is an adv. as well as an adj., and there is accordingly no need of *illy,* which often takes its place in Am. 'Illy considered legislation.' 'We were driven at perilous speed through illy-lighted streets' (H. W. TAFT, Japan and Am. 100). 'Adequate appreciation can be but illy expressed' (A. A. ETTINGER, The Mission to Spain of Pierre Soulé, pref.). 'To meet a crisis of this kind labor was illy prepared' (C. A. and M. R. BEARD, The Rise of Am. Civilization, ii. 213).

impractical. In Eng. one speaks of (1) an *unpractical* person and (2) an *impracticable* thing. In Am. *impractical* serves the purpose of both these epithets. (1) 'He argued that a professor must necessarily be theoretical and impractical' (Prof. C. E. MERRIAM, Chicago, 270). 'The modern school is not wholly the development of impractical theorists' (P. E. SARGENT, Handbook of Am. Private Schools, 23). (2) 'It proved a constructive, statesmanlike document of high order but impractical' (Prof. A. E. MARTIN, Hist. of U.S. i. 83). 'The details of Eliot's scheme of government were quite impractical' (Prof. H. W. SCHNEIDER, The Puritan Mind, 25). 'The making of all laws by direct action of the people would be hopelessly impractical' (Prof. H. L. McBAIN, The Living Constitution, 202).

in. 'Taking his first vacation in four years.' 'The most comprehensive statement that has appeared in many a long day.' 'The worst wreck that has occurred in this part of New Jersey in some time.' 'Some of the greatest works in the repertory of German opera have not been heard

here in years and years.' 'He had not eaten a substantial meal in so long that he had forgotten the taste of food.' In all these examples, Eng. idiom would have required *for* instead of *in,* wherever the preposition is used to govern a word denoting a space of time.

inaugural, inauguration. The ceremony which takes place when a new Pres. of the U.S. enters upon his office is called his *inauguration,* and the day on which it is held is *inauguration day.* His formal allocution on this occasion is known as an *inaugural address,* often abbrev. to *inaugural.* 'All the relations came to Washington for the Inauguration.' 'The Rough Riders supplied the principal motif at the inauguration in 1905' (H. F. PRINGLE, Theodore Roosevelt, 362). 'The wintry days of the Taft inauguration four years before' (D. LAWRENCE, The True Story of Woodrow Wilson, 85). 'The following March, when he [Lincoln] delivered his second inaugural, the surrender at Appomattox was scarcely a month away' (J. TRUSLOW ADAMS, The Epic of Am. 268). 'The civil-service reform pledges of the platform, which Pres. Hayes repeated with great emphasis in the inaugural' (Prof. J. W. BURGESS, The Administration of Pres. Hayes, 58).

The same terms are used in connexion with entrance upon the governorship of an Am. State or the headship of an Am. university.

Independence Day. It was on July 4th, 1776, that the Declaration of Independence was adopted by the Continental Congress. The anniversary of that date is observed as a legal holiday throughout the U.S. under the official name of *Independence Day.*

The term in most general use, however, is *the Fourth of July,* often abbrev. to *the Fourth.* 'The book is worth about ten Fourth of July orations in showing the reader his duty to be a worthy citizen.' 'The tremendous display of fireworks which Vesuvius is sending up every night may lead the inhabitants of Mars to think that every day is the Fourth of July in Italy at the present time.' 'The courts are acting wisely in undertaking to prevent the use of dangerous explosives by making their sale an offense likely to be punished. It is not the small boy, but his elders, who have given us a deadly Fourth.' 'There were four great public holidays: the Fourth, the Grange picnic, the circus and the country fair' (A. NEVINS, The Emergence of Modern Am. 156).

initiation. In Am. clubs, *initiation fee* = Eng. *entrance fee.* 'Unique among clubs, it levies no initiation fee and no annual dues' (Advt.). 'Honorary members pay no dues or initiation fees' (Rotary? 115). The Eng. term is also used in Am. See DUES.

inn. In Eng. *innholder* is now obs., having been superseded by *innkeeper.* The latter is the more usual term in Am. also, but a visitor to Atlantic City will find on the door of his room in the hotel a notice containing extracts from 'an act concerning innholders, boarding-house keepers and their guests, in the State of New Jersey'.

inning. In Eng. the plur. form, *innings,* is invariably used, whether the sense is sing. or plur. In Am. the sing. form, *inning,* is employed for the sing. sense. 'The Ambassador's team won by 12 runs and one inning.' 'The woman with pretty arms is enjoying an inning these days.' 'As he had done all the talking the night before, so now I was to have an inning' (HAMLIN GARLAND, Roadside Meetings, 433). 'The man of action had his inning' (Dr. FRANKLIN H. MARTIN, The Joy of Living, i. 5).

instal(l)ment. Am. *installment selling* = Eng. *hire purchase.* It may, or may not, be significant that this kind of business transaction is ordi-

narily regarded in Am. from the point of view of the seller but in Eng. from that of the buyer. 'It was the time of mergers, mass production, common stocks, and installment selling.'

institute. In Eng. an *institute* is as permanent a thing as an institution. In Am. it may be a temporary affair— a series of lectures and classes, esp. for the training of teachers, similar to a summer school exc. that it may be held at any time of year. 'Sunday-school institutes have recently been held in the dioceses of Pittsburgh and Maryland. At the former the principal address was delivered by . . . The Maryland Institute heard addresses from. . . .' 'The burden of this campaign was education. The Legislature had provided the machinery in the shape of so-called "teachers' institutes"—essentially roving commissions to improve educational conditions. Wherever these young exhorters could assemble an audience —in mountain cabins, in rural schools, in open fields, at the crossroads—they forced their theme' (B. J. HENDRICK, Earlier Life of Walter H. Page, 401). 'The public health nurses of the Connecticut valley opened a three-day institute at Carnegie hall, Northampton, this morning.'
For a full account of the *institutes* recently introduced into the system of many Am. universities, see Dr. Abraham Flexner's *Universities,* p. 110. In this connexion, he says, the word 'may mean something or nothing'.

†institution. The adj. *institutional* is spec. used in Am. as a descriptive epithet for a church which includes many social organizations among its activities. 'Rainsford was known to the general public in his own generation as the pioneer of the institutional church. He found the church a building for worship, he left it an organization for service.'

instruct has a spec. meaning in the vocab. of Am. politics. When delegates are sent from a minor party organization to a major convention where nominations to office are to be made, they are often appointed on the understanding that they will vote for certain candidates. They are then said to be *instructed to vote for* or *instructed for* such candidates. 'The Democrats of Texas instructed their delegates to vote for him' (W. G. McADOO, Crowded Years, 129). 'As a delegate from Nebraska, he was instructed to vote for Clark' (Prof. A. E. MARTIN, Hist. of U.S. ii. 515). 'We were instructed for Bryan. We would all vote for him on the first ballot' (F. J. STIMSON, My U.S. 135).

The term *instruct* is similarly used in other cases where a delegate's action is prescribed for him by those who appointed him. 'In 1877 he became Senator from Mississippi. Being instructed in 1878 by the legislature of Mississippi how to vote on the Bland Bill, he refused to obey, and his course was ultimately sanctioned by the people of the State' (Prof. W. P. TRENT, Southern Writers, 388).

Hence *instructions*, in a corresponding sense. 'The state convention will send 78 delegates to St. Louis with ironclad instructions for him.' 'There are two kinds of instructions: one, "First, last, and all the time", which binds the delegates in the national convention to vote all the time for their candidate; the other, simple instructions, which only binds them to vote for him on the first ballot or two' (F. J. STIMSON, My U.S. 134).

In Am. colleges an *instructor* is a junior teacher inferior in rank to a professor. He is of lower status than a tutor in a college of Oxford or Cambridge or a lecturer at other Eng. universities. 'After spending a year as a fellow at Princeton in physics, he was made instructor in mathematics' (Dict. Am. Biog. vi. 386). 'He went through Harvard College mainly as a matter of form, and remained in that institution after graduation as instructor and as an assistant in the library' (W. M. PAYNE, Editorial Echoes, 270). 'Dr. Wilfred P. Mustard was appointed Instructor in Latin and later raised to the position of Professor' (Dr. RUFUS M. JONES, Haverford College, 77).

Insular. The term *insular cases* denotes a series of important cases decided by the U.S. Supreme Court in 1901. The question at issue was whether the Constitution of the U.S. applied to Porto Rico and the Philippines, which had recently been annexed. If it did, the inhabitants of these islands would be entitled to the constitutional guarantees enjoyed by Am. citizens, and their products would enter the ports of the U.S. unrestricted by any tariff. In answer to the basic question, "Does the Constitution follow the flag?" the Court decided "yes", but with important and sweeping qualifications. The Constitution was held to consist of two kinds of provisions, "fundamental" and "formal", only the former of which applied to the dependencies. The Court intimated that it would declare from time to time, as specific cases arose, which provisions possessed this fundamental quality. In deciding the concrete issues then before it, the trend of the Court's thinking became apparent. Acc. to the "Insular Cases", the inhabitants of these scattered possessions are not citizens of the U.S. unless and until Congress expressly confers citizenship upon them' (Prof. A. M. SCHLESINGER, Political and Social Hist. of the U.S. 479).

Interference is a technical term of the Am. Patent Office. See first quotation. 'If there is a prior application for substantially the same invention a proceeding called interference is instituted for the purpose of determining the question of priority of invention' (Encycl. Soc. Sci. xii. 21). 'The Commissioner of Patents is by statute made the tribunal of last resort in the Patent Office, and has appellate jurisdiction in the trial of interference cases' (Congressional Directory). 'The Patent Office thereupon declared an interference between the two patentees and a bitter fight was precipitated' (Dict. Am. Biog. vii. 408).

It is also an Am. football term, defined by the *O.E.D.* as 'the act of interposing between a runner and a tackler to obstruct the latter.' 'Much that seemed intentional rough play was the "interference" which, forbidden by the Eng. rules, is the most characteristic feature of our game.' 'New rules were adopted as regards downs, tackling and interference' (Prof. A. M. SCHLESINGER, The Rise of the City, 317).

intermission has two spec. uses in Am. It may denote (1) an interval between lessons in school, such as in Eng. schools is usually called a *break*, or (2) an *interval* between the acts at a dramatic performance.

(1) 'Every girl is given a half-hour intermission morning and afternoon to lounge in the rest-room and read or gossip.' 'The pupils meet in the auditorium for general exercises, after which, except for brief periods of intermission, the day is spent in classrooms' (Dr. C. C. BOYER, Hist. of Education, 447).

(2) 'When the curtain descended for the intermission, Dan stepped into the little corridor back of the boxes to smoke a cigarette' (H. FOOTNER, The Ring of Eyes, 97).

internal. Am. *internal revenue* = Eng. *inland revenue*. 'These percentages stood at 14·7 per cent. for customs and 68·78 per cent. for internal revenue' (Prof. A. E. MARTIN, Hist. of U.S. ii. 719).

inure. In Eng. this word is seldom employed intrans. exc. as a legal term. In Am. it is in everyday use in the sense of *work out, be operative*. 'Much of this expense inures to nobody's advantage.' 'It would be a singular thing if the tariff laws inured mainly to the benefit of the working

man.' 'In this they were aided by the profits inuring to shrewd manipulators of corporate finance' (H. O'CONNOR, Mellon's Millions, 273).

inventory. In addition to its normal Eng. use, *inventory* is in Am. a business term corresponding to the Eng. *stock-taking.* Thus one may see advertisements of 'pre-inventory sales' or of sales 'after inventory clearance'. 'Take advantage of this pre-inventory price and stock up your stationery supply at a great saving' (Advt.).

investment. The Am. term *investment bank* denotes what is called in Eng. a *merchant bank* (because firms of this kind were evolved from mercantile concerns) and in France a *banque industrielle*; i.e. a firm which does not conduct ordinary banking business, but confines itself mainly to acceptance and loan issuing. 'A restraint on boom-time extravagance which will enrage the promoters, the merger experts, the investment bankers, the high-pressure sales managers.'

†**iron.** In Am. *iron out* is often used fig., in the sense of *smooth out*. 'The prospects of ironing out these differences are at present not bright' (C. P. HOWLAND, Survey of Am. Foreign Relations for 1931, 384). 'The inner differences in credit standing between the various branches and the parent bank were speedily ironed out' (Prof. T. J. GRAYSON, Leaders and Periods of Am. Finance, 175). 'The President interposed to iron out the differences between Secretary Mellon and those congressmen who thought him too tender of great aggregations of wealth' (Dict. Am. Biog. viii. 255).

issue. In Eng. *issue* sometimes denotes the *act of issuing*. In Am. *issuance* is commonly preferred in this sense. 'Much revenue is lost to the railroads by the issuance of these free passes.' 'A case decided immediately after the issuance of these rules' (T. C. BLAISDELL, The Federal

Trade Commission, 86). 'The suit to compel the issuance of the bonds voted by the people of San Francisco' (G. T. CLARK, Leland Stanford, 214). 'Having much to do with the issuance in Norwegian and Eng. of popular editions' (Dict. Am. Biog. ix. 269). 'These election results were not wholly caused by the issuance of the Emancipation Proclamation' (Prof. A. E. MARTIN, Hist. of U.S. i. 720).

ivy. See LAUREL.

J

jag means in Eng. a *sharp projection*, such as the point of a rock. In Am., as formerly in Eng., and still in certain Eng. dial., it commonly denotes a *load*, and esp. a *load of liquor* that is more than the drinker can carry. Hence it sometimes means also a *state of drunkenness.* 'A jag acquired in a model saloon will be called a condition of cerebral excitement superinduced by undue indulgence in fermented beverages.' 'Those who overeat of starches and sweets often manufacture much alcohol in the digestive tract. They go on a jag without knowing what makes them feel gay' (Dr. R. L. ALSAKER, Eating for Health and Efficiency, 479).

jail delivery. In Eng. the clearing a jail of prisoners by bringing them to trial. In Am. a concerted escape of several prisoners from jail. 'The most daring jail delivery in the history of Delaware occurred in the Georgetown jail to-day, when the aged Deputy Sheriff was murderously assaulted by eleven negro criminals, who, after beating him into insensibility, made their escape.' 'In an attempted jail delivery in the Camden County jail to-day six prisoners escaped from the institution.' 'There was a jail delivery at Lockport yesterday, while the sheriff and most of his deputies were doing police duty at

Olcott. Probably the jail will be more strongly guarded hereafter.'

janitor is in much more frequent use in Am. than in Eng., where *doorkeeper* or *caretaker* is commonly preferred. 'Most of the school janitors are paid according to the floor space they must attend to. In addition, they receive pay acc. to the number and kind of steam-heating boilers in the school.' 'He thought of the expense of maintaining church worship—paid choirs and organists, salaried janitors, &c.' 'At the factory do you charge the boss's time at the same rate you charge for the janitor's?' (L. F. CARR, Am. Challenged, 15). 'Under the old method of cleaning a schoolroom, the janitors would sweep with an ordinary broom' (H. M. POLLOCK and W. S. MORGAN, Modern Cities, 279). 'At St. Giles's, Cripplegate, the janitor is a woman' (W. WINTER, Shakespeare's England, 180).

jar. As a trans. verb *jar* is now rare in Eng., but is still in constant use in Am. in both (1) the literal and (2) the fig. sense. (1) 'A man was jarred by the sudden stopping of the car and dropped his false teeth on the footboard.' (2) 'It may jar romantic souls by its tone of superiority toward the alluring world of dreams.' 'A centralized organization would take care of the regular party workers and would jar as little as possible the conservative and settled ideas of the people themselves' (J. KERNEY, Political Education of Woodrow Wilson, 32). 'N. Carolina had never before been so angered, so jarred, so instructed, so entertained' (B. J. HENDRICK, Earlier Life of Walter H. Page, 168).

jay. In Eng. the habits of the bird called *jay* have given rise to the fig. use of the word to denote an *impertinent chatterer*. The *O.E.D.* gives examples from Shakespeare. In Am. it means rather a *simpleton* or *gullible person.* 'The trouble with the reputation of Kansas abroad is that the

State's representatives in public life are "jays", though Kansas has as many men of culture and refinement and capacity as any State in the Union.'

††The compound *jaywalker* denotes a person who is foolish enough to attempt to cross the street without sufficient circumspection.

jeer. The earlier Eng. usage, now obs., of making *jeer* a trans., thus dispensing with the need of a following *at*, still survives in Am., as in Scotland. 'The sidewalks were jammed with a noisy crowd that started to jeer the brokers.' 'The Dewey who was jeered in April of 1900 was precisely the same Dewey who was idolized in May of 1898' (M. SULLIVAN, Our Times, 341). 'When the name of the Am. President was jeered in the House of Commons' (L. DENNY, Am. Conquers Britain, 15). 'He was repeatedly jeered and pelted by unfriendly audiences' (Dict. Am. Biog. vi. 558).

jeopard, jeopardy. In Am. *jeopard* is preferred to *jeopardize*, the common term in Eng. 'He would not in any way jeopard his future interests by taking the chairmanship.' 'He would by that act banish himself from communion with his fellows and jeopard his possessions to the last dime' (W. J. GHENT, Our Benevolent Feudalism, 180).

The U.S. Constitution provides that no person shall be subject 'to be twice put in jeopardy of life or limb' for the same offence. This guarantee against a second trial is commonly spoken of as a guarantee against *double jeopardy*. 'There is no specific state constitutional provision prohibiting double jeopardy' (G. R. SHERRILL, Criminal Procedure in N. Carolina, 20). 'The guaranty against double jeopardy was extended by Congress to the Philippines' (Prof. F. M. BURDICK, Law of Am. Constitution, 398). 'He held that one conviction for possessing liquor and another conviction for selling the same liquor did not violate the constitutional protection against double jeopardy' (A. T. MASON, Brandeis, 171).

jerk. No process of violent shaking is involved in the preparation of what is called in Am. *jerked beef* or *jerked meat.* This term denotes meat that has been cured by being cut into long thin slices and dried in the sun. Acc. to the *Century Dict.*, the word is a corruption of a Chilian word *charqui* meaning *dried beef.* John Bradbury, in his *Travels in the Interior of Am.*, published in 1817, writes: 'We found that the Fort was but ill supplied with provisions, having little of anything but jerked meat.' 'Supplies of bread from the government bakery were issued every noontime, and they brought what they chose from home to supplement it. Most of them brought jerked beef or some such thing.'

The *O.E.D.* Suppl. says of the Am. compound *jerkwater* that it is 'used attrib. as a term of depreciation' and compares FRESHWATER (q.v.). 'Andrews, with 21 picked soldiers, stole the train under the eyes of the crew, who were breakfasting at a jerkwater station.'

Jersey. In writing of certain residents in N.Y. City, Mr. Hamlin Garland remarks that 'their ways were quite as remote from the so-called captains of industry as from the farmers of Jersey' (The Tyranny of the Dark, 108). One might naturally wonder why the manners and customs of the Channel Islanders should thus be dragged in to point a contrast. The *Jersey*, however, to which Mr. Garland is referring is *New Jersey*, the State which is separated from N.Y. City by no more than the breadth of the Hudson River. It is frequently mentioned in Am. without its distinguishing adj. 'Nothing does the Jersey commuter enjoy more than his country drives.' 'Sir Henry Clinton had crossed the Delaware with a huge train of waggons and artillery, and was scudding away in hot haste over the plains of Jersey in full retreat from N.Y.' (Prof. J. A. HARRISON, George Washington, 317). 'A New Jersey reception at the White House was planned for Feb. 13, 1914. . . . The Jersey folks had a gala night in the White House' (J. KERNEY, Political Education of Woodrow Wilson, 282). *Jerseyman* is similarly used.

The reputation of the State of New Jersey as an exception to the general slowness of criminal procedure in Am. has been crystallized in the term *Jersey justice*. 'Once again has Jersey justice vindicated its potentiality; once again has the machinery of the law given proof that it can move with terrible swiftness.'

The name of *Jersey wagon* is given to a low basket carriage formerly much used in New Jersey.

jimmy. In Eng. a burglar's crowbar is called a *jemmy*, although the familiar form of the name *James*, from which it is believed to be derived, is not *Jemmy* but *Jimmy*. In Am. this tool is known as a *jimmy*. 'Lock picks, a jimmy, a safe punch, and a revolver were there.' 'Rob a miser's safe and he's broke; but you can't break a big merchant with a jimmy and a stick of dynamite' (G. H. LORIMER, Old Gorgon Graham, 159).

Hence the verb *jimmy*. 'The two sleuths found that the front door had been jimmied.'

joiner. In Am., not only a variety of carpenter, but also a man of such strong gregarious instincts that he becomes a member of many societies or fraternal orders. 'Always a joiner, Jim early became an Elk.' 'Of all the leaders Martin Behrman appears to have been the greatest "joiner". He belonged to at least 16 business, social, and religious societies' (Dr. H. ZINK, City Bosses of U.S. 30). 'The Am. of the Machine Age was a "joiner": never, apparently, was he so happy as when banded together with his neighbors and acquaintances in an association for the common furtherance of fraternal, business, moral, or athletic purposes' (L. M. HACKER and B. B. KENDRICK, The U.S. since 1865, 695).

joint is in Am. a colloq. name for a low drinking-place or opium den—a meaning which gives an obvious opportunity for newspaper humour. Thus: '"At which joint did your friend have his arm amputated?" "That's a mighty disrespectful way to speak of a hospital."' Again: 'Champion Jeffries is laid up with a crippled knee. This is not the first case on record of a prizefighter's being disabled through the influence of a "bad joint".' 'Despite stringent enforcement laws, there were numerous "joints" where liquor was sold more or less openly' (Dict. Am. Biog. xiii. 394).

The word is infrequent in Am. as applied to meat served at table.

joker has a spec. meaning in Am. politics. It is defined by Webster as 'a clause that is ambiguous or apparently immaterial inserted in a legislative bill to render it inoperative or uncertain in some respect without arousing opposition at the time of its passage'. 'The committee will eliminate from the measure the lumber "joker", first exposed by Representative Tawney. This "joker", in practice, would have restored the Dingley rate of $2 on rough lumber, despite the fact that the bill was supposed to reduce the duty 50 per cent. The "joker" was concealed in a proviso that exacted the maximum rates on forest products coming from any country that imposed any restrictions whatsoever upon the shipment or manufacture of lumber.' 'At the last moment the bill was imperilled by discovering a "joker"—a provision believed to be surreptitious, which had escaped attention in the heat of debate—that was held to vitiate the hides-leather compromise' (Prof. N. W. STEPHENSON, Nelson W. Aldrich). 'The closing days of a long and laborious session were at hand·

At such times it is necessary to exercise unusual caution, as legislation becomes hurried, and frequently is stacked with "jokers" that nullify the fundamental purpose of the bills' (D. LAWRENCE, True Story of Woodrow Wilson, 113).

jolly. †In Am. *jolly* may be used colloq. as a verb, in a sense that would be approximately expressed in Eng. by *chaff*. 'The clubmen had a good time jollying the Senator in order to get his responses.' 'When the hard-worked business man has jollied the professor on having such a lazy time of it in summer, the ready answer has been that the three months of leisure are part of his salary.' 'Flood knew it was useless to rally the boys, for a wet, hungry man is not to be jollied' (ANDY ADAMS, Log of a Cowboy, 154). The verb is also used in Am. in the sense of *wheedle, cajole, keep in good humour*. In a speech made at a N.Y. club shortly after his appointment to the London Embassy, Mr. Whitelaw Reid said: 'Some one spoke the other day of the duty of our embassy as consisting merely in "jollying the English". In so far as this means that whenever an ambassador has to say anything he should say a friendly thing if he can, the remark is well enough.'

jolt is used fig. in Am. much more commonly than in Eng. 'As the feud now stands it is one of the most malodorous in the history of the turf, and the game at Ascot has suffered a severe jolt.' 'But Hogg's supremacy now received a severe jolt' (S. H. ACHESON, Joe Bailey, 69). 'The antiquated banking system received a terrific jolt in 1907. That year there was a disastrous money panic' (W. G. McADOO, Crowded Years, 212). 'This final step of our reflation would perhaps soften the jolt to international exchange' (Prof. IRVING FISHER, Mastering the Crisis, 65).

joy is sometimes used in Am. as equivalent to mere *pleasure* or *com-fort*, without any suggestion of ecstatic emotions. 'The club houses have kitchenettes, tea-rooms, and many other pleasant arrangements that add much to the joy and efficiency of the members' (Advt.).

†The Am. term *joy ride*, introduced after motoring became popular, originally denoted a ride taken for pleasure in a car that is intended to be used for business purposes, or in a car that is used by an employee without his employer's knowledge. 'The Acting Mayor vetoed, this afternoon, the ordinance passed last week to prevent city officers from taking "joy rides", providing for conspicuous marking of city automobiles.' 'A "joy ride" early Sunday morning ended fatally for a chauffeur, who, it is said, was in his employer's car without leave when it collided with a milk wagon.' Nowadays the term commonly denotes any ride taken for pleasure, whatever the car.

When this term was first introduced, its unfamiliarity in Eng. occasioned a curious instance of the misinterpretation of cablegrams. A London paper reported that 'another chauffeur was killed in what is known as the Joyride, N.Y., as the result of a collision'.

The term *joy-ride* is sometimes used fig. 'The shrewd politicians of Europe saw to it that the President of the U.S. had a great joy-ride when he came to put the finishing touches on his vision of everlasting peace' (J. KERNEY, Political Education of Woodrow Wilson, 426).

judge carries with it in Am. by no means such dignified associations as it possesses in Eng. It may mean no more than a *magistrate* of a police court. 'The magistrate's court located in Manhattan and the Bronx is organized into a city-wide system with more than 40 judges and a Chief Magistrate.' 'He was a justice of the peace and hence was commonly known as Judge Wilson' (Prof. H. J. FORD, Woodrow Wilson, 2). 'Lyman

Beecher caught the thief, brought him back to his room, and made him lie on the floor by his bed until morning, when he carried him before the judge' (A. Fields, Life and Letters of H. B. Stowe, 5). See also TRY.

judiciary. When, in 1932, one Eng. judge publicly criticized another from the bench, an M.P. announced his intention of proposing in the House of Commons a motion declaring that such conduct was 'calculated to lower the prestige of the judicature'. If a similar incident had occurred in Am., the word *judiciary* would have been preferred to *judicature.* 'A committee of attorneys waited upon him to see if they could influence him to increase the judiciary in their district.' 'The final debate in the Senate was whether rates were to be regulated by an extension of the executive branch or by the judiciary' (H. F. Pringle, Theodore Roosevelt, 423). 'A fair and impartial judiciary has never been better represented than by Judge Frank Murphy at this trial' (A. G. Hays, Let Freedom Ring, 231).

jug. The handle of a jug is placed on one side of it. Hence the term *jug-handled* is used fig. in Am. as a synonym for *one-sided, inequitable.* 'A great many Canadians are of the opinion that at the present time the trade between Canada and the U.S. is distinctly jug-handled, with the handle altogether on the side of our people. . . . Is it not jug-handled to have an average duty of 50 per cent. imposed upon what we import from good customers and consider that they are only treating us with common fairness when they impose a duty of about 25 per cent. on the merchandise which we send to them for sale?' See also PITCHER.

jump. The compound *jumping-rope* is peculiar to Am. It denotes what is known in Eng. as a *skipping-rope.*

junior. Within an Am. household a son who bears the same name as his father is often addressed or desig-

nated as *Junior* instead of by his Christian name. 'A little ingenuity and care will make Dad and Junior, yes, and Mother too, eat the alkaline-rich fruits and vegetables for taste as well as for health.' In public references the son may retain the appendage *Junior* long after the death of his father has made such a distinguishing mark unnecessary. Thus, the N.Y. *Times* of March 6, 1932, announced the death of a railroad president, Eppa Hunton, Jr., in his 77th year.

In Am. colleges *junior* is the technical term for a student in his third year. 'Finally, the sophomores, in despair, made a wild charge down the stairs and proceeded to bundle juniors and freshmen out of the hall.' 'The question at once starts itself, Why is the "Junior" so called in his third year and not in his first? The answer is that "Junior" and "Senior" are short for "Junior Sophist" and "Senior Sophist". We have here in short the *Generalis Sophista*, the man of two years' standing who has passed his "responsions", who was not quite forgotten at Oxford in my younger days, and who, I believe, is better known both at Cambridge and at Dublin' (E. A. Freeman, Some Impressions of the U.S. 194). 'When he was only a junior at Cornell, his knowledge of botany was such that he was appointed an instructor in that department' (Dict. Am. Biog. x. 211). The *junior college* is a recent development in Am. education. It is an institution that offers a general two-years' course, such as is normally given in the earlier years of the older colleges. 'This phenomenal growth of the junior college has come about in four ways: University amputation; high-school elongation; college decapitation; and independent creation' (Prof. M. A. May, The Education of Am. Ministers, iii. 336).

junk. †In Eng. the associations of this word are mainly nautical. It denotes primarily the old and discarded ropes of a ship, and secondarily salt meat, as being of the consistence of such ropes. In Am. it is the generic term for any kind of material that has been thrown away as useless. 'The machine was hurled against a telegraph pole, a mass of twisted junk.' 'After an hour's search through trays which were overloaded with junk, I came upon a large quarto volume of Don Quixote' (W. D. ORCUTT, Kingdom of Books, 85). 'The railroad and its equipment was, as a piece of physical property, not much better than junk' (H. CROLY, Marcus Alonzo Hanna, 79). The following quotation illustrates the fig. use of the word. 'The promised time when musty old precedents shall have been relegated to the junk heap.'

Hence the verb *junk = discard, throw away as rubbish.* 'It does not follow that all unremunerative lines should be junked.' 'The Am. wants action and results. If they are not forthcoming he turns to something else, a trait that has helped to junk so many hopeful third-party beginnings' (L. SYMES and T. CLEMENT, Rebel Am. 371).

jurist. The *O.E.D.* defines a *jurist* as 'one who professes or treats of law, one versed in the science of law, a legal writer', and it mentions as obs. the use of the term to denote 'one who practises in law, a lawyer'. In Am., however, the word is still used in the latter sense. The *Dict. Am. Biog.* describes as jurists many men whose qualifications, if they had been Englishmen, would not have entitled them to that description in the *Dict. Nat. Biog.* 'Sixty-one of them [members of the last Senate] were jurists, eighteen were business men, three were farmers, and two had been journalists. As to the jurists, they are not men who are still active as attorneys or judges. Generally men are in question who went over early from the legal profession into politics, and who have lived almost entirely in politics. Indeed, not a few of these lawyers who have become legislators have been for some years in commercial life at the head of great industrial or railroad corporations, so that the majority of jurists is no indication whatsoever of any legal petrifaction' (Dr. E. B. HOLT, in his trans. of Hugo Munsterberg's The Americans, 88). 'Someone has observed that the District Judge has greater power and jurisdiction than any other Am. jurist' (B. A. KONKLE, Joseph Hopkinson, 10). 'A well-known jurist at that time [at Chattanooga] was Judge Trewhitt, who presided over the Circuit Court' (W. G. McADOO, Crowded Years, 41).

In one instance, at least, this difference between Eng. and Am. usage was a matter of some importance. When, after refusing arbitration, the U.S. consented to refer the Alaskan boundary dispute to a Joint Commission consisting of three Am. and three British representatives, it was provided that this tribunal should consist of 'impartial jurists of repute'. Two of the three chosen by the U.S. were admittedly jurists in no other sense than that they had been admitted to the Bar. They had made no contribution to legal studies, and even their active careers had been in politics rather than in the practice of the law. (See ALLAN NEVINS's biog. of Henry White, 194, and H. F. PRINGLE's biog. of Theodore Roosevelt, 291.)

†**just** is sometimes used in Am. (1) as an intensive and (2) in the sense of *precisely.* (1) 'Everyone was so busy and happy that time just flew.' (2) 'A controversy arose as to just what was the difference between a "central bank" and "a system of central banking"' (Prof. N. W. STEPHENSON, Nelson W. Aldrich, 414). 'Under these circumstances just what do you mean by a "materialistic conception of history"?' (NORMAN THOMAS, America's Way Out, 137).

K

kangaroo. For *kangaroo court*, see quotation. 'An additional disciplinary feature found in one fourth of the jails of Virginia is the "kangaroo court", an organization of prisoners for the purpose of holding mock trials. In 13 jails the court is held only intermittently and is without continuous organization. In 15 jails, however, there is a permanent organization having, in most cases, written rules and holding sessions whenever there is "business" to come before the court. . . . The "kangaroo court" is approved and encouraged by a considerable number of jailers who find it helpful in the running of the jail. One jailer reports that he leaves all matters of discipline to the court' (Professors F. W. Hoffer, D. M. Mann, and F. N. House, The Jails of Virginia, 130). Elsewhere in the same book we are told that the officials of the court are elected by prisoners from among their number. The rules of a typical court are reproduced in full.

†**keep.** In Am. *for keeps* is a colloquial expression meaning *as a permanency, for good*. 'His personal opinion is that the gold standard has been established for keeps.' 'The Senator says he is "out of politics" for the present, but in fishing for keeps.' The leader of a strike is reported in a newspaper as saying: 'But as soon as his hired men began to prod us we made up our minds to prod back, and the fight is on for keeps.' 'There was no unrest over the fact that the curtain did not rise until 8.30. Once it did go up it atoned for the delay by not going down again for keeps until 2 o'clock Sunday morning.' 'I read more than was required, and I read for keeps too. I know these subjects to this day' (L. Steffens, Autobiog. i. 112).

key has two senses peculiar to Am. (1) A low sandy island or reef; e.g.

Key West, off the coast of Florida. 'On the Florida Keys hundreds of railroad laborers were overwhelmed by the combined results of hurricane and tide.' 'On one of the keys of Alligator Bay is the principal plume-bird rookery left in Florida.' The word in this sense is a variant of *cay*, from the Spanish *cayo*.

(2) A watch-key, used as the badge of Phi Beta Kappa, the most distinguished of college societies. 'If we made the key stand more for real intellectual power and less for mere faithful drudgery.' 'He graduated with a Phi Beta Kappa key before he was quite twenty' (Dr. C. R. Brown, They Were Giants, 150).

A *keyman* is a *telegraphist*. 'In connection with the visit of the international president of the Commercial Telegraphers' Union to this city, some of the leading keymen are sounding as their shibboleth the cry of "government ownership of the telegraph systems of this country".'

†A *key man* is a controlling or essential person in an enterprise. 'Big business was alarmed at the prospect of losing its key men, from both the managerial and industrial sides, as many were intent upon enlisting' (Dr. Franklin H. Martin, The Joy of Living, ii. 146).

kick. In Am. *kick*, both as verb and as noun, is commonly used in a fig. sense = *criticise* or *criticism*, generally with the implication that such criticism is opinionated or perverse. 'He had about the same comment to make on the treaty. He said he expected a strong vigorous kick from the barley growers of the Northwest, but he did not say whether or not he would respond to this kick by opposing the treaty.' 'Together with it there grew up naturally another Am. trait, that of "boosting" and of objecting to criticism as "kicking"' (J. Truslow Adams, The Epic of Am. 217).

Hence *kicker* = *critic*, *objector*. '"Kickers" who seem to think everything has gone wrong and the country is going to the demnition bow-wows because their wishes have not been consulted.' The reform forces, to whom the speaker gave most of his attention, were classified by him as "kickers".' 'One word of blame sinks deeper, spreads farther, and is longer remembered than the most florid hymn of praise. It is not surprising, then, that in the popular conception "critic" and "kicker" are one and the same.' 'The man who criticized or went back East was considered not only a "kicker", but a dangerous enemy to growth' (J. TRUSLOW ADAMS, The Epic of Am. 218).

††The noun *kick* may also denote 'a sharp stimulant effect, e.g. that of strong liquor or pungent seasoning; also, a thrill of excitement, fear, &c.' (O.E.D. Suppl.). 'At least one could toss off a few drinks and get a kick out of physical passion and forget that the world was crumbling' (F. L. ALLEN, Only Yesterday, 122).

For *kick-back*, noun and verb, see the following quotation. 'The kick-back operates in the following manner. A wage scale is set either by law, as in government contracts, or by agreement between capital and labor. The worker assumes that he is to get so much per day or per hour for his work. At the end of the week, he is required to return or kick-back part of his wages to a designated person, often a foreman or a book-keeper' (G. E. SOKOLSKY, in Atlantic Monthly, Aug. 1934, 139).

kill. In Am. newspaper offices 'copy' is said to be *killed* when the responsible editor decides that it is not to be published. 'The leading theme on which he [the Am. court reporter] builds a sensational, inadequate and misleading "story", which his city editor seldom kills' (H. W. TAFT, Japan and Am. 81). 'The editor can make room by killing the last paragraphs of the other stories' (E. L. SHUMAN, Practical Journalism, 62).

kindle. Wood used for lighting fires is commonly known in Am. as *kindling wood, kindling,* or *kindlings.* In Eng. these terms are not unknown, but *firewood* is much more usual. 'Every household should know about our dry pine kindling wood' (Advt.). 'Every two-hour period of sawing and splitting of kindling wood was followed by a dip and swim in the Passaic River' (Prof. M. PUPIN, From Immigrant to Inventor, 111). 'Ross split kindling and carried up coal.' 'Friends often met him on the street carrying kindling under his arm to light his office fire' (Dict. Am. Biog. xiv.529). 'He had taken the kindlings out of the wood-basket and piled them up in the fireplace' (E. O. WHITE, Lesley Chilton, 84). 'A large basket full of old parchments, standing on the floor, waiting to serve as kindlings when the next fire should require their use' (G. E. MERRILL, Parchments of the Faith, 181).

In descriptions of the results of collisions and similar accidents, Am. *kindling wood* = Eng. *matchwood*. 'His wagon was smashed into kindling wood.' 'The baggage car half buried itself in the sand on the right side of the locomotive. It was smashed almost to kindling wood.'

knife. One may sometimes read in an Am. paper at election time that such-and-such a candidate has been *knifed* at the polls. This knifing is entirely fig., just as in Eng. one often speaks fig. of stabbing a man in the back. In Am. politics a candidate is knifed when members of his own party endeavour treacherously to defeat him in some underhand way, esp. by voting for his opponent. 'If the Governor is defeated, it will be either because of the defection of Independents, Prohibitionists, and those who have hitherto supported him, or else because of knifing within his own party.' 'Intensity of party faction leads directly to those dreaded political things, "lukewarmness" and "apathy", and often to actual "knifing".' 'If Tammany knifed Cleveland, the Mugwumps played havoc with the following of Blaine' (WILLIS J. ABBOT, Watching the World Go By, 77).

knock. The Am. use of *knock* in the sense of *find fault with, run down,* is described by Webster as vulgar slang. It may be found, nevertheless, in reputable newspapers, though sometimes between apologetic quotemarks. 'The persistent "knocking" to which the Western Pacific Railroad is subjected by the periodical circulation of false reports.' 'Mr. Bryan is not exactly knocking at the White House door, but he is knocking everybody else who wants to knock there.' Hence *knocker = censorious person, captious critic.* 'The municipal "boosters" that are an organized factor in the development of Western cities have no use for what they call "knockers", critical citizens who are figuratively credited with using a "hammer".' '"Booster" organizations were formed to fight the "knockers"' (F. L. BIRD and F. M. RYAN, The Recall of Public Officers, 238). 'Men who in another era would have been denounced as knockers and defamers were acclaimed as heroes and servants of the Republic' (C. C. REGIER, The Era of the Muckrakers, 22).

In Am. *knock down* may mean *embezzle* (*the fares of passengers*). 'Two conductors on surface cars were convicted of petit larceny to-day. The men were accused of "knocking down" fares on their cars.' 'Does the Springfield street railway lose over $100,000 a year in fares "knocked down" by conductors? This claim was made this week by a conductor of that road.'

The auction *knockout*—a combination among dealers by which they obtain articles at auctions at a low price to resell afterward among themselves—seems to be peculiarly Eng. The *knockout blow* is known in Eng. and Am. alike. In Am. *knockout*

drops are drops of some drug put into a man's drink to stupefy him for purposes of robbery. 'He suffered from delusions, principally the conviction that people were putting knock-out drops into his coffee.' 'Bowery thieves were using chloral or "knockout drops" as an aid in robbing victims.' A man addicted to such practices is a *knockout man.* 'He is sometimes dangerous, for he may be one of the new sort of "knockout men" discovered this week.' The verb *knock out* is also used fig., as is *knock on the head* in Eng. 'In power, the Democrats wouldn't knock out protection if they could, and couldn't if they would.'

The derivative *knockabout* denotes a small sailing-boat, esp. used as a pleasure craft. 'Yachts of every size, from the great steam palace to the little 20-foot knockabouts.'

The expression *knocked up* needs a danger signal. In Eng. it means *tired out,* but in Am. *enceinte.*

know. The expression *knowing to = aware of* is now obs. in Eng. but still current in Am. 'Some of the neighbors were knowing to the event, and called to offer their congratulations.'

In spite of the superficial similarity, *knownothingism* is not an Am. variety of *agnosticism.* It is a political term, denoting a party which was organized about the middle of the last century with the object of excluding all foreigners and Roman Catholics from political rights. It was originally a secret organization, and, as its members were required, when asked anything about it, to answer that they did not know, it came to be called *the know-nothing party.* 'The Dem. party was well served by the Knownothing craze which swept the country for a very brief period. This drove the foreign-born voters, the great majority of whom at that time were Irish Catholics, into the Dem. party because it was opposed to the Know-nothings.' 'Since the death of the Know-nothing party, N.Y. has ceased any organized attempt to lessen the power of the foreigner' (M. W. OVINGTON, Half a Man, 196). An alternative name for this organization was *the Am. party.*

L

landscape. The Am. term *landscape architecture* covers what is denoted in Eng. by *landscape gardening* and considerably more. In the 14th edition of the *Encycl. Britann.* an Am. writer says: 'In Eng., where the term *landscape architecture* is at present little used, the term *landscape gardening* persists, partly because much institutional and public work included in the practice of Am. landscape architects is done there by architects.' The *Am. Year Book* includes under the heading of *Landscape Architecture* an account of work carried out during the year not only on private estates but in the laying out of public parks and even in town planning. There is an 'Am. Society of Landscape Architects' whose official organ is entitled *Landscape Architecture.* There are also schools of *Landscape Architecture* in connexion with several Am. universities.

†**landslide.** The term *landslide* is used in Am. in preference to the Eng. *landslip.* 'Landslides blocked the only exit from our territory.' 'The landslides in the canal channel' (Dr. J. H. FREDERICK, The Development of Am. Commerce, 321). This word is fig. used in politics to denote an overwhelming victory at an election. The *Concise Oxford Dict.* is mistaken in defining it as an overwhelming political defeat. The Presidential election of 1932, for instance, was not a Rep. but a Dem. landslide. The party whose name is attached to the word *landslide* is pictured not as a once solid mass that has now crumbled into ruin, but as an irresistible natural force that has swept everything out of its path. 'The so-called silent vote grows larger and larger

every year, swaying majorities and occasionally precipitating landslides.' 'The result of the campaign was a Dem. landslide, in which Jackson received 219 electoral votes to 49 for Clay' (Prof. A. E. MARTIN, Hist. of U.S. i. 406).

large. When we read in an Am. paper that a certain Congressman is a representative *at large*, we are not to understand that he has a sort of roving commission. The term means that he has been chosen by a whole State, not by a particular district (constituency) within that State. In the decennial reapportionment of members of Congress among the States according to population, it may happen that a State that has previously sent five members to Congress is now allotted six. In such cases the State Legislature sometimes saves itself the trouble of 're-districting' by deciding that the additional member shall be elected by the State as a whole. The member thus elected is a representative *at large.*

The term is sometimes used by Am. writers in a similar sense when describing electoral methods abroad. Thus: 'The members of the Small Council [of Zurich] were all delegates from the guilds except six councilmen at large and two burgomasters who acted *ex officio*' (Prof. S. M. JACKSON, Huldreich Zwingli, 42).

See also BY.

lark. The Am. *meadow lark* has little resemblance to the Eng. *lark,* but is more like the Eng. *jackdaw.* Its scientific name is *sturnella magna,* and it belongs to the family of *Icteridae.*

last. In Am. the end of a week or month is often called the *last* of it. This does not necessarily mean the last day of it; it may, indeed, include more than one day. 'The store in which the committee will hold their rummage sale Friday and Saturday is beginning to pile up with a heterogeneous collection of articles that promises a lively scramble of bargain hunters the last of the week.' 'They go to the binders the last of January.' 'The corn will be hard by the last of August' (L. F. CARR, Am. Challenged, 194). 'By the last of May he had formulated his plan and on the 29th he issued two proclamations' (Prof. A. E. MARTIN, Hist. of U.S. ii. 24). See also FIRST.

latchstring. On both sides of the Atlantic the *latchstring* is nowadays an antiquated device, but in Am. the word has a fig. use which seems unlikely to become obs. 'If one hears that Nicholas Murray Butler is in Washington it is a waste of time to look for him at any hotel. The latchstring hangs out for him always at the White House.' 'The Citizens' Union has its latchstring out for voters of this class, but that does not satisfy all of them.' Writing in the days before any policy of restricted immigration was thought of, Lowell made Hosea Biglow boast that his country's 'free latch-string never was drawed in against the poorest child of Adam's kin'.

laurel. The Eng. *laurel* is any tree or shrub of the genus *laurus*; spec., the *laurus nobilis*. In Am. the word may denote an evergreen shrub of either *kalmia* or *rhododendron*. '"The dry-tongued laurel's pattering talk" does not refer to our mountain laurel or kalmia, but to some true laurel or bay.' Cecil Sharp (acc. to his biog., p. 145) found that there was a part of N. Carolina known as the Laurel Country, so named because of the abundance of rhododendrons (called *laurel* by the mountain-people) which grow on the mountain side. The real laurel was called *ivy*, while the ivy became *vine*.

lawn. In Am. *lawn party* is an alternative to *garden party*. 'An Englishwoman at a lawn party' (SINCLAIR LEWIS, Dodsworth, 85).

lay. The distinction between *lay* (trans.) and *lie* (intrans.) is not strictly observed in Am. (It was not observed by Jane Austen, but to-day a confusion between the two words is regarded in Eng. as a solecism.) 'The women wrapped themselves in a bedspread and laid down on the track.' 'If the pistol and bottle were thrown there after use, they must have laid upon the surface of the ground and could hardly have escaped the early searchers.'

Thus, *lay off* has both (1) the trans. sense of *discontinue the service of* = Eng. *stand off*, and (2) the intrans. sense of *take a rest.* (1) 'The company was laying off some of its hands on account of some decrease in the sales.' 'Unemployment insurance would help the workers who are laid off' (NORMAN THOMAS, America's Way Out, 198). (2) 'The doctor told her that, if she did not lay off for several weeks, she might find herself without a voice to use next season.' 'Like other newcomers to industry, the Filipino was inclined, in the earlier stages of his employment, to lay off frequently for small cause. He is now as regular in his attendance as the Japanese' (B. LASKER, Filipino Immigration, 182).

Another Am. use of the verb is illustrated by the invitation to visitors to *lay off* their outer garments when they enter a house.

There is a corresponding noun *lay-off*. 'The men who have been on for a year or more get a vacation of ten days. Those who have been working less than a year have to get along with only a five-day lay-off.' 'The company has distributed its production through the year so that no lay-offs are necessary' (L. ADAMIC, Dynamite, 407).

The derivative *lay-out* may denote (1) a *state of affairs, situation;* (2) a *gambling equipment.* (1) 'This is the lay-out. It is Parker, the Jurist and Patriot, against Roosevelt, the would-be Man-on-Horseback.' (2) 'He hurls back with scorn the charge that he is the angel of a faro lay-out.' 'Every gambling house ran from two to three monte layouts' (ANDY ADAMS, Log of a Cowboy, 260). In the sense of *plan, arrangement* (of ground, factory, &c.), the word is used in Eng. and Am. alike.

††**layer.** The name of *layer cake* is given in Am. to the kind of cake whose ingredients are arranged in layers. It thus corresponds very nearly to what is known in Eng. as a *jam sandwich.* 'Another good fruit layer cake is a banana cake. Take two bananas and grate them into the whipped white of an egg and a cup of sugar. Spread between layers of cake, and decorate with slices of banana.' 'She had brought a tart or a triangle of layer cake with her school luncheon' (K. D. WIGGIN, Rebecca, 78).

leave. †In Am. the past partic. *left* sometimes = Eng. *left behind.* 'The dinner was so good, and we lingered over it so long, that we came near being left, but galloped to the depot just in time to jump on to the last car' (J. H. CHOATE, quoted in his Life by E. S. MARTIN, i. 346).

There is an Am. compound noun *left-over*, used in various obvious senses. 'If every one who wished could not get into the Inaugural Ball, the left-overs did not seem to mourn the lack of the spectacle.' 'It is an excellent way to use up bits of cold boiled vegetables—left-overs that are too small to make a dish in themselves' (M. ELIZABETH, War Time Recipes, 90). 'The dread of this Executive power is a curious left-over from Colonial days' (Dr. LYMAN ABBOTT, Am. in the Making, 94). In the last quotation an Eng. writer would have used the word *survival.* See also HANG and HOLD.

ledger is occasionally used in Am. in the sense, now obs. in Eng., of *register.* 'Listed in the county ledgers as housewife.'

let is commonly used in Am. with *up* in the sense of *slacken.* 'He started a single-handed fight against Boss Tweed, and did not let up until the

famous ring was swept away.' If *let up* is followed by a preposition, that preposition is *on.* 'The doctrinaire, when he gets hold of a good thing, never lets up on it. His favorite idea is produced on all occasions.' 'He never let up on his main hobby of planting trees' (H. J. COOLIDGE and R. H. LORD, Archibald Cary Coolidge, 334).

There is a corresponding noun *let-up.* 'There will be no change in the policy we have steadily pursued, no let-up in the effort to secure the honest observance of the law' (Pres. THEODORE ROOSEVELT, in a speech). 'The months of Mr. Wilson's courtship involved a let-up in his labors of previous years in the White House' (D. LAWRENCE, True Story of Woodrow Wilson, 177).

The Eng. expression *let well alone* appears in Am. as *let well enough alone.* 'Why not let well enough alone, when you can by no possibility hope to better conditions at any point?' 'Two paths there were to follow, one an easy, let well-enough alone passage, the other a laborious, experimental climb.' 'The moderates in the patriot party were willing to let well enough alone' (S. G. FISHER, True Hist. of the Am. Revolution, 97).

letter. 'While a cadet at West Point, Gen. Nolan won his letter in baseball.' The Eng. equivalent to *won his letter* would be *won his cap.* The letter referred to is the initial, worn on the jersey, of the team which the player or athlete represents. Thus, a college president, writing to a N.Y. paper, says that 'so long as father and mother, and brothers and sisters, are more proud of seeing their hero wear an "H", a "Y", or a "P", than a Φ.B.K. just so long will our students strive more in athletics than in scholarship'. The letters in this quotation are the initials of Harvard, Yale, and Princeton respectively. See also FRATERNITY.

levee is used in Am. in two special senses; (1) an embankment to prevent the overflow of a river; (2) a district in which prostitution is segregated. (1) 'The levee problem has become more serious as the forests have been cut away from the headwaters of the Mississippi.' 'Lincoln's hatred of slavery was inborn, but its development began when he saw human beings being sold at auction on the levee at New Orleans' (W. E. CURTIS, The True Abraham Lincoln, 314). 'Sacramento is protected from high water in the rivers by levees which send the overflow off to flood other countries' (L. STEFFENS, Autobiog. i. 26). (2) 'Three levees, one for each of the three leading parts of the city, are to be sanctioned by the city of Chicago.' 'If Fate had condemned me to start in business on th' Levee' (Mr. DOOLEY's Opinions, 211). 'After the partial breakdown of the old levee district many of the persons formerly associated with the licensed vice resorts intrenched themselves in the neighboring cabarets' (M. A. ELLIOTT and F. E. MERRILL, Social Disorganization, 630, footnote).

liable. In Eng. a thing is not said to be *liable* to happen unless the risk of its happening is permanent or frequent. In Am. there is no such restriction in the use of the word. 'Boston is liable to be the ultimate place for holding the convention.' 'If the lawmakers get back before the frosts kill the vegetation, many of them are liable to think it a reproach to the nation that grass should be growing in the streets of the national capital.' In each of these instances *likely* would have been used in Eng. See APT.

lid is used fig. in Am. to denote restrictions on the sale of drink or on other illegal practices. 'The "lid" went down with a bang in Brooklyn yesterday, and some spots in the borough were as so many miniature Saharas for dryness.' 'The war on liquor has begun again at this resort. The sheriff of the county was here last week, and notified the dealers that the "lid" must be put on again.' See WIDE OPEN.

lieutenant. In Am. this rank is given in the police force as well as in the army. 'In addition to the chief of police there are a number of other uniformed ranks above that of patrolman. The commonest are captain, lieutenant, and sergeant. . . . Each captain is assigned a number of lieutenants who perform duties prescribed by him and succeed to command in fixed order when he is off duty' (C. C. MAXEY, Outline of Municipal Government, 162).

The Eng. pronunciation of the word is *leftenant*; the Am. *lewtenant* or *lootenant*. Thus, when 'Mr. Dooley' refers to 'th' loot at th' station', he means the lieutenant at the police station.

The rank of *lieutenant-general* is in Am. much higher than in Eng., where a *lieutenant-general* comes after a *field marshal* and a *general*. It carries with it the post of commander-in-chief of the army (under the President). 'Congress revived the grade of lieutenant-general, a position which carried with it the supreme command of the armies of the U.S., and, on March 9, Lincoln conferred this commission upon Grant (Prof. A. E. MARTIN, Hist. of U.S. i. 745). The rank had previously been held by only Washington and Scott. Since Grant, it has been conferred upon only twelve Am. officers, and to-day it is held by no one. See GENERAL.

life. In Eng. *life guards* are 'two regiments of cavalry, forming, together with the Royal Horse Guards, the household cavalry' (O.E.D.). In Am. they are men employed to keep bathers from drowning, and otherwise to rescue persons in danger along the coast. Accordingly, they correspond to the Royal Humane Society's men in Eng. They are also sometimes called *life savers*. 'A life guard in the employ of the Delavan Bathing Pavilion.' 'The Mayor has instructed the peace officers to prevent bathing at this season as much as possible. The life guards, of course, do not go on duty until June; and their functions are, in the mean time, performed by the police.' 'After 14 hours of being tossed about in my catboat I was taken off by the life guards.'

The term *life-saving* is technically applied in Am. to a government organization which combines many of the functions exercised in Eng. by the coastguard and the Royal Humane Society. 'The U.S. has an elaborate life-saving service, which patrols the coast, warns vessels off dangerous shores, and, in case of wreck, by life-boats and life-lines attempts to save the passengers and the cargo' (Prof. A. B. HART, Actual Government, 449). 'The plight of the sloop had been signalled at the life-saving station at Sandy Hook.' 'The boat had been placed at one of the life-saving stations on the New Jersey coast' (Dict. Am. Biog. vi. 582).

lift. 'The tariff was lifted' (T. BEER, Life of Hanna, 181). An Eng. reader would understand this to mean that the tariff was removed. Actually it means that the rates of duty imposed by the tariff were made higher. 'Nobody will be surprised that the Ways and Means Committee of the House frowns upon the salary-raising plan for members of the Legislature. The people would not stand for it. The committee is not so clear as to other salary-lifting bills.' 'Credit enlargement is the typical method of price lifting by reflation' (Prof. IRVING FISHER, Mastering the Crisis, 55).

†light. The Am. expression *see the light = become converted.* 'He will be formally renominated by all save the Kings County Democrats. And it is altogether likely that they, too, will see the light before another week has passed.' 'Mild reservationists were our bane. Frank Brandegee detailed me to try to make some of them see the light, but it proved a humiliatingly unsuccessful job' (ALICE ROOSE-VELT LONGWORTH, Crowded Hours, 284).

likely. The Am. idiom in the use of this word, as illustrated in the following examples, differs from the Eng. 'There is another factor appearing which may likely favor the Democrats.' 'There is reason why a woman of the stage marries an actor. She is devoted to her art, and he will probably allow her to continue behind the footlights. If she married outside the "profession", the husband would likely protest.' The Eng. idiom would be 'may very likely favour' and 'would very likely protest', or else 'which is likely to favour' and 'would be likely to protest'. 'If the Negro was driving a loaded wagon, he would likely draw out to the side and wait for the white man to pass' (W. T. COUCH, in Culture in the South, 474).

See also LIABLE.

lily white is used spec. in Am. politics as explained in the following quotation. 'The "lily white" movement in the Southern Rep. party was another indication of the South's opposition to Negro suffrage. The term seems to have been coined in Texas in 1888, after riots between white and Negro Republicans struggling for the control of a convention. It was applied to bodies of white Republicans in Southern States determined to purge their party of Negro leadership, Negro control, and a Negro share in the spoils of victory' (P. LEWINSON, Race, Class, and Party, 110).

limit is rarely used in Eng. but commonly in Am. of a physical boundary, esp. in the plur. 'The gathering was arranged particularly as a welcome from the people of Windsor County to the Indiana senator, whose father was born within its limits.' 'The damage on the Lackawanna was caused by the bursting of a dyke in the west city limits.' 'At the navy yard limit the marine escort was withdrawn.' 'Most street car lines started from the center of the town and ran out to some city limit and back' (L. STEFFENS, Autobiog. 474).

†Am. *the limit* = Eng. *the last straw*. 'Making life preservers out of rotten cork chips would seem to be bad enough, but when it comes to putting iron bars in them, just to make them weigh up to the proper standard, that is the limit.' Hence the expression *to the limit*. 'The only possible chance the senator has of re-election is to become Rooseveltian to the limit.' 'The Jeffersonians used federal powers to the limit in purchasing Louisiana' (Dr. C. A. BEARD, The Am. Party Battle, 5).

In Am. a *limited* (*express*) is a train which is restricted to the carrying of passengers who pay an extra fare. 'The St. Paul and Minneapolis Limited was wrecked early to-day.' 'The traveller in Iran must love travel for itself—not the Twentieth Century Limited variety.' 'The day is surely coming when a gentleman will no longer boast of having bowled along our highways at the speed of a limited express.'

The Eng. *Limited* (abbrev. *Ltd.*), as the designation of a trading company in which the liability of partners or shareholders is limited to a certain amount, is unknown in Am., where the nearest equivalent is *Incorporated* (abbrev. *Inc.*).

line. A row of persons waiting their turn is in Eng. a *queue*. In Am. it is a *line*. 'People were herded by policemen into lines stretching away from the marble entrance to the Knickerbocker Trust Co.' (MARK SULLIVAN, Our Times, iii. 502). 'The next morning there was a line of women, six deep, waiting in front of the door' (K. BERCOVICI, Manhattan Side-Show, 271). In times of severe unemployment one reads of *bread lines* consisting of queues of persons waiting for doles of food. 'At the end of a decade of the highest wages in history, the average Am. worker is only a month or so away from the bread

line if he loses his job.' 'I remember talking with him about the "bread lines" which regularly formed each night at certain bakeries which gave away their stale bread' (HAMLIN GARLAND, Roadside Meetings, 198).

Hence *line up* (verb and noun) in both lit. and fig. senses. 'A tall man with a look of settled melancholy lined up at a place in Park Row.' 'The prisoners were brought before witnesses—not in a line-up with others of the same general type, but separately' (A. G. HAYS, Let Freedom Ring, 289). 'The candidates are now lined up for the municipal elections.' 'The telephone industry was lined up, with the Bell Co. on one side and all other interests consolidated under the Independent banner on the other.' 'Thus we have a line-up of corporations against the people.'

The noun *line* may also be used in the sense of *boundary*. 'The police threw a mounted guard along the county line to turn them back.' 'An observant traveller could always tell when he crossed the line from Dutchess County into Berkshire' (F. J. STIMSON, My U.S. 24). 'Only a few men had affairs that took them across state lines' (W. LIPPMANN, Public Opinion, 273).

Another special Am. use of the word is seen in : 'These dressmakers cannot get a line on the styles promoted by the swell 5th Avenue dressmakers except at the Horse Show, so they come here looking for points.' 'It doesn't take the officials long to "get a line" on the damage; then operations begin.' 'The overwhelming victory in Vermont is not conclusive. It gives a good line on what N.Y. State above the Harlem will do, but it but slightly indicates the trend of the urban vote.' Here *a line on* = *an idea of*.

Am. *in line for* = Eng. *in the running for*. 'Sen. Gorman's victory in Maryland placed him in line for the Dem. nomination for the Presidency.' 'My secret ambition had been to teach Church History: but there were few opportunities; I was not a graduate of an Am. seminary and so in line for them' (Dr. F. J. KINSMAN, Salve Mater, 56).

Am. *in line with* = Eng. *in harmony with*. 'The step is unusual and the amount large, but it is in line with the plan of reorganization proposed by the creditors' committee.' 'The terms in which he characterizes sin are in general not theological or ecclesiastical, nor are they always in line with Biblical representations of it' (Prof. L. O. BRASTOW, Representative Modern Preachers, 233).

In the sense of the rails upon which trains run, *track* or *tracks* is preferred in Am. to *line*.

Lo. When Alexander Pope wrote, in his *Essay on Man*,
'LO, the poor Indian! whose untutored mind
Sees God in clouds, or hears him in the wind'
little did he foresee the curious use to which these lines would be put in Am. Some person of a waggish turn of mind hit upon the idea of interpreting the exclamation *Lo* as the name of the Indian to whom the poet was referring. This notion tickled people's fancy, and the use of the word as a synonym for *Indian* has long since become a commonplace. 'The hunting is not very good, and the march of civilization has convinced Lo that fighting is not as profitable as it used to be.' 'On Florida's shield stands a placid buxom Mrs. Lo, with fringed shirt falling to the knee.' 'You remember the Indian and the white man were at a loss to know how to divide the turkey and the buzzard, but in the end poor Lo got the buzzard' (ANDY ADAMS, The Outlet, 344). 'An Indian inspector suggested the thumbprint in addition to the mark, and all new Indian deeds bear this imprint. The result is that Lo is given to understand that no amount of false swearing will serve to disprove his signature as witnessed by the unerring thumbprint' (F. J. HASKIN, The Am. Government, 86).

load. Am. *load down* = Eng. *load up*. 'The scientists returned to Buenos Ayres loaded down with specimens of great zoological value.' 'A pack-train of mules loaded down with tons of ore' (G. D. LYMAN, Saga of the Comstock Lode, 46).

loaf. A cake peculiar to Am. is the *loaf cake*, a plain cake in the form of a loaf. 'Sipping hot tea and tasting with evident approval a large piece of loaf cake.'

†**loan** is in modern Eng. usage a noun only, though it was once a verb also. In Am. it is still a verb. 'The plan was for the government to borrow four million dollars to be loaned to the planters.' 'London remains the great loaning centre of the world.' 'Carlyle loaned me Maurice's novel' (MONCURE D. CONWAY, Autobiog. i. 440). 'I urged that Congress provide $2,500,000 to be loaned to Americans in Europe against letters of credit' (W. G. McADOO, Crowded Years, 294).

lobby. Each House of Congress, like each House of the British Parliament, has a *lobby*. But the implications of both *lobby* and *lobbyist* are widely different at Washington and at Westminster. 'Another force is the lobby, by which is meant those men, and sometimes women, who make it a business to argue with congressmen and to solicit their votes. Some of these lobbyists are paid attorneys of corporations; many of them are former members of Congress, who understand the inner workings of the body' (Prof. A. B. HART, Actual Government, 247). An Eng. Parliamentary *lobbyist* is not a man who seeks to influence legislation. He is a journalist who haunts the lobby in order to talk to members and pick up items of political news for his paper. At Washington the source of such gossip is not the *lobby* but the CLOAK-ROOM (q.v.). The terms *lobby* and *lobbyist* are used in a similar sense in connexion with the State Legislatures. For a full account of the Am. *lobby* see Bryce's *Am. Commonwealth*, Note (B) to Chapter XVI.

Examples follow of the Am. use of (1) *lobby*, as a noun, (2) *lobby*, as a verb, and (3) *lobbyist*. (1) 'Early in the session it was announced by insurance interests that no lobby would be maintained and no important insurance legislation would be asked.' 'The Am. Bankers Association had a lobby at Washington which was one of the potent factors in that unacknowledged congregation of occupational councils which is the fourth estate in federal legislation' (Prof. N. W. STEPHENSON, Life of Sen. Aldrich, 363). 'Committees even of the Am. Bar Association rarely, if ever, bring about the legislation they desire; while a secret lobby will succeed in full half the time' (F. J. STIMSON, My U.S. 153). (2) 'A class of well-informed persons who acquire fortunes by lobbying all sorts of claims through Congress.' 'It was he, more than anyone else in the U.S., who taught clergymen how to lobby for peace, prohibition, and the Bible' (M. R. WERNER, Bryan, 254). 'There should be other machinery for fixing their wages than lobbying before legislative bodies and organizing to exert political pressure' (N. THOMAS, America's Way Out, 161). (3) 'The sop which the President has thrown to the pension lobbyists will, instead of satisfying them, only whet their appetite for more.' 'Of unsavory reputation as a lobbyist in securing government contracts for his friends' (ANDY ADAMS, The Outlet, 327). 'Tariff lobbyists were threatening the political annihilation of Wilson if he persisted in driving through the Tariff Bill without regard to the demands of special interests' (Prof. C. SEYMOUR, Intimate Papers of Col. House, i. 156).

local is in Am. sometimes a noun, meaning a *branch of a trade union*. 'The advisory board of the N.Y. locals of the Amalgamated Meat

Cutters and Butcher Workmen declared a second strike.' 'Each of these national unions is made up of a state organization and of locals' (T. C. PEASE, The U.S. 540). 'There is in N.Y. a colored local, the only colored local in the city, among a few of the carpenters, with regular representation in the Central Federated Union' (M. W. OVINGTON, Half a Man, 98).

The name of *local room* is given to the department of a newspaper office which deals with local news. 'No doubt too many years spent in news writing may unfit a young man in some degree for good critical writing. But the fact remains that almost the only open door to the editorial room is through the local room' (E. L. SHUMAN, Practical Journalism, 90).

locate, location. In Eng. *locate* is a trans. verb, meaning either *discover the position of* or *place*. In Am. it is also intrans., meaning *take up one's residence, settle*. 'He has resigned his position as clerk at the Pope Manufacturing Co., and will locate in Trenton.' 'He says his destiny is to go to Europe and locate along the Mediterranean Sea.' 'The foreign ambassadors located there in order to be accessible to the authorities of Zurich and to be within easy reach of the Confederation as a whole' (Prof. S. M. JACKSON, Huldreich Zwingli, 41).

In the following passage the trans. *locate* seems to have the unusual sense of *plan, lay out*. 'He was appointed principal assistant engineer in the Pennsylvania state service, in which capacity he located a railroad from Gettysburg to the Potomac' (Dict. Am. Biog. viii. 400).

The noun *location* means in Am. either (1) *the act of settling or taking up residence*, or (2) *situation, position*. (1) 'Immigrants were warned against hasty location, and were admonished that they would do well to rent land for a time, pending a more careful scrutiny of the country' (Prof. J. B. HEDGES, Henry Villard, 131). (2) 'A report containing the name of the corporation, the location of its principal office, and the date of its last annual meeting.' 'Its location at the junction of important railroads had made it one of the great trading sections of the Southwest' (B. J. HENDRICK, Earlier Life of Walter H. Page, 130).

loft is commonly used in Am. in the sense, now obs. in Eng., of a *whole upper floor or story.* 'They erected in the lower part of the avenue tall loft buildings to attract the wholesale garment-making trade'; i.e. buildings whose top floors are used as garment-makers' workrooms.

†**log-rolling.** 'In olden times pioneers on the frontier helped one another to cut trees and roll up logs for their cabins. This process was known as "log-rolling"' (Dr. C. A. BEARD, Am. Government and Politics, 258). Hence the fig. use of *log-rolling* in the vocab. of Am. politics. 'General appropriations, like the river-and-harbor and public-building bills, are much affected by log-rolling—that is, a number of members agree each to vote for the item desired by the other' (Prof. A. B. HART, Actual Government, 246). 'The process, with which we have since become so familiar, of "log-rolling", that is of each congressman voting for a duty not wanted in his district if a vote could thereby be obtained for a duty that was wanted, began within the very first week of the national government' (J. TRUSLOW ADAMS, Hist. of the Am. People to the Civil War, 173). The term has been adopted in Eng., in relation not so much to politics —where the opportunities for such mutual assistance are few—as to literary criticism.

long. In the vocab. of the Am. telephone system, *long distance* takes the place of the Eng. *trunk.* 'We have replaced billets doux with long-distance telephone calls.' 'By ten o'clock the Mayor had attended to his mail

and made several long-distance calls.' 'There were frequent conversations over the long distance telephone' (D. LAWRENCE, True Story of Woodrow Wilson, 69). 'He always made it a point to call his wife by long distance if he was too far away to come home for the week-ends' (M. A. ELLIOTT and F. E. MERRILL, Social Disorganization, 487).

look. The expression *look to* or *look toward* is common in Am. with the meaning of *tend toward, point in the direction of, aim at.* 'Suggestions looking to a remedy for this apparent injustice.' 'A scheme looking to ameliorated conditions as to land.' 'The movement looking toward emancipation was growing weaker' (Prof. A. E. MARTIN, Hist. of U.S. i. 439). 'These measures looked to the expansion of the intellectual resources of the college' (H. JAMES, Life of C. W. Eliot, ii. 11).

In Am. *look to be* is often used where an Eng. writer would say *seem to be,* or *look* (without *be*), or *look like.* 'The men are a hard-bitten lot, and look to be perfectly able to take care of themselves.' 'It looked to be about eight feet tall' (K. D. WIGGIN, Rebecca, 133). 'England looks to be the huge well-cared-for farm of a Croesus' (PRICE COLLIER, England and the English, 315).

lose, as an intrans. verb, is often intensified in Am. by the addition of the adv. *out.* 'News comes that he may lose out in his race for renomination.' 'More and more the individual lost out in the conflict with organization' (Prof. A. H. QUINN, The Soul of Am. 104). 'The happy fact is that the tough-minded of the world are losing out, disappearing in the course of evolution' (MARGARET WILSON, The Crime of Punishment, 142).

lot. When the biographer of Harriet Beecher Stowe tells us that one of her ancestors received from the founders of Massachusetts the gift of a lot of land, most Eng. readers will understand this to mean a good deal of land. Actually the Am. writer means only what would be called in Eng. a *plot of ground.* 'The horse ran into an open lot at Kent Avenue.' 'A deed for a house and lot.' 'Here Abraham rendered the last service of his minority by ploughing the 15-acre lot.' 'The lot on which the old Chicago Avenue Church had stood for more than 50 years' (W. R. MOODY, Life of D. L. Moody, 130). Thus Am. *corner lot* = Eng. *corner site.* Acc. to Leon Mead (Word Coinage, 128) the Boston Town Records of 1636 show that the word, in this sense, is an abbrev. of *allotment.*

louder. In Eng. cries of *Speak up!* indicate to a public speaker that he is imperfectly heard. In Am. the usual cry is *Louder!* 'He had hardly begun when cries of "Louder!" were heard from far recesses of the hall.' 'He was apparently in poor voice last night, his address being interrupted by cries of "Louder!" and the scuffle of the feet of those that left the room.' 'Even his [Bryan's] golden voice was to desert him, and the day was to come when he again stood before a national convention and heard cries of "Louder! We can't hear you!" come mockingly down from the galleries where once there had been deathlike silence' (H. F. PRINGLE, Theodore Roosevelt, 161).

lovely. In Am. this word, when applied to persons, is sometimes almost equivalent to *lovable.* It denotes the possession of attractive qualities, among which beauty may not necessarily be included and it may be applied to men as well as women. In a letter written by Matthew Arnold while visiting Boston in 1883, he says: 'I am staying with Mrs. Fields here —a *lovely* woman, as they say here— which means not a sweetly beautiful woman, but what we call a "very nice" woman.'

low is sometimes used in Am. as a noun, in the sense of *low level* of *low figure.* 'What the fate of psychology will be now that it has hit its new low is as difficult to predict as the level to which United Aircraft will some day rise.' 'In 1906 the finances of the Longworths, though they were on the way, had not reached their present "low"' (ALICE ROOSEVELT LONGWORTH, Crowded Hours, 133). Cf. HIGH.

The Am. compound noun *low-down* denotes an opinion based on facts often of an uncomplimentary nature, not possessed by the general public. 'After all, what was the use of getting opinions out of newspapers when he had so many friends willing to give him the absolute low-down on public opinion?' 'As a stranger, you could drop into the tobacco store for a cigar, and get the low-down on half the lawyers in town in 20 minutes.'

††The *lowbrow* is the opposite of the HIGHBROW (q.v.). 'An honest man and an "intellectual" uses his dishonest brain to cover or to discover his honest thinking, which is, really, very like a lowbrow's' (L. STEFFENS, Autobiog. 581).

luggage. While Am. *baggage* = Eng. *luggage,* the latter word is not unknown in Am. It is used there, however, in a sense that differs from its meaning in Eng. In Eng. *luggage* is a collective term for the trunks, bags, &c., that a traveller takes with him. These trunks are not considered luggage until they are packed for the journey. In Am., on the other hand, it is only as long as they are empty that they are called *luggage.* Thus we may read in a newspaper advt. that 'a gift of hand luggage is a substantial evidence of one's esteem for the recipient'. The specific items suggested to prospective purchasers are women's overnight cases, men's travelling bags, and brief cases. A Boston firm which sells travelling bags and similar articles has taken the name of the Boston Luggage Co. A newspaper records a protest made by 'the luggage industries', including the National Luggage and Leather Goods Manufacturers' Association, against the sale of 'prison-made luggage'.

lumber is little used in Eng. exc. to denote *discarded articles of furniture*, &c., such as are stowed away in a *lumber-room*. In Am. it is the common word for *timber*, esp. when sawn for use. Hence *lumberman* = an owner of timber land, or one engaged in producing lumber, and *lumberjack* = one of his employees. 'If a lumberman who owns 1,000 acres of timber land considers only his own interests, he will probably cut down the trees and turn them into lumber as fast as the ax and saw will do it.' 'He said he had no boats with which to cross the Delaware, when the lumber to make boats and rafts was lying in piles before his eyes' (S. G. FISHER, True Hist. of the Am. Revolution, 320). 'Each of the principal lumber producing regions in the U.S. is characterized by the type of timber grown' (T. C. BLAISDELL, The Federal Trade Commission, 148). 'The lumbermen who have grown rich by taking dishonest advantage of the land laws.' 'Ordinarily he was not very profane, for a lumber-jack.'

lunch, luncheon. Am. *lunch* or *luncheon* often = Eng. *snack*. In Eng. a lunch is always a mid-day meal. In Am. it may be a light repast taken at any time in the 24 hours. 'The first of what is expected to become regular monthly informal socials was held Friday evening. A light luncheon was served.' 'Quite as often she was unable to return to Norumbega till ten or eleven at night. Then she took a light lunch' (Prof. G. H. PALMER, Life of Alice Freeman Palmer, 152). 'Most of the operators brought their midnight lunches with them' (Dr. F. T. MILLER, Thomas A. Edison, 98). 'Those who do light work in town or city should eat only one "square" meal a day. The other two should be lunches' (Dr. R. L.

ALSAKER, Eating for Health and Efficiency, 340). See also DUTCH.
In Am. the corresponding verb is similarly exempt from any time limit. 'Those who lunch between meals are giving way to a bad habit' (Dr. R. L. ALSAKER, op. cit. 339).

lyceum denotes in Am. not only a place or a building but also a lecture system, once extremely popular but nowadays superseded by the Chautauqua movement. 'It was the time of the Lyseum, an institution of extraordinary popularity, through which the best minds displayed themselves on the lecture platform to the delight and profit of insatiable audiences' (Dict. Am. Biog. ix. 172). 'The shallow, sensational "lyceum lectures" were the rage immediately after the Civil War' (JULIA B. FORAKER, I Would Live it Again, 59). 'From 1850 to 1870 Emerson went into the West in person as a lyceum-lecturer' (V. F. CALVERTON, The Liberation of Am. Literature, 251).

M

†machine, in the vocab. of Am. politics, is the common term for a *party organization*. 'Philadelphia was the liveliest centre of election day activity, the reformers making strenuous efforts to win a crushing victory over the machine.' 'Lord Randolph Churchill conceived the bold plan of getting control of the popular organization of the party, known as the National Union of Conservative Associations. The attempt of a politician to capture the machine was a surprise in Eng.' 'Roosevelt had wrestled publicly and successfully with the machine element in every State in the Union where the machine had tried to impose upon him for Federal appointment candidates whom Roosevelt regarded as unworthy men' (W. A. WHITE, Masks in a Pageant, 309). 'His methods and purposes were quite different from

those of the party boss, for he never worked through a "machine"' (Prof. C. SEYMOUR, Intimate Papers of Col. House, i. 5). See also ORGANIZE.

mad. The proverb that anger is temporary madness was evidently endorsed by our fathers, for—as many quotations in the *O.E.D.* show—they used *mad* as a synonym for *angry*. In this sense it has almost become an Americanism, for its Eng. use is nowadays colloq. only. 'The book is sure to be mercilessly criticized by the votaries of war. It will make many of them thoroughly mad.' 'Some people are mad with him for what they think he is going to say when he gets ready to speak.' 'The following day I found him in bed, hopping mad. "I have got a cold", he said' (T. B. MOTT, Life of Myron T. Herrick, 370). 'Those financial leaders of Chicago were "mad". All but one became so enraged as they talked that they could not behave decently' (L. STEFFENS, The Shame of the Cities, 269). 'Only about once in four years do I get mad enough to write a political article' (Letters and Memorials of W. P. Garrison, 41). Here *mad = worked up*.

maid of hono(u)r. In Eng. a lady in attendance on the Queen when she appears in public. In Am., the principal bridesmaid at a wedding. 'The maid of honor wore white point d'esprit over white silk and carried yellow roses' (From a newspaper report of a wedding). 'Miss Lyons was maid of honor at Flavia's wedding' (L. N. WRIGHT, Limbs of an Old Family Tree, 160).

mail. In Eng. *mail trains* carry *mail-bags*[1] full of *mails*, which are brought to the railway from the Post Office in *mail-vans*. Otherwise, in striking contrast with Am., the word *mail*, whether noun or verb, is little

[1] *Mail-bag*, however, is in Eng. only an alternative to *post-bag*. Mr. E. V. Lucas has entitled one of his books 'Post-bag Diversions'. An Am. author would certainly have called it 'Mail-bag Diversions'.

used in Eng. An Am. does not post a letter, but mails it. He does not inquire at the hotel desk whether there are any letters for him, but whether there is any mail for him. He does not ask his wife at breakfast if the post has come, but if the mail has come. 'A hastily scribbled note, mailed without any idea that it would be preserved.' 'His desk was covered to the depth of several inches with unopened mail.' (In Eng. this would be 'unopened letters'.) 'They say that all of the details of service cannot be given by mail, but that a representative of the concern will call.' 'Eliot answered his mail with his own hand' (H. JAMES, Life of C. W. Eliot, i. 304).

Hence (1) *mail car*, (2) *mail matter*, (3) *mailman*, and (4) *mail-box*. (1) 'The locomotive and tender and baggage and mail cars were thrown from the tracks.' (2) 'All mail matter for the secretary of the convention should be addressed to etc.' (3) 'There was no telephone and no mail man.' 'One day the mailman brought me a card from Charlie' (K. BERCOVICI, Manhattan Side-Show, 223). (4) 'Thousands of requests for more margin found their way into speculators' mail-boxes' (F. L. ALLEN, Only Yesterday, 308).

major. A student in an Am. college is said to *major* in the subject or subjects to which he gives most of his attention. 'At Christian College at Santa Rosa he majored in modern literature and Christian sociology' (Dr. C. C. REGIER, The Era of the Muckrakers, 151).

majority. At an Eng. election, where more than two candidates are standing, the candidate who heads the poll is said to have a *majority* of so many votes over the second man. In Am. this excess of votes would be called a *plurality*. The word *majority* is reserved for an excess of votes over the total of votes given to all the other candidates; i.e. what in Eng. would be called an *absolute majority* or a *clear majority.* 'We were hasty in assuming that Vardaman had received a majority of the votes. It was only a plurality, and the combined vote of his two competitors was 19,000 more than his own.' 'The Rep. electors [for the Presidency in 1860] did not receive a majority by nearly a million votes, but the division of the Democrats left them a plurality' (W. E. CURTIS, The True Abraham Lincoln, 161). 'When the vote was taken Jackson had the most electoral votes, but not a majority, so the decision had to be made by the House of Representatives' (E. D. ADAMS and J. C. ALMACK, Hist. of U.S. 368).

make is often used in Am., as dial. in Scotland, in the sense of *reach, attain to*; a meaning which is rare in Eng., exc. in such expressions as *make port.* 'She had gone on to the Grand Central Station in order to be in time for the 7.30 train. I had just time to make it, with a minute or two to spare.' 'Field Coach Dickson said to the candidates that every man had a chance to make the eleven, as the veterans would have to prove their right to stay on the team.' 'Two of the girls are good swimmers, and they made shore in good shape.' 'Running swiftly alongside the moving train, she made the door easily' (G. ATHERTON, The Travelling Thirds, 19). 'Roosevelt was a conscientious worker who made Phi Beta Kappa in his senior year' (H. F. PRINGLE, Theodore Roosevelt, 37).

An Eng. speaker *makes* a speech, but *gives* or *delivers* an address. An Am. *makes* an address, as well as a speech. 'As at present arranged, the president of the Rapid Transit Commission will make the address.' 'Aldrich dined with the Merchants' Association and made an address' (Prof. N. W. STEPHENSON, Life of N. W. Aldrich, 477).

Make out has in Eng. a trans. meaning only. In Am. it is also intrans., in the sense of *make shift, get along, get on, manage.* 'They started to walk, but they were met later by Judge Margary with two horses, and so they made out, walking and riding alternately, to get safely to town.' 'Given the environment and the local traditions, the Argentine municipalities make out very well.' 'Without my wife's inspiration and help, I could not have made out at all' (W. G. McADOO, Crowded Years, 55). 'Supposing we could take some man of modern times and put him among those cave-men, how do you suppose that he would make out?' (U. SINCLAIR, Industrial Republic, 54).

manager. The leader of a party in an Am. legislature is sometimes called its *manager.* 'He soon shewed his genius as a leader in the House, becoming a brilliant debater and for a time the Dem. manager' (Prof. W. P. TRENT, Southern Writers, 86).

In some Am. municipalities, the council or commission which is responsible for the local government discharges its executive functions through a *city manager* appointed by it and holding office at its pleasure. He has authority to appoint and remove all heads of departments and their subordinates. The adoption of this plan does not involve the disappearance of the mayor, who usually remains as president of the council but is shorn of many of the powers he ordinarily exercises in an Am. municipality.

mandatory. This term is little used in Eng. but is commonly employed in Am. where *compulsory* or *obligatory* would be used in Eng. 'Now that a court has held a hotel porter's tips are in themselves sufficient compensation, does it become mandatory upon the public to tip?' 'A decent regard for the feelings of his immediate friends should have been mandatory in compelling respect for the deceased statesman's memory.' 'The commission was not given mandatory powers, but had to depend upon publicity and the aid of public opinion for the acceptance of its decrees' (L. M. HACKER and B. B. KENDRICK, The U.S. since 1865, 424). 'It is made mandatory that a child be examined by a physician as to physical fitness before becoming employed' (Prof. C. W. PIPKIN, in Culture in the South, 655). 'At Dublin, the oath of allegiance to King George, mandatory on members of the Free State Dail and Senate, was removed by the Dail' (N.Y. World Almanac for 1934, 102).

mark. The Am. colloq. term *easy mark* denotes a *gullible person.* 'Castle told him that, while he didn't doubt his honesty, he was afraid he was too easy a mark to succeed in Wall Street' (G. H. LORIMER, Old Gorgon Graham, 288). 'The kindly gentleman of Van Hornesville is no easy mark. He is in fact a little terrifying to simple minds' (IDA M. TARBELL, Owen D. Young, 306).

marker. In Eng., not applied to inanimate objects exc. in such compounds as *book-marker* and *bridge-marker.* In Am., a tablet or other permanent memorial. 'The table [used by the Russian and Japanese plenipotentiaries at the Portsmouth Conference], which will be used by the history department at Dartmouth College, contains a large marker, suitably inscribed.' 'The committee appointed to investigate the matter of a marker for the Washington elm reported in favor of a granite marker, six feet long, two feet thick and six feet high, three feet to be above the ground and three feet below; the stone to be Quincy granite, with a polished face for a suitable inscription' (The Washington elm was a tree at Cambridge, Mass., under which George Washington took command of the Am. army). 'When the first woman President of the U.S. is elected, the marker for her birthplace will more likely be in a ward in a hospital than in a log cabin, tenement apartment or single dwelling' (NORMAN THOMAS, America's Way Out, 173).

market. In Am. *market* sometimes denotes the shop of an individual trader in provisions. 'A pair of gunmen relieved Mitchell Jasinskie, proprietor of Mitchell's market at 202 School Street, of $150. A short time before the pair held up Frank Poltenson in his meat market at 221 Birnie Avenue and rifled the cash register of $4.' 'With this much capital he opened a meat market' (Dict. Am. Biog. viii. 204).

To *play the market* is an Am. phrase meaning to *speculate on the Stock Exchange.* 'The man who earns only a pittance in college may become a stockbroker; a pleasant manner and reasonable intelligence in playing the market may make him a millionaire' (E. HUNTINGTON and L. F. WHITNEY, The Builders of Am. 215). 'The reports are originated by persons who are interested in playing the stock market, hoping that the rumor will gain currency and that certain stocks will be affected before the truth can be determined' (D. LAWRENCE, True Story of Woodrow Wilson, 131).

marshal is in Eng. the title of various officials—legal, academic, and so on—whose duties nowadays are mainly formal or ceremonial. The duties of an Am. *marshal* are much more arduous. 'For the execution of its powers each Federal court has attached to it an officer called the U.S. marshal, corresponding to the sheriff in the State governments, whose duty it is to carry out its writs, judgments, and orders by arresting prisoners, levying execution, putting persons in possession, and so forth. He is entitled, if resisted, to call on all good citizens for help; if they will not or cannot render it, he must refer to Washington and obtain the aid of Federal troops' (LORD BRYCE, The Am. Commonwealth, c. 22). There is also a *town marshal,* who similarly exercises the functions of a police officer. 'The marshal with some 15 men rushed into the headquarters of the National Textile

Workers and began searching the rooms.' 'A fight between a band of outlaws and a number of deputy marshals.' 'Every other shanty on the main street either a saloon or a dance-house, and the town marshal easily the hardest worked man in the camp.' 'In *Weeks* v. *U.S.* it appeared that the defendant's house had been entered without any warrant or legal authority by a U.S. marshal, and property and papers taken therefrom' (Prof. C. K. BURDICK, Law of the Am. Constitution, 393). See also FIRE.

masher. In Eng. this is one of many words—*beau, macaroni, fop, swell, dandy,* &c.—that have been used at one time or another to denote a man of affected style and over-fashionable dress. In Am. it carries with it an evil implication, denoting a man who obtrudes unwelcome attentions on women. 'Mashers have become such a nuisance in State Street, Chicago, that all the dry goods stores have entered into an alliance to prosecute and drive them off the street. "Men will not be allowed to stand in front of stores and stare at women shoppers", said Chief of Police O'Neill.' 'Although from time to time the methods of the Brooklyn Bridge masher vary, nevertheless his supreme aim at all times is to startle, annoy, frighten and attract the attention of women.'

mat. In addition to its other meanings, *mat* may denote in Am. a piece of cardboard used as the backing for a picture. It thus = Eng. *mount.*

matter. This word is much used in Am. in the interrogatory formula, *What's the matter with. . . .?* 'What's the matter with the mayor's appointing a committee?' (Why doesn't the mayor appoint a committee?) 'Hawaii's turn comes next; and what's the matter with Alaska?' (Why not Alaska?) 'The members appealed to Senator Fitzgerald, and he said to them: "What's the matter with $10,000? You can get it as easy as

$8,000, and the State has plenty of money' (Why not ask for $10,000?) 'Suppose the iron supply is exhausted; what is the matter with building out of brick, stone and cement?' (Why not build?)

The same question, with the addition of the name of the hero of the moment and followed by the response 'He's all right' affords a means by which excited crowds work off their enthusiasm. 'Then Taft laughed and the applause increased. "What is the matter with Bill?" cried some one in stentorian tones. "He's all right." "Who's all right?" "Bill's all right." It took music by the orchestra and a song by the guests to restore a semblance of quiet' (Report of Mr. Taft's appearance at a political meeting). 'The multitude of people pouring out of the gates divided to let the Chicagoans pass and cheered them with shouts of "What's the matter with Chicago? She's all right".'

maybe. In Eng. *maybe* has almost become an archaism and a dial. word, having been supplanted by *perhaps.* In Am. it is still in everyday use. Indeed, acc. to Dr. Krapp it is more familiar and colloq. in tone than *perhaps.* 'Maybe you can find to-day in the "Little Ads of the People" what you have been looking months for.' 'He had been pondering the matter for weeks—maybe had read some thundering editorials on the subject in the California press' (B. LASKER, Filipino Migration, 361). 'For that reason, maybe, they are not made as frequently as they formerly were' (M. M. MATHEWS, Beginnings of Am. English, 130). 'Mr. Archbold announced that Mr. Rockefeller's health was not good and that maybe if Hadley paid him a visit he would answer his questions' (J. T. FLYNN, God's Gold, 413). 'And I don't mean maybe' is a very common phrase in Am. talkies—usually a threat.

mayflower. In Eng. this name is given locally to various flowers that bloom in May. In Am. it denotes esp. the *trailing arbutus*, or *Epigaea repens*.

mayor. 'The foregoing description of the Eng. mayor will have been very insufficient if it has failed to show how entirely different an official he is from the Am. mayor. Exc. as regards what we may call the "dignity business", the two officials are not even analogous. When essentials are considered, the Am. functionary who corresponds to the Eng. mayor is the president or chairman of the common council' (Dr. ALBERT SHAW, Municipal Government in Great Britain, c. 3). Among the differences are that the Am. mayor is no part of the council but an independent and co-ordinate authority, elected directly by the people; that he has a veto upon ORDINANCES (q.v.) adopted by the council; and that he makes appointments to various municipal offices.

mean. The adj. *mean* has a wider range in Am. than in Eng. A man who is out of sorts or 'seedy' because he has a bad cold will tell you that he is 'feeling rather mean to-night'. If he has sprained his ankle, he may describe it as 'a mean accident'; that is to say, it is not terribly serious, but uncomfortable and inconvenient enough to be a great nuisance. 'These wreaths were rather mean to make'; i.e. making them was a troublesome job. Impure or adulterated whiskey is 'mean whiskey'. 'New Yorkers, who have become accustomed to all sorts of weather, found that of yesterday meaner than any they have experienced for years, for when the rainstorm came along early in the day the wind sent the rain in sheets into the faces of pedestrians, and, within a short time, the mercury began to drop until it seemed as if the zero mark would be reached before nightfall.' 'Threshing clover was one of the meanest jobs I remember, for while it was going on the air was so filled with dust that you couldn't see

three feet beyond your nose' (Dr. W. W. FOLWELL, Autobiog. 26).

measure. In Am. *measure up to* is used in a sense which will be self-evident from the following examples. 'There was a sneaking suspicion that the boys would never quite measure up to the high standards set by their father.' 'Colleges seek students who measure up to the new and exacting requirements.' 'He appears ready to criticize everything that does not measure up to the promises of the president.' 'Stanford ever had in mind the problem of selecting some one who measured up to his ideal as president of his university' (G. T. CLARK, Leland Stanford, 405).

The expression *measure up with* is less frequent. 'The essay measures up well with the articles on the same subject which abound in the reform journals of the time' (V. LOGGINS, The Negro Author, 70).

The derivative *measurably* is often used in Am. in the sense of *to some extent.* 'On the emotional and affectional and measurably on the practical side of his nature he was allied with the so-called Evangelical branch of the church' (Prof. L. O. BRASTOW, Representative Modern Preachers, 59). 'The first necessity of the new government was to provide revenues, and this was measurably accomplished by the passage of the first tariff act' (Dr. J. M. BECK, The Wonderland of Bureaucracy, 10). 'Accentuated by Wilson's administration in handling of matters in the Great War, and only measurably relieved by his Federal Reserve Act' (F. J. STIMSON, My U.S. 74).

meat. A use of this word found only in Am. and in certain Eng. dial. is illustrated in the following quotations. 'A friend who had learned the tinsmith trade and had done a little canning of lobster meat' (Dict. Am. Biog. ix. 366). 'The ptomaine poisoning came, it was said, from eating crab meat on the presidential boat' (F. L. ALLEN, Only Yesterday, 135).

'Instead of turkey meat, Agnes and the children had boiled beef and potatoes for Thanksgiving dinner' (L. ADAMIC, Laughing in the Jungle, 277). In Eng. the addition of the word *meat* to *lobster*, *crab*, and *turkey* would have been thought unnecessary. Cecil Sharp, in a letter to his wife from the Appalachians (quoted in his biog., p. 150) says the only meat the people there ever eat is pig, 'or hog-meat as they call it'.

†medicine is used fig. in Am. to denote anything disagreeable, esp. when it is the natural consequence of folly or error. 'Occasionally, when a Jackie learns that his ship is about to sail for a foreign port, and he does not want to go, he gets ashore on pass, stays there until his boat sails, and then gives himself up to the nearest receiving ship, and takes his medicine.' 'Even if he could summon up courage enough to declare himself positively about anything, he has let his opportunities slip by unutilized. All he can do now is to swallow his medicine as gracefully as he can or else manfully resign.' 'Having suffered the autocratic rule of Czar Reed in the preceding Congress, the Democrats now that they were in the majority proposed to give the Republicans some of their own medicine.'

meeting. In Am. *meeting* often denotes spec. a gathering for religious worship. In Eng. it is so used only in such compounds as *prayer-meeting*, *class-meeting*. Otherwise *Church* or *service* would be used. 'They set out together for evening meeting in the summer twilight.' 'A voice whose roll and cadence told that he had led in family prayers these many years, if not in meeting' (G. ATHERTON, The Travelling Thirds, 3). 'The next day is Sunday, and there is mild excitement in Coniston. For Jethro Bass appeared at meeting!' (W. CHURCHILL, Coniston, 15).

To *speak in meeting* does not necessarily imply vocal utterance, whether at a religious service or elsewhere.

The term may be applied to the expression of one's individual views through any medium. In a letter (printed in Letters and Memorials of W. P. Garrison, 17) declining an invitation to contribute to a magazine, Mr. Garrison says: 'I desire to avoid the appearance of speaking in meeting too often, especially as I generally speak in criticism, if at all.' The idea becomes more emphatic in the expression *speak right out in meeting*.

†melon has a fig. use in Am. in the sense of *profits for distribution*. 'A purse of $25,000 will be distributed by the Interborough Company among employees. About 8,000 men will participate in the cutting of the melon the next time the pay-car goes round.' 'If the executives cut enough melons, what else do the stockholders care?' (NORMAN THOMAS, America's Way Out, 29). 'An industry would have to pay, but the money made could not be wasted in dividends, melons, and big salaries' (L. STEFFENS, Autobiog. 869). 'Behind these formal charges lay a county fight between various supervisors in the matter of slicing the road-fund melon' (F. L. BIRD and F. M. RYAN, Recall of Public Officers, 300).

melt is sometimes followed in Am. by *up* where *down* would be used in Eng. 'Fifty thousand cars have been melted up since the April before last' (E. WILSON, The Am. Jitters, 47).

merchant is now usually restricted in Eng. to a *wholesale trader*, esp. with foreign countries, and, with a few exceptions, such as *coal merchant* and *wine merchant*, is never applied to a retail shopkeeper. In Am., as in Scottish dial., it retains its earlier sense of a *dealer in merchandise*, whether on a large or a small scale. 'In my village the merchants habitually close their shops every Wednesday at one.' 'The growth of the [chain store] system has been accompanied by the failure of thousands of merchants in the small towns' (Prof. A. E. Newton, Hist. of U.S. ii. 771). 'The merchant at the cross-roads store is as much a business man as the merchant of N.Y.' said W. J. Bryan in his famous 'cross of gold' speech at the Dem. convention of 1896.

It is in a corresponding sense that Americans use the verb *merchandise* —a word which in Eng. is a noun only. 'The educated Negro comes out of school to find most white-collar jobs closed to him. He is generally excluded from merchandising.' 'His father ran a general merchandising store' (Upton Sinclair Presents William Fox, 14). 'Because of an efficient merchandizing system, the company is able to offer low prices to its employees' (Bruce Crawford, in Culture in the South, 365).

message is the technical term for an official communication from the President of the U.S. to Congress. 'The message was a verbose document of more than 20,000 words. . . . Out of the excess verbiage of this first presidential state paper grew the more definite principles which he made his own' (H. F. Pringle, Theodore Roosevelt, 245).

The term may similarly denote an official communication from (1) the Governor of a State to the State Legislature or (2) the Mayor to the City Council. (1) 'The Governor of the Commonwealth at once recognized the serious situation in which the banks had placed themselves. His message to both houses of the legislature dealt at length with the financial situation' (G. T. Starnes, 60 Years of Branch Banking in Virginia, 90). (2) 'The Mayor in his message to the aldermen yesterday declared himself in favor of the city's operating its own lighting plant.'

midway. In addition to its other meanings, *midway* is in Am. sometimes a noun, denoting the entertainment section of an exposition or fair. 'Ever since Chicago led the way, the "Mid-way" features of our great fairs have threatened more and more to overshadow the mere educational features.' 'Out in the little "Midway" of tents and booths, where the two-headed baby was on exhibition, where the six-legged calf and the freak horse were housed.' The term was first used in connexion with the Chicago World Fair of 1893, where it indicated the actual position of this feature in relation to the plan of the whole exposition.

mighty is no longer used adverbially in Eng. as it once was, exc. in dial., but this use persists colloq. in Am. 'There will be some mighty interesting conferences to-morrow.' 'It was not only unfair, but it was mighty bad policy.' 'It is a mighty good thing that it is possible now' (Speech of President Theodore Roosevelt). 'He said a mighty good thing about mathematics' (O. W. Holmes, Autocrat of the Breakfast Table, 1). 'We were mighty glad to see the lights of Atlantic City' (F. J. Stimson, My U.S. 439).

mileage. In Eng. distance measured in miles. In Am., as in official circles in India, also a travelling allowance based on distance in miles. 'An officer who is ordered to change station while he is on leave of absence is entitled to mileage from the place of receipt by him of the order to his new station.' 'It is estimated that the allowed mileage about pays the fares of a congressman, his wife, and three children' (Prof. A. B. Hart, Actual Government, 228).

mill has in Am. a meaning which has nothing whatever to do with any mechanical operation. It is a term used in financial calculations to denote *a thousandth part of a dollar*. In this sense it is derived from the Lat. *mille*. 'The Legislature of Missouri gave the St. Louis Board of Education power to use as school money six mills on each dollar of the city's valuation for purposes of taxation.' 'They support the Universities by a direct mill tax levied upon the assessed valuation of the State.' 'The continental paper was bought and sold by speculators at prices ranging all the way from a mill to a quarter of a cent on a dollar' (Prof. D. S. Muzzey, The Am. Adventure, i. 120).

In Eng. the verb *mill* is little used exc. trans. In Am. it is intrans. also, meaning *move round and round in a crowd.* 'Policemen were clearing the sidewalks, and in the City Hall the crowd was milling' (W. A. White, Masks in a Pageant, 480). 'A milling, enthusiastic and hilarious mob gathered at the corner of Park and Tremont streets' (A. G. Hays, Let Freedom Ring, 160).

mine. In Am. *mine worker* is sometimes preferred to the Eng. term *miner.* Thus, the organization known as the United Mine Workers of Am. corresponds to the Miners' Federation of Great Britain.

miss. Prof. Félix Boillot correctly warns his French readers (Le Vrai Ami du Traducteur, 167) that in good Eng. *miss* is not used exc. before a proper name; so that it is as ridiculous for a Frenchman to say 'Nous venons d'engager une miss' as for an Englishman to say 'We have just engaged a mademoiselle'. It might be added that the only exception is to be found in such contemptuous expressions as 'a pert miss'. In Am. there is no such restriction on the use of the word. 'Misses' and Girls' Fall Apparel at very attractive prices' (Advt.). 'The little girl who would like to ride on the Shetland pony when the clown offers any miss in the audience an opportunity' (M. Deland, Dr. Lavender's People, 336). 'They were a regular business vaudeville team—one big and broad-gauged in all his ideas; the other unable to think in anything but boys' and misses' sizes' (G. H. Lorimer, Old Gorgon Graham, 238).

mission. The *mission* style of architecture, furniture, &c., is that which takes as its pattern the type found in the buildings erected by the Spanish Roman Catholic missions in California. 'Soft green pottery that will harmonize well with mission furniture in the favorite green oak.' 'The mission style has been found well adapted to such materials as stucco' (E. D. Adams and J. C. Almack, Hist. of U.S. 724). 'Modern California has done everything to keep the old Spanish province everywhere in mind. There are "mission" plays and "mission" groceries and "mission" garages, and, as all Am. knows to its sorrow, "mission" furniture' (Harrison Rhodes, Am. Towns and People, 168).

The word *mission* is also used in Am. to denote a permanent diplomatic establishment. Thus one may speak of 'the British mission at Washington'. The subject of Dr. A. A. Ettinger's book entitled *The Mission to Spain of Pierre Soulé* is not an appointment outside the regular diplomatic service, such as in Eng. might be called a *mission*, but a normal appointment as U.S. Minister to Madrid.

mistreat is commonly preferred in Am. to the Eng. *maltreat.* 'The fact that negroes are mistreated in the North is no excuse for mistreating them in the South.' 'There is something loathsome about the character of a person who would cruelly mistreat a horse.' 'He shipped on a coastwise sailing vessel but was mistreated by the mate' (Dict. Am. Biog. vi. 425).

Hence Am. *mistreatment* = Eng. *maltreatment.* 'To attack the Administration for its alleged mistreatment of the Philippines.' 'The mistreatment of the mail was due to the carelessness of clerks in the post office.' 'Acc. to decisions in various states [in divorce suits] cruelty may include mistreatment endangering life or health' (M. A. Elliott and F. E. Merrill, Social Disorganization, 521).

†mixer. In Eng. a *mixer* is a person who performs the operation of mixing in various manufactures, &c. In Am. it is also the term for one whose social gifts make him quickly at home with all sorts and conditions of men. 'The ideal president of a university will know how to sympathize with men in every department. He must be a mixer.' 'In this campaign he developed a gift which he was least suspected by the politicians of having —the gift of being a good "mixer". He made votes hand over fist, going around among the people of the district, getting acquainted with them and giving them a chance to get acquainted with him.' 'He was not a mixer. He was never known to slap anyone on the back in jovial fashion' (D. LAWRENCE, True Story of Woodrow Wilson, 86). 'Fat, jolly and a good mixer, he made friends on every hand' (WILLIS J. ABBOT, Watching the World Go By, 200).

moderator. In Eng. *moderator* is the title of certain examiners at Oxford and Cambridge and of the occupants of certain ecclesiastical offices in the Presbyterian and Congregational Churches. In Am. the name is similarly used in an ecclesiastical sense, and in addition it is given to the person elected to preside over a TOWN MEETING (q.v.). 'Deacon Lysander Richardson, the moderator, sits aghast in his high place as they come trooping in, men who have not been to town meeting for ten years' (W. CHURCHILL, Coniston, 58). 'When I came up on the platform I asked for a moderator, as the New Englanders call a chairman' (L. STEFFENS, Autobiog. 595).

monarch. The derivative *monarchial* is sometimes preferred in Am. to the Eng. form *monarchical*. 'It was, indeed, a monarchial government which Hamilton recommended, thinly camouflaged by rep. forms' (Prof. T. J. GRAYSON, Leaders and Periods of Am. Finance, 55). 'An attempt at the establishment of a monarchial scheme in the New World' (L. F. HILL, Diplomatic Relations between the U.S. and Brazil, 105).

†monkey. The reputation of the monkey for playing mischievous tricks has enriched the vocab. of Am. metaphor. 'After a good play the whole team would for a moment cut monkey-shines that would make the grand stand and bleachers roar' (J. W. JOHNSON, Black Manhattan, 64). Here *monkey-shines* = Eng. *capers*. 'The public promulgation of such an order can only mean a warning to Russia that we will not tolerate any undue delay or any monkey business whatsoever.'

Hence Am. *monkey with* = Eng. *play tricks with, meddle with*. 'It is strange what a passion some people have to monkey with that structure. A few years ago we had to pray the legislature to save it from destruction.' 'Too much monkeying with the currency and the coinage has been going on of late at Washington.' '"Hello in there!" came a voice. "Don't monkey with that line!" And it came to me that this rope held the block which held the swing which held the man' (C. MOFFETT, Careers of Danger, 33). 'A common form of error, when you monkey with statistics' (FLORENCE CONVERSE, Efficiency Expert, 157).

monopoly is followed in Eng. by *of* but in Am. by *on*. 'The South no longer has a monopoly on "Dixie". It is national in the broadest sense.' 'No religion has ever held a monopoly on the control of human passions' (W. D. ORCUTT, Kingdom of Books, 31). 'The national banks were given the monopoly on bank note currency' (Prof. E. S. SPARKS, Agricultural Credit in U.S. 336).

moot. In Am. *mooted point* and *mooted question* are alternatives to *moot point* and *moot question*. 'There are, besides, a number of mooted points upon which authorities are not agreed.' 'The questions of seniority and tests for employees are still mooted questions.' 'This reorganization already has caused a great deal of discussion, and probably for generations to come will constitute one of the mooted points of Am. railroad finance' (Prof. T. J. GRAYSON, Leaders and Periods of Am. Finance, 466). In Eng. one might say 'The question was mooted' but not 'It was a mooted question'.

most is commonly used in Am. as an abbrev. of *almost.* 'Most everyone waited to see the finish.' 'The President is capable of being wrong on most all important questions.' 'A better idea of its location can be got by asking most any resident.' 'There was a crowd most everywhere in Nassau County to-day.' The same abbrev. may be found in some Eng. dial.

mourn. The name *mourning-dove* is sometimes given to the common Am. turtle-dove, on account of its plaintive note. 'Toward evening there came from some far-away pot-hole in the woods the cry of the mourning-dove' (M. H. HARTWICK, in Life in the U.S. 7).

††move. The Am. colloq. expression *get a move* (*on*) = Eng. *hurry up, look alive.* 'Four months have passed and not a single case has been called for trial. The District Attorney should imitate the example of the President and get a move on.' 'The frightened passenger was relieved of a watch and his purse, and the robber yelled: "Get a move there, the rest of you. I've no time to wait. Have your money ready when I come."' 'Conservatism doesn't go in Western Yankeedom. When it comes to mottoes, there is a widespread inclination to accept "Get a move on" as the watchword of one's existence.'

mucilage is an unusual word in Eng. but is the common term in Am. for the adhesive known in Eng. as *gum.* 'Blank books, transfer files, inks, mucilage, fine stationery, &c.' (Advt.).

'I bought pencils, crayons, and mucilage of the local stationers' (K. D. WIGGIN, My Garden of Memory, 112). On inquiring at an Am. Post Office whether there was gum on the newspaper wrappers, I received the reply: 'Yes, they're mucilaged.'

muck-rake. Bunyan's well-known character, 'the man with the muck-rake', has long provided a suitable description for one who takes a depraved interest in foul or scandalous things. Pres. Theodore Roosevelt adroitly—but quite unfairly—exploited the implications of this term by denouncing as *muck-rakers* a group of writers who, early in the present century, set themselves to investigate and expose the corruption in Am. political and business life. In the course of time it has become recognized that those who undertake such tasks are actuated by public-spirited rather than unworthy motives, and to *muck-rake* now means simply to investigate and expose shady proceedings, without any suggestion that the investigator takes pleasure in the process. 'To pass legislation increasing the amount spent on pensions would arouse a storm of indignation among the people and cause the pension system as a whole to be muck-raked as it has never been hitherto.' 'Municipal muck-rakers have insisted constantly that the ever-increasing cost of municipal government is due to the waste and corruption of city officials.' 'In the late Wilson and Harding administrations there were obvious grafts, but the Senate itself was doing some muck-raking' (L. STEFFENS, Autobiog. 831). 'The "Home Rulers" turned muck-rakers and charged Behrman with receiving $100 per month from the Edison Electric Co. while state tax assessor' (Dr. H. ZINK, City Bosses in U.S. 322). See Dr. C. C. Regier's study of *The Era of the Muckrakers* (University of N. Carolina Press).

mull. In Eng. to *mull* is to *make*

a mess of. A fielder at cricket mulls a catch if he lets the ball slip from his hands. In Am. this verb is employed (usually with *over*) in the sense of *cogitate, ruminate,* without any suggestion of failure. 'Mr. Bonaparte has been mulling over the constitution, and it is no secret he discovered grave objections to many of its provisions.' 'With Mr. Wilson the art of meditation was not lost. He liked to mull over problems' (D. LAWRENCE, True Story of Woodrow Wilson, 228). 'He was lying ill in bed and mulling over the big deal which meant so much to him' (Prof. T. J. GRAYSON, Leaders and Periods of Am. Finance, 462). 'Canning mulled the problem over and in the summer suggested to our Minister etc.' (J. TRUSLOW ADAMS, Hist. of the Am. People to the Civil War, 279).

mural. In Eng. *mural* was once a noun as well as an adj. It meant a *wall*. In Am. it is to-day a noun, in the sense of *mural decoration.* 'One of a series of murals installed in the Public Library.' 'The growing use of murals as a unifying and significant part of a room's ensemble is rapidly reuniting the fine arts with interior decoration. . . . Especially difficult is the problem of harmonizing a mural with diverse styles of furnishings.' 'The notable murals of the Library of Congress' (Prof. A. M. SCHLESINGER, The Rise of the City, 274). 'He painted historical murals for the Minnesota and Wisconsin capitols' (Dict. Am. Biog. xii. 645).

muscle. In Am. *muscle* may be a verb. The expression *muscle into* = *make one's way into,* with a suggestion of violence. 'An unscientific inflation measure had, for a time, "muscled into" the situation' (Prof. IRVING FISHER, Mastering the Crisis, 53). In the vocab. of the bootleggers, *muscle in* is almost a technical term. '"Muscling in", which was the attempt to appropriate selling territory already sacred to another gang, was responsible for nearly all the remainder [of the conflicts between bootleggers]' (S. B. WHIPPLE, Noble Experiment, 130).

museum. 'Although a museum may include a library (as does the British Museum) or a picture gallery, the word is not in ordinary Eng. use applied to an institution of which either of these is the sole or most prominent feature. On the continent the corresponding word is often used with reference to a collection of works of painting or sculpture' (O.E.D.). The continental practice is followed in Am., where *museum* often = *art gallery.* Thus, the official catalogue of a special exhibition held at the Corcoran Gallery of Art, Washington, in April 1934, refers to the staff of that institution as 'the Museum's staff'. In the August 1934 issue of the *American Mercury* there appears an article which purports to discuss the effect of the economic crisis upon Am. museums, but it actually deals almost entirely with Am. picture galleries. 'Evidence of a country's love of painting is generally found in the number and size and quality of the country's museums' (ULA MILNER GREGORY, in Culture in the South, 279).

mushroom. In Eng. the verb *mushroom,* in the fig. sense of *spread out,* is applied only to bullets. In Am. it may be used of fires also. 'A fire that started in the basement and spread rapidly through the hallway to the top floor, where it mushroomed.'

muslin. What is called *calico* in Eng. is *muslin* in Am. An Am. paper tells the story of an Englishwoman, newly arrived in Am., who was buying some materials with which to make pyjamas for her husband. She found what was shown her too thick, and said so. 'Perhaps, madam,' said the obliging saleslady, 'you would like muslin.' To the mind of the customer, muslin suggested something diaphanous, and the thought of her serious husband so clad was too much for her gravity.

mustard. The Am. term *mustard greens* denotes the tops, i.e. the leaves, of the mustard plant. These leaves, when green and fresh, are boiled and served as part of a meal. The Eng. *mustard and cress* seems to be unknown in Am.

N

name. The verb *name* is rarely used in Eng. but commonly in Am. in the sense of *appoint*. (Cf. French *nommer*.) 'The Board of Education has aroused a color-line agitation by naming a negro as janitor of the public school.' 'Mr. King has been named consul at Aix-la-Chapelle.' 'He was named as the Bampton Lecturer for 1822' (S. W. DUFFIELD, Eng. Hymns, 188).

Am. *name for* = Eng. *name after*. 'Congressman Rockwood Hoar was named for his uncle, the late Ebenezer Rockwood Hoar.' 'A series of lectures at University College, London, named for the late Lord Northcliffe.' 'He organized the Hendricks Club, named for Vice-Pres. Thomas A. Hendricks' (Dr. H. ZINK, City Bosses in U.S. 74). 'Evans now lived in Chicago and later in its suburb which was named for him, Evanston' (Dict. Am. Biog. vi. 205).

nasty. 'The original force of the word, denoting what is disgustingly dirty or foul, has been greatly toned down or altered in Eng. use, but is retained in the U.S., where *nasty* is not commonly used by polite speakers' (O.E.D.). It is perhaps too much to say that the word 'is not commonly used by polite speakers' in Am. The point is that, when they do use it, it is in the sense of *disgustingly dirty*. Thus an Am. seldom speaks of a nasty day (meaning unpleasant weather), or a nasty fall while hunting, or a taste for the cheap and nasty.

naval, navy. The term *naval officer* has in Am. a spec. meaning,

explained in the following quotation. 'More than one reader must have paused abruptly over the headline "Would Abolish Naval Officers" and wondered with a gasp whether the millennium had really come unheralded and our Dreadnoughts were about to be converted into floating hospitals for consumptives. Of course it is not the men who command our warships that the President's Economy Commission has decided to do away with, but the persons technically described as Naval Officers, who form part of the customs machinery in the ports of the U.S.' 'Upon his retirement from legislative work he was appointed naval officer of the port of Boston' (Dict. Am. Biog. ix. 336). Charles Hudson, in whose biog. this statement occurs, was never an officer in the navy but a minister of religion who was also a politician.

The Am. *Navy Department* corresponds to the British *Admiralty*. 'He claims that the Navy Department denied him an opportunity to demonstrate the value of his boat.'

Am. *navy yard* = Eng. *dockyard*. 'They weaken the army and navy by retiring officers and refusing ammunition appropriations instead of abolishing useless army posts and navy yards.' 'Other divisions of the shore establishment include great dry-docks and machine shops at navy yards at the great harbors' (F. J. HASKIN, The Am. Government, 157).

near. In Am. *near* is frequently used, in the sense of *almost*, in combination with (1) adjectives or (2) nouns, either with or without a hyphen. (1) 'The children have been going around near-nude all winter and presumably will not wear much less during warm weather.' 'The Negro man of the near-white type is far more likely to leave the Negro group and align himself with the white than is the near-white Negro girl' (E. B. REUTER, Race Mixture, 70). (2) 'The original idea was that a lot of near-saints, called electors, should wrap their togas around them and after solemn reflection pick out the best man for President.' 'A near duel between Auguste de Staël and Benjamin Constant' (R. L. HAWKINS, Mme. de Staël and the U.S. 40). 'Some alleged labor leaders have been near-racketeers' (N. THOMAS, America's Way Out, 274). 'The danger point will be reached when a near-shortage drives prices upward' (L. DENNY, Am. Conquers Britain, 321). 'Two near-recalls, which have fallen short of official action' (L. F. BIRD and F. M. RYAN, The Recall of Public Officials, 98). 'His near blindness made it almost impossible for him to get about' (Dict. Am. Biog. viii. 486). The passing of the Prohibition Amendment resulted in a demand for a drink known as *near beer*, concerning which a wag remarked that the man who gave it that name must have been a poor judge of distance.

†The word may also be compounded with *by* to form the adj. *near-by.* 'Southey and Coleridge were near-by neighbors.' 'Many had their luncheons at a near-by restaurant' (M. E. WILKINS FREEMAN, By the Light of the Soul, 417). 'Short canals to connect near-by rivers' (Prof. C. R. FISH, The Rise of the Common Man, 76).

neighbo(u)rhood. †*In the neighbourhood of* as a substitute for *about* is described by H. W. Fowler in *Modern Eng. Usage* as 'a repulsive combination of polysyllabic humour and periphrasis'. Until quite recently this expression has been peculiar to Am., where it has been in common use since the beginning of the present century, at any rate. 'The work now in progress is to cost in the neighborhood of $200,000.' 'In the neighborhood of 350 conductors on the different railroad lines.'

A use of *neighborhood* that is still peculiar to Am. is in such terms as *the neighborhood schools*, meaning *the schools of the neighborhood.* One similarly finds *neighborhood gossip, a*

neighborhood row, neighborhood papers, neighborhood meetings, neighborhood stores, neighborhood opinion, and *neighborhood sentiment.*

New Year. In Am. *New Year's Day* is often abbrev. to *New Year's.* 'Within three months, probably before New Year's, direct telegraphic communication will be established.' 'An hysterically gay Christmas and New Year's' (S. E. RODGER, in Life in the U.S. 161).

news. Am. *newsdealer* = Eng. *newsagent.* 'Readers who are unable to secure a copy of any edition of the paper from any newsdealer will confer a favor on the management by reporting the fact promptly.' 'Newspaper carriers and news dealers are really engaged in one form of retail dealing' (H. BEST, Blindness and the Blind in the U.S. 227).

In Eng. a *news-room* is a room, usually connected with a public library, in which various newspapers are available for reading. The Am. *news-room* is that department of a newspaper office which deals with the news section of the paper. 'When *The World* was sold, it was not regarded in the newsrooms of *The World* as a specially big story' (J. W. BARRETT, in The End of *The World*, 3).

For *news-stand,* see STAND.

Am. *newsy* = Eng. *newsboy.* 'Curfew Law for Newsies' (Headline). 'The fair feminine members of the Children's Aid Society who assumed the duties of newsies and sold papers at ridiculously low prices to good-natured buyers.' An alternative to *newsy* is *news-hawk,* apparently an abbrev. of *news-hawker.* 'Whose nerves are jarred and jaded by crowded subways, screaming news-hawks, and dashing taxis' (M. A. ELLIOTT and F. E. MERRILL, Social Disorganization, 439).

next. In Am. *the next man* = *anyone else, the first comer.* 'A Dem. plan of campaign which leaves N.Y. and

New Jersey to the enemy is doomed to failure. Mr. Bryan knows this as well as the next man.' 'We do not surrender our property to the next man who is an abler business manager' (S. G. FISHER, True Hist. Am. Revolution, 146). 'The Am. underdog has been taught to believe that, essentially, he is as good as the next man, and as such has the right to refuse to stay an underdog' (L. ADAMIC, Dynamite, 362).

The colloq. expression *get next to* is sometimes equivalent to another Am. colloq. expression, *get wise to*. (See WISE.) 'The British people are getting next to Dowie; and as a natural consequence his usefulness among them is about at an end.' It may also denote a close acquaintance pursued with the object of profiting by it. 'The art of "getting next" to a State department, the most lucrative practice of "honest graft" at the Capitol.'

nickel, unknown in Eng. except as the name of a metal, is in Am. the usual term for a *five-cent piece.* 'Nickels, dimes, and quarters were tumbling into cash drawers.' 'They worked twelve hours a day, for less than a nickel an hour' (H. N. CASSON, Life of C. H. McCormick, 38).

night. A *night stick* is a truncheon which is part of the equipment of an Am. policeman on night duty. 'The policeman made a tourniquet out of the strap on his night stick, and succeeded in stopping the flow of blood.' 'The policeman kept feeling of, weighing, and finally whirling nervously his long night stick, like a lion waving its tail' (L. STEFFENS, Autobiog. i. 213).

The name of *Night Riders* was given to an organization of farmers in Kentucky and Tennessee, who in 1908–9 resisted the attempt to create a powerful monopoly in the purchase of tobacco for manufacture. They committed attacks by night on tobacco-growers who refused to join them.

See also HAWK.

nine. In Am. a baseball team is a *nine*, as in Eng. a cricket team is an *eleven.* 'Just as men cheer for their own baseball nine.' 'The great ball game of the season was to be played between the Clayton team and the Lexington nine' (ALICE HEGAN RICE, Sandy, 91).

nip. The Am. expression *nip and tuck* has nothing to do with the Eng. *nip* in the sense of *pinch*, but is derived from an Eng. dial. and colloq. word *nip*, which means *move quickly.* (Hence also the modern Eng. term *nippy*, denoting a waitress who is nimble in her service. This term, by the way, is a registered trade mark, so there are probably legal difficulties to prevent its being taken into use in the general sense suggested by its derivation.) The expression sometimes means *at full speed.* 'It began its march in July, and by a nip-and-tuck effort reached Peking in the middle of August' (A. NEVINS, Henry White, 169). More commonly it = Eng. *neck and neck, a close thing.* 'He sat down to rest for a few moments in close proximity to a small tank of gasoline. He lit his pipe to enjoy a smoke, and as they went up through the ceiling a moment or two later it was nip and tuck between him and the tank.' 'Throughout the 14th century it was nip and tuck between the evolving Turk and the dissolving Eastern empire.'

nolle. The legal term *nolle prosequi*, which in Eng. is a noun only, is in Am. a verb also, usually with the omission of *prosequi* or with the substitution of *prosse.* Sometimes *nolle* is contracted to *nol.* 'Case Against Haskell Nolled' is the headline of a newspaper paragraph which begins: 'All cases against Haskell were nolle prossed Friday.' 'A third count in the indictments was nol prossed by the District Attorney.' 'In the two years 14,567 cases were nolle-prossed or dismissed' (D. L. COLVIN, Prohibition in U.S. 505).

none. In the sense of *not at all,* this word is used in Eng. only with *the* and the comparative, or with *so* or *too,* as *none the better, none so good, none too good.* In Am., as in certain Eng. dial., there is no such limitation. 'Has civilization advanced none from the barbaric days of the fifth century?' 'These men suffered none in comparison with their white colleagues' (R. R. Moton, What the Negro Thinks, 160). 'I slept none that night' (Frank Roney's Autobiog. 164).

normal. For the origin of the Am. derivative *normalcy,* see the first quotation. 'At Boston, a few weeks before the Convention [of 1920] he [Warren G. Harding] had correctly expressed the growing desire of the people of the country and at the same time had unwittingly added a new word to the language, when he said, "America's present need is not heroics but healing; not nostrums but normalcy; not revolution but restoration; ... not surgery but serenity"' (F. L. Allen, Only Yesterday, 41). 'Compared with it, the achievements of aviation . . . that hitherto had provided his paper with headlines, faded into the normalcies of a back page.' 'With the return to religious normalcy, there came a general feeling of relief and relaxation' (Prof. H. W. Schneider, The Puritan Mind, 125). 'I never regretted any word more than the word normalcy, because normalcy spells death, the end of all things' (C. Nagel, Speeches and Writings, i. 78).

notch is common in Am. in a fig. sense. 'Its prices are at the lowest notch.' 'An exhibition of collective strength that shall raise us a notch or two in the estimation of the nations.' 'The wages of labor in the building trades have been pushed to the very top notch.' In some parts of the U.S. the word may mean a *mountain pass,* and in this sense it may form part of a place-name. 'Not the least attractive feature of the route is Wilmington Notch, a chasm two miles long formed by a rent in the side of Whiteface.' 'New Hampshire will cover herself with disgrace if she fails to save the magnificent Crawford Notch from the deadly injury threatened by lumbermen who have begun cutting down the forests which clothe its slopes.'

Am. *top-notch* = Eng. *tip-top, first-rate.* 'Several new jackets that are top-notch in style and make' (Advt.). 'The tenant is willing to pay the top-notch rent.' 'The average lawyer earns $2,000 a year; the top-notch lawyer gets $250,000' (E. E. Calkins and R. Holden, The Art of Modern Advertising, 142).

Hence Am. *top-notcher* = Eng. *first-rater.* 'While his ability, with the onslaught of years, had deteriorated, there was a time when he was considered a top-notcher.'

notion. In every Am. department store will be found a *notion department,* where various small and inexpensive articles are for sale. It corresponds broadly to the Eng. *haberdashery.* 'At 8.30 this morning we begin our Fall Sale of Notions and Dressmaking Supplies' (Advt.). 'Valentines and Favors in Notion Department' (Advt.). 'Notion Department: Dress Shields, Pin Cubes and Collar Foundations' (Advt.). 'At the book counter a lady said "Please give me Double Thread" and wanted to complain to the floorwalker when the girl, instead of giving her Miss Fowler's book, told her to go to the notion counter.' 'Prof. Ely has pointed out several branches of industry in which small-shop production is increasing. It is pronounced in the notion trades' (W. J. Ghent, Our Benevolent Feudalism, 18). 'One chain of 5-and-10-cent stores through its 1,800 branches sells annually $72,000,000 worth of "notions"' (Prof. A. E. Martin, Hist. of U.S. ii. 771).

nub. In Eng. a *lump* or *protuberance.* In Am. the *core, kernel,* or *central point* of an affair. 'Let us get at the hard nub of the business' (F. NORRIS, Responsibilities of the Novelist, 51). 'The beginner cannot get far wrong if he gets the nub of the whole story into his first paragraph' (E. L. SHUMAN, Practical Journalism, 61). 'The paramountcy of the constitution may be conceded; but the nub question is: who shall determine what the constitution means?' (Prof. H. L. McBAIN, The Living Constitution, 241).

nullification, nullify. These terms have a spec. meaning in Am. politics, as indicated in the following quotations. 'On many occasions states declared that they themselves had the power to decide when acts of Congress violated the federal Constitution and that they could nullify such laws within their borders no matter what the Supreme Court said. This was the doctrine of defiance and nullification announced from time to time by states, North and South, and made famous by the Kentucky and Virginia resolutions of 1798–99 and the Nullification Ordinance of S. Carolina passed in 1832' (C. A. and W. BEARD, The Am. Leviathan, 65). 'The Alien and Sedition Acts [in 1798] brought forth responses in the form of resolutions passed by the Southern State of Virginia and the Western State of Kentucky, claiming that the Acts were in contravention of the Federal Constitution and calling upon other States to consider them void, thus voicing the doctrine of States' rights and nullification' (J. TRUSLOW ADAMS, The Epic of Am. 134). 'The new S. Carolina legislature summoned a special state convention. This body adopted by an overwhelming vote an "Ordinance of Nullification", declaring the tariff laws of 1828 and 1832 unconstitutional and void within the state' (Prof. A. M. SCHLESINGER, Political and Social Hist. of U.S. 37).

O

oar. The compound *oarlock* is now seldom used in Eng., having been generally superseded by *rowlock.* In Am. it is still the common term. 'Clinker-built boats . . . one pair ash oars and oarlocks' (Advt.). 'She can distinguish the sound of oarlocks a mile away and tell whether the boat is manned by friend or stranger' (G. A. HASTINGS, Happy Journeys to Yesterday, 42).

of is used in Am. in place of the Eng. *to,* in the sense of *before* (a particular hour). 'At five minutes of four I stepped from the Avenue line.' 'The second day I got to bed at a quarter of twelve.' 'Everybody here played bridge last night till 20 minutes of one this morning' (J. H. Choate, quoted in his Life by E. S. MARTIN, ii. 151). 'It was a quarter of three, but there were lights in his cottage' (SINCLAIR LEWIS, Work of Art, 342).

See also ALL, FEEL, OFF, SMELL.

off, as a prep., is in Am. frequently followed by *of.* 'This is illustrated by the use of salt to melt the ice off of sidewalks' (Prof. J. L. HOWE, Inorganic Chemistry, 63). 'You and I have to get off of the ground if we are going to do anything' (Dr. C. H. PARKHURST, A Little Lower than the Angels, 65). 'After the edge had been rubbed off of the struggles and hardships of the early settlers' (H. CROLY, Marcus Alonzo Hanna, 1).

office. In Am. the use of the term *office* is not restricted to places of business. A doctor or dentist sees his patients in an office. 'A physician's office and reception room offers a new problem to the decorator.' 'Behind the drug store was the office of Dr. R. C. Hewett.' 'He opened a dentist's office' (Dict. Am. Biog. vi. 9). The Eng. term *domestic offices,* denoting the parts of a house devoted to household work, storage, &c., is unknown in Am.

In Am. the compound *office-holder*, unknown in Eng., is the normal term to denote the occupant of a post under Government. It thus frequently corresponds to the Eng. *civil servant*. 'Two great leaks in the federal budget are the salaries of federal officeholders and the payments to World War veterans.' 'Federal officeholders were forbidden to solicit or receive, directly or indirectly, political contributions or assessments from one another. . . . The prohibition did not extend to state and local officeholders, whose salaries continued to furnish the main source of funds in the lesser elections' (Prof. A. M. SCHLESINGER, The Rise of the City, 403). 'When he [Jefferson] entered office there was not a single office-holder of his own political beliefs' (J. TRUSLOW ADAMS, Hist. of the Am. People, i. 217).

Another Am. compound, *office-seeker*, similarly denotes an applicant for a Government post. 'The assassination of President Garfield at the hands of a disappointed office seeker' (Prof. R. McELROY, Grover Cleveland, i. 123). 'At the outset, he [Lincoln] was simply besieged by office-seekers' (C. A. and M. R. BEARD, The Rise of Am. Civilization, ii. 95). Robert Henry Newell, an Am. humorous writer, made his reputation by sketches which he published under the name of 'Orpheus C. Kerr', intended as a play upon the term *office-seeker*. In Eng., in the days when the patronage system flourished, this kind of person was called a *place-hunter*.

old. The adj. *old-time* is known in Eng. as well as Am., but the noun *old-timer* is at any rate more frequent in Am. than in Eng. 'The Colonel was too experienced a politician not to know that the old-timers then in control would load the dice heavily against him' (L. EINSTEIN, Roosevelt, 199).

A partly-smoked cigar is sometimes called colloq. an *old soldier*. 'That sign which forbids the carrying into the cars of half-smoked cigars, pipes and cigarettes belongs to the class that is never enforced. Like the signs admonishing the riders not to spit on the floor, the rule about "old soldiers" might as well never have been posted, judging from the good it does.'

The *Old Colony* is Massachusetts. 'All roads lead to Plymouth—you will remark at the very beginning of your pilgrimage through the Old Colony' (K. M. ABBOTT, Old Paths and Legends of New Eng. 357).

The *Old Dominion* is Virginia. 'Virginia, through a veto of the governor, has delayed its long-meditated project of sending a statue of Robert E. Lee. The Old Dominion is unlikely to send anybody else until his statue has been received there.'

Old Glory is a popular name for the national flag. 'A setting of bright blue skies, against which Old Glory can wave in splendor.' 'The smoke stack of the engine swathed in voluminous folds of Old Glory' (J. HAWTHORNE, Hawthorne and his Circle, 48).

Old Hickory is a nickname given to President Andrew Jackson on account of the toughness and sturdiness of his character. 'I should not say that Old Hickory was faultless, but Andrew Jackson was as upright a patriot, as honest an American, as faultless a gentleman as ever any nation had' (Pres. THEODORE ROOSEVELT, in a speech). 'The classes who found democracy incarnated in "Old Hickory" voted solidly for Jackson' (J. TRUSLOW ADAMS, Hist. of the Am. People, i. 295).

The *Old Home Day* or *Old Home Week* is a New Eng. institution whose nature will be understood from the first quotation. 'In about 50 of the towns and cities of Massachusetts this first week of August is being observed as Old Home Week, and preparations have been made for welcoming back in a more or less formal way the visitors who return to their native, or earlier, home to renew acquaintance with former scenes and companions.' 'Old Home Day was observed at Langmaid's Grove with a barbecue of the old-fashioned kind. Two lambs were roasted whole, and baked beans were served in individual pots.' 'None of New Hampshire's towns have given a warmer Old Home Week welcome to their guests than did Epping, which burned three of its buildings yesterday morning.' '"The Washington atmosphere of to-day is like that of Old Home Week or a college class reunion" wrote Edward G. Lowry shortly after Harding took office' (F. L. ALLEN, Only Yesterday, 125).

on is frequently used in Am. where other prepositions would be used in Eng.

Am. *on* = Eng. *about, concerning.* 'I noticed a paragraph in the papers giving the figures on the production of asbestos.' 'Statistics on the birthplaces of notable Americans.'

Am. *on* = Eng. *against.* 'A Charlotte gentleman is telling a good story on one of his country friends.' 'John Alexander Dowie to-day began a legal fight on his opponents.' 'The people openly rejoiced that the laugh was on those whom they often consider their natural enemies.'

Am. *on* = Eng. *in.* 'He is rowing on the freshman crew at Yale.' 'Christians have, presumably, a copyright on the Golden Rule.' 'A volume well enough printed to be read on a railway train.' (In Eng. one would say 'in a railway train' or 'on a railway journey'.) 'The man on the street must acknowledge that he knows little about conditions in the rural sections' (L. F. CARR, Am. Challenged, 10). 'Objects on the street below are described as of life size' (E. H. SPALDING, Principles of Rhetoric, 60). 'Milton's Life on Bread Street' is the title of a chapter in Lucia Ames Mead's *Milton's England.*

Am. *on* = Eng. *of.* 'Hardly anyone tries to take notes on the lectures.'

'Dreamers awake from their lethargy and seem to take a new lease on life.' 'These provisions may be regarded as infringements on the theoretical scope of the power by itself' (D. M. DEWITT, Impeachment and Trial of Andrew Johnson, 181).

See also BRUSH, HAND, MONOPOLY.

The expression *on yesterday* is an example of the Am. use of *on* where it would be considered superfluous in Eng. 'The Rev. W. D. Smith was on yesterday elected to the office of archdeacon.' 'I took occasion to ask the Secretary of State on yesterday' (Sen. H. C. LODGE, reported in the Congressional Record, Dec. 27, 1922). 'I duly received your address on yesterday' (J. F. Rhodes, quoted in his Life by M. A. DE W. HOWE, 326).

†**once.** The Am. compound *once-over* denotes a *cursory survey,* as distinct from a detailed scrutiny. 'Order your meats prepared and served plain, and then you can give them the nasal once-over. If they pass, they are pretty safe' (Dr. R. L. ALSAKER, Eating for Health and Efficiency, 394). 'Jim brought him a little packet of literature, suggesting that Lenard give it the once-over' (L. ADAMIC, Laughing in the Jungle, 278).

open. For Am. *open note,* see quotation. 'The notes are of the open (or, as our English friends term it, minim or semibreve) style.' These notes are presumably so-called because they are written with a loop which is not filled in, as in the case of a crotchet. In Eng. this term denotes a note produced by an organ pipe which is not closed at the top, by a string not stopped by a finger, or by a wind instrument without slide, key, or piston.

See also SHOP and WIDE.

In the vocab. of Am. stores *opening* is a technical term denoting a display of the styles for the new season. 'This is the first week of the annual fall openings in all the shops. . . . At an opening at one of the large stores this week were seen some very original voile gowns.' This use of the word explains the following extract from the comic column of a newspaper. 'Teacher: "What is the meaning of *aperture*?" Class (in chorus): "An opening." Teacher: "Tommy Smith, give a sentence containing the word *aperture*." Tommy: "All the big stores have had their fall apertures."'

operate. In Am. *operate* is a much overworked word, being freely used in place of the Eng. *work, run, conduct, carry on, deal with.* 'A sedan operated by Sidney Begor ran into a car owned and operated by Ned Taylor.' 'Europeans think we operate our institutions greatly to the advantage of the female sex.' 'In 1879 Pierpont Morgan stepped out upon his own and operated sensationally the first underwriting in Am. railway securities' (J. K. WINKLER, J. Pierpont Morgan, 97). 'Closing machines now operate 120 to 125 cans per minute where previously they operated 60' (B. LASKER, Filipino Immigration, 74). 'The National Research Council is not an organization which operates scientific laboratories' (Prof. M. PUPIN, From Immigrant to Inventor, 373). Other extracts might be given to show that in Am. one may operate a railway, a bank, a factory, a mill, a wagon, a boat, a farm, a newspaper, a school, a café, a college, a theatre, a canal, an oil reserve, a play ground, a park.

There is a similar freedom in the intrans. use of the word. 'The saving in operating expense for the church for the year is 42 per cent.' 'The man who invented the first prepared cereal food operated in an empty barn, without machinery.' 'The skill with which he operated in the Senate.' 'Vice appeared to operate rather openly throughout the city' (Dr. H. ZINK, City Bosses in U.S. 86). 'The banks operating under state charters' (Prof. A. E. MARTIN, Hist. of U.S. i. 312). 'Sundry white citizens were

aggrieved that the City Council tolerated a Negro dentist to remain and operate in their midst' (C. S. JOHNSON, The Negro in Am. Civilization, 11). In this last quotation the writer is referring not to the performance of dental operations but to the carrying on of the occupation of a dentist. Hence Am. *operating costs* = Eng. *running expenses, working expenses.*

So, too, with *operation.* 'She had been in charge of the operation of the cafeteria.' 'The bill to prevent the operation of hotels on Sundays.' 'The Bureau supervised the building and operation of schools' (Prof. A. E. MARTIN, Hist. of U.S. ii. 10).

Am. *operator* must be carefully distinguished from Eng. *operative.* It denotes an employer, not an employee. 'After reciting the claims made by the miners and the operators respectively, the report makes the following awards.' 'The demands of the labor organizations for higher wages were rejected by the operators of the mills, mines, factories, and railroads' (Prof. A. E. MARTIN, Hist. of U.S. ii. 216). 'Mark Hanna told the coal operators that it would be the better part of valor to give the men what they wanted' (M. R. WERNER, Bryan, 124). 'The operators in that section were wise enough to realize that the type of farming practiced in that section wouldn't pay modern wages' (C. F. CARR, Am. Challenged, 62).

orchestra. In Am. the name of *orchestra, orchestra chairs,* or *orchestra stalls* is given to that part of a theatre which is known in Eng. as the *stalls.* 'Fitch climbed down from the stage into the orchestra stalls' (Dict. Am. Biog. vi. 430). 'She regarded me much as she would a new play for which she had an orchestra seat' (G. ATHERTON, Adventures of a Novelist, 143). 'A President must always be on his dignity. He cannot sit in the orchestra or in the balcony, away from everybody's staring glasses'

(D. LAWRENCE, True Story of Woodrow Wilson, **117**).

order. In Am. to say that a thing is *in order* does not always mean either that it is in accordance with the rules regulating the proceedings of a meeting, or that its constituent parts are systematically arranged. The meaning of the term has been so extended that it is sometimes equivalent to *permissible, appropriate, fitting,* or even *probable.* 'Surely it is in order time and again to protest against the prevalent notion that literary pleasure is given only by poems and dramas and novels and tales.' 'Mr. Hoover will then discover that reparations and debts are, after all, not a finished fact, and that it will be quite in order for a loyal and patriotic Am. to discuss those questions.' 'Unless between now and next week either side yields, a general tie-up in the shipyards will be in order.' 'But the discussion of specific campaigns and particular situations may be more illuminating than that of common practices, and it is now in order perhaps to discuss in more detail the way in which a few battles have been carried on' (Prof. C. E. MERRIAM, Chicago, 281). 'As the soft Roman days lengthened to spring, *campagna* picnics were in order.'

The expression *call to order* differs in meaning in Eng. and Am. In Eng. a chairman calls a speaker to order if he infringes the rules of procedure. In Am. he calls the meeting to order by formally opening the proceedings. 'The annual meeting of the society of alumni was called to order shortly after 10 o'clock in Jessup Hall.' 'There was a large gathering in response to this announcement. It was called to order by Mr. Crocker, who undertook to define the objects of the meeting' (G. T. CLARK, Leland Stanford, 76). 'The Rep. National Convention of 1900 had been called to order at 12:30 o'clock with the usual formalities' (H. F. PRINGLE, Theodore Roosevelt, 220).

Am. *in short order* = Eng. *immediately, in no time.* 'He would leave a few pills which he assured me would cure the trouble in short order.' 'The fire was put out in short order, and before it could get anywhere near the powder.' 'Professors of Latin, stepping into a college presidency, have had to deal in short order with problems of drainage' (Dr. A. FLEXNER, Universities, 159).

Am. idiom permits an ellipsis of *to be* after the verb *order.* 'The Emperor ordered his bones transported to the New World.' 'The Commissioner became irate and ordered Sulzer impeached' (Dr. H. ZINK, City Bosses in U.S. 155). 'Minister Adams worked steadily and skilfully to prevent the sailing of the vessels on completion, and Russell finally ordered them seized' (J. TRUSLOW ADAMS, Hist. of the Am. People, ii. 58). 'The mayor ordered the railway tracks torn up and the bridges destroyed' (Prof. A. E. MARTIN, Hist. of U.S. i. 665). See also FILL.

ordinance. Except historically (e.g. the Self-Denying Ordinance) and in the phrase *religious ordinances* (meaning *religious rites*) *ordinance* is rarely used in Eng. In Am. it is the technical term for a legislative decision of a municipality, esp. such as in Eng. would be called a *by-law.* 'So far as the city ordinances are concerned, the theatre-goers of Chicago seem to have been well enough protected. It was the failure to enforce the ordinances which made disaster possible.' 'The Philadelphia councils enacted an ordinance which provided for the establishment of a gas works with a capital of $100,000' (Dr. H. ZINK, City Bosses in U.S. 194). 'Defendant was convicted of violating an ordinance of the town of Burlington limiting the speed of automobiles in the fire district to 8 miles per hour' (G. R. SHERRILL, Criminal Procedure in N. Carolina, 116).

The tendency in Am. is to confine the use of *by-law* to the rules and regulations of private companies and associations.

organic. When an Am. TERRITORY (q.v.) is created or when a *territory* becomes a *state*, the law passed by Congress to prescribe the fundamental conditions of its government—the law, that is to say, which organizes it—is called an *organic law* or *organic act.* 'In 1864 the territory of Montana was organized.... Unfortunately the organic act failed to provide a system of law for the territory' (Dict. Am. Biog. ix. 243).

organize, organization. In the vocab. of Am. politics these words have a spec. meaning. A newly elected Congress is said to be *organized* when its principal officers and committees have been elected. Such posts are mainly filled by representatives of the majority party. Even the Speaker of the House of Representatives is avowedly a partisan, who is expected to use his position in the interests of his own party. This explains an otherwise mysterious comment of an Am. paper on the British general election of 1931. 'So great was the strength of the Conservatives', it said, 'that some observers pointed to the possibility of that party being able to organize the House of Commons.' 'When the session opens, the Democrats will organize the House. They will put John N. Garner in the Speaker's chair and take over the committee chairmanships, which are now held by Republicans.' 'The Republicans, who had only an infinitesimal majority, had organized the House with Thomas B. Reed as Speaker' (F. E. LEUPP, Walks about Washington, 103). 'This 14th Congress met on Monday, Dec. 4, and it was not organized by Federalists' [i.e. the Federalists were not in the majority] (B. A. KONKLE, Joseph Hopkinson, 186).

The term *organization* not only denotes the process described above, but is also a synonym for the party

MACHINE (q.v.). 'His administration has been non-partisan. Let the complaints of the baser organization Republicans testify.' '"I'm a customs inspictor," says th' boy. "Tis a good job," says Hannigan. "I thried f'r it wanst mesilf, but I jined th'wrong or-gan-ization", he says' (F. P. DUNNE, Mr. Dooley's Opinions, 163). 'Every official of this Court is at some time touched with the blight of local organization politics' (W. B. and J. B. NORTHROP, The Insolence of Office, 106).

oriole. The Eng. and Am. birds of this name belong to quite different families. The Eng. *oriole* is of the family Oriolidae, but the Am. belongs to the Icteridae, closely allied to finches.

out is commonly used in Am. to intensify a verb: as †*try out, lose out, win out, watch out, test out, perish out.* One may compare the Eng. Prayerbook version of Psalm xxvi. 2: 'Try out my reins and my heart.'

For *take out* (to dinner) see TAKE.

††A person who is eagerly attempting to get something may be said in Am. to be *out* for it, or *out* to get it. 'A band of Revolutionary soldiers who had not received their back pay, and were out to get it by any means, fair or foul' (Prof. T. J. GRAYSON, Leaders and Periods of Am. Finance, 37). 'An *agent provocateur* out to wreck the unions by dividing labor's ranks' (L. SYMES and T. CLEMENT, Rebel Am. 191).

A peculiarly Am. meaning of *out* is *lacking, minus.* 'The ardent enthusiast who stands open-mouthed at the election board discovers long before he knows who is the next President that he is out a watch or a diamond pin.'

In Am. *out* may be used as a noun, in the sense of *drawback, flaw.* 'We don't just know how we are going to feel toward this scheme; we think we see some outs about it.' 'As the campaign developed it became manifest that there were no serious outs in the year's work.' 'He has the advantage of having a political machine ready at hand. The outs about him that you and I should feel would not affect the masses' (Prof. A. C. Coolidge, in a letter quoted in his biography by H. J. COOLIDGE and R. H. LORD, 252). The word may also denote *omission*. '"Outs", or omissions from copy, are detected by means of the trained copy-holder' (T. L. DE VINNE, Modern Methods of Book Composition, 298).

Am. *at outs* = Eng. *at odds*, *at variance*. 'Bishop Barnes is at outs with some of his clergy of the extreme Catholic party in regard to sacramental teachings.' 'She was at outs with her parents because of her marriage, so she went to live with her aunt.' 'Almost every one of the novelists who were ranked most highly by the post-war intellectuals was at outs with the censors' (F. L. ALLEN, Only Yesterday, 119). This expression is found in some Eng. dial.

The compound *outgiving* is of Am. coinage. It denotes a statement made to the public, esp. as a declaration of policy. 'His fixed plan of minimizing the revolutionary character of his fiscal programme is ably continued in his latest outgiving.' 'The political leader knows how to cajole, to influence, even to mislead public opinion, but he seldom attempts to manage it by the disingenuous outgiving, because he knows the dangers of the method.' 'The comedy developed through days of thunderous outgivings from the private letter-files on both sides' (M. SULLIVAN, Our Times, iii. 102).

outfit. In Am. this term may not only denote the material equipment for a journey or expedition but may include the group of persons undertaking it. It is esp. used of a party of men in charge of herds of cattle. 'As the outfit rode away to relieve the last guard, every mother's son was singing' (ANDY ADAMS, The Outlet, 81). 'The outfit consisted of three covered wagons, four tents, eighty saddle horses, three cooks, and about twenty riders' (HAMLIN GARLAND, Roadside Meetings, 286). 'The Rocky Mountain fur trade was carried on much more by parties of white trappers than by outfits of traders, clerks and voyageurs who bartered for furs secured by the Indians' (K. W. PORTER, John Jacob Astor, 768). 'He spent three years with an outfit of 45 men trading and trapping' (Dict. Am. Biog. xiv. 601).

The meaning of the word has been extended to apply to a number of persons combined for any purpose. 'The entire outfit of candidates on the State ticket intend to vote for Peck.' 'There sprang into power the Am. Federation of Labor, an un-idealistic, hard-headed outfit' (L. ADAMIC, Dynamite, 84). 'The Tammany outfit had supported him in the gubernatorial campaign' (W. G. McADOO, Crowded Years, 38).

over. Am. *Over* = Eng. *P.T.O.* (Please Turn Over) at the bottom of a card, as an instruction to read what will be found on the other side.

Am. *over and over* = Eng. *over and over again*. 'Women and children went to see it over and over' (MARK SULLIVAN, Our Times, iii. 463).

††Am. *put over* or *get over* = Eng. *put through*, but commonly with a suggestion of adroitness, not to say sharp practice, that is absent from the Eng. term. 'Some of the bosses helped the reformers put over their anti-graft charter' (L. STEFFENS, Autobiog. 409). 'He cast about for some method by which his object might be attained. The way in which he "put it over" is illustrative of the resourcefulness and ingenuity of a facile and able intellect' (Prof. T. J. GRAYSON, Leaders and Periods of Am. Finance, 67). 'One of the greatest hoaxes ever planned was put over by a French forger' (Dr. A. S. W. ROSENBACH, Books and Bidders, 117). 'He rather delights in taking pains with what he wants to get

over' (IDA M. TARBELL, Owen D. Young, 246). See ACROSS.

†*overall*. In Eng. this is a loose outer garment worn by women— e.g. domestic servants—to keep their clothes from being soiled while they are at work. In Am. the plur. form *overalls* denotes an outer garment worn by men for a similar purpose. In a review of the *O.E.D.*, the N.Y. *Nation* (Jan. 21, 1904) remarks: 'Dr. Murray is misled by Bancroft into making mere trousers of it; it is all but what would be called nowadays a "union garment", lacking the sleeves, and 50 years ago was worn by boys at play to protect their jackets as well as their trousers.' 'The workman likes his pipe while he's working, but when he takes off his overalls and goes home he wants a cigar.' 'There advanced toward him beside a heavily laden baggage-truck a stout man, wearing the silk cap and the oily overalls of a railroad employee.' 'His audience was made up almost entirely of workmen from the factories, most of them being in overalls.'

overly. This word, a synonym for *excessively*, is now rare in the British Isles, exc. dial. in Scotland and Ireland. In Am. it is still in frequent use. 'In a majority of instances the bridegroom is not overly blessed with funds.' 'In our magazine we have repeatedly harped on the evil of consuming overly refined foods.' 'Nor is my purpose an overly zealous one' (M. E. CHASE, A Goodly Heritage, 8).

overseer was formerly used in Am. to denote a man in charge of slaves on a plantation. It has to-day a spec. use at Harvard, defined in the following quotation. 'Storey's official connection with the University was for many years that of a member of the Board of Overseers, a body of 30 men chosen by the alumni literally, if in practice somewhat leniently, to oversee (with large powers of veto) the smaller body of seven to whose hands the active conduct of the University is entrusted. Storey was not a man to take his overseeing lightly, and in that chief function of an Overseer, which is to serve on committees to "visit" departments of the University, and to conduct special investigations, he took his work with all seriousness' (M. A. DE W. HOWE, Portrait of an Independent, 174).

The *overseer of the poor* is a local government official in both Eng. and Am., but with different functions. In Eng. he assesses, collects, and distributes the poor rate, and makes out jury lists and lists of voters for parliamentary and municipal elections. The actual relief of the poor, which was once part of his duties, is now carried out by other officers. In Am., on the contrary, this is the one duty of the overseers of the poor.

In Am. the noun *overturn* often takes the place of *overthrow* or *revolution*. 'The object of the fray is neither the overturn of government nor the ending of private property.' 'Then came the political overturn which brought in Thomas Jefferson' (Prof. T. J. GRAYSON, Leaders and Periods of Am. Finance, 215). 'It is probable that the extreme depression will pass in a year or two, barring social and political overturn in some countries, which might delay recovery' (J. TRUSLOW ADAMS, The Epic of Am. 405).

owl. The nocturnal habits of the owl have suggested in Am. an appropriate name for trains that run in the small hours of the night. 'The engine of the "owl train"—for by this term the one leaving N.Y. after midnight is called—went off the track.' 'The mail car that comes up to this city from N.Y. on the owl train, due at 3.20 a.m.'

P

pack. The verb *pack* is specialized in Am. to mean *prepare food for preservation* (i.e. canning or tinning). Acc. to the article on the subject in the *Encycl. Soc. Sci.* (x. 244) this use of the term dates from the colonial period. From Boston and other seaboard cities there sailed, to the West Indies and the Southern plantations, vessels carrying pickled meat, which was barrelled or packed for the journey. 'Hence,' says the *Encycl.*, 'although the greater part of the meat prepared each year continued to be shipped in bulk, the term packing came to be applied to the entire procedure of preparing various kinds of meat for market.' 'The invention of the refrigerator completely changed the meat business of the U.S., resulting in great packing centers from which meat was sent in all directions instead of being slaughtered for local use in each little community' (E. D. ADAMS and J. C. ALMACK, Hist. of U.S. 576). 'The word "packing" is sometimes misunderstood. Packing connotes slaughtering, the preparation of the slaughtered meat for the market, and then packing, shipment and eventual distribution' (Prof. J. T. GRAYSON, Leaders and Periods of Am. Finance, 393). 'White farm laborers, displaced by Filipino workers in their jobs of packing peas and lettuce' (B. LASKER, Filipino Immigration, 17).

Hence the noun *pack* is used to denote the product of such an industry. 'The salmon pack on the Frazer River this year is practically a failure. The total pack this season to date is 68,804 cases.'

In Eng. a *packer* is a workman who puts things together in boxes, bundles, &c., for transport. Publishers' packers, for instance, are men who make up books in bales for dispatch to retail booksellers. In Am. a *packer* is usually a person engaged in the packing industry above-mentioned. Sometimes he is a labourer. Thus, B. Lasker (Filipino Immigration, 18) writes of 'peach and apple growers who were planning to employ Filipino packers'. More frequently the term is applied to the head of a packing business. 'In reply to the

demands, the packers have declared that they will grant the wage increase if the men will agree to do 10 per cent. more work.' 'Packers coming within this legal classification are subject to severe penalties when found guilty of attempts to monopolize business, manipulate prices, or discriminate unjustly against any person' (C. A. and W. BEARD, The Am. Leviathan, 545).

In Am. the word *package* is commonly used to denote what in Eng. would be called a *packet*. It is also generally equivalent to the Eng. *parcel*. 'A car parked near Main Street yesterday was filled with Christmas packages, purchased during the day by a Winchester woman.' 'A bushel of wheat will buy just one package of cigarettes and one package of gum.' 'The internal revenue law fixes the size of packages of tobacco' (T. C. BLAISDELL, The Federal Trade Commission, 217). 'Their expresses carried gold-dust, mail, packages and passengers' (Dict. Am. Biog. vi. 271). 'There are too many people whose idea of a summer's literary provision becomes embodied in a package of ephemeral novels' (W. M. PAYNE, Little Leaders, 165). Important legal questions have arisen in connexion with what is known as the *original package* doctrine; i.e. the theory 'that when goods imported from another State or country are still in the hands of the importer unsold and in their original packages they are still a part of interstate commerce. But if the goods have been taken from the original packages in which they were imported, though for the purpose of sale by the importer, the interstate or foreign commerce has terminated' (Prof. C. K. BURDICK, Law of the Am. Constitution, 213).

The word *package* may also be used as a verb. 'This applies not only to eggs, oranges, buns, but to nearly all packaged goods.' 'The exorbitant prices for packaged spirits and wines' (S. B. WHIPPLE, Noble Experiment, 173).

pad. 'Most of the peculation took the form of padded bills rendered in connection with the construction of a new court house' (Dr. H. ZINK, City Bosses in U.S. 108). In this passage there is an extension of the normal sense of *pad = stuff*. What is meant is that the bills presented were for larger sums than were honestly due.

paddle. In addition to its normal aquatic meaning, the verb *paddle*, in Am., may mean *spank*, *smack*. 'A secret society of girls initiated some neophytes by blindfolding them, pushing them into a briar bush, paddling them, and then rolling them down a steep hill.' '"I'll paddle you!" is the threat used by despairing mothers and teachers [in Texas] in case of necessary discipline; and sure enough they do, with a regular wooden paddle constructed for the purpose.'

page, as a verb, has in Am. an additional meaning to that recognized in Eng. dictionaries. See the first quotation. 'The practice of calling guests in the large hotels has added another word to the language. When a visitor steps to the desk and asks for Mr. Smith and Mr. Smith is not in his room, a bell boy is called. "Here, page Mr. Smith, Room 186" the clerk will say. The process of "paging" Mr. Smith consists of calling out his name in the dining and other public rooms of the hotel' (N.Y. Sun, Aug. 21, 1904). 'Mr. Hurley and I were having dinner at the Willard Hotel. We were discussing a personal matter when Mr. Hurley was paged' (Dr. FRANKLIN H. MARTIN, The Joy of Living, ii. 205).

pail. To Eng. readers Mrs. Wharton is one of the most intelligible of Am. writers, but many of them must have failed to catch her meaning when she remarked that at present the demand made of novelists by critics was that 'only the man with the dinner pail shall be deemed worthy of attention' (A Backward Glance, 206). Who is 'the man with the dinner pail'? In Eng. the word *pail* is never used exc. of a vessel for carrying liquids, but there is no such restriction in Am., where it may denote a vessel for carrying solids also. Hence, the compound *dinner-pail* is the conventional term for the vessel containing a workman's mid-day meal. It was originally a contrivance about a foot high, elliptical in shape, and having a cup screwed into the centre of the closed top. Nowadays a thermos kit usually serves the purpose. 'Thousands of men with their dinner-pails on the way to work.' 'Protection may not fill the dinner-pail, and yet its incautious withdrawal may empty it.' 'I was not much better dressed than the workers, and found that, by the simple device of carrying a dinner-pail, I could go anywhere' (UPTON SINCLAIR, Candid Reminiscences, 138). 'Carrying dinner in a pail to his father at a woolen mill' (D. DUDLEY, Dreiser and the Land of the Free, 30).

The *full dinner-pail* is accordingly a common symbol of industrial prosperity, much as the *big loaf* once was in Eng. 'The numerous persons who up to this time have believed that crops, prosperity, stable finances, and the full dinner pail all depended upon the Rep. party.' 'A good deal of doubt existed as to the paramount issue of the campaign. To Mark Hanna it was the Full Dinner Pail' (H. F. PRINGLE, Theodore Roosevelt, 224). 'If peace means dull stagnation, selfish ease, the prosperity that can be measured in dollars and cents, there is sure to come a revulsion against it. The gospel of the full dinner-pail and the plethoric pocketbook does not satisfy' (Dr. S. McC. CROTHERS, The Pardoner's Wallet, 139).

The *dinner-pail* is used also by children who take their lunch with them to school instead of returning home for it. 'Small boys on their way to school with their dinner pails'

(DAVID GRAYSON, The Friendly Road, 173).

panhandle has a curious fig. use in Am., denoting a narrow strip of land, included within the boundaries of a State but projecting from the main body of that State very much as the handle of a pan projects from the pan itself. 'Your atlas will show that Idaho has a panhandle jutting up to the Canadian border.' 'The storm now extends from the panhandle of Texas to central Wyoming.' 'We know from Roosevelt's letter to Lodge that he was ready to fight rather than give up the Alaskan panhandle' (A. NEVINS, Henry White, 197). West Virginia, which affords an example of this peculiarity, is sometimes called *the Panhandle State*.

For some unknown reason a street beggar is said to *panhandle* and is called a *panhandler*. 'On Hart's island at the present time are housed a large number of "panhandlers" who have been arrested for begging.' '*I* watched the tramps and "panhandlers" on Union Square during my luncheon hour' (L. LEWISOHN, Up Stream, 130).

paragrapher. In Am. *paragrapher* is preferred to *paragraphist*, which is more usual in Eng. 'The world-wide extent of the country newspaper paragrapher's knowledge.' 'A very rich man with us is the meat of the paragrapher.' 'It was a jest for paragraphers and actors' (H. JUSTIN SMITH, Chicago, 139).

parish, parochial. In the early days of New Eng., the Eng. parish system was among the institutions adopted by the settlers, but it disappeared when the union of Church and State was dissolved. Nowadays there exists in Am. no ecclesiastical division of territory known as a *parish*, but the word is sometimes loosely used by an Am. minister of religion to denote his field of labour or his congregation. In Louisiana, the territorial division corresponding to the county in other States is called a *parish*.

Hence Am. *parochial* corresponds closely to Eng. *denominational*, esp. in the term *parochial school*, which denotes a school organized and maintained by a religious body, as distinct from the common or public school. 'Plans have been filed for a four-story parochial school, to be erected for St. Paul's Roman Catholic Church in East 117th Street.' 'Generally speaking, the races of the Roman Catholic religion have much larger numbers in the parochial schools than do the races with the Protestant religion or esp. the Hebrews' (J. W. JENKS and W. J. LAUCK, The Immigration Problem, 289). 'Not being an established church, the Am. Presbyterian churches have no parishes in the old-world sense, and there were those who pointed out to them that the term "parochial" could be used only by a loose analogy. Nevertheless, the first official list of schools was headed "Parochial Schools in the Presbyterian Church". . . . A parochial school was one controlled by an ecclesiastical "court"; i.e. by the session of a particular church' (Prof. L. J. SHERRILL, Presbyterian Parochial Schools, 1846–70, 69).

park, as sometimes used in Am., esp. in the term *national park*, does not necessarily carry with it the suggestion of a 'tame' piece of land, as in Eng. It may be of vast area—the Yellowstone Park, for instance, is 3,426 sq. miles in extent—and may include mountain ranges, hundreds of lakes, numerous waterfalls, and many deep canyons. The essential idea of it is that it is a territory set apart for public use and preserved from exploitation by private interests.

The word *park* may also denote a *playing field*; e.g. *baseball park, ball park*. 'It required some persuasion on her part to convince Mama that it was proper to go to a public ball park on a holiday' (Dr. FRANKLIN H.

MARTIN, The Joy of Living, i. 247).
†An *amusement park* is an open-air
place of entertainment at which
various popular amusements, such as
a switchback railway, are provided.
'The amusement park is neither
bathing beach, picnic ground, Chautauqua, nor roof-garden, but partakes of the qualities of all. Its direct
ancestor was the Chicago Midway.'
'Many theatres, dance halls, amusement parks, beaches, etc., refuse to
admit Negroes' (Prof. T. J. WOOFTER,
Jr., Races and Ethnic Groups in Am.
Life, 198). 'The sort of visceral delight which comes from heaving
baseballs at crockery in an amusement park' (F. L. ALLEN, Only
Yesterday, 233).

††The verb *park*, now familiar in
Eng., is a recent importation from
Am. It was first used in connexion
with automobiles, but often has a
much wider application. 'The train
was parked near the Union Station,
and was visited by hundreds of
townsfolk.' 'High-school girls told
my informant that they "park"
their corsets when they go to dances,
because they have been taught that
to wear them is unfavorable to deep
breathing.'

parley. This word, now usually
restricted in Eng. to a discussion of
terms between representatives of
contending forces, originally had the
general sense of *talk, conversation,
conference*. In Am. it retains much
of this wider meaning. 'Episcopal
Leaders Busy with Parley' (Headline
of newspaper report of arrangements
for the holding of a Protestant
Episcopal Diocesan Convention). 'On
Thursday and Friday the college body
of Wesleyan university will hold its
10th annual parley. The topic under
consideration will be "Race Relations". The Jewish, Negro and
oriental problems will be the major
points of discussion.'

parliamentarian. In Eng. either
(1) an adherent of the Parliamentary
cause in the Civil War of the 17th
century, or (2) a member of Parliament who is skilled and experienced
in debate. In Am. it may also denote
an official appointed to regulate the
proceedings of an assembly. 'Whether
the annual congress of the Daughters
of the Am. Revolution shall have a
parliamentarian, is a subject that
aroused the interest of the delegates
last night. Around the hotels where
the Daughters are stopping it was
rumored that a parliamentarian will be
employed.... Coming, as it does, after
the president general had said no such
position was necessary, because of
her knowledge of the laws governing
such meetings, many of the Daughters
did not know what to think.'

parlo(u)r. In Eng. *parlour* has
largely been superseded by *drawing-
room* or *sitting-room* though retained
in certain technical senses, such as
bank parlour and *Mayor's parlour*, and
in combination, as in *parlourmaid*.
It is more common in Am., where it is
also employed as a grandiose name
for a room that is showily fitted up
to attract customers; e.g. a barber
will advertise his shop as a *tonsorial
parlor*. 'In 1904 there were but
three shoe-shine parlors in the hands
of Greeks. . . . But the line in which
the Greeks have made their greatest
success is the fruit stores, candy
kitchens and ice-cream parlors' (Dr.
H. P. FAIRCHILD, Greek Immigration
to U.S. 127). 'Devotees of the
delicatessen, the sandwich shop, the
chop-suey parlor, and the beauty
saloon' (H. JUSTIN SMITH, Chicago,
220). The name is commonly given to
a mortuary in an undertaker's establishment. 'One of the Largest Under-
takers in the World. 6 Chapels, 12
Parlors, 18 Hearses, Ambulances and
Cars' (Advt.).
A *parlor car* is a railway car which
is more luxuriously fitted up than the
ordinary car, and for which, of course,
higher fares are charged. 'The parlor
car and baggage car were dragged
from the rails, and several passengers
in the former hurt by flying glass.'

A *parlor match* is defined by Webster as 'a friction match which contains little or no sulphur'. 'In striking a parlor match the head fell off and fell upon the fringe of a couch cover, which flared up.'

Am. *parlor socialist* = Eng. *armchair socialist*. 'Radicals, parlor socialists, and that "lunatic fringe" he had so often ridiculed' (L. EINSTEIN, Roosevelt, 202). Similarly, *parlor sansculotte*. 'He almost invariably expressed his radicalism in such a way that it became innocuous. . . . He was what might be called a parlor sansculotte' (V. F. CALVERTON, The Liberation of Am. Literature, 379). Also *parlor democrat*. 'Although Bancroft was politically a Dem., he was rather a parlor dem. "I love to observe the bustle of the world," he wrote in an early letter, "but I detest mixing in it"' (J. TRUSLOW ADAMS, Hist. of the Am. People to the Civil War, 334). Examples might also be quoted of *parlor Bolshevist*.

parole. For the Am. use of this word see the following quotation. 'Parole is a term commonly used in the U.S. to designate conditional release granted to a prisoner who has served a part of his sentence in a penal institution' (Encycl. Soc. Sci. xii. 437). In Eng. this term is used in relation to prisoners of war only, and an ordinary convict, when released conditionally before completing his term of imprisonment, is said to be not *on parole* but *on ticket-of-leave*. 'The parole of —— —— has again awakened discussion of the question whether laws should not be enacted making it much more difficult for long-term convicts to escape the penalties inflicted on them by trial courts.' 'It is enlightening to note the readiness with which a Governor, knowing a dangerous criminal's record, paroled him on the say-so of a man who admittedly knew "none of the details".'

parquet is not used in Eng. exc. to denote a kind of wooden flooring. In Am. it may also mean a part of a theatre. 'There are [in Eng. theatres] the stalls, which occupy one-half of the lower floor, our parquet.'

parterre. In Am. this word does not always mean an arrangement of flower beds. It is sometimes used in the French sense of the *pit* of a theatre. 'The Opera House was packed from parterre to roof' (G. ATHERTON, Adventures of a Novelist, 123). The *O.E.D.* defines it as 'the part of the ground-floor of the auditorium of a theatre behind the orchestra; later, in U.S., the part beneath the galleries'. The latest Eng. example quoted is dated 1756.

partridge. Acc. to Webster, this word, when used without qualification, denotes in the Northeastern States the *ruffed grouse*, and in the Southern and parts of the Western States the *bobwhite*. With a qualifying word, such as *mountain, Gambel's, Massena*, &c., it is applied to the other members of the sub-family (Odontophorinae) to which the bobwhite belongs.

pass, passage. In Am. there are many persons with a strain of Negro blood in whom this heritage of colour is so inconspicuous that they might easily be supposed to be of pure white lineage. If such persons leave their Negro associations and succeed in becoming accepted as Whites, they are said to *pass*. 'Very much of "passing" is more a matter of acceptance or indifference than of actual and successful concealment' (E. B. REUTER, Race Mixture, 56).

†A business company which does not pay a dividend is said in Am. to *pass* it. 'Concerns which not only passed dividends in the hard times of the nineties, but went bankrupt.' 'The losses to the Pennsylvania Railroad were appalling. For the first time in its history the road had to pass its dividend' (J. T. FLYNN, God's Gold, 196).

Am. *pass up* = Eng. *decline, refuse.*
'He was sent to the Senate as a
Rep., but on his own terms, having
previously passed up the Senator-
ship rather than take it on the terms
of others.' 'With the cue he became
exceedingly proficient, but the game
never absorbed him to the extent
that he could pass up the opportunity
for conversation or badinage' (F. F.
Bond, Mr. Miller of the *Times*, 56).

In Eng. one usually speaks of the
passing of a legislative measure, but
in Am. of its *passage.* 'Democrats
joined with the Republicans in en-
dorsing the measure, the vote upon
its passage being 326 to 17.' 'The
passage of a more stringent fugitive-
slave law' (J. Truslow Adams, The
Epic of Am. 240). 'He secured the
passage of a law which revised city
assessments' (Dr. H. Zink, City
Bosses in U.S. 232).

In Eng. *pass-key* denotes either a
private key, entrusted to a person for
a special purpose, or a *master-key*
which will open several locks. In
Am. it sometimes means also a
skeleton-key, such as is used by a
burglar.

Hence *pass-key man.* 'A pass-key
man visited North Adams Saturday
afternoon, and as a result of his visit
three house owners have reported
to the police department that about
$500 worth of goods is missing.'

pasteboard is sometimes used in
Am. where *cardboard* would be used
in Eng. 'The crowd brings its lunch
in paper bags or pasteboard boxes.'
'One spring, I bought myself a little,
cool, green snake. Eventually I
started out on a series of visits, the
snake accompanying me in a pasteboard box' (Alice Roosevelt Longworth, Crowded Hours, 59).

pastor. When Mr. Hilaire Belloc
visited the U.S., he received 'a very
great shock' on hearing a Roman
Catholic priest called a *pastor*. 'To
the travelled Catholic Englishman',
he comments, 'there rises up with
that word a hideous vision of the

4079

Huguenots. It is as though an Am.
Baptist visiting Eng., were to hear
one of his Ministers called Monsignor'
(The Contrast, 260). Here is an
example of the usage that affected
him so painfully. 'He [Father
McGlynn] held several pastorates in
the poor sections of the city . . . and
finally became pastor of St. Stephen's
Church' (Prof. G. R. Geiger, The
Philosophy of Henry George, 344).
In its record of the career of J. N.
Neumann, a Roman Catholic bishop,
the *Dict. Am. Biog.* mentions that
at one time he was pastor of the
church of St. Alphonsus, Baltimore.

patrol is in Eng. mainly a military
term. In Am. it is commonly used
as a police term also, corresponding
to Eng. *beat.* Hence (1) *patrol wagon*
= Eng. *prison van, Black Maria,* and
(2) *patrolman.* (1) 'The county detectives then went in the patrol wagon
to the Criminal Courts Building.' 'I
was given the choice of riding in the
patrol wagon or walking to the police
station' (E. Goldman, Living My
Life, 124). (2) 'Work on the new
apartment hotel was continued to-day
under the guard of three patrolmen
and a roundsman.' 'The pressure
formerly brought to bear on Washington and upon state capitals has now
been transferred to the simplest unit
of government, the patrolman on his
beat' (Jane Addams, The Second 20
Years at Hull-House, 238). 'Uniformed patrolmen assigned to foot-
patrol duty constitute the great
majority of the personnel of the police
force in all cities. . . . The traditional
method of patrol is to divide the city
into precincts or districts, each of
which is in turn divided into patrol
posts or "beats". To each post a
patrolman is assigned' (Dr. C. C.
Maxey, Outline of Municipal Government, 167).

pavement. The paved footpath by
the side of a street, which in Eng. is
called the *pavement*, is in Am. the *sidewalk.* The Am. *pavement* is the Eng.
roadway. Thus, when preparations

were being made in Washington for a procession of several thousand members of a fraternal order, the newspapers of the city complained that in Pennsylvania Avenue the grandstands filled the sidewalk and compelled pedestrians to walk on the pavement. 'It is a terrible task to pull a ponderous engine or water tower on wheels through streets where the going is as difficult as it still is over many miles of our pavements.' 'You could see the sidewalks on either hand, but the dark wooden pavement of the street was almost lost in shadows' (ERNEST POOLF, The Dark People, 4).

pay is often used attrib. in Am. 'The total number of calls for each book during three months in a pay library.' 'Five men were killed in a collision between a pay train and a passenger train. The pay train, consisting of a locomotive and one coach, was going west to pay the men along the division.' 'Enough pay patients will be taken to assist the hospital management in carrying on its work.' 'A five-dollar gold piece was placed in the pay envelope of every employee' (H. CROLY, Marcus Alonzo Hanna, 89). 'He gave illustrated lectures to pay audiences' (Dict. Am. Biog. xiii. 373).

When a miner turns up earth in which he finds gold, he calls it *pay dirt*. 'Pay dirt had been discovered near the confluence of the South Platte and Cherry Creek' (H. V. FAULKNER, Economic Hist. of U.S. 205). This term sometimes has an extension of meaning; e.g. 'The German archaeological expedition to Babylon, which was at first disappointing in the small number of inscriptions discovered, has now struck "pay dirt" and has unearthed a mass of cuneiform tablets.'

A compound in everyday use in Am. is *pay-roll*, corresponding to the Eng. *wages sheet* or *salary sheet*. 'The bulk of the names on construction crew pay-rolls began with "O" or "Mc"' (MARK SULLIVAN, Our Times, iii. 395).

'The first move [of Chicago ringsters] is to scan the list of the payroll and either fill it with old friends, or compel enemies and neutrals to take a new oath of allegiance' (Prof. C. E. MERRIAM, Chicago, 29). 'The increased production was accomplished without equal increase in factory pay-rolls, since neither hours nor wages were yet changed' (G. SOULE, The Coming Am. Revolution, 223).

peanut is not an exclusively Am. word, though the nut it denotes is more commonly known in Eng. as the *monkey-nut*. The term *peanut politics*, however, needs interpretation for Eng. readers. It is applied to political tactics of a mean and paltry type, and the man who is accustomed to practise them is dubbed a *peanut politician*. 'An overgrown village governed by the proverbial peanut politicians and dominated by a typical political boss' (F. L. BIRD and F. M. RYAN, Recall of Public Officers, 125). 'If the Rep. party has all the really good brains, then it follows as a matter of course that any Dem. Cabinet, if not actually deficient mentally, consists of adolescents and small peanut politicians' (W. G. McADOO, Crowded Years, 191). Dr. C. A. Beard, in discussing the proper size for a Congressional district, says that, if it is too small, its representative 'is likely to be what is called in political slang "a peanut politician", that is, one narrow in mind, devoted to petty business, and incapable of taking a large view of things' (Am. Government and Politics, 24).

This employment of *peanut* as a term of derogatory political metaphor explains an otherwise mysterious allusion in the following extract from an Am. newspaper: 'His acceptance of the chairmanship is a guarantee that the Dem. campaign will not be knee-deep in peanut shells.'

†**pedal.** The function of the soft pedal of a pianoforte has suggested in Am. the employment of a verb *soft-pedal* in a fig. sense. 'The leading

educational centres tended to stress the utilitarian studies and soft-pedal those courses which sought merely cultural ends' (F. F. BOND, Mr. Miller of *The Times*, 170). 'The Dem. managers urged Wilson to soft-pedal his reply' (J. KERNEY, Political Education of Woodrow Wilson, 72). 'The interview had become the big story of the evening, and even those who wanted to soft pedal it had to treat it as such' (High Low Washington, 122).

peek. In the *O.E.D.* the latest Eng. example of the verb *peek = peep* is dated 1739. The word is still current in Am. 'Peeking through windows, listening at keyholes.' 'A shabby curtain moved and a black head peeked out cautiously' (C. G. WILSON, Chinatown Quest, 84).

The Am. noun *peek =* Eng. *glimpse.* 'The "George Washington" reveals Woodrow Wilson just as the essays on Burke and Gladstone and Lee reveal him. But they give us a peek at only one phase of him' (WILLIAM ALLEN WHITE, Woodrow Wilson, 123).

Am. *peek-a-boo =* Eng. *hide and seek.* 'The budding flowers were playing peek-a-boo with one another.' The name has been applied to an article of attire, for a reason given in the next following quotation. 'A shirt-waist, supposed to be an extreme of daring, in which embroidered perforations permitted sight of female epidermis upon the arms and as much as two inches below the nape of the neck, was called the peek-a-boo' (MARK SULLIVAN, Our Times, iii. 499). 'In San Francisco there is no winter suit and summer suit. The same medium-weight garment is worn the year round and the peek-a-boo waist is unknown.'

penalty. The Am. term *penalty envelope* denotes an official envelope used for letters on Government business and thus corresponding to an Eng. envelope marked *O.H.M.S.* (On His Majesty's Service). It derives its name from the fact that a penalty is imposed for its unauthorized use. 'The officials of the District Government were not entitled to the use of the mails like other Federal officials who use penalty envelopes.'

penitentiary. A *penitentiary* was originally a place of monastic discipline. Later it came to have the two meanings now attached to it in Eng.; (1) an asylum for prostitutes seeking an amendment of life, and (2) a reformatory prison or house of correction. In Am. it commonly denotes a *prison,* without any suggestion of reformation of character. 'Swindles that should land the promoters in the penitentiary.' 'When the fact that the Post Office Department harbored a nest of thieves was brought to his attention, he inaugurated an investigation which eventually placed the offenders in the penitentiary.' 'Such things are done not only by better men, but even by many of those who have been, or deserve to be, in the penitentiary' (Prof. N. S. SHALER, The Citizen, 122). In his biography of Senator Aldrich, Prof. N. W. Stephenson quotes Senator Quay as saying that 'Harrison would never learn how close a number of men were compelled to approach the gates of the penitentiary to make him President.'

pennant. In Am. a *pennant* is more than a flag; it is a flag awarded as a sign of victory in an athletic championship contest. 'The champions took a little stronger hold on first place in the race for the pennant.' 'The Yankees [a baseball team], organized in 1903, had never won a pennant. In the 12 years of Huggins's leadership the Yankees won three world's championships and six Am. League pennants' (Dict. Am. Biog. ix. 346).

penny is popularly used in Am. to denote the *one-cent piece,* which corresponds not to the Eng. *penny* but to the Eng. *halfpenny.* 'A hotel clerk bet $10 with a friend that the Athletics would take two games out of the first three. The friend carried a large bag to Wynecoop to-day and poured out 1,000 pennies on the counter. "Here's the money I lost," he said.' 'One of the most widely desired improvements in the postal service that is indicated for the early future is the adoption of one-cent letter postage. It has been asserted by Congressional leaders that, as soon as the Post Office Department could make itself a self-supporting institution, Congress would grant penny postage to the people of the U.S.' (F. J. HASKIN, The Am. Government, 77). The Am. author of a guide-book to Europe warns the visitor to London that, when a bus conductor asks him for a penny, he means two of them (F. L. COLLINS, Travelcharts and Travel Chats, 14).

In the plur., *pennies* is used in Am. where *pence* would be used in Eng. 'The despised material, worth only three or four pennies a yard' (K. D. WIGGIN, Rebecca, 286).

†pepper, in the fig. sense, is in Am. commonly abbreviated to *pep*. 'The captain is a little fellow, resourceful, full of "pep", information, and nautical lore' (Sen. H. B. HAWES, Philippine Uncertainty, 20). 'When the mind is sick, the soul lacks spiritual pep' (R. B. H. BELL, The Life Abundant, 182).

period is little used in Eng., but commonly in Am., in the sense of *full stop*. 'This final drafting in which men haggle over a word, a phrase, a comma, a period' (IDA M. TARBELL, Owen D. Young, 199). 'Throughout his mature life he was known to his friends by the initials only of his given names, and always signed himself W J McGee, without periods' (Dict. Am. Biog. xii. 48).

pet. The Am. colloq. term *petting party* denotes a 'social gathering of young people at which hugging, kissing, &c., are indulged in' (Concise Oxford Dict.). 'In the more dimly lighted palm-room there may be a juvenile petting party or two going on' (F. L. ALLEN, Only Yesterday, 11). 'Apparently the "petting party" had been current as early as 1916, and was now [1920] widely established as an indoor sport' (op. cit. 90).

pheasant. Acc. to the *Century Dict.*, in the Southern and Middle States this word denotes the *ruffed grouse.*

physician has a much more popular use in Am. than in Eng. E.g. an Am. might say: 'My physician tells me I smoke too much.' 'If this pain continues, I must consult a physician.' 'My son intends to become a physician.' In such cases an Englishman would use the word *doctor* instead of *physician*. See also OFFICE.

piazza. The Italian word *piazza* properly denotes a public square or market place. In Eng., where it is now rare, it means a *colonnade*; e.g. the piazza on the North side of Covent Garden, London. In Am. it is the *verandah* of a house. 'The most effective missionary work may often be done over the teacups and on the summer hotel piazza.' 'The piazza politician, sipping his toddy, spreading his legs, and discussing constitutional questions on the spacious verandahs of open-air Virginia' (Prof. J. A. HARRISON, George Washington, 198). 'I sat on the piazza in front of that little cottage' (Prof. M. PUPIN, From Immigrant to Inventor, 323). 'From our piazza and many parlor windows we overlooked the town' (F. J. STIMSON, My U.S. 7).

†pick. Am. *pick on* = Eng. *single out, select*, esp. for the purpose of passing censure or causing annoyance. 'Governor Dawson picked on Judge Nesbitt to succeed the late Judge Melvin.' 'Some of the early California laws picked on certain aspects, such as cubic air space in laundries, in order to hit the Chinese; but all such acts have been declared illegal because of the obvious discriminatory features' (Prof. E. G. MEARS, Resi-

dent Orientals on the Am. Pacific Coast, 192).

pie. The Am. *pie* corresponds nearly to the Eng. *tart*. The Eng. *pie* is sometimes known in Am. as a *deep pie*. The word is used fig. in the vocab. of politics, to denote the spoils of office, esp. in the term *pie counter*. 'This representative was looked upon as the dispenser of patronage in Virginia because of the promise of the President that he would allow the pie to be handed out by the men who did the fighting.' 'Tammany leaders gathered together to-day for the cutting of the political pie. The distribution of pieces was discussed with Murphy, who runs the pie counter.' 'When his constituents asked him why he could not secure more [postal] routes, the only reply he could make was that he could not get up to the pie counter.' Cf. PORK.

The use of the word in Am. is not restricted to pastry. The *Eskimo pie*, a popular delicacy in hot weather, may be described either as a bar of chocolate filled with ice-cream or as a bar of ice-cream coated with chocolate. 'Munching an Eskimo pie in an effort to keep cool between the acts.' 'Such was the sudden and overwhelming craze for Eskimo Pie that in three months the price of cocoa beans on the N.Y. market rose 50 per cent.' (F. L. ALLEN, Only Yesterday, 80). See also POT.

piedmont is in Eng. a proper name only, denoting a district in Italy at the foot of the Alps. In Am. it is a common name also. 'This middle group and the agricultural proletariat (the "poor whites") shared the piedmont' (P. LEWINSON, Race, Class and Party, 6). 'The territory was practically covered with rocky hills reaching nearly to the ocean, with but a narrow piedmont region, and with no coastal plain' (Dr. J. H. FREDERICK, The Development of Am. Commerce, 4). 'The Albemarle pippin of the Virginia piedmont'

(Prof. A. M. SCHLESINGER, The Rise of the City, 3).

pig. In Am. this word retains its original meaning of the young of swine. In Eng. it has come to mean a swine of any age. Acc. to the *O.E.D.* clear examples of this later use are rare before the 19th century. See HOG. For *blind pig*, see BLIND.

The Am. term *pig Latin* has nothing to do with *dog Latin*. It denotes what is known in Eng. as *back-slang*; i.e. a kind of secret language in which the first consonant of an ordinary word is taken off and placed at the end, a vowel sound being then added. 'Some of the patrons of her school considered Flavia "stuck up" because she didn't approve of their listening in on their party telephones when she talked home evenings to Alta. She talked in pig Latin, she and Alta both speaking and understanding it as if it were a native tongue. Unable to keep up with them, the neighbors missed the drift of the conversation' (L. N. WRIGHT, Limbs of an Old Family Tree, 102).

pilot. In Eng. a railway engine sent to clear the way for another—before a royal train, for instance—is known as a *pilot engine*. On Am. railways a *pilot* (also called *cowcatcher*) is an apparatus fixed in front of an engine to remove obstacles. 'A portion of the track was destroyed, and the pilot and headlight of the engine were blown off.'

pin. In Scotland, acc. to Wright's *Dial. Dict.*, this word may denote an iron or wooden peg and in Eng. it has the same meaning in certain connexions. In Am. the compound *clothes-pin* = Eng. *clothes-peg*. See also ROW.

pint. In using Am. recipes, Eng. cooks must remember that the *pint* is in Eng. a measure of 20 fluid ounces but in Am. of only 16. See also GALLON and QUART.

pipe. In the vocab. of Am. politics,

pipe-laying is an alternative term for *wire-pulling*. 'He was elected to Congress, but refused to serve a second term. He was disgusted by the wire-pulling, the office brokerage, and the pipe-laying which went on around him.' 'Through the instrumentality of William H. Seward, who introduced [into the N.Y. Legislature] a system called "pipe laying", the whole political atmosphere was changed. "Pipe laying" was an organized scheme for controlling votes, and derived its name from certain political manipulations connected with the introduction of Croton water in N.Y. City' (MARIAN GOUVERNEUR, As I Remember, 12).

pit has in Am. the spec. meaning of 'that part of the floor of an exchange where a special kind of business is carried on' (Century Dict.). A famous novel by Frank Norris is entitled *The Pit* in this sense. 'It has been regarded as the most important crop report of the season, and some time before the report was due the pit became crowded to the last foot of standing room with anxious brokers.' 'Through an initial misjudgment of the future prospects of the market, the [Farm] Board seems to have gotten into the grain pit by the back door' (CASSIUS M. CLAY, The Mainstay of Am. Individualism, 124). 'Henry Morgenthau, Jr., chairman of the Federal Farm Board, sold in the Chicago pit the remaining 1,100,000 bushels of Sept. wheat' (N.Y. World Almanac for 1934, 101). In Am. *pit*, as denoting part of a theatre, has been superseded by *orchestra* or *parquet.*

pitcher is nowadays an archaic or poetical word in Eng. In Am. it is the everyday substitute for the Eng. *jug*. Acc. to Gilbert M. Tucker (Am. Eng. 164) a *pitcher*, in Am. usage, is a vessel of any material but having a comparatively wide mouth, perhaps covered but never tightly closed, whereas a *jug* is made of earthenware and has a small mouth

intended for a cork or some other sort of stopper. 'Serve the after-dinner coffee on a tray with a coffee-pot, cream-pitcher, and sugar-bowl, all matching.' 'Symphony Hall platform was bare of all furnishings but a stand with glasses and a water pitcher.' 'A clean towel laid across the top of the wash pitcher.' 'She came back with a pitcher of hot tea' (K. D. WIGGIN, My Garden of Memory, 161). 'Cocktails mixed in a glass pitcher' (SINCLAIR LEWIS, Dodsworth, 261). 'The steward brought me a large pitcher of ice water' (ANITA LOOS, Gentlemen Prefer Blondes, 43).

In Am. *pitcher* is also a baseball term, denoting the player who throws the ball to the batter, in an effort to 'strike' him out, or 'fan' him, i.e. to cause the batter to fail in three attempts to hit the ball. 'A baseball enthusiast has invented a pneumatic gun to take the place of the pitcher.' 'He came along during the transition from the original "straight arm" delivery, from which the words "pitching" and "pitcher" were derived, to the unhampered throw that made the curve so effective.' 'He served as pitcher of the student ball team' (Dict. Am. Biog. x. 211).

place, when used in Am. to denote a property in the country, usually indicates something on a much smaller scale than when used in the same sense in Eng. 'Scattered among the large farms are a few little "places". These little patches of land, ranging in size from an acre or so to ten or twenty acres, have in them the making of summer-home sites.' The owner's name is often prefixed to it. 'Charlotte and Emory Blake lived at the old Blake place, on the little plateau at the foot of the Colton hill, in a vine-covered cottage.' 'The property which he had purchased the year before—the Hoppin place—included fourteen acres of land and a comfortable old house'

(Prof. N. W. STEPHENSON, Nelson W. Aldrich, 145).

plan. In Am. the verb *plan* may mean not only *devise* but *intend*, *hope*. It may accordingly be followed by *to*, so that one may not only plan a thing, but plan to do or make a thing. 'The trip that he and his wife had planned to take abroad has been postponed.' 'The Bishop plans to keep the third anniversary of his consecration on Monday.' 'When her mother sent her a Christmas present of a Paris gown, she danced with delight. There was to be a Christmas tree in the academy chapel, and she planned to wear it' (M. E. WILKINS FREEMAN, By the Light of the Soul, 422). 'A land in which they planned to do as they chose' (J. TRUSLOW ADAMS, The Epic of Am. 115).

plank. In the vocab. of Am. politics, a *plank* is a single item in the PLATFORM (q.v.). 'The principal feature of the platform will be the tariff plank.' 'In response to public opinion, the Rep. party put into its platform a plank in favor of giving enlarged powers to the Commission.' 'When the plank against injunctions was put in the Kansas City platform in 1900 it was resented by the public as an impeachment of the courts.' 'Throughout California during the eighties the question of Chinese immigration was particularly acute. No political party platform was complete without a plank in favor of restriction or exclusion' (G. T. CLARK, Leland Stanford, 452).

A favourite Am. method of cooking fish (esp. shad) is by splitting it open, fixing it on a board, and roasting at a hot fire. Fish thus treated is said to be *planked*. 'Lots of sunshine, baseball, and an abundance of steaming planked shad made the fire underwriters a happy and jovial bunch at their annual outing yesterday. . . . All this time a hundred shad were being baked in the open just behind the dining hall. Long planks, cut fresh from oak trees, were set on the ground about three feet apart. On these were skewered the shad, while between them green wood was burned, which slowly turned the fish into the delicious morsels which have made these annual feasts famous.' 'Most fish is planked too long, that's why it's dry and flavorless.' 'Any white fleshed fish is good planked' (Mrs. RORER's New Cook Book, 108).

The use of this process is not limited to fish. 'The planked chicken was served on the plank, which was garnished with mashed potatoes browned, cut up carrots, chopped green peppers, asparagus tips, string beans, and green peas, arranged in a garland around the chicken.'

plantation, planter. An Eng. *plantation* is a piece of land on which young and growing trees have been planted. The word is also used in Eng. to denote an estate, in tropical or sub-tropical regions, on which tea, sugar, rubber, &c., are grown. It is in the latter sense that the word is used in the Southern States of Am., with special reference to the growing of cotton, tobacco, and sugar.

In an earlier sense the word practically = *colony*, i.e. a settlement planted in a new country. Thus, some of the first settlements in New Eng. were called the Rhode Island or Providence plantations.

Accordingly, *planter* may mean either (1) a pioneer colonist, or (2) the owner of a large estate in the South.

plate. A distinctively Am. term is *plate dinner* or *plate lunch*. This denotes a meal at which, in order to save time and trouble, the whole of a course—e.g. meat and several vegetables—is set before one simultaneously on a plate, instead of its various items being offered separately. 'His pork-chop plate lunch seemed singularly tasteless.'

In the vocab. of Am. journalism the term *plate matter* is used as explained in the first of the following quotations. '"Plate matter" was the invention of a noble genius who saw in this device the way to profit from the parsimonious instincts of rural journalism. Columns of "literature" were written in N.Y., set up and stereotyped, and large sheets of metal, of newspaper size, were sent by the thousands into the provinces. The newspapers receiving these Greek gifts thus had a complete page—pictures and all—without the investment of a dollar' (B. J. HEN-DRICK, Earlier Life of Walter H. Page, 198). 'Most of the space of the four-sheet *Kemper Herald* is taken up by advertisements and plate matter' (A. F. RAPER, Tragedy of Lynching, 89).

An alternative term for the same thing is *boiler plate*. 'Barrages of boiler plate, clip sheets, and so on descended on 10,000 newspapers from the Legion News Service.' 'Newspapers and magazines had been supplied with articles, news releases, and "boiler plate" favorable to the ideas of those in charge of the corporations in the industry' (T. C. BLAISDELL, The Federal Trade Commission, 261). 'He was distributing boiler-plate propaganda to the press' (F. L. ALLEN, Only Yesterday, 58).

See also HOME and SILVER.

platform. There is a familiar and somewhat cynical saying in Am. politics that a platform is not something to stand on but something to get in on. The point of this remark is blunted for any one who is not aware of the spec. Am. uses of the word *platform*. In the vocab. of Am. politics it denotes the programme of a political party, as adopted at its national convention, esp. in the year of a Presidential election. Thus: 'The issues of the campaign have been enunciated, as far as possible, in the platforms of the respective parties.' 'As the platforms indicated, the presidential contest between the two political parties was waged on the question of repudiation' (Prof. D. C. BARRETT, Greenbanks and Specie Payments, 168). 'A party convention choosing a candidate and

writing a platform' (W. LIPPMANN, Public Opinion, 24). Accordingly, to say that a candidate has a *strong platform* does not mean the same thing in Am. as in Eng. In Eng. it means that he has an able group of speakers to support him at his meetings; in Am. that his programme is likely to be attractive to voters.

An account of the Am. political *platform* will be found in Bryce (Am. Commonwealth, cc. LXX and LXXXIII). He remarks that the nearest Eng. parallel to an Am. platform is to be found in the addresses to their respective constituencies issued at a general election by the Prime Minister and the Leader of the Opposition. Such addresses, however, as he points out, do not formally bind the whole party, as an Am. platform is supposed to do. See PLANK.

But when this difference is noted, the saying quoted above still needs explanation. For, at an Eng. railway station, a platform *is* something to stand on. Am. railway stations, however, usually have no platforms in the Eng. sense, but passengers enter the trains from the ground level. An Am. platform is one of the projecting ends of a railway car, on which passengers must step when they enter the train. As they are not allowed to remain here, but are required to proceed at once to their seats, it becomes true that in Am. a platform is not something to stand on but something to get in on. 'The Japanese envoy waved good-bye to N.Y. at 10 o'clock this morning from the rear platform of the Montreal Express.' 'Jig boarded the train. He stood alone on the back platform, waving to me' (S. GLASPELL, The Road to the Temple, 199). 'That afternoon the train was crowded. I gave my seat to a lady and went to the rear platform' (W. G. McADOO, Crowded Years, 115). 'Passengers must keep off the platform until the train stops' is a notice one may often find inside the cars.

platoon is in Eng. a military term only. In Am. it is also used to denote a posse of police. 'It has been charged that the division of the force into three platoons made it impossible to maintain proper reserves in the station houses.' 'She looks out of the window and sees the platoon of policemen on a run to quell a riot.' 'The depot was packed solid, and a platoon of police had to clear the way with clubs' (U. SINCLAIR, Manassas, 351).

platter is nowadays a rather archaic term in Eng., but is still in current use in Am. 'Mrs. Frake replenished the platter, and put more eggs and bacon on the skillet' (P. STONG, State Fair, 80). 'Great platters of fricasee chicken' (Dr. FRANKLIN H. MARTIN, The Joy of Living, i. 12). 'Charley placed a platter before him on which lay an even dozen speckled trout freshly caught, fried crisp brown in corn meal' (E. HILTS, in Life in the U.S. 124).

plead. In Am. pled, now obs. in Eng., exc. in dial., is still used as the past tense and past participle of this verb. 'He pled for whatever bases of harmony might be attained among the dissident churches' (Dr. L. N. RICHARDSON, Hist. of Early Am. Magazines, 107). 'He begged and pled with his young associate not to throw up a good connection' (Prof. T. J. GRAYSON, Leaders and Periods of Am. Finance, 311). 'The conventional forms under which divorce cases are pled' (R. S. and H. M. LYND, Middletown, 122). 'The superficial facts of the steel situation at that time pled strongly on their side' (B. J. HENDRICK, Life of Andrew Carnegie, 165).

plenty. Shakespeare used this word as an adj., but nowadays in Eng., exc. in dial., it is a noun only. In Am. it may still = plentiful. 'Opportunities for advancement do not seem to be as plenty as they were.' 'Hickories and plums and peaches—just as young and just as plenty' (WILBUR D. NESBIT, The Trail to Boyland, 2). 'Maps of the West Indies are now plenty' (Dr. E. E. HALE, Lowell and his Friends, 219). 'In the early days, when land had been plenty' (J. TRUSLOW ADAMS, Hist. of the Am. People to the Civil War, 76).

plug has in Am. the additional meaning of an overworked or worn-out horse, a jade. 'Indignant that the poor beast must serve not only as a butcher's plug in the day but also as a riding nag at night' (K. W. PORTER, John Jacob Astor, 19). Am. plug-hat = Eng. silk hat. 'In Hawick, as in most of Scotland, men go to church in plug-hats and frock-coats' (J. KERNEY, Political Education of Woodrow Wilson, 94). 'The plug-hat brigade felt no twinges in its heart; it took privilege as its right' (W. A. WHITE, Masks in a Pageant, 241). See also SPARK.

plum is sometimes used fig. in Eng. to denote a piece of good fortune, or one of the prizes of a profession. In the vocab. of Am. politics it is spec. used of a stroke of luck of a particular kind—appointment to a public office, esp. as a reward for party services. 'At this time of the year the word "plum", in its political significance, is conspicuous in the newspapers. The "plum" is, of course, a luscious fruit in the shape of an office under the State government, which many people are on the lookout to secure, and which is supposed to fall to some fortunate individual as the result of a process in which the "pull" bears an important part.' 'Juicy plums in the form of public offices and jobs' (Dr. H. ZINK, City Bosses in U.S. 49). The source of such emoluments is, accordingly, often described as a plum tree. 'This is to be a bad year for small fruits. The apple crop is below the average. The San Jose scale is ravaging the Jersey peach orchards. And—worst of all—the State Civil Service Commission has just lopped off a goodly number of blossoms from the local political plum tree. Into the competitive basket have fallen 16 examiners of accounts in this city, 26 clerkships in the Board of Elections, and sundry sanitary superintendencies.' 'The "boys" have taken rather kindly to the new boss. They believe that, if he once gets a mayor of his own, there will be a chance for them to "shake the plum tree".'

plurality. See MAJORITY.

pocket. 'The measure passed House and Senate, but Lincoln pocketed it' (Prof. T. C. PEASE, The U.S. 471). This would seem a careless, not to say disrespectful, way for a President to treat an important Congressional document. What Prof. Pease actually means, however, is that Lincoln exercised what is known as a *pocket veto*. When the President of the U.S. wishes to veto a bill that has been passed by Congress, his normal procedure is to return it with a written statement of his reasons for disapproval. If the bill has been passed within ten days before adjournment, he may exercise a *pocket veto*; i.e. he may refuse to sign, and at the next session of Congress may communicate his reasons. The verb denoting this act is either *pocket*, as in the above quotation, or, more commonly, *pocket veto*. 'When in 1912 Congress passed it, it was pocket vetoed by President Taft' (Dr. M. C. CAHILL, Shorter Hours, 92).

pocket-book. Although the material purse has largely gone out of service in Eng., the change has not yet affected popular usage in such expressions as 'a well-filled purse', 'to tighten one's purse', 'to hold the purse-strings', &c. In Am., where for several generations money of as low a denomination as a dollar has been issued in the form of paper, *pocket-book* has long corresponded, in this sense, to the Eng. *purse*. 'They are brought

within reach of the woman with a modest pocket-book.' 'He contributed $2,000 to the campaign fund, but the others are keeping their hands on their pocket-books.' 'The laws go deep into the pocket-books of the citizens' (Dr. C. A. BEARD, Am. Government and Politics, 258). 'Vegetarian menus are easy to make up to suit the taste and the pocket-book' (Dr. R. L. ALSAKER, Eating for Health and Efficiency, 107).

point. Several uses of this word are peculiar to Am. (1) It is often employed, esp. in relation to railway travel, where *place* or *station* would be used in Eng. 'The number here [arriving for a convention] is now estimated at 21,000 persons from Eastern points.' 'It is a standing indignity to the millions of people who go between N.Y. and New Eng. points to make them endure the annoyances of that station.' 'They have taken a cottage on Lake St. Clair and one at Mackinac, and will divide their summer between those two points.' 'Under the consolidation it has become possible to run cars direct to distant points' (T. DREISER, Tragic Am. 120).

(2) Its meaning in the vocab. of the Am. college is sufficiently indicated by the following quotations. 'For university credit, each 30 hours' course counts one point, and laboratory work at the rate of 60 hours to one point. Fifteen points represent the minimum amount of work required of every resident student.' 'Neither the German nor the Eng. student can obtain a degree or qualify for examination by arithmetical accumulation of points or hours or credits' (Dr. A. FLEXNER, Universities, 321). 'Plastic youths who sought education found it graded and measured by "points"' (Dr. C. A. and MARY R. BEARD, The Rise of Am. Civilization, ii. 729).

(3) Am. *point* or *pen-point* = Eng. *nib*. When the compiler of this dictionary asked in a Washington store

for a new nib for his fountain pen, the shop assistant did not know what he meant, but offered to supply him with a new point. '14-karat solid gold pen point tipped with iridium' (Advt.).

(4) Am. *exclamation point* = Eng. *note* or *mark of exclamation.* 'The exclamation point subtly conveys an emotional, rhetorical hint to the reader.' 'The exclamation point is sometimes used by job-printers at the end of displayed lines, for no other reason than its convenience in filling up an otherwise short line' (T. L. DE VINNE, Correct Composition, 283).

The Eng. railway term *points* is unknown in Am., where this apparatus is called a *switch.*

†pointer. In Eng. a teacher or lecturer gives this name to the rod by means of which he calls attention to something on a map or blackboard. In Am., as in some Eng. dial., the word is used fig. of a *hint* or *suggestion.* 'We shall give some pointers about the care of the eyes that will be helpful to various readers.' 'Pointers on Sensible Shoes. Hints to the Woman Troubled With Aching Feet' (Advt.). 'He was joined by a number of business men from China, who talked over the industrial system there and gave him some pointers of value to the U.S. and her policies in the Far East' (R. L. DUNN, William Howard Taft, 71).

police. In the discussion of Am. constitutional problems a question of great importance is that of the exercise of the *police power*, a spec. term which is explained in the following quotations. 'The police power is that broad and undefined power, which is inherent in all governments, to restrain individual freedom both as to person and property in order to safeguard and promote public interest in such fundamental matters as public safety, health, morals, and the like' (Prof. C. C. MAXEY, Outline of Municipal Government, 198). 'The power to enact laws in the interest of such matters as the public morals, health, and safety—in short, the police power—belongs primarily to the States' (Prof. H. L. McBAIN, The Living Constitution, 50). 'We have never been accustomed to thinking of land as subject to the exercise of "the police power"—that convenient Am. term for the avoidance of constitutional difficulties' (C. P. HOWLAND, Survey of Am. Foreign Relations, 1931, 107).

policy. When W. J. Ghent refers to 'policy and race-betting' as 'the special refuges of the desperately poor and the desperately fatuous' (Our Benevolent Feudalism, 172), the word *policy,* as he uses it, has nothing to do with either politics or prudence. It is the term in Am. for a form of gambling, by betting on numbers, of which a detailed account is given by W. B. and J. B. Northrop (The Insolence of Office, 59–61). 'Detectives last evening raided an alleged policy headquarters where the drawings were printed on the blank side of Rep. primary ballots.' 'Policy rackets have been unearthed even in public schools.'

politician, politics. The following passage is taken from a leading article in the N.Y. *Evening Post* of March 2, 1923: 'The Chancellor of the British Exchequer remarked at the Pilgrims' dinner Wednesday that our common language carries an impediment to full Anglo-American amity because it makes people of the two lands feel that they have nothing more to learn about each other. Mr. Baldwin of all men should know that it has still another grave disadvantage. The slight differences in our speech open up many pitfalls of misunderstanding. He recently referred to the fact that the debt agreement would have to be submitted to "politicians" from "pastoral districts" of the West. In Britain the word "politician" is applied without a thought of reproach, while Mr. Baldwin meant the word "pastoral" in simple literalness. In Am. "politician" carries a tinge of opprobrium, while we think raillery implied in any reference to the "pastoral" regions. Hence indignation in Congress, consternation in Mr. Baldwin's breast. Editors of the *Britannica* hardly understood the anger of some Americans at finding Newton D. Baker described as a "politician" therein.' A striking confirmation of the 'tinge of opprobrium' attaching to the word in Am. was given by Miss Ellen Wilkinson, M.P., in the *Star* of March 25, 1931. 'Once,' she says, 'when lecturing in Am., I made the obvious statement that I was a politician. I felt my audience stiffen. My anxious chairwoman-cum-hostess said to me in tones of agony afterwards, "My dear, *don't* say that again. It sounds so *dreadful*".' A former Cabinet minister records a similar experience. 'Speaking to an Am. audience a few months ago I referred to myself as a politician. I saw that they were shocked' (H. B. LEES-SMITH, in Daily Herald, Nov. 9, 1934).

Perhaps one may best understand the difference between Eng. and Am. usage by means of some further quotations. (1) 'However much Blaine was a politician, it seems to be a fact that from 1876 he was the choice of the majority, or of the largest faction, of Republicans, who believed that he had been kept from nomination by political expedients and who felt that his time had now come' (Dict. Am. Biog. ii. 325). It is quite safe to say that this sentence would be absolutely unintelligible in Eng. Why should it be thought strange that a politician should be the choice of the majority of his party, and why should there be any objection to the use of political expedients to prevent his nomination for the Presidency? The explanation is that *politician* is here almost a synonym for *intriguer* or *wire-puller*, and that *political expedients = intrigues.*

(2) 'Some of President Taft's best friends are said to be urging upon him the selection of an astute politician to act as "arbiter" in directing his political fortunes. They give the reason that politics is very distasteful to him. The real unstated reason is of course that he has not the slightest aptitude for politics.' This is from a paper that at the time was warmly supporting Pres. Taft and his policies! Here *politics* evidently means *tactical skill* or *manoeuvring.*

(3) 'Northern enemies [of Pres. Theodore Roosevelt] were quick to draw a conclusion; the expulsion of the Brownsville soldiers was mere politics, a play to the gallery to make sure the hold of the administration on the Southern Rep. machine' (Prof. N. W. STEPHENSON, Life of Senator Aldrich, 327). Here the word means very much the same as in (2).

(4) 'At that time I had no experience which, in a technical sense, could be called political. I had held no public office, and I had never worked my way through a party organization in the manner regarded by regulars as a pre-requisite to office-holding' (G. W. PEPPER, In the Senate, 8). We learn, however, from the same book that, although Mr. Pepper had had no political experience, he had been a leader, outside the Senate, in the fight against the unconditional acceptance of the League of Nations and had served on a Commission on Constitutional Amendment and Revision.

(5) In his autobiography, 'Up To Now', ex-Governor 'Al' Smith thus explains why a former Mayor of N.Y. was a failure in public life. 'The loose cog in the wheel happened to be that he held a political position and was 1,000 miles away from being a politician. He did not know how to handle people and did not know how to deal with them or how to get along with them. . . . Not being a politician, he was lacking in knowledge of the human element.' Here the essential qualification of a politician is not

competence in dealing with the problems of government, but the temperament of a good 'mixer' who is adroit in obtaining and retaining votes.

(6) Must not every Congress necessarily be a political body as every Parliament must be a political body? Apparently not, as the two following quotations suggest. 'This is a political Congress, as well as a do-nothing Congress; or, rather, it is a do-nothing Congress, because it is a political Congress. The whole present idea of the Rep. members in the two Houses is to do nothing or say nothing that will injure the party in the campaign next summer.' 'The present session might fitly be called a do-nothing Congress. Members have done nothing of large import to the dear ones at home. They are too busy talking politics and writing politics and thinking politics and working politics.' Or, as would be said in Eng., they are doing everything with an eye to the next election.

The peculiar senses thus attached to *politics* in Am.—esp. in connexion with office-seeking—have led to its use in matters that are far remote from *politics* in its Eng. sense. 'The retirement of Col. Shumway from the Second Regiment has stirred up interest in regimental politics, and his successor is already being discussed. The general opinion among militiamen in this locality is that Major Fairbanks will be chosen to that position.' 'Never had I known such fun in a newspaper office as I had the first few years on the *World*. Whatever office politics there may have been, I was unaffected, for nobody wanted my job and I didn't want anybody's' (F. P. ADAMS, The End of *The World*, 21). '"I thought I was out of politics for good when I completed my four-year term and started a bank", remarked a former office-holder, "but I find that I never knew what politics was until I got into the banking business. The many clashing interests to harmonize, the

differences between business men to heal, the rivalry for the good accounts and the distaste for the bad ones, together with the effort to avoid losses without making enemies, give to the country banker's life a piquancy that to the public servant is unknown.' 'In the South the Greek-letter fraternity system dominated student social life and campus politics as well' (Prof. A. M. SCHLESIN-GER, The Rise of the City, 208).

In Am. tactical manœuvring in public affairs is often described as *playing politics* (not *playing at politics*). 'The people of the country as a whole are tired of seeing political parties trying to play politics. They will insist on square dealing with all public questions. Any party that attempts to do a thing simply for the purpose of gaining a political advantage is not likely to be sustained by the people.' 'The Governor himself to-day occupies a most unenviable position and will find himself faced with the charge of playing politics.' 'While professing to believe that some sort of emergency legislation was immediately necessary, the Senate played politics and talked to the country on all these issues by turns' (Prof. N. W. STEPHENSON, Life of Senator Aldrich, 327). 'No doubt can exist that Theodore Roosevelt, as the 1904 election drew near, was playing politics in his own behalf. Expediency dictated certain of his appointments' (H. F. PRINGLE, Theodore Roosevelt, 343). See also PEANUT.

pony. 'Many a college youth rides through his Greek and Latin recitations on a pony' (LEON MEAD, Word-Coinage, 188). This indoor equestrian feat is likely to puzzle any Eng. reader who is not aware that *pony* is used fig. in Am. to denote a translation for the assistance (esp. illegitimate) of students—the kind of book that in Eng. is commonly called a *crib*. See TROT. For *cow pony*, see COW.

poor. In articles and books dealing with the Southern States one often comes across references to a class of persons known as *poor whites*. Thus: 'The poor whites of the black belt, a numerous folk who had always formed the very dregs of Southern white society' (Prof. A. M. SCHLESINGER, The Rise of the City, 4). 'The "poor whites" in the South, although they belonged to the same race as the slave holders, were looked upon as almost a different species' (C. S. JOHNSON, The Negro in Am. Civilization, 356).

In a valuable essay on this subject contributed to 'Culture in the South' Dr. A. N. J. Den Hollander complains that this term is commonly employed loosely and incorrectly by non-Southern writers. It has come to be used—of course, in a derogatory sense—of all non-slaveholding white people in the South, and has thus been responsible for much misunderstanding. There was a considerable group of non-slaveholding small yeoman farmers, artisans, &c., who did not belong to the class of *poor whites*. In discriminating Southern speech, the term was not used to apply to all white persons who were poor, but was spec. applied to those who were not only poor but conspicuously lacking in the common social and economic virtues—people characterized by 'laziness, carelessness, unreliability, lack of foresight and ambition, habitual failure, and general incompetence' (Culture in the South, 414).

pop. The verb *pop* has a spec. use in Am. in connexion with CORN (q.v.). To *pop corn* is to parch or roast it until it bursts open with a pop. A variety of corn suitable for this treatment is known as *popcorn*. 'The popping of corn', acc. to a statement of the U.S. Department of Agriculture, 'is due to volatilization of the oil contained in the kernel. Field corn does not pop as easily as popcorn pops, because the outer portion of the kernel is more porous, permitting the escape of the oil as it volatilizes,

while in the case of popcorn a great pressure is developed in the kernel by the confined oil and the kernel is suddenly exploded and turned wrong side out. In composition popcorn differs from ordinary corn in having a larger proportion of corneous element and a greater per cent. of oil.' 'Eight acres have been sown with green corn and one with popcorn for popping at open fires in the winter.' 'I do not imagine that anywhere else in the world is there a half, or a tenth part, so much fiction consumed as in the Eng. summer resorts. It is probably of the innutritious lightness of pop-corn' (W. D. HOWELLS, in North Am. Rev.).

The Am. compound *pop-eyed* is an epithet for a person who is so startled that his eyes seem almost to be popping out of his head. 'Half an hour later he was before a magistrate in the police court pop-eyed with alarm.' 'The class was open-mouthed, and the professor pop-eyed with wonder.'

porch. The *porch* of an Am. house is not a covered approach to the front door but a *verandah*. 'He paced the back porch slowly.' 'Broad porches ran the length of the house on both sides.' 'I can picture him in that last autumn of his life, seated on the porch of his beloved Mount Vernon in the gathering twilight' (J. M. BECK, May it Please the Court, 83).

Hence Am. *porch climber* = Eng. *cat burglar*. 'For years before he became a convict he had led the life of a thief, a pickpocket, a yeggman, and a porch climber.' 'Confidence men, porch climbers, burglars, and all sorts of thieves were permitted to operate' (L. STEFFENS, Autobiog. 377).

pork. 'Patronage and pork amalgamate and stabilize thousands of special opinions, local discontents, private ambitions' (W. LIPPMANN, Public Opinion, 291). On the face of it, the connexion of pork with political patronage seems comparable to that of Monmouth with Macedon. The actual association between the two is revealed by Dr. C. A. Beard in his account of Congress at work (Am. Government and Politics, 257), where he tells us that the fortunes of the ordinary Congressman are likely to depend on his success in obtaining, from the Federal treasury, appropriations for Post Office buildings, river and harbour improvements, and pensions, for the benefit of his own constituency. 'Legislation of this character', continues Dr. Beard, 'is called "pork-barrel legislation", a term reminiscent of plantation days. It was the old custom on Southern estates to allot periodically a certain amount of pork to the slaves; at the appointed time the pork-barrel was rolled into view, the head knocked in, and the contents distributed among eager beneficiaries. The applicability of the figure of speech to the legislative process above described needs no elucidation.' A different, and less likely, account of the origin of the term is given by Prof. A. E. Martin (Hist. of U.S. ii. 235, footnote).

The metaphor is obviously capable of being extended to cover similar transactions outside Congress. 'The policy of the architects is always to prefer a nearby building material where the conditions are favorable. They do this, not to give somebody a piece of "pork" that is going around, but for artistic reasons.' 'When there is a party bond between the mayor and the majority of the council, it is quite possible for the mayor to exercise a constructive influence in legislative matters, provided he is willing to pay the price in patronage and "pork"' (C. C. MAXEY, Outline of Municipal Government, 55). 'Denominational representatives habitually act upon the formula, "You favor me here and I'll favor you there." In brief, a trading psychology, like that of Congressmen, is added to the watch-

dog psychology. This tends to create a pork-barrel atmosphere' (H. P. DOUGLASS, Church Comity, 63).

portfolio. This word has a spec. use in the vocab. of Am. finance, where it denotes the collection of securities possessed by a financial institution, a bill-broker, &c. 'The portfolio of the three largest Insull holding companies consisted of three types of investments: securities of operating companies, securities of sub-holding companies, and each other's stocks.' 'When the J. M. Guffey Petroleum Company stock graced the Mellon portfolio' (H. O'CONNOR, Mellon's Millions, 100). 'In the member banks of the Federal Reserve System, discountable paper in its portfolio, when converted into reserve notes, makes credit elastic' (Prof. J. L. LAUGHLIN, The Federal Reserve Act, 242). 'In the exercise of his functions as a middleman, the dealer is compelled to maintain a certain portfolio, as are investment banks, commercial paper houses, and all like institutions exercising intermediate functions in the money market' (B. H. BECKHART, The N.Y. Money Market, iii. 382).

post. In the terminology of the Am. army, a *post* is (1) a place where a body of troops is stationed, or (2) the body of troops occupying such a station. 'At some of the posts the desertions have reached as high as 30 per cent.' 'The canteen was a saloon kept by military authority in camps, posts and garrisons to sell liquor to the soldiers. Officially in the army it was usually referred to as the "post exchange", which was the army name for the general store' (D. L. COLVIN, Prohibition in U.S. 304). 'A tour of inspection of frontier army posts' (Dict. Am. Biog. ix. 263). A *garrison* is apparently distinguished from a *post* by being fortified for defence.

A spec. use of the verb is current in certain States where land is said to be *posted* when the owner puts up signs prohibiting the shooting of game thereon. 'A report comes from Granville to the effect that farmers have posted their land in all directions and are expressing dissatisfaction at the slaughter of the deer.'

In Am. the notice *post no bills* takes the place of the Eng. *stick no bills.*

In Eng. cards sent by post are alike called *post cards*, whether they are issued by the Post Office itself or are of private manufacture. The Am. Post Office distinguishes between *postal cards*, issued by itself, and privately manufactured *post cards*, though both are transmitted at the same rates. The term *postal card* is commonly abbrev. to *postal.* 'On Monday night the company sent out 500 postals, asking men to return to work yesterday.'

See also MAIL.

pot. The Am. compound *pot-pie* is defined by the *Century Dict.* as 'a dish of stewed meat with pieces of steamed pastry or dumplings served in it'. 'Whether these lovely creatures are killed to adorn women's bonnets or to furnish pot-pie for the half-civilized immigrants, their slaughter equally deprives the earth of beauty.'

> 'On Thursday as turkey
> He cutteth a dash;
> He's potpie on Friday,
> On Saturday hash.'

The term is sometimes used fig. 'If a paper has more than one editor, if its editorial page is an intellectual pot-pie, then "we" is not inappropriate' (J. R. BUCHANAN, Story of a Labor Agitator, 346).

potato. In Am. the common potato is often called the *white potato* or the *Irish potato*, to distinguish it from the *sweet potato.* 'Sweet potatoes, cooked with fat, are much more objectionable than white potatoes under the same conditions' (Mrs. RORER'S New Cook Book, 312). 'The cultivation of white potatoes and peanuts has increased slightly,

but there was a marked decrease in the acreage devoted to corn, wheat, hay, and sweet potatoes' (Prof. T. J. WOOFTER, Jr., Races and Ethnic Groups in Am. Life, 99). The *sweet potato* is sometimes called a *yam*; e.g. 'Sweet potatoes from Florida are the latest arrivals in Centre Market, where a good supply of yams are received this week.' It belongs, however, to the Morning Glory family (Ipomoea Batatas), while the yam is a Dioscorea. Acc. to Greenough and Kittredge (Words and Their Ways, 138) the *sweet potato* has the best of rights to its name, for it was called *potato* before this name was given to the white tuber that is now called the true *potato.*

preceptor is a term which is now antiquated in Eng. It survives only in the College of Preceptors, a London educational institution dating from 1846, which would certainly have had a different name if it had been founded in the present century. The word may still be occasionally met with in Am., as may also *preceptress.* 'For a short time he was preceptor of the academy in Fairfield' (Dict. Am. Biog. vi. 565). 'I felt a little as if I had escaped from an exacting preceptress' (WILLA CATHER in *Atlantic Monthly*). 'A certain Mrs. Williams is the fictional preceptress of a very select boarding-school admitting only seven pupils at a time' (Dict. Am. Biog. vi. 548).

Of late years the word has acquired in Am. a new and spec. meaning in connexion with a reform introduced at Princeton by Woodrow Wilson. The *preceptorial system* which he instituted there corresponds largely to the *tutorial system* at Oxford and Cambridge. The *preceptors* he appointed were young men of distinguished scholarship who were to meet groups of students, discuss with them the subjects of their study, and generally advise them with regard to their work.

precinct. In Eng. an enclosed

space, esp. including a place of worship. In Am. a subdivision of a ward, for election and police purposes. 'The city is usually divided into a number of precincts or districts for police administration with a captain as chief commanding officer in each' (C. C. MAXEY, Outline of Municipal Government, 162). 'Now it is necessary to call up Police Headquarters, which in turn notifies the precinct.' 'Others require the sanction of the precinct committeeman' (Prof. C. E. MERRIAM, Chicago, 262). 'The speakers expressed the feelings of the listeners, and the precinct police were for dispersing them' (L. STEFFENS, Autobiog. 640).

The term is also used of a similar electoral division in rural districts. 'A precinct may include but a single block, as in a big city, or it may cover a township, as in the more sparsely settled districts. In some cases it contains only a handful of voting inhabitants; in others, several hundred' (C. E. ROBINSON, Straw Votes, 1).

pre-empt, pre-emption. In Am. *pre-empt* has the spec. meaning of 'occupy (public land) so as to establish a pre-emptive title' (O.E.D.) and *pre-emption* denotes 'the purchase, or right of purchase, in preference and at a nominal price, of public land by an actual occupant, on condition of his improving it' (O.E.D.). 'Coupled with this attitude of neglect was the more positive Federal policy of reckless land grants to private individuals. The lands of the State [California] were admitted to preëmption by the act of March 3, 1863' (Prof. G. R. GEIGER, The Philosophy of Henry George, 220).

prelate is sometimes loosely used in Am. as a synonym for *parson* or *priest*. 'An Episcopal clergyman of Asbury Park announced from his pulpit that women without headgear were not wanted in his church. It is said that other prelates of the Episcopal church sympathize with

him in the position he has taken.' 'Like a flash the Father [a priest in a mining camp in Nevada] grappled with the man, grabbed the gun, overpowered him and threw him on the floor. "Now stay there", ordered the prelate, "until I have finished"' (Dr. G. D. LYMAN, The Saga of the Comstock Lode, 81).

premier. During Sir Austen Chamberlain's tenure of the Foreign Secretaryship an important N.Y. daily happened to refer to him as 'British Premier'. This was commented on by an Eng. writer as an example of an Am. journalist's ignorance of Eng. affairs. The real explanation is that the N.Y. newspaper was employing the word in the Am. sense. In the U.S., *premier* denotes the Secretary of State, whose functions correspond to those of the British Foreign Secretary. 'The Department of State has always been the most important of the executive departments of the U.S. government. Its chief, called sometimes though loosely "the Am. premier", is first among the cabinet officers.' 'Mr. Roosevelt all along hoped that Mr. Hay would continue as his Premier.'

Hence *premiership = secretaryship of state.* 'Madison had his cabinet troubles, too. Monroe accepted the premiership in March, 1811, but not until being specifically assured that the foreign policy of the administration was open to change' (H. MINOR, Story of the Dem. Party, 69).

president is in Am. the title not only of the head of the Federal Administration but of the head of almost any kind of business organization, from the most important banks and railways downwards. 'Walking on Fifth Avenue one day, I met President Mellon of the N.Y., New Haven and Hartford Railroad' (L. STEFFENS, Autobiog. 631). 'President Pulliam of the National League says emphatically that there will be no changes in the baseball rules this season.' 'President Sigismund Schwartz, of the Pushcart Men's Union, was at the City Hall to-day to complain to the Borough President of continued interference with his men.'

In the academic world of Am., *President* is the usual designation for the head of a college or university. The heads of four colleges at Oxford and of one at Cambridge are called Presidents, but the name is not given to the head of any university in Great Britain.

†There is a corresponding freedom in the Am. use of the verb *preside*. 'A particularly inoffensive looking young man presided over the blanket counter.' 'No Am. youth is worth while who does not register a daily vow to preside over something, from a railroad corporation to a labor organization, from a bank to a saloon.' 'Learn shorthand from expert shorthand reporters. The Success Shorthand School is presided over by the most expert reporters' (Advt.).

primary. 'Prior to the adoption in 1913 of the amendment providing for popular election of U.S. senators, numerous states by primary laws had in fact deprived their legislatures of the power to choose senators' (Prof. H. L. McBain, The Living Constitution, 27). Of what nature, then, are primary laws, as distinct from secondary and, possibly, tertiary laws? Actually there exists no such classification of Am. laws as seems here to be implied. By *primary laws* Prof. McBain means *laws regulating primaries.*

For in Am. *primary* is a noun as well as an adj. It was originally a contraction of *primary meeting*, a local party assembly which is so called because it is the basic unit in the machinery of party politics. Its delegates constitute the larger groups called CONVENTIONS (q.v.). 'The primaries have become so completely subjected to "boss" manipulation that the average citizen has ceased to attend them.' 'In order to secure pliant tools as delegates to conventions and mem-

bers of committees, political directors resorted to tactics which excluded the honest voters from participation in the party primaries. . . . They packed primaries with their henchmen, who drove out or overwhelmed dangerous opponents' (Dr. C. A. BEARD, Am. Government and Politics, 152).

In most instances nowadays *primary* is a contraction of *primary election*, i.e. a local election within a political party. Such an election does not necessarily take place in connexion with a meeting. Although these elections are purely a party matter, they are regulated in Am. by statute, i.e. by *primary laws*, which vary from State to State. 'Having defined the type of organization which should be deemed a party and laid down the rules determining membership in the party, legislatures next provide for safe-guarding the balloting at primaries; in this connection they have regulated the dates of primaries, polling places, size and shape of ballots, the conduct of the balloting, the count, and the payment of expenses' (Dr. C. A. BEARD, Am. Government and Politics, 544).

Where the *direct primary* system has been adopted, those who take part in a primary themselves express their choice of candidates for office instead of leaving the matter to the discretion of the delegates they send to a convention. 'Before the World War checked the movement for reform, the direct primary was established by law in most of the states of the Union. This served to break in a measure the tight grip of the bosses on the personnel in office' (Dict. Am. Biog. x. 544). 'The direct primary has increased the popular interest in nominations to some extent. It gives the independent candidate and the independent voter a chance to be heard. It makes the grip of the boss somewhat less secure by occasionally upsetting his calculations' (Dr. C. A. BEARD, Am. Government and Politics, 552).

Prince Albert. In 1860 the Prince of Wales, afterwards King Edward VII, visited the U.S. That event is perpetually commemorated by the Am. use of the term *Prince Albert coat* or *Prince Albert* to denote a *frock-coat*, as that was the kind of coat he commonly wore during his travels. 'With his silk hat, his Prince Albert coat and his fresh boutonnière one would never suspect him of being a beggar.' 'He was himself what is called an "elegant dresser"—always wearing a Prince Albert' (IDA M. TARBELL, Owen D. Young, 54). 'There we found the First Assistant Secretary of the Embassy, in his silk hat and Prince Albert coat' (Dr. FRANKLIN H. MARTIN, The Joy of Living, ii. 9).

probe. The noun *probe* is much more commonly used in Am. than in Eng. in the general sense of *investigation*, without any surgical implication. The classical example is the newspaper headline, 'Oyster Bars Jam Probe', which so startled Eng. visitors on the day of their arrival in Washington for the Arms Conference of 1921. It prefaced an announcement that Mr. J. F. Oyster, one of the Commissioners of the District of Columbia, had refused to institute an investigation of the local traffic congestion.

process, as a verb, has in Am. an additional spec. use in the term *processing tax.* This is a tax imposed on basic agricultural commodities at the point at which they go through the first process after the farmer has disposed of them. 'A processing tax of 30 cents a bushel was put on wheat milled after July 1' (N.Y. World Alm. for 1934, 160). 'Upon the Secretary's proclamation that rental or benefit payments are to be made with respect to any basic agricultural commodity, "a processing tax shall be in effect with respect to such commodity from the beginning of the marketing year"' (Dr. C. A. BEARD and G. H. E. SMITH, The Future Comes, 78). 'The processing tax was not to be collected on goods destined for free distribution

to the unemployed' (G. SOULE, The Coming Am. Revolution, 212).

Hence the noun *processor*, in a corresponding sense. 'The power given to the Secretary to enter into market agreements with processors and distributors of any agricultural commodity or product' (C. M. CLAY, The Mainstay of Am. Individualism, 189).

procurement is in Am. a spec. term for the purchase or collection of material, supplies, &c., by Government departments. 'Work will be started on construction of Holyoke's new post-office within two weeks, it was announced at the procurement division of the treasury at Washington.' 'The department had quite a sizable job of procurement. Departmental activities requiring materials purchased include normally etc.' (R. W. BABSON, Washington and the Revolutionists, 129). 'The procurement policies of the War Department differ somewhat from those of the Navy, where purchasing is largely centralized. . . . In procurement plans the U.S. is districted into four areas. Each area has a central purchasing bureau to procure local requirements' (op. cit. 177).

producer. 'The word *producer* has a different meaning for an Am. from what it has for a Briton. To him it means *manager* or *proprietor* of the theatre. The person whom we call a *producer* is called a *director* in Am.' (ST. JOHN ERVINE, in the *Observer*, May 8, 1932). The following quotation illustrates this Am. usage: 'In 1916 he took his play to Arthur Hopkins, a courageous producer in N.Y. In Dec. of that year Mr. Hopkins accepted it' (D. DUDLEY, Dreiser and the Land of the Free, 395).

professor. This title is popularly given in Am. to all male teachers, regardless of the kind of institution in which they teach. (Cf. the French use of *professeur*.) 'Prof. Emory L. Mead, new principal of the Utica Free

Academy.' 'Prof. B. E. Solomon, principal of the High School.' 'The principal of the Normal School in Westbridge had been a certain Professor Lane'(M. E. WILKINS FREEMAN, By the Light of the Soul, 385). 'An old-time school-master, carrying, of course, the title of professor, had opened his school within walking distance of the town' (S. H. ACHESON, Joe Bailey, 6).

promenade, often colloq. shortened (as in Eng.) to *prom.,* is spec. used in Am. to denote a dance given at a college or school by the members of a CLASS (q.v.). 'Yale men assumed the rôle of host this afternoon for the vanguard of fair guests invited to the Junior Promenade, the gayest event of the college year. . . . The "prom" will be danced Tuesday evening in the Second Regiment Armory.' 'The senior "prom" of the central and technical high schools crowded the armory with 1,100 young people Friday night, the dancing beginning at 8.30 p.m.'

proponent. While *exponent* and *opponent* are everyday words in Eng., *proponent* is nowadays extremely rare, having been supplanted by *proposer,* or, more frequently, *advocate.* In Am. it is still in common use. 'Senator Borah makes the perfect reply to the proponents of a political truce.' 'No agreement can be reached so long as proponents and opponents of a measure select only those facts that suit their own case' (B. LASKER, Filipino Immigration, xi). 'The opponents and proponents of the Treaty had already gathered their ammunition' (C. P. HOWLAND, Survey of Am. Foreign Relations, 1931, 409). 'The year 1814 began inauspiciously for proponents of a national bank' (K. W. PORTER, John Jacob Astor, 958).

proposal is sometimes used in Am. in the sense of *tender.* 'Sealed Proposals, plainly marked on the outside of the envelope: "Proposals for coal",

and addressed to the Commissioner of Indian Affairs, will be received at the Indian Office until 2 o'clock of Tuesday' (Advt.). See BID.

†**proposition.** In Am. this word has lost its spec. meaning of *something propounded,* and has come to be loosely and lazily used as a synonym for *task, affair, matter.* 'Wanted— An intelligent man of genteel appearance for strictly high-grade proposition' (Advt.). 'To hold together without external pressure the Rajput, the Mahratta, the Bengali and the Tamil is scarcely a sane proposition.' 'Quit worrying about being thin, if you feel well. If you are thin and ill, it is a different proposition' (Dr. R. L. ALSAKER, Eating for Health and Efficiency, 236). 'The steamship combination did not justify itself nor become a paying proposition until dowered with the artificial profits of the Great War' (J. K. WINKLER, J. Pierpont Morgan, 190). 'Government is no longer the simple proposition it was in the days of Andrew Jackson' (J. M. BECK, Our Wonderland of Bureaucracy, 124).

proselyte. In Eng. *proselyte* is a noun only. In Am. it has supplanted *proselytize* as a verb also. 'The Church must approach them with a great compassion, recognizing not an occasion to proselyte, but a great opportunity for service.' 'Christianity has always been a proselyting faith' (Prof. C. R. FISH, Rise of the Common Man, 192). 'The older proselyting worked more slowly, perhaps more surely, but never so inclusively' (W. LIPPMANN, Public Opinion, 47). The word may sometimes mean *gain proselytes for.* 'In the early 50's Joseph Weydemeyer had sought to proselyte the new faith among his fellow exiles' (L. SYMES and T. CLEMENT, Rebel Am. 100).

prospect. In the lingo of Am. advertising, *prospect = prospective customer.* 'Obviously the first step in getting circulation is to list prospects to whom the paper is to be offered' (H. M. SWETLAND, Industrial Publishing, 124). 'Motor-busses roared down Flagler Street, carrying "prospects" on free trips' (F. L. ALLEN, Only Yesterday, 271). This use of the word seems to be on the way to acquiring more reputable associations. 'Governors, judges, Congressmen, and the like were poor prospects for printed propaganda' (Prof. G. H. BARNES, The Antislavery Impulse, 100).

protest. In Eng. one protests against things of which one complains. In Am. *against* is omitted, and the verb thus becomes trans. 'The award was immediately protested by a competing bidder.' 'The thinking Negro does not protest the restricted franchise as such, but he does protest its unequal application' (R. R. MOTON, What the Negro Thinks, 132). 'A committee of clergymen called on him to protest his policy on vice' (L. STEFFENS, Autobiog. 480). 'The Germans protested the sale of munitions to the Allies' (Prof. C. SEYMOUR, Am. Diplomacy during the World War, 85). Cf. APPEAL.
In Eng. the verb is trans. in the technical phrase, 'protest a bill of exchange'.

proud. 'Too proud to fight.' These famous words of President Wilson's, uttered in connexion with the attitude of the U.S. to the Great War, aroused much strong feeling. Perhaps, however, they did not mean quite what they were commonly supposed to mean. 'Mr. Wilson is a Southerner by birth, descent and tradition, and, although all his life from early manhood has been lived in the North, heredity is ineradicable. To the Southerner, esp. the Southerner of the generation of Mr. Wilson's childhood, "proud" has a different meaning and is used in a different sense than it is by the Northerner. Men of the North seldom talk about their pride; men of the South frequently do, and they mean not pride in the

Shaksperian sense, but in the same sense that the Am. of the North or the Englishman does self-respect. A Southerner will say, "I am too proud to do it", a Northerner or an Englishman would say, "My self-respect will not allow it". It was undoubtedly in that sense Mr. Wilson, subconsciously reacting to his Southern heritage, used "proud", meaning that there are occasions when a nation, no matter how great the temptation, must not fight, just as an individual, to save his own self-respect, must not engage in a brawl' (Sir A. MAURICE LOW, Woodrow Wilson, 172).

prove. The past participle *proven* is archaic in Eng. but in current use in Am. 'Practices which, if proven, will lead to expulsion or suspension.' 'How little he understood the will of the Am. people is proven by their unyielding demand for this service' (C. KELLY, U.S. Postal Policy, 81). 'That he deliberately took the most difficult side of a question in order to stimulate his study is sufficiently proven by his progress both in his thought and in his style' (B. A. KONKLE, Joseph Hopkinson, 24). 'He had already proven himself a bold operator in various speculative fields' (Dict. Am. Biog. xiv. 531).
In Am., when a grant of land is made under certain conditions (e.g. a HOMESTEAD), a person who has fulfilled those conditions is said to *prove up* on his claim. 'With only a preëmption title to my land, I now planned to "prove up" on it' (HAMLIN GARLAND, Roadside Meetings, 3).

prudential has a spec. use in Am., esp. in New Eng., in the term *prudential committee*, which denotes a managing committee esp. concerned with the administration of business affairs. Thus the prudential committee of a church or college is the body responsible in matters of finance and other affairs not primarily religious or educational. 'His resignation takes away an old and useful member of the Yale Corporation.

During his 30 years of service—25 years as member of the prudential committee—he has missed but one meeting and that while travelling abroad.'

public enemy. Among the anti-crime laws passed by the 73rd Congress for the purpose of extending and strengthening the Federal police power was one which authorized the Attorney-General to offer a reward up to $25,000 for the capture of any person who had been declared a *public enemy*. The first person to be designated *public enemy No. 1* was Al Capone. The next holder of the title was Dillinger, who was killed by Federal agents in Chicago in July 1934.

††**publicity**, which properly means *the quality or state of being public*, is specialized in Am. as a synonym for *advertising*. 'A bureau of publicity for the purpose of advertising Springfield in the newspapers of the state will be maintained by the board of trade.' 'It is of the utmost importance that every advertiser know what other advertisers are thinking and doing. Only in this way can the art of publicity be intelligently developed.' 'In the same paper he had a half-column advertisement of his hillside plow. This was publicity on a large scale, acc. to the ideas of advertising that were then prevalent' (H. N. CASSON, Life of C. H. McCormick, 81). 'Smith would to-day be called a good "advertiser" or "publicity man", for the whole purpose of taking Pocahontas to Eng. was to excite interest in the colony' (E. D. ADAMS and J. C. ALMACK, Hist. of U.S. 32).

publisher. In discussing (Public Opinion, 43) the methods by which a Government exercises its censorship of news in time of war, Walter Lippmann mentions its 'legal power over publishers' as one of the expedients available. This comment is mysterious unless the reader is aware that, whereas in Eng. the word *publisher*, when used without qualification, always means a *book publisher*, in Am. it quite as often denotes a *newspaper proprietor*. Thus, Lord Northcliffe is frequently referred to as 'the noted publisher', and an organization consisting of various newspapers bears the name of 'The Publishers' Association of N.Y. City'. 'Connecticut Publisher Dead. F. R. Swift, owner of the Bridgeport and Waterbury Herald, died at his home last week.' 'The Am. newspaper publisher has discovered that he can get rich by catering to the tastes of the vulgar and vicious and unlettered' (W. M. PAYNE, Little Leaders, 182).

Every Eng. newspaper also has its *publisher*. He is not, however, the proprietor, but an agent of the proprietor. He is the person responsible for issuing and distributing the paper when the printer has finished his part in its production.

In a letter, written in 1920 and printed in W. F. Johnson's biog. of George Harvey, Lord Northcliffe says: 'Misunderstandings due to different meanings of the same words are among the basic difficulties of Anglo-Am. relations. Just now there is a discussion about the price of paper in which the use of the word *publisher* for *newspaper owner* confuses our people.'

†**pull.** The noun *pull* is used fig. in Am. to denote *influence* (esp. secret or illegitimate) *employed for one's individual advantage*. 'The frauds were possible only owing to the spoils system and the sway of political pull.' 'There are "pulls" in business as well as in politics, and, while virtue may be its own reward, it cannot count on getting all it deserves.' 'He had no pull of any sort. Only natural wit, good habits and unfailing industry were behind his start in business' (Prof. N. W. STEPHENSON, Life of Senator Aldrich, 8). 'There is no essential difference between the pull that gets

your wife into society or for your book a favorable review, and that which gets a heeler into office, a thief out of jail, and a rich man's son on the board of directors of a corporation' (L. STEFFENS, The Shame of the Cities, 10). 'Financial and political pull are more powerful in our courts than a good cause' (NORMAN THOMAS, America's Way Out, 211).

†punch, which in Eng. means a *blow with the fist*, is used fig. in Am. to denote an *incisive energy*. 'He felt real respect for an organization like Tammany, with its brawn, its punch, and its good-nature' (L. EINSTEIN, Roosevelt, 19). 'His later evolution was one of power and punch rather than of breadth and idea' (op. cit. 28). 'He was able to feel satisfaction for the punch he could put into his work' (op. cit. 48). 'He himself could write a better editorial, one with more "punch", a greater clarity of expression, a more direct appeal to the classes he wished to reach' (WILLIS J. ABBOT, Watching the World Go By, 135).

See also COW.

puncheon. In Eng. *puncheon* denotes, in one of its meanings, a short piece of timber, used as a supporting post; e.g. for a roof in a coal mine. In Am. it may also denote a piece of split timber used for flooring in the absence of sawed boards. 'The puncheon floor is kept snowy white by frequent scourings with homemade soap and sand' (J. W. HATCHER, in Culture in the South, 382).

push. The compound *push-cart* has been coined in Am. to denote a costermonger's or peddler's *barrow*. 'Seedless fruits will be at a high premium. But in ten years they ought to reach the push-cart.' 'Out of the narrow streets came the peddlers and venders, with their push-carts, eager for a bargain.' 'Both sides are lined with push-carts, which groan with wares of all kinds' (K. BERCOVICI Around the World in

N.Y. 76). 'As contrasted with him, many of the other "great" bankers had the souls of push-cart peddlers' (J. TRUSLOW ADAMS, Epic of Am. 346).

Am. *push-pin* = Eng. *drawing-pin*. 'The foot-rules, push-pins, plotting sectors' (FLORENCE CONVERSE, Efficiency Expert, 14). See also THUMB.

puss. The game of *puss-in-the-corner* is usually played by Am. children under the name of *pussy-wants-a-corner*. 'The folks no more anticipated that at 50 he was to begin gadding about the earth than they expected the big old sycamore in front of the Cedarton House to commence playing pussy-wants-a-corner with the Water Street willows.' 'Every householder returned us the same pantomimic answer—he never sold food, but he was sure his next door neighbor did, and the neighbor was as sure that it was in the next hovel that our money would make us welcome. We played this game of pussy-wants-a-corner for an hour, and we were still "it" when we reached the last dwelling' (H. A. FRANCK, Vagabond Journey, 427).

pussyfoot. The application of the nickname *pussyfoot* to an Am. who has visited Eng. in connexion with the prohibitionist movement has led to a widespread belief in Eng. that this is an Am. term for a temperance propagandist. E.g., George Saintsbury fell into this error in his *Scrap Book*, where he used the word in this sense in the paragraph-heading 'Wordsworth and the Pussyfoots'. Actually, its connexion with the advocacy of prohibition is purely accidental. The nickname was given to this particular individual by his fellow-countrymen not on account of his opinions but on account of his methods. Acc. to his biog. in *Who's Who in Am.*, he was so called 'because of his catlike policies in pursuing lawbreakers in the Indian Territory'. 'The more numerous and more outspoken the candidates the better, because the more difficult it will then be for the party in power to sidestep and pussyfoot.' 'When asked to pussyfoot on the gold question to insure his election, he declined and publicly affirmed his belief in gold unequivocally.' 'He was apprehensive over what he scented as "pussyfooting" in the attitude of the Republicans. Their tactics, he thought, were mapped out to beat Wilson by keeping neutral as to the international duty, supporting him in what seemed to Roosevelt a sham preparedness programme and trusting to the tariff and some understanding with the German vote to defeat him' (L. EINSTEIN, Roosevelt, 233). 'He was an opportunist if you will—bitter Mr. Ingalls said that he was so pussy-footed that he could walk from N.Y. to San Francisco on the keys of a piano and never strike a note' (Prof. N. W. STEPHENSON, Nelson W. Aldrich, 136).

Hence, *pussyfooter*. 'The conditions which are attached to its operation make plain its insincerity. It is, therefore, on that very account beginning to attract the favorable attention of the trimmers and the pussyfooters' (Dr. N. M. BUTLER, Between Two Worlds, 109).

Q

quail is a colloq. term in some Am. colleges for a *girl student*. 'Because she was hazed and snubbed some by the young women students, one "quail", as the boys call them, who was a freshman here last year, did not return this fall.'

Quaker. An Eng. reader may easily draw wrong conclusions from reports in the Am. press of the achievements of *Quaker* football or baseball teams. These athletic activities have only a remote historical connexion with the Society of Friends. Philadelphia, founded by William Penn, is to-day often called the Quaker City, although Friends now form only a small pro-

portion of its population. 'In spite of the apparent slump which the University of Pennsylvania football team took during the first part of the week, there is more reason than ever for the belief that the Quakers will this year have one of the most formidable elevens in their history.' 'Quaker Bluecoat Injured' is the heading of a news item reporting an injury to a Philadelphia policeman.

quart. Alike in Eng. and in Am. a quart is one-fourth of a gallon, but as the gallon differs in the two countries the quart differs also. See GALLON and PINT.

quarter is the name popularly given in Am. to the 25-cent piece, which is a quarter of a dollar. 'It is the advertiser's business to persuade the buyer that he will be interested or instructed or amused by the volume to the value of his outlay, be it a quarter or 50 dollars' (V. BURNETT, in The Building of a Book, 281). The ambiguity of *quarters* gives point to the following story: 'All the room in a sleeping car appears to be used for the passengers,' said the inquisitive old gentleman to the Pullman porter. 'Where are your quarters?' 'Well, suh,' was the answer, 'Ah totes 'em in a suit case till we comes to de end ob de trip, an' den Ah invests 'em in real estate.' The use of *quarter* to denote a measure of wheat is unknown in Am.

In Eng., the *quarter-days* fall on March 25, June 24, Sept. 29, and Dec. 25. Acc. to Webster, in matters influenced by U.S. statutes the Am. quarter-days are the first days of Jan., April, July, and Oct., but otherwise in N.Y. and many other cities they are the first days of May, Aug., Nov., and Feb. The term, however, is little used in Am.

quit. Exc. in the legal term *notice to quit* and in its reflexive use (e.g. *quit oneself well*) the verb *quit* is nowadays almost obs. in Eng. Wright's *Dial. Dict.* recognizes it as still current in Scotland. In Am. it is in everyday use, both (1) trans. and (2) intrans., in the sense of *give up*, *leave*. Its past tense is *quit*, not *quitted*.

(1) 'Five of the crack teams quit the race at two o'clock.' 'In the evening, when they quit work, the iron-workers were assaulted.' 'His great-grandfather quit Ulster in the troublous days of 1735' (H. N. CASSON, Life of C. H. McCormick, 22).

(2) 'The man who does 16 hours work in 8 is usually the man who can afford to quit at 40.' 'The Montana farmer let the place run down to almost a raw land before he quit.' 'After nine months at King and Baird's, he quarrelled with the foreman and quit' (Dict. Am. Biog. vii. 212). 'Seamen cannot quit in mid-ocean whenever they are dissatisfied' (C. A. and W. BEARD, The Am. Leviathan, 498). 'If the muscles get a little sore and stiff at first, do not quit, for by continuing the exercises the soreness soon leaves' (Dr. R. L. ALSAKER, Maintaining Health, 249). 'John P. O'Brien quit as a County Surrogate at N.Y. City and was sworn in as Mayor' (N.Y. World Almanac for 1934, 92).

†Hence Am. *quitter* = Eng. *shirker*. 'They were ready to fight to the last ditch. Not a quitter was there in this collection of America's bravest youths.' 'A man may shirk and be a "quitter", as they call him, in the class room, if he pleases, but he cannot be a "quitter" on the football field and retain his position on the team.'

†quite is often used colloq. in Am. to give a slight additional emphasis to a statement. 'Harvard was employed by Mr. Howells as a background for fiction quite some time ago.' 'Brattleboro farmers have made quite a little maple sugar during the past few days.' 'He had got for himself a hoof and part of the shinbone, to which quite a bit of meat was attached' (JACK LONDON, White Fang, 159). 'She had stuck to this hobby quite a while' (E. POOLE, The Harbor, 230). In telling us of her mother's care for the purity of her Eng., Mrs. Wharton says: 'I still wince under my mother's ironic smile when I said that some visitor had stayed "quite a while", and her dry: "Where did you pick that up?"' (A Backward Glance, 49).

quiz. In Eng. the verb *quiz* means either *banter*, *make fun of*, or *look inquisitively or curiously at*. A *quiz* is a person given to such practices, esp. the former. In Am. to *quiz* is to *interrogate* or *examine*, and a *quiz* is an *interrogation* or *examination*, esp. viva voce. The CATALOGUE (q.v.) of the University of Southern California has a 'quiz master in Clinical Medicine' in the list of the faculty of its Medical School. 'To Quiz Rhodes Candidates. Examination for Scholarships to be Held Today and To-Morrow' (Newspaper headline). 'Twelve candidates took the examinations for pure food inspectorships and two for chemists' work in the agriculture department. For the food chemists the quiz included a study of both the French and German languages.' 'The practice of examining boys [at Harvard] by quizzing them before a committee of the Board of Overseers' (H. JAMES, Life of C. W. Eliot, i. 68). 'First-cabin immigrants are hereafter to be quizzed like other immigrants.' In more than one of his letters, Col. House speaks of his being 'quizzed' by newspaper correspondents. 'The teacher's neat pile of quiz papers' (M. A. ELLIOTT and F. E. MERRILL, Social Disorganization, 490). The Senate's investigation of the munitions industry is called an 'arms quiz' in newspaper headlines.

Hence *quizzical* = *critical*, and *quizzically* = *critically*. 'There is more of profound glance into the eternal unknown in one poet than in all the quizzical philosophers from Aristotle down to Herbert Spencer' (Dr. C. H. PARKHURST, A Little Lower than the

Angels, 223). 'Revolution in China will bring us a hundred articles dealing quizzically with the Missions, the Treaties, or the Yellow Menace.'

R

race. A man who bets on horse races in Am. is said to *play the races.* 'All three men tried to induce the clerk to play the races, telling him of wonderful "sure things".' 'The remaining $10,000 he said was won in gambling, playing the races, and shooting craps' (W. B. and J. B. NORTHROP, The Insolence of Office, 38). The term *race-horse bill* is used in Am. to denote a bill drawn to pay another bill and not based on an actual sale of goods. 'While branches ceased to discount, they increased their purchase of "race-horse" or fictitious bills, as a device for renewing past debts' (Prof. E. S. SPARKS, Agricultural Credit in U.S. 265). 'Another feature of this early period was the initiation of so-called "race-horse bills". These were bills sent from one branch to another for collection, and owing to general indisposition to pay would not be settled but instead the debtor would meet the obligation by drawing a bill on another branch bank. In this way the debt would be passed from branch to branch, in some cases almost indefinitely' (Prof. T. J. GRAYSON, Leaders and Periods of Am. Finance, 171).

Am. *raceway* = Eng. *mill-race,* or any artificial passage for water. 'An attempt to destroy a feed gate constructed . . . with a view of depriving the Crane Felt Manufacturing Co. of a water supply which it claims as its right, resulted in serious complications last night. . . . Several men were assaulted and injured, and some were thrown into the raceway.'
See also TRACK.

racket has acquired in Am. a spec. and sinister meaning. In the N.Y.

Times of Aug. 9, 1931, Prof. Raymond Moley quotes and endorses the following definition of it as given by Col. Robert Isham Randolph, President of the Chicago Association of Commerce: 'A conspiracy to commit extortion by intimidation, force, violence, blackmail, arson, murder, kidnapping, bombing, or undue influence.' The word is sometimes loosely used to denote something that is scarcely more than GRAFT, but the *racket* proper always involves some kind of threat which hangs continuously over its victim, and it is practised for the sake of some unfair and / or illegitimate profit. 'Those countless customers who demand their money back on every conceivable pretext and make a racket of returning things they buy.' 'The power-and-light industry is essentially a racket whose immense profits depend on the power people's ability to block the enforcement of law.' 'Unquestionably some alleged labor leaders have run their unions more or less as rackets' (NORMAN THOMAS, America's Way Out, 274). 'Brady represented a company in which the officers of the New Haven and other railroads held shares; the company had the exclusive privilege of selling supplies to those railroads. It was a racket, of course, but the ramifications of its business, influence, and power were so complex that even Morgan dared not touch it' (L. STEFFENS, Autobiog. 590).

This peculiar Am. use of the word may possibly have some connexion with its use in Eng. slang in the sense of *trick, dodge, scheme, line of business.* For its Am. history see the following quotation. 'The word "racket", in the general sense of an occupation which produces easy money, is of venerable age: it was employed over fifty years ago in Tammany circles in N.Y. But it was not widely used in its present meaning until the middle nineteen-twenties, and the derived term "racketeering" did not enter the Am. vocab. until the year 1927.

The name was a product of the Post-War Decade, and so was the activity to which it was attached' (F. L. ALLEN, Only Yesterday, 266).

Hence *racketeer*, noun and verb. 'In a broad sense, anyone is a racketeer who has a "racket", just as anyone is a grafter who has a special "graft". But in a more special way the racketeer is a regulator of competitive business by means of pressure of an illegal and violent nature' (Prof. C. E. MERRIAM, Chicago, 48). 'To racketeer is illegitimately to get something for nothing, often by violence' (NORMAN THOMAS, America's Way Out, 31). 'In the great cities millions of dollars were wrested from the citizenry through racketeering and other criminal methods' (Prof. A. E. MARTIN, Hist. of U.S. ii. 746). For a full account, see the article on the subject in the *Encycl. Soc. Sci.* xiii. 45–50. This includes a brief bibliography.

racy. Am. *racy* = Eng. *salacious*. 'The authorities of Kansas City have begun a crusade along lines which should be of interest to this city. It is directed against the display of racy and catchy pictures in store windows and other public places.' 'Most people want their amateur theatricals pure though they enjoy the spicy sort of stuff when done on the professional stage. It is like reading a racy book—one doesn't do it in public.' In Eng. *racy* has no sinister implications, but means simply *piquant* or *pungent*.

radical. In Eng. *radical* was the term applied, esp. toward the end of the 19th century, to the advanced wing of the Liberal party, of which Chamberlain and Dilke were leading members. See the index to Morley's life of Gladstone. The Radical Club was founded in 1870 with Sir Charles Dilke as secretary, and John Stuart Mill, John Morley, Leslie Stephen, and Henry Fawcett among its original members.

Since the Great War the word has come to be applied in Am. to an extremist of a disorderly, not to say anarchistic, type. Possibly its being preferred to *revolutionary* is partly due to the fact that, for historical reasons, the word *revolution* has acquired a sacrosanct connotation; e.g. Daughters of the American Revolution is the name of a society that in Eng. would be described as ultra-Conservative. The Am. Yearbook for 1919 speaks of the apprehension with which the Government looks upon 'the radical agitation' which has appeared in Russia, Germany, and other countries. 'In the U.S.', it says, 'this radicalism not only sought to subvert the existing industrial system of the country, but advocated violent methods to attain this end.' Again: 'On June 3 the country was startled by what was apparently a general attempt on the part of anarchists and other radicals to murder a large number of prominent persons by means of bombs sent through the mails.' 'Radical is the bad name which opponents of any plan of social change give to it with a view to defeating it' (Encycl. Soc. Sci. xiii. 52).

During the Reconstruction period the word had another spec. meaning. 'In the years following the Civil War the word "Radical" was employed to designate that wing of the Union-Rep. party which desired the complete discomfiture of the old planter element in the South and substitution therefor of a ruling group who, in return for such local political rewards as were to be had, would support the policies of the Union-Rep. party in national affairs. Generally speaking, the Radicals of 1865–75 were not radicals at all, but were really the spokesmen of those very interests which today are most bitterly antagonistic to the theories advanced by contemporary radicals' (L. M. HACKER and B. B. KENDRICK, The U.S. since 1865, 13).

raft is used colloq. in Am., as in some Eng. dial., to denote a *large* *number,* an *abundance,* a *shoal* (fig.). 'The N.Y *Times* is getting a raft of communications in answer to its question.' 'This is bargain day, and there'll be a raft of women downtown wanting to go home for lunch.' 'This bill will be rushed through with a raft of other bills.' 'There were rafts of people I knew on the boat' (ALICE ROOSEVELT LONGWORTH, Crowded Hours, 175).

railroad. In Am. *railroad* is not only a noun (in more frequent use than *railway*) but a verb. 'The high standard set in street railroading in Massachusetts.' 'His coal-shipping interests took him into railroading.' 'Wall Street never appealed to him, however; constructive railroading was far more to his liking' (Dict. Am. Biog. vi. 402).

Hence the derivative noun, *railroader.* 'The skill shown by the men in handling the locomotive convinced the detectives that they were railroaders of considerable experience.' 'With its attack upon the financier and the railroader—the latter was one of the greatest employers of labor in the decade—the Greenback movement struck a responsive chord' (L. SYMES and T. CLEMENT, Rebel Am. 130).

The verb is used fig. (esp. with *through*) to denote a hurried and peremptory movement—where, so to speak, the track has been cleared of all possible obstacles. 'The determination of Republicans to railroad the bill through the House by shutting off all amendments.' 'Discriminating measures are often railroaded through at the will of an aggressive minority' (R. R. MOTON, What the Negro Thinks, 56). 'He was absolutely certain, since the day of Mrs. Surratt's execution, that he would be railroaded to the gallows by the same methods' (T. DIXON, The Clansman, 110).

raise. In Eng. one *grows* farm or garden products, *breeds* animals, and *rears* children. In Am. one *raises*

them all. 'Wheat is no longer much raised as a crop in Iowa; it is cheaper to raise corn, cattle, or hogs, or all three, and buy Minnesota flour.' 'Fresh vegetables can be raised by many who think they must go without' (Dr. R. L. ALSAKER, Eating for Health and Efficiency, 170). 'Mr. Choate had but one idea about raising boys; that was to put them through the same course that had been profitable to himself' (E. S. MARTIN, Life of J. H. Choate, i. 402). 'In that house for 27 years he lived his life and raised his children' (H. JUSTIN SMITH, Chicago, 169). Acc. to Wright's *Dial. Dict., raise* in the sense of *rear, bring up,* may be heard in certain Eng. dial. and in Scotland.

Hence Am. *raiser* = Eng. *grower* or *breeder.* 'He said the potato raisers of his State were greatly alarmed over the possibility of higher prices for fertilizer.' 'Zwingli's father was a farmer and raiser of flocks and herds' (Prof. S. M. JACKSON, Huldreich Zwingli, 50).

The name of *raised biscuit* is sometimes given in Am. to biscuit (in the Am. sense, of course) made with baking powder. 'The everlasting repetition of salt meats, potatoes, and raised biscuit in their bill of fare makes them esp. susceptible to rheumatism.'

In Am. to *raise a check* (Eng. *cheque*) is to alter it fraudulently so that it denotes a larger sum than was intended by the drawer. 'Later these checks came back to the banks, when it was learned that they had been raised to large amounts.'

In Eng., exc. in certain card games, *raise* is a verb only. In Am. it is a noun also, in the sense of the Eng. *rise.* 'If we keep our business ideals high, we shall have no need to worry about a raise in salary. A raise in salary is very apt to follow a raise in ideals.' 'The men demanded a raise in wages' (L. ADAMIC, Dynamite, 54). 'He secured an engagement at fifteen dollars a week, and kept the job till he asked for a raise' (Dict. Am.

Biog. xii. 259). 'If he is an employer on a high tide of prices, he will not grant a raise of wages if he can help it' (Prof. IRVING FISHER, Mastering the Crisis, 114).

rake. The derivative *rake-off* has been coined in Am. to denote an *illegitimate commission.* 'Their wages are subject to so large a rake-off by the contractors that only a trifle ever gets into the boys' own pockets.' 'The members of the ring demanded a rake-off of 55 per cent. on all amounts paid by the supervisors' (Dr. H. ZINK, City Bosses in U.S. 108). 'There was a rumor current that somebody in the Administration was going to make a handsome rake-off, or piece of graft, from the sale of the German vessels' (W. G. McADOO, Crowded Years, 309).

†**rally.** The kind of religious or polit. gathering that in Eng. would be called a *mass meeting* (itself a term imported from Am.) or a *demonstration* is in Am. sometimes called a *rally,* without any suggestion that it is a reassembling of forces after a defeat. 'An evangelistic rally will be held in the 5th Avenue Presbyterian Church, when a full report on the tent work done in this city during the summer will be presented.' 'The work that is being done in behalf of the candidate for the Rep. nomination will culminate in a rally in the Court Square theater.' 'Mr. Wilson on April 13th was the chief figure at a big Dem. rally in Indiana' (D. LAWRENCE, True Story of Woodrow Wilson, 48). 'Enthusiastic rallies were held at which orators pointed to Assemblyman Roosevelt as their champion' (H. F. PRINGLE, Theodore Roosevelt, 132).

rank. In Eng. *rank* is not used trans. exc. when meaning *classify* or *give a certain status to.* In Am. it may mean *outrank, take precedence of.* 'There is not a Congressman who would dissent from the opinion that Burton is in the front rank, though many would dissent from the proposition that he ranks all the rest.' 'The Secretary of State ranks all other members of the Cabinet.' 'Complicity with another officer in the publication of an article reflecting discreditably upon an officer who ranked both of them.'

Hence the word has come to be used intrans. in the sense of *hold the first place.* 'Sen. Daniel is now the ranking Dem. member of the Senate committee.' 'Admiral Fisher, ranking officer of the British navy.' 'The group of captains of industry attains a daily increasing power, and becomes the ranking order in a vast series of gradations' (W. J. GHENT, Our Benevolent Feudalism, 8). 'Hamilton regarded himself somewhat in the light of an Eng. Prime Minister, and not merely the ranking member of the President's Cabinet' (J. TRUSLOW ADAMS, Hist. of the Am. People to the Civil War, 181).

rap. In Eng. *rap on the knuckles* is a common expression in the sense of *reprove, criticize.* In Am. *rap,* simply, is used in the same sense. 'He rapped Judge Parker for favoring the gold standard.' 'At a private meeting of the Royal Institute his remarks included a criticism of the NRA. His address there also rapped international bankers and financiers.' 'In screamer headlines the conference was rapped as a secret and reprehensible thing' (J. KERNEY, Political Education of Woodrow Wilson, 105).

rare is still commonly used in Am. in the sense, now obs. in Eng., exc. in dial., of *underdone.* 'The waiter took his order for a sirloin rare.' 'You have no idea how you crave good old rare and bloody meat after a month or two in the desert air.' 'Lowell was not punning, of course, when he asked the world, "What is so rare as a day in June?" But these June days and the latter end of May have certainly been rare in the sense of "underdone".' 'The Am. fashion of serving meat rare or in a rather purple condition is certainly objectionable' (Mrs. RORER's New Cook Book, 138).

rate. In Am. the verb *rate* = Eng. *mark.* 'I know how to train you to get highest ratings in Civil Service examinations' (Advt.). 'He prescribed a number of licenses both in spelling and in syntax, which examiners should tolerate in rating for certificates.' 'In philosophy, ethics, history, political science, and Eng. literature he always received a high rating, but in scientific branches he received lower ratings, and these brought down his average. The poorest showing he made was in astronomy, in which his senior rating [i.e. marking in his senior year] was 73' (Prof. H. J. FORD, Woodrow Wilson, 9).

The noun *rates* in the sense of *local taxes* is unknown in Am.

††**rattle** is used fig. in Am. in the sense of *scare, fluster.* 'The horse had evidently become nervous and rattled.' 'The attempt to rattle the players in college games.' 'He went calmly on, neither rattled nor discouraged.' 'Who are the scholars who get "rattled" in the recitation-room? Those who think of the possibilities of failure and feel the great importance of the act' (Prof. W. JAMES, Talks to Students, 221).

†**ready.** Am. *ready-to-wear* or *ready-for-service* = Eng. *ready-made.* 'Clerical Clothing and Vestments. Ready-to-Wear and Made-to-Measure' (Advt.). 'An advertiser's legend informing me whose ready-to-wear clothing I must purchase to masquerade as a prosperous man of fashion.' 'Acquire some opinions—not ready-to-wear ones manufactured in the sweat-shop of some propaganda factory' (IDA C. CLARKE, Uncle Sam Needs a Wife, 92). 'Through this store's efforts a new attitude toward ready-for-service clothing has been adopted by hundreds of men in the past few seasons' (Advt.).

real. In Am. *real* often serves colloq. as an adv. 'He considered the article real funny.' 'If a child is real robust and healthy' (Dr. R. L. ALSAKER, Eating for Health and Efficiency, 274).

In Eng. *real estate* is a legal term only. In Am. it is an everyday business term also. 'In recommending the purchase of real estate, either as an investment or a speculation, our primary aim is not to earn a commission.' 'Every large town wants a handsome post office at a place that will adorn its "civic center" and enhance its real estate values' (C. A. and W. BEARD, The Am. Leviathan, 311). 'N.Y., from the Battery to Canal Street, is history; from Canal Street upward, it is real estate' (K. BERCOVICI, Around the World in N.Y. 8). 'Ernest Thompson Seton came along one year looking at the landscape as real estate. He was after a piece of land to make a park of' (L. STEFFENS, Autobiog. 440). 'He devised the system of land survey by townships, ranges, and sections, that has done so much to make Am. real estate more thoroughly a commodity than the land of any other country' (A. M. SIMONS, Social Forces in Am. Hist. 128).

Hence there has been coined the hideous word *realtor* to denote what in Eng. is called an *estate agent.* 'The immense activities of realtors, subdivision men and landowners' (NORMAN THOMAS, America's Way Out, 175). 'The realtors and insurance brokers no longer sell to each other at a profit' (F. J. STIMSON, My U.S. 63). Acc. to Dr. Krapp, this word was first adopted by the National Association of Real Estate Boards in 1916 for the use of its members only.

recall. For a spec. Am. use, see the first quotation. 'Not content with bringing the legislature under the direct control of the electorate, the advocates of popular government have contrived a new device, or rather reconstructed an old institution, known as the recall. The principle upon which it is based is simple, namely, that elected officers are merely agents of the popular will, and that the voters should have at all times an opportunity to pass upon the conduct of their representatives. The device itself is a plan whereby a certain number of voters, whenever they are dissatisfied with the services of a public officer (usually elective officers only) may, on petition, compel him to stand for a new election, and thus submit his claims to the judgment of the electors' (Dr. C. A. BEARD, Am. Government and Politics, 515). 'The first effect of the recall will be to discourage competent men even more than is now the case from consenting to serve the public' (C. NAGEL, Speeches and Writings, i. 35). Acc. to the *Encycl. Soc. Sci.*, the *recall* originated in certain Swiss cantons, appeared in Am. in the Articles of Confederation, and was discussed in the Constitutional Convention. Its present use in the U.S., however, is the result of an entirely independent political movement. It was first introduced in the Los Angeles charter of 1903.

This special meaning of the noun has affected the Am. use of the verb. 'The amendment passed and the following year Haywood was recalled from the Socialist Executive Committee' (L. SYMES and T. CLEMENT, Rebel Am. 276). The context shows that *recalled from* means here *dropped from, not re-elected to.* Haywood had opposed the amendment.

recess is in Am. not only a noun but an intrans. verb, meaning *take a recess, adjourn.* 'Senator Robinson moved that the Senate recess until 11 a.m. Monday.' 'The convention was thrown into confusion. It recessed almost in a riot' (WILLIS J. ABBOT, Watching the World Go By, 315). 'The World Economic Conference, at London, recessed without date' (N.Y. World Almanac for 1934, 108).

recitation, recite. In the terminology of Am. schools, a *recitation* does not necessarily mean the declaiming of a poem or other passage that has been committed to memory. It is equivalent to what in an Eng. school would be called the *hearing of a lesson,* and may thus include the putting and answering of questions. The term is applied in the same sense to the methods of instruction in a college. 'The recitations [at West Point] are not merely occasional or scattered questions, but a demonstration of principle at the blackboard, or a solution of problems.' 'The work for the most part will consist of extensive reading, brief reports, timely questioning, pointed discussions, and brief talks or lectures by the instructor in which the scattered threads are united. To conduct a recitation in this manner requires strength and energy' (Dr. G. W. A. LUCKEY, Training of Secondary Teachers, 195). 'She recited arithmetic with lisping little Thuthan Thimpthon; geography with Emma Jane Perkins, and grammar after school hours to Miss Dearborn alone' (K. D. WIGGIN, Rebecca, 54).

Hence Am. *recitation room* = Eng. *class room.* 'I feel a reasonable confidence that I could learn to teach well in a recitation room' (C. W. Eliot, in a letter published in H. JAMES's biography of him, i. 63). 'The recitation room brought the student into touch with the personalities of the professors' (Prof. M. PUPIN, From Immigrant to Inventor, 129).

The French *réciter* appears to be more nearly akin to the Am. than to the Eng. *recite.* Acc. to Prof. Félix Boillot (Le Vrai Ami du Traducteur, 208) the Eng. *recite = déclamer,* not *réciter,* and 'Récite-moi ta leçon' = 'Let me hear your lesson'.

reconstruction is in Am. the technical term for the process, beginning with the Reconstruction Act of 1867, by which the States which had seceded during the Civil War were restored to the rights and privileges of the Union. 'Ever since the period of chaos known as the Reconstruction era, the negro has been the under dog in Southern Republicanism.' 'With his prestige Lincoln might have averted some of the horrors of Reconstruction' (Prof. A. H. QUINN, The Soul of Am. 79). 'The South in Reconstruction times offered few opportunities to musician or author' (Prof. W. P. TRENT, Southern Writers, 403).

A Southerner who in later days still cherishes the sentiments common in the South during the Reconstruction period is sometimes described as *unreconstructed*. 'In time, however, even unreconstructed Georgians became proud of Booker Washington' (WILLIS J. ABBOT, Watching the World Go By, 113). 'In the midst of this warlike atmosphere sat the unreconstructed little doctor, wearing his gray uniform and his gray felt hat, which was reluctantly removed only at bedtime' (ALICE HEGAN RICE, Sandy, 98). On the other hand, a Southerner who accepts the postwar régime may be described as *reconstructed*. '"In case of any trouble with Spain remember that my tender of service is on file at the War Department" wrote this Dem. and reconstructed Rebel officer' (S. H. ACHESON, Joe Bailey, 91). The reference is to Joe Wheeler, once a Confederate general.

record. Such expressions as *go on record*, *place oneself on record* are much more common in Am. than in Eng., where the same sense would ordinarily be conveyed by *definitely commit oneself*. 'The Legislature was persuaded to go on record as refusing to indorse the predominant sentiments on this question.' 'The Rep. party, along with the other parties in the notable campaign of 1912, went on record as favoring a federal trade commission' (T. C. BLAISDELL, Federal Trade Commission, 6). 'The Dem.

party in Alabama went on record with pledges to disfranchise no whites save for crime' (P. LEWINSON, Race, Class and Party, 86). 'Mrs. Unwin goes on record as the only woman known to have disliked him' (AGNES REPPLIER, To Think of Tea, 116).

When President Roosevelt receives newspaper representatives at the White House, he sometimes prefaces or supplements a statement by remarking: 'This is *off the record*.' That is to say, it is for their private information, and not for publication.

See also SPREAD.

rector. In Eng. this term is reserved for the parson of a parish whose tithes are not impropriate. In Am. it may be applied to any Protestant Episcopal clergyman in charge of a PARISH (q.v.).

red. Am. accountants are accustomed to record debit balances in red ink. Hence an account that shows a loss is said to *be in (the) red* or *go into (the) red*. 'Books of which a modest edition could be sold out at no expense and with a small profit to the publisher, are loaded down with an advertising charge too small to sell any copies, but large enough to put the book in the red.' 'All the time the Haverford budget was balancing on the wrong side, or, as we should say today, "was going into red"' (Prof. RUFUS M. JONES, Haverford College, 22). 'The problem is not with those businesses which now have profits. It is with those that are on the edge of the red or on the deficit side already.' 'We undertook to take the National Treasury out of the red and put it into the black' (Pres. FRANKLIN D. ROOSEVELT, addressing the Am. Legion, Oct. 2, 1933).

The *red-head* is an Am. bird of the woodpecker class. 'Who will ever again taste anything to equal their . . . broiled red-heads?' (EDITH WHARTON, A Backward Glance, 59).

regent. At Oxford and Cambridge *regent* once denoted a Master of Arts who presided over disputations in the schools. It is still an academic term in current use in Am., where it may denote a member of the governing body of a State University or of the Smithsonian Institution at Washington. 'The Republicans of Nebraska met to-day in State convention to nominate a candidate for Supreme Court and candidates for University Regents.' 'The regents of the Smithsonian Institution assemble for their annual meeting next Tuesday.'

At Harvard the *regent* is a university officer who supervises the conduct of the undergraduates. 'In 1849 on the creation of the office of Regent under President Sparks, he was chosen as the first incumbent. The purpose of this office, like that of the more recent Dean, was to relieve the President of much of the detail of personal dealing with students' (Dict. Am. Biog. vi. 317).

register, registration, registry.
††On entering an Am. hotel as a guest, one *registers* (intrans.) by entering one's name in a book kept in the office. 'It would be shown they registered at a Coney Island hotel on the day the assault was committed.' 'Whenever prominent men, strangers or not, registered at the hotel, Mr. Hanna always managed to meet them' (H. CROLY, Marcus Alonzo Hanna, 459). 'By himself, he would doubtless have registered and taken meekly whatever room was given him' (SINCLAIR LEWIS, Dodsworth, 127).

The word is similarly used in Am., intrans., of entries of personal names in other records. 'With less than 20 students to register, the founders of this beneficent work opened the school doors in Nov.' 'The shipkeeper of the old Constitution reports that 5450 visitors have taken the trouble to register in the log-book in the 21 days that the ship has been open to the public.' The use of the word is further extended in such examples as the following. 'The Senate passed the bill, Aldrich and Platt registering against it' (Prof. N. W. STEPHENSON, Life of Nelson W. Aldrich, 48). 'The enormous increase of interest in foreign affairs was registered in the U.S. the very day before the Armistice was declared, when the Foreign Policy Association was founded in N.Y. City' (JANE ADDAMS, The 2nd 20 Years at Hull-House, 212).

Hence *registration*, in a corresponding sense. 'In the Maine woods the hotels were one-room log houses, and a registration of five in some cases taxed their capacity.' 'The recent meeting of the National Educational Association was enormous in point of registration' (= Eng. in point of attendance).

In the vocab. of Am. politics *register* and *registration* have a spec. meaning. In many States an intending voter is required to present himself in person, on one of certain prescribed days a few weeks before the election, and apply to have his name entered on the list of qualified voters. In so doing, he is said to *register*. 'Acc. to the figures of the census bureau there are 3975 men in the city who are able to vote, but are too indifferent to register.' 'There is little doubt that the full registered vote will be polled, but the registration is more than 3,000 short of that of two years ago.' 'During all the years that I have lived in Macon County, I have never had the slightest trouble in either registering or casting my vote at any election' (BOOKER WASHINGTON, My Larger Education, 46). 'Of course the annual registration practically requires a man to appear twice, once to register and once to vote, and therefore probably somewhat reduces the vote; but preliminary registration is in cities the only possible safeguard against illegal voting on a large scale' (Prof. A. B. HART, Actual Government, 73).

In Eng., *registrar* is now the normal term to denote an official charged with the duty of keeping a register. In Am., *register*, now obs. in this sense in Eng., is still in common use. There is a Register of the Treasury, a copy of whose autograph may be seen on every dollar bill. One of the officials of the Library of Congress is a Register of Copyright. 'A basis for equalizing the compensation of the different judges and registers.' 'Forquer had been a Whig, but changed his politics, and was rewarded by the Democrats with an appointment as Register of the U.S. Land Office' (W. E. CURTIS, The True Abraham Lincoln, 96).

On registering a letter at an Am. Post Office, one pays a *registry fee*, not a *registration fee*, as in Eng.

A by-product of the Securities Act of 1933 is the technical term *registration statement*. 'What are the liabilities imposed on the seller of securities by the Securities Act and by the British Companies Act with which it is so often compared? Both Acts demand a statement describing the securities to be sold, and in the statement certain specified information is required. Under the Am. Act this is called the registration statement, and has to be filed with the Federal Trade Commission 20 days before the security can be offered for sale to the public. Under the British Act this basic statement is called the prospectus' (BERNARD FLEXNER in Atlantic Monthly, Feb. 1934).

regular, regularity. In Am. politics the word *regular* (noun and adj.) is applied to a *thick-and-thin adherent of a party*. 'Even in the last two presidential contests he has been "regular", having voted for Bryan and announced the fact publicly.' 'Whole-heartedly to support Taft was out of question, and anything short of this would have been resented by the regulars' (L. EINSTEIN, Roosevelt, 193). 'Mr. Pinchot saw reason for great hope in the fact that party regularity is no longer as binding as it once was. "The man in the street", said Mr. Pinchot, "no longer asks about a measure or a policy merely whether it is good Rep. or good Dem. doctrine."' See also GUY.

†**release** is the technical term in Am. journalism for the publication of a speech or document that has been supplied to a newspaper office in advance. 'The report was given to the press associations in the usual manner of such official publications— that is, labelled "confidential", with a fixed date for "release", before which no part of it was to be used.' 'The temporary chairman will make the opening address. Possibly that speech will be "released" in time for the Commercial to print it this afternoon.' 'Both the Yale and the Hopkins Institutes are issuing through the press and directly from the universities a series of "releases" for publicity purposes' (Dr. A. FLEXNER, Universities, 124). 'On Thursday evening of each week the statement of condition of each of the Federal Reserve banks and the consolidated statement of all twelve are released to the press, for publication on Friday' (Dr. B. H. BECKHART, The N.Y. Money Market, ii. 110).

remember. The *O.E.D.* gives examples from Chaucer, Shakespeare, and Milton of *remember* followed by *of*, but adds that this usage is now rare. That remark would scarcely apply to Am. practice. 'Do you remember of ever making a purchase as the result of an advertisement?' (H. M. SHAW, Profitable Advertising, 500). 'She couldn't remember of any time when she wouldn't have preferred to live in an expensive hotel' (L. N. WRIGHT, Limbs of an Old Family Tree, 144).

rent. In Eng. one may pay *rent* for land, houses, offices, and rooms, but most other commodities are *hired*. In Am. no such distinction is observed. The subscription libraries advertise 'latest fiction for rent', and are themselves called rental libraries.

'We rent only new pianos of the most modern design. We take excellent care of the piano while you rent, and should you decide to purchase we will allow a liberal amount of the rent to apply toward the purchase price' (Advt.). 'He rented a motor, and toured along the old Roman road through Kent' (SINCLAIR LEWIS, Dodsworth, 388). 'Controversies as to whether rental libraries and book clubs cut off retail sales through bookstores have agitated the trade' (Encycl. Soc. Sci. xii. 413).

Apart from this distinction *rent* is much more commonly used in Am. than in Eng. Thus Am. *for rent* = Eng. *to let*. 'For Rent—completely and handsomely furnished residence' (Advt.). 'Its large hall is always for rent for public meetings, concerts, and balls' (A. SHAW, Municipal Government in Great Britain, 160). The verb *rent*, in particular, often takes the place of the Eng. *let*. 'Large numbers of farmers sold or rented their farms and moved to town.' 'The renting season left several cottages untenanted this year at Southampton.'

Hence the Am. *renter*, a word seldom used in Eng. exc. in connexion with the cinema. It may mean either (1) one who lets out for rent, or (2) one who uses by payment of rent. (1) 'One of the largest firms of apartment renters up town.' 'All of which is a sad blow to many hotelkeepers, proprietors of luxury shops, renters of fast and beautifully upholstered automobiles.' (2) 'This is all cultivated by renters, who pay $7 an acre.'

repeater is a term spec. applied in Am. politics to a person who votes, or attempts to vote, more than once at an election. 'The repeaters go from one polling-place to another, voting on slips, and on their return rounds change coats, hats, etc.' 'Mr. Morgan has silenced the Tammany howl by showing that he was acting under the law in stopping attempts to have repeaters register in the names of dead men and absent electors.' 'In some cities scores of thousands of illegal registrations stand from year to year, and are voted by repeaters, who go from ward to ward' (Prof. A. B. HART, Actual Government, 73). This practice nearly corresponds to what is called in Eng. *personation*. Cf. FLOAT.

The following newspaper extracts illustrate other varieties of *repeater*. 'The Women's Prison Association believes that a large percentage of the persons committed to the city institutions are "repeaters", who spend their lives in the jails and workhouses of different counties.' 'Major-Gen. Greely, telegraphing from San Francisco, says that systematic arrangements are being made to distribute clothing and other like materials to homeless and destitute. He reports that robberies are practically at an end. The present trouble, he says, lies in repeaters and imposters.'

require. In Am. colleges and schools *required* is the technical term to denote a subject of study that in Eng. would be called *compulsory* or *prescribed*. 'In our freshman year all the studies were required. . . . Afterwards, with increasing freedom from year to year, our programme of studies was made more and more liberal, and the elective system began to show its effect, although not nearly so much as in later years, for still many subjects were required' (J. H. CHOATE, Autobiog. i. 74). 'He made the courses of his department the most conspicuous in the curriculum. Since they were required courses, directly and indirectly he touched the whole student body' (Dict. Am. Biog. x. 564). See also ELECTIVE.

reservation. Those who have followed what has happened since the Great War to proposed treaties when brought before the Senate will not need to be reminded that the most common Eng. sense of *reservation* is current in Am. also. It has in addition two special Am. meanings: (1) a tract of land set apart by the Government for some special purpose, e.g. for the occupation of Indian tribes or for a public park, and (2) esp. in the plur., personal accommodation booked in advance.

(1) 'For ten years and more Jones had kept the peace of the small Osage reservation.' 'Apart from the public lands open to entry, there are reservations—national forests, national parks, game refuges, Indian holdings, and military camps—which all require surveying and mapping' (C. A. and W. BEARD, The Am. Leviathan, 624).

(2) 'A considerable number of N.Y. people have made reservations at the Curtis hotel for the holiday season.' 'Lucile had told Fran that Hémisphères was "such a nice, quiet hotel", and Sam had wired for reservations from London' (SINCLAIR LEWIS, Dodsworth, 127). 'A number of persons who were booked for passage on the Lusitania were called anonymously on the telephone and were urged to cancel their reservations' (Prof. A. E. MARTIN, Hist. of U.S. ii. 598).

resign. In Eng. a politician resigns from the Cabinet, but resigns the Home Secretaryship. So, too, a business man resigns from a board, but resigns his directorship. In Am., *from* would be used in either case. 'Mackenzie resigned from the headmastership of Lawrenceville School in 1899' (Dict. Am. Biog. xii. 93).

rest. In an Am. court of law, when the lawyer on either side has completed the presentation of his evidence, he is said to *rest the* (or *his*) *case*, or, simply, to *rest.* 'All the evidence for the plaintiffs was before the court, and Greyhurst sat down, stating that the plaintiff rested the case' (Dr. S. WEIR MITCHELL, Constance Prescot, 183). 'The prosecution having rested on Friday afternoon, the defence began' (O. G. VILLARD, Life of John Brown, 491). The expression is also used fig.

'With this third volume of "Modern Chivalry" Brackenridge rested his case against the ignorant interlopers in Am. social institutions' (Dr. C. M. NEWLIN, Life of H. H. Brackenridge, 123).

retraction. In Am., *retraction* is the more usual form of the word which in Eng. commonly appears as *retractation.* 'The Massachusetts government condemned the book, and Eliot had to make a public retraction' (Dict. Am. Biog. vi. 80). 'Next day his paper published a generous retraction' (MARK SULLIVAN, Our Times, iii. 328).

rhetoric. As its etymology suggests, *rhetoric* has to do primarily with speaking, and it is in this sense that the word is almost exclusively used in Eng. At the Summer School of Music Teachers at Oxford in 1931, one of the lecturers lamented that rhetoric was a lost art in Eng., and urged that this defect should be remedied by introducing into schools the teaching of the spoken as well as the written language. Moreover, the word is commonly employed in disparagement. A *rhetorician*—often a *mere rhetorician*—is a speaker whose eloquence is of a flashy and *ad captandum* variety, employed to hide the flimsiness of his argument or the superficiality of his matter. If *rhetorical* is used of a written composition, it suggests a meretricious style, more in keeping with the arts of an oratorical trickster than with the canons of good literature.

In Am., on the other hand, *rhetoric* has about it no taint of the disreputable, and it is used quite as often of literary as of oratorical productions. It is, indeed, practically equivalent to *Eng. composition.* In the biography of Prof. J. F. Genung in *Dict. Am. Biog.* (vii. 210) we are told that his book, *The Working Principles of Rhetoric,* was 'a masterly treatment of the philosophy of composition'. In his biography of Prof. Barrett Wendell, M. A. de Wolfe

Howe says that his book entitled *English Composition* took its proper place beside the 'Rhetoric' of Prof. A. S. Hill, 'the earlier contribution of Wendell's senior and chief to the cause of good English'. In the preface to his *Southern Writers*, Prof. W. P. Trent hopes that this volume 'may serve the purposes of a reading book, as well as of a supplementary collection of specimens for use in classes in composition and rhetoric'. The *Dict. Am. Biog.* tells us that the arrival of Hammond Lamont at Brown University as Professor of Rhetoric was 'the beginning of a revolution in the teaching of English composition there'. In his *Better Writing* H. S. Canby refers to 'the broader questions of arrangement of words which we call rhetoric'. 'Do you know what a paragraph is?' he asks his readers, and tells them: 'If not, find out from the nearest rhetoric.' He mentions, as a typically arbitrary rule given in text-books of rhetoric, the instruction that a sentence should never end with a preposition. 'The only way in which a writer may gain and constantly develop good style is by making use consciously and subconsciously of the principles of grammar and rhetoric' (H. M. SWETLAND, Industrial Publishing, 89). 'The study of manuals of composition and of formal treatises on the art of writing is an important aid to methodical knowledge; but it is absurd to believe that rhetorical rules alone will suffice to teach a man a flawless style' (L. MEAD, Word-Coinage, 27).

ride. As long ago as 1828 James Fenimore Cooper, when visiting Eng., noted a difference between the Eng. and the Am. use of *ride*. 'The men here', he reports, 'are a great deal in the saddle. This they call "riding"; going in a vehicle of any sort is "driving". The distinction is arbitrary, though an innovation on the language. Were one to say he had been "riding" in the park, the infer-

ence would be inevitable that he had been in the saddle.' He illustrates by the case of an Am. lady, no longer young nor a featherweight, who told an Eng. acquaintance that she had been riding in the Bois de Boulogne in Paris. 'Good heavens!' remarked this acquaintance in telling this piece of news to Fenimore Cooper; 'does Mrs. —— actually exhibit her person on horseback, at her time of life, and in so public a place as the Bois de Boulogne?' Cooper explained that the Am. lady had doubtless traversed the Bois in a carriage, and defended her use of the word as 'undeniably right'. 'But if you ride in a coach, what do you do when you go on a horse?' he was asked. 'And if you drive in a carriage,' he replied, 'what does the coachman do out of it?' (See COOPER's Gleanings in Europe: England, Oxford University Press reprint, 85.)

The current Eng. usage is thus set forth by the *O.E.D.* (s.v. *Drive*). 'One drives in a vehicle of which the course is under one's control, as one's own or a friend's private carriage, or a hired carriage or cab; one rides in a vehicle the course of which one does not control, as a public stage-coach, omnibus, or tram-car, or the cart of a friendly farmer who gives one a "lift" on the way.' This account of the matter, however, seems to need some qualification. In Eng., no doubt, one rides in an omnibus, but does one ride in a train? An Am. paper speaks of 'a 200-mile train ride through the Deerfield Valley'. In an Eng. paper this would be a *railway journey* rather than a *train ride*.

In Eng. *ride* is seldom used of a journey by water, but in Am. this use of the word is quite common. 'The new steamers are suitable only for service in the warm months, the result being that no one would ride in them in winter.' 'Besides tennis and boating, there have been many picnics, drives, and launch rides' (in Eng., *excursions* or *outings* would be used here rather than *rides*). 'His estate, Mount Vernon, lay only a short boat-ride down the Potomac' (F. E. LEUPP, Walks about Washington, 3). Prof. Sumner is quoted as saying that he hankered after a private yacht, because 'I'd like to take my friends a ride and give them a good time' (Prof. A. G. KELLER, Reminiscences of William Graham Sumner, 71). For the new and sinister meaning of *take for a ride*, see the following quotation. 'Another favorite method [of Chicago gangsters in disposing of a rival] was to take a victim "for a ride": in other words, to lure him into a supposedly friendly car, shoot him at leisure, drive to some distant and deserted part of the city, and quietly throw his body overboard' (F. L. ALLEN, Only Yesterday, 261).

For *joy-ride*, see JOY.

rig. A spec. Am. meaning of this word is *horse and vehicle, turn-out.* 'He stole a horse and wagon and drove home. On the outskirts of the city he offered to sell the rig to a grocer for 50 cents.' 'The man who hires a rig and takes a girl buggy-riding.' 'Old man Hatch and his one-horse rig' (S. GLASPELL, The Road to the Temple, 16). 'In a few minutes Bill was driving a handsome rig into his dooryard' (J. T. FLYNN, God's Gold, 31).

right. In Eng. *right* is used as an adv. in such expressions as *right on, right round, right well.* In Am. this intensive use may be seen also in (1) *right along*, (2)† *right away*, (3) *right here*, (4) *right now*, and (5) *right there*. Some of these expressions, as examples in the *O.E.D.* show, were once common in Eng. (1) 'There is every evidence of a constant development of a good business right along.' (2) 'Mr. Edwards said he did not apprehend any great difficulty in clearing away the snow. "We are getting busy, right away," he said.' (3) 'Let me say right here that I've never known a place where reliable information is as hard to get as it is

in Persia.' 'Right here in the midst of writing my memoirs, I pause to send greeting to the members of that staff' (ELIZABETH BANKS, Autobiog. of a Newspaper Girl, 20). (4) 'Never did we need a world market more than right now.' 'Right now, farmers are getting 90 cents for their wheat' (L. F. CARR, Am. Challenged, 4). (5) 'Right there is the main principle of the Japanese national policy.' 'This caused a great stir in the banking circles of Philadelphia, and the conspiracy died right there' (Prof. T. J. GRAYSON, Leaders and Periods of Am. Finance, 123). The usual Eng. equivalents would be (1) *all the way along*, (2) *straight away*, (3) *here and now*, (4) *at this moment*, and (5) *just there*.

right of way is in Eng. a legal term for the privilege, established through long usage, of passing through another person's ground, and hence for the path itself. In Am. it is a railway term for what in Eng. is called the *permanent way.* 'One reason for the safety of railroads in Great Britain is simple. No outsider is allowed on the right of way.' 'The inquisitive bull-pup who started out to smell the third rail on the trolley right-of-way' (G. H. LORIMER, Old Gorgon Graham, 3). 'For their rights-of-way, early railroad builders needed narrow strips of land' (MARK SULLIVAN, Our Times, iii. 194).

ring is used both in Eng. and in Am. to denote a sinister combination in business or politics, but the derivative *ringster*, denoting a member of such a ring, is peculiar to Am. 'During his term of office he had to contend against the opposition and enmity of ringsters and seekers after political office.'

riot. Sending a riot call in Am. does not correspond to reading the Riot Act in Eng. A *riot call* is a message sent by police or other authorities asking for help in order to quell disorder that is beyond their own power to deal with. 'Charges of illegal voting at one precinct resulted in a disturbance which the police were unable to subdue, and a riot call was sent in.'

river. When mention is made of the name of a river, in Eng. the word *river*, with either a small or a capital initial, precedes the proper name, but in Am. it follows it, and a capital initial is always used. Thus in Eng. one writes of the river (or River) Thames, but in Am. of the Hudson River, the Mississippi River, or the Charles River.

road. 'Statistics of Roads in the U.S.' This headline in an Indianapolis paper introduces a statistical report concerning not highways but railways. For in Am. *road* is commonly used as an abbrev. of *railroad*. It often takes the place of the Eng. *line*, as in the notice, at a railway junction: 'Change for the Ulster and Delaware and Walkill Valley roads.' 'Congress will consider the matter of granting to the President a special appropriation for travelling expenses, thus relieving him of the necessity or the temptation to accept any favors from the roads.' 'Those railways were once so prosperous that men actually thought the roads would own the country unless curbed.' 'Crawling like great snakes under the straddling spans of the elevated road' (W. P. EATON and E. M. UNDERHILL, Runaway Place, 91). 'In a few years the road had become one of the best equipped and most profitably run railroads in the country' (Dict. Am. Biog. vi. 318).

This use of the word is thus explained by Prof. E. A. Freeman (Some Impressions of the U.S. 59): 'In Eng. we had everywhere roads before we had railroads; the railroad needed a qualifying syllable to distinguish it from the older and better known kind of road. But in a large part of Am. the railroad is actually the oldest road; there is therefore no such need to distinguish it from any other. To us this seems rather like

a state of things in which printing should be familiar but writing unknown; but it is a state of things which the circumstances of our time have brought about in a large part of the U.S.'

roast is more commonly used in Am. than in Eng. to denote a piece of meat intended for roasting. In Eng. *joint* is preferred. 'One of the students seized the great roast of meat which lay in the kitchen waiting for the cook to put it in the oven, and buried it under the roots of the newly planted vine' (Dr. RUFUS M. JONES, Haverford College, 54).

The verb *roast* is nowadays little used in Eng. in the fig. sense of *banter* or *criticize mercilessly*, but it is still frequent in Am. with this meaning. 'At a meeting on Friday night he proposed a set of resolutions roasting the leader of the district.' The noun *roast* is similarly used. 'Public opinion will sustain the coroner in the official roast which he took occasion to administer to the police judges.'

robe. In Am. this word does not necessarily denote a garment. It may mean a rug or wrap, esp. for use in driving. Thus, in a description of the crowds at a football match, we are told that 'they had to sit on carriage robes spread along the ground behind the goal posts.' 'Those were the days when there was not a sleigh without two buffalo robes' (T. W. LAMONT, Henry P. Davison, 16).

Hence Am. *lap-robe* = Eng. *carriage rug*. 'She had given him her hand to hold under cover of the lap-robe' (D. G. PHILLIPS, Golden Fleece, 69). 'Aldao threw back his lap-robe and revealed a perfect arsenal of blunderbusses' (F. J. STIMSON, My U.S. 421).

Am. alternatives to *dressing-gown* are *bath-robe*, *slumber-robe*, and *slumbering-robe*. 'Wrapped in Red's bathrobe and in a luxury of fatigue, I sat and ate' (M. H. HARTWICK, in Life in the U.S. 3). 'He stretched out on a couch, covered himself with a slumbering robe, and was soon in the land of dreams' (J. KERNEY, Political Education of Woodrow Wilson, 123).

Am. *night robes* = Eng. *night clothes*. 'They have no night robes and go many days without a change in underwear' (Prof. J. DOWD, The Negro in Am. Life, 98).

robin. The Eng. *robin* is a bird of the genus Erithacus. The Am. is the *red-breasted thrush*, Turdus migratorius. Accordingly, an Am. songwriter refers to

A tree that may in summer wear
A nest of robins in her hair.
This allusion is likely to puzzle an Eng. bird-lover who knows that it is the habit of the robin to nest in banks and never in bushes or trees. The Am. robin, being really a thrush, nests usually in apple-trees.

rock. In Eng., exc. in schoolboy slang, a *rock* is a *large stone* or *boulder*. In Am. it may be a *stone of any size*, esp. when used as a missile. 'The assemblage grew as verbal repartee changed into that of rocks and rifle shots' (B. LASKER, Filipino Immigration, 363). 'With a big rock in one hand and my bridle in the other, I climbed the fence' (HAMLIN GARLAND, Roadside Meetings, 285). 'She heard the tread of a horse climbing the hill, and the flung rocks from its hooves go trickling down the roadway' (M. CHAPMAN, Homeplace, 14). Also a colloq. term for *money*. 'It is known who are the men with a large accumulation of rocks behind them and who are the ones who are merely bluffing. As a rule, the most extravagant are not the richest.' 'One might think we were still living in the stone age, judging from the fact that most of us are out for the rocks.'

rod. Eng. schoolboys are sometimes taught that there is a measure of length called a *rod*, equivalent to 5½ yards, but when they grow up they speedily forget it, as the word is no longer in common use. In Am. it is still current in calculations and statements of distances. 'Who would guess that we, a few hundred rods away, are in the heart of fairyland?' (W. P. EATON and E. M. UNDERHILL, Runaway Place, 237). 'A few rods from the house was a little one-room school house' (J. T. FLYNN, God's Gold, 20). 'When I walked out into the meadow I saw, not 40 rods away, the back of a barn' (DAVID GRAYSON, The Friendly Road, 147).

room is in Am. not only a noun but a verb, meaning to *occupy lodgings*. 'The transportation, hotel, rooming and boarding facilities promise to be adequate.' 'The woman in whose house he roomed while trying to find work' (HAMLIN GARLAND, Roadside Meetings, 346).

Hence *rooming house*, *roomer*, and *room-mate*. 'One lady told me that it is impossible to keep a rooming house as clean as a private house, and that the majority of roomers would not appreciate cleanliness and order.' 'Unstable or broken families in rooming houses' (H. P. DOUGLASS, Church Comity, 147). 'Those excessively mobile individuals, rooming-house dwellers' (M. A. ELLIOTT and F. E. MERRILL, Social Disorganization, 579). 'The presence of outsiders as boarders at the family table is somewhat less sanctioned today, though roomers are still not uncommon' (R. S. and H. M. LYND, Middletown, 110). 'His room-mate paused in the difficult task of getting the dust of a N.Y. summer off the keys of an unused piano.' 'Mr. Crocker had been a room-mate at Harvard of Charles Young' (IDA M. TARBELL, Owen D. Young, 251).

A *roomer* usually takes his meals outside the house in which he *rooms*.

rooster, a word little used in Eng., exc. in dial., is the normal Am. term for the domestic *cock*. 'Hens and roosters escape to unexpected liberty.' 'The family whose neighbor's roosters crow too early in the morning' (Prof. C. E. MERRIAM, Chicago, 232),

'Clipped cypresses in the shape of roosters, crescents, pyramids' (SINCLAIR LEWIS, Dodsworth, 88). 'The officer's gold braid and rooster feather got no homage from the President' (W. A. WHITE, Masks in a Pageant, 307).

root. From the verb *root* in the sense of *turn up with the snout* comes the Am. proverbial expression *root, hog, or die* which is an exhortation 'used of or addressed to persons, implying the necessity of labour or exertion to maintain life or prosperity' (O.E.D.). 'The school and college cannot use the method of Nature—root, hog, or die—and the more elaborate the schools and colleges become, and the more ingenious their methods of teaching and helping, the less they can use the compulsions which depend on fear of pain, poverty, obscurity and dependence' (Pres. C. W. ELIOT, of Harvard). 'At the beginning of most settlements it was "root, hog, or die" for all' (J. TRUSLOW ADAMS, The Epic of Am. 37).

Hence the Am. expression *root about* = Eng. *rummage about, poke about*. 'He went to his study table and rooted about for a thin, shabby, blue book' (M. DELAND, Dr. Lavendar's People, 121). In Eng. this expression is dial. only.

In Am., too, the partisans of an athletic team are said to *root for* it when they encourage it by their shouts and cheers. 'Near him sat a very fat and puffy lady, who rooted industriously and vigorously for Pittsburg.' 'It was a refreshing experience to accompany him to a ball game and root for the Washington team' (G. W. PEPPER, In the Senate, 34). Hence the noun *rooter*. 'Yale may outplay Harvard, but if Harvard sufficiently out-cheers Yale she wins, and to the rooters belongs the praise' (J. CORBIN, An Am. at Oxford, 153).

rough. †Am. *rough house* = Eng. *disturbance, row, bear garden*. 'The conductor of the car reported that a crowd of students was having a rough house on the car. Many fares had been rung up by the boisterous youths, signs torn from the interior of the car, the bellcord cut, the trolley frequently pulled down and several incandescent lamps broken.' '"You're a liar" shouted Congressman Y——, jumping to his feet. The only reply was a chair hurled from the hand of Sutton at the head of the offender, instantly followed by a rough house' (ANDY ADAMS, The Outlet, 351).

The term is sometimes used as a verb. 'After the rush the classes adjourned to Massachusetts Avenue and began to rough house the passing street cars.'

Am. *roughneck* = Eng. *rowdy*. 'Why the average mild-tempered and decent-mannered individual is metamorphosed into a roughneck by the act of getting off his feet and on wheels is a question for the psychiatrist to answer.' 'During the years as leader of this gang of young roughnecks Tim took part in many a barroom free-for-all' (Dr. H. ZINK, City Bosses of the U.S. 87).

In the sense of *irregular cavalrymen* the term *rough riders* has long been known in Eng. It was introduced into Am. during the Spanish-Am. War, when it came to be popularly and spec. applied to the regiment officially called the First U.S. Volunteer Cavalry, of which Leonard Wood was appointed Col. and Theodore Roosevelt Lieut.-Col.

round. In the vocab. of Am. railways and steamships, *round trip* = Eng. *return*. 'The round-trip railroad fare will be $6.80.' A *round-trip ticket*, as distinct from the *one-way ticket* (Eng. *single ticket*), entitles the passenger to travel the double journey, as he would in Eng. with a *return ticket*. 'The highly wrought emotion with which I bought my round-trip ticket to Ordway that summer morning' (HAMLIN GARLAND, Roadside Meetings, 110). In Eng. the term is used of a circular tour only.

In Eng. one may speak of 'a perfectly rounded life', but *rounded* would not be used as in the following passage by an Am. author. 'Dr. Ewing was considered one of the best rounded scholars in all fields' (B. A. KONKLE, Joseph Hopkinson, 18). Apparently the writer does not mean that Dr. Ewing was an all-round scholar but that he was what would be called in Eng. a finished scholar.

The derivative *roundabout* is not used in Eng. as a noun exc. in the sense of a *merry-go-round* or as a technical term with respect to traffic regulation. In Am. it may mean a *short jacket*, worn by boys. 'It seems only yesterday that this young man was playing about the streets of Washington, a schoolboy in roundabouts.' 'The little boys looked startlingly clean with their freshly scrubbed faces and their Sunday knickers and roundabouts.'

In Eng. a tradesman's employee who goes the rounds of his customers to solicit orders or deliver goods is called a *roundsman*. In Am. the name is esp. given to a police officer, of a grade below a sergeant, who periodically goes his rounds within an appointed district to see that the ordinary police are attending to their duties. 'Several hundred patrolmen reported to-day at the office of the Civil Service Commission for examination for promotion to the rank of roundsman.' 'Another roundsman was on trial for neglecting to detect irregularities on the part of patrolmen.'

††The cowboys on an Am. ranch collect a herd of cattle by riding round them and driving them together. Hence the verb *round up* and the noun *round-up*. 'Our round-up and general treatment of the cattle of the plains resembles to-day and always has in wildness and cruelty the buffalo hunt of the red men.' 'It made me feel as if I had actually been with him in his ranching days, and taken part in what went on at the round-ups that he used to tell us about' (ALICE

ROOSEVELT LONGWORTH, Crowded Hours, 3). This nomenclature has been adopted as suitable for similar manœuvres elsewhere, esp. on the part of the police. 'The captain of the Jamaica precinct believes that he has succeeded in rounding up a gang of thieves that have been stealing bicycles.' 'Thirty-three alleged members of East Side gangs were arrested by detectives in a round-up Monday night.'

route, as a verb, is more frequent in Am. than in Eng., where it is seldom used exc. in connexion with railway traffic and military operations. 'He became acquainted with mail clerks that run on the trains and from conversation with them he became familiar with the routing of the mails.' 'The letters are routed according to their requirements for attention' (H. M. SWETLAND, Industrial Publishing, 228, in a chapter describing how the morning's mail, when received by a firm, is distributed to the heads of the various departments). 'If a request for information comes to the Secretary or Assistant Secretaries of the departments, the letter is routed down the line to the subordinate clerk or officer who had the matter in charge' (Dr. J. M. BECK, Our Wonderland of Bureaucracy, 105). 'The defense claimed that the parade had been deliberately routed past the hall' (L. SYMES and T. CLEMENT, Rebel America, 330). 'There can be no doubt that these boyish sensations had been enlarged and routed by memory before they were set down as memoirs' (Dict. Am. Biog. ix. 579).

Whether noun or verb, *route* is often pronounced in Am. to rhyme with *out*.

row. The Am. expression *doesn't amount to a row of beans* (or *pins*) = Eng. *doesn't matter a straw*. 'One of the delegates said yesterday: "The letter of Buchanan suspending us doesn't amount to a row of beans."' 'The work doing from Ann Street to

Bowling Green does not amount to a row of pins.'

A person who has a big job to tackle is said in Am. to have *a hard row to hoe*. 'If I am to maintain both my household and my self-respect, I have indeed a hard row to hoe.' 'Industrially, the negro has a hard row to hoe. The more menial positions he is permitted to fill, but beyond that he is confronted with a stone wall of prejudice or race feeling.'

†Am. *rowboat* = Eng. *rowing-boat*. 'We build from a rowboat to a cruiser in our own factory' (Advt.). Francis succeeded in building there a fast rowboat with this unsinkable feature in it' (Dict. Am. Biog. vi. 582). 'I declared that I would some day do the Neckar over again in a rowboat slowly' (L. STEFFENS, Autobiog. 138). See also SAIL.

rubber. In some parts of Am. *overshoes* are called *rubbers*. 'How willingly would he exchange his rubbers and his ulster for the bathing-suit or the cool garments worn in Florida !' 'About the only weather question we ask is—must I take an umbrella or wear rubbers?' (C. W. ELIOT, in a letter quoted in his Life by H. JAMES, ii. 243). See GUM.

A person who projects his neck forward to see or hear (as though it were made of elastic) is said to *rubber*. 'It was a crowd in motion that well-nigh filled the streets [to see an air-ship]. Occasionally a too eager man who could not run and "rubber" at the same time would fall down.' 'The quartermaster cut that clipping out of the paper and stuck it to the bulletin board. The bluejackets took turns rubbering at it.' The use of the word is extended to include an exercise of curiosity that does not require any physical contortions. 'While rubbering in the old man's cabin he overheard the old man naming the next port to the navigating officer.' 'He [the valet] rubs th'millyionaire's head an' rubbers on his love affairs' (F. P. DUNNE, Mr. Dooley's Opinions, 119).

Hence the noun *rubberneck*. 'Trolley cars stopped in front of the hotel and curious folks jumped out to see what was doing. Along came Cop Rodihan, elbowing the rubbernecks aside.' 'Novelty shops with a lot of things the "rubberneck" coming to visit Chinatown in one of the sight-seeing cars is bound to buy as souvenirs' (K. BERCOVICI, Around the World in N.Y. 105).

ruby. The type so called in Eng. is $5\frac{1}{2}$-point, intermediate between nonpareil and pearl. This is known in Am. as AGATE. The Am. *ruby* is $3\frac{1}{2}$-point, known in Eng. as *brilliant*.

run. An Eng. politician *stands* for Parliament; an Am. *runs* for Congress or for office. One may, perhaps, regard as the classical example Mr. Coolidge's famous declaration in Aug. 1927: 'I do not choose to run for President in 1928.' 'It was while Roosevelt was running for re-election in 1904' (MARK SULLIVAN, Our Times, iii. 18). 'He ran for the office of governor on two occasions' (Dr. H. ZINK, City Bosses in U.S. 337).

For the Am. use of *run* to denote a certain kind of stream, see the following quotation. Writing of the neighbourhood of Boston, Prof. G. H. Palmer says: 'Our largest current is Topsfield River; in the second grade of things that flow we put our many brooks; and that which runs swiftly a part of the year, and shows a dry bed for the remainder we fittingly call a run' (Life of Alice Freeman Palmer, 277). The word is used in this sense in the name of Bull Run, the scene of two battles of the Civil War.

The kind of defect in stockings which in Eng. is called a *ladder* is known in Am. as a *run*. 'An unknown admirer wrote her that one of her stockings in the Smithsonian had a run in it.' 'My bargain stockings began to wear out; not gradually and decently, with a small hole here and a run there so that they can be mended.' 'A pebble in her dancing-slipper or runs in her stockings' (SINCLAIR LEWIS, Work of Art, 247). For *home run*, see HOME.

†The Am. derivative *runway* denotes a path over which anything runs. 'Deer never make trails without an object. Their runways lead somewhere.' 'These beaches are interrupted by little inlets into which the tide runs at high water, running out again when the tide fails. Standing on a bridge over one of these runways, I happened to see etc.' 'The woman became hysterical, and stampeded for the wagon runway in the middle of the [ferry] boat.' 'A hundred ladies appeared on the stage and romped up and down two runways that ran through the lower part of the theater' (K. BERCOVICI, Manhattan Side-Show, 259). 'He stood at a gate in the Grand Central Station watching his son lope up the inclined cement runway from the New Haven train' (SINCLAIR LEWIS, Dodsworth, 188).

rush is used attrib. much more freely in Am. than in Eng. *Rush hour* has by this time become familiar in Eng. to denote the period of the day when street traffic is most congested. Other examples, not yet acclimatized, are: 'Six weeks' rush work would be required to repair the boilers.' 'The people of Hartford have had very short notice to give a proper welcome to the Rep. candidate. It will be a rush meeting.' 'Out in the Yellowstone National Park, beyond the reach of a rush telegram.' 'The cruiser left to-day under rush orders from the Navy Department.'

Similarly the verb *rush*, as a trans., is used more freely in Am. 'The construction company received an order to rush 175 cottages for the earthquake sufferers.' 'The officials of the Fair made a tour of inspection to see whether every exhibitor was doing all in his power to rush the work.' 'Some would emigrate, but the rest would rush their labor into the remaining industries.'

The noun is used spec. of a scrim-mage between the various CLASSES (q.v.) at a college. 'The annual rush at Tufts College between the sophomores and the freshmen was particularly violent.' Sometimes the struggle is for the possession of a flag or a CANE (q.v.). 'The annual flag rush between the sophomores and freshmen of Williams College followed their baseball game. The flag was nailed to the flagpole, and the sophomores were formed in a solid mass around the pole to protect it. The freshmen struggled for three minutes to get it, but were unable to lay hands on it, and at the end of the time it still swung in the breeze.' 'He was so closely hemmed in by the escort, and the escort so crowded the platform that the body of men, as it moved, looked more like a cane rush than a President's escort.' A cane rush at Columbia University is thus described in a newspaper report: 'The freshmen proceeded to South Field, and the sophomores followed. The two classes were placed 50 feet apart in columns 15 abreast. Between them five freshmen held a cane. At a given signal the two classes rushed together. When two minutes had expired, the men were pulled away from the pile, and the freshmen were found to have the greater number of hands on the cane.'

rustle is used in Am. in a sense that has nothing to do with the sound produced by dry leaves or silk dresses. The *Century Dict.* defines it as 'to make, do, secure, obtain, etc., in a lively energetic manner'. 'When all the range was free, and the rich, nourishing buffalo-grass grew knee-high, there was no need to have a supply of hay on hand to winter the stock, as the animals could rustle enough off the range to get through the winter months in good shape.' 'The cows were allowed to rustle their own feed and produce what milk such handling would give' (Dr. F. S. HARRIS, Scientific Research and Human Welfare, 160). 'The tramp who cares to play the camper, and who will rustle for his food in farms and gardens and occasionally in the hen houses of the open country' (Here *rustle for* = Eng. *forage for*).

The last of these quotations suggests that theft is often part of the rustling process. Accordingly, in the West *rustler* has come to be the spec. term for a man who steals cattle and puts his own brand on them. 'Where cow herders have to ride the range for 50 or 75 miles they are likely to be forestalled in branding a calf by some vigilant rustler whose little mountain ranch is near the usual grazing place of a bunch of cattle.'

S

sabbatic(al). In the Mosaic legislation the Israelites were required, every seventh year, to let their land rest and lie fallow. This practice has suggested the use of the adj. *sabbatic* or *sabbatical* to describe the year's vacation that it is customary to allow to professors, every seventh year, in some Am. colleges and universities. 'Professors Willcox and Kendall will be absent during the year on sabbatical leave.' 'Professors Hull and Durham are spending their sabbatic year in Europe.' 'He utilized his sabbatical year in translating his notes on this subject from Norwegian into English' (Dict. Am. Biog. ix. 269). The term is sometimes used as a noun. 'A Greek sabbatical resulted in his *Aegean Days*' (Dict. Am. Biog. xii. 229).

saddler. In Eng. a *harness-maker*. In Am. also a *saddle-horse*. 'The President was astride Wyoming, and Mrs. Roosevelt rode her favorite saddler, Yganka.'

†sail. Am. *sailboat* = Eng. *sailing-boat*. 'It is difficult to say which is the more dangerous, the rowboat or the sailboat, without a master.' 'A lagoon on which sailboats floated' (H. JUSTIN SMITH, Chicago, 286).
See ROW.

sale. In Eng. *salesman* ordinarily means either a middleman between the producer and the retailer or a man who sells goods over the counter. In Am. it may also mean a *commercial traveller* or *business canvasser*. 'To the earlier generation of storekeepers the salesman was less an emissary of the manufacturer than a sort of oral digest of current events. . . . To buy to any large extent from his samples was against the principles upon which that early merchant did business.' 'At the writing-tables [in a hotel] are seated several salesmen engaged in writing up reports and orders to home offices' (E. HILTS, in Life in the U.S. 117). For *bond salesman*, see BOND.

In Am. *saleswoman* has *saleslady* as an alternative. 'The host of salesladies and female clerks and stenographers.' 'Wanted — experienced saleslady for our suit department' (Advt.). 'By this time the saleslady had become quite hysterical' (WINSTON CHURCHILL, Coniston, 311). 'Salesladies of assorted ages, sizes, and salaries' (FLORENCE CONVERSE, Efficiency Expert, 37).

The term *salespeople* is also peculiar to Am. 'Wanted—the services of experienced salespeople for every department' (Advt.). 'She found salespeople incompetent and department managers negligent.' 'Members of the lower ranks of the business class, such as retail salespeople and clerical workers' (R. S. and H. M. LYND, Middletown, 35).

saloon. In Am. this word denotes a *public-house*. 'The soldier had a considerable sum of money when he entered the saloon, and he continued drinking there until two o'clock.' 'He was a vigorous advocate of temperance, and was soon instrumental in clearing the town of two saloons that had thrived there' (Prof. L. O. BRASTOW, Representative Modern Preachers, 317).

Hence Am. *saloon-keeper* = Eng. *publican*. 'A widely circulated story that Lincoln was once a saloon-keeper was based upon the fact that the firm of Berry & Lincoln obtained a license to sell liquors, which was the practice of all country store-keepers in those days' (W. E. CURTIS, The True Abraham Lincoln, 34).

In Eng. *saloon* is unknown in this sense, yet the Eng. public-house has a *saloon bar*. The use of the word in *billiard saloon, boxing saloon, dancing saloon, hairdressing saloon,* &c., is peculiar to Eng. In Am. *hall* or *parlor* takes its place in such connexions, e.g. *tonsorial parlor* for *hairdressing saloon*. See also SEDAN.

salt. In Am. *salt down* is colloq. used fig. in the same sense as the fig. Eng. expression *dress down*. 'Senator Depew salts down William Allen White, who has stated in a magazine article that the senator tried to bully the president into etc.'

The Am. compound *salt-rising* is defined by the *Century Dict.* as 'a leaven or yeast for raising bread, consisting of a salted batter of flour or meal.' The term is also used as an adj. 'She hoped that the beau would like salt-rising bread, but she feared that he would not, surmising that outside the Ridge the stylish world was abandoned to yeast.' 'There are alien-born dishes put in nomination, but the general suffrage seems to go to those of the homelier sort, like Virginia ham, salt-rising biscuits, apple dumpling.' 'There is made in this country a light bread called salt rising or "emptyings" bread, in which the housewife depends entirely upon the wild yeast plants of the air and the accompanying bacteria. This is called "leaven" bread. The "leaven" is the salt-rising' (Mrs. RORER's New Cook Book, 490).

salutatory, which in Eng. is an adj. only, is in Am. a noun also, with a spec. meaning. It denotes an oration delivered, formerly in Latin, at a college commencement by the student who is second in rank at graduation, and who is accordingly called the *salutatorian*. 'The annual class day exercises of the University of Pennsylvania were held to-day. . . . H. B. Taylor delivered the salutatory.' 'By vote of the Yale faculty there will be no appointment of valedictorian and salutatorian after the present year.' 'He graduated in 1831, salutatorian of his class, delivering the address in Latin' (Dict. Am. Biog. xiv. 130). See VALEDICTORY.

sand. In Am. *sand* may take the place of the Eng. *grit* as a fig. expression for *firmness of purpose*. 'It takes sand to go into a football scrimmage a dozen times in quick succession, and know that each time somebody is going to get hurt.' A former Secretary of the Navy declared in his report that 'we want such a navy in size, style and sand that no other navy will ever desire an engagement with us.' 'If one had plenty of sand, if he was quick on the trigger, no questions were asked' (Dr. G. D. LYMAN, The Saga of the Comstock Lode, 109).

†The compound *sand-bag* has become in Am. almost the typical word for a weapon intended to stun its victim. 'They came for gold, the gold of the mines, but they were no knights of the pick and the pan; for them it was the sandbag and the bludgeon to wrest the dust from the belts of the miners.' 'If I knock you down with a sand-bag and rob you, is that to be called competition?' (Prof. R. T. ELY, Evolution of Industrial Society, 127).

†Hence the verb *sand-bag*. 'Having sandbagged and drugged him, he ships him before the mast in a merchant vessel.' It is often used fig. 'The resolution might be sandbagged by reference to a committee which would obey the orders of politicians.' 'He has been sandbagged with stock from influential quarters where there still is antagonism to advancing market prices.'

The compound *sand-hog* denotes a

worker in a caisson or other underground tunnelling. 'A sand-hog or high-pressure man, who was at work in the tunnel under the East River, died in the tunnel yesterday as a result of "caisson disease".' See BENDS.

say. A distinctively Am. idiom is the use of *say*, followed by *to*, as in the following examples. 'A medical journal says to take your time in getting up'; i.e. tells you to take, says you should take. 'Sophia told her to be sure and see the display of preserves. Her brother said not to miss inspecting the stock.' 'Two youths told me I must apply for any information I needed to the Archbishop. They said to telephone.' '"Where is she, Jepson?" "She didn't say, sir. She said to say, when you arrived, that she was from home"' (LILIAN BELL, The Dowager Countess, 14). Curiously enough, in the last example, this quite un-Eng. expression is put into the mouth of a butler in an Eng. country-house.
The exclamation *Say!* is preferred in Am. to the Eng. *I say!* 'One of them called out after me: "Say! Don't you worry"' (ELIZABETH BANKS, Autobiog. of a Newspaper Girl, 40). 'Say! Your room is simply too cute for words' (K. D. WIGGIN, Rebecca, 224).
The noun *say-so = ipse dixit* is now obs. in Eng. but still in common use in Am. 'Of course all this metaphysics is devised simply to maintain the say-so of Mr. Taft.' 'This is not our say-so. The sad truth is now officially established.' 'Don't take the say-so of any typewriter advertisement as truth. Investigate for yourself.'

†scab. The unpleasant word *scab* is used fig. in Am. to denote what in Eng. is called a *blackleg*; i.e. a man who works for an employer whose usual employees are on strike or are locked out. 'The McCormick Reaper Works locked out hundreds of its men who were union members and hired scabs' (L. ADAMIC, Dynamite,

68). 'A battle between miners who were trying to organize and mine-guards and deputy sheriffs who were trying to bring in scabs' (E. WILSON, The Am. Jitters, 160).
Hence the verb *scab*. 'The Negro has attained a firm footing in most of the leading industries. It is no longer so necessary for him to scab in order to get employment' (S. D. SPERO and A. L. HARRIS, The Black Worker, 145). 'Several speakers protest with bitterness that the companies only want to get them out so that they can scab the job' (E. WILSON, The Am. Jitters, 223).

scalawag. Both in Eng. and in Am. a *good-for-nothing fellow*. In Am. the term is also spec. applied to those white Southerners who, during the Reconstruction period, co-operated with the Rep. party. The *scalawag* was thus commonly bracketed with the CARPET-BAGGER (q.v.), who was a Northerner. 'The forcing of the amendment on the unwilling South by means of negroes, scalawags, bayonets and carpet-baggers' (L. P. STRYKER, Andrew Johnson, 750).

scalper. On the London Stock Exchange this term is applied to a man who buys at very low rates so as to sell at lower than the official rates. In Am. it has the same meaning, but is much more frequently applied to a person who profits similarly by irregular transactions with railway or theatre tickets. 'He thinks the ticket scalpers have deterred the railways from selling low-rate tickets to stimulate special and unusual travel.'

scare. The roundabout expression *throw a scare into* is common in Am. in place of the verb *scare*. 'Five or six million votes for Thomas this fall would not be thrown away; they would throw a scare into one or both of the old parties and bring Am. politics a little closer to reality.' 'His whole plan of campaign seems to be to throw a scare into the Democrats in order to bring them to the support of his ticket.' 'This quaint old man loves to throw scares into the hearts of his friends' (K. BERCOVICI, Manhattan Side-Show, 229). 'I saw an opportunity to throw a reverberating scare into the whole swarm of propagandists' (W. G. McADOO, Crowded Years, 328).

schedule is in Eng. a rather formidable official term, not in everyday use. It may denote an appendix to an Act of Parliament giving details that could not be conveniently inserted in the Act itself, or a formal tabulated statement, such as an income-tax return. In Am. the name is given to a great variety of lists; e.g. a price schedule, a schedule of advertising rates, a schedule of speakers at a meeting. Most frequently it denotes a *time-table*. 'Their names appear in guide-books and train schedules' (Prof. T. R. LOUNSBURY, The Standard of Pronunciation in English, 203). In her Cook Book Mrs. Rorer has 'Schedule for Fish and Game' as the heading for her statement of the time that should be taken in cooking various dishes. 'With the exception of the opening date of Sept. 29, the schedule of Georgetown football team for next season has been completed.' 'Bible study was included in the schedule of everyone' (W. R. MOODY, Life of D. L. Moody, 315).

†*Schedule time* is a common expression. 'The Empire State Express will not wait beyond its schedule time for connecting trains.' 'It was half an hour after the schedule time when Chairman Quinn called the convention to order.'

Am. *according to schedule* = Eng. *as arranged*. 'The banquet was held according to schedule' (G. T. CLARK, Leland Stanford, 273). *On schedule* has a rather different meaning, as it = *punctually*. 'The hopes are universal that each race will be run on schedule.' 'The victualling fleets did not always arrive on schedule, and these supplies

often failed' (Dr. O. T. BARCK, N.Y. City During the War for Independence, 100). 'On schedule to the minute, the flagship Connecticut came abreast of the Mayflower' (ALICE ROOSEVELT LONGWORTH, Crowded Hours, 164).

Hence the verb *schedule*, which nearly = *appoint, set down definitely*. 'Chauncey M. Depew is scheduled for a speech.' (Here *scheduled* = Eng. *on the programme*.) 'Something happened at the matinee yesterday that was not scheduled.' 'The doors of the theatre were scheduled to be opened at three o'clock.' 'It had taken me more than four weeks to go a distance on those rivers which was scheduled for eight days' (A. J. BEVERIDGE, The Russian Advance, 55). 'The Western trip was scheduled for May' (D. LAWRENCE, True Story of Woodrow Wilson, 47).

By a slight extension of meaning *scheduled* comes to mean *practically certain*. 'The storm of sectional strife and party bickering is scheduled to break the minute that committee assembles.' 'N.Y. State is scheduled to go the way of Ohio politically unless the factional quarrel in the Rep. party is settled.'

In Am. the *ch* of *schedule* is pronounced hard.

school. The various types of school in Am. are known by different names from those which denote similar institutions in Eng. In Am. *public school* carries with it no suggestion of an establishment on the lines of Eton or Harrow. It corresponds to the Eng. *council school* or former *board school*, denoting as it does a school, whether elementary or secondary, that is under public management. It is thus distinguished from the *private school* (see below) and from the *parochial school* (see PARISH). 'The withdrawal of hundreds of thousands of children into parochial schools is unfortunate, because the public school is the greatest democratic influence in our country' (Prof. A. B. HART, Actual Government, 549). In an article in the *Educational Review* of Sept. 1902, may be found the following ludicrous example of a misunderstanding apparently due to ignorance of the difference between the Eng. and the Am. use of this term. 'In the rural districts [of Eng.] the board schools are regarded with increasing favor from people of rank and culture. I was told that the Duchess of Devonshire sends her children to the public school.'

The Am. *public school* is also known as a *common school*. 'A comparative summary showing the increase in what are called common schools, including under this designation schools of the elementary and secondary grades supported from public funds' (Report of U.S. Commissioner of Education). 'The first aim of our schools—that which gives them the name of common schools—is to give to the mass of the people a training which will serve the needs of citizenship' (Prof. N. S. SHALER, The Citizen, 174). 'Belief in the right of every individual to start equal in the race of life with other individuals was a marked force in the spread of a universal and unified system of common schools' (Prof. J. DEWEY, in The Educational Frontier, 46).

Another name for it is *district school*, esp. in rural neighbourhoods. This term thus frequently denotes what would be called in Eng. a *village school*. 'The district school opens about the middle of July, and closes the first week in Feb.' 'Owen Young could not have been more than six when he was going down the hill to the little district school' (IDA M. TARBELL, Owen D. Young, 11).

In Am. the name of *private school* is given to hundreds of schools that would not come within this category in Eng. For it denotes any kind of school that is not maintained by public funds and controlled by a public authority. Thus, even Eton and Harrow would be considered private schools in Am. In Eng. this term is restricted to such schools as

are conducted for the profit of the owner. For examples of the various types of school that bear this name in Am. see Porter E. Sargent's annual *Handbook of Am. Private Schools*.

In Eng. a *preparatory school* is a school where young boys are prepared for a public school (in the Eng. sense), but in Am. it is a school where much older boys are prepared for college. It thus corresponds in many respects to the Eng. public school or to the Eng. secondary school whose curriculum prepares for entrance to a university. Indeed, a New Eng. newspaper refers to Eton as 'England's most celebrated preparatory school'. 'As the preparatory schools are designed to fit boys for college, they cannot materially alter their curricula until the colleges change their entrance and graduation requirements.' 'He had a fine education, having attended the best preparatory schools of New Eng., and later Bowdoin College' (E. D. ADAMS and J. C. ALMACK, Hist. of U.S. 490). 'As my family had steadily planned to have me go to college, the time came when they saw that I must go to a preparatory school' (Dr. W. W. FOLWELL, Autobiog. 35). The term is often abbrev., as in Eng., to *prep school*. 'The fact that our secondary schools are so universally called throughout the country "prep" schools sufficiently indicates our attitude toward them.'

See also FIT, GRADE, TEACH.

In Am. *schoolma'am* is a common term for a woman teacher. 'Among the passengers on that steamer was a young schoolma'am from Massachusetts.' 'The dictionary does not set up a schoolma'am theory of elegant English.' 'Miss Sadler was by no means the type which we have come to recognize in the cartoons as the Boston schoolma'am' (W. CHURCHILL, Coniston, 323).

A man engaged in the teaching profession is sometimes called a *schoolman*. 'There is among schoolmen no hard and fast agreement even concerning the most elementary details of everyday practice.' 'The Dayton trial of 1925 of a young schoolman who had violated the anti-evolution law' (L. M. HACKER and B. B. KENDRICK, The U.S. since 1865, 686).

schooner. This word has no nautical associations in the Am. term *prairie schooner*, which denotes the wagon in which a family of pioneers would cross the prairies in the early days of the settlement of the West. 'The canvas-covered prairie schooner, drawn by horses, followed by cattle, loaded with household goods and the rising generation, set out on its voyage' (T. C. PEASE, The U.S. 392). 'The prairie schooners were ferried across the Mississippi in the spring of '36' (SUSAN GLASPELL, The Road to the Temple, 2). 'Clumsy, broad-wheeled bullock carts, in appearance like our "prairie schooners", creaked by behind humped oxen' (H. A. FRANCK, Vagabond Journey, 259).

scooter. The Eng. *scooter* is a child's toy, consisting of a small board with two tandem wheels. One foot rests on the board while the other propels the vehicle by striking the ground, with the guidance of a long handle attached to the front wheel. That is the usual sense of the word in Am. also, but it has there an additional meaning, thus given by a N.Y. paper. 'The scooter is at home on water or ice. It is not a bird or a beast, but a boat. It is built with a bottom and a deck which are duplicates of each other. . . . A scooter of the most modern type is 14 feet long and its greatest width is 4 feet. . . . A mast 9 feet high and 3 inches thick is big enough to carry a sufficient area of canvas for the stiff winter winds.'

score. In Eng. one person *scores off* another by getting the better of him, esp. in argument or repartee. In Am. that use is unknown, but the verb is used (without *off*) in the sense of *slate, rebuke, censure.* 'Judge West gave him a severe scoring, and then imposed a fine.' 'The Suprema takes every official in turn, from inquisitors down to messengers, specifies their misdeeds, and scores them mercilessly, showing that the whole organization was solely intent on making dishonest gains, on magnifying its privileges, and on tyrannizing over the community' (H. C. LEA, Hist. of the Inquisition of Spain, i. 530). 'Wilson, in one of his speeches, scored both of the old party machines, declaring that government under them was an illegitimate and abominable partnership between business and politics' (J. KERNEY, Political Education of Woodrow Wilson, 70). 'He scored Pres. Cleveland's administration for cutting off the increase of money by the repeal of the Sherman Act when money was most needed' (A. B. DARLING, Public Papers of F. G. Newlands, i. 48).

scratch. There has been formed in Am. the compound word *scratch-pad* = Eng. *scribbling-block.* 'He called it "a scratch-pad draft", and remarked that it was not to be taken as final' (W. G. McADOO, Crowded Years, 220). An alternative, less common, is *scratch-block.* 'His writing he did on large yellow scratch-blocks' (WILLIS J. ABBOT, Watching the World Go By, 95).

scrub is in Eng. a noun and a verb only. In Am. it is an adj. also, not precisely in the sense of *scrubby*, though generally with a certain suggestion of inferiority. 'The same man may be field marshal at home, second lieutenant at the office, and scrub private in politics' (W. LIPPMANN, Public Opinion, 225). A *scrub team* at a college is a junior team against which the college team practises throughout the football season. The noun *scrub* thus comes to be used of such a team, or of a single member of it. 'The rest were from last year's freshmen and scrub team.' 'A goal that lured the sore, disheartened little quarter-back to let himself be battered about on the scrub.' 'At the University as a "scrub", an outsider, a non-fraternity man, he endured experiences of a sort that most boys ultimately forget' (MARK SULLIVAN, Our Times, iii. 214).

Where *scrubbing-* is used in an Eng. compound, *scrub-* is used in an Am. Thus Am. *scrub-brush* = Eng. *scrubbing-brush.* 'He discovered Sandy lying on his face in the passageway, his right hand still wielding the scrub-brush' (ALICE HEGAN RICE, Sandy, 13). The Am. compound *scrubwoman* = Eng. *charwoman.* (The *char* in this word, by the way, is etymologically akin to the Am. *chore.*) 'No one works in Wall Street at night except scrubwomen.' 'There is a scrubwomen's cupboard upstairs, formerly used to store mops and pails and aprons' (C. MORLEY, John Mistletoe, 258).

In Am. the compound *hand-scrub* is an alternative to *nail-brush.*

sea. The compound *sea-food* is in common use in Am., where it is applied to any kind of edible fish, esp. shell-fish. 'N.Y. City is experiencing a scarcity of sea-food, and as a result prices are higher than the oldest dealers in the Fulton Market can recall.' 'Alleged wholesale leases of oyster beds illegally held by certain large seafood corporations' (P. LEWINSON, Race, Class, and Party, 178). See SHORE.

secret service. The functions of the *secret service* in Am. differ considerably from those of the service which bears the same name in Eng. 'The U.S. Secret Service is frequently confused by the public with the special agents' division of the Department of Justice. They are entirely different. The U.S. Secret Service was organized in Lincoln's time for the purpose of running down counterfeiters, and that is still its main activity, though the scope of its operations was widened considerably during the World War. Another duty of the Service is to protect the President and his family' (W. G. McADOO, Crowded

Years, 317). 'The secret-service men are by act of Congress ordered to guard the life of the President. . . . The secret-service men are at his side wherever the President goes' (D. LAWRENCE, True Story of Woodrow Wilson, 119). 'President Hopkins of Williams College was giving a small dinner at which the President of the U.S. was guest of honor. On the grounds outside lurked secret service men and newspaper correspondents' (H. F. PRINGLE, Theodore Roosevelt, 3). 'In the afternoon we [President T. Roosevelt and F. J. S.] took a point-to-point walk through swamp and thicket to the great discomfort of the Secret Service men, whom he delighted in dodging' (F. J. STIMSON, My U.S. 169).

section. In Eng. when a certain portion of a town or city is distinguished from the rest by the special characteristics of its population, it is called the so-and-so *quarter* or *district*; e.g. the Italian quarter, the business district. In Am. the word *section* is applied to a similar division. 'From 82nd to 86th streets, the German-Austrian section of the town' (K. BERCOVICI, Manhattan Side-Show, 275). 'A committee of citizens from the best residence sections' (L. STEFFENS, The Shame of the Cities, 137). 'Because of a belief in the undesirability of Negro neighbors the whites felt impelled to seek houses in other sections of the city' (S. D. SPERO and A. L. HARRIS, The Black Worker, 385). 'Born in the Hampstead section of London' (Dict. Am. Biog. xi. 206).

On a large scale the same term is applied to a region of the U.S., often comprising several States, which has certain interests in common. 'The hope is universal that Mr. Taft will select a strong, broad, experienced man to take charge of the Treasury Department. No one cares what section he may hail from, as long as he measures up to the requirements of that great office.' 'Large stock farms are bringing back to Middle Tennessee some of the prestige in fine cattle that characterized this section in ante-bellum days' (Prof. E. MIMS, Adventurous America, 106). 'After the formal religious elements had largely passed from the New Eng. schools, they persisted in elementary schools in other sections' (Prof. L. J. SHERRILL, Presbyterian Parochial Schools, 1).

Hence *sectional* and *sectionalism*. 'Rivalry for horse show honors between the East and the West has become keen even to the edge bordering upon sectional feeling.' 'Humanity compels us to think first of the injustice and cruelty perpetrated on the blacks in the name of sectionalism.' 'By sectionalism is meant not the rivalry between the North and South culminating in the civil war or the hatred and jealousy of parties representative of different portions of the country, but rather the struggle, often unconscious, between regions of smaller area—sometimes included within the boundaries of a single State and sometimes embracing parts of many States—that represent common racial, economic, or religious interests. Such sections are the tidewater and the back country in colonial times, the Trans-Alleghany country, the Ohio and Mississippi Valleys, the lake region, and the Western plains later.' 'In the first part of the decade the dominant note was still that of sectionalism. There was a literature of New England, a literature of the South, and a literature of the West' (C. C. REGIER, The Era of the Muckrakers, 45). Accordingly, a *sectional conflict*, which in Eng. would mean a conflict between different classes of the community, would mean in Am. a conflict between different parts of the country geographically.

In the vocab. of Am. railways *section* has two spec. meanings. (1) A division of a sleeping-car. 'Coming from the West, I shared a section with a well-built, well-dressed young man.' 'The Western Limited trailed wearily across the continent. The Henrys, the collie, and a mass of charts and records occupied a drawing-room section in the rear sleeper.' (2) A portion of the permanent way, kept in good order by a *section crew*, consisting of *section hands* living in a *section house*. 'Beginning life as a water carrier to the section hands' (E. L. MASTERS, Spoon River Anthology, 108). 'He had been a section hand and a railway superintendent' (SINCLAIR LEWIS, Dodsworth, 26). 'Crowbars and tolls were identified as having been taken from the railroad section house.'

A further technical use of *section* is to denote one of the squares, each of 640 acres, into which the public lands have been divided. See HOMESTEAD.

secular. In Eng. *secular*, as a noun, has only the spec. ecclesiastical meaning. In Am. it is also used to denote a secular song, sung by the Negroes, as distinct from a SPIRITUAL (q.v.). 'The increasing power of the Negro churches had a strong repressive effect upon the singing of seculars by church members' (GUY B. JOHNSON, in Culture in the South, 549).

†**sedan.** In Eng. a now obs. vehicle of the palanquin type, carried by bearers. In Am. the closed motor-car known in Eng. as a *saloon*. 'The sedan he was driving was hit at an unprotected grade crossing.' 'Then some one took us in his sedan and drove us to the hotel.' 'Your business men drive out to the golf club in closed sedans' (SINCLAIR LEWIS, Dodsworth, 382). 'The chances are nine to one that Mr. Smith's automobile is open. The vogue of the sedan is just beginning' (F. L. ALLEN, Only Yesterday, 6).

see is sometimes in Am. a euphemism to denote the kind of interview which includes the passing of a bribe. Thus Lord Bryce (Am. Commonwealth, ii. 699) tells us that the president of a great Am. railroad 'must have adroit agents at the State capitals, well sup-

plied with the sinews of war, ready to "see" leading legislators and to defeat any legislative attacks that may be made by blackmailers or the tools of rival presidents.' 'When a corporation desires legislation, that is, legislation that requires that legislators should be "seen", it sends its bill to Albany.'
See here! is the Am. equivalent of the Eng. *Look here!* or *I say!* 'Halting in front of me, he held me up. "See here," he said aggressively; "you know so much more than I do about running a railroad, let me give you a problem"' (L. STEFFENS, Autobiog. 631).

select. 'The selectmen of an African kraal-village would have had more respect for their ancestors' (O. W. HOLMES, Autocrat of the Breakfast Table, 216). The Autocrat's reference to *selectmen* will need interpretation for most Eng. readers. This compound word is a technical term of the New Eng. political system, denoting members of the executive committee of a town meeting. (See TOWN.) Lord Bryce describes them as corresponding in a way 'to the churchwardens, or select vestrymen, called back by the conditions of colonial life into an activity fuller than they exerted in Eng. even in the 17th century, and far fuller than they retained in the 19th'. 'The selectmen of Montague and Erving held a joint meeting at Millers Falls Tuesday for a conference with the active promoter of the Orange, Erving and Northfield street railway.' 'The selectmen of Nantucket, backed by a commanding sentiment, have passed an automobile regulation which excludes all motor-propelled vehicles from the town of Nantucket.' 'He sat through the [town] meeting with the air of an amused outsider. He paid little attention to the weighty arguments of the selectmen, but noted down all their slips in grammar' (S. McC. CROTHERS, The Pardoner's Wallet, 32).

sell is nowadays often used in Am. in the sense of *popularize, secure the acceptance of,* without any suggestion that a financial transaction is directly involved. 'By steadily pounding away at programs that once were considered caviar, symphony orchestra and concert promoters have "sold" that type of music very widely' (H. JUSTIN SMITH, Chicago, 319). 'The work of the committee began on Jan. 14, with Gen. Dawes as chairman, and it was Gen. Dawes who without a manner of doubt sold the Experts Committee to the listening world' (IDA M. TARBELL, Owen D. Young, 167). 'Then I had to "sell" the idea [i.e. his scheme for a Hudson River Tunnel] to men like the elder J. P. Morgan and E. H. Gary' (W. G. McADOO, Crowded Years, 41). This does not mean that Messrs. Morgan and Gary bought the plan at a price, but that Mr. McAdoo succeeded in getting them to take it up and push it. 'The Belgian Relief had to be "sold" to millions throughout the warring and neutral nations; it had to be floated upon the tides of world opinion by arts not differing in their fundamentals from those used to float mining securities on the London Stock Exchange' (W. MILLIS, in Atlantic Monthly). 'No amount of exhortations of pastors, recruiting rallies, or any other form of high-pressure salesmanship will be very effective in "selling" the ministry and keeping it "sold" to any great proportion of highly intelligent students' (Prof. M. A. MAY, The Education of Am. Ministers, iii. 322).

semi-. This prefix is in much more frequent use in Am. than in Eng. In Am. one never comes across the word *half-yearly,* for *semi-annual* invariably takes its place. So, too, a *jubilee* usually becomes a *semi-centennial* In a great many instances *semi-* is loosely used as an equivalent of *partly, largely,* or *approximately,* rather than *half.* 'Her return to the

New Empire Theatre assumed the proportions of a semi-national event.' 'The manager of the Amusement Park will resume his semi-open-air lyric opera season next summer.' 'Semi-wild coffee is the chief crop.' 'As a result of the controversy, Tammany Hall was in a condition of semi-panic last night.'

A favourite Am. word is *semi-occasionally*, meaning *every now and then*. 'He had notes, but referred to them only semi-occasionally.' 'To still a third group the Christian Church seems to be a loose society of those who are interested in listening, semioccasionally, in an atmosphere of intense respectability, to discussions of the good, the true, the beautiful' (Dr. B. I. BELL, in Atlantic Monthly). 'The strangest post office from which the Am. postal service receives mail is one on the Galapagos Island. It is nothing but a barrel in which letters are dispatched semi-occasionally' (F. J. HASKIN, The Am. Government, 73).

seminary. In Eng. this word, when denoting an institution for the professional training of students for the ministry, is restricted to institutions preparing for the Roman Catholic priesthood. In Am. it is a normal term for a theological college connected with any Church or combination of Churches; e.g. Auburn Seminary (Presbyterian), Bangor Seminary (Congregational), Crozer Seminary (Baptist), Drew Seminary (Methodist), General Seminary (Protestant Episcopal), Meadville Seminary (Unitarian), New Brunswick Seminary (Reformed), Pacific Seminary (Lutheran), and Union Seminary (Undenominational).

senior is the spec. term in Am. for a college student in his fourth and final year. 'At the beginning of my senior year I was still undecided as to what I was to do after graduation' (Prof. M. PUPIN, From Immigrant to Inventor, 126). 'Student disorders [at Harvard] culminated in the "Great Rebellion" of 1823, when half the senior class were expelled just before Commencement' (Dict. Am. Biog. x. 431). 'Three years of college were behind us, for his course was open to seniors only' (Prof. A. G. KELLER, Reminiscences of William Graham Sumner, 2).

sergeant. In some States there is an official known as a *city* or *town ser-geant*. 'A sergeant is elected by the qualified voters of every town and city unless otherwise provided by its charter. Sergeants of towns are elected for a two-year term and have the same powers and discharge the same duties as constables within the corporate limits of the said towns, and to a distance of one mile beyond the same. The sergeant of a city, elected for a four-year term, bears much the same relationship to the corporation court of the city that the sheriff bears to the circuit court of the county. . . . In some cities he also executes the processes and orders of the court of law and chancery. Where there is a city jail, the sergeant is the keeper' (Professors F. W. HOFFER, D. M. MANN, and F. N. HOUSE, The Jails of Virginia, 154).

The Am. compound *top-sergeant* is not officially recognized in the U.S. Army, but came into general colloq. use, during the Great War, as a suitable term for a person who enforces rigorous discipline. Its connotation thus corresponds largely to that of *sergeant-major*. 'Sumner was no more conciliatory than a top-sergeant' (Prof. A. G. KELLER, Reminiscences of William Graham Sumner, 21). 'Top sergeants might remark that the only good Hun was a dead one' (F. L. ALLEN, Only Yesterday, 21).

series. 'His death came suddenly in Washington, whither he had gone on invitation of Judge K. M. Landis to see the world series' (Dict. Am. Biog. x. 490). Few Eng. readers would have the least idea of what is meant by *world series* in this sentence. It is the name given to the most important series of competitions among Am. baseball teams. 'The Eng. may bemoan the decline of cricket, but as the world series between the N.Y. National league team and the Washington Am. league team approaches, the climax of the season, there seems no reason to bemoan the decline of baseball.' 'The N.Y. Am. League Club defeated the Chicago National League Club in the World Series of 1932 in fou₁ games' (World Almanac for 1933, 838).

session. In the vocab. of Am. schools session is spec. used to denote that part of (1) the day or (2) the year during which teaching is given. (1) 'A school that holds a twelve-hour a day session for twelve months in the year' (Advt.). 'When he is six years old he enters the first grade, which is usually a half-day session.' 'Up to the time he was 17 he had attended school but one year, and that only for half-day sessions' (Dr. C. R. BROWN, They Were Giants, 81). (2) 'The rural child receives only about 65 per cent. as much schooling as the city child. This is due to the slack attendance and shorter school session. The average daily attendance in the country is 67·6 per cent.; in the city, 79·3 per cent. The school year in the former is 137·7 days, and in the latter 184·3 days' (W. E. SMYTHE, City Homes on Country Lanes, 24). See also EXECUTIVE.

set. The Am. compound *set-up* means *structure* in the fig. sense. 'Included in the proposed capital set-up were 210,000 shares of common stock' (W. B. and J. B. NORTHROP, The Insolence of Office, 250). 'Mr. Morgan was an adept when it came to re-adjusting financial set-ups' (Prof. T. J. GRAYSON, Leaders and Periods of Am. Finance, 465). 'The Negro in politics cannot be considered in a framework of abstract considerations, or of merely general political conditions. He must be studied with reference to the particular set-ups in the white politics about him' (P.

LEWINSON, Race, Class, and Party, 163). 'The problems that these writers have to confront are problems connected with the class structure of our society, the economic set-up of our life' (V. F. CALVERTON, The Liberation of Am. Literature, 40).

See also FIRE.

shade has in Am., as in some Eng. dial., the additional meaning of a *window-blind*. 'Curious people gathered in front of the residence, but the shades were drawn, and there was nothing to be seen.' 'Window Shades at the lowest prices. Opaque shades in all the popular colors, mounted on good spring rollers' (Advt.). 'Draw the shades and light the lamp' (STRUTHERS BURT, When I Grew up to Middle Age, 76).

In Am. the convenient term *shade tree* is used to denote a tree that is planted for the sake of its shade, as distinct from its fruit, beauty, or commercial value. 'A beautiful feast was spread under the large friendly shade trees which are so numerous about the old home.' 'There are more shade trees in Washington than in any other city in the world' (F. J. HASKIN, The Am. Government, 376).

†A seller who lowers his prices slightly is said in Am. to *shade* them. 'Shading Steel Prices Further. Considerable Concessions Being Made by Western Manufacturers' (Newspaper headline). 'To spur his freight traffic manager to get business without shading rates.' 'Macy originated the shaded price policy—$1.98 instead of $2' (Encycl. Soc. Sci. x. 33).

shake. The only meaning of *shake-down* in Eng. is that of a *makeshift bed*. In Am. it has another use, defined in the following quotation. 'He [a N.Y. policeman] was fined 30 days' pay because he would not stand for a "shake-down", which means that he had refused to give from time to time upon demand five or ten dollars from his meagre salary to his superiors to be used for purposes unknown' (A. HODDER, A Fight for the City, 219).

The usual term in Am. for a shuffling of positions in an official group is *shake-up*. 'Shake-up of Chicago Police' (headline of a newspaper paragraph reporting several transfers and discharges). 'It was a characteristically thorough shake-up of the diplomatic service in which Roosevelt indulged at the beginning of his second term. In one day he nominated no fewer than five ambassadors and eleven ministers to new posts' (A. NEVINS, Life of Henry White, 243). In Eng. *reshuffle* would be used in such connexions.

In Am. the word *shake* also qualifies a variety of roof. 'The houses, built by government contractors of rough logs, consisted of a single room with a shake roof' (C. H. STERNBERG, Life of a Fossil Hunter, 149).

shape. †Commonly used in Am. as a synonym for *condition*, without any suggestion of *form* or *configuration*. 'The banks are in much better shape than at this time last year.' 'The picture was apparently in fair shape, though a close inspection revealed long and deep fissures.' 'The street was in bad shape, even swampy in spots' (H. JUSTIN SMITH, Chicago, 50). 'The Spanish navy was old and in bad shape' (J. TRUSLOW ADAMS, The Epic of Am. 337). 'Soon he felt his business affairs were in such shape that he could ask Miss Murray to be his wife' (S. H. ACHESON, Joe Bailey, 28). Hence the expression *in . . . shape to*. 'Lewis County is in fairly good shape to give the Rep. candidates the normal Rep. vote.'

Hence Am. *shape up* (intrans.) = Eng. *work out* (intrans.). 'It is not at all certain that matters will shape up so as to permit them to do this.'

shark, when used fig. in Eng., denotes only a person of predatory habits. In Am. it may mean an exceptionally clever person. 'The instructor stood amazed as he saw the two boys who were sharks in

mathematics standing puzzled with the problem less than half solved, while Flavia was rapidly filling the blackboard' (L. N. WRIGHT, Limbs of an Old Family Tree, 85). In Eng. *whale* is sometimes used in a similar sense.

sharp. In Am. a popular term for *expert*. 'Naval Sharps in Session' is the heading of a newspaper report of a meeting of the Society of Naval Architects. A former Speaker of the House of Representatives was quoted in the press as saying that he was not 'a schedule sharp' and as adding that, when he first came to Congress he would not have known the merits of a schedule if he picked it up in the street. 'A mechanical sharp from the factory has been going over the machine.' 'The surface indications point to his triumphant election. The majority of political sharps are forecasting it.' 'The boating sharps, who early left their beds for a sizing-up of wind and water conditions, came back to breakfast with smiling faces.'

sheepman is now obs. in Eng., where it meant *shepherd*. In Am. today it means a *breeder or owner of sheep*. 'A substantial Western sheepman who is afraid that the overcrowded conditions of the Western ranges will soon ruin his business is now looking to the wilds of Vermont for better pastures. He hopes by transporting his 10,000 sheep across the continent to escape the intense competition of the Western business.' 'At a meeting of the sheepmen and wool growers, held at Walla Walla, a committee of sheepmen were allowed to allot the range. Cf. CATTLEMAN and COWMAN.

shell. In addition to its other meanings *shell* may denote in Am. a *light racing-boat*. 'Few former college oarsmen from this side of the Atlantic have sat in the Oxford shell during the last unhappy decade.' 'Is it really obligatory for the Yale crew to row in a $10,000 shell?'

The compound *shell-game* denotes a

sleight-of-hand gambling trick in which a small object is concealed under one of a number of walnut shells and bets are made as to which shell is covering it. It is thus an Am. variant of *thimble-rigging*. 'The police reported that during the day the shell-game man had ceased from troubling.' 'Deception was a jugglery he would hardly have tried. Cleveland might throw the hammer or put the shot, but he could never work a shell-game on man or woman' (W. A. WHITE, Masks in a Pageant, 116).

sherbet. The Eng. cooling drink to which this name is applied is only a distant reminder of the true Oriental *sherbet*. It is a concoction of bicarbonate of soda, tartaric acid, sugar, &c., and is usually more pleasing to a juvenile than to an adult palate. In Am. the word has a still different sense, as it denotes a variety of water ice. Mrs. Rorer, in her Cook Book, describes it as a water ice stirred rapidly during the freezing, and distinguishes it from a *sorbet*, which is a stirred water ice with a one-egg meringue added after the mixture is frozen.

sheriff. Eng. readers of Am. detective fiction must sometimes be puzzled to know why, when a murder is discovered, the sheriff is so often the first person to whom the news is communicated. Here is the explanation. 'The sheriff', says Lord Bryce (The Am. Commonwealth, i. 606) 'is everywhere in Am. neither an ornamental person, as he has become in Eng., nor a judge with certain executive functions, as in Scotland, but the chief executive officer attached to the judicial machinery of the county.' 'The general police officer in every county (and in all cities included within the county) is the sheriff. Whether freely exercised or not, the historic police powers of the sheriff survive unless they have been expressly curtailed by statute; and this often leads to serious jurisdictional conflicts between the sheriff of the

county and the police departments of the cities within his bailiwick' (C. C. MAXEY, Outline of Municipal Government, 136). 'The sheriff's proclamation of yesterday declaring the village under state of riot has been rescinded.' 'Behind every law stands the sheriff, and behind the sheriff the militia, and behind the militia the whole military power of the Federal Government.' 'Sheriffs in some instances went so far as to supply themselves with machine guns and took other measures to protect the community against possible violence' (Dr. R. R. MOTON, What the Negro Thinks, 66). 'The disorder was checked by a posse hastily organized by the sheriff' (B. LASKER, Filipino Immigration, 18). See DEPUTY.

shield. In Am. this word is used to denote a policeman's official badge. 'Two men called upon him and stated that they were detectives, both showing him shields in support of their claim.' 'The ex-policeman who turned in his shield in Sept.' 'A Police Department surgeon said the policeman was unfit for duty, and the lieutenant stripped him of his shield and service revolver.'

The compound *windshield* takes the place of the Eng. *windscreen* to denote a part of the equipment of a motor-car. 'The driver's eye level in relation to the top of the wheel and the windshield has a bearing on safety.' 'He was in the back seat holding on, and not sheltered by the windshield' (CHRISTOPHER MORLEY, John Mistletoe, 283).

shilling. Although Am. has adopted a decimal currency and the shilling has thus disappeared from its coinage, it may still be heard of in the calculations of people living in certain backward regions. 'To this day', wrote Prof. J. A. Harrison in a *Life of George Washington* (p. 405) published in 1906, 'the mountain people of Virginia rudely reckon in shillings ($16\frac{2}{3}$ cents) ninepences ($12\frac{1}{2}$) and fourpences.'

The *pine-tree, Boston,* or *Bay shilling* was a silver coin of Massachusetts, struck in the latter half of the 17th century and bearing the device of a pine-tree. 'Its shrewd common sense, its learning, its idealism, its canniness, its poetry, its prosiness, its queer blend of piety and protest—all are here minted into something that is as unalloyed, rare, and racy of the soil as a pine-tree shilling.' (FERRIS GREENSLET, J. R. Lowell, 83, with reference to the Biglow Papers).

shine. An Englishman has his boots or shoes *blacked,* or *cleaned.* An Am. has his shoes *shined.* 'Thousands of Italian bootblacks are earning an industrious living by shining shoes.' 'A row of men reading the tabloids as they have their shoes shined' (E. WILSON, The Am. Jitters, 44). In the last ten years the Greeks have practically appropriated the whole shoe-shine trade of the city' (K. BERCOVICI, Around the World in N.Y. 61).

shingle. In Am. the sign-board of a professional man. Hence Am. *hang out one's shingle* = Eng. *put up one's brass plate.* 'When a man once assumes the full title of architect and hangs out his shingle.' 'Won't Hang Out a Shingle' is the headline of a newspaper announcement that a certain ex-ambassador does not intend to resume his law practice when he returns to N.Y. 'He hung out his shingle as Dr. Kennedy' (Dict. Am. Biog. vi. 9). 'Bailey was admitted to the bar of Copiah County, and hung out his shingle at the county seat of Hazelhurst' (S. H. ACHESON, Joe Bailey, 18).

The term is also sometimes used in connexion with the announcement of occupations of a lower than professional rank. 'We hung out a shingle: "Goldman and Minikin, Dressmakers", but we were soon compelled to realize that customers were not exactly standing in line on the corner' (E. GOLDMAN, Living My Life, 71).

ship. In Eng. the verb *ship,* in the sense of *transport,* bears only its natural meaning of *send goods by water.* In Am. it is used quite as frequently of sending goods by land. 'Over 2,000 barrels of apples have already been shipped out of Conway over the street railway.' 'They have to ship goods by rail from Boston to N.Y.' (F. J. STIMSON, My U.S. 77). 'A world in which a Kansas farmer shipped his wheat 1,500 miles by railroad and then 3,000 by steamer' (J. TRUSLOW ADAMS, The Epic of Am. 354).

A similar dilution of meaning has been suffered by *shipper* and *shipment.* 'The granting by railroads of rebates to favored shippers' (MARK SULLIVAN, Our Times, iii. 223). In enumerating the various ways in which 'inequality of opportunity in transportation' may arise, Prof. R. T. Ely (Evolution of Industrial Society, 210) mentions 'rushing through the freight of the favored shipper while that of another is sidetracked' and 'maintenance of such relations between various modes of shipment—as, for example, between tank-cars and barrels, and between rail, water, and pipe-line transportation—that advantages come to some which others do not enjoy.'

See FREIGHT.

shoot. Am. *shoot to death* = Eng. *shoot dead.* 'Three bandits were shot to death after a three-mile chase.' 'His eldest son had recently been shot to death in a disgraceful fracas' (G. ATHERTON, Adventures of a Novelist, 204). 'A reporter was shot to death in a crowded subway' (F. L. ALLEN, Only Yesterday, 263). 'On May 21, he surrendered, only to be shot to death while he lay asleep' (L. M. HACKER and B. B. KENDRICK, The U.S. since 1865, 479).

shop is in Am. a place where certain things are made, or where certain mechanical operations are performed, rather than, as in Eng. (exc. in such terms as *workshop, engineering shop, shop steward*), a place where things are sold, which is usually called a STORE (q.v.). Thus, when Morris Hillquit, in his autobiog., tells us that in his youth he was employed in a *shirt shop*, he means a place where shirts were made, not where they were sold. H. L. Mencken points out, however, that for years *shop* has been used in Am. in the Eng. sense in such terms as *shopper, shopgirl, shopping, shoplifter, shopworn*, and *pawnshop*. Am. idiom omits the *'s* in the defining word that usually precedes *shop*; e.g. a blacksmith shop, a barber shop, a carpenter shop, a tailor shop—not a blacksmith's shop, a barber's shop, a carpenter's shop, a tailor's shop.

Accordingly *shopman* does not mean in Am. as in Eng. a man who sells articles over the counter, but a worker in a machine shop or repair shop. 'On Aug. 2 a strike of railroad shopmen was called' (Am. Year Book for 1919, 457).

In the vocab. of Am. labor a *closed shop* is a shop in which only trade unionists are employed, as distinct from an *open shop*, where unionists and non-unionists work side by side. 'Two thousand cloakmakers went on strike to-day. An increase in wages, recognition of the union, and closed shops are demanded.' 'Otis had become the most savage and effective enemy of labor unionism in the country, and as a result of his doings Los Angeles was the outstanding open-shop town in the U.S.' (L. ADAMIC, Dynamite, 204). 'Organized labor generally seems to have felt that this would be the strategic moment to demand full recognition—a closed shop in all the industries' (IDA M. TARBELL, Owen D. Young, 124).

For *shop chairman* see the following quotation. 'The shop steward of British industry is analogous to the shop chairman of Am. trade unionism, but in Am. the shop chairman of such industries as the men's clothing industry has more power and recogni

tion than was ever accorded to the shop stewards of Eng.' (P. BLANSHARD, Outline of the British Labor Movement, 75).

The verb *shop* does not always mean quite the same thing in Am. as in Eng. An Am. woman sometimes distinguishes between a buying expedition, undertaken with a deliberate intention of making purchases, and a shopping expedition, which may involve nothing more than a tour of inspection. Thus a N.Y. clothier advertises: 'Shop around first at all the sales going on about town—then see these remarkable suits.' 'With Bertha Spinney she went window-shopping' (SINCLAIR LEWIS, Work of Art, 261).

shore. The term *shore dinner* is used in Am. to denote a dinner of SEA FOOD (q.v.), usually partaken near the coast. 'The repast was a typical Rhode Island shore dinner, and many of the visitors found the clambake a novelty.' 'There will doubtless be other Sundays before the end of the season when thousands of excursionists will seek to satiate their appetite with the succulent clam, but it will be surprising if a greater number go to the dining halls on any one day than were fed with shore dinners yesterday.'

The compound *longshoreman* is much less commonly used in Eng. than in Am. 'Longshoremen is the Am. term for workers customarily called dockers in Eng. . . . It includes all workers engaged in the loading or discharging of vessels' cargoes' (Encycl. Soc. Sci. ix. 606). Thus, the Am. *longshoremen's unions* correspond to the Eng. *dockers' unions.*

shout. In the vocab. of Am. politics *shout for* is used fig. in the sense of *support enthusiastically.* 'The Tammany leader is good enough to say that he is not opposed to him; but he is not shouting for him.' 'Thus far most of the enthusiastic shouting for Gorman can be traced to the Gorman press bureau.'

Hence *shouter*, in a corresponding

sense. 'The canvass of the state was very thorough, Hearst shouters being busily engaged in every city and village.'

†**show.** In card-playing, the act of laying down one's cards with their faces upward is called a *show-down.* In Am. this term is in common use fig. 'A show-down disclosed the fact that all the district leaders but Doyle and Kehoe of the Ninth were with him.' 'The controversy in regard to the unlimited coinage of silver, at a ratio of 16 to 1, came to a show-down in both national conventions' (Dr. FRANKLIN H. MARTIN, The Joy of Living, i. 357). 'I suggested to my colleagues that the finance and economic questions would meet us at every turn and that we might as well face them and have a show-down with our associates of the Allied Governments' (Intimate Papers of Col. HOUSE, iv. 279).

shower. In Eng. you shower missiles or compliments on a person. In Am. you shower him with the missiles or compliments. 'Natives who had a grudge against North Americans showered the parade with rocks.' 'They showered Aaron Burr with special honors' (Prof. A. E. MARTIN, Hist. of U.S. i. 192). 'The delegates were showered with telegrams from their constituents approving Bryan's course' (M. R. WERNER, Bryan, 190). 'A youth whose parents have been showered with this world's goods' (H. E. BUCHHOLZ, U.S. 86).

In Am. a *shower party*, esp. in connexion with a wedding, is a party at which the hostess is thus showered with presents from her friends. The *showers* are often specialized; e.g. *apron showers, bag showers, doyley showers,* or *kitchen showers* (when each guest brings a kitchen utensil). 'There is poor expression of good will in a shower of old shoes or a rice bath. The "shower parties" that through mistaken hospitality the wedded couple, who desire most of all to be let alone, are forced to attend, and there be made sport of, differ from the riotous shower of stale vegetables in Philadelphia only in degree.' Similar *showers* are sometimes organized for the benefit of charities. 'The managers of the Home for the Friendless invite the public to a linen shower and reception. . . . The managers desire to furnish the dormitories and dining rooms for the coming year, and the sizes of table linen and bedding needed are as follows.'

shut. ††Am. *shut down* = Eng. *close.* 'The Hamilton Cotton Mills shut down to-day because of the state of the cotton market.' 'In the evenings, long after the quick Am. twilight has shut down on the heated earth, the Eng. horizon gives light for recreation' (J. CORBIN, An Am. at Oxford, 145). 'If the farmers had been able to shut down as the factories did, the restriction of output would have brought their prices up' (G. SOULE, The Coming Am. Revolution, 211).

†Hence the noun *shut-down.* 'The official announcement states that the shut-down is made to give the operatives a vacation.' 'Then they decided on a 30-day shut-down of all flowing wells. In ten days not a barrel of oil was being pumped' (J. T. FLYNN, God's Gold, 181).

A person who is confined to the house by illness or other cause is called in Am. a *shut-in.* 'People all over the city are asked to contribute flowers for distribution among the sick and shut-ins in the hospitals and homes.' 'The Red Box put there to receive magazines and books for shut-ins' (CHRISTOPHER MORLEY, John Mistletoe, 175). Organizations established in order to minister to invalids in such ways are called *Shut-in Societies.*

shuttle. In Am. this term is applied to a train or car that runs to and fro, like a weaver's shuttle, over a short supplementary line. 'They also have many shuttle cars, or cars that make short runs' (E. E. CALKINS and R. HOLDEN, The Art of Modern Advertising, 89).

shy. In Am. *shy* or *shy of* = Eng. *lacking, short of*. 'The Topeka councilman walked off the edge into four feet of water. But for the prompt action of Mr. Price, the Fourth Ward would have been shy one councilman.' 'Even if either man should obtain the fifteen votes remaining unpledged, he would still be shy of nomination by just three votes.' 'If he finds a house with a butler's pantry it is shy a bathroom, or if it has two bathrooms it is invariably shy a butler's pantry.' 'We sympathize with the village justice who may have been a little shy in the matter of international law but who was a whole encyclopedia of information concerning the automobile speed limit.' 'Philadelphia Shy of Funds' is the heading of a newspaper report of a deficiency in the city treasury, and 'Ohio Shy on Speed' of a statement that the battleship *Ohio* failed to reach the stipulated speed requirements. In Eng. this use of *shy* is restricted to betting slang.

sick. The difference between Eng. and Am. idiom is thus stated by H. W. Fowler in his *Modern Eng. Usage*: 'The original and more general sense of *sick*, which has now been transferred for the most part to *ill*, was suffering from any bodily disorder. That sense remains to it in attrib. use (*sick people, a sick child*, &c.) but is now uncommon in predicative use (*be, feel sick*), in which it means vomiting or ready to vomit. In U.S. and Scotch use the wider sense is still common, and cf. *go sick* as the army phrase for declaring oneself ill.' Accordingly, 'I'm afraid I'm going to be sick' means in Eng. 'I'm afraid I'm going to vomit' but in Am. 'I'm afraid I'm going to be ill'. Many examples of the earlier Eng. use will be found in the A.V.

of the Bible and in the Book of Common Prayer. Here are some examples of the survival of this use in Am. In a letter (quoted in ALLAN NEVINS's Life of Henry White, 234) Pres. Theodore Roosevelt writes: 'Poor Hanna has just died. Thank heaven, before he became sick the whole opposition to me had collapsed.' 'The President's friends did not know how sick he was. They knew only that he needed rest and freedom from worry' (D. LAWRENCE, True Story of Woodrow Wilson, 289). 'The parents have it in their power to keep the children well, sick half the time, or half sick all the time' (Dr. R. L. ALSAKER, Eating for Health and Efficiency, 281).

In Am. the word may be applied to spec. parts of the body, in the sense of *diseased*. 'Death lurks in sick kidneys' (Advt.). 'When the hair begins to fall out, it is sick. It needs a tonic and proper care, or the sick hair will spread the trouble until the whole scalp is involved' (Advt.). 'Sick nerves seem to be the great Am. disease' (A. A. CAREY, New Nerves for Old, 1).

In Eng. the original and more general meaning survives in compounds, such as *sick-bay, sick-bed, sick-berth, sick-leave, sick-list, sick-nurse, sick-pay,* and *sick-room,* as well as *homesick, heartsick,* and *lovesick.*

side. †The Am. expression *on the side* is equivalent to such Eng. expressions as *by the way, into the bargain, as an extra.* 'The invitation from the managers of the exposition to attend the big fair in a body and receive the entertainments of St. Louis on the side.' 'The rest of us plod on, working at any one of a hundred jobs, and, on the side, scrimping from week-ends, holidays, and our night's sleep the precious time for our writing.' 'My father put me into the best private school in San Francisco, and he retained one of the teachers there to tutor me on the side' (L. STEFFENS, Autobiog. 112).

'Although by far the most important reason for Astor's trip to Montreal was the purchase of furs, he sometimes engaged in other enterprises on the side' (K. W. PORTER, John Jacob Astor, 68).

In N.Y. one does not speak, as in London, of the *East End* and the *West End*, but of the *East Side* and the *West Side*. Why these parts of the city are called sides and not ends will be clear to any one who glances at a map of Manhattan Island. 'The abysmal craving of N.Y.—West Side and East Side, hotel and apartment, boarding-house and flat—is for friends.' 'The Church would no longer be a class organization, with its rich congregation meeting on the avenue and its poor members gathering in some East Side chapel.' 'To the men and women of the East Side he was speaking of the details of their daily life' (A. HODDER, A Fight for the City, 51). 'One would like to think of the Jewish quarter in N.Y., the East Side especially, as if it were Palestine' (K. BERCOVICI, Around the World in N.Y. 68).

Hence Am. *East Sider* = Eng. *East Ender*, and Am. *West Sider* = Eng. *West Ender*. 'Fifteen thousand East Siders attended the final dedication ceremonies at William H. Seward Park.' 'The persistence with which West Siders have followed up this question of the Broadway trees.'

The Am. term *side-burns* denotes short side-whiskers, esp. when worn with a moustache and a clean-shaven chin. 'They saw that he had sideburns, that his hair was sandy and his eyes blue' (H. F. PRINGLE, Theodore Roosevelt, 65). 'With his white sideburns and high silk hat, he himself was in keeping with the possessions with which he surrounded himself' (L. N. WRIGHT, Limbs of an Old Family Tree, 43). 'With his sideburns and his passionate air, "the sheik" [Rudolph Valentino] had set the standard for masculine sex appeal' (F. L. ALLEN, Only Yesterday, 212). For the origin of this curious term see

the following quotation: 'Gen. Burnside gave his name to a type of whiskers but to no great victory [in the Civil War]' (J. TRUSLOW ADAMS, America's Tragedy, 285). The derivation is more likely to be remembered when, as often happens, the alternative term *burnsides* is used. Cf. the origin of *dundreary*.

Am. *side-check* = Eng. *bearing-rein*. 'An Englishman lately arrived in this country, and no doubt one of the patrons of the Horse Show in N.Y., protests against the side-check, or, as it is called in Eng., the bearing-rein.'

Am. *sidewalk* = Eng. *pavement* (in towns) or *footpath* (in the country). 'He spoke from a platform hastily erected on the sidewalk of the main street.' 'The rule that men meeting on the sidewalk shall pass to the right' (R. LUCE, Congress, 38). 'All questions as to the width of sidewalks and the specifications for their construction should be settled with reference to the character of the street and the use of abutting property' (C. C. MAXEY, Outline of Municipal Government, 215). See also PAVEMENT.

†In Am. *side-step* is commonly used as a verb in a fig. sense, meaning *evade, steer clear of.* 'The Idaho Republicans are deftly side-stepping the anti-Mormon issue, hoping thereby to gain Mormon votes, while the Democrats are side-stepping the "law and order" issue, hoping so to gain the votes of the labor unionists.' 'Imminent issues are often deliberately dodged or side-stepped in party platforms and campaigns' (Prof. H. L. McBAIN, The Living Constitution, 210). 'He vigorously assailed the Am. Tract Society for its attempt to sidestep the slavery issue in the interest of harmony' (Dict. Am. Biog. x. 12).

†Actually, to *side-track* an issue often amounts to very much the same thing as to *side-step* it, but the metaphor is different. You side-step something by getting out of its way, but you side-track it by putting it out of your way. 'Dr. Dowie had

been able to sidetrack his taxes on much of his Zion property, presumably on the ground that Zion City was a religious institution.' 'The rules have now grown so numerous that only those who are in the habit of using them daily understand just how to bring up or to sidetrack a motion' (Prof. A. B. HART, Actual Government, 241). 'The result was the sidetracking of the question of protection until the political status of the restored Southern states could be determined satisfactorily' (Prof. A. E. MARTIN, Hist. of U.S. ii. 46).

Am. *side-wheeler* = Eng. *paddle-boat.* 'The side-wheelers to Staten Island pass close to the engineering work.' 'They went in the comfortable side-wheeler *Argo*, with a fair voyage of a fortnight before they reached Havre' (A. NEVINS, Henry White, 9). An alternative is *side-wheel steamer.* 'Our recent ancestors were amazed by . . . the locomotive and the side-wheel steamer' (G. SOULE, The Coming Am. Revolution, 75).

sight unseen. In Am. a commodity is said to be sold *sight unseen* when it is purchased without being actually inspected. 'Any man who can sell a half million Model A automobiles, sight unseen, price unset, has a convincing argument in support of his economic philosophy.' 'This land was sold sight unseen by John Jacob to his brother George' (K. W. PORTER, John Jacob Astor, 82).

Signer. 'The grandson of a President and the great-grandson of a Signer' (WILLIAM ALLEN WHITE, Masks in a Pageant, 67). 'Mr. Maltby Gelston told me that Mrs. Harper was the only child of a Signer then living. He was an authority upon the subject, having married the granddaughter of Philip Livingston, a New York Signer' (M. GOUVERNEUR, As I Remember, 101). 'Thus Joseph Hewes was the second Signer born in Princeton' (Prof. V. L. COLLINS, Princeton Past and Present, 90). A signer of what? When the word is

thus used in Am., without qualification and with a capital initial, it denotes one of the 56 signatories to the Declaration of Independence. Those who put their names to this document are regarded as the patriotic élite of their period; so much so that autograph collectors have given as much as $28,500 for individual specimens of their signatures to other papers.

silent. Am. *silent partner* = Eng. *sleeping partner.* 'Men's wear apparel manufacturer, reputable growing concern, desires silent or active partner' (Advt.). 'Rockefeller proposed that Flagler should become a partner in his firm and that Harkness should put a lot of money into it as a silent partner' (J. T. FLYNN, God's Gold, 134). For the application of this term to Col. House, see his *Intimate Papers*, vol. 1, c. 5.

silk stocking. In Am., a few generations ago, the wearing of silk stockings was a sign of luxurious and extravagant habits. Hence the term *silk stocking* came to be applied to a person or district of a fashionable and ostensibly (not to say, ostentatiously) aristocratic type. 'The mass of voters look upon him as a "silk stocking"— as one who neither understands nor sympathises with their life.' 'Roosevelt was an unknown young silk-stocking in the Civil Service Commission' (W. A. WHITE, Masks in a Pageant, 233). 'Labor decided to teach the silk-stockinged profiteering employer a lesson' (F. L. ALLEN, Only Yesterday, 20). 'This eagerness to vote was marked in every part of the city—on the lower east side, in the silk stocking upper west side, and in the Bronx.'

silver. In Am. the compound *silverware* = Eng. *plate,* in the sense of a collection of table and domestic utensils. 'Nothing was taken so far as could be learned, jewelry and silverware being left, the thieve apparently looking for money.'

Similarly, Am. *silver basket* = Eng. *plate basket*. 'The head of the household climbed the stairs and set the silver basket on its shelf with the revolver and the watchman's rattle.'
See also CERTIFICATE and FLAT.

sir is sometimes used colloq. in Am. as an intensive adverb, to make a *Yes!* or *No!* more emphatic, and with no reference in mind to the sex or number of those addressed. '"You don't mean to say they did all that?" said the other woman, in a tone of admiration. "Yes, sir, they did"' (M. E. WILKINS FREEMAN, By the Light of the Soul, 398).

sit. Am. *sit down hard on* = Eng. *set one's face firmly against.* 'While the conservatives called for a tariff war with the U.S., Laurier was doing what he could to show his determination that Canada should break loose from Great Britain. He sat down hard on the proposition that Canada should meet a penny of the imperial expenses.'
†Am. *sit up and take notice* = Eng. *wake up to the situation.* 'Tammany politicians sat up and took notice this morning when the city clerk announced the appointment of William S. Andrews as commissioner of records. The first comment heard was one betokening bewilderment.' 'The crowd that fell upon Washington was of such a size that the District authorities sat up and took serious notice. "What will we do four years from now", they asked each other, "if the number of visitors is proportionately larger?"'

skill. In Eng. one can no longer speak of *a skill,* i.e. a craft, an accomplishment, but this obs. sense survives in Am. In their 'Middletown' Mr. and Mrs. R. S. Lynd speak of 'the leisure-time skills of singing and drawing' (190) and of 'the facts and skills constituting the present-day high-school curriculum' (192). 'Reading, spelling and arithmetic,' they say, 'exhibit at certain points less emphasis upon elaboration of symbols and formal drill and more on the practical application of these skills' (191). 'Subject-matter, like Latin, mathematics, or history, and skills, like typewriting or cooking, are ingeniously combined on an utterly fallacious theory into "units", "points" and "counts"' (A. FLEXNER, Universities, 46).

slant is used in Am. metaphorically as well as literally. 'The titles of articles on this subject from the magazines bear an extremely pessimistic slant.' 'The controversy has been given a personal slant that is scarcely relevant.' 'This home-town journal was looking for a fresh "news slant" after having exhausted almost every other' (E. F. DAKIN, Life of Mrs. Eddy, 380). 'The brief Fox ministry in Eng., with its pro-Am. slant' (Prof. C. R. FISH, The U.S. and Great Britain, 21). 'A brilliant little book containing many new slants on the relation between senatorial powers and the powers of the executive' (Prof. H. L. McBAIN, The Living Constitution, 277).

slash is often used in Am. in the sense of *cut down, reduce.* 'Senator La Follette hammered away in opposition to the Hoover plan to put through an emergency tax reduction. Slashing taxes was no way, as he saw it, to prevent depression.' 'A disposition was manifested in the Senate Committee to slash the salaries of members of the commission.' 'This message as elsewhere printed is little more than one-third of the original. It is not a pleasant thing to slash a presidential message to this extent, but it will have to be done to an even greater extent if such lengths as this continue to be maintained.' 'Mollison's Wife Slashes His Time On Capetown Hop' is the headline given by an Am. paper to its report of Mrs. Mollison's feat in beating her husband's record. 'Munsey slashed the price of his magazine to ten cents a copy' (C. C. REGIER, The Era of the Muckrakers, 14).

A contributor to the Women's Page of the *Manchester Guardian* noted the other day that Am. instructions to dressmaking neophytes tell them to *slash*, as though they were engaged upon some murderous occupation, instead of merely cutting the material.

slate is the name given fig. in Am. to a list of candidates adopted by a party organization before an election; i.e. a proposed TICKET (q.v.). 'There was no suggestion made last night concerning a sub-committee to work out the slate, and the ticket will be prepared, therefore, by the complete Fusion Conference Committee.' 'The Rep. Convention assembled in Philadelphia and selected its slate of nominees for the Presidency and Vice-Presidency' (J. T. CARPENTER, The South as a Conscious Minority, 124).

The word may also denote a provisional list of persons to be appointed to various offices by a new President, Governor, Mayor, &c. 'When the Mayor returns from Princeton, where he intends spending Christmas, he will probably bring his completed slate with him.' 'During the few days before the inauguration it seemed that the entire Cabinet slate would be destroyed if either Blair or Davis received an appointment' (W. E. CURTIS, The True Abraham Lincoln, 187).

Similarly, a list of nominations to office in a club or similar organization may be called a *slate*. 'The By-Laws [of the Chicago Rotary Club] provide full opportunity to challenge nominations or to add nominations from the floor to the regular slate [prepared by a committee]' (Rotary? 176).

Hence the verb *slate*. 'Although it is several months before the spring primaries, the Rep. organization is slating candidates for the county offices.' 'Henry Ash is now slated for the chairmanship of the Rep. convention.' The following are examples of the use of the word in a somewhat wider meaning. 'These phases of the

situation are understood to be slated for attention later.' 'The amount of painstaking labor consumed in the preparation of the paper must have been enormous. It should have been slated for a morning session.' 'It is reported that the Kitchener plan for the reorganization of the Indian army is slated to pass the Commons.'

slaughter has a fig. use in the vocab. of Am. politics. 'His lieutenants are openly declaring that they will "slaughter" the McClellan ticket.' 'After being mayor four times, he was hopelessly beaten by Dunne in the primaries of 1907; and again slaughtered by Sweitzer in the primaries of 1915' (Prof. C. E. MERRIAM, Chicago, 280).

slay is in Eng. a poetical or rhetorical word only. In Am. it is an ordinary alternative to *kill*. Thus, in the record of the previous year's events published in the *World Almanac* for 1933 one finds: 'At Tokio, the Japanese Premier was assassinated at his home. An attempt was made also to slay Count Makino.' 'A two-day pursuit of armed men suspected of having slain and robbed Mrs. Sharp.' 'In Alabama one convict was slain and 24 were wounded by gunfire when an attempted escape was followed by a general uprising.' 'To obtain valid explanations of the South's homicide record it is first necessary to classify slayings into three major groups' (Prof. H. C. BREARLEY, in Culture in the South, 684).

Hence, *slayer* is also used in the same way. 'George Grant, Negro, alleged slayer of the Brunswick Chief of Police' (A. F. RAPER, Tragedy of Lynching, 203).

sled. In Eng. there is so little occasion for the use of the *sleigh* or *sled* that it has left no trace on popular metaphor. In Am. a difficult task is often called *hard sledding*. 'The companies building steel vessels have had hard sledding, owing to the

decline in the demand for freights.'
'The bill was passed unanimously in
the House; in the Senate there was
one vote against it. But, for all that,
the measure had hard sledding in
both houses' (J. T. FLYNN, God's
Gold, 286). 'The situation made hard
sledding for all branches of the labor
movement' (NORMAN THOMAS, America's Way Out, 259). 'It was a severe
system; often the *Privatdozent* had
for years hard sledding' (Dr. A.
FLEXNER, Universities, 326).
On the cotton plantations the word
has a spec. meaning also. 'There has
grown up a mechanized method of
picking cotton called "sledding".
These sleds are run across the level
fields, plucking the fruited fiber and
unopened bolls' (R. B. VANCE,
Human Factors in Cotton Culture,
132). 'In parts of Texas and Oklahoma where "sledding" instead of
hand-picking has been practiced as
a method of harvesting, large-scale
machine methods of cotton culture
have been introduced' (CLARENCE
POE, in Culture in the South, 339).

sleep. For *sleeping charter*, see
quotation. 'The Governor's latest
veto is of an act postponing for a
third time the date at which work
must be begun on a railway. These
"sleeping charters", as they are
sometimes called, are a fruitful source
of corruption. A man or a clique of
men obtains a charter for a route
which may some day be profitable, or
may form a link in a larger system.
They do not build; perhaps they
never intended to build; often they
have gone into the enterprise as a
mere speculation, hoping to sell their
right to some existing railway; and
to this end they petition for one extension of time after another.'
In the vocab. of Am. railways
sleeper always denotes a *sleeping-car*,
and never the material used as a
support for the rails, which is known
in Am. as a TIE (q.v.). The name is
also sometimes given to a trunk which
is brought into the country by a

steamship without being accompanied by the owner.
See also SILENT.

slick is in Am. sometimes a verb,
esp. in the expression *slick up = tidy
up, brighten up*. 'Denver has been
having her period of spring slicking
up, and during three days citizens
labored to make their premises clean
and attractive.' 'Pictures which were
often garish in color and feebly
slicked up' (Dict. Am. Biog. xii. 339).

slim. In 1716, acc. to the *O.E.D.*,
Barrow could write of 'a very slim
benefit', but the use of the word in
the sense of *poor, small, of little substance* is now obs. in Eng. In Am. it
is still not unusual. 'The replies were
founded on rather slim documentary
evidence.' 'Owing to a heavy downpour of rain, the gathering was very
slimly attended.' 'The chance of
being President seemed slim' (L.
EINSTEIN, Roosevelt, 83). In a letter
published in his biography by E. S.
Martin, Joseph H. Choate writes of
a sumptuous supper to which he did
entire justice because he had had 'a
slim dinner'. 'These were, however,
slim arguments with which to urge
the Negro citizen towards the registration office' (P. LEWINSON, Race,
Class, and Party, 127). 'A nice old
lady who was raising a lot of orphan
grandchildren on a mighty slim income' (G. H. LORIMER, Old Gorgon
Graham, 301). 'This is slim evidence
on which to condemn Jackson'
(Prof. D. S. MUZZEY, The Am. Adventure, i. 413).

sling. The compound *slingshot* has
been coined in Am. to denote the
kind of sling, used by boys, which in
Eng. is commonly called a *catapult*.
'A keeper in Central Park charged
the boy with shooting birds and
squirrels in the park with a powerful
slingshot.' 'I could hunt mud-hens
with my slingshot' (L. STEFFENS, in
recollections of his boyhood in Autobiog. 13). 'Boy children kill birds,
rabbits and squirrels with slingshots'

(J. Peterkin, Roll, Jordan, Roll, 176).

slip. Am. *slip up* = Eng. *fall short, err.* 'There has resulted the huge irony of a country which boasts of being able to prepare a boy exactly for any profession, trade or art he may choose, slipping up on the most important of all professions—that of governing.' 'The Dem. party must carry practically all of these centres, while the Republicans can slip up on all except any one and still win.'

Hence the noun *slip-up* = Eng. *mischance, error.* 'With the fishermen a slip-up meant the loss of a vessel.' 'His secretary recalls a feat of memory, involving the introduction by name of 50 persons, most of whom he had merely casually met, without a single slip-up' (Dr. H. Zink, City Bosses in U.S. 330). 'There was to be no slip-up in his administration' (J. Kerney, Political Education of Woodrow Wilson, 421).

slug. In Am. the noun *slug* denotes, in addition to its other senses, a gold coin, of the value of $50, privately minted in San Francisco during the California gold-mining rush. The word is in common use to-day to denote a piece of metal sold for five cents and resembling a NICKEL (q.v.) in size and shape. It is used in the slots of telephone booths and sometimes of private telephones also. Some telephones are so constructed that only *slugs* can be used in them.

There is in Am. a verb *slug*, which means *strike violently*, and is presumably akin to the Eng. *slog.* 'The slugging of strike breakers continued. A driver employed by a department store was reported to the police to-day as having been attacked by three men and left unconscious.'

Hence *slugger.* 'What claim can the strikers in Chicago make upon public sympathy when they have formed bands of sluggers for the express purpose of beating—killing, if need be—the men who have taken their places?'

slur. In Eng. the verb *slur* is now used only in its technical musical and phonetic signification, and, with *over*, in the sense of *pass lightly over, minimize.* In Am. it retains the archaic meaning of *depreciate, disparage.* '"Under new management" slurs the past for the benefit of the present.'

Am. *cast* (or *throw*) *slurs at* = Eng. *put a slur on.* 'If it was intended to try the case on the testimony, it was their bounden duty, after throwing slurs at the defendants, to have introduced it.'

slush. In reviewing Dr. Krappe's translation of Eisler's *The Messiah Jesus* the *Manchester Guardian* (April 14, 1931) remarks that 'Dr. Krappe's country of origin is amusingly betrayed when he makes Dr. Eisler say that Josephus's name "was put on the pension list of the slush fund" of the Roman Emperor.' The word *slush* is sometimes used fig. in Eng. to denote *silly sentiment*, but the term *slush fund* is peculiar to Am. A newspaper, for instance, speaks of 'slush funds to corrupt the voters at the primaries'. In the *Dict. Am. Biog.* (viii. 257) the biographer of Pres. Harding refers to 'the enormous slush fund connected with the oil-lease transactions'. 'The impeachers circulated the story that Senators were being bought, and that a huge slush fund for Johnson had appeared in the capital' (C. G. Bowers, The Tragic Era, 192).

smell. In Am., as in some Eng. dial., the verb *smell* in the sense of *take a smell at* is followed by *of.* 'It really seemed as if none of those directors took the pains which Vespasian declined to take and smelled of their money before they banked it.' 'He drew the bottle from its resting place, took out the cork, smelled of it, and then replaced it' (F. J. Haskin, The Am. Government, 276). 'Mrs. Kossuth was unable to overcome her distrust of Am. cooking, and used to scandalize her neighbors at table by ostentatiously smelling of every new dish before tasting it' (F. E. LEUPP, Walks about Washington, 187). Cf. FEEL.

snake. The sinuosity of the snake has suggested in Am. the term *snake fence* to denote a rough fence of split rails laid zigzag. 'Her wasted fields with straggling "snake" fences' (U. SINCLAIR, Manassas, 48).

For *snake-head*, see STRAP.

snap. There are three uses of this word that can be described as Am., though two of them are nowadays becoming familiar in Eng. †(1) It may denote *vivacity, energy, 'go'*. 'The tales are written with a combined snap and humor that make them a very safe investment as a source of entertainment.' 'We must change ourselves from a race that admires jerk and snap for their own sakes to one that, on the contrary, has calm for its ideal' (Prof. W. JAMES, Talks to Students, 217). 'Negro women as cooks, and Negro men as waiters in private homes, in hotels, and on dining cars, work with astonishing snap and dexterity' (Prof. J. DOWD, The Negro in Am. Life, 86). Hence the adj. *snappy*. 'There was a snappy readiness in the marching gait that could only characterize a picked body of men.' 'Should Yale invite him here, he would find a snappy game of football, such as Eng. does not afford a sight of.' 'These new shoes comprise all the new and snappy designs.' 'Too many speeches and not enough striking cartoons, snappy editorials and effective interviews' (WILLIS J. ABBOT, Watching the World Go By, 182).

†(2) Am. *cold snap* = Eng. *cold spell* exc. that a *snap* is of shorter duration than a *spell*. 'The extent of the damage done by the late cold snap.'

(3) Another use, unknown in Eng., is defined by Webster as 'any task, labor, set of circumstances or the like, that yields satisfactory results or gives pleasure with little trouble or effort, as an easy course of study,

a job where work is light, a bargain, etc.' Thus: 'For sale—a sure snap, 160-acre farm on instalments.' 'Under such a system of indirect control, the students are perpetually on a strike for a sufficiency and variety of snaps.' 'Office was considered as a goal to be fought for. Public office was a private snap' (A. M. SIMONS, Social Forces in Am. Hist. 210). The term *soft snap* is esp. common in this sense. 'The average politician seemed to regard that office as a soft snap, for the performance of whose duties no training was required.' 'The men and women I have met upon the streets are not there because as a mode of life it may be considered a soft snap' (JACK LONDON, People of the Abyss, 194).

†In Am. *snap* is also an adj., as an epithet for something that is suddenly sprung upon one. 'The initiative, referendum and recall under restrictions which will prevent snap and flippant action have much to commend them.' 'Many Tammany men expressed indignation to-day over last night's snap meeting of the general committee. It appears that notices of the meeting were not sent out until yesterday morning, and that the friends of the candidates other than Welsh did not hear of it until a few hours before the time set.'

The term *snap beans* is used in Am. for what are known in Eng. as *French beans* or *scarlet runners*. 'By raising early potatoes, egg plant, snap beans, and cucumbers, they reap large profits.'

snarl is now archaic in Eng., exc. in certain dial., in the sense of *snare, tangle* or *ensnare, entangle*, but is commonly so used in Am., both lit. and fig.

Examples of the noun: 'Uncle Jerry took down a gingham bag of strings and occupied himself in taking the snarls out of them' (K. D. WIGGIN, Rebecca, 122). 'A veritable snarl of street urchins took possession of several benches in Lincoln Park.'

'Doubtless the snarl will be unravelled; but, as it stands, it is the final touch in a policy of blunder.' 'The San Domingo snarl has been the subject of sage debate' (Prof. N. W. STEPHENSON, Nelson W. Aldrich, 259).

Examples of the verb: 'The Paris police never seemed to interfere with traffic unless it was badly snarled.' 'Where the ocean frequently snarls itself into lumps which impart emotions not at all pleasant to passengers.' 'His train became snarled several miles outside of Long Island City and he had to get out and walk.' 'The basic conflict in attitudes that snarls up our social order' (Prof. H. G. HULLFISH, in The Educational Frontier, 181).

snipe. In addition to its other meanings, *snipe* is used colloq. in Am. to denote a *half-smoked cigar* or *cigarette*. 'As each caller departs Mr. Ickes empties the ash tray into the waste basket. He smokes, too, but he detests the smell of cold snipes.'

†**snow.** In Am. *snow under* has the fig. meaning of *overwhelm*, esp. in an election contest. 'Snowed under by Rep. votes.' 'He was snowed under when he ran in the election as an independent' (P. LEWINSON, Race, Class, and Party, 167). 'Greely was snowed under, and died a few days after the election' (J. TRUSLOW ADAMS, Hist. of the Am. People, ii. 145).

so is frequently used in Am. with an ellipsis of *that*. 'Turning it from time to time so it may be cooked alike on both sides.' 'Patching up a truck temporarily, so it will support the car until the shops are reached.' 'One of the books in front of mine was 6*s*. I bought it, so mine would show' (E. L. BANKS, Autobiog. of a Newspaper Girl, 143). 'His ability to state them so everybody easily understood his meaning' (IDA M. TARBELL, Owen D. Young, 249). 'He desires to enlarge them [i.e. profits] by scientific

management so the share of labor may be increased' (A. T. MASON, Brandeis, 75).

Am. *every so often* = Eng. *every now and then*. 'Old Donal was employed by the Dominion Government to take a look at us every so often.' Compare also: 'A number of us had joined together for the purpose of studying the history of the art. We met once in so often' (W. D. ORCUTT, Kingdom of Books, 64).

soak has certain fig. uses peculiar to Am. It may denote *strike hard, pummel.* 'There was a grocer who didn't like the Elder's way of preaching. Wanted him to soak the Amalekites in his sermons, and to leave the grocery business alone' (G. H. LORIMER, Old Gorgon Graham, 14). 'A Communist, grabbing apples from an unemployed apple vendor, soaks the policemen with them' (E. WILSON, The Am. Jitters, 44).

It may also mean *charge exorbitantly, swindle.* An Am. paper relates how a foreign prince, visiting N.Y., is charged $1,000 by a dentist for a few hours' work. He pays the bill without complaint, but some of his friends tell him he has been soaked and persuade him to bring the matter to the attention of a consul.

†**soap-box.** An empty box is often a convenient pedestal for a propagandist in the open air, and the *soapbox* has been adopted in Am. as the symbol of this type of public speaking. 'He sees the dream of the soapbox orator in process of fulfillment.' 'Soap-box orators denounced the Government, the capitalists, the police' (H. JUSTIN SMITH, Chicago, 239). 'In nearly every open forum of the country and from most of the soap boxes one hears the same slogans and shibboleths' (E. B. CHAFFEE, The Protestant Churches and the Industrial Crisis, 158).

Hence the verb *soapbox* and the derivative *soap-boxer* = Eng. *tubthumper*. 'When still in her teens, she soapboxed on street corners in

N.Y.' (L. ADAMIC, Dynamite, 161).
'He did not have to listen to the
polemics of soap-boxers in order to
realize that a civilization which reduced men and women to such levels
of degradation should not be permitted to survive' (V. F. CALVERTON,
The Liberation of Am. Lit. 419).

sociable. In Eng. the adj. *social* is
sometimes used as a noun, to denote
a social gathering, esp. one arranged
by a church or other organization.
In Am. *sociable* is preferred for this
purpose. 'All the clergy present
favored entertainments, sociables,
and receptions for which admission
is not charged.' 'Church sociables
and hayrack rides varied the monotony of winter' (H. JUSTIN SMITH,
Chicago, 112). 'One marked feature
of their life in Washington was the
Sunday evening sociables at the
White House, when Cabinet officers
and other dignitaries would come in
and pass a couple of hours singing
hymns, with light conversation between' (F. E. LEUPP, Walks About
Washington, 221).

soft. In Am. a non-alcoholic
beverage is commonly called a *soft
drink.* 'The object of his remarks
went into the adjoining room, where
drinks, mostly "soft", were being
served. Both of them took ginger
ale.' 'The Italians consider a wedding
at which there is no wine for drinking
the health of the bride to be an absolutely unnatural affair, and the substitute of "soft drinks" to be most
unsatisfactory' (JANE ADDAMS, Second 20 Years of Hull-House, 228).
'The shares of soft drink concerns
were selling on a basis to yield half
as much as the obligations of the
U.S. government' (B. H. BECKHART,
N.Y. Money Market, iv. 96).
  See HARD, and also COAL and PEDAL.

solicitor. Lawyers have long since
become hardened to gibes at their
profession, but they may reasonably
think the joke is being carried too
far when they find Bruno Lasker

saying (Filipino Immigration, 391)
that one object of a careful watch
over outsiders visiting the plantations
in Hawaii is 'to keep out solicitors,
labor agitators, and immoral women.'
The offensiveness of this statement is
transferred to another occupation
when one learns the difference between an Eng. and an Am. *solicitor.*
In Eng. he is a legal practitioner who
advises clients and instructs barristers,
but does not appear as an advocate
exc. in the lower courts. In Am. he
is a person who solicits business or
help of any kind—an advertising
agent, a canvasser, or even a beggar.
'No Solicitors or Peddlers Allowed in
This Building' is a notice that one may
frequently see outside an Am. office.
  Thus a guide-book informs visitors
to Boston that on all important trains
entering the city from a distance
'there will be found a responsible
solicitor through whom baggage may
be sent to any part of the city'.
'President McCall of the New York
Life declared that, to increase the
business of the companies, good
solicitors must be obtained, and that,
to obtain good solicitors, large commission must be paid.' 'It would be
easier for all classes of publications
to hold their advertisers if the solicitors did not paint the prospect so
rosily. Most solicitors promise altogether too much.' 'A woman was
indicted under the Espionage Act for
a discourteous reception to a Red
Cross solicitor' (L. SYMES and T.
CLEMENT, Rebel Am. 301).
  The legal associations of the word
solicitor are retained, however, in the
title of the *solicitor-general* of the
U.S., who is the second officer of
the Department of Justice. He assists
the attorney-general, and usually
takes charge of Government cases in
the Supreme Court. In some of the
States the chief law officer is called
solicitor-general.

Solon. In Am. to apply this term to
a legislator is by no means to pay
him an esp. high compliment, for the

newspapers have come to use it freely of any member of Congress. 'Civic Body Offers Aid to New Solons' is the heading, in a Washington paper, of a report of the welcome to be given by the Washington Board of Trade to new members of Congress. A Springfield (Massachusetts) paper announces the death of two members of Congress under the heading 'Two Solons Die at the Capital'.

some is in Am., as in Scottish dial., a frequent substitute for *somewhat, to some extent.* 'The sea had gone down some during the night.' 'Bryan Some Better' (Newspaper headline). 'The Western boy has the grit and the intelligence, even if he may have lacked some in the atmosphere of culture at home.' 'These men helped matters some' (L. STEFFENS, The Shame of the Cities, 237).

The word has also a laudatory use. 'I call that some picture' means 'I call that something like a picture', 'I call that a fine picture'. 'Furthermore, Dern [former Governor of Utah] is a Congregationalist in Salt Lake City, which is controlled by Mormons! Some record!' (R. W. BABSON, Washington and the Revolutionists, 172). For an acute comment on this difference betw. Eng. and Am. usage, see the chapter entitled 'Is the Atlantic Narrowing?' in Mr. G. K. Chesterton's *What I Saw in Am.*

sooner enjoys in Am. the rare distinction of being a comparative adv. that is sometimes used as a noun. It may denote a man who, when a territory is thrown open for settlement, endeavours to stake out a claim before the appointed date. 'Although the Uintah Indian reservation is not to be thrown open for settlement until next March, prospective settlers are already beginning to camp on its boundaries and trouble with "sooners" is expected.' 'It's like what happened at the opening of Oklahoma Territory. Be-

fore the day set by the government when they were all to start fair in their race for farms, a band of adventurers called "sooners" smuggled themselves across the line. When the bona fide settler arrived on his quarter section, he found an independent sooner in possession' (Dr. S. McC. CROTHERS, The Pardoner's Wallet, 86). 'Two of my friends were on the famous dash for settlement across the frontier—one shot a "sooner" but kept his claim' (F. J. STIMSON, My U.S. 184).

It is interesting, by the way, to note that this Am. usage does not exhaust the capacity of the word to meet a special need, for it was employed in a peculiar sense by the members of a British Antarctic Expedition in 1902. In writing home about a trial trip for the testing of their dogs, Dr. Edward Wilson says: 'We took two pullers and two "sooners" as they are called. Why? because they'd sooner do anything than pull.'

sound. In Eng. in financial matters, *sound* is a synonym of *solvent* or *safe;* e.g. 'the banks are sound', 'I am afraid that is not a sound investment'. In Am. the word came into use at the time of W. J. Bryan's bimetallist agitation as a question-begging epithet for the orthodox doctrine of the currency. 'The latter running as a Tammany and sound-money Dem.' 'The Fabians have been in favor of what is called with us sound currency' (Prof. R. T. ELY, Evolution of Industrial Society, 482). 'Within less than a year the cause of sound money, and all that it stands for, was fighting for existence' (C. NAGEL, Speeches and Writings, i. 211). 'In 1868, both the Dem. and Rep. parties split between sound money and the "cheap money" heresy' (J. TRUSLOW ADAMS, The Epic of Am. 300). 'Past economic experience would seem to indicate that "sound money", that is, money that is redeemable in a fixed unit of value, is the best instrumentality of trade' (CASSIUS M. CLAY, The Mainstay of Am. Individualism, 223).

sour. The Am. compound *sourdough* denotes a person who has spent one or more winters in Alaska. 'This is a private enterprise, there being only two shareholders, one an old "sour-dough" from the Yukon, the other a Philadelphia capitalist.' 'Most of the settlements in Alaska are so new that it requires only two or three years for the "Cheechawka" to become a "Sour Dough Boy". In the vernacular "Cheechawka" means a tenderfoot—any new-comer. "Sour Dough Boy" is the euphonious appellation bestowed upon the veteran or old settler, and is derived from the curious custom followed to secure leavened bread. The Alaskan, when he bakes a batch of bread, cuts off a small lump of dough and carries it about in his pocket to keep it warm until he needs to bake again; then he uses the lump as leaven for the new batch, from which in turn he cuts another lump to be saved for future use.' 'A small number of white men lived in Fort Yukon. These men had been long in the country. They called themselves Sour-doughs, and took great pride in so classifying themselves. . . . The men who came ashore from the steamers were new-comers. They were known as chechaquos, and they always wilted at the application of the name. They made their bread with baking-powder. This was the invidious distinction between them and the Sour-doughs, who, forsooth, made their bread from sour dough because they had no baking-powder' (JACK LONDON, White Fang, 186).

spa is sometimes used in New Eng. to denote a drug-store or other place where SOFT drinks are served. 'I took him into the nearest spa and gave him a glass of orange phosphate' is a quotation from a Boston paper.

space. In Am. a *space writer* or *space man* is a journalist who does not receive a salary but is paid at *space rates,* i.e. according to the space occupied by his contributions. He differs from a *free lance* in being definitely engaged to work for a particular paper. 'Most of his editors and space writers also retire.' 'The early reports of the storm which went abroad were telegraphed by newspaper men on the spot, who colored their reports in order to command space rates.' 'Though he was always on space compensation his prolific pen brought him moderate wealth' (Dict. Am. Biog. viii. 475). 'I was put among a crowd of "space men" employed to help out the regular salaried reporters' (W. H. RIDEING, Many Celebrities, 41).

spark. Am. *spark guard* = Eng. *fire guard.* 'Fire Irons and Brasses, Spark Guards, &c.' (Advt.).
Am. *spark plug* = Eng. *sparking plug.* 'The motorist might sally forth for the day without fear of being crippled by a dead spark plug' (F. L. ALLEN, Only Yesterday, 161). 'Some applicants for the job of repair thought the trouble was in the spark plugs' (G. SOULE, The Coming Am. Revolution, 190).

spat. In Am. this word means not only a *splash* of something, e.g. of rain, but also a *tiff,* or *slight quarrel.* 'Roosevelt and Spring Rice, both with sharp tongues and irascible natures, had many a spat together in the days when the former was still a Civil Service Commissioner and the latter a Second Secretary. But their friendship never wavered' (L. EINSTEIN, Roosevelt, 134). 'Morley and Carnegie would have their spats, like quarrelling schoolboys' (B. J. HENDRICK, Life of Andrew Carnegie, 516).

speakeasy. There is a general impression in Eng. that this curious Am. compound, denoting an *illicit drinking-place,* is a coinage of the Prohibition era. The word was, however, in common use long before the passing of the 18th Amendment. 'Persons against whom warrants had been issued for keeping disorderly houses, speakeasies, and other notorious resorts' is a quotation from a Philadelphia newspaper of 1904, and other examples might easily be found in the press of the time.

Speaker. The House of Representatives at Washington has borrowed from the House of Commons the term *Speaker* as the title of its presiding officer. In two respects, however, there is a notable difference of function. (1) In Am. the term naturally lacks the historical signification it has at Westminster, where the Speaker is so called because he is the mouthpiece of the House in its communications with the Sovereign. (2) The connotation of the term is also radically different in the two Houses. In Eng. the Speaker is a symbol of neutrality and impartiality. In Am., on the other hand, he is an avowedly partisan officer, elected by the majority party and expected to promote its interests by assigning to its members special privileges in committee assignments, recognition, and other matters affecting legislation.

special. A *special bill* in Congress corresponds roughly to a *private bill* in the House of Commons. 'Some of the measures [laid before Congress] are general in nature; these we may call "public bills". Others pertain to particular persons, localities, or claims; these are "special bills"' (C. A. and W. BEARD, The Am. Leviathan, 178).

In Post Office terminology Am. *special delivery* = Eng. *express delivery.* 'I felt like a parcel marked "Special Delivery—Rush".' 'It is a simple matter to go to a post office and purchase and apply a "special delivery" stamp, yet that service is one of the important facilities of the post office' (C. KELLY, U.S. Postal Policy, 176). 'Will you not write the letter to-morrow and send it by special delivery?' (Intimate Papers of Col. House, ii. 350). See EXPRESS.

†**speed.** In Am. the compound *speedway* has been coined to denote a road so constructed as to be suitable for fast traffic. 'The owners of rapid roadsters are devoting no inconsiderable portion of their summer leisure to spirited brushes on the new speedway.' 'He hurried across the white glare of the speedway into the river-garden' (FLORENCE CONVERSE, Efficiency Expert, 65).

spell. The *O.E.D.* gives a quotation from Raleigh, dated 1595, as an example of the use of *spell = relieve* (another person) *by taking a turn at some work.* This use is now confined to Am. 'James C. Marriott, the N.Y. Senate stenographer, and W. A. Jones spelled each other in taking Mr. Hughes's speeches.' 'I was deputed to go on at ten; Davis spelled me at lunch; and Busk went on at tea time' (F. J. STIMSON, My U.S. 68).

For the origin and meaning of the Am. compound *spellbinder,* see the following quotation from a Cleveland newspaper. 'There are two classes of orators in a national campaign—the speakers and the spellbinders. The speakers are men of position who give their services to the committee; men of eminence, who perhaps hold office or expect to, whose services are free, and who are assigned only to important engagements. The spellbinder receives his name from the fact that his friends always describe him as having "held his audience spellbound" on this occasion or on that. He is a man possessing a good flow of language, much atmospheric power, and well posted as to the issues of the campaign. In many cases a young lawyer who needs the money while waiting for the clients who are coming, or an old lawyer who needs the money because his clients have departed.' This distinction between the two types of political oratory is implied in the following comment by a Springfield paper on a speech of Theodore Roosevelt's: 'Col. Roosevelt has made his expected address in Boston to a large and enthusiastic audience, but it was chiefly notable beyond this for the absence of any reference to the policies of the new nationalism. Indeed it was an effort such as any partisan spellbinder might have made, warmly eulogistic of Governor Draper and Senator Lodge but not progressive in a way to interfere with such advocacy.' 'The national committee generally maintains a special bureau which prepares a list of available statesmen and "spellbinders". These orators are of every rank, from the person with the strong voice who can harangue a crowd on a street corner to the finished speaker whose very name will draw multitudes' (C. A. and W. BEARD, The Am. Leviathan, 235).

The verb *spellbind* appears to have been created by back-formation from *spellbinder*. 'Campaign spellbinders are warned that in the coming campaign they must either travel and spellbind at their own expense or remain at home with their surging eloquence pent up in their own bosoms.' 'There will be plenty of resounding political appeal this week, with both Governor Guild and Candidate Moran spellbinding every night.'

spindle. In Am. this word has certain spec. uses. It may denote the skewer on which MSS. or proof sheets are impaled in a newspaper office. In Eng. this implement is called a *spike*. 'If he wants the article, he puts it on a spindle or in a pigeonhole' (E. L. BANKS, Autobiog. of a Newspaper Girl, 194).

It may also denote 'a round, usually iron pile or pipe placed on a rock or shoal as an aid to navigation' (Webster). 'During the last week some of the visitors awoke one morning to see a man a short distance off shore apparently standing on the water and driving nails into the sea. What this man was really doing was simply placing a spindle on Magazine Rock. Magazine is a large boulder

directly off the point which is often seen at low tide, but at high water becomes a dangerous obstacle to all sailors, and which should long ago have been marked.'

spiritual, which in Eng. is an adj. only, is in Am. a noun also, denoting a religious song, sung by the Negroes. The *spiritual* is not a hymn, but a song of a spec. type, such as 'Swing low, sweet chariot' and 'Roll, Jordan, roll'. 'Until recently the prevailing opinion was that the spirituals were, of all Negro songs, the most distinctive, because they grew out of the Negro's trials and tribulations in slavery.... Now it has been discovered that the structure, the ideology, in fact, the whole complex of factors making up the spirituals, were borrowed from the revival songs of the common white people' (GUY B. JOHNSON, in Culture in the South, 550). See also SECULAR.

spit. The Am. compound *spitball* is defined by Webster as 'paper chewed and rolled into a ball to be thrown as a missile'. The word is often used fig. 'Their vitriolic comments on the floor of the national legislature and in the press consisted chiefly of mere verbal spitballs thrown in a prevailing mood of political sabotage' (W. G. McADOO, Crowded Years, 225).

spite. The meaning of the Am. term *spite fence* will be sufficiently understood from the following quotations. 'A "spite fence" was hurried into place last evening separating the Commerce building from the Traders', the Imperial, and the Western Union buildings on the north. Instead of a wide court flanked on the south by buffets, cages and safety deposit vaults the tenants of the north side will find this morning a solid iron railing 8 feet high and 90 feet long. And it is a long walk around. "It is built simply to protect our property rights" was the declaration of the owners of the Traders' and Imperial buildings. "It is built because all the trade in this neighbourhood was coming to the Commerce tenants" insisted the agent of the Commerce.' 'To protect his place at Atlantic City, Mr. Vare engaged in a long legal battle with A. S. Lambert who erected a spite fence on a narrow strip of ground which separated the Vare place from the ocean' (Dr. H. ZINK, City Bosses in the U.S. 226).

spoils has a spec. use in Am. politics, esp. in the term *spoils system.* 'In a strict sense the spoils system is defined as the practice of filling public offices in consideration of partizan service rather than of merit, but in a broader sense the term connotes any improper or illegal use of public position for political or personal purposes' (C. C. MAXEY, Outline of Municipal Government, 76). 'It was not till the introduction of the so-called spoils system into the national government in Jackson's administration that the principle was adopted of systematically displacing federal employees of all kinds because they did not agree in politics with the president for the time being' (Prof. A. B. HART, Actual Government, 287). 'The wholesale introduction of the spoils system [by Jackson] demoralized the federal administrative service as a whole, and established a baneful precedent which continued to be more or less regularly followed until the present civil service law began the substitution of a merit svstem' (Dr. W. MacDONALD, Three Centuries of Am. Democracy, 147).

Hence *spoilsman.* 'However excellent such a scheme may be in theory, it is impossible of execution in practice without turning the army over to political spoilsmen.' 'The party system, when turned over to spoilsmen, makes government merely an agency of priests of prosperity' (W. A. WHITE, Masks in a Pageant, 315).

spool. In Eng. a weaver's yarn, or a photographic film, or a typewriter ribbon, or an angler's line may be wound on a *spool.* In Am. the word is also used, in the term *spool of thread,* to denote what in Eng. is called a *reel of cotton.* 'Wildly hoping that she [a cardinal bird] might want to build again, I dropped my work, snatched up a spool of thread, and hurried outside to tempt her.' 'A farmer's wife can hardly buy three spools of thread with the money received from the sale of a dozen eggs.' Acc. to Wright's *Dial. Dict. spool* is used in the same sense in certain Eng. dial. and in Scotland and Ireland.

spoon. For the meaning of *spoon bread,* see the first quotation. 'Virginia produced spoon bread, which one still sees on Southern menus—a soft batter bread, partly corn meal, which was baked in a baking dish. Instead of being cut with a knife, which would have made the delicate mixture turn soggy, it was dished out with a spoon.' 'It was time for me to speed back to the spoon bread and young broiled turkey that were being prepared for me now in Edith's kitchen' (M. P. CIMINO, in Life in the U.S. 27).

At Cambridge it was formerly the custom, on the day when successful candidates at the mathematical tripos were admitted to their degrees, for some one in the gallery to lower a wooden spoon as a present to the candidate who had taken the last place in the third class. Yale also once had its *spoon man,* who was awarded a similar distinction as the most popular man in the graduating CLASS (q.v.).

sport. In Eng. *sport* is often used as an abbrev. of *sportsman.* In Am. it has also a bad sense, usually denoting a gambler or a man of a flashy or dissipated type. 'He is not a sport, though a sportsman, and not a swell, though an epicurean. This means that he cannot spend his money on dissipation or ostentation.'

In an Am. department store, what in Eng. are called *sports requisites* will be found described as *sporting goods.*

'When Miss Applebee first introduced hockey in the U.S. she found it impossible to secure the correct sort of sticks even from the best dealers in sporting goods.' 'Acc. to a noted economist approximately a quarter of the national income is expended for play. The outlay for sporting goods alone exceeds $200,000,000 a year' (Prof. A. E. MARTIN, Hist. of U.S. ii. 773).

†**spotlight.** The glare of publicity is represented in Am. by the *spotlight* as well as by the *limelight*. 'In the drama that was enacted he was not in the spotlight at any time, but it cannot be denied that his was an important part.' 'If he [a diplomatist] sought personal glory and tried to keep a spotlight somewhere within reach, his negotiations would be likely to fail' (A. NEVINS, Henry White, 494). 'Already the spotlight, for the country at large, had switched to the impending presidential election' (S. H. ACHESON, Joe Bailey, 54). 'Under the spotlight of other revelations the separation of powers simply disappears' (C. A. and W. BEARD, The Am. Leviathan, 260).

spread. An expression peculiar to Am. is *spread on the records*, meaning *enter on the records*, without any suggestion of wide distribution. 'The law requires that the names of the members of the jury be spread on the records.' 'To this extraordinary power over railway finance and the money market, Wall Street added implicit belief in Harriman as a Stock Exchange speculator on an extensive scale. Achievements in that field are naturally not spread on the record as are exploits in railway financing.' 'Spread on the records of Congress is a letter from Ebenezer Hazard' (C. KELLY, U.S. Postal Policy, 25). 'The Senate retorted by denying the right of the President to protest and refused to spread the protest upon its records' (Dr. W. MACDONALD, Three Centuries of Am. Democracy, 152).

sprinkle. Am. *sprinkling-can* = Eng. *watering-pot* or *watering-can*, and Am. *sprinkling-cart* = Eng. *watering-cart*.

spur. In the vocab. of Am. railways the term *spur line* is sometimes used to denote a *branch line*. 'The terms of the law did not include train crews gathering up loaded cars from spur lines and placing them for movement by an interstate train' (Dr. M. C. CAHILL, Shorter Hours, 85).

squad. In Eng. rarely used exc. as a military or police term, but in Am. commonly applied also to a football or other sporting team. 'Reynolds, a halfback who played a fine game last season, has injured his knee, and has been told by Dr. Nichols that he must leave the squad.' 'Candidates for the rowing squad at Yale reported at the gymnasium this afternoon.' 'Members of the basketball squad underwent medical examination to-day.' 'His powerful physique won him a seat in the university crew and a place on the football squad' (Dict. Am. Biog. xiv. 154).

square. Eng. once had her *roundheads*. Am. to-day has her *squareheads*, esp. in the parlance of sailors. 'All North Europeans are known as "squareheads" or "Dutchmen", whether they be Swedes, Norwegians, Danes, Russians, Germans, or real Dutchmen.'

squat. The verb *squat* has a spec. use in Am., where it may mean *occupy land*, esp. without legal title. 'They [the "poor whites" of Virginia] squatted where they could and lived as they could' (M. D. CONWAY, Autobiog. i. 14).

Hence *squatter*, in a corresponding sense. 'U.S. Marshal Palmer found a disposition among the squatters to resist, as some of them had occupied the ground nearly 30 years and thought they owned it.' 'The district is a valuable tract of land on the Chicago lake front and is claimed by Streeter under squatter rights.'

For *squatter sovereignty* see the following quotation. 'His [Senator Douglas's] doctrine of "squatter sovereignty", i.e. the theory that the inhabitants of each territory should elect for themselves whether it should be free or slave' (J. TRUSLOW ADAMS, America's Tragedy, 131).

squint. The fig. use of this word, whether verb or noun, is now obs. in Eng. but is still common in Am. 'The application of a superseded section of the 14th Amendment, as squinted at in the Rep. national platform.' 'Some significant paragraphs in the daily papers, squinting at the possibility of a scandal.' 'In such a philosophy there could be no room for any hypothesis which even so much as squinted towards dualism' (HAMLIN GARLAND, Tyranny of the Dark, 123). 'A certain whimsical fancy, he complained, gave this reporter's stories both a color and a squint that often proved embarrassing' (F. F. BOND, Mr. Miller of *The Times*, 118).

squire. The *squire* in an Eng. country district is usually both a landowner and a magistrate, but it is in the former rather than the latter capacity that he is given that name. In Am. the *squire* is primarily a justice of the peace, but the name is loosely given, most commonly as a title, to any prominent resident in a village.

staff. In Eng., as in Am., a pole on which a flag is hoisted on shore is called a *flag-staff*. But when such a flag is lowered half-way in sign of mourning, the nautical term *mast* is adopted in Eng., and it is said to be at *half-mast*. In Am. it is often said to be at *half-staff*. 'Within five minutes after word of death reached the capital, the flags on government buildings were hauled to half-staff.'

†**stag** is used attrib. in Am., with such words as *dance, dinner, party*, to indicate that the gathering is attended by men only. 'A stag dinner was tendered the secretary of the company last evening by a number of friends as a farewell to his bachelorhood days.' 'One of Forrest's boys had a fiddle, and bringing it along, the festivities opened with a stag dance, the "ladies" being designated by wearing a horse-hobble loosely around their necks' (ANDY ADAMS, The Outlet, 232).

†**stage.** From the normal meaning of the verb *stage*, i.e. *place on the stage of a theatre*, there has developed in Am. the use of the word to denote the deliberate organization of any kind of incident of a more or less sensational nature. 'In combating rum-running, bootlegging, and illegal transportation and possession in the earlier years of Prohibition, Federal agents staged raids that revealed, &c.' (F. J. HASKIN, The Am. Government, 437). 'Attempts of Am. Filipino organizations to stage a demonstration at the bier of Tobera in Honolulu as it passed through that port failed to materialize' (B. LASKER, Filipino Immigration, 364). 'In a few years just before the disaster of 1884, the market, just as before the panic of 1873, was staging a boom' (R. I. WARSHOW, The Story of Wall Street, 207). 'Some of the farm organizations of the middle west recently staged something like a forcible rebellion' (Prof. IRVING FISHER, Mastering the Crisis, 20).

stair. Am. *stairway* = Eng. *staircase* or *stairs*. 'The guests of the hotel had begun to stream down the stairways and elevators.' 'Signs telling the tenants not to blow out the gas on the stairways and in the rooms' (K. BERCOVICI, Manhattan Side-show, 256).

stall. The verb *stall*, in the sense of *bring to a standstill*, is obs. in Eng., exc. in dial., but still current in Am. 'Some of the trains are stalled between washouts.' 'The highways became nearly impassable for mud. It was not uncommon for a heavy vehicle like a fire-engine to get stalled when it most needed to hurry' (F. E. LEUPP, Walks about Washington, 47). 'That lack of self-confidence which psychologists call our inferiority complex, and which stalls so many honest writers half-way along the road of their thoughts' (H. S. CANBY, Better Writing, 18).

stand. The noun *stand* has a few Am. uses unknown in Eng.

(1) The witness-box in a court of justice. 'The Assistant Postmaster-General took the stand this afternoon as a witness for the Government.' 'Morgan's view of the Northern Pacific contest was given a year later on the witness stand in a stockholders' suit' (J. K. WINKLER, J. Pierpont Morgan, 209). 'The defendant was not put on the stand in his own behalf' (O. K. FRAENKEL, The Sacco-Vanzetti Case, 14). Cf. CHAIR.

(2) Rank in marking at college. 'The highest stand man of the non-elective scholastic period was Dean Wright of 1868, who attained a stand of 3·71 on a scale of 4·00.'

(3) 'The stand (or frame, as it is called in Eng.) is an open framework of pine wood made to support the cases of type' (T. L. DE VINNE, Modern Methods of Book Composition, 5).

(4) A stall for the sale of goods, esp. in the street or by the roadside. 'Sometimes they can retail part of their production from a road-side stand.' 'There are others who bathe in the ocean, far from crowds and hot-dog stands.' 'The sidewalks littered with fruit and vegetable stands' (K. BERCOVICI, Around the World in N.Y. 16). Thus Am. *news-stand* = Eng. *book-stall.* 'The railroad station news-stands.' 'The paper-covered fiction of the news-stand' (W. M. PAYNE, Little Leaders, 64).

†The verb *stand for* = *be responsible for, countenance, tolerate.* 'Other Southern newspapers refuse to stand for the brutal lynching of the two negroes.' 'The bishop will not stand for such a marriage on the part of a clergyman.' 'The Alabama slave power would stand for no agitation for the restriction of the "peculiar institution", and Tharin was driven from the state' (S. D. SPERO and A. L. HARRIS, The Black Worker, 10).

A distinctively Am. term is *stand pat.* It is taken from the game of poker, where a person who plays, or signifies his intention of playing, his hand as dealt, without resorting to the draw, is said to stand pat. It is roughly equivalent to *sit tight,* and it is accordingly used to describe the attitude of a politician who opposes change, esp. a reduction in the tariff. The verb *stand pat* has given rise to the adj. *stand-pat,* and also to the nouns *stand-patter* and *stand-pattism.* 'It is now officially announced that the President will not summon Congress in extraordinary session to revise the tariff. That decision will undoubtedly stiffen stand-patting.' 'The Rep. party, even with its stand-pat doctrine, has learned that there is danger in upholding the principle of protection in its extreme.' 'The declaration on the tariff will satisfy stand-patters, but will not be agreeable to those who believe customs duties should be revised from time to time.' 'In 1902 he [Senator Hanna] declared himself the champion of that "stand-pattism" which soon carried all the connotations of reactionary politics' (Dict. Am. Biog. viii. 228). The reference in this last quotation is to the introduction of the phrase into the Am. political vocab. by Senator Hanna. For a full account of the circumstances and a discussion of the applicability of the term, see Herbert Croly's biography of him, pp. 417–19.

star. For *star route* see the following quotations. 'Another form of delivery is through Star route carriers, many of whom serve individual patrons along their routes . . . The appellation "Star route" dates back to the early Departmental practice of designating routes open to bids by asterisks in correspondence and reports' (C. KELLY, U.S. Postal Policy, 116). 'The persistent rumors of graft in the awarding of contracts to carry the mail over the "star routes"; namely, those on which the mails were carried by private contract in certain parts of the thinly settled West' (Prof. A. E. MARTIN, Hist. of U.S. ii. 178).

start. The intrans. verb *start* is often intensified in Am. by the addition of *in* or *out*. 'The college-bred man, who makes good use of his opportunities, starts in with an advantage.' 'Jackson shot Ambrister, and then in true Jacksonian style started in to take possession of the Spanish posts' (J. TRUSLOW ADAMS, Hist. of the Am. People, i. 276). 'The phenomena bear close relation to the inquiry with which we started out.' 'We have seen statesmen start out as radicals and end as conservatives.' 'It was one of those settlements that started out to be a big city and then apparently, for no good reason, stopped short in its career' (Prof. T. J. GRAYSON, Leaders and Periods of Am. Finance, 21).

State, Secretary of. In Eng. several members of the Cabinet hold the office of *Secretary of State*—for Foreign Affairs, for Home Affairs, &c. In Am. there is only one *Secretary of State*. His duties are primarily, though by no means exclusively, concerned with foreign affairs, so he is virtually the Am. *Foreign Minister*. 'Thomas Jefferson was chosen Secretary of Foreign Affairs because of his experience and acquaintance abroad, but the name was soon changed to Secretary of State' (E. D. ADAMS and J. C. ALMACK, Hist. of U.S. 267). 'His tastes ran to diplomacy, and Secretaries of State had given him numerous secret missions to both Europe and South Am.' (J. R. SCOTT, Colonel of Red Huzzars, 16).

The office of which he is the head is

called the *State Department*, which thus corresponds largely to the Eng. *Foreign Office*. 'Our State Department has ordered the Am. minister to Constantinople to do everything possible for the early release of the prisoner.' 'His tenure [of the ambassadorship to London] though diplomatically one of the most routine character, has been personally very acceptable to both our State Department and to Downing Street.'

stated. In Eng. this term, in the sense of *regular, ordinary, occurring at prescribed times*, is now old-fashioned and little used. In Am. it may still be met with. 'The stated meetings of the Committee on Admissions shall be monthly and shall occur on the first Monday of each month' (Rules of a Washington club). 'He became stated supply, and subsequently pastor, of the Presbyterian Church at Rye' (Dict. Am. Biog. x. 475).

Hence the adv. *statedly*. 'The provision of ways and means by which the irreducible minimum of unemployed may be statedly cared for' (Dr. N. M. BUTLER, Looking Forward, 118).

statesman. The *O.E.D.* defines a *statesman* as 'one who takes a leading part in the affairs of a state or body politic; esp. one who is skilled in the management of public affairs'. A similar definition may be found in the *Century Dict.*, which adds 'a politician in the highest sense of the term'. The word, however, may be applied in Am. to a politician in senses a long way below the highest. 'The reception rooms were thronged with the Dem. statesmen of King's County and many from Manhattan and the other boroughs.' 'Senator James J. Davis is contemplating the abandonment of his career as a statesman to accept a high position in the motion picture industry.' 'It was on entrance to Blackwell's Island to serve out the prison term that Mr. Tweed returned the now historic replies to the questions of the warden: "Occupation?" "Statesman"' (Dr. H. ZINK, City Bosses of U.S. 111).

station. Branch post offices in Am. are usually called *stations* (or *substations*). 'The Post Office Department has decided to establish a substation in or about Times Square. The purpose is to relieve the pressure of business on stations E and G.' Am. *station house* = Eng. *police station.* 'A complaint against a criminal may come to one station house and on the same day similar complaints may be received in other station houses.' 'In the station house we were presented with the warrant' (E. GOLDMAN, Living My Life, 443). 'He [Theodore Roosevelt when Police Commissioner of N.Y.] arrived one drowsy June afternoon at a station house in the lower part of the city, and interrupted the meditations of the sergeant on the desk' (H. F. PRINGLE, Theodore Roosevelt, 138). For *station agent*, see AGENT.

stay. †A use of this term peculiar to Am. is in the expressive term *stay put*, meaning *remain where*, or *as, placed.* 'The old blatant jingoism, which demanded that the flag should ever stay put in the Philippines.' 'The London Daily News has made the prediction that when the time comes to vote on the budget he will be in seclusion at his villa in Naples. But that is nothing but a radical fling at his lordship's propensity not to stay put.' 'Men of his breadth are peculiarly hard to label because they do not stay put in hard-and-fast compartments'(R. W. BABSON, Washington and the Revolutionists, 131). Analogous uses of *stay* are illustrated in the following: 'The Am. voter can be bought, but he will not stay bought.' 'The case may be regarded by some as a closed incident, but it seems that it will not stay closed.' 'Through Mr. Bryan's influence the Nebraska legislature has rejected a bill. . . . It is decidedly uncertain, however, whether that honorable body will stay hitched where Mr. Bryan seems to have left it.' 'Many contrasts are deeply rooted here, and they are going to stay rooted' (J. D. WADE, in Culture in the South, 628). For *come to stay*, see COME.

steady is a colloq. term in Am. for a *fiancé(e)* or *sweetheart.* 'Fifty-one needles have just been removed from the body of an Ohio girl, and her "steady" now ventures to sit on the same sofa with her for half an hour at a time.' 'We all know that Saturday means a trip to the nearest beach by trolley with a "steady", to the girl who bends over a loom during the preceding five days.' 'She earned enough to buy herself some showy clothes, and she had a lover, a "steady", as she called him' (MARY E. WILKINS FREEMAN, By the Light of the Soul, 41).

steer (noun). In Eng. a *steer* is a young male ox, esp. one which has been castrated and is used for beef. In Am., acc. to the *Century Dict.*, the term is extended to include male beef-cattle of any age.

steer (verb). A term peculiar to Am. is *steering committee*, which denotes a committee charged with the duty of regulating the business of the body that appoints it. 'The Rep. floor leader has called a caucus of the Rep. members [of the Senate] this afternoon to name a steering committee which will prepare the party programme for the winter's legislation.' 'It is apparent that the Senate steering committee has not found it easy to agree on a bill.' 'He had won the confidence of almost all his colleagues in the Senate and the warm affection of many of them. He was thoroughly established as one of the steering committee of the Upper House' (H. CROLY, Marcus Alonzo Hanna, 342). 'The majority leader [in the House of Representatives] is subject more or less to the direction of a "steering committee" chosen by the caucus for the purpose of exercising general supervisory powers. . . . Floor leaders and steering committees are to be found also in the Senate; their function, however, is not dictation; their business is to secure party harmony by informal methods' (Dr. C. A. BEARD, Am. Government and Politics, 265). 'I had been appointed a member of the Chicago Charter Convention of 1906, and was a member of the Steering Committee of that body' (Prof. C. E. MERRIAM, Chicago, 223). In his account of the Disarmament Conference at Geneva, Walter Lippmann speaks of 'a steering committee called the Bureau of the conference' (The U.S. in World Affairs in 1932, 230), and the same term is used by Col. House in connexion with the proceedings of the Allied Council at Versailles (Intimate Papers of Col. House, iv. 99).

stem. Am. *stem from* or *out of* = Eng. *spring from, originate in.* 'The policy of vigorous intervention in the affairs of the nations bordering on the Caribbean Sea stems from Roosevelt's administration' (Prof. A. H. QUINN, The Soul of Am. 131). 'The Bailey controversy in Texas stemming out of the Waters-Pierce Oil Company episode' (S. H. ACHESON, Joe Bailey, pref.). 'Clay's theory, stemming from Hamiltonianism, was that by means of a protective tariff manufactures would be deliberately built up' (J. TRUSLOW ADAMS, Hist. of the Am. People to the Civil War, 270).

The compound *stem-winder* denotes in Am. what is called in Eng. a *keyless watch.* It is curious to note that, while Eng. usage contents itself with a negative statement, telling us no more than how such a watch is not wound, Am. usage gives positive information about the method employed. A similar objection to negatives may be noted in the Am. preference of *radio* to *wireless.*

step. In Am. the verb *step* may be trans. as well as intrans., esp. in *step up.* 'It has stultified disarmament conferences and stepped up

military expenditures to ridiculous altitudes.' 'By the artifice of a statute, the law can be stepped up into line with the more urgent needs of the social order when it is strongly pushed from behind.' 'He stepped his engine up to 60 as they sped into the blackness of the night' (C. G. WILSON, Chinatown Quest, 1).

The exhortation *'Step lively!'* is frequently addressed by an Am. car conductor to passengers whose movements he wishes to accelerate. The Eng. equivalent would be *'Hurry up, please!'* 'Zeal for efficiency is all very well in its place, but this "step lively!" of the N.Y. conductor is enough to make anarchists of us all.' 'The passengers alighting at this station had just left the train, and the guards had shouted to the passengers getting on to "step lively", when the crash came.' 'When she was told to step lively on the trolley-car, her true self asserted its endurance. "I am not going to step in front of a team for you or any other person", she told one conductor, and she spoke with such emphasis that even he was intimidated, and held the car meekly until the team had passed' (M. E. WILKINS FREEMAN, By the Light of the Soul, 41).

The warning *Watch your step!* is sometimes given in Am. to persons entering a lift or alighting from a car or in other situations where a mis-step might lead to an accident. The expression has also a fig. use, where *watch one's step* = Eng. *take care.* 'Visitors to London must watch their step lest they transgress one or another of the thousand and one curious commandments that are imposed on residents.' 'If Cousin Sue writes a book of verse, Cousin John, who edits the book-page, had better watch his step in commenting thereon.'

For *step on the gas,* see GAS.

stick. The fig. use of *big stick* owed its vogue to Pres. Theodore Roosevelt, but did not originate with him. In

1900, when he was engaged in a conflict with the Rep. machine of N.Y. State, he wrote to a friend: 'I have always been fond of the West African proverb: "Speak softly and carry a big stick, you will go far."' (See H. F. PRINGLE, Theodore Roosevelt, 214.) This phrase 'afterward became his slogan in dealing with the governments of Europe and South Am.' (op. cit. 279). His first public use of the term was in a speech delivered in Chicago in 1902 when he said: 'There is a homely old adage which runs: "Speak softly and carry a big stick, you will go far." If the Am. nation will speak softly and yet build and keep at a pitch of the highest training a thoroughly efficient navy, the Monroe Doctrine will go far.' For the popular use of the term, see the following extracts from Am. newspapers. 'There is something in the rough-and-ready, short-cut, "big stick" policy of Mr. Roosevelt that appeals to the Irish temperament.' 'The armored cruisers Pennsylvania and California have left Panama, and will arrive at Amapala, Honduras, tomorrow, to swing the big stick over Central Am.'

In Am. any printed matter that is affixed by gum or other adhesive is often called a *sticker*. Thus an Am. newspaper correspondent, describing the revolution at Madrid in 1931, writes: 'Several youths hold armfuls of red stickers 15 inches long, while others rub sponges across the gummed backs of stickers and slap them against the cars.' 'The Supreme Court holds that a telegraph company is obliged to accept a sticker on a message intended to fix additional liability on the telegraph company in the event of delay in transmission.' 'James P. Kennedy, John F. Allen, and Frederick Hanks are the new board of aldermen of Greenfield. John E. Burke, who was to run on stickers, withdrew from the contest.'

Am. *stick-pin* = Eng. *breast-pin*; i.e. a pin that is merely stuck in as an ornament, as distinct from a pin that is intended to fasten things together.

'He is met by a keen-eyed man, dressed smartly and wearing a large diamond stick-pin in his cravat.' 'A dozen tie-clips and stick-pins' (ELLERY QUEEN, The Siamese Twin Mystery, 165).

still. The stealthy pursuit of game, which in Eng. is called *stalking*, is known in Am. as a *still-hunt* or *still-hunting*, and the man engaged in it is a *still-hunter*. 'Lacy, a seasoned sportsman at 22, had still-hunted many a deer.' 'Still-hunting is the only form permitted under the law, and the best still-hunter that ever struck the woods will not average one deer knocked down to five followed.' The term is sometimes used fig. 'In appearance the Baron is the typical titled foreigner supposed to be on a still hunt for the Am. heiress.' 'Although the trustees of the University are showing no concern regarding the election of a president, a still hunt has been organizing for a head for that institution and prospective presidents have been suggested for the consideration of the board. The utmost secrecy is being maintained in regard to the names of the men suggested.'

†**sting** is used colloq. in Am. in the sense of *overcharge*, *cheat*. 'Very often you may have the feeling that you paid too much for some book—in other words, you were stung' (Dr. A. S. W. ROSENBACH, Books and Bidders, 76).

stock. In Am. *stock* is the normal term for investments which in Eng. would be called *shares*. 'Perhaps they could not have publicly used their influence to check the orgy of stock issues.' 'Despite the efforts made by the enemies of the bank to prejudice public opinion against it and to prevent the sale of sufficient stock to enable the bank to begin operations, the stock selling campaign was a great success' (G. T. STARNES, 60 Years of Branch Banking in Virginia, 23). 'Issues of stocks and bonds have been determined by railway managers acc. to their own notions of duty and convenience' (Prof. H. J. Ford, Woodrow Wilson, 309).

The terms *common stock* and *preferred stock* correspond in Am. to the usual Eng. terms *ordinary stock* (or *shares*) and *preference stock* (or *shares*). 'At the time when the sale was consummated, the bonds and preferred stock were at par and the common stock sold at 50' (Prof. T. J. Grayson, Leaders and Periods of Am. Finance, 419). 'The controlling group, having the majority of the common stock, could redeem the preferred and retain control by virtue of their present holdings' (R. I. Warshow, Story of Wall Street, 261).

Am. *stockholder* = Eng. *shareholder*. 'It is impossible to run a corporation by discussion in a stockholders' meeting.' 'A temperamental genius, he soon quarrelled with his associates and later on with the stockholders of other enterprises in which he was interested' (Dict. Am. Biog. ix. 617). 'The management of the company was committed to nine directors, to be annually elected by the stockholders' (K. W. Porter, John Jacob Astor, 167). 'The Pilgrims soon bought out the English stockholders in the company which financed them' (G. Soule, The Coming Am. Revolution, 33).

Similarly Am. *stock-list* = Eng. *share-list*. 'Supposing he had seen a N.Y. stock-list of 1900 and had studied the statistics of railways, telegraphs, coal and steel' (Education of Henry Adams, 22).

The Eng. distinction between *stock-broking* and *stock-jobbing* does not hold in Am., where *stock-jobbing* means carrying out some *job*, in the discreditable sense of the word, in connexion with the stock of a company. 'The watering of the stock and other forms of stock-jobbing intensified public anxiety and hostility' (Prof. A. E. Martin, Hist. of U.S. ii. 223).

The Am. fig. expression *take stock in* is quite different in meaning from *take stock of*. One does not invest in enterprises in which one has little confidence, so this term comes to mean *believe in, pay attention to, set store by.* 'Political malcontents, in whose sincerity the voters declined to take stock.' 'I take no stock in the alleged precious "values" cultivated by aristocratic societies and destroyed in democratic ones' (E. Wilson, The Am. Jitters, 312). 'Mr. Wilson took no stock in these aspersions; he did not believe them for a moment' (W. G. McAdoo, Crowded Years, 182).

stockade. In the Southern States *stockade* has the spec. meaning of a *convict prison.* 'The county stockade is insecure. It is a wooden structure, with a wire fence about it not strong enough or well enough constructed to hold or delay escaping prisoners' (A. F. Raper, The Tragedy of Lynching, 257). 'Two lanterns hung from the wooden cross driven deep in the red soil of the convict camp stockade' (J. L. Spivak, Georgia Nigger, 1).

stoop. 'At Robey Street lived Kendig in a small frame house with a long stoop' (E. L. Masters, The Tale of Chicago, 235). Does this mean that the angle of the house was something after the fashion of the leaning tower of Pisa? Not at all, for the word *stoop*, as used here, is a variant of the Dutch *stoep*, introduced into Am. at the time when N.Y. was New Amsterdam. This stoop is properly the platform, if one may so call it, at the top of a flight of steps (i.e. the French *perron*) leading up to the front door of a house. Sometimes the word denotes the whole flight of steps. 'Sitting on a stoop, surrounded by small boys.' 'She ran up the stoop and rang the bell.' 'The U.S. has said plump and plain to Spain and Columbia, "You cannot fight on our stoop".'

Hence *stoop line.* 'Magistrate Barlow said the Captain had no right to station men inside the stoop lines. He must get inside the house to secure evidence.'

In Am. the verb *stoop* seems to be trans. as well as intrans. At any rate, it has a past participle, *stooped* = Eng. *stooping*. 'A tall, gaunt stooped man.' 'He emerged a white-haired stooped figure' (Dr. H. ZINK, City Bosses in U.S. 349).

stop. In Am. the verb *stop*, followed by *off* or *over* = Eng. *break one's journey*. 'The Secretary of War, who was on his way from Ithaca to N.Y., stopped off in Syracuse this afternoon and attended the meeting.' 'On the way to the convention most of the leaders stopped off at Fairview to visit Bryan' (M. R. WERNER, Bryan, 158). 'Passing through Albany while he was governor, I stopped over to pay my respects' (CHAUNCEY M. DEPEW, Memories of 80 Years, 220).
Hence the noun *stop-over*. 'On through tickets to or from the West, stop-over will be allowed at Niagara Falls, on deposit of ticket with the ticket agent at Niagara Falls Station immediately on arrival' (Advt.). 'At the station next morning four yen more than sufficed for a ticket to Tokyo, with unlimited stop-overs' (H. A. FRANCK, Vagabond Journey, 478).
Am. *stop by* or *stop in* = Eng. *call, look in, drop in*. 'Time and again he spoke of stopping by some day on his way to town.' 'While on a business trip to N.Y. he chanced to see the street sign of the Roxbury India Rubber Co. and stopped in' (Dict. Am. Biog. vii. 413). 'On his way to her hotel he had stopped in at the Luxembourg' (E. WHARTON, Here and Beyond, 228). 'When the neighbors stopped by, you heard nothing else talked of but that' (U. SINCLAIR, Manassas, 16).

store. In Eng. *store* has normally much the same meaning as *storehouse*. The Co-operative movement introduced the application of the word to a place for the sale of goods by retail; a *co-operative store* meaning a shop in which a co-operative trading society offers goods for sale to its members.

Then *the stores* came to be used of a large shop divided into several departments. Hence one came to hear of the way in which the small shopkeeper was suffering from the competition of the stores. This complaint would scarcely be intelligible in Am., where the smallest village shop is itself called a *store*, the word being practically = the Eng. *shop*. Thus, an Am. speaks not of a chemist's shop but of a drugstore; not of a book-shop but of a book-store. 'There are only two ways by which goods can be sold to the consumer; one through the retail stores, the other directly by the manufacturer' (E. E. CALKINS and R. HOLDEN, Art of Modern Advertising, 33). 'My father owned a farm some two miles out but was keeping a general store at this time' (HAMLIN GARLAND, Roadside Meetings, 1).
'A perfectly good reason for the difference,' explains Prof. E. A. Freeman (Some Impressions of the U.S. 63) 'can be found in some circumstance of early colonial life. In the early settlements a shop was really a "store", in a sense in which it hardly is now on either side of the ocean.' So, too, Prof. J. B. Greenough and Prof. G. L. Kittredge (Words and their Ways, 134) remark that 'this is not mere provincial grandiloquence, as is often supposed, but results from the fact that, when the use grew up, the places in question were really storehouses, as every "shop" in a new country must necessarily be'. See DEPARTMENT.
Hence Am. *storekeeper* = Eng. *shopkeeper*. 'The independent storekeeper is competing with the manager of the chain store in his territory' (S. D. SPERO and A. L. HARRIS, The Black Worker, 7).
Am. *chain stores* = Eng. *multiple shops*. 'Hotels and chain stores can take only a limited percentage of the total vegetable production' (L. F. CARR, Am. Challenged, 249). 'Small towns in the West, where the chain stores were threatening the retail livings of the local merchants' (L.

STEFFENS, Autobiog. 870). It is curious to come across a mention of *chain shirt stores*, which, of course, does not mean shops where one may buy chain shirts.

The word *store* is often used attrib. to distinguish articles purchased in shops from home-made or natural products. Thus *store bed*: 'Our beds were of spruce, and no "store bed" was ever so refreshing' (S. GLASPELL, The Road to the Temple, 260). *Store cake* and *store food*: 'A decent meal of pork, eggs, hot bread, sorghum, and store cake.' 'Louise patched their clothes by the kerosene lamp and they did with little store food that winter, for so much depended upon finishing the season clear of debt' (J. L. SPIVAK, Georgia Nigger, 23). *Store clothes = ready-made clothes.* 'He wore cheap store clothes' (ALICE HEGAN RICE, Sandy, 224). 'They dressed as the Mexicans in Arizona dressed—cotton shirt and trousers for field work, a suit of "store clothes" for dances, Sundays, feast days, &c.' (B. DAVIS, The Truth about Geronimo, 62). *Store tooth = artificial tooth.* 'The "store teeth" of to-day have become marvels of usefulness and artistic verisimilitude.'

story. When an Am. newspaper man speaks of a *story*, he does not necessarily mean a *tale*. It may be a piece of news 'copy' of any kind, even a report of the proceedings at a bankers' convention. '"Newspaper English" has come to mean all that is slovenly, wooden, facetious, or bombastic in written speech. It is not for nothing that fact becomes "story" in the jargon of the newspaper office.' 'Many papers carried a story which gave the impression that this was the only Gutenberg Bible in existence' (Dr. A. S. W. ROSENBACH, Books and Bidders, 17). 'The Committee [of the Chicago Rotary Club] proposed to contact Chicago newspapers and periodicals more regularly and to send them stories on general activities, interesting personalities,

incidents of the weekly programs, etc.' (Rotary ? 184).

straddle. In the vocab. of Am. politics the verb *straddle* is used fig. in the sense of the Eng. expression *sit on the fence*, and the noun *straddle* has a corresponding meaning. 'On the question to elect U.S. Senators by popular vote, eleven Senators answered yes, four no, and four straddled.' 'A compromise between free trade and protection that in Am. would be contemptuously characterized as a straddle.' 'The major parties almost invariably straddle major issues. They do not divide on prohibition, woman suffrage, the League of Nations' (Prof. H. L. McBAIN, The Living Constitution, 141). 'A frequent form of statement on serious questions is the so-called straddle—that is, a declaration which means anything to anybody' (Prof. A. B. HART, Actual Government, 97). 'A "hard money" Dem. was nominated on a "soft money" platform. The straddle ended any hope of winning' (T. BEER, Hanna, 59).

straight. In Eng. this adj., when applied to a person, means only *honest, upright, free from crooked ways*. In Am. it may also be an epithet for a politician who, whatever his personal character, is unwavering in his support of his party. 'They will put forward a straight Rep. for mayor.' 'There was an element of conciliation on the part of some, but an element of Parker men declared for a straight Parker delegation.' 'The Third District at Stony Point is said to be the straightest Dem. district in the State. It normally gives 22 Rep. and 140 Dem. votes.' See also TICKET.

It is not in politics only that *straight* is used as a synonym for *undiluted*. 'Franklin County Republicans vote their ticket as they drink their whisky—straight.' In the case of the drink, the corresponding Eng. term would be *neat*. 'The frontier scout and his men drank their whisky straight and considered all other tipples unmanly' (S. B. WHIPPLE, Noble Experiment, 10).

strap. The Am. term *strap rail* is defined by *Webster's Dict.* as 'a metal strap placed upon a wooden rail to provide a more durable surface for the vehicle.' 'The State built a road to Springfield in 1838. The road was built with strap rails on on wooden stringers.' In the early days of Am. railways these strap rails gave considerable trouble. They had a way of getting loose on their wooden supports, and the ends of them would not infrequently come up, as a car was passing over them, and get inside the car, tearing out some of the floor and proving very dangerous to passengers. The end of a strap rail that behaved in this fashion was known as a *snake-head*.

straw. The common saying that a straw will show which way the wind blows has suggested in Am. the term *straw vote* to denote a vote taken unofficially, some time before the election proper, in order to discover the trend of public opinion. 'The *Chicago Tribune* has taken a straw vote in Chicago to indicate the preferences of the voters, and finds a cheerful outlook for the Republicans. It employed professional canvassers, who did not tell anyone who their employer was and who took every precaution to ensure a fair vote. In this way it ascertained the Presidential preferences of 3,605 Chicago voters.' 'The *Harvard Republican* contains the result of a straw vote taken by that paper among the Harvard faculty, which gives Roosevelt a majority of six in a total vote of 66.' An exhaustive study of the subject will be found in a volume of 200 pages, entitled *Straw Votes: a Study of Political Prediction* (Columbia University Press), by Dr. Claude E. Robinson.

street. In Am. *the Street* is often spec. used to denote *Wall Street.* 'Though the Street has never received any direct information as to the identity of those now in control, it is generally believed that the latest combination is the purchaser.' 'Then dawned the ninth of May, 1901, a day which will be remembered on the Street for many generations' (Prof. T. J. GRAYSON, Leaders and Periods of Am. Finance, 464). Occasionally it has a wider application, as a generic term for the financial districts of other cities besides N.Y. 'The country at large is now thoroughly suspicious of and effectively angry with the Street to a degree never before known. . . . When I speak of the Street—meaning not only Wall Street, but State, La Salle, Montgomery, South Broad, and Carondelet—I refer only to the dominant class in the Street.'

strike. †'Unfortunately for him in this instance, he struck a President who knew him.' This statement does not, as might be supposed, refer to a personal assault. In Am. *strike* may be a synonym for *happen upon, come across, arrive at.* 'The heat waves from that stove were the most comforting thing I had struck in a long time.' 'We seemed to have struck a late season.' 'The prospective Yale graduates who were slated to "do" N.Y. under the protecting wing of Prof. Bailey struck town at 9.30 yesterday morning.' 'Then we struck federal officials, and they made trouble' (F. J. STIMSON, My U.S. 148).

In Am. political terminology a *strike* is a form of blackmail. A member of a legislature may introduce a bill hostile to some wealthy interests, not with any desire to secure its enactment but in the hope of being paid to withdraw it. 'Local Rep. politicians were surprised to-day when they read the reports from Albany that there was a serious intention of passing Assemblyman Wainwright's bill providing for local option. A bill of this sort has been before the Legislature for years, but it was generally considered a "strike" or a threat which was not meant to be executed.' 'A bill to reduce the fare on N.Y. City elevated railroads from ten to five cents was one of the familiar "strike bills", so named because its purpose was to extort bribes from the traction interests in return for negative votes' (H. F. PRINGLE, Theodore Roosevelt, 74).

The name is also given to a miner's lucky discovery of precious metal. 'Six months ago his time came, and he made a first-class strike down in the Southern Hills.' 'He was now cannily working a vein which had a streak of gold in it, and, like all miners, was just on the point of making a strike' (HAMLIN GARLAND, Tyranny of the Dark, 50).

The past participle *stricken* is now obs. in Eng. exc. in a few such phrases as 'stricken with paralysis'. In Am. it survives also in the sense of *deleted*, usually with the addition of *out*. 'The ward and precinct clauses of the bill were stricken out.' 'As a result of their telephone conversation the item was stricken out' (G. W. PEPPER, In the Senate, 91). 'In October the case was stricken from the docket of the U.S. Supreme Court' (O. K. FRAENKEL, The Sacco-Vanzetti Case, 182).

string is more commonly used in Am. than in Eng. as a synonym for *series* or *row*. 'Writing football and baseball news for a string of western papers' (E. POOLE, The Harbor, 60). 'In pioneer days Sheridan Road had a string of taverns' (H. JUSTIN SMITH, Chicago, 216).

What is called in Eng. a *bootlace* or *shoelace* is in Am. a *string* or *shoestring*. 'All kinds of strings for sale' is a notice one may see in a 'shoeshine parlor' at a railway station. 'The gopher dashed up to me at full speed and grabbed my shoestring with his teeth.' 'Young children on the streets selling matches, shoestrings and other trifles.' The name of *shoestring* may also be given fig. to a very thin strip. 'Roll together in a long piece and slice into shoestrings'

(M. ELIZABETH, War Time Recipes, 49). To do business *on a shoestring* is to attempt it with small capital at one's back. 'It was possible to put up a magnificent building upon the merest financial shoestring.' 'They told me that I could not hope for success unless I had at least $100,000 capital. "You can't do it on a shoestring", they told me' (IDA C. CLARKE, Uncle Sam Needs a Wife, 164). 'Shoestring theatrical producers' (K. BERCOVICI, Manhattan Side-Show, 267).

A fig. use of *string*, peculiar to Am., once puzzled John Morley. When he returned to N.Y. after spending the week following the 1904 election with President Theodore Roosevelt at the White House, he wanted his friends to tell him what a proposition with a string tied to it was. He explained that Mr. Roosevelt, when speaking of his declaration that he would not again be a candidate for the Presidency, had told him that he had tried to make this declaration as plain as possible, so that the Am. people would see that there was no string tied to it. A statement with a string tied to it is one to which some condition is attached—often a condition that is only implied, or one that would be likely to escape the notice of a casual hearer or reader. Thus, a newspaper remarks, in discussing a similar matter: 'The refusal seems to have a very strong string attached to it, and it would be no contradiction if he were to let his friends go ahead and make the most of a campaign they could, and, if he were the most available candidate, he could consistently accept the nomination.'

Here are some further examples. 'Woodrow Wilson turned the gift down. His defense was that the gift had "strings tied to it"' (D. LAWRENCE, True Story of Woodrow Wilson, 28). 'Money beckons and lures even where there is a string attached. And every national gift to the States is dangled upon a string. If they accept they must conform to the national requirements' (Prof. H. L. McBain, The Living Constitution, 57). 'Much to the mortification of the Cubans, we tied a string to their sovereignty, and forced them to add an amendment to their Constitution by which the U.S. could in part control their foreign policy and finances' (J. Truslow Adams, Hist. of the Am. People, ii. 258).

The beans known in Eng. as *French beans* are called in Am. *string beans*. 'String beans are not rich in nourishment, and may well be placed with the green or succulent vegetables' (Mrs. Rorer's New Cook Book, 321).

Another term peculiar to Am. is *string tie*. It denotes a narrow tie, of equal width throughout, which is tied in front in a small flat bow. This kind of tie is nowadays rather outmoded. 'He usually wore a black string tie, tied in a single knot with the long ends hanging loose.' (Dr. Rufus M. Jones, Haverford College, 62). 'Bryan in his professional black suit and white string tie' (M. R. Werner, Bryan, 181). 'He was clad in a long frockcoat of ancient fashion with a high, open, white collar and a thin string tie of glossy black' (T. J. Grayson, Leaders and Periods of Am. Finance, 268).

stripe is used fig. in Am. to denote a particular variety of opinion or type of character. It thus often corresponds to the fig. Eng. use of *kidney*. 'The passing of control in Am. railway enterprises from adventurers of the Jay Gould stripe to banking interests.' 'Cleveland was not the manageable sort of statesman that politicians of the Tammany stripe desire' (T. C. Pease, The U.S. 530). 'It is not well to have teachers all of one stripe' (A letter of President Eliot's quoted in James's biography of him, i. 249). 'The commission invariably consists of two partizans of one stripe and one of the other' (C. C. Maxey, Outline of Municipal Government, 92). 'Some of the first Stevens's grandsons, probably not being of the stripe

of religious fanatic or political reformer to breathe easily in that passionate province, transferred their activities to the easier-going N.Y.' (Edith Wharton, A Backward Glance, 9).

stub may denote in Am. not only a *stump* but a *counterfoil*; e.g. of a cheque or a theatre ticket. 'The stubs of current checkbooks give his financial history' (W. B. and J. B. Northrop, The Insolence of Office, 23). 'Letters, theater stubs, dance programs, photographs, and the like become fetishes' (M. A. Elliott and F. E. Merrill, Social Disorganization, 470).

subsistence. The term *subsistence farm* is one of the additions made to the Am. vocab. by Pres. Franklin Roosevelt's 'recovery' policies in connexion with his plans for helping the unemployed. It denotes a small holding in which a family grows food for its own consumption and not for the market. These farms are grouped together, with the houses in a cluster and the fields a little distance away. In some cases adult members of the farm household work part-time in handicraft factories of various types established in the immediate neighbourhood. 'Some of them [industrialists] therefore envisaged a large permanent residue of unemployed, to be cast off into the middle ages by being settled on "subsistence farms". Such a programme would be disastrous socially, and would also make impossible 1929 production itself, since millions of former buyers would be removed from the markets for industrial goods' (G. Soule, The Coming Am. Revolution, 220). An alternative is *subsistence homestead*.

substitute. In addition to its trans. meaning the verb *substitute* has in Am. an intrans. use, in the sense of *act as substitute*. 'The license to substitute qualifies the holder to act as substitute in an elementary day school.' 'The unemployed Japanese army was to man the front, substituting for the Russian' (W. LIPPMANN, Public Opinion, 133).

subway. In Eng. a tunnel for pedestrians, usually from one side of a street to the other or from one railway platform to another. In Am., an underground railway, whether at home or abroad. 'Every man on the train had a personal interest in the time made by the train, for it would decide once for all the rival time-saving advantages of the subway over the elevated road.' 'The kind of book which is heard of for a season above the din of subway travel.' 'For a time steam was the motive power on the elevated roads of N.Y. as well as in the subways of London.' 'The electrical power transmission system employed to-day in the N.Y. subways' (Prof. M. PUPIN, From Immigrant to Inventor, 286). 'The question of a proper fare on a municipal subway is symbolized as an issue between the People and the Interests' (W. LIPPMANN, Public Opinion, 235).

The Eng. *subway* is called an *underpass* in Am. 'All Springfield men and families returning from their summer outings have been doubly and trebly impressed this year with the need of an underpass at the union railroad station in this city. Bad as the state of things is to all who are familiar with the station and the trains, it is an even more flagrant scandal when experienced by strangers bewildered in a maze of trains, with the way to the station or to another train blocked on either side.'

succeed. In Am. a man may not only succeed another person in an office; he may even *succeed himself*, i.e. be re-elected or re-appointed. 'The Rev. Dr. Parke was nominated to succeed himself as Archdeacon of the Susquehanna.' 'The mayor is elected by the people for a term of four years. He is not eligible to succeed himself.' 'Tyler had the ambition to succeed himself in the presidency' (T. C. PEASE, The U.S. 354).

'Thrice after 1905 La Follette was elected to succeed himself' (Dict. Am. Biog. x. 544). 'Germany had first of all to vote on the question whether von Hindenburg should succeed himself as President of the Reich' (W. LIPPMANN, The U.S. in World Affairs in 1932, 133).

suck. In Eng. a person who is deceived by a plausible tale may be colloq. said to be *sucked in*. In Am. the victim himself is represented as sucking; i.e. swallowing too readily what is told him. Thus the Am. *sucker* = Eng. *greenhorn*. 'Showman Barnum's theory that a sucker is born every minute.' 'He liked to tell tales of his own smartness—to laugh at the work of suckers he seemed to meet everywhere' (J. T. FLYNN, God's Gold, 14). 'An expert at cards, who swindled "suckers" by playing stud poker and stacking the hands' (L. STEFFENS, Autobiog. 377). 'I am one of the hundred and ten million suckers who swallowed the hook of the British official propaganda' (UPTON SINCLAIR, Money Writes, 27).

suit. The legal term *suit* is sometimes preferred in Am. where *action* would be used in Eng. For examples, see under AMBULANCE.

sulky is now in Eng. an adj. only, being obs. in the sense of a light two-wheeled one-horse carriage for one person. This use survives in Am. 'Trained and shod in the modern manner and drawing the modern sulky.' 'Arion's record stood unbeaten for 18 years, and then it was lowered by a horse drawing a sulky equipped with pneumatic-tired, ball-bearing bicycle wheels' (G. T. CLARK, Leland Stanford, 358).

sulphur. The medicinal dose known to Eng. boys and girls (mostly of a previous generation) as *brimstone and treacle* is, or was, administered to Am. children under the name of *sulphur and molasses*. A writer in a N.Y. paper, recalling the administration of sulphur and molasses as among the memories of his childhood, says of himself and his brothers: 'How keen their appreciation of the tortures suffered by Smike and his fellows at Dotheboys Hall, when they learned that Mrs. Squeers's morning dose of brimstone and treacle was only their own spring medicine under another name.' 'The sulphur and molasses which with the coming of spring was always dealt out to us on the principle of three mornings in succession followed by a skipping of the three ensuing' (Prof. MARY E. CHASE, A Goodly Heritage, 83).

sun. The compound *sunburst* is an Am. term for a set of jewels so constructed as to imitate the sun with its rays. 'The sunburst is regarded as a valuable one, and consists of a large centre diamond with 30 smaller stones set in a double row around it.' 'It would be more logical to arrange the whole article in the form of a sunburst or a starfish' (J. B. GREENOUGH and G. L. KITTREDGE, Words and Their Ways in Eng. Speech, 260).

In Am., as in some Eng. dial., *sunup* and *sundown* are alternatives for *sunrise* and *sunset* respectively. 'By sunup I was six or seven miles from the hills.' 'Early the next morning he rode to the nearest elevation which would give him a view of his cattle. Within an hour after sunup he returned' (ANDY ADAMS, The Outlet, 172). 'Whatever credit facilities they may have in daytime, they start in at sundown to demand tickets.' 'Fifth Avenue was wholly blocked with a procession from sundown till late in the night' (L. ADAMIC, Dynamite, 149).

Though sometimes used in Am., *sundowner* seems to be not of Am. but of Australian origin. It denotes a tramp who arrives at a farm at sunset and asks food and lodging.

superintendent. In Eng. the head of a Sunday school is called its *superintendent*, but otherwise the term is used only in connexion with certain spec. schools, e.g. those preparing for

the navy or the mercantile marine. In Am. it is the normal title of the person responsible for the administration of a local school system. 'The localities elect boards of education, which in turn choose superintendents' (Prof. A. B. HART, Actual Government, 540). 'The functions of the superintendent of schools comprise the selection of principals, supervisors, teachers, and other members of the educational staff, the assignment of teachers to their duties, the regulation and supervision of methods of teaching, the determination of the content of the course of study subject to the restrictions of state law, the administration of discipline in the teaching force, and the responsibility for promotions among the teachers' (C. C. MAXEY, Outline of Municipal Government, 294). 'There is never any lack of doctrinaires among superintendents and committeemen to devise programmes that are calculated to destroy the nascent liking for literature that is the normal possession of healthy young minds' (W. M. PAYNE, Editorial Echoes, 154).

supervisor may denote in Eng. a certain Excise or telephone official and the word has a few other special meanings, but it is mostly used in a general sense. In Am. *supervisor* may denote an elected officer of a county or town having principal charge of its administrative business, or a member of a board that has a similar responsibility. 'He had been a supervisor of his county for 16 years, and for 12 years chairman of the board of supervisors. As a member of this board, he became well acquainted, naturally, with the farmers of his section.' 'We had the very unbecoming spectacle of boards of aldermen and county supervisors and state legislatures passing resolutions as to what Great Britain ought to do about Ireland' (Dr. N. M. BUTLER, Between Two Worlds, 155).

In Am. some of the larger school systems have *supervisors*, whose function it is to supervise the courses and the teachers, rather than to teach.

sure. The Am. exclamation '*Sure!*' or '*Sure thing!*' = Eng. '*Certainly!*' 'I sent for the chef and asked him if anybody could make that kind of a salad if he had the ingredients and knew how. "Sure!" he said' (W. E. SMYTHE, City Homes on Country Lanes, 198). '"Do you think she is sixteen?" he asked. "Sure!" said I' (F. J. STIMSON, My U.S. 144). The same expression is found in some Eng. dial.

Am. *would sure* = Eng. *would be sure to.* 'He had a scheme which would sure put us all on Easy Street' (R. CRAWFORD, in Life in the U.S. 256).

In Am. *surely* is often used where *certainly* or *undoubtedly* would be preferred in Eng. 'You surely have accomplished what I thought was impossible.' '"It was surely the first time that these two men met" Dr. Erdman recently wrote me' (J. KERNEY, Political Education of Woodrow Wilson, 163). This sentence would have been possible in Eng. usage, but with a different meaning; i.e. 'I cannot believe that these two men had ever met before', with the implication that the speaker might, however, possibly be mistaken. The context shows that Dr. Erdman intended to state it as an indisputable fact that they had not met before. 'He [a certain member of President Franklin Roosevelt's cabinet] married Miss McKenzie, who has surely made him a good wife' (R. W. BABSON, Washington and the Revolutionists, 207). It is not implied here, as an Eng. reader might suppose, that her wifely excellence has been, or is likely to be, challenged.

There is an Am. adj. *sure-fire*, which means *infallible, certain to succeed.* 'Each has tried to establish a sure-fire method of keeping his popularity fires working both ways.'

surface. In Am. a tram-car running through the streets is often called a *surface car*, to distinguish it from cars running on the Elevated Railroad or the Subway. 'It became necessary to call out the police reserves to force a lane through the crowd to permit the Third Avenue surface cars to move.' 'On streets leading to these ferries surface travel was blocked by heavily laden vehicles stalled.'

surrogate. In Eng. an ecclesiastical official, esp. one who grants licences to marry without banns. In Am. a civil judge with jurisdiction over the probate of wills and the administration of estates. 'The surrogate subsequently handed down an opinion, which in effect construed the will as being elastic' (The End of *The World*, 12). 'Surrogate James A. Foley settled the estate of Miss Ella V. von E. Wendell under an agreement which upholds her charity and church bequests and divides $2,125,000 among four distant relatives' (N.Y. World Almanac for 1934, 106).

suspenders denotes in Eng. attachments to the top of stockings or socks to hold them in place. In Am. it=Eng. *braces.* 'The dress of the public links is the dress of democracy. Suspenders excite no comment.' 'The colonel spoke without suspenders, and the manner in which he pulled up his pantaloons from time to time added much zest to his oratory.' 'Until collar and coat have been stripped off and he stands in suspenders and shirt sleeves' (Dr. H. ZINK, City Bosses in U.S. 76).

swallow. In Eng. the common swallow is *Hirundo rustica.* In Am., acc. to the *Century Dict.*, it is *Hirundo erythrogastra.*

swarm. In Am. *swarm* may be a trans. as well as an intrans. verb. 'Thousands were pouring from the tracks and swarming the cars.' 'Great crowds swarmed the streets and open spaces' (Senator H. B. HAWES, Philippine Uncertainty, 24).

sweat, as a trans. verb, is used fig., in Eng., where workers employed at low wages or excessively long hours are said to be *sweated*. In Am. it is a police term also. A suspected offender, or even a witness, is said to be *sweated* when the police use third degree methods on him to induce him to make the statements they want. 'He confessed, under sweating, that he broke into several offices in the Commercial Building to get the checks he afterward filled out with forged names.' 'The negro who is held at Elkton as a witness has made several conflicting statements, and it is believed that after a little more "sweating" something tangible will be gleaned from him.' This process is sometimes called the *sweat-box* method.

sweet. The Am. compound *sweet-bough* denotes a variety of apple-tree. 'Once he halted under the sweet-bough and gave one branch a shake.'

swing. The verb *swing* is often used fig. in Am., esp. in descriptions of political movements. 'The Democrats are making every effort to swing the State in the last weeks of the campaign.' 'The patrolmen are popularly supposed to swing a considerable vote.' 'Some doubt is expressed whether the President will be able to swing a majority to support his view.' 'He attended the sheriff's convention and swung his fellow-delegates for William H. Kern' (Dr. H. ZINK, City Bosses in U.S. 196). 'The Negro primary electorate was this time swung for Tobin, and Tobin was elected' (P. LEWINSON, Race, Class, and Party, 113).

An Am. alternative to *swing-bridge* is *swing-span*. 'Where lake captains used to bluff their way through old swing-spans while truckmen cursed and pedestrians waited' (H. JUSTIN SMITH, Chicago, 41).

switch is a word whose meaning would be understood by Eng. railwaymen, but it is in much more general use on Am. railways. It is the common term in Am. for what is called the *points* on Eng. railways. 'The cars run by gravity down the gentle grade, to be shunted by the man at the switches to the proper sidings.' 'The crush was reduced by putting on more trains at the Franklin Street switch and running them back empty to Fourteenth.'

In Am. the verb *switch* commonly takes the place of the Eng. *shunt* or *be shunted*. 'The two private cars of the army officers were switched from the Burlington to the Pennsylvania.' 'There is only a single track on the bridge, and the freight was switched to this track as the passenger train was leaving it.' Both the noun and the verb are frequent in polit. metaphor. 'Pre-election drifts, ground swells and last-minute switches are very real campaign phenomena' (C. E. ROBINSON, Straw Votes, 112). 'In the senatorial election of 1885, the Democrats switched their votes to him in a last effort to stave off the election of John A. Logan' (Dict. Am. Biog. vi. 295). 'He bolted the regulars and switched to reform groups' (Dr. H. ZINK, City Bosses in U.S. 207).

Am. *switchman* = Eng. *pointsman*. 'On Sept. 1 the pay will be increased for all trainmen and switchmen on the Illinois lines of the road.' 'The switchmen of the Michigan Central struck against the threat of another cut in their wages' (L. ADAMIC, Dynamite, 33). 'Paul, Athanasius, Luther, Calvin, Wesley were switchmen, who set the moving train of spiritual and moral progress on right lines.'

Am. *switch-tower* = Eng. *signal-box*. 'A slight blaze occurred to-day in an elevated road switch-tower at Myrtle and Hudson Avenues.'

Am. *switchyard* = Eng. *shunting-yard*. 'The commission changed the plans so as to provide for great switchyards at this point.'

There is another and very different kind of *switch* that also needs a note. As CANE (q.v.) has not the same meaning in Am. as in Eng., *switch* has come to be used in its place to denote an instrument of chastisement. 'The children of parents who

TAB   317   TAKE

are themselves too weak to use either the switch or modern methods' (E. Huntington and L. F. Whitney, The Builders of Am. 92). 'The willow switch was a dismal failure in attempts to discipline him' (Dr. F. T. Miller, Thomas A. Edison, 41).

Hence the verb *switch* = Eng. *cane*. 'She made him take off his coat, and switched him sharply on his bare arms' (H. Croly, Marcus Alonzo Hanna, 19).

T

tab. The only *tab* known in Eng. is a small flap or strip, as part of a garment. In Am. it has a different meaning in the phrase *keep tab on* = Eng. *keep check on*. 'It is customary for the best class of banks to keep close tab on their customers, and throw an account out whenever it gives evidence of anything wrong.' '"We see so many people that it's hard to keep tab," remarked the friendly platform guard.' 'How on earth do the owners of a freight car keep tab on it in its truancies?' 'After all, the newspapermen did keep close tab on Mr. Wilson's movements after he came to the White House' (D. Lawrence, True Story of Woodrow Wilson, 131).

table. In Eng. a motion is tabled when it is submitted for discussion, without any suggestion of its subsequent fate. In Am. tabling a motion is equivalent to shelving it or postponing it indefinitely. It corresponds to the British Parliamentary euphemism of deciding to read a bill 'this day six months'—a date which falls at a time when the House is not sitting. 'The Wyoming Legislature has tabled the inquiry; but neither the U.S. Senate nor Senator Warren himself can afford to do so. A senator ought not to be a skulker.' 'The matter was tabled, and the convention adjourned sine die' (S. D. Spero and A. L. Harris, The Black Worker,

26). 'Their documents may be presented and filed in the Congressional waste basket. Indeed, under a precedent now long buried petitions may be tabled without being referred to committees or receiving any further consideration' (C. A. and W. Beard, The Am. Leviathan, 60).

Although the meaning of the verb *table* differs in Eng. and Am., in Eng. the expression *lay on the table* sometimes = Am. *table*.

tabloid. An Eng. reader may naturally be puzzled at finding an Am. newspaper refer to 'the public's voracious appetite for literature in the form of tabloids'. For the only *tabloid* he knows is a drug prepared in a condensed form. In Am. it may also mean a newspaper much smaller than the standard size, and usually of a sensational type. 'The advertising significance of the large mass circulations of the tabloids.' 'The "tabloid" newspapers representing scenes far more lurid than the stage play' (Prof. A. H. Quinn, The Soul of Am. 196). 'The cars are packed with Negroes returning from work; some reading the tabloids' (Dr. C. V. Kiser, Sea Island to City, 27). 'A sample of preëlection sentiment derived from tabloid readers would give very different results than a sample taken from the readers of the N.Y. *Times*' (C. E. Robinson, Straw Votes, 90).

tag is often used in Am. where *label* would be used in Eng. Thus Am. *baggage tag* = Eng. *luggage label*.

Am. *tag day* = Eng. *flag day*. 'Feb. 22 has been designated as "tag day" in Alexandria, and the proceeds will be used to improve the children's playgrounds in George Washington park.' 'A tag day was on in La Fayette, and all the female beauty, eight to thirty, was out selling tags for the local hospital' (Dr. Franklin H. Martin, The Joy of Living, ii. 327).

take. Am. *take in* = Eng. *visit*, '*do*', *attend*. 'Not a few of the conventionists visited the South End ground and took in the baseball game.' 'As we left, we continued to take in the town, strolling by pairs' (ANDY ADAMS, Log of a Cowboy, 336). 'Occasionally he took in a matinee or a lecture' (L. ADAMIC, Laughing in the Jungle, 283). 'Mr. Miller took occasion to attend most of the President's public appearances in N.Y. He took in among others the famous Gridiron Club dinner in 1906' (F. F. BOND, Mr. Miller of *The Times*, 112). 'I left England for a week-end jaunt to Paris, to take in the Grand Prix' (ALICE ROOSEVELT LONGWORTH, Crowded Hours, 234).

In Am. a gentleman *takes* a lady *out*, not *in*, to dinner. When on a visit to Windsor Castle, the Am. Ambassador, J. H. Choate, writes to his son that 'the King took Mama out to dinner' (E. S. MARTIN, Life of J. H. Choate, ii. 272). 'He [Walter Hines Page when Ambassador in London] considered taking a duchess or royalty out to dinner was hard sledding. They refused to exert themselves in the slightest to keep up the conversation' (Intimate Papers of Col. House, i. 193).

tally. The verb *tally* is now used in Eng. in the intrans. sense only. In Am. it may still be found in the trans. sense, now obs. in Eng., of comparing for the purpose of verifying an account or a list of figures. 'Essex County had been tallied for them by the earlier estimates, but the returns when more fully counted up revealed a majority of 1,000 against them.'

tap. At Yale there is an annual event known as *Tap Day*, when the three leading undergraduate societies —Skull and Bones, Scroll and Keys, and Wolfshead—elect their new members. The day derives its name from the fact that a successful candidate is notified of his election by being tapped on the shoulder.

In the U.S. Army the name *taps* is given to the *lights out* signal. The term may also denote a similar signal at schools and elsewhere. 'At ten all the Grotonians [i.e. boys at Groton School] had sounded taps and were off to the land of Nod' (B. MOSES, Franklin Delano Roosevelt, 26).

The word *tap*, in the everyday sense of a cock through which liquid is drawn, is little used in Am., the synonym FAUCET being preferred.

tape. The domestic implement known in Eng. as a *bodkin* is called in Am. a *tape needle*.

tar. 'N.Y. found itself greatly amused by tar-heel O. Henry' (J. D. WADE, in Culture in the South, 626). The application of so curious an epithet to this popular novelist might puzzle any Eng. reader who did not know that *tar-heel = native or inhabitant of North Carolina*. The gibe may be due to the fact that tar is one of the principal products of that State, but its application is said to date, on the *lucus a non lucendo* principle, from an incident in the Civil War. In one of the battles a brigade of North Carolinians failed to hold a certain hill, and were laughed at by the Mississippians for having forgotten to tar their heels that morning. 'He has the name of being very hard on North Carolina negroes when they get in his court. It is said that he desires very little additional evidence after he discovers that a defendant of color is a Tar Heel.' 'Greensboro, N. C. Three hundred guests, including Republicans of prominence from North Carolina and other States, attended the banquet of the Tarheel Club here to-night.'

tardy. 'Too swift arrives as tardy as too slow' declares Friar Laurence in *Romeo and Juliet*. In this sense of *behind time, late, unpunctual*, the word is now rare in Eng., where it usually means *moving at a slow pace, sluggish, dilatory*. Even so, it is a literary word, not in common use. The Shakespearian meaning is retained in Am. (Cf. French *tardif*.) 'Don't shoot your husband when he is two hours tardy for supper.' 'Principal Mead said that different excuses for tardiness were presented. He felt when a girl told him that she was detained at home by the illness of her mother that he might well say, "Well done". This is entirely different from the case of the fellow loitering along the street, but they are marked tardy just the same.' 'All this brings recollections of the paternal roof, where tardiness at breakfast meant, perhaps, the loss of dessert, and bedtime an hour earlier' (J. CORBIN, An Am. at Oxford, 17). The punishment mentioned in this last quotation is not for dilatoriness in eating one's breakfast—as it would mean in Eng.—but for coming down late.

target. 'The crossing is unprotected by either targets or interlocking apparatus.' The only protective *target* known in Eng. is a shield or buckler. What is referred to here is a disk attached to a railway signal and indicating by its position, shape, or colour whether the points are open or closed. 'The target was against the Erie freight train. . . . As his train reached the crossing he stopped it. A moment later the target was lowered, giving him the right of way.'

tariff. For *tariff reform*, see the first quotation. 'At 70 years of age Mr. Chamberlain feels that he must lose no opportunity to advance the dear cause of tariff reform, which means in Eng. exactly the opposite of what it does in this country' (Springfield Weekly Republican, July 12, 1906). The biographer of Walter H. Page tells us that the Reform Club of N.Y. was organized 'for promoting tariff reform and similarly improving causes'. He then mentions among its 'guiding spirits' John de Witt Warner, 'a N.Y. Congressman who was one of the leaders of the fight for Cobdenism in Am.' (BURTON J. HENDRICK, Earlier Life and Letters of Walter H. Page, 198).

The word *tariff* is not used in Am. to denote a list of charges at a hotel or restaurant.

taxi-dance hall. See quotation. 'Accompanying this improvement of the public dance-hall, a totally new institution has arisen which has taken on many of its pristine and objectionable characteristics. We refer to the 'taxi-dance' hall, a dingy institution for public entertainment, which caters solely to male customers. Women partners, known as hostesses, are provided by the management and are paid by the dance. . . . Facilities for rapid transportation furnish the opportunity both to the patron and to the dancer herself to slip in and out of the twilight zone from areas of greater stability and a lower degree of mobility' (M. A. ELLIOTT and F. E. MERRILL, Social Disorganization, 638).

teach. Am. *teach school* = Eng. bv *a teacher, be engaged in teaching.* 'She was educated at the Wilbraham Academy and afterward taught school at Florence.' 'At the age of twenty she had had an offer to teach school in Harwich' (W. CHURCHILL, Coniston, 8). 'For a time she taught school' (Biog. of Mrs. Eddy, in Dict. Am. Biog. vi. 8). 'Before going to the University, he had taught school for several years' (W. G. McADOO, Crowded Years, 2).

team. In Eng. a *team* consists of two or more draught animals. In Am. it may include the vehicle they draw, and may thus = Eng. *turnout.* '"We are short a hand to-day", suggested the florist's decorator, "and I have got a reception on at the West End. Jump into my team and I will take you over."' 'Young Woman Thrown from a Team and Hurt' (Newspaper headline). 'People began arriving early from all of the surrounding towns. The larger number came in teams, but the street railway brought many.' 'I tried to hire a team; but no team was to be had on short notice, and I determined to walk.'

Teaming is restricted to mean transport by carriers' vans or heavy wagons. 'Through the shopping district

there must be room for carriages, street cars, and pedestrians, with as little teaming as possible.' 'The Employers' Teaming Co. has to-day 2,100 wagons making deliveries.'
In Am. the verb *team* is used fig. in *team up with* = Eng. *join forces with.* 'It was during the middle eighties that Carnegie teamed up with H. C. Frick' (Prof. T. J. GRAYSON, Leaders and Periods of Am. Finance, 412). 'Whetmore was not Rockefeller's agent, but a lawyer and independent promoter who teamed up with the Merritts and worked with them' (J. T. FLYNN, God's Gold, 314). Cf. TRAIN.

telegrapher. In Am. the form *telegrapher* is preferred to the Eng. *telegraphist.* 'The telegraphers who constitute the connecting link between the conventions and the great Am. public.' 'Telegraphers gossiped in dots and dashes over private wires' (H. F. PRINGLE, Theodore Roosevelt, 237). 'While still a boy Kennan developed expert proficiency as a telegrapher' (Dict. Am. Biog. x. 331). Cf. CYCLER.

tell. An expression peculiar to Am. is *tell good-by* = Eng. *bid good-bye.* 'A dozen of my students were gathered there to tell me good-by.' 'As soon as the country cousins had breakfast this morning, they made a straight line for the White House. They all wanted to see the President and tell him good-by.' 'Those who had been unsympathetic told her goodbye with tears streaming out of their eyes' (J. PETERKIN, Roll, Jordan, Roll, 113).

ten. The Am. game of *tenpins* corresponds to the Eng. *ninepins.* 'There was a rush of such overpowering fumes that the firemen were toppled over like tenpins.' 'It seemed almost as if the business world were a set of tenpins, ready to knock one another over as they fell' (F. L. ALLEN, Only Yesterday, 343). 'When a real crisis arrived, they were soon helpless and passed into the hands of receivers so

rapidly as to remind one of a game of tenpins' (Prof. T. J. GRAYSON, Leaders and Periods of Am. Finance, 20).
The feat of the player who knocks down all the pins at once is called a *ten-strike.* This word, like the name of the game itself, is often used fig. Thus, a Congressman is reported to have made a ten-strike by a speech which carries the House with him in support of the Bill under debate. 'Bob reported him as having made a ten-strike with the officers' mess, not being afraid to spend his money' (ANDY ADAMS, The Outlet, 317). 'Trollope made his first ten strike with "Framley Parsonage"' (Dr. C. R. BROWN, They Were Giants, 60).

tender. The verb *tender* is little used in Eng. except in legal or formal phrases; e.g. tender one's resignation, tender for a contract. In Am. it is much more common. 'As the Senator entered the hall, the first ovation was tendered.' 'The Rev. Dr. A. M. Dulles has been tendered the chair of apologetics.' 'He was tendered a public banquet in N.Y.' (J. K. WINKLER, Life of J. Pierpont Morgan, 96). 'The degree of D.D. was tendered by the University of Edinburgh' (G. E. MERRILL, Parchments of the Faith, 167). 'This group in 1872 tendered its nomination for the Presidency to Supreme Court Justice David Davis' (L. M. HACKER and B. B. KENDRICK, The U.S. since 1865, 297). 'It is painful to recall an injury which I once tendered her' (Prof. MARY E. CHASE, A Goodly Heritage, 58).
From the adj. *tender* comes the Am. compound *tenderloin,* which denotes primarily an *undercut of sirloin.* 'In camp we were rarely out of antelope meat, and even now my mouth waters at the thought of the delicious tenderloin' (C. H. STERNBERG, Life of a Fossil Hunter, 10). The name of *the Tenderloin* is applied to a district of N.Y. distinguished for its evil reputation. 'One of those antiquated cabmen who knew the Tenderloin in its

palmy days.' 'All these prospered in such a hotbed of evil as N.Y.'s Tenderloin, bounded by 24th and 40th streets and 5th and 7th avenues' (Prof. A. M. SCHLESINGER, The Rise of the City, 112). 'The N.Y. Tenderloin was a model of order and virtue compared with the badly regulated, police-paid criminal lawlessness of the Chicago Loop' (L. STEFFENS, Autobiog. 425). This label originated in 1876 when a certain policeman, shortly after being transferred to the West 30th Street Station, was asked how he liked his new assignment. 'Well,' he replied, 'I like it fine. I've had chuck steak for a long time, and I'm glad now to eat tenderloin for a while.' He was referring to the profit a policeman in such a district could derive from the protection of disorderly houses and from other illegitimate sources of income.

The name is sometimes attached to similar districts in other Am. cities. 'Portland is not a puritanic city. In fact, its tenderloin is extensive and worse than anything in San Francisco.' 'Innumerable charges for treats, lunches to officials, dinners, circuses, and visits to the Tenderloins of the various Texas cities.'

terminal. In the vocab. of Eng. railways this word is used in the plur. to denote the charges made for the use of a terminus, for services rendered in loading or unloading goods there, &c. In Am. it is also used, in the sing., as the equivalent of the Eng. *terminus*. 'A N.Y. street is scarcely safer as a playground for infants than a railroad terminal.' 'The traffic of the Erie road converges to the Jersey City terminal from six different branch lines.' 'Railroad earnings sufficient to justify the building of a great terminal' (L. F. CARR, Am. Challenged, 221). 'We must keep the trains running while we change the tracks and rebuild the terminal' (NORMAN THOMAS, America's Way Out, 151).

territory. This word is specialized in Am. as the legal term for an area of the U.S. to which such full powers of self-government have not been granted as are enjoyed by areas that have been admitted to statehood. At present the only territories are Alaska and Hawaii. They are to be distinguished from the dependencies, such as the Philippines and Porto Rico, which are of an inferior status.

Thanksgiving. An Eng. reader may naturally be puzzled if he reads in an Am. book of a *Thanksgiving turkey*, and he will get no enlightenment from looking up this unknown variety in a manual of ornithology. It denotes no special breed, but signifies the turkey which is usually the most substantial dish at a *Thanksgiving dinner*, i.e. the dinner which forms part of the traditional celebration of Thanksgiving Day. *Thanksgiving Day* (or *Thanksgiving* simply) is a national festival held annually on the last Thursday in Nov. It originated among the early settlers in Massachusetts, as a devout expression of their gratitude to God for preserving them from the perils of their adventure. Nowadays it is preceded by a proclamation from the President, in which he calls attention to the reasons which should move modern Americans to a recognition of Divine Providence. 'On this Thanksgiving, I like to think that many more fathers and mothers and children will partake of turkey than for many years past' (Pres. F. D. ROOSEVELT, On Our Way, 203). 'Preparation for Christmas starts soon after Thanksgiving' (J. PETERKIN, Roll, Jordan, Roll, 244).

A ludicrous misunderstanding of the history of this feast occurred shortly after the institution of the Rhodes Scholarships. A correspondent of the *Oxford Magazine*, signing himself 'Loyalist', protested in that journal against the holding of a Thanksgiving Day service in the Cathedral, on the ground that it was unseemly to celebrate in this fashion the defeat of the British arms. He was evidently confusing Thanksgiving Day with INDEPENDENCE DAY (the Fourth of July).

This confusion seems very persistent. On the morning after the Duke of Kent's wedding, which had happened to synchronize with Thanksgiving Day, 1934, a London newspaper reported that Covent Garden salesmen, in preparing to meet the special demand, 'had not overlooked Am. Independence celebrations' and had therefore procured large supplies of sweet potatoes and cranberries.

thank-you-ma'am. 'George Miller has a plan that, if carried out, may seriously impede automobile speeding. This is to place thank-you-ma'ams at frequent intervals along the public roads frequented by automobilists. It is impossible to speed with safety over thank-you-ma'ams.' What is this device which, while nominally so polite, is actually so troublesome? The *thank-you-ma'am*, only to be found in the more primitive roads in Am. rural districts, is thus described in another newspaper extract. 'To protect the roads from wash-outs in the spring and during the sudden summer showers, it is the custom to construct water-bars, familiarly known as thank-you-ma'ams, across the roads on grades. These serve also to give the horses an opportunity to rest during the long up-hill pulls. They are, however, the bane of the motorist's existence, for they are fatal to springs, if passed over at speed, and they are not conducive to comfort in riding under any circumstances.' The peculiar name is said to have been suggested by the fact that, when a vehicle passes over such an obstruction, the passengers bob their heads as though they were making a courteous bow. 'The broad, smooth turnpike without so much as a loitering curve to whet one's curiosity, nor a thank-you-ma'am to laugh over' (DAVID GRAYSON, The Friendly Road, 93).

That's right! In Eng. this expression is not used exc. (vulgarly) in conversation, where it is an indication of assent, equivalent to *Yes* or *Just so.*

In Am. it is the term by which members of an audience show their agreement with the speaker, and is thus equivalent to the Eng. *Hear, hear!* 'When he spoke kind words of the Bryanites and urged that they be given credit for what they were doing to elect the ticket, there was real enthusiasm and cries of "That's right!"' 'The President's address was frequently interrupted with applause and cries of "That's right!"'

theme may have in Am. the sense, now rare in Eng., of a *composition* or *essay* written as a school or college task. Cf. the French *thème.* 'The only relief a teacher can be sure of in reading themes is the amusement which comes from some colossal blunder.' 'No doubt his college themes and orations were solemn pronouncements on weighty subjects' (C. M. NEWLIN, Life of H. H. Brackenridge, 22). 'The students found him a rigid disciplinarian. Themes two minutes late were not received, whatever the accompanying excuse' (Dict. Am. Biog. x. 564).

thread. In Eng. *thread*, when used spec., denotes 'flaxen or linen thread as distinct from silk or cotton' (O.E.D.). In Am. it commonly denotes cotton thread. 'Upon such little things as good needles and thread the small merchant had built his reputation.' See also SPOOL.

thrifty retains in Am. the sense of *thriving, prosperous*, which is now obs. in Eng. exc. in some dial. 'The plants appear to be thrifty and perfectly free from the bugs.' 'The author skims from the cleaning of oil paintings to the way to kill evil odor or to keep a palm thrifty.'

†**thrilled**, as used in Am., often means no more than *excited* or even *interested.* 'There was no doubt that Owen Young was tremendously thrilled by the prospect of going with the General Electric' (IDA M. TARBELL, Owen D. Young, 103).

through. The difference between the Eng. and Am. uses of this word caused some confusion when the Anglo-Am. telephone was introduced. When the London operators put the question 'Are you through?', meaning 'Are you connected?', they were understood in N.Y. to mean 'Have you finished?' Similarly: 'The legal courts come into operation only after the police are through.' 'The socialist orators had reasoned out their position, and, when they were through, the conference showed that it was impressed.' 'The Negroes were waiting until the white people were through before partaking of the communion' (M. W. OVINGTON, Half a Man, 19).

This use of *through*, which is also found in Northern Eng. and Scottish dial., is esp. common in *through with* = *finished with*. 'He was most anxious to get through with his examination' (Note that this does not = get through his examination). 'The speaker hoped that they were through with revision of the Prayer Book' (i.e. that they would hear no more of any proposals to revise it). 'The ripeness of a society which had gotten through with foundation-laying' (H. W. MABIE, Backgrounds of Literature, 106). 'Vaguely we felt that we had left Europe because we or our ancestors were through with it' (J. TRUSLOW ADAMS, The Epic of Am. 373). One may find a Shakespearian precedent for *through with* in an utterance of Falstaff's (2 Henry IV, Act I, Scene ii). In one of his published letters, Matthew Arnold says he gets as sick of a certain lecture he has been giving several times 'as Lord Hartington is said to get of his own speeches before he is through with them.' An interesting question arises: was Arnold's use of this expression due to a reminiscence of early Eng. idiom, or was it an example of the ease with which one may catch the tone of a new environment? He was writing from Boston, and had then been in the U.S. less than two months.

throw. In Am. *throw down* is used fig. in the sense of *reject, defeat.* 'Even the Supreme Court will not attempt to throw down that proposition.' 'He had thrown down Shevlin in a financial deal while he was Controller.' 'He finds plenty of Republicans who are only waiting for a good chance to throw down Lodge' (i.e. to prevent his re-election to the Senate).

Hence the noun *throw-down.* 'A Camden preacher has secured water from the River Jordan for his baptismal ceremonies. This is certainly a throw-down for Camden's boasted water supply.'

Am. *throw in with* = Eng. *throw in one's lot with.* 'He had decided to throw in with us, but for lack of an interpreter had been unable to explain his coöperation' (B. DAVIS, The Truth about Geronimo, 10).

For *throw a scare*, see SCARE.

thug. In Am. this term is used to denote a *ruffian* or *cutthroat*, without any suggestion of his membership of the infamous Indian organization of assassins. 'The Republicans in Minneapolis won considerable sympathy by charging the Amesites with hiring thugs to attack them' (Dr. H. ZINK, City Bosses in U.S. 340). 'Any thug can readily procure a revolver by the simple process of going across the river to New Jersey and buying one' (J. TRUSLOW ADAMS, A Searchlight on Am. 109).

thumb. Am. *thumb-tacks* = Eng. *drawing-pins.* See PUSH.

thus. The expression *thus and so is* peculiar to Am. In Eng. either *thus* or *so*, by itself, would be considered sufficient. 'Most of us assume that we know why we stand thus and so in the tangle of conflicting faiths.' (Here the most idiomatic Eng. equivalent would perhaps be *where we do.*) 'The majority feel that if they did not do thus and so early in life, it is too late after a few decades have passed.' 'He made it clear to us that, on what evidence he had, an issue looked thus-and-so' (Prof. A. G. KELLER, Reminiscences of William Graham Sumner, 29).

ticket. The voter at an Am. election is seldom called upon to elect to one office only. There are usually several offices to be filled at the same time. The list of such candidates for these offices as are adopted by any party is called that party's *ticket*. 'There was no discussion of any candidates for any office exc. the head of the ticket' (i.e. the candidate for the most important office, whose name, of course, appears at the head of the list). 'The broad church ticket was successful in a stubborn contest over the election of delegates to the Episcopal Triennial General Convention.' 'If there are two tickets in the field in his city, one composed of honest men and the other of notorious blatherskites and criminals, he will not hesitate to vote for the blatherskites if his "party honor" shall exact it' (MARK TWAIN, Christian Science, 359). The elector votes a ticket, not *for* a ticket. 'A very large number of Democrats voted the Rep. ticket outright.' 'Thousands who regularly vote a ticket devote no thought or time to party debates and conferences' (Dr. C. A. BEARD, The Am. Party Battle, 14).

To vote a *straight ticket* is to vote for all the candidates of one's party. 'Franklin county Republicans vote their ticket as they drink their whisky—straight.' 'The avowed intention of the club is to support the straight Tammany ticket.' 'To vote a straight ticket, which is one to cover all the candidates of one party, the voter need only mark a cross in the circle set at the head of the ballot between the emblem and the name of that party.' 'They were initiated into the mysteries of Am. politics sufficiently to learn how to vote the straight Dem. ticket' (E. F. ROBERTS, Ireland in Am. 179).

To *split a ticket* or *vote a split ticket* is to vote for some candidates on one list and some on another. 'To vote a split ticket, which is one for candidates of different parties, the voter should make a cross mark before the name of every candidate for whom he desires to cast a vote.' 'Never before was there as much splitting of tickets. Thus the electors in New Hampshire chose the Rep. candidate for governor, but declined to re-elect Sen. Moses, long one of the most prominent Rep. Senators.'

A candidate runs *ahead of his ticket* if he obtains more votes than the other candidates of his party, and *behind his ticket* if he obtains fewer. 'Roosevelt swept the district. His Dem. opponent received only 1,989 votes to 3,490 cast for Roosevelt. Since the normal Rep. majority in the 21st [district] was about 900, he had run well ahead of the rest of his ticket' (H. F. PRINGLE, Theodore Roosevelt, 61).

tickle. In Eng. *tickled* has sometimes the sense of *amused* or *diverted*. In Am. it means rather *gratified*. 'This result might easily be brought to pass with the most sorrowful consequences to our national prosperity. Yet Am. protectionists appear immensely tickled over the development of this sentiment in Eng.' 'The President is vastly tickled over the prospect of seeing two more huge battleships well under way before his Administration comes to a close.' ' "Well, I s'pose Lily told you the news this morning?" she said, presently. "I s'pose that was why she wanted to see you. I s'pose she was so tickled she couldn't wait to tell of it." "You mean her engagement to Mr. Ramsey?" said Maria. "Yes." ' (M. E. WILKINS FREEMAN, By the Light of the Soul, 342).

The idea is often intensified by the addition of *to death*. 'Adeline is tickled to death to get Lily out of the way' (A New Eng. character in M. E. WILKINS FREEMAN, op. cit., 342).

tide. The compound *tidewater* is a common term in Am. to denote a coastal region, esp. in the South. 'He aspires to be the Rep. boss of the Old Dominion, from mountains to tidewater.' The word is often used attrib. 'The tidewater counties of Virginia.' 'The college was established at Ashland in the tidewater section of Virginia' (B. J. HENDRICK, Earlier Life of Walter H. Page, 51). 'The tidewater population of Virginia differed profoundly from that of the western part of the State' (MADISON GRANT, Conquest of a Continent, 73). 'But when Bill's mountain practice became demanding, Bill abandoned tidewater California without a pang' (G. D. LYMAN, Saga of the Comstock Lode, 50).

tie may denote in Am. a low-cut foot-covering of the kind called in Eng. a *shoe*. 'Latest Summer Footwear for Ladies. One-eyelet Ties in Dull Black Kid' (Advt.). An *ankletie* is a low shoe with straps fastening round the ankle. 'There is also a very dim and evasive memory of a "dame school", where I see myself sitting on a low bench in the company of three or four other children with brief legs, white stockings, and ankle-ties' (K. D. WIGGIN, My Garden of Memory, 5).

It is also the Am. term for a railway *sleeper* used for the support of the rails. 'The car left the rails and jolted over the ties for several feet.' 'Railroads were planned to connect these paper towns. Stock was bought before a spadeful of earth had been turned to lay the first tie' (E. D. ADAMS and J. C. ALMACK, Hist. of U.S. 436). In this sense *tie* is an abbrev. of *crosstie*. 'The consumption of timber for railway cross-ties.' 'Rails, cross-ties, replacements, and the thousand and one things that a railroad needs' (W. G. McADOO, Crowded Years, 466).

For *string-tie*, see STRING. For *Windsor tie*, see WINDSOR.

Am. *tie to, tie up to, tie up with* = Eng. *join forces with, associate oneself closely with*. 'These gentlemen have associated themselves with his fortunes because he was the likeliest man to tie to in a campaign which

they hope may bring them opportunities for activity and prominence.' 'The college must offer in its faculty men whom students can tie to, men who can evoke personal devotion and enthusiasm.' 'The practical assurance that he is to have a good post in the reorganization of the Rep. national committee may be the reason that so many fellows want to tie up to him.' 'When a representative has a navy yard in his district, it becomes his first business to make business for that yard. He can best do this by tying up with the other navy yard representatives on the committee.'

Hence the noun *tie-up* = Eng. *connexion, association*. 'This educational tie-up with religion is what has given fundamentalism its foothold in the South' (V. F. CALVERTON, The Liberation of Am. Literature, 109).

Am. *tie-up* also = Eng. *stoppage, deadlock*. 'The delegate said the tie-up in the building trades was responsible for this state of affairs.' 'An accident to one of the motor cars caused a tie-up of the southbound trains.' 'A dispute over the hours of labor brought on a crisis that threatened a general strike and a consequent nation-wide tie-up of the railroads' (W. G. McADOO, Crowded Years, 450). There is a corresponding verb *tie up* in this sense. 'Traffic for all through trains was tied up through the wrecking of an eastbound freight train.'

tier is often employed in Am. as a geographical term, esp. in the expression *tier of counties*. 'The Rep. leaders say that any defection in the northern end of the State will be more than offset by the big Rep. majorities in the lower tier of counties.' 'The route lay through the sparsely populated southern tier of Pennsylvania counties' (H. O'CONNOR, Mellon's Millions, 99). 'The tier of counties north of this belt and along the borders of New York was comparatively neglected by them' (MADISON GRANT, Conquest of a Continent, 121).

tiger is in Am. a symbol for (1) Princeton University and (2) Tammany Hall. (1) 'It had been settled that Foulke, the Tiger's half-back, would not start the game.' (2) 'Tammany may change its leaders and its candidate, but it cannot change its nature, for the Tiger remains the Tiger, let it wear what mask it will.' 'As for Mayor Walker, he is Tammany's darling. He is not one of those sometimes troublesome Al Smiths who on occasion desire the Tiger to reform.' 'The Socialists caught the Tammany Tiger napping and sent ten legislators to Albany' (L. SYMES and T. CLEMENT, Rebel Am. 302).

The word may also denote a yell supplementing the giving of three cheers. 'At the end of six minutes Mr. Robb secured partial quiet, and when three cheers and a tiger had been given he was able to make himself heard.' 'It choked them to "hurrah" for Lincoln when they had planned a "tiger" for Seward' (Dr. G. D. LYMAN, The Saga of the Comstock Lode, 123). See also BLIND.

timber is used fig. in Am. to denote personal quality, esp. as making a man suitable for a particular office. It thus becomes virtually equivalent to *calibre*. 'In age, attainments, experience, habit of mind, and public services, he is Presidential timber.' 'The Legislature will have enough of the best timber to ensure the speedy dispatch of business.' 'Fate had little of private life in store for William Howard Taft. She had found him to be the right sort of timber' (R. L. DUNN, Life of W. H. Taft, 8). 'He had seen Presidential timber in Wilson while the latter was still President of Princeton University' (Dict. Am. Biog. vii. 503). When a London paper describes a certain Eng. politician as 'of real Ministerial timbre', it is, of course, using a quite different metaphor.

†**time.** Am. *on time* = Eng. *up to time, punctually.* 'Meals were served, not only on time, but in a style that pleased the family.' 'The train arrived on time' (G. ATHERTON, The Travelling Thirds, 139). 'The opposition herds had been detained, which would force them to drive over 20 miles a day in order to reach Buford on time' (ANDY ADAMS, The Outlet, 314). 'I kept at it, and finished and delivered my novel on time' (EDITH WHARTON, A Backward Glance, 208).

tipple. As in Eng., *tipple* is in Am. a colloquialism for *strong drink*. It is also used in one of the senses of the Eng. *tip*, i.e. a place where coal, &c., may be dumped. 'They were clearing the track near the Glendale coal tipple, and the escaping steam from the tipple obscured the view of the approaching train.' 'The old detective who as superintendent has to short-weight the miners at the tipple' (E. WILSON, The Am. Jitters, 285). 'The gunny sack which he was about to use for filching coal from the tipple' (M. Ross, Machine Age in the Hills, 24).

tired. When an Am. tells you that such-and-such a thing makes him *tired* he does not necessarily wish you to understand that he feels exhausted. He uses the word as a synonym for *bored, annoyed,* or *disgusted.* 'In the language of the day the Filipinos make us tired. Here they are bobbing up again with their incessant prayers for the abolition of the tariff on Philippine products.' 'It must make them rather tired to turn over the book publication of this novel to another firm, but that is what they have to do.'

†**to.** In Am. *to* takes the place of Eng. *about* or *in* in such examples as follow. 'We took it full and they didn't, and that is all there is to it.' 'The imponderabilia are all there is to civilization.' 'People have instinctively felt that the tune and its associations are all there is to "The Star-Spangled Banner" for the uses to which it has been put.' 'There is

more to the Library of Congress for the Am. dream than merely the wise appropriation of public money' (J. TRUSLOW ADAMS, The Epic of Am. 414). 'Owen Young has not yet tapped the full potentialities of his mind and spirit, and I am curious to know how much more there is to him and where and how he will demonstrate it' (IDA M. TARBELL, Owen D. Young, 311).

toga. The *toga*, as the garb of a Senator in ancient Rome, is fig. used in Am. of the attire of a Senator in modern Washington also. 'Who will succeed Fairbanks as U.S. Senator from Indiana? There are a number in Indiana who would be glad to wear the toga.' Apropos of an attempt to prevent the re-election of Senator Bailey, his biographer says that 'Bailey's response was packed with stinging words and phrases for those who sought to snatch the toga from him' (S. H. ACHESON, Joe Bailey, 227).

Less frequently the *toga* serves fig. to denote the attire of other officials. In the same book Mr. Acheson tells us that 'young Charles A. Culberson of Dallas had received the toga of Attorney General [of Texas]' (op. cit. 40).

Tombs. The city prison of N.Y. is known as *The Tombs*. It inherits the name from a previous building, which it superseded in 1898, and which was so called on account of its gloomy appearance. 'The magistrate decided to hold him for trial, and he was committed to the Tombs.' 'There is no home environment about this fifth flat at No. 6 just as there is none about cell No. 6 in the fifth tier of the west corridor of the Tombs.'

ton. The Am. *ton*, like the Eng., = 20 hundredweight, and accordingly = 2,240 lb. in Eng. but 2,000 in Am.

too, in the sense of *moreover*, is never used in Eng. as the first word of a clause or sentence, but in Am. there is no objection to its occupying this place. 'Too, the commission's schedules of rates were to be considered prima facie evidence of reasonableness' (L. M. HACKER and B. B. KENDRICK, The U.S. since 1865, 272). 'Too, there were rumors of his incorruptibility' (H. F. PRINGLE, Theodore Roosevelt, 135).

Am. *too bad* = Eng. *a great pity.* 'The investors in South Am. bonds have lost most of their money. That is too bad, but relatively unimportant.' 'When told of Mathews' suicide, he started, turned pale, and exclaimed: "My God, my God; that's too bad, too bad."'

Tory denotes in Am. a Loyalist of the Revolutionary period; i.e. one who opposed the severing of the connexion with Great Britain. It is true that the use of the word in this sense is sometimes challenged. 'It will be observed that I invariably speak of those colonists who were opposed to the revolution as loyalists, and not as Tories. They never fully accepted the name Tory, either in its contemptuous sense or as meaning a member of the Tory party in Eng. They were not entirely in accord with that party. They regarded themselves as Americans who were loyal to what they called the empire, and this distinction was, in their minds, of vast importance' (S. G. FISHER, True Hist. of the Am. Revolution, 10). The term, however, is commonly so used by Am. writers. 'The distractions of the time were further enhanced by the rude treatment of the Tories, 100,000 of whom, it is reckoned, were driven out of the country between 1783 and 1785, despite the most solemn treaty obligation' (Prof. J. A. HARRISON, George Washington, 404). 'Though a man of much property he declined to take the apparently safe course and become a Tory. From the beginning of the contest Morris never wavered in his attachment to the colonial cause' (Prof. T. J. GRAYSON, Leaders and Periods of Am. Finance, 23). See WHIG.

toss. Am. *toss and catch* = Eng. *pitch and toss*. 'Playing at toss and catch with his conscience and honor.'

tough. In Am. the adj. *tough*, when applied to a person, has a sinister meaning unknown in Eng. It is a synonym not for *stubborn* or *intractable*, as in the Eng. expression 'a tough customer,' but for *ruffianly, criminal*. 'Columbus and the Pinzon brothers found it hard to get any but rather tough fellows for the crew. Some, so the story goes, were released from prison on promise to go on this voyage of discovery' (E. D. ADAMS and J. C. ALMACK, Hist. of U.S. 12). The word is used in Am. as a noun also, in a corresponding sense, thus becoming nearly equivalent to the Eng. noun *rough*. 'The N.Y. broker who is accused of hiring two East Side toughs to assault his coachman.' 'The Irish boss who, beginning with a gang of toughs, branches out into the tumble of ward politics' (Dr. H. ZINK, City Bosses in U.S. 275).

tout has sometimes in Am., as in Scotland (but not in Eng.) the sense of *discuss*. 'One much-touted episode of his later career belongs to legend rather than history; namely, his relation to the "Pacific Republic" in aid of the Confederacy' (Dict. Am. Biog. x. 580).

tower. In the vocab. of Am. railways a *signal-tower* or *tower* is a *signal-box*. 'The plan in vogue on railways employing the block-system is to place at the end of each block signals that are usually operated from towers.' 'The man in the tower cannot, by any manipulation or any precipitation, make the mechanism which he operates by pushing buttons produce a collision.' 'A man in the neighbouring tower opened the block, and the diminutive freight screamed by us' (H. A. FRANCK, Vagabond Journey, 328). See also SWITCH. Hence Am. *tower man* or *tower operator* = Eng. *signalman*. 'A powerful statement of the causes of our railroad accidents, written by a tower man of long experience.' 'Four men were seen by the tower operator near the point where he discovered the bar of iron wedged beside the rail.' See also WATER.

town. Chaucer's 'poore persoun of a towne' was a village priest. In New Eng. (but not in other parts of the U.S., where *township* usually takes its place) *town* still denotes a rural, not urban, community, and is nearly equivalent to the Eng. *parish*. In a quite recent guide-book (So You're Going to England, 139) Miss Clara E. Laughlin refers to Hawarden as 'this town'. 'The town of Coniston, it must be explained for the benefit of those who do not understand the word "town" in the New Eng. sense, was a tract of country about ten miles by ten, the most thickly settled portion of which was the village of Coniston, consisting of twelve houses' (W. CHURCHILL, Coniston, 49). 'The New Eng. towns vary in size from 20 to 40 sq. miles. The town is usually a rural region containing one or more villages, varying in size from very small hamlets to settlements containing three or four thousand inhabitants' (Prof. C. A. BEARD, Am. Government and Politics, 776). See also CITY and PARISH.

Hence *on the town* = Eng. *on the parish*. 'Miss Sawyer remarked that no member of her family ever had been "on the town", and she guessed they wouldn't begin at this late day' (K. D. WIGGIN, Rebecca, 255).

The *town farm* in New Eng. is a *poorhouse*. 'Her nearest neighbor wished her to go to the town farm' (S. O. JEWETT, The Queen's Twin and other stories, 225).

The affairs of a New Eng. *town* are administered by a *town meeting*, of which every inhabitant is a member. 'Diplomacy cannot be conducted by town meeting.' 'If the town-meeting principle of legislation directly by the people is a sound and good one, as all admit, why not extend it so far as practicable to the cities and the state, as through the initiative and referendum?' 'Samuel Adams lived at town meeting rather than at home, and, when he slept, doubtless dreamt resolutions and amendments' (Prof. J. A. HARRISON, George Washington, 251). 'Did we not see him at the town meeting when a very serious question concerning the management of the town poor-house was to be settled?' (Dr. S. McC. CROTHERS, The Pardoner's Wallet, 32). For a full discussion of the Am. *town* and *town meeting*, see Bryce's *Am. Commonwealth*, cc. xlviii and xlix. See also MODERATOR and SELECT.

For *township*, see quotation. 'In most of the Western states there is also some form of town or township government, but the unit of those states is almost invariably a "public land township",—that is, an area of six miles square, not having the historical coherence of the old New Eng. towns' (Prof. A. B. HART, Actual Government, 172).

The Am. compounds *down-town* and *up-town* do not indicate any difference in elevation. Whether as nouns, adjectives, or adverbs, they are applied to the business and the residential district, respectively, of an Am. city. 'The sudden turning on of electric lights in the downtown office buildings overtaxed the output of electricity from the power stations'. 'One of the diversions of downtown yesterday was watching the sure movements of a steeplejack'. 'Many uptown banks have been kept busy supplying their customers with small cash for the occasion'. 'Since Dr. Rainsford came to N.Y. 40 churches below 20th Street have moved uptown'. 'It used to take him about 20 minutes to walk from his house to his office; and so as he went downtown every morning he mentally delivered the first half of his speech and as he came up-town in the afternoon he mentally delivered the second half' (Prof. BRANDER MATTHEWS, Notes on Speech-making, 42).

track. In the vocab. of Am. railways *the track* or *the tracks* is commonly used where in Eng. one would speak of *the line* or *the rails*. 'I crossed the tracks, climbed over freight-cars, and came upon the river bank.' 'The congestion at the tunnel has become intolerable. It is due to the fact that upon its two tracks has to be carried both a large through express and a freight traffic.' Hence Am. *jump the track* or *leave the track* = Eng. *run off the line*. 'Several passenger cars left the track and crashed into the station buildings.' 'Trolley car 415, while on its way to Jersey City to-day, jumped the track.'

Hence (1) *trackage*, (2) *tracklayer* (= Eng. *platelayer*) and (3) *trackman*. (1) 'The double tracking of the Erie railroad between Jersey City and Newark has been completed. By means of the additional trackage the handling of all freight and passenger traffic on the Newark branch will be greatly facilitated.' 'Crooked or unduly sanguine promoters had built double the needed amount of trackage in the U.S.' (J. K. WINKLER, J. Pierpont Morgan, 105). (2) 'A good tracklayer cannot be made in a week or a month' (W. G. McADOO, Crowded Years, 451). (3) 'The shopmen and trackmen of the Denver and Rio Grande Railway.'

Am. *race-track* = Eng. *racecourse*. 'The Louisiana Legislature prohibited race-track gambling in that State' (MARK SULLIVAN, Our Times, iii. 536). 'He added to his notoriety by being ruled off every race-track in Eng. as a cheat and a blackguard' (PRICE COLLIER, England and the English, 114). 'The disreputable race-track and gambling crowds' (J. KERNEY, Political Education of Woodrow Wilson, 70).

traction. In Am. this word is spec. applied to street railways (i.e. tramways). 'Plans are being worked out for the consolidation of the traction systems of this city.' 'The reservoir broke, flooding paper mills and tying up railway and traction lines.' 'If a poor man needed a job, he would find one with the street-cleaning force or in city traction' (L. EINSTEIN, Roosevelt, 18). 'In Chicago even the notorious Thompson machine received the support of large traction and corporate interests' (NORMAN THOMAS, America's Way Out, 157).

trade. In Am. the give-and-take between polit. parties or factions is often called *trading*. 'A judgeship has more than once been disposed of by combinations and trades effected to secure nomination for some minor office.' 'There was none of the petty bargaining, the trading, that disgraces so much legislation' (Prof. N. W. STEPHENSON, Life of N. W. Aldrich, 308). 'Since the two traditional parties are on the whole rather evenly balanced, it is necessary for them to bid for votes among the independents, and to make concessions in return for ballots. No doubt this policy of trading is partly responsible for the failure of every third party to reach a dominating position' (C. A. and W. BEARD, The Am. Leviathan, 87). 'This stupendous bill was lobbied through the legislature by trade and barter, by giving to counties and towns money for improvements in them, in consideration that they would vote for Springfield as the new capital of Illinois' (E. L. MASTERS, The Tale of Chicago, 89). Cf. DEAL. The *coupon* which a trader sometimes gives away with an article purchased, as a voucher contributing toward the acquisition of another article—as when, e.g. a packet of cigarettes contains a coupon that will help pay for a book—is called in Am. a *trading stamp*. 'The trading stamp craze which prevails in Brooklyn has at last extended to the local burglars. Early yesterday morning two thieves broke into a store and made off with 5,000 trading stamps, taking nothing else. Green envy seized upon every housewife in that borough when she heard of the haul, and figured out

what it meant in the way of real hand-painted sofa pillows and decorated porcelain mantel clocks.' 'In 1916 the Supreme Court settled a controversy which had been going on in the lower courts as to whether a State could prohibit the use of trading stamps. In the cases which came before the court the legislation involved had put a prohibitive license fee upon the use of trading stamps, and the court held this constitutional, since a State could entirely prohibit the use of such stamps. The court's decision was not put upon the ground that such devises actually tend to defraud purchasers, but the court declared that "by an appeal to cupidity" they "lure to improvidence", and that the State is justified in protecting its citizens against such seduction' (Prof. C. K. BURDICK, Law of the Am. Constitution, 575).

tradesman. In Eng., exc. in certain dial., this word is nowadays used only of *a man who sells commodities*, esp. a shopkeeper. It could once mean a *craftsman* or *artisan*. The expression *learn a trade* is a relic of this meaning. In Am. the word *tradesman* may still be occasionally found in this earlier sense. 'Whereas the Negro carpenter and mason of 25 years ago was a highly competent man, having served an apprenticeship under competent tradesmen, a large proportion of the tradesmen of today have picked up their trade hurriedly and consequently are not given preference for the well paid and steady construction jobs' (Prof. T. J. WOOFTER, Jr., Races and Ethnic Groups in Am. Life, 120).

train forms part of several terms in use on Am. railways but unknown in Eng.; e.g. (1) *train dispatcher*, (2) *trainman*, and (3) *trainmaster*. (1) 'The accident was the result of a misdirection by a train dispatcher. He ordered a westbound train held at Chicago Junction to allow an eastbound passenger to pass. The passenger train was running in two sections, but the conductor of the westbound train was not notified of this.' (2) 'Two trainmen were killed and six passengers severely injured in the wreck of a Big Four fast passenger train.' 'A trainman, stepping from car to car with lighted lantern, saw us huddled between the bumpers' (O. KILDARE, My Mamie Rose, 176). (3) 'The men chiefly concerned are the signalmen, who attend the signal stations, the train-masters, who superintend the train-men, and the superintendent, or higher officer, who is responsible for the general policy.' 'He was succes-sively switchman, yardmaster, con-ductor and chief clerk and trainmaster for the Cincinnati-Indianapolis division of this road' (Dict. Am. Biog. ix. 63).

The intrans. verb *train* is used in a sense peculiar to Am. in the expres-sion *train with = ally oneself with*. It is a metaphor derived from the practice of members of an athletic team who go into training together. 'He represents a certain class that will never openly train with radical elements in politics.' 'That he does not train with the extreme radical theologians is plain from the fact that he has but recently attacked two of the newest school of radicals.' Cf. TEAM.

transfer. In most Am. cities a tram or bus passenger, paying a single fare, may begin his journey on one line and complete it on another—an arrangement which is not unknown but much less common in Eng. The conductor of the first vehicle gives him a †*transfer ticket*, or *transfer*, which is accepted as a voucher by the conductor of the second. 'It has long been a pleasant intellectual exer-cise for the newcomer to memorize the points and the lines at which, and from which, he can obtain transfers, and those where he cannot.' 'Almost everybody collects nowadays. If it isn't books, it is chewing-gum tags; if it isn't coins, it is street-car trans-fers.' 'To Let. Front office facing busiest transfer corner in city' (Advt.).

In such cases the verb *transfer* is used as well as the noun. (In Eng. one would say *change*.) 'The man was transferring from the Queens car to the Jamaica car when he was struck.' 'It will be better to take a cross-town car and transfer at Seventh Avenue' (M. E. WILKINS FREEMAN, By the Light of the Soul, 160).

The word is also applied to the con-veyance of passengers or baggage from one railway station to another in the same city, or from a railway station to a ferry. 'The transfer of passengers and baggage between rail-way stations in many Am. cities' (Prof. R. T. ELY, Evolution of In-dustrial Society, 198). Hence *transfer company* and *transfer wagon*. 'The transfer companies are running extra wagons, which clear out the depot rooms as quickly as possible after the arrival of each train.' 'A depot hack with an omnibus behind, and a transfer wagon on the other side.' The intrans. use of *transfer* is not limited to changes made during a journey. 'Finding the instruction here inadequate, he transferred the next year to the Berkeley Divinity School' (Dict. Am. Biog. ix. 100).

transient is a book word in Eng., but in Am. it is in everyday use, both as noun and as adj. The hotels offer different rates for residents and for *transient guests* or *transients*. 'There are two hotels in Irving Place where South Am. transients with money in their purses like to go.' 'Charles F. Rogers will build a 12-story transient hotel at East 27th Street.' (This means, of course, not a hotel that will soon be demolished—though many N.Y. hotels would come in that cate-gory—but a hotel for temporary guests.) 'A family house for transient or permanent residence.' 'The city of Washington is, in fact, the home town of few, being simply a house of transients' (D. LAWRENCE, True Story of Woodrow Wilson, 108). The word is even applied to horses, as in the advt. 'boarding stables for transients'.

An official notice in a Post Office reads: 'Letters to strangers or to visitors in a town or city, whose special address may be unknown, should be marked in the lower left-hand corner with the word "Transient".' The Post Office also discriminates in its rates between *transient news-papers*, sent occasionally by one private person to another, and the newspapers that are dispatched regularly from the publication office to subscribers.

In some of the above instances *temporary* would be the corresponding word in Eng. usage. The equivalent would be *casual* in 'Filipinos were employed in the harvesting of figs, a job held in previous years by white transient laborers' (B. LASKER, Filipino Immigration, 14) and in 'The real safeguard for the collector is to buy his books, not from the transient individual who has two or three bargains to offer, but from the man who is known first of all for his reputable dealing' (Dr. A. S. W. ROSENBACH, Books and Bidders, 133). It corresponds to *periodical* in 'The Russian counterpart of the Am. newsvender boards these far-Siberian craft and sells daily papers, magazines, and other current and transient literature' (Sen. A. J. BEVERIDGE, The Russian Advance, 407) and to *ephemeral* in 'They retain the elements of transient journalism though now bound between dignified and durable covers'. An Am. newspaper announces: 'Advertizing rates. For transient advertisements, 5 cents per line. For longer insertion, reduced rates.' In an Eng. paper *for transient advertisements* would be *for a single insertion*.

transom. In Eng. a horizontal cross-bar separating a door from a fanlight above it. In Am. the fanlight itself. 'A clergyman in the next room had early morning prayers with his family, which were distinctly audible through the transom.' 'A small can of thick black paint to smear over the transom to keep the hall light out.'

'Fire-crackers were sometimes tossed in over the door through the transom, which had to be open for the sake of ventilation' (Prof. E. G. SIHLER, From Maumee to Thames and Tiber, 148).

transportation. In Eng. *transportation* was the term used for the system of sending convicts to a penal settlement overseas. Though the system itself has long been abandoned, the word still retains its Botany Bay associations, and much merriment is apt to be caused among visitors from Eng. when their Am. friends speak of making arrangements for their transportation. In Am. *transportation = Eng. transport, conveyance.* The University of Pennsylvania has a Chair of Transportation and Commerce. 'The prevailing opinion was that a railway was a commercial concern engaged in selling an article—transportation.' 'Transportation was a vital question in a region where roads were often quagmires' (Dict. Am. Biog. vi. 525). 'The new means of transportation have made of travel at once a delight and an easily-attainable method of self-cultivation' (W. M. PAYNE, Editorial Echoes, 38).

trash, which in Eng. is mostly used fig., is in Am. common in its literal sense. When it refers to domestic refuse, it is distinguished from GARBAGE (q.v.). 'Broken bottles go with garbage and not with trash.' 'The building was just as the plasterers had left it, the floors being covered with trash' (Myron T. Herrick, quoted in his biog. by T. B. MOTT, 135). 'In its center stood the abandoned capitol building. Its steps were littered with trash' (W. G. McADOO, Crowded Years, 12). In the last two quotations, *rubbish* would have been the word used by an Eng. writer.

trifling, in the sense of *good-for-nothing, worthless,* is used in Eng. of things only. In some parts of Am. it may be applied to persons also.

'The certainty that idleness will be tolerated no longer has driven trifling negroes and shiftless whites from their hovels and induced them to apply for work.'

trillion denotes in Eng. a million million millions, but in Am., as in France, a million millions. It is thus exactly equivalent to the Eng. *billion*. See also BILLION.

trim. In Eng. *trim*, as a noun, means *trimness* or *good order*. In Am. it is also the name for the *woodwork of a house*, esp. in the compound *door-trim*=Eng. *door-case* or *door-frame*, i.e. the frame, lining a doorway, in which the door is hung. 'The corridors, floors, stairways, and doortrims are of marble' (Advt.).

tripe may be found in Am. in the plur. form *tripes*. 'The motors are cleaned out like a bull's tripes' (E. WILSON, The Am. Jitters, 46).

trolley. In Eng. a low truck without sides or ends, such as that used by porters on the platform of a railway station. In Am. a moveable pulley receiving current from an overhead electric wire; hence, also, a car driven by means of such a trolley. The word is used in Eng. also to denote a pulley of this type, but its application to a car is peculiar to Am. The term *trolley-bus*, however, denoting a vehicle introduced into London in 1931, is becoming current Eng. 'Much of this country is within easy reach by trolley.' 'Then he caught the next trolley and was carried as far as it went in the direction of Englewood' (E. WHARTON, Hudson River Bracketed, 373). Mr. G. K. Chesterton tells us (What I Saw in Am. 66) that, after he had given an interview on the Labour question to an Am. reporter, he found it published under the heading 'Chesterton Takes Sides in Trolley Strike'. 'This,' he comments, 'was inaccurate. When I spoke I not only did not know that there was any trolley strike, but I did not know what a trolley strike

was. I should have had an indistinct idea that a large number of citizens earned their living by carrying things about in wheel-barrows, and that they had desisted from these beneficent activities.'

trot has in Am. the same fig. sense as PONY (q.v.). 'An edict against "cribs"—the words "pony" and "trot" are more common in this country—has been issued by the head master of Eton.'

truck, which in Eng. usually denotes an open railway wagon or a porter's barrow, is the common term in Am. for the kind of commercial road vehicle which in Eng. would be called a *lorry* or *van*. 'A huge white delivery truck of a wholesale ice cream company stops in front of a restaurant.' 'The language of Sandburg's brutal poems is that of stevedores and truck-drivers' (Prof. J. M. MANLY and E. RICKERT, Contemporary Am. Lit. 52). Hence a firm of haulage contractors is called in Am. a *trucking corporation*.

The use of this word to denote *garden produce* is peculiar to Am. 'The principal growers of truck say that all small fruit have been damaged to a great extent, and that corn, peas and vegetables have all suffered greatly.' 'This country generally produces about twice as much fruit and truck as the market can consume' (L. F. CARR, Am. Challenged, 50). Hence Am. *truck farmer* = Eng. *market gardener*. 'A truck farmer is able to reduce his expenditure by raising his own food' (C. S. JOHNSON, The Negro in Am. Civilization, 18).

There is a verb *truck* in a corresponding sense. 'Neither trucking nor fruit growing is a universal panacea for a decadent agriculture' (R. B. VANCE, in Culture in the South, 32).

trunk. A *main line* of railway is alternatively called in Am. a *trunk line* or *trunk road*. 'Soon these tiny roads became links in the trunk lines' (J. K. WINKLER, Life of J. Pierpont Morgan,

106). 'To have unlimited opportunities to make money, and to be hindered in giving it away, seems to him like building a trunk line of railroad and then being denied terminal facilities' (Dr. S. McC. CROTHERS, The Pardoner's Wallet, 164). 'Gould reported to Miller that the trunk road had possibilities under proper management' (R. I. WARSHOW, Story of Wall Street, 106).

The *trunk call* of the Eng. telephone system becomes in Am. a *long-distance-call*. See LONG.

trust. The commercial combination known as the *trust* is as familiar in Eng. as in Am. Am. has originated and developed also an institution called the *trust company*. 'Trust companies undertake the administration of large transactions, such as the refunding of a corporate loan or the amalgamation of corporations; they act as trustees and investors for estates; and most of them receive deposits, subject to check, although none of them have any privileges of note issue' (Prof. A. B. HART, Actual Government, 489).

The derivative *trustee* is sometime used in Am. as a verb. 'Cyrus H. K. Curtis, newspaper and magazine owner, died. He trusteed his publications, which were left to his daughter and other heirs' (N.Y. World Almanac for 1934, 105).

trusty is in Eng. an adj. only. In Am. it is a noun also, meaning a convict to whom special privileges are given and certain tasks entrusted as a reward for good behaviour. 'He was in all respects a model prisoner, so he had become a "trusty".' 'He had arranged with a trusty to obtain the dynamite on the outside and bring it in to him.' 'In the "chain gang" camps in the southern states the "trusties" or honor prisoners are very often murderers' (Prof. H. C. BREARLEY, Homicide in the U.S. 87). A curious slip is made by the author of a recent book of travel, who tells us that in Am. such convicts are

called *trustees*. For a full account of the system, see *The Jails of Virginia*, by F. W. Hoffer, D. M. Mann, and F. N. House.

try, trial. In the legal sense the verb *try* properly means 'to examine and determine (a cause or question) judicially; to determine the guilt or otherwise of (an accused person) by consideration of the evidence' (O.E.D.) Hence in Eng. a case is correctly said to be tried by the judge and jury only. In Am. it is also said to be tried by the lawyers who are engaged in it. 'The barristers in London keep their places until their cases are reached, and then try them from the same seats. . . . The bar is divided into two separate parts, the common law bar and the chancery bar, and a barrister does not, as in Am., try cases of both kinds.' 'This was one of eight cases he tried in his first year, and he was for the defense in every one. This was striking enough to deserve the application of the title "defender" to the young attorney' (B. A. KONKLE, Life of Joseph Hopkinson, 45). 'His great ability lay in the trial of jury cases. He had a rare gift for eliciting information from friendly or reluctant witnesses, perceiving the drift of a jury's mind, revealing the drama of fact' (Dict. Am. Biog. vi. 66, in a biography of a lawyer who was never a judge).

Hence a *trial lawyer* is a lawyer who conducts cases in court, as distinct from one whose work is confined to his office. 'The defendants were represented by experienced trial lawyers.' 'His practice is seldom that of a trial lawyer, but rather as an adjuster of cases and an adviser in civil processes' (R. R. MOTON, What the Negro Thinks, 146). 'Excelling in cross-examination and in addressing a jury, he was unequaled by any of the Connecticut bar as a trial lawyer' (Dict. Am. Biog. ix. 154).

The Eng. sense of the word is retained in *trial judge*, which is nevertheless a term peculiar to Am. and has a spec. meaning, indicated in one of the following quotations. 'It may be equally effective to play upon the frailties of the trial judge until he betrays a partisan attitude.' 'We first went into the chambers [in Tokyo] of a judge of first instance, i.e. a trial judge' (H. W. TAFT, Japan and Am. 80). 'In ten years as a trial judge he conducted more than 1,200 trials. As an appellate judge in the course of a decade he participated in the hearing of 2,047 cases' (Dict. Am. Biog. ix. 249).

†In Elizabethan times *try*, in the sense of *test*, was often intensified by *out*. This usage has persisted in the U.S., and is now coming into vogue again in Eng. through Am. example. 'He **is** apparently a capable man, but he has not yet had time to be thoroughly **tried** out.' 'A famous army post, where the airplane invented by the Wright brothers was tried out' (F. J. HASKIN, The Am. Government, 484). '**The** professor tried out his **theory** on the members of the State legislature' (D. LAWRENCE, True Story of Woodrow Wilson, 39). Sometimes *try out* is used intrans. 'He also tried **out** as a reporter and on occasion **was** called upon to report proceedings of the legislature' (Dict. Am. Biog. xii. 249). Hence the noun *try-out*. 'Rushing off to other cities for the try-out of new plays' (Dict. Am. Biog. vi. 430). 'I was to have a try out on the Globe as a reporter at \$15 a week' (T. DREISER, A Book about Myself, 43).

tube. The *valves* of a *wireless set* become in Am. the *tubes* of a *radio set*. 'Poor reception is often caused by weak tubes or loose connections' (Advt.). 'Those in high places have preached to the people that it was their destiny to have two-car garages and eight-tube radio sets.' 'Whether the listener would rather pay a small annual fee, which might amount to the cost of a new tube for his set' (C. A. and W. BEARD, The Am. Leviathan, 444).

turkey. In Am. not every dish is *turkey* that is so described on the menu. 'In the western part of the U.S., in nearly all the hotels, restaurants, and private houses, Belgian hare is looked upon as a great delicacy. It is canned and sold under the name of "boned turkey"' (Mrs. RORER's New Cook Book, 208). 'Our Saturday dinner consisted of salt fish boiled in a cloth bag and in a pot well filled with potatoes. This sustenance, commonly known in New Eng. as "Cape Cod turkey", was served with a generous supply of hot pork scraps floating in a bowl of equally hot grease' (Prof. MARY E. CHASE, A Goodly Heritage, 139). See also THANKSGIVING.

††**turn.** Am. *turn down* = Eng. *refuse, reject*. 'It is said that all proposed appropriations for the state reservations are to be turned down by the sapient economists of the Legislature.' 'If Alderman Gass is turned down, his defeat will be due to his name, rather than to lack of support.' 'The proposition was a tempting one. But it was turned down' (J. T. FLYNN, God's Gold, 226). 'We sat around, making suggestions and getting them accepted or turned down' (Prof. A. G. KELLER, Reminiscences of William Graham Sumner, 78). Hence the noun *turndown*. 'The turndown of the labor candidates, who had been refused places on the Independence League ticket, was a part of the deal made at the convention.'

turner. The only *turner* known in Eng. is a man who works with a lathe. In Am. it may mean a member of one of the *turnvereine* (gymnastic societies introduced from Germany). 'It was largely due to the activity of the turners that physical training had become so general in educational institutions.'

tutor, as a verb, is frequently intrans. in Am. 'He wintered in Munich, eking out an existence by tutoring' (Dict. Am. Biog. vi. 384). 'In the first two summers I fairly filled the weekdays tutoring in the summer houses of the patrons of the Collegiate Institute' (Prof. E. G. SIHLER, From Maumee to Thames and Tiber, 133). Occasionally it means not *teach* but *receive tuition*. 'Oliver T. Morton and I had become fast friends and we agreed to tutor together and go to Cornell instead of Yale' (Intimate Papers of Col. House, i. 14).

Many Americans give to the first syllable of *tutor* the pronunciation of *too*, as in Carolyn Wells's amusing limerick:

A tutor who tooted the flute
Tried to tutor two tooters to toot.
  Said the two to the tutor,
  'Is it harder to toot or
To tutor two tooters to toot?'

twist has a spec. sense in Am., as set forth in the following quotation from a N.Y. newspaper. 'The proposal to make "twisting" an indictable offence, which has been seriously discussed in connection with the new legislation affecting the management of life insurance companies, has led many people to ask what "twisting" really is. By "twisting" is meant the persuading of policy holders in one company to transfer their insurance to another.'

typesetter commonly takes in Am. the place of the Eng. *compositor*. 'It is said he could work on two or three editorials at once, dashing off alternate pages of them to send to the typesetters' (Dict. Am. Biog. ix. 424). 'Ford, who was a type-setter in a Hoboken newspaper office, did not aspire to be public printer' (J. KENNEY, Political Education of Woodrow Wilson, 185).

U

underground. The railway which in Eng. is called the *underground* is in Am. the SUBWAY (q.v.). In Am.

underground railroad is the popular term for a system, organized by Abolitionists in the days of slavery, by which slaves were secretly passed along from one sympathizer to another until they could reach Canada or some other free territory. It was underground in a fig. sense only, and it was imagination, not historical research, that prompted the statement in a London paper a few years ago that the method most generally used was to cross the borders by means of subterranean tunnels, the mouths of which were carefully concealed in the thick local brushwood. 'While Brown had taken two slaves out of Kansas to freedom before this wholesale liberation and was throughout his life an ever-ready agent of the Underground Railroad, he was at no time especially interested in this piecemeal method of weakening slavery' (O. G. VILLARD, Life of John Brown, 367). 'These Quakers became a soil for the growth of anti-slavery feeling in Ohio; and when the underground railroad was started the majority of the stations were situated in their houses' (H. CROLY, Life of Sen. Hanna, 12). 'He helped negroes to reach Canada, his house being a station on the Underground Railroad' (Dict. Am. Biog. xii. 447).

Union, Unionist. In Am. *the Union* is a common synonym for *the U.S.* 'The experiment which is being tried here is under scrutiny from almost every city of the Union.'

There are two spec. Am. meanings of *Unionist*. It may denote an opponent of the secession of the Southern States from the Union at the outbreak of the Civil War. 'The mountaineers in Kentucky and Tennessee were largely unionists and this provided an additional strong incentive for the federals to control the region.' 'President Roosevelt's father forbade the boys and girls to discuss the war at home for fear of hurting their mother. And in return for this chivalry she brought up her children loyal Unionists, though her heart was with her father's people and the lost cause' (W. A. WHITE, Woodrow Wilson, 54). 'Houston was opposed to secession, and during the ten years preceding the Civil War worked without ceasing to prevent the destruction of the Union. In 1850 he was the Unionist candidate for Congress' (Dict. Am. Biog. ix. 262).

It may also mean a member of a trade union. 'We must perceive and admit that before the law the capitalist, the unionist, and the non-union man are exactly the same.' The fact that in Am. *unionist*, without prefix, commonly means *trade unionist* led to a report in an Am. paper some years ago of certain action that was about to be taken by Mr. Balfour, Sir Michael Hicks-Beach and 'other Trade Unionist members' of the House of Commons. No doubt the cablegram said simply *Unionist*, and some sapient person at the Am. end of the wire expanded the message in the light of Am. usage.

A railway station used by two or more companies and known in Eng. as a *joint station* is called in Am. a *union station*. 'On the west the N.Y. Central will meet the subway at Marble Hill, where the two roads will have a union station.'

For *company union*, see COMPANY.

unit. In Am. *a unit* often takes the place of the Eng. *united, unanimous, agreed.* 'The experts at the yard are not yet a unit as to the cause of the mishap.' 'The object of the pamphlet is to prove that he and the President are a unit on the question.' 'Trumbull and his Rep. colleagues were a unit against his right to vote' (D. M. DEWITT, Impeachment of Andrew Johnson, 76). 'The legal profession in the province was a unit in support of his position' (Dict. Am. Biog. ix. 237).

The word *unit* is also a term in the vocab. of Am. education relating to the requirements for admission to a college. 'When a college catalogue states that 15 units of high school

work are required for matriculation, a unit, as defined by the College Entrance Examination Board, represents one year's study in any one subject in a high school' (Dr. A. FLEXNER, Universities, 47).

In Am. politics the *unit rule* is a regulation, sometimes adopted at national conventions, that the vote of all the delegates from a State shall be cast for the candidate whom the majority wishes to support. 'It is not likely that he has lost anything by the unit rule tradition of the Dem. party. Just as many delegates would have escaped from him in the States which he now controls absolutely, as would have been gained by him where he was a minority candidate.'

unpleasantness. In Am. books of the end of the last century one may sometimes come across references to *the late unpleasantness*. This facetious euphemism for the Civil War has suggested a similar use of *unpleasantness* as a synonym for subsequent wars. 'The recent "unpleasantness" in the Philippines gave some of our Am. volunteers a chance to study the native dialect' (L. MEAD, Word-Coinage, 62). 'In time of war, when a free press in a democracy would be a real safeguard, there is repression. During the recent unpleasantness [i.e. the Great War] this repression was practised sometimes directly by the Federal Government' (A. G. HAYS, Let Freedom Ring, 158).

up. ††Am. *up against* = Eng. *confronted with, face to face with.* 'Canadians frequently abandon Eng. for their own beautiful country after trying it as a place of residence and going up against fog, rain, and gloom.' 'This proposition brings the standpatters in Congress squarely up against the argument for tariff revision.' 'Now that the magic had gone abruptly from him, and there was nothing to take its place, he felt himself up against the barren rocks of life' (G. ATHERTON, Rulers of Kings, 25).

†† Am. *up to* = Eng. *incumbent on, the turn of.* 'Each party says that it is up to the other side to ask for a conference.' 'It is up to the police now to decide whether the laws against dangerous fireworks shall be enforced.' 'As to the method of action, I am not certain, and that is immaterial. That would be up to the big banking houses; they probably know already how they could do it' (L. F. CARR, Am. Challenged, 281). This expression is said to be borrowed from the game of poker.

The Am. term *up-and-coming* is not precisely equivalent to *wide-awake* or to *pushing*, but it partakes of the meaning of both these epithets. It is frequently applied to a young person who has abundant self-confidence, and who is keenly alert to every opportunity of getting on. 'The bumptious, effervescent, up-and-coming youth of small-town Am.' 'East-ward from sedate Cowes is the up-and-coming resort town of Ryde.' 'It stopped the eight-hour movement; not permanently, of course, but all that the up-and-coming industrialists cared about was the immediate situation and results' (L. ADAMIC, Dynamite, 84). 'That pleased the old man —that his shrewd, up-and-coming young son John could go out and get the money' (J. T. FLYNN, God's Gold, 71). 'Good salesmen, up-and-coming authorities on cash registers and motor tires' (SINCLAIR LEWIS, Dodsworth, 106).

† The compound *uplift* is a favourite term in Am. to denote an elevating or inspiring influence. 'No great moral uplift can derive from a source which has done so much to degrade Am. journalism.' 'Another year and they could withdraw from business to return to poetry and uplift work' (K. BERCOVICI, Around the World in N.Y. 59). 'Their zeal for the uplift of the Chinese people' (Am. Foreign Relations in 1930, 80).

For *up-town*, see TOWN.

use. † The Am. locution *have no use for* is an under-statement. It really indicates actual dislike or disapproval. 'The Prince of Montenegro has no use for libel laws to restrain the newspapers.' 'The Employers' Association has no use for him or for his union.' 'They exchanged the careful salutations of men who had no use for one another' (R. W. CHAMBERS, The Fighting Chance, 421). 'He had no use for M. Klotz's mixture of greediness and timidity in approaching the problems of reparations and taxes' (A. NEVINS, Henry White, 378).

In Am. *used* is a common euphemism for *second-hand*, as in advts. of 'used books'. 'Used cars and trucks were being marketed in this fashion' (L. M. HACKER and B. B. KENDRICK, The U.S. since 1865, 619). 'She was tempted to go into the business of dealing in used furniture' (L. N. WRIGHT, Limbs of an Old Family Tree, 184).

† usher is in Am. used particularly to denote a friend of the bride or bridegroom who shows guests to their seats at a church wedding. 'At weddings it is generally understood that the bridegroom, his best man, and the ushers should wear the conventional Prince Albert coat.' 'At the Philadelphia wedding of young Mrs. Goelet, the uninvited irrepressibles pelted with stale vegetables the ushers who sought to drive them back.' 'Four of the bride's summer friends were the ushers' (K. D. WIGGIN, My Garden of Memory, 379). The word may also be used in connexion with a funeral. 'When Barnum died, Harry was an usher at his funeral' (T. W. LAMONT, Henry P. Davison, 38).

utility. 'Mr. Insull, a utility magnate, had made contributions to his campaign fund' (Dr. J. M. BECK, May it Please the Court, 269). The utility man is a familiar figure on the Eng. stage, but no one would ever think of calling him a magnate. It is, indeed, an entirely different kind of person that is referred to here. In this quotation *utility = public utility*, a term which is of Am. origin but is nowadays coming into use in Eng. also. It denotes a public service, such as an electric light company, a gas company, a water company, a telephone company, and so on. As in the above quotation, the word *public* is often left to be supplied by the intelligence of the reader. 'By the time he had become a member of the firm he was one of the best informed advisors on utilities at the Boston bar' (IDA M. TARBELL, Owen D. Young, 91). 'Through faith in him many millions had been invested in the railroads, the utilities, and the great industrial corporations' (Prof. T. J. GRAYSON, Leaders and Periods of Am. Finance, 473).

V

vacation is in Eng. applied only to cessation of work at the Law Courts and Universities, but in Am. to any period of holiday from a regular job, even a domestic servant's. 'The policemen are on their vacation.' 'A number of employees of the works took a day's vacation on Labor Day.' Seaside and mountain resorts, tourist agents, and steamship companies invariably use *vacation*, not *holiday*, in their advts. Newspapers announce their terms for *vacation subscriptions*. The word *holiday*, indeed, is almost entirely restricted to the one-day public or legal holidays —Washington's Birthday, Independence Day, Columbus Day, and so on —that correspond to the Eng. bank holidays. Accordingly, *vacationist* is a much more common term in Am. than *holiday-maker*. 'The vacationists who are at the seashore.' 'New York had entered into competition with Niagara Falls for honeymooners and vacationists' (K. BERCOVICI, Manhattan Side-Show, 257).

Hence the verb *vacation = take holiday*. 'That type of unforced,

continuously relaxing, and pleasurable vacationing which the President happens to prefer.'

Another sense of the word is illustrated in the following quotation: 'The merchants were kept well in hand by many little municipal grants and privileges, such as switches, wharf rights, and street and alley vacations. These street vacations are a tremendous power in most cities. A foundry occupies a block, spreads to the next block, and wants the street between. In St. Louis the business man boodled for his street. In Pittsburg he went to Magee' (L. STEFFENS, The Shame of the Cities, 157).

valedictory, as a noun, has in Am. the spec. sense of an oration delivered at a college or university by a picked student from the graduating class. 'When it came to his own graduation, young Hopkinson did not make a brilliant record like his father, for he had neither valedictory nor salutatory' (B. A. KONKLE, Life of Joseph Hopkinson, 18).

The student chosen to deliver the valedictory is called a *valedictorian*. 'He graduated from Illinois College in 1881 with high honors as valedictorian of his class' (Prof. A. E. MARTIN, Hist. of U.S. ii. 336). The term may be used in connexion with schools as well as colleges. 'It was in 1889 when he was 14 years old that Owen Young graduated from the East Springfield Academy, the valedictorian of his class' (IDA M. TARBELL, Owen D. Young, 16). See also SALUTATORY.

valise is a word seldom used in Eng. The dictionaries define it as a case for carrying a soldier's kit. In Am. it retains the meaning, now obs. in Eng., of a travelling case carried by hand. 'He found the bonds in a valise which was left in his hotel.' 'Stiles packed a valise, and left at once' (MARK SULLIVAN, Our Times, iii. 328). 'The colored boy carried to the platform a valise of the documents' (L. STEFFENS, Autobiog. 595).

'Tracts were brought to our doors by dusty men with valises from which they extricated their pamphlets' (Prof. MARY E. CHASE, A Goodly Heritage, 86).

velvet. The Am. term *velvet bean* denotes 'a cultivated form of cowhage, grown for forage and green manure in the southern U.S.' (WEBSTER). Its botanical name is *Stizolobium pruriens utile*. 'The gulf states have made unsuccessful attempts to create a permanent agriculture of the velvet beans and peanuts type' (R. B. VANCE, in Culture in the South, 31).

vest. That part of a man's underclothing which in Eng. is known as a *vest* is called in Am. an *undershirt*, or simply a *shirt*. The use of *vest* in Am. to denote underclothing is limited to that of infants, children, and women. A man's *vest* in Am. is a *waistcoat*—a sense of the word which is unknown in Eng. exc. in tailors' advts. 'This London physician has called the world's attention to the fact that the waistcoat (known in Am. as the vest) is a preposterous and pernicious article of apparel.' 'He wears double-breasted gray vests.' 'The Journeymen Tailors assert that there are few Negro tailors capable of making coat, vest, and pants of a suit' (C. S. JOHNSON, The Negro in Am. Civilization, 110). 'A thin gold watch chain stretched from the top of a vest pocket to a lower vest pocket on the same side' (E. WILSON, The Am. Jitters, 106).

Acc. to Prof. Frederick Newton Scott (School Review, June 1912) '*waistcoat* is to the great body of Americans as bookish as *glebe*.'

vestibule. In Eng. an ante-chamber near the front door of a house, or the porch of a church. In Am. part of the platform at the end of a railway car, which is so enclosed that one may easily pass from one car to the next. A train whose cars are thus constructed is called in Am. a *vestibule* (or *vestibuled*) train. Accordingly, though a vestibule is not a corridor, the Am. *vestibule train* practically corresponds to the Eng. *corridor train*. 'The more costly the train, as, for example, a vestibule train, the worse the ventilation.' 'You may now board a vestibuled train of sleeping-cars at Port Arthur and go to Moscow without change' (Sen. A. J. BEVERIDGE, The Russian Advance, 7).

veteran. The distinctive meaning of this word has entirely disappeared in Am., where it has come to be applied to any *ex-service man*, however young or however brief his military experience. The Spanish War was in 1898, but in 1903 the Boston *Transcript* could refer to 'all existing organizations of the veterans of the Spanish and Philippine Wars'. The Government agency for the relief of men disabled in the Great War is officially called the Veterans' Bureau. 'That large proportion of War's young veterans who came unscathed from the battlefields' (W. E. SMYTHE, City Homes on Country Lanes, 203).

In Am. *vet*—which in Eng. is a colloquial abbrev. of *veterinary surgeon* —is an abbrev. of *veteran*. 'All the old vets have returned from the reunion [of Confederate veterans].' 'The bill to extend to World War vets loans up to 50 per cent. of the value of their adjusted compensation certificates' (World Almanac for 1932, 99).

vine. Exc. in a few compounds such as *hop-vine*, this word is in Eng. restricted to the plant that bears grapes. In Am. it is the generic term for any kind of creeper. 'The trimmed hedge, the gravel walk, the clipped lawn, the neat flower beds, the trailing vines over the porch.' 'I missed the climbing rose vines that cover the piazzas of the Charleston houses.' 'Pulling up dried pea vines for the cow.' 'The old purple wisteria vine which covers the south wall with its clusters' (Prof. V. L. COLLINS, Princeton Past and Present, 177).

Accordingly the vine that bears grapes is distinguished in Am. by the term *grapevine*. 'One nurseryman advertised fifty million grapevines for sale' (A. NEVINS, The Emergence of Modern Am. 156). 'He brought grapevines and mulberry trees from France' (R. L. HAWKINS, Mme. de Stael and the U.S. 18).

See also LAUREL.

visit. The Eng. use of this word seems to be in a transitional stage. Jane Austen, as noted by Dr. R. W. Chapman in the vocab. appended to his edition of her works, could write of a tea-visit and of dinner-visiting. This would be impossible to-day. A doctor still visits his patients, a pastor visits his flock, and officials pay visits of inspection, but in social intercourse *visit* has been largely superseded by *call*, exc. when it denotes a stay of some duration. There are survivals, however, of the earlier meaning. A door-bell retains its traditional label, 'Visitors', although, if it is rung many times in the course of an afternoon, we say there has been a stream of callers. The Englishwoman still keeps a visiting list, although, when new-comers arrive in the neighbourhood, she considers not whether she shall visit them but whether she shall call on them.

In Am. *visit* is used more commonly than in Eng. without any suggestion of duration. A more remarkable difference is that in Am. you may visit your friends without even entering their doors, for all that is necessary to constitute a visit is a meeting of two persons, however brief and in whatever place, for the purpose of social converse. A *visit* is thus often equivalent to a mere *chat*. If two friends happen to meet in the train and talk together for half an hour, one of them may remark as they separate: 'I have much enjoyed this pleasant visit.' A member of the audience at a concert remarks, when she returns home: 'I *visited* with the pianist and

the first violin.' This means that she had a little chat with them when the concert was over. In reporting a horse show, a newspaper says that 'visiting among the boxes was as frequent as heretofore'. A farmer writing in *Foreign Affairs* for Jan. 1933 on the agricultural situation says: 'Frequently we [the farmers of the district] discuss it all, following the Grange and Farm Bureau meetings, while we are visiting before starting for home.' A journalist thus describes what happened when she sought an interview with ex-President Coolidge: 'Calvin Coolidge sat in his old law office and talked. He had refused to be formally interviewed, he forbade quotation, but at 9 o'clock in the morning, having disposed of a batch of correspondence, he was willing to visit in an informal and utterly friendly fashion. It was good talk.' Here we can see how far the word has escaped from the limitations of its meaning in Eng. For the person described as visiting is not the journalist, who calls, but Mr. Coolidge, who stays in his office. In their study of the life of a Middle West town, R. S. and H. M. Lynd state that 'the attenuation of visiting to telephone visiting is one of the phenomena that has appeared since 1890' (Middletown, 275); i.e. nowadays people ring up their friends for a conversation to save the trouble of calling.

It should be noted that, as in one of the examples quoted above, *visit* is in Am. often followed by *with*. 'My visit with Edward Carpenter lasted the greater part of an afternoon' (E. GOLDMAN, Living My Life, 979). 'The Faculty had many informal gatherings in the President's outer office, where they wandered in to get their mail and remained to visit with one another' (L. N. WRIGHT, Limbs of an Old Family Tree, 137).

In view of the difference between Eng. and Am. usage, one would naturally expect that the card one leaves on making a call would be known in

Eng. as a *calling card* and in Am. as a *visiting card*. Actually, it is the other way about. 'We'll execute calling cards to your order in conformity with the very latest requirements of fashion' (Advt.). 'The unsuccessful became "expectant officials", as the young scholars in Peking used to write on their calling cards' (Survey of Am. Foreign Relations for 1930, 73). 'A calling-card which was supposed to have Willie Stevens's fingerprint on it' (F. L. ALLEN, Only Yesterday, 214).

volley. The Am. compound *volley-ball* is defined by Webster as 'a game played by volleying a large inflated ball with the hands over a net 7 ft. 6 in. high.' 'Thirty-five institutions provide a gymnasium . . . and five a volley-ball court' (Prof. W. ADAMS BROWN, Ministerial Education in Am. 152).

vote. When a voter casts his vote in Am., he is sometimes said to *be voted*. 'Twenty-five men were in line in many places, and they were voted at a rate of nearly one a minute after the clerks began work.' 'The Philadelphia delegation was voted solidly for Mr. Pennypacker.'

A party organization is said in Am. to *get out a* or *the vote* when it succeeds in inducing its prospective supporters to exercise the right of voting. 'The Republicans are exerting themselves strenuously to get out their own vote, and are not bothering to convert Democrats.' 'No one outside the members of the inner councils of the great political organization knows what it costs Tammany to get out the vote, but it was reported that the organization distributed more Monday than in some previous elections.' 'The carriages contained district leaders, each of whom carried away a large roll of money with which to get out the vote.' 'He devised an efficient system for getting out 100 per cent. of the vote' (Dr. H. ZINK, City Bosses in U.S 224).

W

wad. In Eng. a lump of soft material used to stuff an opening. In Am. also a roll of paper money. Thus Am. *wad of bills* = Eng. *sheaf of notes*. 'The man who comes to the city with a wad to spend, and wakes up one morning moneyless, in some cheap lodging-house.' 'And then you'd slide into the ring and pick up the wad that was coming to you on account of your foreknowledge.' '"Here, boys," said old man Don, throwing the roll of money on the bed, "divide this wad between you"' (ANDY ADAMS, The Outlet, 277).

Accordingly, a miserly person, who in Eng. would be described as *close-fisted*, is called in Am. a *tightwad*.

wade. The expression *wade into* is used fig. in Am. in the sense of *denounce vigorously, criticize severely*. 'Father spoke in Chicago, wading into the N.Y. and Indiana machine crowd' (ALICE ROOSEVELT LONGWORTH, Crowded Hours, 189).

wage. In Am. a *wage-earner* is sometimes called a *wage-worker*. 'The speaker went further than was necessary in his laudable effort to do justice to the wage-worker.' 'The only persons who gain by our tariff on wheat are the millers, railways, steamships, and wage-workers of foreign countries.' 'Taking the ministry as a whole the average income in 1928 was about on a par with that of wage workers in the gas, electricity, stone, clay, and glass industries' (Prof. W. ADAMS BROWN, Ministerial Education in Am. 47).

wagon. In Am. *wagon* (never spelt *waggon*) generally takes the place of the Eng. *van*. It does not, however, necessarily mean a vehicle used for commercial purposes or for carrying heavy loads. 'The rector had arranged that some of his young ladies should take me on a scientific ramble. They appeared in a handsome wagon, all in pretty gowns, each armed with her little hammer' (M. D. CONWAY, Autobiog. ii. 196). Here the term apparently = Eng. *wagonette*.

Am. dictionaries record as distinctively Eng. the use of the word to denote a railway car carrying freight.

See BAND, DEMOCRAT, DIRT, EXPRESS, GARBAGE, JERSEY, PATROL, and TRANSFER.

waist is sometimes used in Am. to denote a *blouse*. An alternative is *shirtwaist*. 'She wears a black garb consisting of a waist buttoned close to the neck, but without a collar, and a long full skirt.' 'N.Y. dress and waist makers struck on Jan. 26' (Am. Year Book for 1919, 455). 'Gwendoline took a letter from the bosom of her shirtwaist' (D. G. PHILLIPS, Golden Fleece, 2). 'They had sent their mothers' sturdy shawls and "hoods" to the attic and wore shirt-waists and picture hats' (MARK SULLIVAN, Our Times, iii. 400).

Hence *waisting*, as in 'The dotted effects which are to be seen in everything this year are to be found in the heavy cotton waistings'.

waitress. In Eng. this word is never used of a domestic servant in a private house, but only of a woman who waits at meals in a hotel or restaurant. In Am. there is no such limitation. Thus, one reads in Am. papers such advertisements as: 'Wanted: One cook and one waitress for same family.' 'A competent girl as waitress and to take charge of parlor floor; private family.' 'The hostess should hand her bill of fare to the cook at least four days before the dinner party. If she has a waitress of whom she is not sure, let the instructions for her also be carefully written' (Mrs. RORER's New Cook Book, 654).

walk. In the vocab. of Am. labour, *walk out* has the spec. sense of *go on strike*. 'The Mine Workers announced their intention to walk out on May 1, but on the eve of the strike the leaders suddenly realized that the union was in no position to do so, and ordered the men to stay on the job' (L. ADAMIC, Dynamite, 103).

Hence the noun *walkout*. 'If the laborers threatened strikes, the employers shut down the plants before a walkout could be organized' (L. ADAMIC, Dynamite, 85). 'The Lawrence strike began with the spontaneous walkout of thousands of unorganized textile workers' (L. SYMES and T. CLEMENT, Rebel Am. 271).

walnut. In Eng. *walnut* means the *juglans regia*. 'In some parts of Am. the name walnut is given to the "shagbark", a kind of hickory nut, and the true walnut is known as the "Eng. walnut"—a term which involves a curious etymological contradiction' (Prof. J. B. GREENOUGH and Prof. G. L. KITTREDGE, Words and Their Ways in Eng. Speech, 340). This term, they explain, is an 'etymological contradiction' because the first syllable of *walnut* is related to *Welsh*, which originally meant *foreign*.

want. 'If you have a bud on your rose-bush that you want should blossom' (Dr. C. H. PARKHURST, A Little Lower than the Angels, 195). '"I want you should take her to my sisters", she said' (K. D. WIGGIN, Rebecca, 4). In such instances Eng. usage would require *to* instead of *should*.

Am. *want of* = Eng. *want with*. 'He has a $6,000,000 house, entirely new, in N.Y. But what on earth does he want of a $6,000,000 house?' 'What do you want of a guide? Don't you know where the sun rises?' 'Now we hear again the same familiar strain: "What do we want of a navy? Nobody is going to attack us."'

ward. Alike in Eng. and in Am. a *ward* is an administrative division of the city, but the terms *ward politics* and *ward politician* are peculiar to Am. They always connote professional political activities of the Tammany type. 'Although he had been associated with ward politics, he was familiar with the best forms of N.Y.

club life' (Prof. A. E. MARTIN, Hist. of U.S. ii. 181). 'He had not been trained in the hurly-burly of ward politics, but was a product of academic groves' (L. M. HACKER and B. B. KENDRICK, The U.S. since 1865, 456).

A ward politician is sometimes called a *ward heeler*, the suggestion being that he comes to heel when his boss issues orders. 'He used to go to the business men of his ward individually, and try to persuade them that they ought to be more actively interested in local municipal affairs—that they, the taxpayers and not the ward heelers, should rule the city' (H. CROLY, Marcus Alonzo Hanna, 114). 'They were ward-heelers, saloon-keepers, a cheap lawyer or two, perhaps a bail-bond shark' (H. F. PRINGLE, Theodore Roosevelt, 59).

warden. 'Many of my young friends, who have never heard of the Warden of All Souls, Oxford, insist that the only wardens they have ever seen have been wardens of jails and penitentiaries' (Dr. J. R. OLIVER, Foursquare, 221). The Am. prison *warden* corresponds to the Eng. prison *governor*, and must not be confused with the Eng. prison *warder*. 'All governors of mankind, from doctors and jail-wardens to demagogues and statesmen' (Prof. W. JAMES, Talks to Teachers, 89). 'I know a man who turned a corner in life when, with the warden's permission, he brought away with him after a jail sentence two or three books from the prison library that had meant much to him during a dark time' (CHRISTOPHER MORLEY, John Mistletoe, 229). This meaning is a survival of an old Eng. use; e.g. the governor of the Fleet Prison was called its *warden*.

In some parts of New Eng. the term = *mayor*. 'The news that Warden John F. Wade will go to Germany next month and thus leave the office of warden vacant caused much comment in town to-day. . . . It is a conceded fact that no other Dem. in town can carry the borough for

warden, and that the Republicans have the chance of a lifetime to get back the head of the borough government.'

Am. *port warden* = Eng. *harbour master*. 'Notice is hereby given that the following vessels are now under examination by the Port Wardens' (Official advt.). Is this, possibly, a survival of the Eng. use of the term now confined to the wardens of the Cinque Ports?

wash. In certain compounds Eng. usage prefers *washing*, while Am. prefers *wash*. Thus, Am. *wash-day* = Eng. *washing day*. 'They can be folded up and put away till next wash-day.' 'Rose Standish said the very first act of colonization ought to be wash-day, using fresh water, for all the soiled clothing of the long voyage' (E. D. ADAMS and J. C. ALMACK, Hist. of U.S. 40).

So, too, Am. *wash water* = Eng. *washing water*. 'Pure Refined Paraffine serves a useful purpose almost every day. Add a little (melted) to Monday's wash water, and wash easier' (Advt.).

At the same time, Eng. usage allows *wash-boiler*, *wash-house*, *wash-leather*, *wash-stand*, and *wash-tub*.

The compound *wash-board* is of Am. origin. It denotes a board with a corrugated surface used by washerwomen when they are scrubbing clothes. 'He wants to see washing machines in place of wash tubs and washboards' (IDA M. TARBELL, Owen D. Young, 222). 'Addison's pony, whose ribs resembled two washboards' (Dr. FRANKLIN H. MARTIN, The Joy of Living, i. 7).

Am. *washroom* = Eng. *lavatory*. 'Adjoining his office is a washroom with a large clothes closet.' 'The magazine had appeared when I took the train for St. Louis, and I remember hearing men in the washroom talking about it' (L. STEFFENS, Autobiog. 389).

Am. *washwoman* or *washlady* = Eng. *washerwoman*. 'Negro Washwoman Demands Extra Dollar for Cleansing

344 Pieces in One Week' (Newspaper headline). 'She didn't think that her maid or washwoman would work for her for nothing in order to help win the war' (L. N. WRIGHT, Limbs of an Old Family Tree, 188). '"Blanchiseuses", what some folks here call "washladies".'

Am. *wash-bowl* = Eng. *wash-hand basin* and Am. *wash-rag* = Eng. *facecloth*.

The collapse of a portion of a railway line, road, &c., through floods or other destructive causes is called in Am. a *washout*. 'Extremely heavy rains have caused numerous washouts on the Great Northern Railroad.' There is a corresponding verb *wash out*, which is used both (1) trans. and (2) intrans. (1) 'Bridges have been swept away, railroad tracks washed out, telegraph wires torn down.' (2) 'It was a tough trip this time of the year on desert roads that washed right out from under you if a rain storm came' (H. CAHILL, in Life in the U.S. 79). In Eng. *washout* is a spec. term of mining engineering, but it is not commonly used in this Am. sense.

In the vocab. of the Am. Stock Exchanges *wash* has a fig. use. The meaning of a *wash sale* or *washed sale* may be understood by combining the following definitions given by Am. dictionaries. 'A mere transfer by a broker of the stock or commodity which one principal had instructed him to sell to another customer who had given instructions to purchase a similar quantity of the same stock or commodity' (Century Dict.). 'The operation of simultaneously buying and selling the same stock for the purpose of manipulating the market' (Webster's Dict.). 'A sale of stock or other securities at a stock exchange between parties of one interest, in order to attract attention by reason of the apparent activity of the market, or to create a market price, or both. When the latter only is aimed at, the transaction is referred to as *matched orders*' (Standard Dict.).

waste. Am. *waste basket* = Eng. *waste paper basket*. 'The House at the last moment threw the whole batch of bills into the waste basket and substituted one of its own devising.' 'That lecture is best tossed into the waste basket' (H. S. CANBY, Better Writing, 48). 'Aldrich advised Roosevelt to throw the treaties into the waste basket' (Prof. N. W. STEPHENSON, Nelson W. Aldrich, 179).

watch. Am. *watch out* = Eng. *look out, be on one's guard*. 'We advise the golfers to watch out, or else they may find themselves locked up.' 'If Venezuela doesn't watch out, we may have to give her the punishment ourselves which we prevented Eng. from giving her not so long ago.' '"The bogey man will catch you if you don't watch out!" is the cry that has at last roused Democrats from their apathy.'

In Am. electioneering *watcher* is the technical term for a candidate's friend who looks after his interests at the polling-place. 'That Dem. and Rep. henchmen combined on Election Day to defeat Henry George is possible. He had few, if any, watchers at the polls and no influence whatever with the police and election officials' (H. F. PRINGLE, Theodore Roosevelt, 114). 'I was probably never in greater danger in my life, for it was a common enough thing to knock an election watcher over the head and dump him into the gutter' (UPTON SINCLAIR, Candid Reminiscences, 86).

water. †The term *water tower* denotes in Eng. 'a tower serving as a reservoir to deliver water at a required head' (O.E.D.). Thus, a prominent structure near the Victoria Gate of Kew Gardens is known as the Water Tower, as it contains, at the top, a reservoir originally used to give sufficient pressure for the palms &c., to be watered overhead. In Am. a *water tower* is an apparatus used by fire brigades in extinguishing fires at a great height. 'It was nearly four hours before the water tower ceased playing.' 'An odd incident of the fire was the appearance of the water tower on the scene when a few pails of water could have put out the fire.'

The Am. compound *waterboy* denotes a boy who fetches and carries water for the use of workmen. 'He assisted himself in securing an education by working as a waterboy on the railroad in the summer.' 'From all over the county came offers of support, and he avers that not only will he carry his home town but that he will run like a waterboy in the bailiwicks of his opponents as well.' 'His first position as waterboy in a quarry opened a career in the stone business' (Dict. Am. Biog. xii. 180).

The derivative *waterway* is not exclusively Am., but the use of the term as part of the name of a canal is peculiar to Am. Thus: 'The Illinois Waterway, linking the Great Lakes and the Gulf of Mexico, was officially opened' (N.Y. World Almanac for 1934, 106). In a list of 'Federal Canals in the U.S.' given in the same handbook, one finds Florida Waterway, Intracoastal Waterway, &c.

See FRESH and JERK.

way. In Am. *way* has several uses unknown in Eng. It is an abbrev. of *away* in such expressions as *way above, way aft, way ahead, way back, way behind, way below, way down, way off, way out, way over,* and *way up.* It is also a common suffix, as in *areaway, bargeway, crossway, driveway, entranceway, entryway, fishway, hallway, launchway, parkway, passageway, raceway, runway, shipway, skidway, speedway, spillway, trafficway, walkway,* and *waterway*; though, curiously enough, *railway* is less frequently used in Am. than *railroad.*

A *way station* is a station of minor importance on a railway line, and a *way train* is a train that stops at such stations. 'The car was quite full at first, but the passengers got off at the way stations' (M. E. WILKINS FREEMAN, By the Light of the Soul,

173). 'A transcontinental which made of Portland a way station was not acceptable to Chapman, who wished to see her a terminal city' (J. B. HEDGES, Henry Villard, 53). 'To attempt to run way trains through the middle of the day while running express trains in the crowded hours would result in endless confusion.'

The compound *waywisdom* means skill in finding one's way, either lit. or fig. 'Her motives and her action, except for its lack of waywisdom, were above reproach.'

In Am. the use of *ways* as a singular, in such expressions as *a long ways,* is not a solecism, as it would be in Eng. 'He is a long ways from thinking himself out of the running as a candidate for mayor.' 'Copley Hall, a little ways from the church, will be the business headquarters.' 'We are a good ways apart' (Dr. C. H. PARKHURST, The Sunny Side of Christianity, 112). The *O.E.D.* gives Eng. examples of this use of *ways,* dated 1588 and 1594, as well as from *Tom Jones,* but notes it as now dial. only. 'The origin,' it says, 'of the use of *ways* for *way* is obscure. It might possibly have arisen from the analogy of the phrases containing the adv. genitive.'

Am. *all the way from* or *to* = Eng. *anywhere* or *anything from* or *to, anywhere* or *anything between.* 'Enterprises valued all the way from 20,000 to 500,000 dollars.' 'The organized labor vote of the State is variously estimated all the way from 22,000 up to 40,000.' 'One notary took 280 acknowledgments in one day from persons living all the way from 81st Street to Spuyten Duyvil.' (This does not mean that each of these persons lived in a house that stretched for the whole of this distance.) 'The periodicals pay all the way from half a cent to 15 cents a word.'

††**wear,** in such combinations as *footwear* and *neck-wear,* is a modern Am. usage, now well established in Eng. also.

weasel. The weasel has the reputation of being a sinuous and wriggling animal, and in Am. the metaphor of *weasel words* has been hit upon to denote utterances of a convenient ambiguity. 'At a time when 99 out of 100 words uttered for public consumption are mealy-mouthed, cautious, weasel, and with an eye to the main chance, plain speaking is as refreshing as spring showers on packed winter earth.' 'The members of the convention were master draftsmen. They never wasted a word. They never indulged in "weasel words"' (J. M. BECK, May it Please the Court, 290).

week. In Am. *fortnight* is almost as archaic a term as *sennight* in Eng. Its place is commonly taken by *two weeks*. 'The plant of the Washington Cotton Mills shut down to-day for two weeks.' 'A tired boulevardier has come down from Paris for his two-weeks' holiday' (F. J. STIMSON, My U.S. 215). 'Some leaders ask for reports every two weeks' (C. E. ROBINSON, Straw Votes, 5). 'Coming for a two weeks' visit among you my neighbors' (Pres. FRANKLIN D. ROOSEVELT, On Our Way, 200).

well. As the *O.E.D.* shows, *well* was used as an attrib. adj. by Pepys and Dryden. It is now so used in Am. only. 'Her hope that she might at last be strong enough to bear a well child.' 'During the last year of his term Blaine was by no means a well man' (Prof. A. E. MARTIN, Hist. of U.S. ii. 296).

In Am. a point (whether a point of order or an argument) is often said to be *well taken*, in the sense of *justified*. 'The point of our correspondent appears to be well taken.' 'We are inclined to think that Harvard's point about Princeton's too raucous cheering at the recent baseball game is not well taken.' 'If these points be well taken, it follows that etc.' (Prof. W. P. TRENT, Hist. of Am. Lit. 100). 'Presently they showed their fairness by cheering points which were well taken, even when the argument scored against themselves' (Dr. C. R. BROWN, They Were Giants, 218).

See also LET.

Wesleyan. 'Two Wesleyan professors lectured on Wednesday at Hartford.' It must not be understood that these professors were Methodists. They may, or may not, have been, but all that the report means to say about them is that they were professors at Wesleyan University (not *the* Wesleyan University), an institution at Middletown, Connecticut. Woodrow Wilson was at one time a Wesleyan professor, though he was never a Methodist. So, too, the headline 'Wesleyan Parley on Race Relations' does not refer to negotiations by any body or group of Methodists. It appears above a report of a discussion on the racial problem at a meeting held at Wesleyan University.

West. *The West,* meaning *the Western States,* is a geographical term that in Am. carries certain implications with it. '"The West" is not merely a geographical expression; it is a state of mind which is most distinctive of the national consciousness. It is a feeling, an irresistible impulse. It is the sense of undeveloped resources and limitless opportunities. It is associated with the verb "to go". To the Am. the West is the natural place to go to, as the East is the place to come from. It is synonymous with freedom from restraint. It is always "out West"' (Dr. S. McC. CROTHERS, The Pardoner's Wallet, 151). See also EAST and SIDE.

wet. Both as adj. and as noun, *wet* is in Am. a common synonym for *anti-prohibitionist,* as DRY (q.v.) is for *prohibitionist.* 'In Finland a referendum vote on prohibition was won by the wets.' 'The wet vote in New Jersey was a powerful factor in the Dem. party' (J. KERNEY, Political

Education of Woodrow Wilson, 186). 'The Reed Amendment, without interfering with the freedom of "wet" states, made the prohibition states more prohibitory than they had elected to be' (Prof. H. L. McBAIN, The Living Constitution, 53). 'Almost any wet could tell you that prohibition had nothing to do with prosperity but had caused the crime wave' (F. L. ALLEN, Only Yesterday, 254).

wheel. †In Am., by the figure which classical grammarians call synecdoche, *wheel* often = *bicycle*. W. D. Howells writes (Harper's Monthly, July, 1906): 'The drive from Bath to our destination was 12 miles, and the friend who was to be our host for the day had come as far on his wheel to ask us.' In a letter published in H. James's biography of him (ii. 249) Dr. C. W. Eliot, of Harvard, writes: 'We have had but few bicycle rides, because of snow, rain, and mud. This morning we had to walk instead of riding our wheels.' 'Our greatest novelty was our bicycling. One year we carried our wheels from Am., and rode through Normandy' (Prof. G. H. PALMER, Life of Alice Freeman Palmer, 201).

Hence *wheelman* and *wheel suit*. 'It is entirely easy for a wheelman to see approaching vehicles in time to slow up or dismount.' 'Surely that was Winifred Stowe in her new wheel suit.' 'On Roosevelt's behalf State Chairman Odell denounced a canard whereby the Democrats had attempted to capture the bicycle vote. Odell said that the Republican nominee was an enthusiastic wheelman and would work actively for good roads' (H. F. PRINGLE, Theodore Roosevelt, 206). The principal organization of Am. cyclists is called the League of Am. Wheelmen.

The *O.E.D.* gives an example from Evelyn's Diary of *wheel chair*. This term has been superseded in Eng. by *Bath chair* and *invalid's chair*, but it is still used in Am. 'His pride would not permit him to use a wheel chair'

(J. K. WINKLER, J. Pierpont Morgan, 337). 'He could not even be moved down to the wharf in a wheel chair' (H. JAMES, Life of C. W. Eliot, ii. 331).

Whig. This once familiar term of Eng. political history has been adopted in Am. to denote the Am. colonists who supported the Am. Revolution, as against the pro-Eng. Tories. See TORY.

It also denotes the party opposed to Andrew Jackson. 'Since they agreed only in an implacable antagonism to "King Andrew I", in 1833 or 1834 they adopted the name of "Whigs". Reminiscent of the Whig party in Eng., the new Whigs stood for Congressional supremacy and against "executive usurpation"' (Prof. A. M. SCHLESINGER, Polit. and Social Hist. of U.S. 53). 'Opponents of that popular hero called themselves "Whigs", after the manner of the Eng. adversaries of royal prerogative' (C. A. and M. R. BEARD, Rise of Am. Civilization, i. 573). 'When he [Webster] spoke in the Senate chamber it was his custom to wear the Whig uniform, a blue coat with metal buttons and a brass waistcoat' (Dr. T. L. CUYLER, Recollections, 126).

whipsaw. The fig. use of this word, whether noun or verb—i.e. as applied to something that cuts both ways— seems to be peculiar to Am. 'These speculators have subjected themselves to the process known in Wall Street as whipsawing; that is, they have bought when the market was strong and sold when the market was weak, and found each time that they have bought at the top and sold at the bottom.' 'The whip-saw of paying high prices for what they bought and being forced to receive low prices for what they sold' (L. F. CARR, Am. Challenged, 79).

white. In Am. the *white collar* takes the place of the Eng. *black coat* in typifying occupations of the class that is socially above manual labour.

During the severe unemployment of 1931 a White Collar Bureau was opened in N.Y. for the relief of unemployed clerks, typists, &c. 'Educating a boy of the working-classes beyond his mental capacities and into the white-collar proletariat is individual and social waste.' 'The ascent of the Irish to white-collar occupations' (MARK SULLIVAN, Our Times, iii. 400). 'One hears it frequently said that the high schools prepare students for "white collar" jobs rather than for a life on the agricultural lands' (B. LASKER, Filipino Immigration, 224). 'The postwar years have seen a steady shift in the proportion of "white collar" workers to overall workers' (NORMAN THOMAS, America's Way Out, 258). 'High-paid, white-collar men, not asked to punch the time-clock' (FLORENCE CONVERSE, Efficiency Expert, 21).

An allusion to *white wings* in the streets of N.Y. does not point to an invasion by flocks of gulls from the Bay. This is the common term for *street cleaners*. It was suggested by their white uniforms. 'Commissioner Woodbury, of the Street Cleaning Department, this morning began the quarterly inspection of the "White Wings" brigade.' 'Constantinople existed long centuries before Manhattan Island had streets, and yet the only "white wings" had been the hungry pariah dogs.' 'A white wings was pushing his broom along Park Row.' 'One of the D.S.C. offices, where the white wings leave their brooms and shovels after work' (K. BERCOVICI, Around the World in N.Y. 153).

The White House is now the official designation of the President's residence at Washington. (See EXECUTIVE.) 'The White House was not originally intended to be a white house. It was built of a buff sandstone which proved to be so affected by exposure to the weather that as an afterthought it was covered with a thick coat of white paint. From its nearness to several red brick buildings, many persons fell into the way of distinguishing it by its color, and after its repainting to conceal the stains of the fire of 1814 this practice became general. Presidents have referred to it in their messages variously as the President's House, the Executive Mansion, and the White House. Among the people it was also sometimes known, in the early days, as the Palace. The Roosevelt administration made the White House both the official and the social designation, and fastened the label so tight that there is little reason to expect a change by any successor' (F. E. LEUPP, Walks About Washington, 115). The above reference to 'the fire of 1814' recalls an incident of the War of 1812, when British troops set fire to the building.

During the summer, when Washington becomes unbearably hot, the President and his staff often escape for a time to a cooler climate, esp. New Eng. His temporary residence is popularly called *the summer White House*.

For another use of *White House*, see the following quotation: 'It is not without interest to note that the charming old house [at Richmond] with its white columns, in which the President [Jefferson Davis] took up his residence, became known as the "White House" of the Confederacy. With all the feeling there was against the North, there was a curious running close in many ways to old names and symbols' (J. TRUSLOW ADAMS, America's Tragedy, 204).

See LILY.

whole. The metaphor in the Am. phrase, 'a lie out of *whole cloth*', appears to be analogous to that in the Eng. expression, 'a *tissue* of lies'. 'Yet there are travellers who aver that Hermann and his followers saw only the common jugglers of India, and that the tales of Oriental marvels are not all lies out of whole cloth.' 'On one or other of these two lines almost all folk-legends have been developed; leaving only a very small residuum which, starting out boldly by perverting some entirely commonplace occurrence into a marvel, are cut from the whole cloth.'

Other expressions peculiar to Am. are *the whole show* and *the whole thing*. 'This statement was intended as an answer to the criticism that the President is endeavoring to be the whole show, and that the delegates to the National Convention will have nothing to do but ratify a programme prepared in advance at the White House.' 'The Am. farmer may not be the whole thing, but he is so important a part of the industrial machine that he cannot suffer a serious injury without affecting all the running gear.'

whoop. In Am. the verb *whoop* or *whoop up* has very much the same meaning as *boost*. 'The bail was later reduced to $10,000, but was whooped up to $15,000 when Larry was re-arrested.' 'The spectacle of members of the Cabinet whooping up their chief on the hustings in doubtful States is not an inspiring one.' It may sometimes mean *excite, arouse*. 'The purpose of the hearing is not primarily to get information for legislation, but to whoop up public sentiment on some subject or another so that legislation can be passed easily through Congress'.

Am. *whoop it up for* = Eng. *hurrah for, huzza for*. 'They were whooping it up for the war which brought such expanded pay envelopes' (L. SYMES and T. CLEMENT, Rebel Am. 303).

Am. *whoop things up* = Eng. *make things lively*. 'Three boys broke into the Garden, and began to whoop things up. They rolled about, bumping into men and women.'

The noun *whoop* in Am. = the Eng. *rap* in such expressions as: 'The voting public as a whole doesn't care a whoop about the question.'

wide open. An Am. town is said to be *wide open* when there is laxity in the enforcement of the laws against drink selling, disorderly houses, &c.

'"I have had 25 years of experience in this community", said the magistrate, "and never in all that time has the town been so wide open as now. There are violations of the excise law and other violations being flaunted that are degrading this city."' 'The enforcement of the Sunday closing law alienated the support of the people of the city and opened the way to the election of an inferior mayor on a wide-open town basis.' See LID.

wigwam. Reports in N.Y. papers of proceedings at a local wigwam do not indicate the presence of a considerable Indian population. The Dem. organization in N.Y. City calls itself by the name of an Indian chieftain, Tammany, and its headquarters are appropriately known as *the wigwam*. 'The first mass meeting to ratify the Tammany ticket will be held at the wigwam next Thursday night.' 'Although he had taken no active part in city politics for several years, he maintained a keen interest in the affairs of the wigwam.'

†win, in its intrans. sense, is often intensified in Am. by the addition of *out*. 'In real life, the man equipped, able, and shrewd usually wins out.' 'There was a desperate struggle between a stout heart and the dreaded pneumonia. The heart won out' (Prof. M. PUPIN, From Immigrant to Inventor, 322). 'The wild extremists always win out' (F. J. STIMSON, My U.S. 63). An Eng. equivalent would be *pull through* or *carry the day*.

wind. For the Am. compound *windbreak*, less commonly *windbrake*, see the first quotation. 'On the plains and the prairies they establish a local climate anywhere by planting trees, dense as a hedge, round a farmstead, and growing a wind-brake, which is proof against the heaviest blizzard.' 'My cheeks were flaming and my heart was thumping as I passed him at the sycamore windbreak.' 'Over the flat plains of the new world, breezes blow unchecked; no windbreak stops them or lessens their force' (Dr. A. FLEXNER, Universities, 39).

Windsor. The name of the royal borough is best known in Am. to-day through the *Windsor tie*, defined by Webster as 'a kind of broad silk necktie, tied in a double bow, and worn esp. by children'. 'A seedy individual wearing a Prince Albert frock coat, a plaid Windsor tie, and a broad-brimmed hat' (HAMLIN GARLAND, Roadside Meetings, 80). 'A black-bearded gentleman in evening dress and Windsor tie' (UPTON SINCLAIR, Candid Reminiscences, 129). 'The artists abandoned their Windsor ties and velvet jackets' (K. BERCOVICI, Manhattan Side-Show, 282).

†**wise.** The *O.E.D.* gives several quotations, from the year 1200 onwards, illustrating the use of this word in the sense of *informed or aware of something specified or implied,* but adds that it is now used only in such phrases as *none the wiser, as wise as before.* In Am. it is still common, esp. in *get* or *be wise to = become aware of,* and *put* (one) *wise to = inform* (one) *of.* 'Others in the Senate were wise to the situation and the amendment was adopted without opposition.' 'He was fortunately "wise" enough to the purposes of the bill to explain them to Mr. Rockefeller.' 'In the favored locution of the hour, he "put them wise", and helped them to a clear understanding of the situation.'

The compound *wise-crack* has recently been coined in Am. to denote a saying notable for pretentious smartness rather than real wisdom. 'The press crowded round them, firing questions, making wise-cracks.' 'In 1929, *The Pathfinder Magazine* conducted a contest in the invention of a type of aphorism which the slang of the day called "wise-cracks"' (MARK SULLIVAN, Our Times, iii. 339). 'Nor can I believe that the wisecrack of the smart set is the acme of human wisdom' (Prof. E. MIMS,

Adventurous Am. 13). 'There is a grain of truth in the trite wisecrack that "figures don't lie but liars do figure"' (Prof. M. A. MAY, The Education of Am. Ministers, ii. 8).

Hence the verb *wise-crack.* 'These characters speak an entertaining sort of wise-cracking jargon that very much resembles the speech of magazine story cowboys.'

wood. In the polit. vocab. of Am. a politician is said to *saw wood* when he refrains from committing himself on an important issue or taking an active part in propaganda or electioneering, but simply attends to the normal routine or looks after his private affairs. 'Meanwhile the Senator simply sawed wood, contenting himself with the simple statement that he was satisfied with the situation.' 'While there is some disposition to criticise the Judge because of his silence, all are willing to admit that he is doing a beautiful job of sawing wood.' 'He is not only saying nothing, but up to date he is even leaving the wood-sawing to others.'

Another Am. polit. metaphor is that of *taking to the woods,* which denotes running away from one's responsibilities, esp. the responsibility of voting. 'Conservative Gold Democrats cannot be got to support Mr. Johnson, and are preparing to take to the woods on election day.' 'The loyal Democrats who have not "taken to the woods", but fought for the election of the regularly nominated candidates of their party.'

work. In *Our Misunderstood Bible* Dr. H. Clay Turnbull mentions that St. Paul's exhortation, 'Work out your own salvation', is misunderstood in New Eng. owing to a special meaning given to *work out* in that region. A man pays his road-tax either in money or in work. If he pays it in work, he is said to work out his share of the road-tax. Thus he thinks of working out his salvation as meaning that what he has to do is to pay his share of the penalty due for sin. That this use of *work out* is not confined to New Eng. is evident from the following quotations: 'Texas is trying to make local Federal officials work out their road-taxes' (A N.Y. paper). 'I was given a shovel and put on the street to work out the poll-tax, not only of the merchant but of two other clerks in the store' (ANDY ADAMS, Log of a Cowboy, 7).

The Eng. *workday* is a *weekday*, in contrast with Sunday. The Am. *workday* = the Eng. *working day*. 'A grumbling demand from the rank and file of the unions for a shorter workday' (L. ADAMIC, Dynamite, 103). 'The party stood for a shorter workday (10 hours as the first step in factories)' (A. NEVINS, The Emergence of Modern Am. 384). 'Laws which attempted to restrict the length of the workday of men in factories' (Prof. A. E. MARTIN, Hist. of U.S. ii. 220).

In Eng. *workhouse* was formerly the name for what is now called a *public assistance institution*; i.e. a public institution for the reception of paupers. In Am. it denotes a house of correction in which the prisoners perform work of various sorts. 'He was released from the workhouse Thursday after serving three months for petty larceny.' 'Three leading business men of the city have been convicted of violating the state laws against conspiracies in restraint of trade, and sentenced to six months in the workhouse.' 'They were condemned to short terms in the workhouse for "disturbing the peace"' (E. GOLDMAN, Living My Life, 562).

worth. In Am. *worth* has been compounded with *while* to form the adj. *worth-while*. 'The correspondence was typical of Mr. Wilson's attitude of appreciation of worth-while friends' (D. LAWRENCE, True Story of Woodrow Wilson, 133). 'Innumerable worth-while candidates for the Vice-presidency were available' (H. F. PRINGLE, Theodore Roosevelt, 220).

'Sidney Lanier, one of the few worthwhile Am. authors to come out of the South' (V. F. CALVERTON, Liberation of Am. Literature, 111). 'In whose house one met most of the worthwhile in Paris' (EDITH WHARTON, A Backward Glance, 283).

wrangle. There is no implication of quarrelling or strife in the spec. Am. use of *wrangle*, a Western term meaning *take charge of* (horses). 'Rather than have missed the trip, I would have gladly cooked or wrangled the horses for one of the outfits' (ANDY ADAMS, The Outlet, 9).

Hence *wrangler*, in a corresponding sense. 'The remuda and team were taken in charge by the wrangler and cook' (ANDY ADAMS, op. cit. 93). 'The wrangler rounded the drove toward the tents' (HAMLIN GARLAND, Roadside Meetings, 288).

wreck. While the verb *wreck* primarily means *destroy*, the noun *wrecker* is sometimes used, both in Eng. and in Am., to denote a person who salves the contents of a wrecked vessel. In Am. such words are commonly employed in this sense in connexion with disasters on land as well as at sea. Thus, a *wrecking train*, containing *wreckers* or a *wrecking crew* (= Eng. *breakdown gang*), is sent to the scene of a railway accident. 'Two hours after the dust of the crash had settled, the division wrecking train was on the ground and hard at work.' 'The cars were thrown in all directions, several being turned crosswise. Wreckers were sent for from Scranton.' 'After two hours' work the wrecking crew recovered the bodies from under the engine and baggage car.' The official in charge of such a train is called a *wreck-master*. 'When the wreck-master and his gang reach the scene, this is the first question that arises: Is there anyone, living or dead, under the debris?'

In Am. the word is also used in connexion with the demolition of old buildings, called in Eng. *house-breaking*. 'Under the Low administration, he had the Building Department's wrecking contract. The contract is a lucrative one.'

†write. Am. *write-up* = Eng. *descriptive report*. 'The appetite that leads the masses to consume sensational "write-ups" in the newspapers.' 'The names of my employers, the neighborhoods in which they lived, their professions and the position which they occupied in London society, I carefully concealed in my write-up' (E. L. BANKS, Autobiog. of a Newspaper Girl, 90). 'His first job was a write-up of the Galveston commission form of government, an article which was intended to display the more constructive side of muckraking' (Dr. C. C. REGIER, The Era of the Muckrakers, 150).

Y

Yankee. In Eng., an inhabitant of any part of the U.S. In Am., a New Englander. 'The most populous southern section of Illinois was inhabited by men most of whom came from south of Ohio and who had a violent prejudice against Yankee preachers, Yankee politicians, and Yankees in general. As several of the men prominent in the foundation of the college were New Englanders, it was impossible for several years to get a charter from the legislature.' 'Yankees, straight from Down East, settled the town [of Minneapolis] and their New England spirit predominates' (L. STEFFENS, The Shame of the Cities, 64). 'Yankee as he appeared, he was in truth a native of St. Louis' (H. GARLAND, Roadside Meetings, 242).

yea. 'His motion was defeated by a vote of 29 yeas to 32 nays' (A. B. DARLING, Public Papers of Francis G. Newlands, ii. 249). 'When the momentous measure came before the House for the final roll call, the yeas were 119, the nays 56' (Prof. D. S. MUZZEY, The Am. Adventure, i. 598).

In these reports of votes taken in Congress the *yeas* and *nays* apparently correspond to the *ayes* and *noes* of the British Parliament. But there is an important distinction. There are four methods of taking a vote in Congress. (1) The simplest is known as the *ayes and noes* method. When the question is put, members cry *aye* or *no*, and the presiding officer decides according to the sound of their voices. (2) If he is in doubt, or if his decision is challenged, a *division* is taken. This term means something quite different from a division in the British Parliament. First the members supporting the motion and then those opposing it rise in their places and are counted. (3) If the result is again doubtful, or is challenged by a prescribed proportion of members present, there is a vote by *tellers*; i.e. the supporters and opponents file between tellers, as in a division at Westminster. (4) The most formal method is a vote by *yeas and nays*, when the clerk calls the roll, and each member responds *aye* or *no*. The importance of this method lies in the fact that the votes of individual members are recorded in the journals. As this process consumes a great deal of time—there are now 435 members in the lower House, and the roll is called twice in order to give an opportunity to those who were absent at the first call, as well as to allow members to change their votes—it is also a useful means of obstruction.

yell. In Am. *yell* is the name given to a sort of distinctive war-whoop used by students of a college or school, esp. to encourage their own sides in athletic contests; e.g. 'Rah rah rah! rah rah rah! rah rah rah! Harvard!' 'Hurrah! hurrah! hurrah! tiger! sis! boom! ah! Princeton!' 'Cornell! I yell yell yell! Cornell!' 'Rah rah rah! bow wow wow! Rutgers!' The *World Almanac* was formerly wont to publish annually a list of such yells, amounting to over 200. There is a story of a student who was once found sticking a stamp on a letter upside down. He explained that he had just joined a correspondence class, and sticking the stamp on upside down was the college yell. 'At the conclusion of the exercises the students sang the college song and gave the 'varsity yell from the steps of the library.' 'If you never went to college you can not appreciate the immense importance of the college yell. . . . In this modern age it has become an axiom that to found a college one must first secure a yell, and then see some millionaire about the donation.'

yellow. †This epithet is applied in Am. to newspapers of a sensational and unscrupulous type—and to their editors and contributors. 'The yellowness of yellow papers consists in their falsehoods, their sensations, their brag, their vulgarity.' 'Even the yellow journal critics, while affecting flippancy of tone and vulgar meretriciousness of style, are capable of keen, synthetic analysis.' 'Our morals are no longer under the management of teachers and philosophers, but of yellow editors.' 'A whirlwind of popular criticism in which the yellow journals of the time played a leading part' (Prof. T. J. GRAYSON, Leaders and Periods of Am. Finance, 230). 'Your true yellow journalist can work himself into quite as fiery a fever of enthusiasm over a Christmas fund or a squalid murder, as over a war or a presidential campaign' (WILLIS J. ABBOT, Watching the World Go By, 207).

The unlovely appearance of a *yellow dog* has suggested in Am. its fig. use to describe something utterly contemptible. 'A determined fight was made on him from the opening of the campaign, and how effective it was is shown by his defeat in a year when a yellow dog running on a Rep. ticket ought to have been able to win.' 'In preference to a "yellow dog" ticket his organization would support the Fusion candidate.'

For *yellow-dog contract* see the following quotations. 'The measure then proceeds to outlaw the yellow-dog contract—whereby an employee engages, as one of the terms of his employment, not to join a specific labor union.' 'Trade unionists may not agitate among non-union employees who have an agreement with their employer not to join a union—a pledge called by labor leaders a "yellow dog" contract' (C. A. and W. BEARD, The Am. Leviathan, 509). 'Workers, to get jobs, were obliged to sign the so-called "yellow dog" contracts' (L. ADAMIC, Dynamite, 326).

A *yellow-dog fund* is a fund used for bribery or some other discreditable purpose. 'Tuesday the Metropolitan street railway was put into the hands of receivers, and at the same time the counsel for the public service commission began the uncovering of what appears to be a "yellow-dog fund" in connection with that company, similar to the mysterious fund of the big life companies. Payments of some $800,000 charged to the construction account of the company appear to have been made to persons and for purposes whose identity every effort was made to conceal.' 'While here and there agents of the insurance companies are watching the Legislatures, there appears to be a noteworthy absence of "yellow dog" funds in most of the capitals, and also a great falling off in the number of "strike" bills introduced for the purpose of tapping the "yellow dog" funds.'

†yes. The term *yes-man* has recently been coined in Am. to denote the man who never takes an independent stand but agrees with the opinion or complies with the policy of some more important or influential person. 'Steadily we are tending toward becoming a nation of employees. The "yes-men" are as new to our national life as to our vocab., but they are real. It is no longer merely the laborer or factory hand who is dependent on the whim of his employer, but men all the way up the economic and social scales' (J. TRUSLOW ADAMS, The Epic of Am. 409). 'The people of the country became convinced that he was nothing more than Jackson's "yes man", a sycophant and a flatterer who would let nothing stand in the way of his overweening desire to succeed a greater man in the presidency' (Prof. T. J. GRAYSON, Leaders and Periods of Am. Finance, 230). 'The result of all this is that Ford is to-day surrounded by yes-men who live in deadly fear of disagreeing with him' (E. WILSON, The Am. Jitters, 80).

you all. It is commonly alleged and believed in the North that in some parts of the South *you all* (with the accent on the *you*) is frequently used with a singular meaning. Thus, a correspondent of the N.Y. *Times Saturday Review* (Nov. 21, 1903) says: 'It is a most common greeting to have a Southern gentleman greet you in Kentucky, Tennessee, Alabama, Arkansas, and Mississippi with the question "Good morning! Where are you all going this morning?" notwithstanding that you are quite alone.' Another correspondent of the same paper (Dec. 5, 1903) reports that when he first heard the phrase ' I want you all to come over' he thought it meant the entire family, but when the conveyance arrived to carry 'you all' over, he found there was only room for two —the person to whom the invitation had been given and the driver.

On the other hand, most Southerners emphatically, not to say indignantly, deny that this expression is ever employed in the South with reference to a single individual. They assert that they always have in mind other persons in addition to the one they are addressing. Thus, if they ask a man, 'How are you all to-day?' they mean 'How are you and the other members of your household?' If an employee

in a country store is asked 'Do you all have any lard?' the meaning is, 'Have you and the owner of the store any lard?' The controversy on this point has lasted for 50 years at least, and seems likely to continue as long as the Eng. language is spoken in the U.S.

yours. In Am. *yours* is often omitted from *yours faithfully*, *yours sincerely*, *yours cordially*, &c., in the conventional ending of a letter. For published examples, see The Intimate Papers of Col. House, i. 146, iii. 400, and iv. 118.

Z

zone. For the Am. use of this word as a technical term, see the following quotations. 'By "zoning" is meant the districting of the city so as to set apart specifically designated sections of the city to be used principally or exclusively for certain purposes, as heavy industries, light industries, wholesale trade, retail trade, residence, and so on. When such districts or zones are blocked out and designated to a certain use, restrictions are imposed upon the use of property within each district, which are designed to preserve its character and encourage its use for the purpose for which it is set apart' (C. C. MAXEY, Outline of Municipal Government, 186). 'The division of cities into zones for the grouping of like industries and the separation of residential sections from those devoted to commerce and manufacturing' (H. M. POLLOCK and W. S. MORGAN, Modern Cities, 15). 'Sheer necessity has brought us to an age of zoning and city planning' (NORMAN THOMAS, America's Way Out, 175).

The word is also a technical term of the U.S. parcel post system. The rates of payment vary not only acc. to weight but acc. to distance, which is reckoned in *zones*. See also BELT.

INDEX

THIS index does not include words that appear in the titles or sub-titles of articles. For derivatives, see the words from which they are derived. Thus *available* will be found under *avail*, *blinder* under *blind*, *bouncer* under *bounce*, and so on. Compound terms are dealt with under one or other of the words of which they are compounded; e.g., *accommodation train* under *accommodation*, *road agent* under *agent*, and *baggageman* under *baggage*.

I. AMERICAN INDEX

II. ENGLISH INDEX

PRINTED IN GREAT BRITAIN AT THE UNIVERSITY PRESS, OXFORD
BY VIVIAN RIDLER, PRINTER TO THE UNIVERSITY